KU-255-085

Social History of Africa

WORK, CULTURE, AND IDENTITY

SOCIAL HISTORY OF AFRICA
Series Editors:
Allen Isaacman and Jean Hay

BURYING SM
The Politics of Knowledge and the Sociology of Power in Africa
David William Cohen and E.S. Atieno Odhiambo

COLONIAL CONSCRIPTS
The Tirailleurs Sénégalais *in French West Africa, 1875–1960*
Myron Echenberg

CUTTING DOWN TREES
Gender, Nutrition, and Agricultural Change in the
Northern Province of Zambia, 1890–1990
Henrietta L. Moore and Megan Vaughan

LAW IN COLONIAL AFRICA
Kristin Mann and Richard Roberts (editors)

THE MOON IS DEAD! GIVE US OUR MONEY!
The Cultural Origins of an African Work Ethic,
Natal, South Africa, 1843–1900
Keletso E. Atkins

PEASANTS, TRADERS, AND WIVES
Shona Women in the History of Zimbabwe, 1870–1939
Elizabeth Schmidt

"WE SPEND OUR YEARS AS A TALE THAT IS TOLD"
Oral Historical Narrative in a South African Chiefdom
Isabel Hofmeyr

WOMEN OF PHOKENG
Consciousness, Life Strategy, and Migrancy in South Africa, 1900–1983
Belinda Bozzoli
(with the assistance of Mmantho Nkotsoe)

WORK, CULTURE, AND IDENTITY
Migrant Laborers in Mozambique and South Africa, 1860–1910
Patrick Harries

WORK, CULTURE, AND IDENTITY

MIGRANT LABORERS IN MOZAMBIQUE AND SOUTH AFRICA, c. 1860–1910

Patrick Harries
History Department
University of Cape Town
South Africa

HEINEMANN
Portsmouth, NH

WITWATERSRAND
UNIVERSITY PRESS
Johannesburg

JAMES CURREY
London

Heinemann
A division of Reed Elsevier Inc.
361 Hanover Street
Portsmouth, NH 03801-3959

James Currey Ltd
54b Thornhill Square
Islington
London N1 1BE

Witwatersrand University Press
University of Witwatersrand
Johannesburg
PO Wits 2050
South Africa

© 1994 by Patrick Harries. All rights reserved. No part of this book may be reproduced in any form or by electronic or mechanical means, including information storage and retrieval systems, without permission in writing from the publisher, except by a reviewer, who may quote brief passages in a review.

ISBN 0-435-08092-X (Heinemann cloth)
ISBN 0-435-08094-6 (Heinemann paper)
ISBN 0-85255-663-2 (James Currey cloth)
ISBN 0-85255-613-6 (James Currey paper)
ISBN 1-86814-253-1 (Witwatersrand University Press paper)

First published 1994.

Photo credits: pp. 44, 126, 142—Cape Archives; pp. 107, 116, 117—Cory Library, Rhodes University, Grahamstown; pp. 123, 125, 148, 210, 211, 212, 218—Département évangelique (former Swiss Mission), Lausanne; p. 178—*The Graphic*, 17 April 1903; p. 36—Killie Campbell Collection, University of Natal, Durban; p. 20—Local History Museum, Durban; pp. 29, 51, 52, 67, 75—South African Library, Cape Town; p. 87—South African Museum, Cape Town.

Library of Congress Cataloging-in-Publication Data
Harries, Patrick.
    Work culture and identity : migrant laborers in Mozambique and
South Africa, c. 1860–1910 / Patrick Harries.
       p.   cm. — (Social history of Africa series)
    Includes bibliographical references and index.
    ISBN 0-435-08094-6 (paper). — ISBN 0-435-08092-X (cloth)
    1. Migrant labor—South Africa—History.   2. Migrant labor-
-Mozambique—History.   3. Alien labor, Mozambican—South Africa-
-History. I. Title. II. Series.
HD5856.S6H37   1993
331.54′4′0968—dc20   93-26448
                                                  CIP

British Library Cataloguing in Publication Data
Harries, Patrick
    Work, Culture and Identity: Migrant
    Laborers in Mozambique and South Africa,
    c. 1860–1910.—(Social History of Africa
    Series)
    I. Title II. Series
    331.5096

Cover design by Jenny Greenleaf.
Printed in the United States of America on acid-free paper.
97 96 95 94 93 BB 1 2 3 4 5 6

CONTENTS

Abbreviations

ABM	American Board of Commissioners for Foreign Missions
ACU	Annaes do Conselho Ultramarino
AGH	Africa's Golden Harvest
AHS	International Journal of African Historical Studies
AHU	Arquivo Histórico Ultramarino
ASM	Archives of the Swiss Mission, Johannesburg
BMB	Berliner Missionsberichte
BMSAS	Bulletin de la Mission Suisse en Afrique du Sud
BO	Boletim Oficial de Moçambique
BPP	British Parliamentary Papers
BSGL	Boletim da Sociedade de Geografia de Lisboa
BSNG	Bulletin de la Société Neuchâteloise de Géographie
CA	Cape Archives
CCL	(Cape) Commissioner for Crown Lands
CG	Correspondência de Governadors
CGP	Consulate-General of Portugal, Pretoria
CMAR	Transvaal Chamber of Mines, Annual Reports
Col.Sec.	Colonial Secretary, Natal
CPWD	Cape Public Works department
CSO	Colonial Secretary's office, Natal
DNL	Director of Native Labor
EMJ	Engineering and Mining Journal
FHS	Fondation pour l'Histoire des Suisses
FO	Foreign Office
GH	Government House, Natal
GLM	Governor of Lourenço Marques
GNLB	Government Native Labour Bureau
GGM	Governor-General of Mozambique
Gov.	Governor's Office, Transvaal
HA	House of Assembly, Cape Town
HE	Herman Eckstein archives, Wernher-Beit Group
IAC	Immigration Agent, Cape Town
ICE	Industrial Commission of Enquiry, Transvaal 1897
II	Indian Immigration department, Natal
JAH	Journal of African History
JC	Junod Collection, University of South Africa

JRGS	Journal Royal Geographical Society
JSA	James Stuart Archive, KCL
JSAS	Journal of Southern African Studies
KCL	Killie Campbell Library, Durban
LC	Legislative Council, Natal
MIC	Mining Industry Commission of 1908
MMS	Methodist Missionary Society Archives, London
MNE	Ministério dos Negócios Estrangeiros (Foreign Office), Lisbon
Moç	Mozambique
MSMU	Ministerio e Secretariado de Marinha e Ultramar (Colonial Office), Lisbon
NA	Natal Archives
NAD	Native Affairs Department
NC	Native Commissioner
n.d.	no date
NGC	Native Grievances Commission, 1913–14
NGG	Natal Government Gazette
NPP	Natal Parliamentary Papers
OT	Oral testimony
PI	Protector of Immigrants, Natal
PRO	Public Records Office
QBBM	Quarterly Bulletin of the Bloemfontein Mission
RGS	Royal Geographical Society
Rep	Repartiçao
RM	Resident Magistrate
SAAR	South African Archival Records
SAAS	South African Association for the Advancement of Science
SAAYB	South African Archival Yearbook
SAJS	South African Journal of Science
SANAC	South African Native Affairs Commission, 1904–5
SBA	Standard Bank Archives, Johannesburg
SGO	Surveyor-General's office, Natal
SMA	Swiss Mission Archive, Lausanne
SN	Secretary for Native Affairs, Transvaal
SNA	Secretary for Native Affairs, Natal
SP	Smalberger Papers, University of Cape Town
SS	State Secretary, Transvaal
SSa	State Secretary, Foreign Affairs, Transvaal
Supt	Superintendent
TA	Transvaal Archive
TLC	Transvaal Labour Commission, 1904
UNISA	University of South Africa
USPG	United Society for the Propagation of the Gospel
WUL	Witwatersrand University Library
ZGH	Government House, Zululand

Acknowledgments

This book owes a great deal to the mental energy of several generations of scholars. As an undergraduate at the University of Cape Town, Francis Wilson made me aware of the importance of migrant labour and Robin Hallett inspired me, and a generation of students, to study the African past. At the School of Oriental and African Studies in London I was fortunate enough to have David Birmingham as a thesis supervisor. I hope that some of his knowledge and understanding of Lusophone Africa has found its way into this book. I owe an equal debt to Shula Marks who, over the years, has provided me with criticism and inspiration. In the United States I learnt a great deal from Jeanne Penvenne, Marcia Wright and, especially, Leroy Vail. In Switzerland I benefitted from the friendship and assistance of Laurent Monier of the IUED in Geneva, François Jecquier of the University of Lausanne and Mariette Ouwerhand of the *département évangélique* (the former Swiss Mission).

In South Africa, Patricia Davison of the South African Museum introduced me to material culture and made me aware of the richness of difference; the late Monica Wilson taught me the fundamentals of anthropology and Andrew Spiegel and Robert Thornton struggled to keep me abreast of changes in the discipline; Sue Newton-King and Nigel Penn brought shafts of light from the eighteenth-century to bear on early industrialism. Charles van Onselen laid a major part of the intellectual foundations on which I attempt to build. I must also pay tribute to the late F.M. Maboko, who introduced me to the joys and tribulations of fieldwork; I hope that many of the concerns of the old miners we interviewed have found a place in this work.

The long period of gestation that finally resulted in the birth of this book would not have been possible without the financial support of various institutions. A Rondebosch Overseas Scholarship, generously provided by my old High School, allowed me to study in Britain. Funds from the University of Cape Town assisted my research at various stages, and a fellowship from the DDA of the Swiss Confederation permitted me to ransack the mission archives in Lausanne. I hope my mentors and sponsors will draw pleasure from what merits they may find in this book—its defaults remain the responsibility of the author.

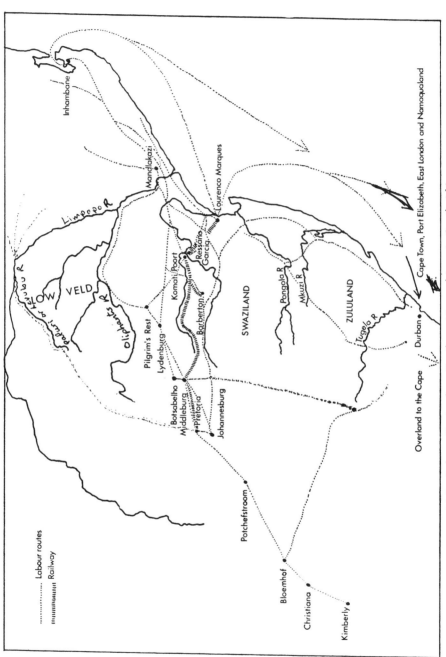

Major Labour Routes from Southern Mozambique to South Africa

Introduction

This book is a history of the Mozambican workers who, in the half-century spanning 1860–1910, tramped to the sugar plantations, diamond fields and gold mines of South Africa. Part one deals with the origins and early history of migration, part two examines the changes effected during the first decade of mining on the Witwatersrand, and part three is concerned with the impact of the first fifteen years of Portuguese colonial rule. The story closes in 1910, one year after the conclusion of the formal treaty that was to systematize migrant labour, and the year of the downfall of the Portuguese monarchy. I focus on several traditional themes; the causes and consequences of migrant labour, the social history of the migrants, and their changing relations with employers and the state. But I am also concerned with the manner in which workers constructed new ways of seeing themselves and others through innovative rituals, traditions and beliefs. Culture, identity and interpretation are central themes in this book. I also hope to contribute to the methodology of writing the history of workers who have left no written records and whose experiences are no longer within the sphere of living memory. I believe I can best clarify my perspective by situating myself within the changing historiography of labour in Southern Africa.

Historiography

The writer who probably knew more than any other about the lives of Mozambican migrant workers was the missionary Henri-Alexandre Junod who lived in or near Lourenço Marques during the years 1889–95 and 1907–21. Junod used the evolutionist ideas of his generation to portray Africans as primitives who would fall victim to a racial degeneration if they were not protected from the malevolent forces of industrialisation by evangelical Christianity. As an anthropologist Junod was primarily interested in recording rural customs and beliefs threatened with extinction and he purposely excluded migrant workers from his published work.[1] This tradition of salvage anthropology, representing African societies as timeless reflections of the lost European past, dovetailed with the concerns of many contemporary critics of industrialisation at Kimberley and Johannesburg. These authors brought to their narratives the assumptions and convictions, and the rhetorical

conventions, of novelists and poets who had discovered, in the space of a generation, the beauty and tranquility of the Lake District and the Alps, and the squalor
and meanness of the industrial city. They condemned the corruption of mining cities in biblical metaphors, through the stark juxtaposition of pastoral and industrial
imagery, and in plots that recounted the downfall of tribesmen at the hands of
town women and evil employers. African miners, they believed, were severed
from their sustaining rural culture, crushed and degraded by an oppressive industrial landscape. Their pastoral imagery presented a radical, organic alternative to
the alienation of industrial society, but it was an alternative that fixed real Africans
to an unspoilt countryside.[2] This view was entrenched by Malinowski, Radcliffe-
Brown and their students who, in the process of seeking to understand and defend
the colonised, stressed the harmony and equilibrium of tribal societies. Function-
alism provided anthropology as a discipline with clear boundaries that distinguished it from the works of amateurs like Junod. The methodology of participant
observation seemed to provide a more scientific approach than archival work in the
papers of colonial officials, and a less peremptory view of African society emerged
as the native's eye supplanted that of the administrator.

The modernisation and intensification of colonial rule following the depression of the 1930s created new openings for an applied anthropology, particularly in
Northern Rhodesia where it was recognized that social planning could assist industrial development.[3] One of the central areas of study of the remarkable group
of anthropologists gathered at the Rhodes-Livingstone Institute was the examination of the causes and effects of migrant labour in the rural areas. Some anthropologists traced the export of labour to an unstable environment, seasonal food
shortages, new consumer demands and the monetisation of bridewealth, and held
that the repatriation of migrants' wages reinforced sagging political structures and
improved rural standards of living. Others started to treat industrial workers as a
legitimate unit of study. But it was difficult for government anthropologists to take
a critical position on the conflict generated by capitalism and colonialism and they
seldom moved beyond a concern for colonial justice, good government, and the
colourful practices through which mineworkers gave meaning to their lives. This
work gave a new visibility and humanity to migrant labourers but its failure to
tackle the sensitive issues of colonial policy and capitalist exploitation was later to
lay it open to anti-imperialist criticism.[4] Significantly, it was an American anthropologist, Marvin Harris, who in 1959 brought these themes to the study of migrant
labour in Southern Mozambique.[5] A more critical perspective of colonialism
emerged in the 1960s as the rapid growth of university education swelled the acad-
emy and gave anthropologists a new independence, and the first decade of African
independence created a political climate critical of colonialism. A growing body of
opinion discerned in migrant labour the development of a vicious cycle of impoverishment as men were forced onto the labour market by colonial policies, rural
production declined, and the reserves were obliged to carry the cost of below-
subsistence industrial wages. Research findings polarised as development econo-
mists came to see migrant labour either as a means of capital redistribution and
modernisation or, increasingly, as a source of underdevelopment.[6]

In the 1960s the history of migrant labour was dominated by two literary
genres that established powerful conventions of expression and approach. What
Richard Johnson has called the "history of social policy", written by the "prudent

administrator", was a literature of empire aimed at the improvement of colonial government. Within that genre the economist Sheila van der Horst had established an extremely high standard with the 1942 publication of her *Native Labour in South Africa*. This was a careful history of state policy towards labour; it reflected the morality and conscience of the liberal wing of the Smuts government and, in the hands of an enlightened administrator, could facilitate judicious government.[7] Like the work of the government anthropologists in Northern Rhodesia, Van der Horst's work was reformist but muted in its criticism of white supremacy and the exploitation of labour. The second genre, with deep roots in the tradition of anti-slavery exposés, was spearheaded by James Duffy, who traced the origins of migrant labour to the export of slaves.[8] Unlike the earlier "prudent administrators", Duffy implicitly rejected the legitimacy of white rule and reinforced the censorious approach of his fellow American, Marvin Harris. But both the "prudent administrator" and the "anti-slavery" genres of writing were informed by a powerful strain of moral superiority and by a reliance on official, archival sources. The Africans at the centre of these works were shadowy and anonymous figures; almost always acted upon rather than acting, they were the innocent victims of employers and colonial officials. In this way, the literary heritage passed on to a new generation of writers and readers reinforced an old picture, as African workers remained passive and depersonalized objects of history rather than subjects capable of assuming command of their destiny. This image was to maintain a tenacious grip on the history of labour in Southern Africa.

Francis Wilson's *Labour in the South African Gold Mines, 1911–1969*, published in 1972, was the consummation of earlier approaches. In a work that combined economics with anthropology and history, he carefully traced the relationship between gold mining and rural society and outlined the costs and benefits of migrant labour. But South Africa in the 1970s was no longer the country that had produced the reform-minded anthropologists and administrators of empire. The universities had been segregated, academics banned and detained, many had left the country and, perhaps most importantly, their influence on government had been reduced to nothing. In the meantime, the real wages of black miners had been falling for seventy-five years and industry was reaping profits that, with the help of apartheid, had lifted white living standards to amongst the highest in the world. Beyond the borders of Southern Africa the end of colonialism had initiated an intellectual decolonisation and there seemed little justification for the perpetuation of white rule.

In this political climate two canonical works, published in 1976, were to transform the study of labour history. In *Class, Race and Gold* Frederick Johnstone examined the structural conditions of capital accumulation and impoverishment on the early Witwatersrand and brought exploitation and conflict to the centre of his work. He argued convincingly that the profitability of gold mining depended on a supply of migrant labour as this drove a wedge between proletarianized white workers and black migrants, and depressed wages by passing to the reserves the costs of reproducing the family.[9] But the picture of "ultra-exploitation" developed by Johnstone was based on a sharp delineation of antagonistic classes and the "downtrodden Black labour army" characterized by "rightlessness, powerlessness" was, ultimately, indistinguishable from the faceless victims of earlier generations of historians.[10] Influenced by slave studies and the new labour history,

Charles van Onselen was far more concerned to present a rich and varied history "from below" and he concurred with labour historians like Herb Gutman in stressing that the power exerted by workers could not be separated from their culture. But as Bozzoli and Delius have recently pointed out, Van Onselen's work was also strongly influenced by the dominant structuralist paradigm of the period.[11] Capital accumulation and social control are dominant themes in *Chibaro*, almost organising principles of the narrative, and black workers are frequently protrayed as victims of an omnipotent capitalist class. "The compound" wrote Van Onselen, was "the college of colonialism, that did much to rob Africans of their dignity and help mould servile black personalities."[12] Yet Van Onselen was far too good a historian to portray workers as passive and suppliant beings and he stressed that their drab and dehumanised conditions created common grievances that engendered "silent and unorganised responses".[13] Whereas Johnstone's black workers were little more than a linguistic category, Van Onselen's were imbued with a vibrant culture. But this culture was largely either the product of drawn-out struggles with capital or the result of the capitalists' strategy of social control. Drunkenness, loafing, theft, desertion, witchcraft and Watchtower were the "hidden struggles" with capital through which workers constructed a class consciousness; at the same time, employers saw mine dancing and sport as a means of defusing class consciousness, liquor drew men to the mines and held them there by raising their consumer needs, education and religion produced a disciplined and acquiescent workforce, and even sex serviced the needs of industry.[14]

Van Onselen's work opened new horizons for the history of labour in Africa. But the revisionist fervour with which he and Johnstone searched for conflict caused them to virulently reject anthropological studies of mine labour which, in the 1970s, were tarred with the label of reformism.[15] By focusing their analyses on the exploitation and conflict found in the work place, Van Onselen (except for a vivid and memorable description of witchcraft in the Bonsor mine) and Johnstone treated migrant workers arriving on the mines as cultural cyphers or blank slates on whom the experience of work left a common inscription. Alternatively they saw human beings produce, like chemicals, a fixed and common reaction in response to certain stimuli. "For Africans to resist spontaneously and directly", asserted Van Onselen, "they simply needed to perceive the single dimension involved in the relationship of exploiter and exploited".[16] This reduced motivation for social action to a single dimension and underestimated the range of experiences and cultural resources that shaped the world view of migrating mineworkers.[17] As he saw resistance as the black miner's natural response to his environment, Van Onselen inverted into working class values the vices, such as drunkenness, theft and laziness, through which Europeans had given a visibility to Africans. At the same time, by portraying culture in terms of response rather than initiative, or in terms of employers' strategies, he ultimately subordinated the workers' lived experience to the rhythms of capital accumulation.

In the early 1980s a number of historians, influenced by the new French economic anthropology, found the dynamics of migrant labour less in the needs of industrial capitalism than in the subsistence crises and social conflicts that beset pre-capitalist, rural societies. Historical studies of specific regions indicated that migrant labour could not be seen as a holistic "system" responsible for either modernisation or underdevelopment.[18] In 1987 much of the approach to labour developed over the previous decade was reflected and refined in two important books on the early history of Kimberley. In *South Africa's City of Diamonds: Mine workers and monopoly capitalism in Kimberley, 1867–1895* William Worger expanded the miners' world to include urban locations and areas of recruitment in the countryside.[19] In *Capital and Labour on the Kimberley Diamond Fields*, Robert Turrell documented the development of the compounds and stressed their importance in disciplining a migrant labour force. Turrell was particularly critical of the concept of class that Van Onselen had linked to everyday forms of "resistance", and candidly admitted that most of the evidence for a grassroots labour history evaporated once he had abandoned this approach.[20] Nevertheless, both he and Worger carefully detailed important aspects of workers' lives; the legal constraints on drinking and the movement of labour, the dangers of mine work and, particularly, changes in the labour process that were a prelude to deep-level gold mining. But Turrell and Worger were only partly concerned with the history of labour and their studies left unchallenged some of the basic canons of the discipline, particularly the central role in the narrative given to the notion of social control. Associated with this was the view of capitalism as a purely violating, penetrating force, bringing in its wake only exploitation and cognitive dislocation.[21] The result was a largely administrative history according to which Europeans built institutions and took decisions that shaped and molded the outlines of workers' lives; the compound remained a prison, drinking purely a problem, leisure and Christianity functioned to assist the accumulation of capital, and coercion was the most visible aspect of everyday labour relations. Migrant labour was viewed at best as an appendage rather than an integral, if not dominant, part of workers' lives on the fields, and the systems of signification brought from the rural areas and developed by miners in and around their places of work were subsumed in an anonymous, industrial homogeneity. As Colin Newbury noted, black workers on the early diamond fields remained "a cast of silent thousands".[22]

Culture

Social history has developed in an original manner in South Africa.[23] In a society where culture is often a synonym for race, and "separate but equal" is a euphemism for apartheid, liberal and radical historians have been cautious in their treatment of cultural differences.[24] Historians who deduce mentality and meaning from a social and economic context often take it for granted that African migrants share the values and beliefs of workers in Europe or the United States or limit their studies to the more "rational" field of trade union history.[25] Another tendency has been for historians, particularly those who reacted against the abstractions of structuralism, to turn to the study of social history. Influenced by Gramsci and E.P.Thompson, they were eager to rescue the historical experiences of working people from 'the enormous condescension of posterity'. But they were more cautious, in their response to the accompanying appeal made by Thompson for historians to recognise that class 'experiences are handled in cultural terms', that workers' 'aspirations were valid in terms of their own experience', and that workers often had 'an alternative definition of reality.'[26] Nor was there criticism of universal values that sometimes hide a strategy of domination beneath a thick discourse of equality.[27]

Instead, radical historians initially viewed culture as a source of raw data that would provide the narrative with "nuance and texture", allow history to "resonate with the lives of ordinary people" and, in general, result in what Paul Thompson has called a "democratisation" of the past.[28] Oral testimony became a crucial part of this enterprise, partly so as to "reconstruct and record" the lives of "obscure, ill-educated people", but also to examine consciousness as a product of everyday experience.[29] But by the late 1980s there was also an increasing move away from socio-economic causality as some historians came to see consciousness not as the product of an "objective reality", or even a lens through which reality is perceived, but as the product of a repertoire of signs through which experience is ordered and arranged, and infused with meaning. From this perspective, experience is symbolically mediated and different individuals, groups and societies (including authors and actors) may interpret the same incidents in very different ways. Dunbar Moodie pioneered this approach in a series of remarkable studies on the social networks, forms of identity and moral economy constructed by black workers on the gold mines.[30] Beinart, Delius and others stressed the deep rural roots of the migrant workers' culture, and Guy and Tabane examined the notions of ethnicity and gender created by Sotho shaft sinkers on the Witwatersrand.[31] Beyond Africa, this concern with the ways in which pre-capitalist miners interpreted their experiences produced startlingly innovative anthropological studies.[32]

The oral testimony of retired miners had an important influence on my approach. They spoke to me of the brutality, fear and exploitation in the mines, but they also directed my attention to other topics with which I was unfamiliar; the deep fear of witchcraft, of being transformed into zombies, of being waylaid on the way to the mines by bush spirits, of the folk medicines and practices that protected the miner. What I had always thought of as "obscurantisms" were quite obviously very central to the lives of these old men. So too was the sense of comradeship and the dignity derived from wage work. They also expressed a pride in virtues and values that were sometimes foreign to me—heavy drinking, an initiatory homosexuality, and a comraderie that often slipped into a brutal chauvinism. Alerted to these differences, my view of the situation at the turn of the century became more opaque as I grappled with the notion of work held by migrants drawn from societies that practised domestic slavery; nor did I have more success with the ideas relating to causation of miners who, at home, sometimes, albeit rarely, practised "unspeakable rites" like human sacrifice.[33] It was not just fieldwork that challenged my universalistic interpretations. The decline of university segregation in the 1980s created a new, heterogeneous intellectual climate in South Africa, while the legalization of the trade unions and the reemergence of mass-based political organisations encouraged a wider, less institutional, approach to labour history. Elsewhere in the world, the rise of Moslem fundamentalism challenged evolutionary models that saw secularism replace the religious or one mode of production supersede another. In the United States, the assimilationist model of national integration was increasingly challenged by historians concerned to reevaluate and legitimate culture and difference. Deindustrialization in the northern hemisphere also tended to highlight the pit and the factory as places of social communion rather than purely sites of exploitation and struggle.

Although I was able to draw on the ideas and experiences of old miners, their accounts were limited to the period of living memory and I was obliged to rely, for my evidence, almost entirely on documentary sources. This incurred a problem of interpretation of which social historians have long been aware. If the past is another country, the historian enters it with all the bias and prejudice of the foreigner.[34] As early as 1959 Eric Hobsbawm had called on historians, "being mainly educated townsmen", to be aware of their alterity and to "think and feel themselves into the skins . . . of people who are unlike them".[35] Others believed that, once historians had established the social and economic context of their studies, they could work out the interests of ordinary people and, by means of the conditional tense, deduce the motivation for their actions.[36] But many anthropologists would now agree that this is to attempt an impossible task; even long spells of participant observation in the field are no longer thought sufficient to strip a trained anthropologist of the preconceptions that will structure both the investigation and the final text.[37] "By getting into the natives' heads and allowing them to speak", writes Renato Rosaldo, "the historian cannot contain a schoolmasterly impulse to correct their speech."[38]

In the northern hemisphere, a growing number of historians have attempted to arrive at the imagery of self and others constructed by workers by analysing the language of labour, particularly as presented in dialect literature.[39] In Africa, where such written traditions are rare, particularly for the popular classes, historians have started to treat local systems of signification as "texts" that may be "read".[40] I follow this practice by means of a close reading of the symbolic forms (behaviour, institutions, language and images) through which people situated themselves in time and space. The "African voices" that inform this work extend from rituals and rites of passage to everyday, mundane habits and gestures; the symbolism produced by changes in dress, cuisine, drink and other forms of consumption; recorded folklore, proverbs and songs, metaphors, aphorisms and other rhetorical devices; religious and secular beliefs. I have also used documented (auto)biographies of migrant workers, their evidence before government commissions and, I hope without too much extrapolation, oral evidence in the final chapters. The reason for the emphasis on the rural areas, in a book on labour history, is not just to account for the causes and consequences of migrancy, or even the bands of solidarity created by migrant workers in South Africa; by examining the webs of signification spun in the homestead and the chiefdom, I stress the importance of the cultural norms through which migrants gave meaning to their lives. My object is only partly to 'reconstruct' or 'recall' their everyday experiences or to document the social condition of labour. I attempt, rather, to interpret the themes, genres and conventions through which people, including historians, created their own meaning and reality. This form of cultural history calls for an awareness of literary criticism and cultural anthropology and conflates economic history with the history of ideas; it particularly rejects a notion of ideology that draws a dichotomy between appearance and reality, base and superstructure.[41] Hence the meaning and value of specific material objects is dependent on the symbols and signifying practices with which they are invested. This makes culture a source of capital and, as the Comaroffs have recently emphasised, a preeminent site of struggle.[42] Social practices such as drinking or fighting on the mines were interpreted in different ways by migrant workers, labour recruiters, mine managers or temperance activists. Because of a mixture of socialization, belief, and material interest, the members of each group struggled to have accepted as the norm their interpretation of these activities. The concept of work, or the borders of identity, or the value attributed to labour or marriage hoes, were all the product of shifting and tacit agreements between people. Meaning is not lodged in the mind, has no single, true essence, is never static, and is indissoluble from the material. Hence interpreting the practices through which men, brought up in the countryside, assembled and rearranged their symbolic world provides an alternative "reading" of, for instance, systems of naming or sexuality that were decried as foolish or immoral by Europeans. This alternative reading also indicates how migrants mobilized, adapted and shaped available cultural resources to construct their own notions of social inclusion and exclusion, mutuality, morality and self-worth; it also speaks about the relations of power, status and exploitation that divided and weakened the miners' community.

Both historians and the authors of their primary sources bring to their understanding of social agency specific preconceptions and narrative conventions.[43] A primary example is the use of binary oppositions that impose on the subject a narrative imagery based on post-enlightenment ways of thinking.[44] To avoid this problem, I attempt to see the balance of power in the pre-colonial rural areas other than in terms of war or peace. Similarly, the Christianity spread from the mines was not an homogeneous system of thought and practice defined in opposition to paganism; the literacy carried home by mine workers cannot be divorced from the orality that dominated their world view; sexual relations developed on the mines cannot be bracketed as either heterosexual or homosexual. Nor can resistance be cleanly separated from collaboration, exploitation from cooperation, or the worker from the peasant. As Geertz has suggested, a blurring of (post-Enlightenment) genres is required in order to approach the world view of the Other.[45] I have found a similar problem with essentialist categories, frequently reified into fixed givens, that condense information while ordering the text in a manageable way. Rather than accept such categories as ethnicity, race, age, gender, class and nation as unquestioned, or foundational, timeless syntheses, I treat them as social constructions with a complex history of development.[46] Working from another perspective, Alan Jeeves has confronted this problem in the form of the image of the omnipotent capitalist class on the Witwatersrand. Through a careful historical analysis he had shown that a labour monopsony was far from automatic and that a fratricidal competitiveness divided and weakened the Randlords.[47] I want to suggest that even where the capitalist class was in a monopolistic position, such as at Kimberley during the last decade of the twentieth century, workers had sufficient bargaining power to oblige management to enter into daily negotiations and reach compromises over such aspects of the labour process as the pace and duration of work, levels of remuneration, personal and social freedoms and, perhaps, the gender and age composition of the work force.[48] It is only when the traditions based on these compromises were unilaterally broken that a seismic faultline emerged between workers and employers; otherwise worker solidarity was ephemeral and often submerged by other, imbricating identities. When migrant labour is stripped of its South African exceptionalism, is seen in the long term and from the perspective of the workers, it becomes a logical way for rural producers to participate in an industrial economy; and a logical response from management was the attempt to curb the freedom with which workers moved, and to impose upon them a new and relentless discipline.[49] In the long term, what is at issue is not the "one hundred years of continuous, severe and systematic labour exploitation, probably unparalleled anywhere in the modern world" claimed by Johnstone for the Witwatersrand, but rather, I suggest in chapter five, a drawnout struggle marked by a serious defeat for black workers during the final years of the Kruger regime.[50]

A major point made throughout this book is that the very real harshness of the migrant workers' lives should not obscure their fundamental humanity. It is important that the image of conflict and exploitation should exist alongside the very different images presented by the workplace as a community; the pride of the miners in their work, their experience and courage, and their dignity as their wages allowed them to overcome the autocracy of nature.[51] Work is a source of tension and conflict between management and labour, but it is equally a common enterprise.

All this does not mean that people simply make history, or that the historian should be concerned only with agency and local, personal motivation. Understanding social action in terms of motives and intentions is not incompatible with causal explanations linked to impersonal forces. Important sections of this book are devoted to the ways in which human action was constrained by climate and environment, prices, demography, kinship and politics, the state, and mental structures. By approaching culture as a range (or repertoire) of resources that may be assembled and asserted or repressed in different situations, I take the view that identity is situational and fluid rather than the organic product of a bounded community. Nevertheless, culture cannot be adopted or abandoned at will as it is learnt and internalized over time and within a specific social and environmental situation. Mozambican migrants arrived in South Africa with the values, signs and rituals of authority they had learnt at home, and it was through their encounter with other blacks, as well as Europeans and colonists, that a new and dynamic culture emerged. This is the history of the making of that culture.

Glossary

amabutho	military regiments
amapisi	professional hunters
baloyi	witches, practitioners of black magic
beja hoe	iron hoe employed as bridewealth
degredados	convicts shipped from Portugal to Africa
gangisa	socially acceptable premarital sexual relations
liberto	indentured, former slave
Mabuyandlela	people who have taken on the culture of the Gaza Ngoni. Also called *Shangaans* or *Vatualizados*
mafura	edible fat obtained from the fruit of the Natal Mahogany
numzane	elders, homestead heads
panja	measurement equal to slightly over ¾ of a bushel
real/reis	unit of currency officially exchanged at about 4$500 to £1 sterling. In 1913 the escudo was introduced and valued at one thousand reis (1$000).
sertanejo	backlander
Vatualizado	see *Mabuyandlela*

NOTES

———————

1. I attempt to read Junod in the context of his times in Harries, "The anthropologist as historian and liberal: H.A.Junod and the Thonga" *Journal of Southern African Studies (JSAS)* VIII, 1, 1981; Harries "The roots of ethnicity: discourse and the politics of language construction in south-east Africa" *African Affairs*, no.346, January 1988.
2. Novels written in this genre include H.A.Junod, *Zidji: étude de moeurs sud-africaines* (Lausanne, 1911) and W.Scully, *Daniel Vananda: the Life Story of a Human Being* (Cape Town, 1923). Works of journalism stretch from Scully, *The Ridge of White Water* (London, 1912) to A.Pratt, *The Real South Africa* (London, 1913).
3. R.Brown, "Anthropology and Colonial Rule: Godfrey Wilson and the Rhodes-Livingstone Institute, Northern Rhodesia" in *Anthropology and the Colonial Encounter* (London, 1973) ed., T.Asad; Ibid.,"Passages in the Life of a White Anthropologist: Max Gluckman in Northern Rhodesia" *Journal of African History* 20, 4, 1979.
4. B.Magubane "A Critical look at Indices used in the Study of Social Change in Colonial Africa" *Current Anthropology* 4-5, 12, 1971, reprinted in J.Copans, ed., *Anthropologie et Impérialisme* (Paris, 1975).
5. Marvin Harris, "Labour emigration among the Mozambique Thonga: cultural and political factors" *Africa* 20, 1959. See the equally important reply by A.Rita Ferreira, "Labour emigration among the Mozambique Thonga: comments on a study by Marvin Harris" *Africa* 30, 1960. An excellent survey of the anthropological literature is presented by F.Wilson in his *Labour in the South African Gold Mines, 1911–1969* (Cambridge, 1972), ch7.
6. The two poles are represented by D.Hobart Houghton 'Men of two worlds: some aspects of migratory labour' *South African Journal of Economics* 3, 28, 1960, and H. Wolpe 'Capitalism and cheap labour power: from segregation to apartheid' *Economy and Society,* 1, 4, 1972.
7. R.Johnson 'Culture and the historians' in *Working Class Culture: Studies in History and Theory* (London, 1979) eds., J.Clarke, C.Critcher and R.Johnson, 46. The leaders in the field were Margery Perham and Lords Lugard and Hailey.
8. Particularly his *A Question of Slavery: Labour Policies in Portuguese Africa and the British Protest 1850–1920* (Oxford, 1967).
9. See also R.Davies, *Capital, State and White Labour in South Africa, 1900–1960* (Brighton, 1979) and N.Levy, *The Foundations of the South African Cheap Labour System* (London, 1982)
10. Johnstone, "The labour history of the Witwatersrand in the context of South African studies, and with reflections on the new school" *Social Dynamics* 4, 1978, 102–3.
11. 'Radical history and South African society' *Radical History Review* 46/7, 1990, 41. Van Onselen, a professor at the University of the Witwatersrand, provided the master narrative for a range of works on early industrialisation in South Africa, most notably those of S.Moroney.

12. *Chibaro, African Mine Labour in Southern Rhodesia, 1900–1933* (London, 1976) 157, 153. Environmental determinism was an important aspect of influential contemporary works by Elkins, Goffman and Braverman, a view that has reemerged recently in V.L.Allen, *The History of Black Mineworkers in South Africa* (Keighly, U.K., 1992), vol.I.

13. *Chibaro*, 244.

14. *Chibaro*, chapters six and seven. Herskovits, Stamp and Genovese had drawn attention to these forms of resistance on slave plantations.

15. 'Black workers in Central African Industry' *JSAS* 1, 2, 1975, 236, 243; *Chibaro*, 159. Johnstone " 'Most painful to our hearts': South Africa through the eyes of the new school" *Canadian Journal of African Studies* 16, 1, 1982, 18. See also M.Legassick, "The northern frontier to c.1840" in R.Elphick and H.Giliomee, eds., *The Shaping of South African Society, 1652–1840* (Cape Town, 1989) 368.

16. *Chibaro*, 244, 157.

17. A point made by S.Marks and R.Rathbone, eds, *Industrialisation and Social Change in South Africa: African class formation, culture and consciousness 1870–1930* (London, 1982), 27.

18. W.Beinart, *The Political Economy of Pondoland* (Cambridge, 1983); P.Delius, *The Land Belongs to Us* (Berkeley, 1984); P.Harries, 'Kinship, ideology and the nature of pre-colonial labour migration' in Marks and Rathbone, eds, *Industrialisation and Social Change*.

19. Less successful attempts to integrate migrant workers into the history of industrialisation were A.Rita Ferreira *O Movimento Migratório de Trabalhadores entre Moçambique é a Africa do Sul* (Lisbon, 1963) and Harries "Labour migration from Mozambique to South Africa; with special reference to the Delagoa Bay hinterland, c. 1862 to 1897" (unpublished PhD., University of London, 1983). The most successful attempts to combine an anthropological history of migrant labour with an administrative history of mining are J.Crush, *The Struggle for Swazi Labour, 1890–1920* (Kingston and Montreal, 1987) and Allen, *Black Mineworkers*.

20. *Capital and Labour on the Kimberley Diamond Fields, 1871–1890* (Cambridge, 1987) xii.

21. Worger emphasizes that conditions on the mines, particularly before the mid-1880s, were the product of struggle between employers and workers. But ultimately both he and Turrell stress the triumph of the capitalists' system of labor control. Worger, *City of Diamonds: mine workers and monopoly capitalism in Kimberley, 1867–1895* (New Haven, 1987) 5, 108, 146, but see also 269, 284; Turrell, *Capital and Labour*, 171–72.

22. *The Diamond Ring: Business, Politics and Precious Stones in South Africa, 1867–1947* (Oxford, 1989) 61.

23. Bozzoli and Delius refer to an "indigenous and eclectic synthesis", "Radical History", 42n66.

24. S.Dubow, "Race, civilisation and culture: the elaboration of segregationist discourse in the inter-war years" in S.Marks and S.Trapido, eds., *The Politics of Race, Class and Nationalism in Twentieth Century South Africa* (London, 1987), 87; E.Boonzaaier, "Race and the race paradigm" in Boonzaaier and Sharp, eds., *South African Keywords* (Cape Town, 1988) 67.

25. cf. J.Lewis "South African Labor History: a historiographical assessment" *Radical History Review* 46/47, 1990, esp.221. The exclusion of migrant labourers from the field of labour history has also been endorsed, if not created, by the politics of publishing. Cf. the Cambridge University Press series on "African Society Today" in which a book on *Migrant Labourers* (by Sharon Stichter, 1985) is separated from *The African Worker* (by Bill Freund, 1988).

26. E.P.Thompson, *Whigs and Hunters* (London, 1975) 183; *ibid.* "Class consciousness" in *History and Class*, (Oxford, 1983) ed., R.S.Neale, 115–16, 118. Ibid., *The Making of the English Working Class* (Harmonsworth, 1963), 11. In his history of East African dockworkers, F. Cooper showed great sensitivity to cultural issues, *On the African Waterfront* (New Haven, 1987).

27. R.Darnton "Intellectual and Cultural History" in *The Past Before Us: contemporary historical writing in the United States* (Ithaca, 1980), ed., M.Kammen, 340. J.Scott "Interview" *Radical History Review*, 45, 1989, 55.

28. S.Marks, 'The historiography of South Africa: recent developments' in *African Historiographies* (Beverly Hills, 1986), eds., B.Jewsiewicki and D.Newbury, 174; B.Bozzoli, 'History, eperience and culture' in her, ed., *Town and Countryside in the Transvaal: capitalist penetration and popular response* (Johannesburg, 1983), 8. P.Thompson, *The Voice of the Past: Oral History* (Oxford, 1988)

29. The quote is from T.Keegan, *Facing the Storm: Portraits of Black Lives in Rural South Africa* (Cape Town and London, 1988) p.v; B.Bozzoli, *Women of Phokeng: Consciousness, Life Strategy, and Migrancy in South Africa, 1900–1983* (Portsmouth, NH., 1991) 2, 3n10.

30. Dunbar Moodie, 'The moral economy of the black miners' strike of 1946', *JSAS* 13, 1, 1986; Moodie, 'Migrancy and male gender relations on the South African gold mines' *JSAS* 14, 2, 1988. From a more sociological perspective, see Moodie "Social existence and the practice of personal integrity: narratives of resistance on the South African Gold Mines" *African Studies* 50, 1&2, 1991 and A.Sitas "Moral formations and struggles amongst migrant workers on the East Rand" *Labour, Capital and Society* 18, 2, 1985.

31. W.Beinart, "Worker Consciousness, ethnic particularism and nationalism: the experience of a South African migrant, 1930–60" in Marks and Trapido, eds., *Race, Class and Nationalism; J.Guy and M.Tabane "Technology, Ethnicity and Ideology: Basotho Miners and Shaft Sinking on the South African Gold Mines" *JSAS* 14, 2, 1988. P.Delius "Sebatakgomo; Migrant Organisation, the ANC and the Sekhukhuneland Revolt" *JSAS* 15, 4, 1989.

32. See particularly M.Taussig, *The Devil and Commodity Fetishism in South America* (Chapel Hill, 1980); J.Nash, *We Eat the Mines and the Mines Eat Us; Dependency and Exploitation in Bolivian Tin Mines* (New York, 1979).

33. On human sacrifice, cf. Fondation pour l'Histoire des Suisses à l'Etranger, Geneva (FHS), Liengme diary 20 July 1893 and 24 December 1893; Junod, "Les Baronga" *Bulletin de la Société Neuchâteloise de Géographie (BSNG)* X, 1898, 390; Junod, *Life of a South African Tribe* (London, first ed., 1912, new ed., 1927) II,383, 405, 413n.1.

34. A point made by John and Jean Comaroff, citing Hobsbawm, in their *Ethnography and the Historical Imagination* (Boulder, Colo. and London, 1992) 14.

35. *Primitive Rebels* (London, 1959), pp.2–3, 175.

36. Cobb, *Promenades* (Oxford, 1980) 3.

37. C.Geertz, *Local Knowledge* (Basic Books, New York, 1983) 44. See also J. Clifford, *The Predicament of Culture* (Havard U.P., Cambridge, Mass., 1988).

38. 'From the door of his tent: the fieldworker and the inquisition' in J.Clifford and G.Marcus *Writing Culture: The poetics and politics of ethnography* (Berkeley and Los Angeles, 1986) 83. G.Marcus and M.Fischer, *Anthropology as Cultural Critique* (Chicago, 1986)30–31; Geertz, *Local Knowledge* 58–9.

39. cf. W.Sewell, *Work and Revolution in France: the language of labour from the Old Regime to 1848* (Cambridge, 1980); C.Koepp and L.Kaplan, *Work in France: representations, meaning, organisation, and practice* (Ithaca, 1986); J.Scott, *Gender and the Politics of History* (New York, 1988); P. Joyce, *Visions of the People: Industrial England and the Question of Class, 1840–1914* (Cambridge, 1991).

40. R.Darnton, "Intellectual and Cultural History", 346; ibid., *The Great Cat Massacre* (New York, 1984); D.W.Cohen "Doing social history from Pim's doorway" in O.Zunz, *Reliving the Past: the Worlds of Social History* (Chapel Hill, 1985) 207, 228; T.Ranger, *Dance and Society in East Africa* (London, 1975), 13, 105, 122–23, 164–66; D.W.Cohen and E.S.Atieno Odhiambo, *Siaya: the Historical Anthropology of an African Landscape* (London, 1989).

41. Two important recent collections on cultural history are L.Hunt, ed., *The New Cultural History* (Berkeley and Los Angeles, London, 1989) and R.Chartier, *Cultural History: Between Practices and Representations* (Oxford, 1988).

42. Jean and John Comaroff, *Of Revelation and Revolution: Christianity, Colonialism, and Consciousness in South Africa* (Chicago, 1991); Cohen, "Pim's doorway", 222. On the notion of cultural capital, see P.Bourdieu, *Distinction: a social critique of the judgement of taste* (London, 1984).
43. Q.Skinner, "Hermeneutics and the role of history" *New Literary History* 7, 1, 1975, 216. F.Jameson, *The Political Unconscious: Narratives as a Socially Symbolic Art* (Ithaca, 1975) 129.
44. Cf. J.Vansina, "Knowledge and perceptions of the African past" in B.Jewsiewicki and D.Newbury, eds., *African Historiographies: What History for Which Africa?* (Beverley Hills, 1986) 31–2, 40.
45. Geertz, "Blurred genres: the refiguration of social thought" in his *Local Knowledge*.
46. An approach stressed by M.Foucault, *The Archaeology of Knowledge* (New York, 1972) 22.
47. Jeeves, *Mining Labour in South Africa's Mining Economy: the Struggle for the Gold Mines' Labour Supply, 1890–1920* (Kingston and Johannesburg, 1985).
48. On the subtle dialectic of accommodation and resistance, and the need for industrial employers to gain the consent of wage workers, see particularly Joyce, *Visions of the People* and M.Burawoy, *The Politics of Production* (London, 1985).
49. From a vast literature on migrant labour, I cite M.Burawoy, *Politics of Production*, 103ff; R.Johnson, *Peasant and Proletarian: The Working Class of Moscow in the late Nineteenth Century* (Leicester, 1979); I.Katznelson, and A. Zolberg eds., *Working Class Formation* (Princeton, 1986); M.Hanagan, *Nascent Proletarians: class formation in post-revolutionary France* (Cambridge, Mass., 1989).
50. The quote is from Johnstone, "Labour history", 103.
51. For workers in the northern hemisphere, see P.Joyce, ed., *The Historical Meanings of Work* (Cambridge, 1987). J.Fabian makes the same point in his "Kazi: the conceptualisation of labor in a charismatic movement among Swahili-speaking workers" *Cahiers d'Etudes Africaines* 50, 1971.

1

Environment, Culture
and Migration

Well over three hundred years after the first Portuguese set foot on the shores of Delagoa Bay, the Lusitanian empire retained only a fragile presence in the area. In 1843 the governor of Lourenço Marques wrote despondently that the outpost perched on the northern edge of the bay "lay at the mercy of the blacks, who are acquainted with our weaknesses and have hemmed us within the confines of our fort."[1] The obscure trading settlement was manned by an unruly garrison, was visited by only a handful of vessels every year, and was a source of plunder for neighbouring chiefdoms. Some 280 miles to the north life was equally turbulent at Inhambane, a notorious centre for the export of slaves.[2] Slavery experienced a slow death at these "outposts of progress." In 1863 well over a third of the population at Lourenço Marques was made up of slaves and *degredado* convicts shipped from Lisbon to Africa; at Inhambane some 3,200 slaves laboured on the plantations around the town.[3]

In the years immediately after the Gaza civil war of 1858–1862, Lourenço Marques fell under an expansionist Swazi kingdom, the shadow of which fell over most of the central and northern Delagoa Bay hinterland. To the south of the Bay the Tembe and Maputo chiefdoms were under the sway of their powerful Zulu neighbour, while to the north of the Limpopo the Gaza established an empire stretching to the Sabi, Buzi, and even Zambezi rivers. Sandwiched between the Gaza empire and the sea, a number of small chiefdoms retained a shaky independence; those people living around the Portuguese settlement at Inhambane were generally termed Tongas while the bowmen living in stockades along the coast to the south of the settlement were called Chopis.[4] The two largest chiefdoms in the Delagoa Bay region, each numbering about 20,000 people, were the Khosa, who faced the Gaza across the Limpopo River, and the Maputo. Between them lay several other smaller chiefdoms.[5]

Anthropologists and historians have used the boundaries of ethnic classification to bring a neat, Cartesian logic to our understanding of the peoples of southern Mozambique. The Ndau living north of the Save River have become Shona, the Amatonga have become Tsonga, and the Tonga and Chopi are portrayed as distinct

1

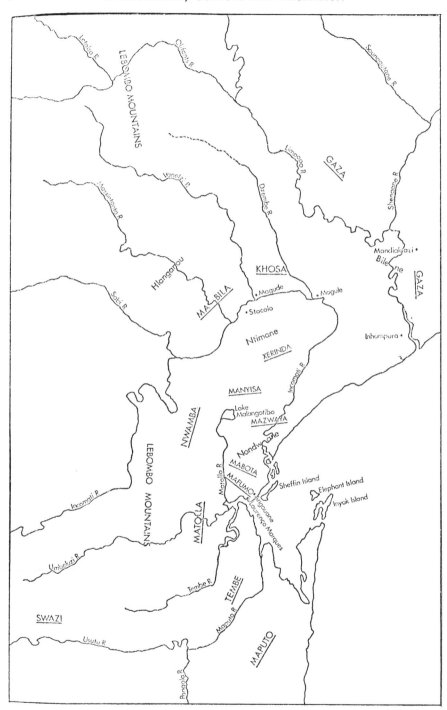

"The Delagoa Bay Region"

cultural groups separated by historical boundaries. Yet most of these terms were originally employed by the Gaza Nguni as a means of delineating themselves from surrounding people who had not adopted their customs. It was only around the turn of the century that these imposed labels took on a new unity and logic as linguists and later anthropologists and administrators erected boundaries, fixed in space and rooted in a mythological past, that separated people into distinct communities. Migrant labour was to play a crucial role in transforming these imagined communities into ethnic groups whose members were conscious of their shared interests. Thus, although classificatory terms like Chopi, Tonga, and Amatonga make society more intellectually manageable, they should be treated with some caution and one should avoid extrapolating into the past the form and function of ethnic groups that were only to emerge in the twentieth century.[6] It is tempting, for instance, to give a term like *amatonga* the bounded inclusiveness of a modern ethnic category. But the Gaza, Zulu, and others employed the word to distinguish themselves from subject neighbours, and gradually the term became a synonym for inferiority and meanness. It was impossible "to define the limits of Amatongas, Butongas, Tongas etc," wrote the explorer St. Vincent Erskine. "These are not tribal appellations and one might as well try to define the limits of the 'Kafirs.' Tonga simply means something which is not Zulu."[7] Nevertheless the word "amatonga" became a social label employed by colonists in Natal and, according to what Amselle has called the "ethnological reason" of the period, entered their rudimentary system of ethnic classification;[8] Amatongas were distinguishable from Natal and Cape Kafirs and from the Sotho to the west. But the people given this appellation had a very different sense of identity, tied to clan and chief, and they considered the word "amatonga" a term of denigration.[9]

Politics and Identity

By the 1860s many people living in Gazaland had adopted aspects of the culture of their Ngoni rulers. These acculturated Ngoni were called Mabuyandlelas or Shangaans, and sometimes, by the Portuguese, Vatualizados. They were able to acquire high office in the Gaza administration and at one stage, both the governor of Bilene on the lower Limpopo, and the head of the Gaza army were drawn from their ranks. The process of acculturation was fluid and complex and many individuals who claimed to be of Gaza descent were unable to hide their lowly origins.[10] The most durable cultural traits distinguishing Gazas from Mabuyandlelas were food taboos on fish, pork, and fowls, differences of dialect, and the inability of indigenous women to speak chiNgoni, the Ngoni language.[11] Nor did the Gaza, like some autochthones, tattoo themselves or file their teeth. Although it was unusual for people to abandon their old culture entirely, it was important to be seen to be Gaza, for people who had not accepted the Ngoni culture were set apart, denigrated, and taxed as Amatongas.

The Gaza were themselves divided into two groups: the Jamene, the royal family and its relatives on the male side, and the Ngoni commoners who could trace their descent back to the lands south of the Pongola River.[12] Marriage and kinship were central to these divisions. Although commoner Ngoni women could only marry Gaza men, the latter could enter into several marriages by taking Mabuyandlela wives. Ngoni men were also encouraged to marry Zulu and Swazi women from other parts of Southern Africa, and the Gaza kings pursued an active policy of enticing Nguni immigrants northwards with presents, political positions, and brides.[13] Cattle were "all owned by the King, his relatives and a few notables," wrote St. Vincent Erskine, and men wishing to marry with cattle needed to be clients of the Gaza Nguni.[14] It was difficult for men to accumulate wealth independently of the king and even raiding was restricted by their sovereign's attempts to control access to guns and ammunition.[15]

Despite these aspects of centralized rule, the sprawling Gaza empire was not highly unified. The missionary linguist Henri Berthoud was to remark that it was only the Gaza, and those Mabuyandlelas who were often "more royalist than the king," who had any notion of being members of a unified state. The Gaza monarch did not have the power of his Zulu or Swazi peers. He had no military regiments (amabutho), through which young men laboured for the royal lineage rather than for their father's homestead, and he kept only a few hundred soldiers permanently at the Gaza capital, where they served as bodyguards and tax collectors.[16] Women of the royal family had to marry Jamene men. The Gaza king had marriage links with the major chiefs of his empire and it was these men, together with his regional governors and travelling representatives, who ruled the provinces.[17] They also supplied him with food, workers, and presents. The people paid official taxes (hlabisa) to local chiefs and separate taxes to the king's emissaries. But from an Amatonga perspective, there was frequently little distinction between tax-gathering and pillage. The sheer extent and poor communications of the Gaza kingdom encouraged men, often posing as Gazas, to emulate their superiors and defraud the powerless Amatonga. The Gaza king and his chiefs could only warn against, but seldom prevent, pillaging that became particularly ferocious during periods of food shortage.[18]

In Gazaland, as well as in the region south of the Limpopo, the following of each individual chief was made up of the members of various clans or kin groups. The unity of the clan was created and reinforced by various symbols; members shared a patronymic or xibongo, a common myth of origin, a marriage pattern stressing preferred endogamy, and they excluded non-kin, even within the same homestead, from worshiping at their ancestral altars or from drinking milk together. The clan was an ideological construct that provided its members with a sense of temporal and spatial belonging by fitting them into a range of accepted social relationships, and by situating them in a line of descent eight to ten generations deep. But a high degree of social segmentation and migration ensured that no clan was of "pure" descent or occupied one contiguous territory.[19]

In a society with a seasonal demand for labour and a low level of technological development, land and capital goods were less important as factors of production than labour. A high birth rate was fostered by such practices as polygamy, the levirate, and partible inheritance; celibacy was discouraged and sexual practices that did not lead to pregnancy were strictly controlled. But a high birth rate was offset by a mortality rate inflated by an extremely unhealthy climate, fluctuating food supplies, and an inveterate political instability. The consequent relative shortage of labour put a premium on the ability of a chief to attract followers to cultivate his fields, look after his cattle, increase his military strength, and provide him with payments in labour and kind. By attracting manpower from outside his clan, the chief was able to increase the amount of food produced under his supervision. It was also through his capacity to distribute food and provide security against the vagaries of climate and environment that the chief sustained the loyalty of his dependents and increased the size of his following.[20] Although there is often a thin line between migration and indigency, strong social and economic pressures discouraged vagabondage and pushed people to join a local chiefdom. Without a familiar patronym that placed them within the locally recognized system of social classification, outsiders were effectively nameless and lived beyond the pale of society in the manner of slaves who entered the community as aliens stripped of all identity.[21] In a society where the notion of moral economy hardly stretched beyond the clan and the chiefdom, captives were the socially dead, people without names, identities, or a place in the order of society. As outsiders without rights captives, particularly in Gazaland, were subjected to brutal treatment until "reborn" as slaves whose status would improve as they were socialised into their community of forced adoption.[22] In Gazaland rootless *populas* were looked down upon while to be "as poor as an *umfugazan*" was considered "a more heinous sin than in Europe."[23] Throughout most of southern Mozambique, the most institutionalised form of social incorporation was for an in-migrating outsider to *kondza*, or subjugate himself to a chief. This was a form of naturalisation through which, as the English term suggests, an immigrant lost his abnormality and was accepted into local society. In return for payments in labour, military service, and goods, the outsider and his followers were given sufficient land and labour to establish an independent household within a village or homestead.[24] Refugees in a desperate condition could pawn themselves or their children into a servile relationship that might be regarded as slavery. Because of the facility with which immigrants were incorporated into the chiefdom, the following of one individual chief was never restricted to a single clan or extended family.

People constructed a political consciousness of self and the other in various ways. The members of each chiefdom spoke a language form that distinguished them from their neighbours and reinforced the borders of their legal and moral community. The spatial unity of the chiefdom was both physical and intellectual. Its members possessed a knowledge of the minute detail of the landscape and its people, both living and dead, and they shared a fund of folksongs and tales, proverbs and riddles. The chief administered justice and invigilated over the forms of social knowledge and custom that regulated everyday life; he called up and protected the army with his war medicines, interceded with the ancestors, and generally controlled production strategies in such a way as to ensure the prosperity of his followers. He organized various rituals of integration, such as first fruits ceremonies and war rites, and was viewed as the representation and embodiment of the political unity of his followers.[25]

Men and women identified themselves as being "from the land of" the clan dominating a specific chiefdom; a person from the chiefdom ruled by the Maputo clan might refer to himself in the local linguistic form as *vakaTembe* or in Zulu as *abakwaTembe*—of the land of Tembe, the founding ancestor of the Maputo clan. These terms of identification were also sometimes used by a particular corporate group whose members defined their political allegiance within the clan in terms of their real or putative descent from a junior branch of the line started by the founding ancestor. These lineages provided the political ideology for large-scale group segmentation from the clan and chiefdom; a Maputo might refer to himself in a situational manner as a *vakaMaputo* (*abakwaMabudu* in Zulu), of the land of Maputo (Mabudu), the chief (1764–1782) who broke away from the senior house of the Tembe clan, or as *vakaMakasana* (*abakwaMakasana*), the grandson of Maputo, who ruled as chief of the clan from 1800 to 1854. In a similar way, people living in the lower Nkomati area occupied by the Mazwaya clan might refer to themselves in the local linguistic form as *wakaMakaneta* or *wakaMaketshe*, the grandfather of Makaneta.[26] The Portuguese often filled their maps with this form of naming by referring to, for example, the area occupied by the Tembe as "Catembe" or that of the Mfumo chiefdom neighbouring Lourenço Marques as "Camfuma."

The personal names given by parents to their children were abandoned at puberty and replaced by adult names, generally beginning with the personal prefixes Mu and Ma or Shi, or the titles Nwa and Mi, denoting "son of" and "daughter of." These names could change yet again if, for instance, the person moved to a new area or was possessed by a spirit. This system of naming was highly situational and provided the individual with a concept of self that was both spatially and temporally anchored. It was pragmatic and adaptable and allowed men and women to locate themselves within a wide range of social relationships. The chiefdom or *tiko* was referred to by Henri Junod as "the true national unit."[27] Its members were bound by a strong "sense of national spirit," remarked his colleague Arthur Grandjean gloomily from Khosen, for "no-one conceives of the possibility of detaching himself from the rest of the people and thus abandoning all the national customs in order to become a Christian."[28]

The continual movement of people and ideas caused the material culture of the chiefdom to change continually through adaptation, borrowing, and innovation. Political identity was rooted in the chiefdom, but it needs to be stressed that this identity was not based on a shared kinship or membership of a lineage or clan. The chiefdom was an open institution attracting and incorporating outsiders prepared to *kondza* to the chief. It was thus able to absorb the many refugees and other in-migrants displaced by famine, soil exhaustion, and warfare, together with those fleeing from ritual contamination with death, disease, and witchcraft. The point is that political institutions such as the chiefdom, and at a more local level the homestead, were corporate groups well adapted to handle and contain large numbers of uprooted people.

The chiefdom did not just soak up displaced people, it also acted as a turbine in generating the movement of people across the land. The hierarchical divisions within society pushed people disadvantaged by their birth or social position to migrate. The deep-rooted feelings of rivalry, jealousy, and exploitation produced by a narrow social intercourse undermined the unity of both the homestead and chiefdom. The frequency with which people left their home communities to settle in other areas was once perceived by anthropologists as a mechanism of conflict resolution. But the neat, functional coherence of notions of "segmentation" and "fission" often obscured the human dimension of the real, daily problems dividing local communities—problems that pitted sons against fathers and elder brothers; wives against their husbands, mothers-in-law, and senior wives; outsiders against insiders; and, in general, the marginalized against the advantaged members of society. When seen in these terms, the concepts of "segmentation" and "fission" do provide a useful indication of the ease with which people moved away from their old areas of settlement.

Social conflict was an important cause of emigration, particularly when it took the form of raiding and warfare. From the perspective of our place and time in history, only defensive wars are considered legitimate. But to the societies of southern Mozambique, small-scale warfare, or raiding, was a branch of production, a form of foreign policy and a means of advertising political loyalties, masculine virtues, and fighting skills. In a society where legal responsibility was bounded by membership of the clan and the chiefdom, and in the absence of a concept of natural frontiers, relations between the different chiefdoms were based on force. The dominant ideology allowed political alliances but no lasting peace, for man had to be mastered in the same way as the environment. During the frequent periods of food shortage, people turned to raiding to replenish their foodstocks or increased their numbers by seizing neighboring women and children.[29] During the second quarter of the nineteenth century, when the Delagoa Bay region had became a cockpit for the struggles between the Zulu, Gaza, and Swazi, men had adopted new military tactics and raiding had become a more serious business. The result was an ongoing political instability which, in combination with the ecological imbalance, increased the already precarious level of subsistence. People often fled to dry and inhospitable areas, in an attempt to hide from raiding parties in search of livestock and crops, or lived precariously on foods disdained by their persecutors.

Ecology

The coastal plain of southern Mozambique rises gradually from the sea to the Lebombos. To the west of these hills lies the Lowveld, which, in the nineteenth century, formed a parched and feverous zone dividing the coast from the escarpment. In the 1850s and 1860s it was only in the winter months, when the cold discouraged the spread of mosquitoes and tsetse, that pastoralists descended from the Highveld plateau to graze their cattle and hunt game in this region. The Lowveld is cut by a number of rivers that empty into the sea to the north of Delagoa Bay, and it was alongside these waterways that hunters, traders, and waves of emigrants made their way into the interior.

Drought is a frequent visitor to the coastal plain where the light and irregular rainfall is swallowed by sandy soils and intense summer temperatures. The land is generally infertile and acidic but is cut by alluvial flood plains that, as in the case of the lower Limpopo, at some points reach a width of twelve miles. In these areas it was often possible to harvest two crops in one year; the first on the high ground next to the river in summer and the second in autumn after the arrival of flood waters and alluvium.[30] Some good agricultural land existed along the coast and in the marshlands to the south, but even in these areas frequent subsistence crises were triggered by insufficient rain in November or December. This was considered "a dreadful misfortune" by Henri Junod, for "famine will certainly follow as cereals can only be sown during these two months and famine means not only suffering and anguish, but often death."[31]

In most of the Delagoa Bay region, much of the original subtropical forest had been turned into wood and bushland by intensive cultivation and grazing, and the large patches of remaining forest cover were almost entirely uninhabited. These were inhospitable areas where the gods of the bush, the *psikwembu psa Nhoba*, and other malicious and hostile spirits waylaid and attacked travellers.[32] The unpre-

dictable climate and harsh environment forced people to live in enclaves of settlement, most visbly in the Shengane and Limpopo river flood plains.[33] The fertile
plain of the lower Nkomati also supported a particularly dense population estimated, in 1880, to be about 350 inhabitants to the square mile. In the south, water
was again the major consideration, and the Maputo clustered in dense settlements
around rivers and marshes.[34] In sharp contrast, the dry inland areas were almost
deserted while the sandy soils to the south and west of Lourenço Marques supported a population of about six persons per square mile.[35] In all these regions,
adverse climatic conditions could suddenly turn a pattern of dense settlement into
one of critical overpopulation. The most immediate response to famine was for a
large part of the affected population to move, either temporarily or permanently.

The silent, anonymous, and impersonal forces of climate and environment
were not the only pressures that caused people to shift to new areas of settlement.
The concentration of population and wealth in restricted areas, and the instability
of agricultural production, fostered a high degree of political insecurity throughout the region. The problems caused by an upset in the ecological balance were
often magnified by human agency as people sought to replenish their stocks of
food and livestock by seizing those of their neighbours. Through infinite repetition, flight from the tandem of famine and warfare had become a traditional response to adversity, most visibly expressed by the waves of emigration from the
coastal plain to the Highveld, and by the social heterogeneity of the chiefdoms.[36]
Migration was to take a new direction in the 1850s, when the first labour migrants
made their way south.

Emigration was not the only response to a fragile ecological balance. The nutritional trends in the region were marked by cultural flexibility and innovation. In
the mid-nineteenth century various strains of sorghum and especially millet
formed the staple diet of the people of the coastal plain. But newer foodstuffs had
also entered the local diet. Cassava had arrived from Brazil in the 1770s and a century later was cultivated "in small quantities" along the coast. Maize had probably
entered the area at roughly the same time, but was initially limited to areas of fertile soil with regular supplies of water.[37] Cassava, sweet potatoes, and groundnuts
were particularly important as famine-breakers as they grew well in sandy soils.
Rice and low-grade sugar-canes were cultivated in the wetter areas, pumpkins
were grown for their leaves, and fruit and watermelons, bambarra nuts, and cow-
peas were all popular. Mung beans were particularly important because of their
resistance to drought and because, harvested in May, they were the last crop to
ripen. In the drier areas cultivators planted a wide range of crops, moved to areas
of ground water in the dry season, and practised a slash-and-burn, mobile system
of farming.[38]

November and December were frequently months of hunger when little food
was left in the granaries and much energy had to be expended in cultivating the
soil. During this time of the year, and especially during periods of drought, people
could not rely on cultivated crops. The most important famine-breakers were fruits
gathered from the commonage separating the various homesteads and in the dry
interior. The mafureira almond of the Natal mahogany (nkuhlu; Trichilia emetica) ripened in November and December. The pulp of this fruit was an important foodstuff, while the nut was rich in the edible fat called mafura. The pulp of the fruit of
the dull-leaved kwakwa tree (Strychnos innocua) was dried or smoked and then

pounded into a storable flour or baked into a cake. The monkey orange (*nsala; Strychnos spinosa*) was "very invigorating," noted Junod and, as it matured in the early stages of the hunger season, he considered it "a great and precious resource in times of shortage."[39] The fruit of the wild plum (*bukanye; Herpethyllum caffrum*) was made into a nutritious beer whose brief longevity and great popularity resulted in boisterous beer drinks. The plums were also an important source of food as they arrived during the "period of regular famine," explained Junod, "just in time to prevent people from dying of hunger."[40] St. Vincent Erskine caustically remarked that "fruit in a Tonga's mind is synonymous with drink and they turn everything of that kind into liquor." Beer served as a means of storing perishable fruits, and Junod considered it "as much a foodstuff as it is a drink."[41] Various other wild fruits were gathered, almost all of which were transformed into nutritious drinks. At harvest time sorghum, millet, and maize beers were consumed in great quantities and, because of the facility with which cereals were stored, were drunk for much of the year.

Communal drinking was an expression of collective identity that, through the propitiation of the ancestors, bound present and past generations. Beer drinks were also a rite of renewal, marking the passage of the seasons and calling for the ancestors' blessings, and they were a means of commemorating important progressions in life, such as birth, marriage, and death. Drink served as a libation and as a central element in rituals that created community borders. It advertised largesse and hierarchy, marked the passage of time, and punctuated spells of hard labour with periods of rest. But this was not the interpretation of European observers shocked by the inebriation of entire communities, including women and sometimes children, during seasonal festivities. Europeans who had been separated from the preindustrial culture of their grandparents and who gauged their moral and racial superiority in terms of values such as sobriety and discipline, viewed unsympathetically a pattern of work that alternated periods of intense labour, as at harvest time, with long periods of idleness. They saw labour as something distinct from leisure, and interpreted revelries that consumed "the working day," and contradicted the notion of labour discipline, as debauched and "Bacchanalian orgies."[42]

Various plants such as tomatoes, onions, pineapples, water-lily bulbs, and water chestnuts were either cultivated on farmland or, like fruit, were gathered on the communal land of the chiefdom. Trees provided wooden poles for construction, various implements and utensils, mortars, canoes, and, especially, fuel for cooking and heating. Fresh- and sea-water fishing was practised and several kinds of Crustacea and molluscs were gathered throughout the year. Fish were caught in tidal basket traps, in specially constructed weirs, and, often from sailing boats, on a hook and line. The collective fish hunt or *tjeba* often involved several hundred people and was an important source of food during the hungry period preceding the rains of November and December, which brought the flood waters down from the Highveld and replenished the lakes.[43]

The meat derived from hunting small game and from foraging for large land snails, tortoises, lizards, and locusts was an important famine-breaker and source of protein. Men who hunted game in order to provide food for their families were called *bahloti*, and were distinguished from professional hunters called *amapisi*. They generally hunted in the dry winter season when the low bush cover increased visibility and the mobility of wild animals was restricted by the lack of ground water and palatable grasses. This was also the period of the year when men could be spared from agricultural activities, when summer diseases such as malaria, tick-bite fever, and dysentery were less virulent and when rivers, no longer swollen by summer rains, presented fewer obstacles to travellers. Game was hunted for meat and skins, and animal fat was used as a body oil and in the softening of hides.

Cattle pastured on the clan commonage were an important bridewealth medium whose ritual slaughter on special occasions brought prestige to their owners. But their ultimate importance lay in their "convertibility" to beef during times of famine. Cattle provided milk, hides, cleansing fat, horns, dung fertilizer, and a dung cement used in the construction of hut floors and walls. Although beef was a prized famine-breaker, the ecology and political geography of the Delagoa Bay region severely limited cattle-keeping. Five species of tsetse fly, each adapted to a specific floral and faunal environment, made trypansomiasis endemic to the area. The most virulent and widespread fly was *Glossina morsitans*, which lived essentially off ungulates, rather than the water and bush cover favoured by other species.[44] Because of the ease with which tsetse flies moved and multiplied, trypanosomiasis at times took on epidemic proportions and could cause the depopulation of an area.[45] But, because the flies lived in belts or patches that could be circumvented by knowledgeable guides, the presence of trypanosomiasis did not everywhere preclude the importation of cattle.

Cattle diseases like trypanosomiasis, as well as the gall-sickness, heartwater, and biliary fever carried by ticks, were particularly virulent during summer and could decimate herds when the animals' physical resistance was reduced due to drought. As cattle were highly visible, mobile, and valuable, they constituted an ideal form of booty for any raiding party. Because of this, people often preferred to keep pigs and fowls, scavengers avoided by Gaza, Swazi, and Zulu raiders, or goats, which were resistant to the blood parasites carried by the tsetse fly. Despite the broad base of their economy and a varied diet, a precarious balance existed between humans and their environment and food supplies were unpredictable. People had no way of controlling the pattern of rainfall, the migration of game, the raiding habits of their neighbours, or the diseases that suddenly infected an area. The spectre of hunger was ever present and seasons of plenty were followed by years of famine. Yet it would be wrong to see human existence as shaped and determined by the towering forces of climate and environment; people moved, adopted new crops, opened up and colonized forest lands, entered into new political relationships, accumulated goods and followers, and in various other ways blunted the autocracy of nature.

I now want to leave the slow-moving forces of environment, climate, and custom that exercised an important influence on daily life, and turn to the conjuncture of events that were to push the first labour emigrants southwards from the Delagoa Bay region. In 1860–1861 climatic conditions in the vicinity of the bay were sufficiently clement to allow the production of a sizeable agricultural surplus.[46] But the following year the region was struck by the drought gripping most of southern Africa and famine broke out in areas already ravaged by the Gaza civil war. According to the governor of Lourenço Marques, the drought was marked by a "great loss of foodstuffs . . . [and] worsened by war." Oral testimony collected thirty-eight years later recalled a famine lasting five years that, together with war, devastated the land.[47] As statistics on the agricultural output of African producers are nonexistent, the price of cereals remains the best index of the general shortage of food during the drought. From May 1862 to October 1863 the official price of millet at Lourenço Marques rose from 172 neis (or $172 worth approximately 11d) to $590 (neis) per *panja* (a measurement equal to slightly over ¾ bushel). The price of maize multiplied four times, from $172 in May 1862 to $690 in October 1864, before reaching a peak of 1$150 per *panja* in May 1865.[48]

In February 1862 the Gaza king Umzila lost most of his cattle to the Swazi forces led by his exiled brother Mawewe.[49] The animals that escaped the warring armies were soon decimated by a strain of peripneumonia that, by August 1862, had killed "almost all" the Gaza cattle. In the area around Lourenço Marques, more than three thousand cattle succumbed to this "lungsickness" while a further five thousand were thought to have perished because of the drought and war.[50] On the lower Limpopo a cattle epidemic, presumably that of 1862–1863, wiped out the indigenous breed of cattle.[51] The great losses suffered by people throughout southern Africa incited the Swazi to descend from the mountains and plunder the plainsmen of their remaining herds. In two short years, the Delagoa Bay region was stripped of its major source of protein. Death from starvation was rare but patterns of famine and mortality were intimately linked, as hunger bred nutritional deficiencies, weakened human resistance to disease, and triggered an inevitable spate of raiding. The trilogy of famine, war, and disease operated in a circular manner as hunger was both an outcome and a cause of war. This was graphically expressed by a Gaza ambassador sent to Natal when he remarked that "death from the assagai is invariably followed by worse death from fever, for these two kinds of death are the constant companions one of the other."[52] Missionaries familiar with the area also noticed that "famine, locusts, drought and war . . . often go together," and a southern axiom held the arrival of locusts to "announce the Gaza armies."[53]

"Delagoa Bay fever" had always presented the most effective barrier to the colonization of the area. The sickness that struck fear into the hearts of visiting Europeans and Africans was probably made up of three distinct diseases. Malaria and yellow fever were mosquito-borne, while the main vector of typhoid fever was the body louse. The prevalence of these fevers gave the wet, low-lying coastal areas a fearful reputation, particularly in summer. The Gaza king readily acknowledged "General Bush and General Fever" to be his most powerful allies; he "does not fight with arms," St. Vincent Erskine was informed, "but with disease and the elements."[54]

The indigenous inhabitants suffered less from malaria and yellow fever than did foreigners. Nevertheless, many people, especially children, suffered from impaludism which lowered their resistance to disease, induced miscarriages, and could result in death.[55] Unlike many other diseases, malaria was not related to malnutrition and poor living conditions, and it counted among its victims wives of the Gaza king and locally powerful chiefs. The anopheles mosquitoes that acted as host carriers for the malarial blood parasites multiplied rapidly after heavy rains extended their marshy breeding grounds. Malaria and especially yellow fever were also spread by people who, in seeking the most effective remedy in flight from an infected area, carried the parasites to regions where they were quickly spread by formerly uncontaminated anopheles mosquitoes. Because of the facility with which the disease moved and expanded, a sudden outbreak of malaria could lead to the flight of the local population.[56] During the summer months, particularly before the draining of the swamp around Lourenço Marques in 1877, the town was considered a death trap.

The worst epidemic, as opposed to endemic, disease to infect the Delagoa Bay region was smallpox, which swept through the area at least four times in the thirty years following 1862. Between May and August of that year the disease "laid waste the negro population" and killed "hundreds of blacks and some whites" in the Crown lands claimed by the Portuguese.[57] In Lourenço Marques the mortality rate was so appalling that people threw the corpses of the dead into the surf or buried them in shallow graves. By May 1863 the epidemic had retreated to the interior, where it caused a further great loss of life.[58] Other debilitating and widespread diseases afflicting the area were various respiratory problems, measles, bilharzia, tick-bite fever, conjunctivitis, and trachoma. Gastro-intestinal problems known generally as "dysentery" were especially prevalent during the hunger period when people turned to less digestible, contaminated foods and drank polluted water.[59] The tropical leg ulcers know as *leishmaniasis* were caused by parasites that bored into feet and legs, causing sores and gangrene. Trichinosis was carried by pigs infected with the protozoal filaria worm, the cause of elephantiasis. Poor living conditions, when combined with nutritional deficiencies, created the preconditions for the rapid spread of epidemics. Pole-and-dagga dwellings encouraged the proliferation of numerous parasites, such as the typhus-carrying body louse and the plague flea. Poor ventilation fostered respiratory problems and a lack of clean clothing encouraged the spread of contagious diseases. A British official passing through Maputoland towards the end of the century commented on the precariousness of life. "The men and women appear to die young," he remarked,

> We only saw one man and one old woman in the country; these two may have been from 60 to 70 years of age. With these exceptions we did not see a single man or woman, who I should say, was over 45 years of age. The death rate must be enormous during the hot season.[60]

Another traveller passing from Lydenburg to Lourenço Marques commented on the distended bellies of the children he met and compared their physical condition unfavorably with that of children in Swaziland.[61]

A high mortality rate, particularly amongst infants, reduced the size of the population and limited the number of children brought to marriage age by a single father. Various cultural practices indicate the high prevalence of infant mortality, as well as the need to restrict the family to a size that could be supported by local resources. For several months the child was considered *shilo* (a thing) or *khuna* (an incomplete being) and only became *nkulu* (a grown up child) after a recognized rite of passage. Premarital sexual relations (*gangisa*) helped to delay marriage and childbirth by allowing external intercourse and even, although it was frowned upon, full intercourse.[62] Prohibitions on sexual intercourse were imposed when men were away on hunting, trading, or military expeditions, for up to eight days after the onset of menstruation and for three months after a miscarriage, and for as much as eighteen months while mothers breast-fed their children. This protected young infants from the malnutrition and related pneumonia-diarrhea complex brought on when the birth of a younger sibling resulted in early weaning. A similar rationale lay behind the practice, in some chiefdoms, of killing one of the newly born twins.[63]

Mobility as a Resource

Another means of struggling against a fate dominated by nature entailed participating in economic activities that took men far from home. Hunting produced meat, skins, bones, and animal fats. A large market for furs and skins had developed in the second quarter of the nineteenth century with the adoption by males of the dress patterns of the surrounding Zulu, Swazi, and Gaza. The old plaited palm leaf covering used to protect the male genitalia was replaced by two flaps of ox or buck skin and, on special occasions, by an expensive kilt of up to sixty strips of monkey, genet, or civet cat skins, each cut roughly six inches long and half an inch wide, and twisted into a tail. Soldiers hung genet tails from their military and dancing shields, wore blue monkey skin strips over the side of the face with leopard and other skin headbands, and topped these with crane, ostrich, and other bird feathers. Lion and leopard skins and claws were worn by chiefs.[64] A profitable trade in these items also developed with the Gaza, Zulu, and Swazi.

The most important product of the hunt and the major export from mid-nineteenth century Lourenço Marques was elephant ivory. When the Portuguese first opened Lourenço Marques to foreign trade in 1852, a number of European and Indian merchants had established themselves around the fort and their activities had revolutionised the ivory trade.[65] They brought powerful and expensive elephant guns to the Delagoa Bay region, as well as the gun powder, lead, tin, spare parts, percussion caps, and other supplies needed to slaughter elephants. Official ivory exports from Lourenço Marques more than doubled between 1846–1859, increasing from 25,000 to 57,000 lbs.[66] But ivory is a wasting asset and this new firepower caused the ivory frontier to retreat away from the settlement. As late as the 1840s, elephants were still to be found close to the bay, but fifteen years later the best hunting fields were in Maputoland and to the north of the Limpopo.[67] The Zulu chief Mpande was to complain several times that Lourenço Marques hunters were operating in his territory without his permission, and the governor of the settlement warned in 1859 that the uncontrolled slaughter of elephants by "hundreds of hunters" was pushing the animals away from the settlement.[68]

A new professionalism was demanded of hunters as the retreating elephant herds required a greater investment on the part of merchants. It seems that the caste of hunters known as *amapisi* emerged at this time.[69] They developed a distinct material culture which separated them from the *batimba* hippopotamus hunters, the *bahloti* local hunters, and the slaves employed by merchants at Lourenço Marques. The wealth of the *amapisi* was reputedly second only to that of the chiefs, and their exploits were remembered in oral traditions.[70] Their style of dress advertized their high status and their involvement in the world market economy: they wore coats, blankets, and skins, and carried bandoliers, powder horns, and hunting knives. They developed special skills in order to hunt with heavy calibre guns and became renowned for their acumen in purchasing hunting goods. The *amapisi* were united by a strong fellowship of common protective charms, songs, incantations, purification rituals, rites, and taboos, and they employed their own diviners. A recognized hunting code determined ownership in cases where, for example, two men shot the same animal or a wounded beast had to be killed in a thicket. These rules and regulations held the *amapisi* apart from the mainstream of society and minimized the social disruption caused by their foreign experiences. As the *amapisi* could spend sometimes a year or more away from home, they were paid advances before they undertook a journey, and their families, perhaps acting as a security for creditors, were looked after in their absence. Traders generally lent expensive guns and ammunition to the *amapisi* and other elephant hunters on condition that they receive a fixed part of the ivory collected in the interior. The hunting expeditions were often large and rambling affairs, made up of ten to twenty hunters, each of whom was accompanied by as many as twenty porters.[71]

Lourenço Marques ivory merchants were frequently wealthy and had close ties with colleagues in the Transvaal. Many were Portuguese Indians from Gao, Diu, and Damão who were generically called "Banians," although often Muslim or Christian. Together with a number of Portuguese merchants, they established and built upon existing trade routes to the Highveld and constructed shops in rural areas and frontier settlements such as Ohrigstad, Lydenburg, Schoemansdal and Rhenosterpoort. Ignacio and Antonio Paiva de Raposo, João Albasini, and Cassimir Simoëns, who left £40,000 on his death, are perhaps the best known of these traders. But numerous others also played a significant role in the ivory trade and gained political importance through their marriages to the daughters of Boer and African notables; it is regrettable that their history remains so obscure.[72]

Elephant ivory exported through Delagoa Bay was of a good colour, size, and quality for carving and was generally sent to India for manufacture into *galang* marriage bracelets, or re-exported from Bombay to London.[73] Hippopotamus hunting became important at the beginning of the nineteenth century when it was discovered that hippo ivory could be manufactured into dentures and rifle foresights. A bull hippopotamus also produced large quantities of flavour-free fat for casking, as well as numerous hide whips. The rhinoceros was hunted for its horn, which was either exported to the Far East to be manufactured into aphrodisiacs, or was carved into snuffboxes after the Zulu fashion. The depletion of the elephant herds in the Delagoa Bay area was caused by hunters operating out of Lourenço Marques, Boers who had established themselves on the Highveld in the late 1840s, and hunters from Natal. The Boers wrought a "fearful slaughter" of elephants during the tsetse-free winter months when they moved into the Lowveld and crossed the Lebombos with their guns, horses, and wagons. In summer, when trypansomiasis and malaria prevented the use of horses and dogs and long grass obscured the game, the Zoutpansberg Boers employed black hunters, called *swartskuts*, in the "hundreds if not thousands" on a credit basis similar to that practised at Lourenço Marques.[74] By the mid-1850s some two thousand elephants were killed every year in the vicinity of the Zoutpansberg region and about 198,000 lbs of ivory was exported to Durban and, to a lesser extent, to Lourenço Marques.[75]

To the south of Lourenço Marques, groups of well-equipped hunters operated in the Maputo and Tembe areas with the backing of Natal merchants. Much of the product of these hunts was sent back to Natal in vessels such as the *Herald*, the longboat of an emigrant ship converted at Durban into a seaworthy craft. In the late 1850s the *Herald* was joined by a small number of coastal schooners, very few of which ever declared their cargoes at the Portuguese settlement.[76] When the Gaza king, Mawewe, attempted to limit the destruction of the elephant herds by imposing heavy taxes on hunters, he incurred the wrath of the merchants at Lourenço Marques and their allies in the interior.[77] During the Gaza civil war these men provided Umzila with riflemen, guns, money, and a place of refuge. This support was in large measure responsible for Umzila's victory over Mawewe in 1862. By the end of the year, twelve hundred hunters armed with guns were operating out of Lourenço Marques and the slaughter of game was such as to cause the governor to warn that uncontrolled hunting would exterminate or drive away the elephant herds.[78] During the war the amount of ivory exported from Lourenço Marques had fallen, from 72,600 lbs in 1860 to 23,630 lbs in 1862–1863;[79] but by 1863–1864 some 90,000 lbs of ivory, together with large quantities of hippo ivory and rhino horn, were exported through the port.[80]

Hunting was not the only long-distance economic activity, for many people had learnt to capitalize on their position as natural middlemen in the trade with the interior. Parents fostered a respect in their children for the skills, wealth, courage, and knowledge of traders who, like the *amapisi*, had their own songs and rites of incorporation.[81] A well-established commercial network linked the coastal plain with the Highveld and long caravans of hunter-traders and porters made their way along the rivers linking the escarpment to the coast. The mineral springs on the Nkomati River bend served as a meeting ground for traders making their way from Lourenço Marques to the Uanetzi and Olifants rivers. From the Olifants three routes led into the Transvaal. The northern route led to the Olifants-Selati confluence and the rich copper- and iron-producing Phalaborwa area. Another passed up the Great Letaba to salt mines at Eiland and the hunting grounds of Modjadji. The most important route followed the Small Letaba River to salt-producing Soutini, the iron deposits of Tshimbupfe and Magoro Kop, and the Spelonken Hills. From Albasini's fortified farm at Goedewensch, traders made their way to the saltpans of the western Zoutpansberg and the iron- and copper-producing areas to the north. Another route from Goedewensch led up the Levubu or Pafuri River and eastwards to Inhambane, while a third took traders southwards to Delagoa Bay via the northern Uanetzi and Limpopo rivers. Merchants arriving from the interior frequently made their way to riverside entrepots from where they transported their goods in canoes, rafts, or flat-bottomed sailing vessels.[82]

Throughout the eighteenth and early nineteenth centuries large volumes of cloth and beads were imported through Lourenço Marques and Inhambane to be traded throughout the Highveld to the edge of the Kalahari, across the Limpopo, and to the border of the Cape Colony.[83] Imported cloth became a major item of trade on the coast, where it undermined the manufacture of local cloths woven on horizontal looms, while to the east of the Lebombos the Portuguese term *peça* (a piece of cloth two fathoms in length) was of such currency as to be incorporated into various indigenous languages.[84] The lack of ore deposits in the Delagoa Bay region made metals a major article of long-distance trade. Heavy copper and brass rings worn on the arm, ankle, and neck were considered a sign of distinction and were used as a medium of bridewealth and tribute payment. Unworked bars or rings of brass brought through Lourenço Marques found a ready market and imported copper manillas served as a form of currency.[85] The lotus-shaped marriage hoe, brought from its area of production in the northern Transvaal, was readily exchanged over a wide area.[86] The introduction onto the Highveld of sweet potatoes, groundnuts, various millet strains, maize, cassava, and possibly tobacco, provides further evidence of the social intercourse between the peoples of the coast and the interior.[87]

Systems of Representation

The description of the relationship between people and their environment presented in this chapter is not aimed solely at providing a geographical setting. My object is to highlight the indomitable and often brutal struggle between people and nature that will underlie and weave its way through much of this story. People reacted to an immovable environment in ways that, over time, had been incorporated into their world view and daily behaviour. The manner in which they tilled the soil, hunted, fished, or moved to exploit a new environment was cyclical rather than innovative and, like their system of beliefs, changed far more slowly than the history of individuals or events. This is not to argue that human action was determined by the forces of nature, but rather to suggest that the culture and identity constructed by people, a central theme in this book, moved only slowly and gradually.

In this chapter I hope to have established two things. Firstly, that people developed a high degree of in-migration, whether as hunters or traders, or as refugees escaping a capricious environment. Whether in the form of a short, temporary migration or an extended out-migration, geographical movement was embedded within a network of cultural strategies. The practice of moving in search of a better livelihood, which was to become familiar under migrant labour, was nothing new. Secondly, I have attempted to break down the abstractions of structural analysis by looking at the patterns of behaviour of people who have left no written records. This is an approach, I believe, that allows a closer reading of their beliefs, feelings, and personal motivations. Another manner in which we may gain closer access to the way in which people in oral societies interpreted their world is through an analysis of folktales that present local forms of knowledge and wisdom. Behind the nonsense and the fantasy, the tales collected in the late nineteenth century by folklorists in southern Mozambique provide a means of assessing the mental world of "a people without history."[88]

Famine plays a central role in many of the stories.[89] The fear and respect with which famine is recalled is reinforced by other tales which express the common, everyday wish to eat one's fill and ward off hunger. An enchanted hoe tills "large fields in a moment," it produces "a splendid harvest," and fills the good woman's storehouses. Through his craftiness the hare, personified by the title "Mr.," "regales" himself on the lion's venison or the baboon's provisions. He "feasts" when an enchanted tree responds to his singing by dropping its fruit. The frog, who is even craftier than the hare, "gorges" himself on hippo meat with the aid of the loyal chameleon while others "regale themselves on meat." Happiness is synonymous with a full stomach, whether in a tale or in real life. For people living so close to subsistence, a solid meal occupied an important part of their thoughts.[90]

A full stomach is earned by guile or good actions, but, as the tales constantly recall, hard labour is the everyday reality. This is repeated in story after story by the image of people labouring in their fields, herding their cattle, drawing water, cutting wood, and performing other chores.[91] But famine remains an ever-present menace to which people respond by moving—to a nearby hillside or to the commonage where they pick wild fruit and vegetables.[92] Others move much further, and *kondza* to a distant chief whose patronage allows them to grow wealthy and famous; having succeeded in life, they sometimes return to their village of origin.[93] A central theme in the stories is the relationship between travelling and wealth. After a "long journey," a hunter comes upon "a land full of cattle . . . so many that they had eaten up all the grass and only the earth was left to them." Boys who leave home to live with their mother's brothers become wealthy and powerful as do travellers who, in the process of meeting giants, ogres, cannibals, and faceless enemies, acquire the knowledge and skills that produce wealth.[94] Proverbs such as "to travel makes one see" and "if you do not travel, you will marry your own sister" carry the same message.[95] The picture created by folktales reinforces the vision produced by everyday patterns of behaviour. To move was a socially constructed reflex; a natural, accepted way of seeking to exploit the environment.

A tradition of migration was ingrained in the pattern of everyday life long before opportunities emerged for men to sell their labour in Natal. Migrant labour emerged from within the context of local custom and practice. From the perspective of men living in the Delagoa Bay region, to migrate was a common-sense decision that rendered life more secure and predictable, like other economic activities involving travel. Because it was rooted in their lived experience, the decision to migrate required no major social adaptation. Nor was the concept of wage labour entirely unknown in the area, as men had for many years served as hunters, traders, or soldiers, or as sailors employed on the whalers operating in the Mozambique Channel. These work opportunities were limited, and it was only with the rise of a plantation economy several hundred miles to the south that men living in the Delagoa Bay region began actively to seek wage work. It was in the 1850s that hunter/traders first arrived from Natal with reports of the opportunities to earn money that existed in the territory, recently colonized by the British, to the south of Zululand.[96]

2

The Politics of
Sugar and Labour

Almost 300 miles to the south of Lourenço Marques, the British colony of Natal was transformed when 5,000 British colonists entered the region in the early 1850s. Many settled on the coast where a strip of land, 16–20 miles wide, was suitable for the raising of subtropical crops. Unlike most British colonists in the tropics, the Natal planters had no access to a proletariat of slave descent and they soon turned to the government to increase the work force by reducing the size of the African reserves. But the lieutenant-governor and the secretary for native affairs refused these demands, at least partly because the black peasantry provided the administration with its largest source of internal revenue.[1] As an alternative, the government initially apprenticed "Zulu" refugees, a number of whom, together with a handful of free labourers, came from the area north of Zululand. It was to these people, known in Natal as Amatongas, that the planters turned for labour.[2]

The importation of Amatongas was initially opposed by the lieutenant-governor, who refused to allow any immigration without his permission, as well as by the Colonial Office; the latter, mindful of the slavery practised openly at Lourenço Marques and Inhambane, was unwilling to recognise the validity of contracts entered into beyond the borders of Natal.[3] Nor were the up-country sheep and cattle ranchers, who dominated the legislature, prepared to subsidize the importation of plantation labour, and in 1857 they successfully blocked moves in this direction. Amatongas who wished to work in Natal officially had to enter the colony under the refugee scheme or under the charge of recruiters sanctioned by the government. But they were discouraged from seeking work by the low wages and long periods of apprenticeship and by the indiscriminate attacks to which they were subjected when crossing Zululand.[4]

The demand for labour on the coast rocketed with the price of sugar in 1857, a year in which recruiters applied to introduce three hundred Amatonga families into Natal.[5] But it was only two years later, when the monthly wages of fieldhands rose by almost 40 percent, that government sought to intervene directly in the labour market.[6] In that year three new laws were passed to aid the importation of foreign labour. Two dealt with Indian immigration, but the third, Law 13 of 1859, provided for government assistance in the transportation overland and by sea of Amatonga workers and their families. It was only in July 1863, however, as the sale of sugar took Natal into a period of unprecedented boom, that the government appointed John Dunn to supervise an Amatonga immigration scheme. This project never got off the ground, at least partly because workers were unwilling to sign three year contracts and demanded that they be allocated to the employer of their choice.[7] But its demise is attributable largely to the wavering confidence of the Natal government in the future of the coastal plantations. Overproduction and a collapse of the world market caused the price of sugar to drop sharply in 1863, and planters who had borrowed heavily during the boom years found themselves unable to repay the debts incurred by the importation of indentured Indians. Three years later the Natal government halted all Indian immigration and, in 1868, turned down the Gaza king's offers to assist the emigration of labour from his country.[8]

Despite the apathy of government officials, Amatonga and other African migrants continued to arrive in Natal; by the late 1860s, they had come to dominate the labour force on the coast. Without contemporary statistics it is impossible to gauge precisely the size and development of this early labour migration; but there is good impressionistic evidence that it was of some considerable size. In 1863, the Zulu king, Mpande, remarked that the amount of tribute paid to him by the Maputo had declined because of the large number of men working in Natal.[9] Two years later the governor of Lourenço Marques complained of the "great number of Maputo who have abandoned agriculture in favour of wage employment in Natal," and in 1866 he reported that the circulation of currency at the settlement was dependent on the sterling specie brought home by Maputo migrants.[10] According to oral tradition gathered at the turn of the century, labour migration started at the time of the death of the Gaza king Shoshangane (1858) and, during the reign of the Maputo chief Nozingile (1854–1876), "large numbers" of men sought work in various parts of South Africa.[11]

It is often thought that the sugar industry was built, from its earliest days, on indentured Indian labour.[12] Yet between 1866 and 1874 only African migrants entered Natal; in 1872, when there were up to eight thousand of these men on the plantations, only twenty-seven hundred Indians remained under indenture in the colony.[13] New strains of hardy cane had allowed planters to increase the amount of land under sugar from 860 acres in 1855 to 16,000 acres in 1869. Despite the moratorium on Indian immigration, the production of sugar in Natal increased from 1,500 tons in 1860 to almost 8,000 in 1868 and by more than 50 percent between 1866 and 1874.[14] Only a part of the African labour on the plantations was drawn from the coastal areas to the north of Zululand. Some workers were drawn from the Natal reserves, while many others came from the northern and eastern Transvaal and Basutoland.[15] These foreign Africans provided the majority of the labour required by the sugar industry during its crucial formative years.[16] At the end of the 1860s the labour shortage reemerged as Sotho and Pedi workers chose to leave Natal for the better-paid, newly discovered diamond fields of Griqualand West, as the indentures of the original Indian immigrants expired, and a disagreement between the Zulu and Maputo halted the movement of Amatongas.

The initial reaction of the planters to this reappearance of their labour problem was to redouble their demands for the government to force the black peasantry

The *William Shaw*. This 39-ton schooner was a pioneer in the coastal trade between Natal and Delagoa Bay. As Amatonga migrant workers were frequently pillaged of their wages and goods when crossing Zululand on foot, many chose to return home in vessels like the *William Shaw*.

onto the labor market. But the protective segregation practised by the Native Affairs Department under Theophilus Shepstone had been fully vindicated during the depression when customs revenues, claimed by the government to be the major form of European taxation, had more than halved while the hut tax had doubled.[17] But while the lieutenant-governor was unwilling to expel peasants from the reserves, he was equally reluctant to encourage the shipment of labour from "another Portuguese kidnapping station" or protect Amatongas travelling through Zululand, as this might upset Natal's uneasy relationship with the Zulu.[18]

In the face of the government's refusal to take action that would reduce the price of labour, the planters looked to Delagoa Bay as a port from which workers could be sent to Natal without having to pass through Zululand. Starting in mid-1867, hunters and traders operating in the Delagoa Bay region added migrant workers to the ivory, horns, and skins shipped south to Durban in small schooners such as the 39-ton *William Shaw*.[19] In 1871 a Labour League was created by two hundred Natal planters to regularise this labour supply. Their representatives contacted chiefs in the vicinity of Lourenço Marques, established reception huts in the town, and paid the governor of the settlement a 15s passport fee for each worker shipped south. The irony of this situation was not lost on colonial officials in Lisbon, for Britain had played a major role in the suppression of the slave trade from Mozambique and, more recently, had prevented the export of contracted workers to the sugar plantations on the French islands of the Indian Ocean. Nevertheless, the Portuguese were determined to profit from this unexpected but welcome upsurge in a traditional source of revenue, and they sought to control and tax the workers shipped from Delagoa Bay.

In late 1871 Lisbon attempted to force the Natal government into a formal agreement on the export of labour by cracking down on coastal schooners refusing to pass through the customs post at Lourenço Marques; the *Bibsy* was stopped with fifty-two workers on board, the *Roe* carrying about thirty men was threatened with seizure, and the *William Shaw*, which on a previous voyage had disembarked fifty workers on the beach outside Lourenço Marques and had picked up workers on nearby Sheffin Island, was confiscated when it landed workers up the Maputo River.[20] In response to these actions, and under pressure from the Natal planters, Britain laid claim to the southern shores of Delagoa Bay and two neighboring islands. In 1872 the border dispute was submitted for adjudication to the French president and negotiations over the shipment of labour were opened between Britain and Portugal. Meanwhile, the flow of Amatonga workers to Natal increased as steamships like the 160-ton *Pelham* and the 275-ton *Kate Tatham* started to ship workers out of Delagoa Bay. Well over 1,000 men were transported to Natal between October 1871 and September 1873 when, suddenly, the governor of Lourenço Marques was fired for allowing the illegal emigration of workers. The export of labour was then strictly prohibited until a settlement could be reached with the British over the territorial dispute.[21] In the meantime the position of the Natal government on the importation of labour overland had undergone a considerable change.

Migrant Labour: A Debate and a Discourse

Faced by the continuing refusal of the representatives of the imperial authorities in the colony either to import labour or to force local blacks to work, the planters on the coast formed an alliance with the up-country farmers. In late 1870 this coalition successfully precipitated a consitutional crisis when Keate refused to implement the reduction in his staff demanded by the colonial parliament.[22] The lieutenant-governor attempted to extract himself from this situation by modifying his position on labour immigration.[23] Approved labour recruiters were provided with introductions to chiefs and Ceteswayo was persuaded to recognize John Dunn as the representative of Amatonga workers passing through Zululand.[24] In November 1871, in the face of Colonial Office disapproval, the lieutenant-governor allowed the passage of a new law under which workers were escorted from the border to the magistracy in which they were to be employed, informed of the labour conditions in the colony, and registered with an employer for a fee of 10s.[25]

Law 15 of 1871 involved the civil service in the organization and control of labour, but it stopped short of committing government funds to the importation of Amatongas as the up-country farmers, despite their alliance with the planters, remained opposed to any state expenditure that would benefit only the coastal districts.[26] But by 1872 the price of sugar had climbed back to boom-year levels and the new lieutenant-governor, Musgrave, was prepared to cooperate with the planters in order to stimulate an economic recovery and to break the settlers' stranglehold over government.[27]

The decision to support the planters was also the product of a change in thinking by government officials on the role of foreign labour. The evolving character and nature of the immigrant workforce had an important effect on this change in policy. Both the secretary for native affairs and the lieutenant-governor realized that immigrant labourers were more popular with the colonists than blacks drawn from within Natal. Africans coming from beyond the borders of the colony were geographically separated from their means of production and consequently were in the structural position of (temporary) proletarians or bachelors without families to support. This meant that, unlike local blacks, their response to the pull of the labour market was not conditioned by the need to work their own land or by family responsibilities, and they were prepared to work for long periods of up to eighteen to twenty-four months. Amatonga migrants were cheaper to bring into the colony, and their wages lower, than indentured Indians.[28] Shepstone believed that

> Natives coming from beyond the confines of the colony . . . necessarily engage themselves to employers here for longer and more continuous terms of service than they would do if they had location lands or friends of their own race in the colony and they are obliged, in the absence of such alternative modes of supporting themselves, to accept such wages as may be offered.[29]

For the government, after its experience with the first abortive Indian immigration scheme, the prime advantage of migrant labour was that the workers could be removed in accordance with the occasionally violent fluctuations in the fortunes of the sugar industry. The prosperity of the plantations was largely based on the international price of sugar, which in turn was dependent on a variety of extraneous factors ranging from the outcome of harvests in areas as far removed as Queensland and the Caribbean, to the size of the European sugar beet crop. Migrant labour was one of the few price variables over which planters had some control, for an impermanent labour supply allowed planters to rid themselves of their excess and elderly labour.

Migrant labour also allowed the government to rid itself of a potential class of proletarians or mendicants who could become a political threat or a drain on state revenue. By the beginning of the 1870s, the development of the sugar industry had changed the nature of coastal society in Natal. Substantial knots of population had emerged on the plantations and the settlers were anxious to control the growth and development of what might coalesce into a resentful and rebellious underclass. To the Victorian mind with its specific experience of industrialization in Europe, proletarianisation meant not only that workers were dependent for their livelihood on wage labour; it also meant the separation of the worker from his customs and political controls. Cut off from the habits and traditions that had given order and meaning to his life, the proletarian was believed to fall victim to the moral decay afflicting the underclasses of capitalist society. Proletarianization was both a material and a moral problem, and impoverishment was traced as much to moral degeneration as to the material conditions produced by the rise of capitalism. Pauperization slid silently into indigency and begging, social evils that produced petty crime and, when stimulated by political agitation, resulted in demonstrations and popular uprisings. The world view of the settlers and imperial officials was little different from that of their parent society in Europe, where the image of labouring classes was firmly fixed to that of dangerous classes. Already threatened by African armies in Zululand and the reserves, the settlers were unwilling to add the threat of proletarian upheaval to their insecurity.[30]

As rootless foreigners, Amatongas were perceived to live without social or political restraints. Because of their peripatetic existence, they and other labour immigrants scavenged for food, raided chicken runs, stole maize, milked unattended cows and goats, and sometimes resorted to banditry. White men were sexually threatened by the overwhelming numerical superiority of blacks and they saw wandering groups of Amatongas, separated from their womenfolk, as potential rapists. Amatongas had a particularly unsavoury reputation. The *Natal Mercury* considered them "the most immoral, thieving tribe in this part of South Africa." Because they had no local roots or chiefs to restrain them, the editor claimed, they were "faceless" and "notorious for committing much of the petty crime on the coast."[31] The superintendent of the Durban Borough Police went so far as to assert that "the Amatonga has taught our Natal natives to thieve."[32] They were "starving adventurers . . . uninfluenced by the sense of tribal responsibility," wrote Theophilus Shepstone in late 1871, who, "having no domicile, no tribe or family in the colony, are subject to none of the restraints or means of control which are applicable to the permanent native population." Amatongas were "drifters with no tribal controls," and a potential "criminal element."[33] In a similar vein, Keate had expressed his apprehension of the "pauperization" that would accompany proletarianization, while Musgrave, writing in the wake of the Paris Commune, and rioting in British Guiana and Jamaica, feared that "one particularly successful *émeute* among the native tribes on the coast, however it may be suppressed . . . would cause the destruction of property worth thousands of pounds and cause ruin to many [planters]."[34] The use of the French word *émeute* draws on the image of, not a tribal rebellion, but a popular uprising led by a revolutionary mob. This discourse on the social evils of industrialization led Shepstone and Musgrave to forge a labour policy that would take heed of the planters' need for workers, while preventing the development of a restless proletariat. Shepstone supported the importation of African labourers but stipulated that, to prevent the growth of a class of workers dependent solely on wage labour for their survival and reproduction, their families should be prohibited from entering Natal. As Amatonga and other immigrant workers could not be monitored by local chiefs, Shepstone proposed that their movements be controlled by a system of deferred wage payments and a unit of mounted police.[35] From the government's perspective, a system of controlled migrant labour was preferable to turning taxpaying African farmers into potentially dangerous proletarians.

The Natal government initially looked to Gazaland for a solution to the labour shortage. In August 1870 Pietermaritzburg again received a mission from the Gaza king, who hoped to persuade the British to bring pressure on the Swazi to halt their raids into the southern marches of his empire. Umzila stressed that the expansion of the Swazi into the area behind Delagoa Bay had blocked the southward emigration of Gaza workers and that, if the British would allow a friendly chief to settle on the coast, he would encourage his subjects to seek work in Natal.[36] In sharp contrast to the apathy with which they had received a similar request two years previously, government officials then believed the importation of "the Amatonga or noncombatant tribes of Gaza" to be of benefit to the colony and sent an expedition to the Gaza capital under the command of St. Vincent Erskine, the explorer son of the colonial secretary.[37] The expedition proved a failure but provided an insight into the possible mechanisms of recruitment in Gazaland. Erskine emphasized that Amatongas refused to tramp south without the king's blessing for fear that their villages would be pillaged and that, on their return, they would lose their wages and perhaps their lives.[38] Nevertheless, in the early 1870s, when the Zulu reasserted their control over the territory south of Lourenço Marques, and the Swazi relinquished their ambitions in the Delagoa Bay region, a trickle of Gaza labour began to cross the Limpopo and enter Natal along the coastal route.[39]

The meagre results of the Erskine expedition persuaded the legislative council to recommend in November 1872 that the government aid the introduction of workers by constructing shelters along the coast where migrants might be supplied with food and protection.[40] In an effort to reduce the cost to employers of desertion, the workers' registration fee was halved and a payment of 1s was introduced for every month that an Amatonga stayed with his employer.[41] An ideal opportunity to implement the immigration scheme arose in September 1873 when Ceteswayo sought the support of the British, in his conflict with the Transvaal Boers, by asking the Natal government to preside over his coronation. At the crowning ceremony the new Zulu king agreed to the appointment of John Dunn as protector of immigrants in Zululand and to the building of rest stations along the coast.[42]

In February 1874, a month after Shepstone had ordered several magistrates to use forced labour to bring in the sugar crop, Dunn was appointed to his new post at an annual income of £300. His brief was to build five rest stations along the coastal route to Delagoa Bay and to endorse the licences supplied to private recruiters by the protector of immigrants in Durban.[43] The following month an immigration agent was installed at the Lower Tugela to register the names and tribes of all immigrants on their arrival, send a receipt to Dunn, and convey the immigrants to the magistracy in the district of their employment. The cost of returning home was to be borne by the worker. In April the Natal Mounted Police Force was established to patrol the rural areas.[44]

Overtaken by these events, the Portuguese sought to benefit from any flow of labour, from an area only nominally under their sovereignty, by allowing the shipping of workers from Lourenço Marques. A coalition in the Natal legislature, overruling objections from the up-country faction, promised to provide financial support, and Frederick Elton, an ardent imperialist who had served in a temporary capacity as Natal's protector of immigrants, was sent to Mozambique Island to negotiate an agreement with the governor-general.[45] In January 1875 United Steam Ship Co. vessels drew Lourenço Marques into international shipping routes when they stopped to pick up workers at the settlement for the first time. But it was only in July of that year, when the British finally recognised Portuguese sovereignty over southern Delagoa Bay, that the governors of Mozambique and Natal issued decrees regulating the shipment of labour between the two colonies.

Under this agreement a Natal government labour agent was appointed at Lourenço Marques, the passport fee was reduced from 15 to 11s, and a return passage fare was settled at 30s. An extra 1s6d was demanded for "guarding and superintending" and preventing recruits from "running away" while awaiting embarkation.[46] But the expense of the scheme rose uncontrollably and the Natal government was obliged to pay a third of the estimated £4.13s3d it cost to ship a worker from Delagoa Bay to Durban. Because disputes over earnings encouraged workers to desert or to refuse to work, the minimum wage was set at the competitive level of 20s per month, and, if the worker agreed to a two-year contract, the employer was obliged to pay his return passage.[47]

The scheme was particularly valued, as men who entered Natal by sea were prepared to enter into long-term contracts in exchange for the security of a free return passage. The shipment of labour also allowed Chopi and Tonga workers from around Inhambane to enter Natal, as their movement overland was blocked by the Gaza. The governor of Inhambane encouraged the shipment of labour to Natal because of the revenues brought both to himself and to the local treasury, and in February 1876 the first batch of Tonga-Chopi labour was landed at Durban where they were lauded as "pioneers." In August the following year Reuben Beningfield, a Natalian with a long experience of hunting, trading, and recruiting in southern Mozambique, was appointed Natal government labour agent at Inhambane. Beningfield knew the region well, was on friendly terms with the Gaza king Umzila, other local chiefs, and Portuguese officials, and during 1878 was able to send more than five hundred workers to Durban under the scheme.[48] He and other private recruiters also continued to send workers directly to individual employers in Natal.[49]

Railway contractors claimed that the wages and capitation fees of Inhambane workers were half those of men drawn from Delagoa Bay. Two factors would account for the cheap cost of Inhambane labour. Firstly, they had little experience of working for wages, unlike men in the Delagoa Bay area, and consequently little concept of the market value of their labour. But of perhaps greater importance were the dubious conditions under which the men were recruited, for Inhambane had been a major slave centre into the 1850s and it was only in November 1878 that the last vestiges of slavery were abolished. It seems almost certain that *prazo* slaves, taken from the Quelimane hinterland, as well as indentured former slaves at Inhambane and Lourenço Marques, called *libertos*, were sent to Durban.[50] The shipping of labour from Delagoa Bay to Natal was hampered from the beginning by the high rate of desertion. As this entailed a substantial loss of public revenue, government support for the scheme remained lukewarm; in its first three years, only about 850 workers officially embarked at Lourenço Marques for Natal.[51] What was far more important than the number of workers shipped south was the establishment of steamship communications between Durban and the neighbouring Portuguese settlement. Men were far more willing to tramp overland in the knowledge that they could safely repatriate their wages and goods when they returned home on one of the vessels plying between Durban and Lourenço Marques.[52]

The overland scheme started in February 1874 yielded far better results. During the first thirty months, an estimated 7,800 Amatonga migrants officially entered and 5,758 left Natal by way of the Lower Tugela ferry. The scheme also reduced the cost of importing labour, for workers soon learnt to make their way southwards independently of white recruiters. As the accompanying figure indicates, the importation of large numbers of Amatongas in the mid-1870s succeeded in turning around the sharp increase in the wages of field hands brought on by boom conditions in Natal.

The cost of importing Amatongas overland was low—4s10d each compared to the old capitation fees demanded by private recruiters of up to 20s—but the

FIGURE 1: Wages of Field Hands in
Natal 1864–1878.

1864 = 10s	1872 = 9s5d
1865 = 9s9d	1873 = 11s
1866 = 8s3d	1874 = 12s7d
1867 = 7s6d	1875 = 14s3d
1868 = 7s	1876 = 13s7d
1869 = 7s9d	1877 = 13s7d
1870 = 7s7d	1878 = 13s5d
1871 = 8s6d	

scheme soon ran into problems when workers, having arrived safely in Natal, either deserted and entered the labour market as free men, or were lured away by
rival recruiters. Men were also drawn away to the Cape railways and harbours and
to the diamond fields, where they could earn up to four times the average Natal
wage.[53] In 1875 the emigration agent at the Lower Tugela ferry reported that during
one month, 7 percent of the 154 Amatonga workers leaving Natal had worked in
the Cape, and the following year at least one group of seventy Amatongas made its
way to the Cape through Pondoland. The protector of immigrants in Durban complained that the exodus of Amatonga labourers to the diamond fields was a drain
on state resources and that many of the migrants merely used the labour importation scheme as a bridge to get to Kimberley.[54] Newspaper editors and government
officials grumbled that, as Amatonga workers had cost public money to introduce,
they should be obliged to spend a specific amount of time in Natal before quitting
the colony.

In February and March 1876 the resident magistrate of Natal's Upper Tugela
District, which bordered on the Orange Free State, remarked on the "unusual
number of Amatongas passing through this way to the Diamond Fields."[55] What
he was observing was the slow beginning of a massive shift in the movement of
migrant labour, as Amatongas started to replace Pedis and Sothos on the diamond
fields. In 1876 diggers on the Kimberley fields attempted to make up for a sudden
fall in the price of diamonds, and a sharp rise in working costs, by halving the
wages of mine workers. In response, almost half the work force left the fields,
some to take part in the Transvaal-Sukhukuni war and others to work on the Cape
railways.[56] By the end of the year the shortage of labour at Kimberley had pushed
up wages to 30s per week. This was eight times the amount paid to plantation
workers, and Amatongas, benefitting from the new ease with which they entered
Natal under the government immigration scheme, soon made their way to Griqualand West. Others trekked overland to find work on the railways under construction in the eastern and western Cape, while between July 1876 and May 1882, over
thirty-two hundred men were shipped under contract from Lourenço Marques to
Cape Town, where they joined other "Mosbiekers" [Mozambicans] working on the
harbour and surrounding farms.[57]

Attempts by the Natal government to organize the importation of Gaza
labour were only renewed once the British came to control Swazi foreign policy,
through their annexation of the Transvaal in 1877. In January 1878 a third em-

bassy arrived in Pietermaritzburg with the express purpose of opening Gazaland to trade and labour recruitment. The terms obtained by the Gaza ambassadors were never made public. However, we do know that the first batch of Gaza workers to return home embarked at Durban eleven months later and that on their arrival at Lourenço Marques the men were met by one of Umzila's *indunas* who immediately "escorted" them home after "collecting [the king's] dues."[58] Erskine had discussed a similar scheme with Umzila, which entailed Gaza *indunas* accompanying groups of between twenty and one hundred workers, reporting on their treatment, checking their conduct in Natal, and "taking charge of fees due to the chiefs."[59]

By recruiting men through powerful sovereigns, employers were able to batten onto, and feed off, non-capitalist forms of labour exploitation. As early as 1873 labourers, whom the colonists referred to interchangeably as Zulu or Amatonga, had entered Natal from northern chiefdoms paying tribute to the Zulu.[60] About three or four hundred of these men had been "hired out" by Ceteswayo at the low wage of 8s per month. They proved not only cheap but extremely reliable for, as their wages were handed over to Ceteswayo, they dared not desert. A further eight hundred men were supplied in this way to the Natal Government Railways. Although they were described as coming from "a tribe which is subject to the Zulu king and is situated between the Zulus proper and the Amatonga," it seems likely that they came from the Bonambi *ibutho*, or Zulu regiment, on the Upper Pongola.[61] We only know of this case because, when it was claimed that the men had been forced to work in Natal and that their entire wage had been paid to Ceteswayo, their recruiters were prosecuted. But British concepts of free and unfree labour were unknown to the Zulu and Amatonga. It was considered normal for the product of the labour of young bachelors to be funneled through the *ibutho* system into the royal lineage. As the future British resident in Zululand was to express it, the Zulu were "long accustomed to look for and abide by the direction of their chiefs in all matters of a public nature, [and] are not yet enough advanced to labour of their own discretion. Going to work," he added, "especially in large numbers outside the chief's territory, is looked upon as a public act."[62] Viewed from the perspective of British law, this form of labour was close to slavery; but noncapitalist peoples had no concept of a proletariat that was in need of "rights" because it had been "freed" from the means of production. As the colonial courts were governed by an industrial, British interpretation of justice, the Natal Government Railways were obliged to look to sources of labour more acceptable to European sensibilities. However, despite official opprobrium, defined locally as unfree continued to be employed in Natal well into the 1880s.

I feel it is safe to assume that by the end of the 1870s, as many as fifteen thousand men from the coastal plain north of Zululand were employed in South Africa. In Natal, Amatongas were considered "a peacefully inclined and industrious race from whom most of the regular labour supply is drawn"; over one thousand were hired as casual, *togt* (day) labourers in and around Durban, about two thousand on the railways and harbour, and about five thousand on the plantations.[63] By 1880 Amatongas made up about a third of the twenty-two thousand blacks working on the diamond fields and supplied perhaps as many as three thousand men to the eastern Transvaal gold fields and the public works of the western and eastern Cape.[64]

A Tramping System

The journey south was long and dangerous, particularly without the protection of a recruiter. Political upheavals in the Delagoa Bay hinterland frequently caused chiefs to prohibit the emigration of their followers or made the trip so unsafe as to render it suicidal. Under normal conditions a man took at least ten days to walk along the coastal route from Delagoa Bay to Natal; tramping to Kimberley or the Cape was a far longer, more dangerous, and exhausting journey. Amatonga workers followed three major routes south to Natal. The first, oldest, and most direct route, used largely by Maputos, followed the established trade route along the coast to the ferry at the lower Tugela drift. This route had water and good grazing for stock taken home by returning workers, but it was particularly dangerous during the summer months when malaria and later sand fleas infested the area, and when summer rainfall made the lower reaches of rivers impassable. However, the major impediment to using this route was that it passed through Zululand. The Natal planter William Campbell stated that in the early days Amatongas had "frequently died on the [coastal] road from exposure and exhaustion, if not from ill usage" as they had "to skulk from bush to bush at night," for the Zulu thought them "fair game for plunder."[65] Amatongas were easy and profitable targets as they often carried tobacco or wildcat and genet skins, and later guns, to exchange for cattle, food, and shelter. Cattle bought in Zululand were driven into Natal where they were sold to raise the money needed to continue to a particular plantation, or to Kimberley, or to recover sufficient strength to shoulder work on the plantations.[66]

The Dunn scheme eradicated much of the danger of travelling through Zululand. The men made their way independently to the Hluhluwe River where they gathered at the first shelter on the route south. They then travelled in parties to the second station on the Umfolosi before continuing to Inabe, Ungoye, and Manyeti, after which they were lodged by the government labour agent at the Lower Tugela ferry. Because workers were provided at each shelter with water and a pint of maize, they were no longer weighed down by supplies of food or trade goods. They slept at each shelter and complained of any harassment to the station head or to the local chief, all of whom were in Dunn's employ. On their arrival at the Lower Tugela ferry the workers were registered, a receipt was sent to Dunn, and the men, after choosing where they wished to work, were then sent to the local magistracy where they were registered a second time.[67] The scheme was strongly supported by the chiefs, who saw it as the only means of protecting their wandering followers. The Maputo chief, Nozingile, sent a messenger to Pietermaritzburg and

> expressed his satisfaction at the arrangements which had been made and said that many of his people had taken advantage of them and the old practices of killing and robbing his men as they passed through Zululand had now stopped and, since their passages had been made safe, very large numbers of people had gone to Natal.

They had "returned with their earnings, from which," Nozingile's messenger was careful to add, both "they and he received benefit."[68]

The second route used by migrant workers passed about 170 kilometers inland, through territory disputed by the Zulu and Transvaal, before entering the

Kimberly under snow in 1876. The bitter cold on the highveld plateau was only one of the severe obstacles faced by migrant workers coming from the sub-tropical coastlands.

Lower Newcastle division of Natal. This mountain route, although longer and more strenuous, was a good alternative to the coastal route in summer. The third route passed west of Zululand and Swaziland and connected the northern Delagoa Bay region with both Natal and Kimberley. Migrants using this route followed the Olifants and Sabi rivers up to the highveld and gathered in large groups near the Berlin Mission village of Botshabelo before travelling down to the Upper Newcastle division or branching westwards to Kimberley. This was the most difficult route, as it passed through high and inhospitable country with little fuel or shelter. Nevertheless it became a highway for migrant workers as the northern Delagoa Bay region was incorporated into the South African labour catchment area.[69] As increasing numbers of Gaza workers made their way south, established trade paths leading up the Levubu and Olifants rivers also came to function as labour routes.[70]

We would do well to remember the determination and courage with which tens of thousands of early pioneers converged on Natal, Griqualand West, the Cape, and the Transvaal, for their industry built a modern economy and their movements etched, filled in, and made tangible the space that was later to become South Africa. The heroism and determination with which these men made their way south has seldom been recorded. "How these starving, naked creatures lived on the way, conquering rain, frost and hunger, I cannot divine," wrote a Kimberley diamond buyer, "nor does anybody know the small armies of them who left their wasted carcasses on the road to fallen vultures."[71] "Starting with only vague ideas of distance, no money, and but little food, their sufferings were terrible," remembered Richard Southey, the lieutenant governor of Griqualand West.

> In the winter time, when ten or even fifteen degrees of frost prevailed at night, they died in numbers round the scanty fires with which they tried to warm their unclad bodies. On the road they could get no help. Even in the month of October, when warm weather was setting in, twelve of these poor creatures died of hunger and exhaustion in a single night within a day's march of a Transvaal town.[72]

The hot and waterless nature of the lowveld compelled migrants to keep to perennial watercourses and this made them easy targets for bandits and wild animals. Climbing the escarpment, immigrants from the coast entered an entirely different environment. Most had no experience of bitter highveld winters and, clad in little more than threadbare cotton coats and perhaps corduroy trousers, many succumbed to the cold. This was particularly the case in rugged, inhospitable areas where men, unable to find food, shelter, or fuel, were savaged by animals or simply lay down to die. Newspapers and travellers often reported the death from exposure and starvation of whole parties of migrants. An entire group of thirty men, presumably weakened by their journey from the Inhambane interior, was reported to have died crossing the Xingwedzi River in the north-eastern Transvaal. During the widespread famine of 1876 it snowed in Kimberley and bands of up to nineteen men died of hunger and exposure on their way to the mining camp.[73] Four years later, twelve Shangaans died on the Pilgrims' Rest Hill and another twelve near Mount Anderson when it snowed in the mountains around Lydenburg.[74]

One migrant lived to recount, in moving detail in his old age, the story of his expedition to Kimberley in the winter of 1879.[75] Abraham Mavanyici was born in about 1857 in the dry area north-east of the bend in the Limpopo. As a young boy, he moved with his family to the Spelonken, where he learnt to handle a team of oxen and speak the local Dutch patois. In his teens, he had worked for a short while in Pretoria but had always longed to go to Kimberley from where men returned with diamonds and sufficient money to procure a wife. When Mavanyici eventually left for the diamond fields his employer presented him with two blankets, to be carried by his young brother as protection against the winter cold. As a means of protection against wild animals and bandits, the two men chose to set out in the company of eight other work-seekers. After about three weeks on the road, the party reached the summit of the inland plateau. Exhausted and cold after a stiff climb, they bivouacked under the stars. While some of their party went to fetch water, the others collected the few bits of wood they could find. They made a fire, prepared their maize meal, and, wrapped in their threadbare blankets, settled down for the night. Without sufficient fuel the fire soon spluttered out and the men huddled together for warmth.

The temperature fell sharply during the night and in the early morning Abraham Mavanyici awoke to find his companions covered by a thin layer of snow. He managed to wake his brother and another man, but the corpses of seven of his companions were already frozen and stiff. The three survivors, who had never seen snow before, were horrified by their experience and their only idea was to return home. But the inhabitants of the first house they stumbled upon feared they were bandits and roughly sent them away. Exhausted and close to collapse, the men eventually found a farmhouse where they were given hot food and shelter for the night. As they made their way home, the three men found the corpses, rotting and half eaten by hyenas and vultures, of other migrants who had perished along the route. They finally arrived home exhausted and covered in cold sores. Abraham Mavanyici was to suffer from epilepsy for several years after his return home. His experience was sadly not an isolated one. Eight years after the fearful winter of 1879, Ruth Berthoud-Junod noted that, as she and her husband passed through the highlands of the south-eastern Transvaal,

> we often found Africans who had died of cold on the route. Last year fif-
> teen were found in one place where they had lain down on the side of the
> road without being able to raise themselves. It is not surprising. . . . They
> will not find any wood at all in the high mountains and they do not know
> what else to do apart from lying on the ground, rolled up in their blan-
> kets. Everyday there is a heavy morning frost and a cold wind blows. . . .[76]

On the death of one of their companions, a party of migrants would cover his body with a pile of stones, place it in a shallow grave, or thrust the corpse into an ant-bear hole. Others too exhausted to bury their comrade would leave his body as a putrefying beacon marking the route to Kimberley.[77]

Even workers who had safely arrived in Natal were not protected from wild animals and exposure to unseasonable, harsh weather. In the late 1850s plantation workers were threatened by the lions that descended to the coast in winter, and they worked under the constant danger of being bitten by snakes in the canefields.[78] During the severe winter of 1871, six Amatongas out of a party of thirty-one died in the Umvoti division and another eight men, out of a party of thirty "starving and exhausted" Amatongas, perished when overtaken by tropical rains.[79]

Defenceless migrants were press-ganged into service by government officials, white farmers, and black chiefs. The experience of a group of 121 Shangaans, sentenced to a period of forced labour at Pretoria in 1879 because they were unable to produce passes, was by no means rare.[80] Many migrants, particularly those who were sick, injured, or famished, sought work in the villages and farms along their route. Others, perhaps the majority, encountered a recruiter on their way south to whom they contracted themselves in exchange for food, clothing, shelter, and protection. Still others, discouraged by their suffering, turned around and went home.

A man who arrived at Kimberley in an exhausted condition had often to rest for several days, or even weeks, before he could start earning a wage and, during this time, he was obliged to pay exorbitant sums of money for water, fuel, and food.[81] Some migrants, covered in vermin, staggered into Kimberley only to die. The entry into the town of large bands of men, drained of their strength by a long journey, was a dominant feature of life at the Fields. "A great majority of blacks," wrote a German digger, "arrived in a skeletal state, and their appalling emaciation bore witness to the fatigue and privations they had had to endure during a march of several months. Hundreds of them had succumbed to hunger and exhaustion *en route*."[82] Sir Charles Warren remarked in 1877 that migrants entered Griqualand West "from the north in droves, some of them having travelled more than 1000 miles. They are thin and gaunt, naked and abject when they enter."[83] Lionel Phillips remembered "the pathetic specimens of savage manhood [who came] hundreds of miles on foot to the scene of industry and on arrival were usually living skeletons."[84] If the Kimberley labour market were oversupplied, a man simply starved. At times when labour was scarce, wrote Louis Cohen,

> some speculative spirit would leave the fair town of Kimberley and meet, say, a famished horde of 200 attenuated wretches on their way to Eldorado or death. He would engage the lot at 10s per week, and if when they arrived in Kimberley there was a glut in the labour market then these poor descendents of Ham were to be seen on the outskirts of Kimberley starving to death, or rotting like pumpkins in the veldt a few miles away.[85]

The migrant labourers who pioneered the trek to the labour markets of South Africa soon developed various ways of protecting themselves from the perils of their journey. Like Amatonga hunters and traders, they carried charms and protective medicines to ward off the hostile bush spirits lurking along the labour routes. They generally journeyed southwards in small groups of up to a dozen men. But on their homeward journey, when carrying wages or burdened with cattle, guns, and other goods, men grouped together for defensive reasons in bands up to two hundred strong.[86] One Natal magistrate noted that, because blacks were not allowed to carry guns through Natal and the Trekker Republics, migrants from the coast would send "the half of their number home with the arms by a circuitous route north of the Transvaal . . . [while the] other natives return via Natal and proceed to Delagoa Bay from Durban by sea."[87] But the journey north of the Transvaal took six months to complete and was seldom undertaken after the establishment of the overland and maritime labour schemes by the Natal government and after the prohibition of gun sales at Kimberley.

Few men travelled to Natal by ship, for they knew of the islands out at sea where cannibalistic whites fattened their captives.[88] Added to a deep-rooted fear of enslavement, expressed through the metaphor of cannibalism, were the severe working conditions imposed on a recruit in return for a free passage to Natal. He was obliged to enter into a long contract and was given no choice in the matter of his employment. But as individuals came to realize that migrants were not shipped from Mozambique solely for culinary reasons, many paid their own passage south. "Mondisa," who left for Natal with two companions, is perhaps a typical example. As distinct from contract workers who had to be shipped by steamer, he was able to purchase a passage on a small sailing vessel for 25s. He had to supply his own food during the voyage and pay a passport fee of 15s to the Portuguese. This investment qualified him to enter Natal as a voluntary labourer with the right to choose his own employer.[89] Once Amatongas had worked in South Africa, they showed a greater willingness to travel by sea and large numbers bought passages on vessels leaving Natal for Lourenço Marques. They streamed to Durban harbour from Griqualand West and coastal Natal, as well as from Port Elizabeth and Cape Town.[90] Workers valued the safety of the sea voyage and frequently entrusted their goods and savings to kinsmen returning home by ship.[91]

In the days before the maritime labour scheme of 1875, homeward-bound migrants normally disembarked from coastal schooners along the beaches or up the river mouths opening into Delagoa Bay. But after 1875 the men were obliged to disembark at Lourenço Marques where they paid import duties on their purchases and a re-entry fee of 2s. The passage home was tolerable by steamer but the cheaper coastal schooners were vastly overcrowded, insanitary, and far from comfortable. Under good conditions sailing vessels took two or three days but, if becalmed, could take far longer to complete the voyage from Durban to Lourenço Marques. Small schooners or luggers like the 76-ton *Sea Gull*, packed with almost a hundred workers, frequently took eight to ten days to perform the voyage; it was also possible for the captain of a lighter like the *Zulu* to cram the decks of his vessel with far more passengers per ton than the slavers that had once crossed the Atlantic.[92] The conditions migrants had to endure, crowded together for days on end under the tropical sun, rekindled images of the slave trade. A digger sailing between Durban and Lourenço Marques in 1874 recounted that "the passage was very rough for nearly the whole of the journey and the stench from the natives was unbearable at times. Several of the natives died and were immediately consigned to the fishes below and the vessel reached Delagoa Bay after some miserable days and nights."[93]

Men travelled by sea because they had no other choice; it was the only way of circumventing hostile chiefdoms and it was the only sure way of repatriating hard-earned wages. Hence, in the decade before the outbreak of the Anglo-Zulu war, twelve thousand migrant workers travelled by sea from Durban to Delagoa Bay, while only a few hundred were shipped southwards.[94]

During the 1870s the constant ebb and flow of migrants took a shadowy pattern which, over time, became systematised as Amatongas established a network of contacts and labour routes and developed a set of customs and traditions associated with the work place. Tramping from one employer to another was largely powered by the temporary nature of most manual wage labour in Natal and by the growth of far-flung but relatively well-paid labour opportunities during the economic boom of the 1870s. Much as at home, immigrant workers used their geographical mobility to better their material conditions. But labour mobility was not merely a means of avoiding low wages and unemployment; it also served to regulate the labour market, for by circulating, workers discouraged employers from cutting wages or lowering working conditions because of a local oversupply of labour. Temporary gluts in the labour market were a seasonal occurrence in Natal when the hut tax forced blacks out of the reserves and depressed plantation wages by up to 30 percent.[95] The effect on wages of cyclical depressions in specific sectors, such as sugar in 1863 and diamonds in 1876, was regulated by large-scale emigration as men returned home.[96] Tramping also functioned as a stage-by-stage means of immersion into the labour market. One magistrate remarked that many Amatongas, "lately from their homes, had passed through Zululand, remained a short time at Durban or its neighbourhood until they could earn sufficient to purchase food and clothing and then started out for the 'Fields.' "[97] From the Natal coast, with its irregular patchwork of canefields, the men threaded their way through the maize and cattle farms of the Uplands with their large settlements of black tenants. After crossing the Berg, they struck out through the dry flatlands of the Free State for Kimberley. "Jonas" told the magistrate that he had left the Delagoa Bay area with nine other migrants. The men had entered Natal via the government immigration scheme and had worked for six months in Verulam and Durban, where they earned enough money and clothing to complete the journey to the diamond fields. "Maroonga" stated that he had left the vicinity of Delagoa Bay two years previously with five companions. After taking advantage of the government immigration scheme he had worked for six months in Durban before leaving for Kimberley. In the mid-1870s Amatonga migrants travelled fairly easily to the gold fields of the eastern Transvaal by engaging themselves as porters carrying goods from Lourenço Marques. But they seldom spent more than three months on the gold fields before moving on to Kimberley or Natal.[98] As a man became familiar with the routine of labour and the risks of working far from home, he gained more confidence about making his way to areas such as the Cape where monthly wages of up to £4 were offered to men prepared to subject themselves to the iron discipline of railway or harbour work.

The early life of Robert Mashaba, the man who planted Methodism in the Delagoa Bay area, is probably the best documented example of this emerging tramping system.[99] He was born at Ntembi's place near Lourenço Marques in about 1861 and, as a young boy, left Maputoland for Durban with his uncle, "a great hunter." They travelled along the inland labour route to Natal, carrying rolls of tobacco to exchange for food. The two men first found work on a coffee and banana plantation but, dissatisfied with conditions, soon moved on to Durban. There Mashaba was employed at the Bluff Naval Station where he remained for some time before paying £1 for a berth in a coastal schooner that took nine days to return to Delagoa Bay. After a period of time at home, he returned with his uncle to Durban where he found work at the Point, the landing place for ships unable to pass the bar at the entrance to the bay. Here he was placed in charge of the railway tool shed where his duties included ringing the bell and weighing workers' rations, activities that introduced him to new forms of calculating time and weight, and that encouraged him to seek a more extensive knowledge of the world of his European employers. At night he attended a mission school where he gradually acquired a basic literacy.

In 1875 Robert Mashaba boarded a steamer for Port Elizabeth to take advantage of the better wages and educational opportunities offered in the eastern Cape. He initially worked on the construction of the railway from Port Elizabeth to Grahamstown, but later moved to the harbour quarry, where as a gang leader he earned £6 a month. In Port Elizabeth he attended the Methodist church in the location north of Russell Road and, influenced by his reading of the book of Daniel and visions of the fiery furnace, he converted to Christianity. After saving £40 Mashaba entered the Lovedale Presbyterian school at Alice in January 1879. During the holidays he returned to Port Elizabeth to earn the money needed to pay his fees and, with the help of a school bursary, was able to complete three years at the institute. Considered "persevering and successful" by his headmaster, Mashaba was in 1882 employed with other Lovedale graduates as a messenger in the Kimberley Post Office under a two-year contract. Sol Plaatje, who was employed in the same position a decade later, referred to this "Lovedale experiment" as an important stage in his intellectual development.[100] In 1885 Robert Mashaba returned home to start educational and evangelical work in the vicinity of Delagoa Bay. Migrants tramped both long distances, as Mashaba's case indicates, and circulated between local centres of employment. This form of constant tramping and movement produced well-developed lines of communication, stretching back to the coastal areas, along which men carried news and information about working conditions.[101]

Cutting Cane

Work in the canefields also engendered a new solidarity. Preparing the fields and planting the cane was hard work, especially in areas where hills and heavy soils restricted the use of the plough.[102] Fieldhands employed machetes to clear the undergrowth, which was heaped in long rows and burnt; they then felled the remaining trees and worked through the soil with grubbing hoes or mattocks and axes. Flatland was then ploughed and hillsides hoed by hand. It normally took a full day for about forty fieldhands to hoe an acre of land to a depth of ten inches. While the newly cleared land was left to aerate, the plantation workers laid out roads for the heavily laden, ox-drawn carts.

Planting was undertaken in the early summer months of September to December, using plant cane (sucrose-poor cane tops) or ratoons (lengths of freshly-cut cane containing several joints from which new growths emerged). Although the crop produced by plant canes was superior to that of ratoons, the latter had the advantage of maturing about six months earlier than the plant canes. Every twelve to sixteen months after the harvest, the roots of cut cane also produced a ratoon, "a second edition," as one observer called it. However, the amount of juice extracted declined with each ratoon and the original plant had to be removed after about six to ten years. As the canefields ripened at different periods, the work of the cane cutter was spread throughout a long harvesting season. The men were careful in their planting. Holes as long as a man's leg were dug to a depth of 8–10 inches to form long rows separated from each other by a space of about 5–6 feet. After a few days' exposure, two good plants were placed in each hole, the one to support the other against strong wind and heavy rain. A light layer of soil was then thrown over the plants, but not sufficient to fill in the hole. After about three to four weeks the first shoots appeared and the workers set about hoeing and weeding the fields. During the first six months of the growing period, much attention was given to cleaning the fields. This was lighter work than planting but could be disagreeable, for, once the cane started to mature, the foliage harbored snakes and cut and pricked the field hands. Weeders were also often obliged to work in driving rain that turned the soil into a quagmire. Despite the piecework nature of much of field labour, it was normal for men to spend up to twelve hours in the fields.[103] At the end of summer the young canes were stripped of their leaves, or trashed, and the stalks exposed to the sun. Once the workers had removed the trash, the fields required little attention, apart from infrequent hoeing, until about a month before harvesting. The canes were then trashed for a second time and left to grow to a height of ten to twelve feet. But before being cut the cane had to survive the threat of frost, flood, fire, and foraging animals.

Great care was given to harvesting the cane. It had to be cut during the relatively dry months of July to December, when the sun and water absorbed during the summer had pushed the sucrose content to its maximum level. If the cane were cut too late, the sucrose dropped to the roots and the stalks became dry and brittle. Nor could the crop be cut and carted after December, for the summer rains made the rough estate roads impassable. A proficient cane cutter, aided by an assistant who tied the stalks into bundles, knew not to cut the cane too high, for the plant tops retained too much water relative to the more mature and sucrose-rich lower parts; and he knew that the cost of crushing the cane was seriously affected if too

Cutting Cane. During the depression of the 1860s the plantations depended on African migrants drawn from the territories to the north and west of Natal.

many tops were taken to the mill. But he also knew not to cut the cane too low, for this might damage the roots and prevent them from producing ratoons.

The cutting team often worked at a frenetic pace, for they were driven by the ripening crop and pulled by the crushing rate of the mill. In the early 1860s cane was carted to the mill in a lumbering four-wheeled ox-cart managed by a driver and his assistant. On hilly estates, as many as twelve oxen were required to pull a wagon holding up to two tons of cane. But on many plantations, this method of transport proved too cumbersome and uneconomic. Disease and the onerous nature of the work killed such large numbers of draught oxen, that by the mid-1870s horses and mules, capable of drawing two-wheeled carts holding 15–20 cwts, were being introduced on the flatter estates. Men who had formerly worked with anywhere from one hundred fifty to two hundred oxen on an estate were then required to reskill themselves, and work with fifty or sixty horses and mules, or seek new forms of employment in the fields or the mill. On some estates, workers learnt to operate newly installed, narrow-gauge tramways. Carting the harvested crop to the mill was a responsible job, for, after two days, the cut cane started to ferment. As the crop could be ruined if it were not brought in on time, wagon drivers, who also transported fuel and other goods, were under constant pressure throughout the harvesting period.

The seasonal labour needs of the sugar plantation fueled the engine of the tramping system. Workers were particularly required during the spring and summer months when, at various periods, the tasks of planting, weeding, harvesting, carting, and crushing overlapped. But during the autumn months, the length of the working day declined to just over eight hours and a large part of the labour force left the estate, while those remaining did little more than erect fences, drain ditches, and construct and maintain roads. It was only during the late winter months, with the onset of the cane-cutting season, that the plantation experienced an increase in the tempo of production and the size of the labour force. But while seasonal changes dominated the long-term work rhythm, in the short term the pace at which men laboured was driven by the crushing and processing capacity of the mill. It was no use cutting cane if it was going to run into a production bottleneck at the mill, and it was costly to leave mature cane in the ground for an extra season. To achieve maximum profitability, the mill had to work smoothly and effectively, particularly as it only functioned during the dry harvesting season, when the heavily laden carts could move through the fields or along the dirt roads.[104]

The fieldhands unloaded the cane at the carting shed, from where it was taken to the crushing house and fed into the rollers several times to extract the maximum amount of juice. From the crusher the juice was conveyed into a clarifying tank before being passed into a "battery" of boiling pans where much of the non-saccharine liquid was evaporated. The mill hands skimmed impurities from the surface and assisted the constantly thickening juice to pass from one pan to the next before it congealed into a syrup. It was then poured into shallow cooking trays and, once the surface treacle was removed, transferred to perforated buckets from which the molasses dripped. The remaining wet fudge was laid out to dry and, once crystallized, the yellow sugar was packed in gunny bags.

The early mills were relatively inexpensive to construct and the number in operation climbed from twelve in 1855 to sixty-four a decade later.[105] The machinery was not particularly complicated, and black fieldhands were able to move upwards into positions in the mill requiring responsibility and experience. Mill workers had to be skilled to achieve a clear sugar; the work could also be dangerous; before the introduction of feeder trays, for example, workers at the crusher risked having a hand or arm pulled into the rollers. Men working at the crusher also had to be careful not to grind the cane too finely, as this injected impurities into the juice, or to bunch the stalks, as this damaged the machinery. A combination of subtropical heat, flames, and steam made work at the battery difficult, disagreeable, and dangerous. The battery workers had to regulate the fire in such a way as to keep the juice in each pan at a constant temperature and consistency. They also had to know when to add lime or milk, how much scum to take from the boiling pans, and how often the scum could be reprocessed. To one mid-Victorian colonist, the fires, the heat, and the steam combined to produce a diabolical imagery. "There is something infernal in this operation," he wrote, "what with the bubbling of the juice, the naked forms of the Kafirs and Coolies brandishing their enormous ladles, the clouds of steam that arise, and the stifling heat that prevails, to say nothing of a pervading perfume of burning butterscotch."[106] Working conditions that shocked the sensibilities of Europeans in a backward and rural colony such as Natal must have impressed themselves even more firmly on the minds of Amatonga migrant workers. In many ways, the mill was the precursor of the mine, and its harsh working conditions gave a glimpse of what future generations of Amatongas were to experience underground.

The introduction of steam-driven machinery in the mid-1860s increased both the amount of cane crushed and the quantity of juice extracted; by the early 1870s, the average mill was able to crush up to 150 tons a day and manufacture 1lb 5ozs of sugar from one gallon of juice.[107] This rapid modernization of the mill had important effects on the labour process. Mechanization caused the price of installing a mill to rise dramatically. The consequence was that the undercapitalized, small planter-miller was unable to process his sugar at a competitive rate; thus, particularly during the depression years of the mid- and late 1860s, many estates fell into the hands of companies able to build modern mills. As the number of plantations decreased, they grew considerably in size. Whereas in the 1850s no estate was planted with more than 300 acres of cane, by the 1870s nine estates cultivated more than 600 acres.[108] The growth in the extent of the canefields was paralleled by an increase in the size of the plantation work force. On the Craigie Burn estate, the 20 acres of cane cultivated in 1858 grew to 92 a decade later and reached 400 in 1871. In that year Craigie Burn employed 190 men while an estate of similar size, the 300-acre Saccharine Hill, engaged 100 Amatongas and 90 Indians. On a large plantation like Sea Cow Lake, some 300 blacks and 242 Indians worked on over 1,000 acres. A smaller estate of 70 acres typically employed, in 1871, about 45 blacks and 33 Indians.[109]

As the number of workers grew, tasks became more specialized and the relationship between workers more impersonal. The same process was noticeable between workers and employers, particularly in those cases where planter-owners were replaced by company managers. The costs of purchasing and importing mill machinery, of buying land along the coast, and of paying the wage bill increased appreciably during the early 1870s. Yet while running costs grew, the productivity of the soil declined through over-cropping; the result was a greater level of exploitation of the labour force. With steam-driven mills, trash was no longer burnt in the fields. Instead, the leaves stripped from the cane, often knee-deep after a trashing, together with wood cut from the surrounding bushland, were used as fuel to drive the mill. The introduction of a more productive species of "Green Natal" cane required the widespread use of bagasse, the fibre remaining after the cane is crushed, as a fertilizer on some plantations. Terracing was introduced as a means of cultivating less accessible land. As the sugar manufacturing process became dependent on technologically advanced machinery, the nature of mill work became increasingly demanding, and Amatonga millhands were replaced by skilled Mauritian immigrants or by Indians shackled to their jobs by five-year indentures. The construction of small coastal railways in 1879–1880 encouraged the introduction of a central milling system that entirely separated the plantation from the mill. Between 1864 and 1884 the number of mills in operation fell by one-third and large, powerful, and technologically complex mills were fed by the surrounding plantations.[110]

While these specialized factories required a highly skilled and reliable labour force, they also set a faster work rhythm for the field workers. As the size, mechanization, and capitalization of the plantations increased, pressure grew on labourers to speed up the pace and efficiency of their work. Life on the plantations introduced Amatongas to their employers' notion of work. Under capitalism the concept of "real work," Raymond Williams once remarked, has come to mean "steady and timed work or working for a wage salary."[111] But in the Delagoa Bay region, work patterns followed the cycle of nature and the sun rather than the inanimate rhythm of machinery and the chronometer. The length of the working day was determined by the size and urgency of the task at hand and periods of intense labour were followed by long spells of leisure. Work was as much a social activity as a productive effort. It combined leisure and consumption with labour in a manner that reinforced local ties of mutuality and interdependence. There was no hard-and-fast demarcation of "the working day," and production was driven by the environment and weather rather than by the insatiable demands of profit and accumulation. On the sugar estates, workers were coaxed and coerced to labour at a continuous, steady, and disciplined pace. Their relationship with their employers was an impersonal and impermanent one governed by abstract market factors such as wages, market demands, and production costs, rather than social relations of kinship or reciprocity. Amatongas performed specific and repetitive tasks under the disciplined eye of a field overseer, worked in single-sex and often anonymous gangs, and undertook rigorous agricultural work and domestic duties for which they had not been socialized. When planters remarked, in the parlance of the period, on having to "break in" Amatonga workers or wrote of their "great improvement," they were alluding to the willingness and ability of these men to adapt to the rhythm and pressures of wage labour.[112]

Life on the plantations introduced migrants both to the capitalist mode of production and to each other. Amatongas were recruited in batches from specific chiefdoms and often travelled together in "family parties."[113] Those who arrived independently usually contracted themselves to a planter only once they had approached their "brothers" about conditions on the plantation.[114] Isolated from their homes in a foreign country, plantation workers were compelled to forge ties of assistance and comradeship wider than those of the chiefdom and clan. The ideological concept of kinship was extended to include, within the classification of "brothers" and "family parties," men who were seen to share a common repertoire of values and traditions. From the perspective of today, it is possible to discern this new identity as that of a vague ethnicity. Amatonga cultural markers were constantly refuelled and strengthened by new waves of immigrants from home, and they saw themselves reflected, in the eyes of other blacks, as a distinct group. Initially hesitant and vague, a new identity born of a community of interests became stronger as it was carried throughout southern Africa by tramping migrants, as it was tested in the defence of traditional work patterns, and as it was expressed in the network of signs through which people gave meaning to their everyday existence. Amatongas not only laboured shoulder to shoulder; they shared the same lodgings, ate and drank, danced and sang together, became ill and fell prey to the same accidents as their fellows, and turned to their own doctors to explain and cure their maladies.[115] The men experienced little contact with European norms and values, apart from those of the rare white overseer, and their contact with the planter and his family decreased as the estate and its work force grew in size and anonymity. No mission activity was carried out amongst black plantation workers, and their rare contact with European religious and secular teachings was in urban centres like Durban and Pietermaritzburg.

Many employers found it politically expedient to reinforce the cultural differences dividing the work force.[116] Under the terms of their indenture, Indians received a fixed ration, officially worked nine hours a day, were paid every two months, worked under their own *sirdars* [managers], and were bound to their employers for five years. The wages of black plantation workers only overtook those of indentured Indians during the boom of the mid-1870s, and their earnings remained constantly inferior to those of free Indians. African workers were generally hired on an *ad hoc* basis and were required to complete a task rather than labour for a fixed number of hours. Their rations, based on a maize meal staple rather than the imported rice eaten by Indians, were determined by their employer, and they were paid either weekly or monthly.[117] As blacks were legally prohibited from drinking "European" liquor in Natal, Indians were the major beneficiaries of the rum, or cane spirit, by-product of sugar milling. This created an important difference between the two groups, for, as most mills were equipped with a distillery, planters supplied their Indian workers with free rations of rum, a large part of which they then sold to blacks.[118] During the late 1870s the difference between the two groups probably took on a force of its own as Amatongas were replaced in the mills by Indians and were obliged to carry passes.

Amatongas were also cut off from the local African population. Coming from the Delagoa Bay area, much of which had been occupied at various stages by the Zulu, Swazi, and Gaza, many Amatongas shared with local blacks such practices as wearing tail skins and a headring, and slitting the earlobe to hold a snuffbox. But as tramping workers they were rootless and scavenging outsiders, and as "tongas" they were perceived of as lowly individuals whose outlandish customs, including the consumption of fish, poultry, pork, and monkey, were considered disgusting. Although most Amatongas spoke a linguistic form related to Zulu as a second language, it seems unlikely that rootless bachelors who spoke with a strange accent, and about whom little was known, would have been incorporated into local society at other than a servile level.

Resistance, Coercion, and Compromise

Amatongas also forged a social and personal identity through the everyday resistance mounted against the labour discipline of the planters. In looking at worker resistance, it is important to appreciate that Amatongas were migrants who spent only a small part of their lives in South Africa. They did not suffer the extreme alienation of proletarians, separated from both their means of production and their culture, and they were under little pressure to form protective combinations that, in the industrialising parts of the world, provided workers with an assertive voice. The ways in which migrant workers combined, through the experience of tramping, were spontaneous and ephemeral, but the promptness of their responses to specific crises indicates the existence of a continuous, although unofficial, level of organization. Their concept of labour relations was defensive and conservative, resting on what they considered to be a just wage and a familiar pace of work. Rather than binding together to demand better working conditions of employers, Amatonga migrants struggled to defend and preserve customary work patterns that were based on a different experience of labour from that of their employers. While planters demanded a work pace sufficient to stoke the accumulation of capital, and condemned what they perceived as laziness, drunkenness, desertion, and absenteeism, migrants clung tenaciously to a noncapitalist work rhythm. Never fully accepted by either side, the work pace was constantly challenged, defended, and reshaped.

Absenteeism was so common that it entered the settlers' colloquial language as "humbug sickness" and "sham sickness."[119] Working fewer days, or even absconding, was a common means of slowing down or breaking the rigour and rhythm of plantation work. Drunkenness provided another relief from the regimented discipline of the plantation. Workers arriving from the Delagoa Bay area were well versed in the methods of fermenting fruit into alcoholic beverages, and they soon applied these skills to the treacle by-product of sugar milling.[120] Amatongas supplemented their meagre rations by raiding the plantations' poultry yards and sometimes purposefully drove draught oxen to their death as a means of boosting their meat ration. Migrants were also able to supplement their wages by undertaking daily labour on a nearby plantation, a form of employment considered illegal by employers who bore the cost of housing and feeding their labourers.[121]

The planter's desperate need for a regular labour supply was based not only on the requirement that the different fields be harvested at the right moment and that the mill be kept working at maximum capacity; he also needed a semipermanent body of knowledgeable and experienced workers. The importance of skilled labour to the planter was reflected in the wage structure: millhands, ploughmen, and carters earned consistently higher wages than field labourers, while boys, or "young novices," received the lowest pay.[122] Planters were in an ambiguous position; they had to attract and hold workers while at the same time imposing upon them a foreign and demanding work rhythm. Nor could they afford to antagonise the work force, for sugar manufacturing is an industry particularly susceptible to sabotage, from the burning of the standing crop to the wrecking of the manufacturing process, to attacks upon the isolated plantation house. Thus methods of coercion and control had to be finely balanced by incentives and inducements. In their attempt to secure a regular and loyal supply of labour, the planters responded to the guile and resistance of the workers with threats and force on the one hand, and persuasion and encouragement on the other.

Newly arrived migrants were given two or three days to construct their own wattle and daub, thatch-roofed houses. Some estates provided small burnt brick barracks with galvanized iron roofs, but most men preferred the privacy of a hut shared with friends or relatives. These dwellings were clustered in villages at the heart of the plantation, close to the mill and the water supply. Free housing both attracted men to the plantation and allowed employers to exercise an influence over both the leisure and working hours of their fieldhands. The distribution of free rations also served to entice Amatongas to enter service. They were generally given a daily ration of about 2–3 lbs of maize meal, supplemented with beans, pumpkins, and sweet potatoes, and perhaps meat once or twice a week. In the 1870s a fieldhand received food worth about 4s a month alongside his cash wage.[123] Because of the free board and lodging they provided, planters often felt justified in imposing a daily fine of 1s6d on absent workers, a practice that could result in a form of debt peonage. Free housing and rations were not the only incentives that doubled as a means of social control. John Robinson remarked in 1871 that the major function of the recently built hospital on the Craigie Burn Estate was that it would "prevent a good deal of shamming."[124]

One cause of the high degree of absenteeism on the plantations was that workers found Sundays, and three holidays each year (Good Friday, Christmas, and New Year), provided insufficient time for leisure or the cultivation of their own fields. Planters used the allocation of plots, on which men grew fruit and vegetables, as a means of attracting and holding their labourers. On the Merebank Estate, eighty-five Indian workers cultivated 8–10 acres of their own land while, on another estate, one Indian reaped a tobacco crop weighing 1,000 lbs. [125] It seems probable that Amatongas and other Africans were also involved in this gardening. The practice lightened the alienation of wage labour, as field hands worked for themselves at the same time as they worked for their employers. The allocation of piecework was closely tied to the garden allotment system, for after completing an assigned task, the worker was free to cultivate his own land or hunt the cane rats, wild pig, guinea fowl, and small game foraging on the edges of the plantation. [126] Piecework was essentially a compromise negotiated between employers and workers over the pace of labour; planters used the system as a stimulus to productivity, while labourers viewed it as a means of shortening the working day. In addition, by working in gangs, they used songs and chants to further regulate the pace and rhythm of labour.

In struggling to establish their own norms as the accepted standard, employers and workers produced political organisations of unequal weight. Planters combined in formal organisations such as the Labour League and the various employer associations on the coast, and at times they succeeded in obtaining the support of the state. Ranged against the planters, Amatonga workers were bound together by a transient and shadowy tramping system. Yet it was the very obscurity, ephemerality, and flexibility of this form of organization that was their greatest weapon. What was considered desertion by employers was a traditional mechanism of survival to men coming from the coast, brought up to see mobility as a traditional means of coping with adversity. [127] The regularity with which workers deserted or in-migrated was facilitated by their very mobility, for, although most were married, they moved in South Africa as bachelors unhindered by wives and children. Tramping from one place of work to another was a product of both tradition and innovation; but as tramping became systematized and took on a regularity of its own, it grew into a weapon used to defend the workers' conception of fair labour practices. Workers could report any undue harshness or unfairness to the local magistrate or, after the start of the immigration scheme in 1874, to Natal's protector of immigrants, a post modelled on that of the former protector of slaves in the Cape. But while Indians were tied to plantations by their indentures and their families, Amatongas seldom had recourse to white officials and resorted to desertion if mistreated. The planters themselves encouraged and generated much of the "desertion," by recruiting workers from neighboring estates or by harbouring men who had broken contract. As Amatongas had no local families or chiefs, they were largely "faceless," according to William Campbell. "Magistrates had no way of identifying absconders," he complained, "and planters did not like you sending your men through their estates in search of absconders—so Tongas could abscond with impunity." [128]

An unrestricted labour mobility was an essential part of the tramping system. By moving from area to area, migrants exhibited a quick appreciation of wage differences and used their mobility as a bargaining tool. Continuous and widespread desertion served as a form of collective bargaining, combating the effects of employers' combinations and generally improving working conditions. Desertion was often well-organized and planned. "It was an unbearable evil," William Campbell complained, that "frequently 30 or 40 or more [Amatongas] will [sic] leave in a night without notice." When they had first arrived, Amatongas had seemed "timid, shy, fawning people," he observed, "they kept their engagements at first, but soon found it was easy to abscond."[129] This fear of desertion pressed the planters to ameliorate working conditions. According to J. R. Saunders, the manager of the Tongati Plantation, "anyone acquainted with their ways, who treats them justly, pays and feeds them regularly, and gains a reputation as a good master, can always, or nearly always, obtain as many [Amatongas] as he may want."[130] On some plantations employers, in their desire to attract and hold migrant workers, almost condoned a certain indiscipline. William Campbell referred in a jocular way to the Amatongas' "weakness for the poultry yard," while the levying of fines, rather than dismissal, and a lax implementation of the liquor laws, indicates a certain suppleness of response to the Amatongas' notion of work. As Shepstone disdainfully observed, "the planter who ultimately retains the services" of his Amatonga workers, "manages them with the timidity suggested by the fear of losing them should he happen to offend them, so that practically they are more independent than their masters."[131]

To illustrate the way in which desertion could function, let us take as representative the case of twenty-six Amatongas who crossed the Tugela in March 1876. These men were pressganged by policemen who drove them to the Stanger magistracy and finally to the huts at the backyard of the Durban police station. The next day the men were set to work on the railways at 20s per month. Within days fifteen had deserted and the rest "consider themselves prisoners, they are dissatisfied, working with *izinhlizio izibohlungo* [sad hearts] and say that men will no longer come if made *isibalo* [forced labour]."[132] To counter the collective bargaining-by-desertion that was an essential element of the tramping system, employers sought to enlist the support of the state. Magistrates could enforce the Masters and Servants Act, which considered insolence, refusal to work, drunkenness, and "gross misconduct" as criminal offences punishable by up to one month in prison, twelve lashes, and a £5 fine. In extreme cases, a planter could call in a detachment of the Natal Mounted Police. The state also assisted the planters through the passage of Immigration Law No. 1 of 1876, a pass law requiring immigrant workers who used the overland scheme to complete a contract of at least six months before continuing with their tramp. By restricting desertion, the aim of this law was to push down recruiting costs and wages, protect Natal employers from open competition for labour with Kimberley and the Cape, and secure government and private investments in the importation of labour. The migrant was issued with a "ticket" or work pass, carrying his number and year of registration, at the magistracy of the division in which he chose to work. At the end of his contract, he was given a discharge certificate from his employer (stating his registration number and year), which entitled him to a travel pass issued by the local magistrate. Armed with this pass, the man was allowed to seek work outside the magisterial division or beyond the borders of the colony. The punishment for transgressing the pass law was a three-year indenture at the low monthly wage of 6s. In 1878 the law was modified to allow Amatonga immigrants to pay 5s, roughly the cost of their intro-

The *Dunkeld Castle*. Steamships carrying migrant workers drew Lourenço Marques into international trade routes.

duction if they wished to leave Natal without having completed the six-month contract.[133] But the pass law proved incapable of curbing the tramping system. The several thousand Amatongas employed in Natal before the implementation of the law fell outside the act and only Amatongas who wished to work in Natal were obliged to carry passes. It was difficult for Europeans to distinguish between Amatongas and Zulus, and passes could be bought illegally. Nor was it in the interests of the wealthier planters, who attracted Amatongas by means of competitive working conditions, to implement pass laws whose restrictions might frighten away labour. Although deserters were often prosecuted, there were too few officials to implement the pass laws effectively. The inability of these laws to control the movement of foreign workers was underlined in late 1878 when, as war loomed between Zululand and Natal, there was a massive exodus of Amatongas from the colony. Many returned home through fear of being conscripted by the British; others sought to protect their families, while yet others returned to serve in the Maputo regiments fighting alongside the Zulu against their erstwhile employers. In December 1878 the governor of Lourenço Marques noted that

> The large-scale emigration from this district and from the lands to the north has ceased completely. Enormous caravans are to-day returning home by land and sea, almost all were working [in Natal] and enjoying a comfortable living. In one month 1300 have returned by sea and more than 500 overland.[134]

This sudden wave of "desertions" dramatically increased the amount of money lost by government and employers and highlighted the control over the labour market exercised by tramping workers. As the government suffered heavy capital losses because of its inability to prevent the desertion of immigrant workers, it halted the maritime labour importation scheme in October 1878, and in February 1879 ended assisted overland immigration. The movement of Amatonga workers to Natal ended entirely in December 1879 when the Portuguese imperial government prohibited the governor of Inhambane from allowing the emigration of workers until such time as they were covered by an official labour agreement.[135]

But the defeat of the Zulu in the war of 1879 transformed the labour corridor leading south to Natal and Kimberley into a highway. John Dunn was reappointed to his old position as protector of immigrants in Zululand in December 1879, and the following year some 2,540 workers entered Natal along the coastal route. In 1881–1882, some 4,340 Amatongas crossed into Natal while over seven thousand, many of whom had been held back by the war, returned home via the Dunn scheme.[136] The number of workers tramping south was probably much higher, for many of the Amatongas using the two upland routes were never registered on entering Natal and sold their labour on the open market. About two thousand Amatonga migrants travelled south by ship in 1880–1881, while only fifteen hundred returned by sea, which indicates that, after the defeat of the Zulu, the coastal corridor had superseded the northbound passage by steamship as the safest means of travelling home. Workers returning to Lourenço Marques from Cape Town frequently stopped over in Durban before making their way home overland, or by sea to Lourenço Marques and Inhambane. On a typical four-day voyage from Cape Town to Durban, the steamer *Dunkeld Castle* carried 25 Mozambican workers. They were all returning to Gazaland and, although heavily charged with baggage, fifteen intended to make their way home via Inhambane while the others were to disembark at Lourenço Marques and walk across Khosen.[137]

The tramping system constructed by migrant workers in the 1870s was maintained into the following decade. Natal officials continued to complain that Amatongas merely "made a convenience" of the government immigration scheme in order to get to the diamond fields or the Cape.[138] The protector of immigrants in Natal also commented on the adroitness with which Amatongas assessed wage opportunities when he stated that men did not desert "because of a wish to return to their homes but in the hope of obtaining better wages as free men."[139] The government attempted to improve control over the movement of labour by tightening the pass law. In 1884 all Amatongas entering Natal were obliged to carry a pass, and employers who engaged immigrants without the requisite pass were threatened with a £10 fine or three-month jail sentence.[140] But the administration did not have the power to enforce these laws, and a few years later the secretary of native affairs was forced to admit that the government could not hold Amatonga workers on the plantations. It was "a question of wages, the labourer will always go where his labour will be best paid."[141] By 1883 the Amatonga diaspora, held together by the tramping system, had reached its greatest extent in both numerical and geographical terms. But over the next three years the movement of workers from Mozambique almost halted as the labour-receiving areas were shaken by a severe economic depression.

Depression and Decline

Between 1883 and 1884 the price of sugar fell from £27.10s to £17.10s per ton. Planters responded by cutting back savagely on working overheads, and the average monthly wage of a black worker was sliced from 17s.6d in 1882 to a low of 11s5d in 1886. This discouraged Amatonga workers from selling their labour at a time when Zulu workers were beginning to move into Natal. With their economy and society shaken to its roots by the defeat of 1879, and under pressure from chiefs collaborating with the British administration, Zulu males were prepared to work for lower wages than Amatongas who had a long experience, and specific expectations, of the labour market. Amatongas responded to wage cuts by tramping to better-paid areas. This "desertion" of labour deepened the labour problems of the planters as it entailed the loss of recruiting overheads and there were increasing calls for Amatongas to be replaced by indentured Indians. The government subsidy on the importation of Amatonga labour had never been fully accepted by the upcountry farmers and came under increasing attack as, not only were recruiting overheads lost, but the migrants brought a severe smallpox epidemic to Natal from Mozambique and Kimberley.[142]

The immediate cause of the demise of the government overland scheme was political rather than economic. In February 1883, a month after Ceteswayo's restoration, Dunn refused to continue with the scheme. His resignation was motivated as much by his opposition to Ceteswayo as by the practical problems he would face in trying to bring labour through royalist territory. The Zulu civil war that was to flare up intermittently and with great violence between 1883 and 1888 effectively prevented the movement of labour across Zululand. As the coastal route passed through chiefdoms adhering to both factions in the civil war, the protection of tramping workers became politically and financially impossible and, in January 1884, the overland importation scheme responsible for bringing almost twenty thousand Amatongas to Natal was officially terminated.[143] As the depression deepened, Natal planters turned to migrant workers from Zululand or to local black peasants who had been crushed by the sale of crown lands, overcrowding in the reserves, a heavier hut tax, and a sharp drop in the price of maize. Planters particularly looked to Indians, bound by five-year indentures, for their labour supply.[144]

The ending of the government immigration scheme brought about a sharp decline in the numbers of Amatongas tramping to South Africa. The Natal government tried at one stage to circumvent the hostilities in Zululand by reintroducing the maritime labour scheme, but employers were unwilling to risk money in importing labour and workers were loathe to enter into long contracts. An alternative that proved more successful was for workers to tramp overland, around war-torn Zululand. In July 1883, about two hundred men living in the Inhambane interior contracted themselves to Natal recruiters, arriving in the British colony after a two-month journey. The success of this experiment resulted in the emigration of several hundred, if not thousand, to South Africa from the Inhambane District.[145] I know little about the composition and organization of these groups. Because they travelled through Gazaland, and were valued for their reliability, it seems likely that the Gaza king was involved in their recruitment.[146] This would also explain why the men were prepared to undertake a long and dangerous journey, at the end of which they earned historically low wages. But despite this and other experiments, by the end of the 1880s migrant labourers from the east coast no longer saw Natal as a profitable destination. Kimberley had become their major focus, and it is to an examination of their lives on the diamond fields that I now wish to turn.

3

Kimberley: The Cradle of a New Working Class

Shangaans from the Gaza empire were the first men from the coastal plain to make their way to the diamond fields, perhaps because their passage south was blocked by the Swazi and because the well-established paths along which they hunted, traded, and emigrated pointed them towards the highveld.[1] But in the early years following the rush of 1871, they seldom constituted more than about one-tenth of the twenty thousand men, mainly drawn from Basutoland and the eastern Transvaal, employed in excavation work. By the end of 1873 the open cast Kimberley mine had reached a depth of almost 200 feet and was experiencing problems as the surrounding shale slid into the mine and covered the claims with debris. Work was further restricted when summer rainfall turned the pit floor into a quagmire and flooded the deeper claims. Workers lived in fear of someone tapping a "greasy slide" at its base, and in this way causing a great block of earth to slither into the pit, and, after the first great "reef" fall in November 1873, they lived under the shadow of a lengthening wall that threatened to collapse on them.[2] Men from the east coast came to dominate the shallower and marginally safer Dutoitspan and Bultfontein diggings. Although these mines was relatively poor, they received increasing amounts of development capital as reef falls and flooding made large parts of the Kimberley and De Beers mines unworkable. When Pedi and Sotho workers left the fields, in response to the wage cut of 1876, Amatongas or Shangaans quickly took their place. Pushed by a severe drought, and a rapid monetization of their home economy, large numbers took advantage of the newly opened government route through Zululand to tramp across Natal to Kimberley.[3] Others followed the Xingwedsi and Pafuri rivers to the Zoutpansberg and Pretoria, or the Olifants and Sabi rivers to Lydenberg, Botshabelo, and Middelburg; from Pretoria they struck out for Kimberley via Potchefstroom and Christiana.[4]

By 1878 nearly 8,000 so-called Shangaans made up about 30 percent of the work force on the diamond diggings. White employers were far more in evidence at Kimberley than on the lonely railway works or the isolated plantations. At Kimberley most migrants lived with their employers on the small allotment of land bought by the digger along with his claim and, for the first time, they came into contact with Christian missionaries. Without fields to till in their leisure hours, Shangaan and other migrants turned to the crowded world of the mining camps to fill their leisure hours. Because Shangaan workers had to tramp long distances to get home, they tended to remain a part of this heterogeneous population for longer periods of time than other black workers. Pushed into the close social intercourse of this cheek-by-jowl existence for up to six months, and separated from the signs and symbols with which they had made sense of the world at home, migrant workers had to construct a new means of explaining their environment.

Two broad and strongly heterogeneous cultures met at Kimberley, the one largely European and capitalist and the other precapitalist and African. Most migrant workers had little knowledge of the small Portuguese settlements at Lourenço Marques and Inhambane, and their systems of belief and signification were shaped and formed in the world of the clan and the chiefdom. During the six months spent on the fields, their cultural beliefs were reinforced by the arrival of kinsmen and renewed on their return home; but they were also adapted and reoriented to cope with the new geographical and human surroundings. We are not dealing with the imposition of a dominant culture on a rootless proletariat, nor with a simple juxtaposition between European and African cultures. Black workers appropriated, mobilized, forged, and assembled a variety of cultural symbols and markers in their attempt to construct a world that was both familiar and secure. Many of these innovations only made sense from within the migrants' system of values and traditions. Other changes were a product of struggle and negotiation over the meaning of concepts, such as time and work, that had been defined and entrenched in other regions and continents.

Technology and Toil

As on the sugar plantations of Natal, the rhythm of work at Kimberley was closely linked to the level of technological development. In the early days of diamond digging, the claim holder and a handful of workers used little more than a pick, spade, wheelbarrow and sieve to extract the precious stones. Windlasses were originally worked by hand, but, as the quarries deepened, horses and then steam engines hoisted increasing amounts of earth out of the mine along hundreds of wire-rope roadways.[5] From the depositing boxes, the diamondiferous blue ground was carted or trucked to the depositing floor, where, after several months under the sun, it was broken up and wheeled to the washing machine, a piece of equipment that had by 1874 replaced the sieve and cradlewasher. The introduction of the rotary washing machine, driven by horse and later steam power, allowed workers to retrieve small diamonds that had previously been overlooked and left in the tailings. The hugely increased capacity that this machine gave to the processing of blue ground was just as important, for it drove and speeded up the entire rhythm of work in the mines. The daily washing capacity of a single machine rose from about 450 to well over 12,000 cubic feet each day. By 1881 over 300 steam engines worked ceaselessly to pump water out of the mines. The cost of this revolution in the hauling and processing capacity of the mines was prodigious, as the machinery had to be imported from Britain and transported from the coast by cart while the price of fuel rose in proportion to the denuding of the countryside. These technological developments were soon felt on the mine floor, as men who had formerly laboured at the pit head were forced into the quarry. Employers who had invested large amounts of money in the purchase and maintenance of machinery did not want to see it stand idle or even slow down. To realize their investment, they had to drive the workers to keep pace with the machinery, for, despite the introduction of dynamite and steam, workers still used labour-intensive picks and spades to extract the blue ground. In the final analysis, it was the dexterity, discipline, and determination of the workers, and not merely the processing capacity of the machinery, that caused the average annual amount of blue ground extracted at Kimberley to increase twenty-fold in the years between 1872–1877 and 1877–1882.[6]

The continual consolidation of companies after the mid-1870s gnawed at the close relationship between the digger, often working a subdivided or shared claim, and his work force. Although frequently of short duration and brutal, this relationship was based on intimate daily contact and on the digger's need to maintain the services and strength of his workers. As claims were consolidated and capital became available to employ men, a typical digger's outfit consisted of two men working with pick and shovel, and another two filling the bucket under the supervision, and often with the help, of a white digger. Four men worked the windlass while two others received the blue ground and carted it to the depositing floor in the digger's enclosure or "compound," where up to ten blacks were employed in breaking up and sifting the earth. By 1882, the several hundred individual claims that had once made up the Kimberley mine had been consolidated into nine companies, of which the largest, the Kimberley Central, employed over 800 men. Few whites laboured alongside black workers in the fashion of the early diggers and those who remained on the fields had either been absorbed into managerial positions or had become overseers. This stratified the labour market along racial lines, particularly as black claimholders were an early casualty of consolidation. Black workers were registered as so many old or new "hands," African members of a "race that would have found more favour with some people," Dickens had remarked, "if Providence had seen fit to make them only hands, or, like the lower creatures of the sea-shore, only hands and stomachs."[7]

Labour relations changed markedly as individual claims gave way to large companies and surveillance became an integral element of production. Whereas the old claim owner or share worker knew his handful of workers personally, the company overseer was employed to drive the work force and prevent the theft of diamonds. Overseers worked under the fear of losing their jobs if their teams did not produce sufficient diamonds, and were encouraged by a premium of 5 percent of the value of all diamonds handed to management. At the Bultfontein mine, where diamonds were small, one overseer supervised the work of sixteen men, while at the Kimberley mine, where valuable diamonds could be found on the quarry floor, the ratio was 1:8.[8] Mine labour required an unrelenting discipline and regularity. Although many of the Amatongas employed at Kimberley were familiar with working conditions on the plantations of Natal, few had been subordinated to the full rhythm and pace, or the alienation, of machine-driven industry. On the plantation, the separation of workers from their means of production was cushioned by the garden allotment system and the mill was isolated in the fields, or separated from the estate. At Kimberley, workers were surrounded by cacophonous machines driven by horse and steam power. Their working lives were pro-

The Kimberley mine in about 1873. A web of cables leads from the windlasses to the floor of the mine. Men had to manoeuvre with great care from one allotment to another and they lived in fear of landslides.

pelled by the inhuman pace of this machinery and by the constant movement of buckets, carts and washing machines. Black workers had to adapt themselves to a concept of time marked by whistles and sirens and divided sabbatically.

Employers on the diamond fields used various strategies in their attempt to restructure the working habits of migrant labourers. They frequently resorted to the fist, the boot, and the whip, but physical violence often proved counterproductive and costly in terms of desertion and surveillance. To attract and hold a body of itinerant workers, and reshape their work habits, employers had to convince them of the correctness of their vision of the labour process. The imposition of a new definition of work through threats and violence was combined with a set of incentives in such a way that men who had never worked with a pick and shovel became adept at handling windlasses, washing machinery, carts, and wagons.[9] It is now generally accepted by historians that the high wages paid to black workers at Kimberley were a product of the labourers' perspicacity in judging how much employers could afford to pay.[10] Shangaan and other migrant workers were in a strong bargaining position due to their alternative means of production and they could squeeze from employers what they considered a just remuneration for the harrowing trip to Kimberley, the poor food, dismal living conditions, and the dangers and drudgery of diamond mining. But the wage relationship was not born overnight. It emerged out of a constant process of negotiation and contention be-

A team of miners, equipped with picks, shovels, and buckets, prepares to enter the Kimberly mine.

tween worker and employer over the level of income, in cash and kind, and over the daily conditions under which men lived and laboured. To an even greater extent than Amatongas in Natal, Shangaans at Kimberley were locked into a dextrous and subtle struggle with their employers over the profits of diamond mining.

"The interesting feature in the labour question is the Kafir," wrote Antony Trollope of Kimberley in 1877, "this black man, whose body is only partially and most grotesquely clad, and who is what we mean when we speak of a savage, earns more than the average rural labourer in England." William Nelson who, unlike Trollope, was critical of conditions in the mines, also thought black workers "much better to do than the poor agricultural labourers of England."[11] In the early 1880s men could earn a purely cash wage of 20s-30s per week, almost eight times more than plantation wages in Natal. But workers at Kimberley were able to press far more than merely high cash wages from their employers. They demanded and secured a system of weekly wages that kept the pace of labour closer to the rhythm they knew at home, for, once they had received their pay on Saturday, the men could end their engagement or take a few days off before looking for a new employer. During the winter months migrants were pushed from the highveld by cold and the fear of pneumonia and were pulled home by the prospect of hunting. Employers fought this seasonal labour shortfall by cutting the work day from thirteen to nine hours and by providing free board and lodging as a cushion against the exorbitant cost of living at Kimberley. A digger who wished to attract workers had to provide a monthly ration of 100 lbs of maize or maize meal, "coarse Kafir meat" once or twice a week, and a glass of brandy over the weekend.[12] Some employers shot or bought cheap springbok carcasses for their workers, a practice that declined with the decimation of game in the late 1870s.[13] Others provided them with rough "boer" tobacco, cotton blankets, large iron cooking pots, and, an item of growing value as the veld was stripped of trees, the fuel needed for cooking and heating. It was generally reckoned that, because of the high and fluctuating price of food and fuel, it cost more than 10s a week to feed each black worker.[14]

The worker's biggest wage bonus was to find a diamond, as he could earn as much as £20 for a large stone handed to an overseer and considerably more from an illicit diamond buyer.[15] This was the equivalent of more than three months' work and was almost enough to pay for an item of high social status such as a double-barreled shotgun or, on the coast, two brideprices. Stealing a diamond often required a great deal of teamwork to distract the overseer, hide the stone, and successfully sell it to a fence. Black workers had their own network for selling diamonds, which ran to the white buyers, via eating houses and domestic servants. Other men chose to swell their earnings by working as "plants" for illicit diamond buyers—a safer, if less profitable, option to selling a stolen diamond to a stranger. On the other hand, men could earn 30s a week working as "traps" for detectives.[16] It is difficult to determine the extent to which diamonds were stolen. Most employers thought that between one-third and two-thirds of the total annual production disappeared in this manner, but merchants claimed this to be a wild exaggeration aimed at persuading the state to exercise a more direct control over the labour force. However, there can be little doubt that the hope of finding and selling a diamond was Kimberley's strongest attraction. As Charles Warren wrote, it was not just the "huge wages" but also "the prospect of securing diamonds" that lured men to the fields.[17] Working at Kimberley combined a steady and high wage with the element of a lottery: by finding and safely disposing of a valuable diamond a man was catapulted upwards in the social hierarchy. "The chance of acquiring diamonds induces natives," remarked the Kimberley registrar of natives, "to brave the perils connected with coming here, in the shape of accidents in the mines, robbery and violence, entanglement in the meshes of the law, and being occasionally cheated out of his earnings."[18] On the coast, missionaries were worried by the widespread trade in stolen diamonds, and they took it for granted that a man who lived without working was a successful diamond thief.[19] But men living in the shadow of death had their own sense of morality, and Shangaan workers required substantial incentives to undertake a long and dangerous journey and endure the daily insecurity of life on the diamond fields.

Employers attempted to hold down wages by recruiting workers in areas where they could benefit from local forms of unfree labour. Despite the prohibition of the export of labour from Inhambane, decreed by Lisbon in November 1879, Reuben Beningfield succeeded in shipping over five hundred workers from the settlement to Durban in late 1881 to early 1882. All were bound for the Kimberley Central Diamond Mining Company, whose board of directors included one of Reuben's brothers. As Beningfield paid the passport and passage costs of these men, they were bound to him and the government had no control over their recruitment, shipment, or distribution. This labour emigration scheme, from a seedy colonial backwater with a long history of unfree labour, seems to have been built on a strong element of compulsion. Beningfield's agent at Inhambane sent envoys into the interior who, it was claimed, press-ganged workers by "all sorts of pretences." Once in Inhambane, the labourers were chained, or put in stocks, and embarked for Natal, where Beningfield was paid a capitation fee of £6. Out of this sum an undisclosed amount went to the governor of Inhambane, who made out exile passports with false names, and a head fee of 20s to his agent.[20] Up to 200 men were packed into a small coastal schooner on each trip; they were not examined by a medical officer on landing at Durban, and they had no latrines attached to their sleeping quarters.[21] The workers, taken in groups under guard to Kimberley, were contracted for long periods at the low wage of 40s per month for the first six months and 60s for the following six months.[22] Theophilus Shepstone's son, Arthur, who had imported Amatonga workers into Natal for the government railways, successfully brought 300 men from the east coast to the diamond fields. For this he received the handsome sum of £1,200, as the men were prepared to work naked and for a monthly wage of only 30s.[23] But attempts to recruit and import labour were short-lived, because of the facility with which men deserted and slipped into the locations and backyards of Kimberley.[24]

When the British annexed Griqualand West in 1871, they had introduced an elementary pass system, which required work-seeking "servants" to enter their names in a roll kept by the registrar of natives. Once employed, the "servant," who was invariably black, was furnished with a 1s pass carrying his name, wages, and the duration of his contract. When he wished to leave the diamond fields, the worker had to present a discharge certificate, or a pass attesting to his conduct, before the registrar handed him a travel pass. Men convicted of breaking the pass law were liable to three months' imprisonment or a fine of up to £5 or 25 lashes.[25] "Servants" were also disciplined by the Masters and Servants Act and their movements were restricted by a 9 p.m. curfew. But these attempts to control the workers' movements were made almost entirely ineffective by the enormous demand for labour, the fractured and competitive nature of the digger's community, and the weakness of the colonial state.[26]

State intervention in the labour market increased markedly after the 1875 Black Flag Revolt and the removal of the restrictions on the consolidation of claims. As investment money flowed into the diamond fields, the Griqualand West police force was strengthened, almost 1,000 pass arrests were made in 1876, and there was a general crackdown on drunkenness, desertion, and "neglect of duty." At the same time, a government commission talked of establishing rest houses on the labour routes to Kimberley, and a central depot was built to house and feed newly arrived migrants. But these measures were unable to halt the massive efflux of labour caused by the wage cuts of 1876 and the spectre of war in Sekhukhuneland. In an attempt to attract workers back to the fields by addressing their grievances, the government followed the Natal example and appointed a protector of natives in 1877. However, this position was added to that of the registrar of natives in such a way as to ensure that functions of control and protection were combined in the same office. The creation in 1879 of the position of depot master was another gesture aimed at bettering the position of black workers while at the same time increasing the level of control over their lives; while the depot was constructed to provide board and lodging for migrants exhausted after a long journey, it was also the place to which deserters were brought to be claimed by their employers. Yet despite the increasing frequency with which the state intervened in the labour market, in 1880 at least one-third of all black workers remained unregistered. The desertion of labourers, sometimes in bodies twenty to fifty strong, was consequently almost impossible to prevent, particularly as men could reengage at another mine or, in the case of their arrest, find a recruiting agent willing to pay their fines.[27] By deserting, men were able to better their conditions of work; but desertion was also resorted to by men wishing to return home because they had found a diamond or because an employer was unwilling or unable to pay their wages. Opposition to the carrying of passes might also be see as an act of resistance, but it should be remembered that, without a pass, a black labourer was technically illegally at work and had no recourse to the law if, as was frequently the case, his employer refused or was unable to pay his wage, or threw him into the street to die when injured or sick.[28] In late 1880, as Basutoland slid into war with the Cape, the authorities could do little about the thousands of Sotho workers who returned home.[29] Without representative government or controls over the budget, the diggers were unable to follow the example of the colonists in Natal and force the state to bear an important part of the costs of importing and controlling workers. They were, however, able to establish in 1877 an irregular mounted unit made up of white volunteers, the Diamond Field's Horse, whose purpose, like that of the Natal Mounted Police, was to suppress insurrection.[30] The facility with which workers engaged "friends" and "relatives" and deserted "in bodies" suggests the existence of a network of information and organisation that was as informal as it was hidden. Without a great deal more research, one can only discern the lineaments of a developing community that was at once black, foreign, migrant, and working class.

Culture and Community

In the early 1870s, men lived in hastily constructed shelters on their employers' allotments, but, as they became familiar with the fields, many attempted to establish a greater control over their lives by securing their own board and lodging.[31] The sheer demand for labour, particularly after the failure of the wage reduction of 1876, put workers in a powerful bargaining position, and many were able to retain the food supplement to their wages while pushing up its money content from 10s to 15s and even 20s per week; those who supplied their own food earned an extra 10s. Large numbers of workers moved off their employers' allotments and drifted into the black communities on the edge of the mining camps. In these unofficial "locations," they constructed simple huts alongside the clay, stone, and brick houses of the more settled members of the community. In 1880, the Pound and Barkly Road locations contained 72 houses and 148 huts while two small Christian communities formed villages of 15 and 45 houses. Three other locations near Beaconsfield included 86 houses and 282 huts.[32]

By 1882 about 9,000 blacks lived on the fields without working for the mines, and the world they created in the back yards and "native camps" provided a haven for off-duty workers. Men retired to these areas to recuperate between bouts of work and carved a new social space for themselves through communal activities ranging from eating and drinking, dancing and fighting, to church- and school-going. Many constructed an often fragile family existence by living with their womenfolk and children. But while the locations were areas where black workers could escape the unremitting grind of the mine, their employers viewed them as islands of drunkenness, violence, and indiscipline, and as a refuge for illicit diamond buyers and deserters. In an attempt to push their workers onto mine properties, the principal claimholders convinced the local authorities, in July 1879, to levy from location residents a rent of 10s every three months on each of their dwellings.[33] The following month government legislation obliged employers to house their workers on mine property, a measure that hastened a process already under way, for, as the small claimholders were squeezed out and replaced by large companies, the mine owners attempted to centralize the lodgings of their workmen by constructing barracks capable of housing anything from several dozen to several hundred men. However, as these early "compounds" were open, men continued to move freely between their barracks and the locations.

The bounded nature of the community constructed by black workers was most clearly revealed when a band of newcomers arrived at Kimberley. As the exhausted men trudged into the town, they were subjected to a rough local initiation. "The entry into the camp of a column of natives in single file, their pace shaky and their ribs protruding," observed one digger, "was always a curious spectacle."

> As soon as they saw them appear, the Kaffirs who had been living at Kimberley for a long time set up a strident clamour that was immediately repeated by the rest of the black colony. And, on every hillock of debris gathered a crowd, breathless with curiosity, which greeted the newly arrived with a deafening *gouba* and a hail of stones and gravel: such was the salutation that these unfortunate people, twisted by hunger and fatigue, received from their friends as a form of welcome.[34]

This initiation into life on the fields was a common occurrence and, because it broke the drabness of everyday life, was frequently commented upon. An American digger described how newcomers were set upon, "hooted at, and pelted with dirt and stones by their better-initiated countrymen. This reception of the neophyte is a daily occurrence, and the ear can readily follow the direction pursued by the entering band by listening for the succession of derisive yells which greets it at every step of its progress."[35] Gardner Williams, the American general manager of De Beers, saw this custom as a form of "hazing," the boisterous initiation practised at some North American colleges. Despite this "pelting with rotten fruit and stones," wrote Williams, "the natives were not churlish at heart, and might, afterward, share their last crust with the strangers."[36]

The rough manner of this harsh welcome is typical of the "degradation ceremonies" described by Irving Goffman or the ritual that Victor Turner has associated with rites of initiation.[37] In the rural areas a person undergoing a change of status or place often had to pass through a period of purification marked by the ritual inversion of normal social practices, a form of symbolic behaviour that detached him from his former life.[38] A liminal stage then served to level and homogenize people of different origins and status. As they entered the third stage, of ritual incorporation and aggregation, the initiates acquired a new set of rights and obligations and were expected to behave in accordance with the norms and standards of their new position.

Migrant workers uprooted from their home society were in sore need of a social and personal identity that would allow them to adapt to an alien, industrial
environment. By 1883 the Kimberley mine had been quarried over an area of nine
acres and to a depth of 420 feet. The mine was filled with the noise of thousands
of men digging, shouting, and singing; the wires hummed overhead as buckets
creaked and rattled in and out of the mine. At the edge of the quarry, depositing
boxes, windlasses, steam engines, and teams of workers contributed to the disturbing cacophony. A great deal of socializing took place around the evening fire when
quantities of maize meal, liquor, and tobacco were shared and consumed. A digger
complained that it was "difficult to break them of the habit of keeping up big fires
all the evening, round which they sit and smoke, and sing and talk with other
Kafirs who 'just drop in,' making a fearful hubbub until 8 or 9 o'clock." He remarked that "visitors were generally very frequent, both morning and evening,
and my 'boys' used to always exercise the duties of hospitality by helping them
liberally to mealie-meal 'pap.' " When the digger remonstrated over the largesse
with which his supplies were distributed, it was explained to him that the visitors
were "brothers" who had a right to be entertained.[39] It was common for black
workers to share a bottle of liquor "with their brothers" and to eat in "parties,"
huddled around a maize meal pot until late at night.[40] These meals were an important activity through which men advertised, as they did at home, their social
belonging and powers of patronage.[41] Through the conviviality of a shared meal,
stories, and songs, migrants built the fellowship and loyalty that was to constitute
the girders of a new social relationship. They were linked together as much by the
public statement of commensality as by the contents of a shared meal.[42] They ate
distinctively "African" food; maize meal, coarse "Kafir meat," venison and offal,
that was clearly different from the tinned foods, bread, and beef consumed by
whites. Men also met and mixed in "Kafir eating houses" that, along with make-
shift canteens, became the focus of their social life. The eating houses were places
where they could socialize without feeling harassed by their employers and were
important centers for the distribution of news about events at home and on the
fields. In the early 1880s there were about twenty-six of these establishments catering to black workers at Kimberley.[43]

To the mine company officials, the eating houses were dens of iniquity and
indiscipline where men were lured by illicit diamond dealing and strong drink.
One of the first acts passed by the British administration after the annexation
of Griqualand West had been a liquor law preventing "servants" from purchasing
liquor without the written permission of their employers. This restriction was
waived in practice, however, partly because merchants did not question the provenance of the chits of paper produced when buying drink, and partly because
the law was seldom enforced: a liberal liquor policy attracted workers and held
them on the mines. As long as there was competition for labour between the
different mining houses, there was little chance of implementing the liquor law;
the result, stated J.W. Mathews, was "practically a free trade in liquor."[44] Large
quantities of liquor were imported to Kimberley from the coastal towns. As there
were no controls on the quality of these brandies, gins, and rums, they were
frequently watered down and then fortified with additives ranging from tobacco,
cannabis, red pepper, and lime, to fusel oil and vitriol.[45] This produced a low-
priced liquor with a high ability to intoxicate that proved particularly popular

with consumers unfamiliar with European alcohol. Drink supplemented and brightened an often dreary diet, served as a physical stimulant and, if taken in temperate amounts, provided a concentrated dose of calories without inducing inebriation. A quart bottle of pure brandy sold at Kimberley for the same price as a one-pound loaf of bread. As in mining communities throughout the world, workers valued liquor as a quick and concentrated nutritional supplement. This was particularly the case in winter, when men, who worked long hours under near-freezing conditions in muddy, open-pit mines, were re-energized by means of unofficial tots of "brandy" and "gin."[46]

As in the rural areas, drinking at Kimberley had a particularly important social function.[47] Through the everyday ritual of communal drinking, individuals won respect through their generosity, participated in reciprocal gift-giving, exchanged news, and found a camaraderie in the bluster of inebriation. Communal drinking was a focal point for leisure activities like dancing, singing, and fighting, that delineated and reinforced gender and group identity. Sorghum beer was "prepared in large quantities for sale and consumed on Sundays," wrote the Rev. George Mitchell, when it leads to "*dancing,* either to Kafir music or the concertina. The Kaffir music is very uproarious, arrogant and heathenish. The concertina is quieter, and the more popular. There is also a deal of brandy drinking. . . ."[48] Adulterated liquor and sorghum beer became almost cultural markers, binding black workers together as effectively as they separated them from their superiors.

On Saturday nights, after receiving their pay, bands of carousing workers took over the "greater portions of Kimberley" and turned them into "a perfect hell" for their white employers.[49] "Every Saturday night and all through Sunday, frightful orgies went on," wrote an Anglican clergyman who associated this revelry with "tribal fights and murders."[50] From his location, the Rev. Mitchell wrote that Sunday mornings brought "unwelcome sounds."

> By 10 o'clock it is like a time of some races or fair. All the week is quiet enough. But no sooner does the noise of the machinery of the camp stop on Saturday afternoon than it begins here, and goes on more or less violently until Sunday night. Sometimes, especially when there is moonlight, it is simply (to a Christian) dreadful. . . . People from different parts of the camp resort on Sundays to this location in shoals.[51]

Men commonly bought several bottles of liquor before the bars closed on Saturday night and hawked their contents on Sunday. The result was a large absentee rate on Mondays when as many as 50 percent of the men failed to report for work. The miners were incapacitated as much by the violence that accompanied drunkenness as by alcohol itself.[52] One compound manager recalled that, "every Monday morning our labour was completely disorganised through boys being in gaol and others intoxicated. We had to lose Monday in arranging new gangs for the work."[53] It often took more than one day to recover from the weekend binge and the inspector of diamond mines considered that "Mondays and part of Tuesdays were usually considered as lost and partly lost days."[54] This Kimberley equivalent of the European "Saint Monday" slowed down expensive machinery, reduced the amount of labour power on the fields, and pushed up the overall cost of labour. As in other parts of the industrializing world, the tenacity of the "St. Monday " phenomenon suggests a rejection of employers' Sabbatarian habits and the enduring strength of noncapitalist concepts and beliefs.[55]

As I pointed out in Chapter 1, on the coastal plain the consumption of alcohol did not carry the moral opprobrium of industrial society. Liquor was viewed as an important source of nutrients, and rituals of public drinking served to bind communities and outline structures of authority. This drinking pattern accepted carnival-like revelry as a relief from heavy bouts of labour and obscured the separation between work and leisure. Monday absenteeism showed a sturdy determination on the part of the worker to cling to his own sense of generosity and respect, leadership and community, and to his own work pattern. But this drinking culture was abhorred by employers who saw in it the theft of their time and the conquest of large parts of the mining camps by disorderly and menacing crowds. However, employers competing for labour had tacitly to accept this break in labour discipline or see their workers move elsewhere.

The singing, dancing, and playing of musical instruments that defiled the Rev. Mitchell's sabbath were favourite pastimes on the diamond fields.[56] The songs were polyphonic and linked the soloist and chorus into an inclusive group. Although we know nothing about the content of these early mine songs, it is highly likely that, in the genre of more recent migrants' songs, they conjured up a bounded world filled with references to home, as well as to local incidents, places and personalities, symbols and images that created spatial and temporal reference points.[57] Songs also provided an outlet for a range of deeply held and often repressed emotions, while affirming shared interests and values. Outsiders frequently have difficulty in understanding unfamiliar cultural expressions and the Rev. Mitchell's remarks on the "uproarious, arrogant and heathenish" nature of "Kaffir music," merely serve to underscore the bounded worlds within which we create meaning. The performance of music, dance, and song was continually reinvigorated by new recruits arriving from home and the quotidian contact with the heterogeneneous population on the fields. Many blacks made their first acquaintance with church singing at Kimberley and, under the influence of composers like Sankey and Moodie, a new genre of liturgical songs was to emerge.[58]

The black worker's practice of adopting a European name seems to have started on the diamond fields. J. W. Mathews was one of the first to remark on these "strikingly curious names."[59] Migrants were required by an 1872 law to register with the police on their arrival at Kimberley, and those who complied with this ruling, perhaps half the black labour force, were given an official European name. These names ranged from terms for local coins, such as Sixpence and Shilling, to popular brands of liquor like Cape Smoke and Pontac, to expletives such as Bloody Fool and God Damn. It is tempting to ascribe what we perceive as the absurdity of these names to the practices of racist whites seeking to infantilize blacks and legitimate their exploitation. While there is some truth in this perspective, I believe it ignores the way in which workers constructed their own vision of the world. Migrants arrived at Kimberley with a highly flexible and adaptive system of naming through which they created a situational identity.[60] To whites, 'Jim" or "Booi" or "April" slid into an amorphous anonymity, and "Woolsack" and "Diamond" into a perplexing incongruity. But to men who took on new forms of address as a mark of their passage through life, these names signified membership of a new and stridently assertive community. At home men were situated in time and space through names that associated them with a clan, a chiefdom, and a specific place in life's passage. Names were metaphors for the range of identities and social relations held simultaneously by the individual. A name carried recognition and status and to be nameless was to be socially dead, worthless, and beyond the protection of society. But the logic behind this system of ordering lost much of its power on the diamond fields, where migrants entered a complex and heterogeneous society. Names that carried a specific meaning at home, and provided their bearers with a temporal and spatial identity, were met with incomprehension on the mines. By adopting the names and ethnic labels applied to them by others, migrants situated themselves within a new social context. They were not anonymous "boys," and their identity was not confined to narrow and far-off clans and chiefdoms; by adopting "European" names they located themselves within a community of workers and adopted labels that, in a rural context, served as badges of self-worth and achievement. "All those returning home," wrote the Rev. Richter from Kimberley, "are happy to have added to their previous name another one by which the whites call them."[61] By extending this system of naming to white officials, traders, miners, and other points of reference, black workers appropriated the other's symbolic system and, by turning it into their own, ordered their lives on the mines.

The black worker's clothing formed another important cultural marker. Migrants generally arrived at Kimberley in heavy, tattered overcoats and corduroy trousers. On the mines they were scantily dressed and normally wore, no doubt with the encouragement of their employers, light kilts of cloth or skin. But on weekends the men dressed in clothing more expressive of their new status. While Christian workers frequently turned out in trousers and tails, most migrants preferred what whites considered a garish, if not bizarre attire. The cast-off, colourful military tunics of Imperial regiments were frequently worn with a range of second-hand garments and footwear.[62] "Everything the White man wears is to them in the light of ornament," wrote one digger.

> One stalwart fellow wears only a vest; another has found and put on an abandoned tall hat. One wears a gaiter-boot, or no boot, or simply a shirt. Another struts proudly by in the bright-buttoned uniform of a soldier's coat, his brown legs in marked contrast to its bright red. Even a cast-aside paper collar is seized and donned, and all this soberly and demurely, and in ignorance of its comicality.[63]

To Africans little concerned with the utility of garments, and unfamiliar with the coordinated signs that made up the clothing codes of white people, this "eccentric dress" had its own specific logic and signification. Like their European names, it was a visible marker of their passage into a new community; their clothing distinguished them from both inexperienced, novice miners and their employers, advertised their wealth and experience, and proclaimed their new status. As early as 1877 the governor of Lourenço Marques remarked on the "more or less extravagant European dress" with which migrants returned home, and an Englishwoman living at Lourenço Marques in the 1870s-1880s observed that men came back from the Cape and Natal "in complete European costume, looking anything but nice in it."[64] As initiates to European forms of dress, many black workers were unrestricted in the manner in which they assembled their clothes, and they dressed to impress their peers rather than their employers.[65] The worker's understanding of the accumulation of capital was essentially different from that of his employers. For while whites valued capital in economic terms, migrants perceived capital in terms of its symbolic and social power.[66] Through his generosity in the distribution of food and drink, and his knowledge in the domains of naming, dress, music, dancing, and other spheres of life on the fields, the worker won the respect and admiration of his fellows. As black migrants established their own norms and expectations, they accepted the control and surveillance of peers whose local knowledge counteracted employers' attempts to impose their cultural hegemony.

The identity that black migrants created for themselves at Kimberley was not merely that of a fractured, racially defined working class reacting against the imposed labour routine of industrial capitalism; they also adopted and developed a consciousness of themselves as Christians, and as members of what whites called a tribe or nation. In 1883 the Congregational Church saw Kimberley, a place "thronged with people of all races," as "the most important missionary center in South Africa." The Congregationalists had two churches on the diamond fields; one under Gwaai Tyamzashe at Kimberley and the other at Dutoitspan under James Poot. Church membership stood at 172, with another 230 attending Sunday services.[67] The Methodists believed that Kimberley offered "a splendid opportunity . . . for scattering the seeds of truth among the native tribes of South Africa." They had seven ministers on the fields, of whom two were black, and their membership stood at almost 200 in 1885, with 61 on trial. Of the three Anglican churches on the diamond fields, two were frequented largely by blacks; the Lutheran, Dutch Reformed, and Catholic churches also served black congregations. As the churchmen realized, men were more susceptible to conversion at Kimberley because, separated from the tight controls of their home communities, they exercised a greater individual choice over their religious and other beliefs. Brass bands, magic lantern shows, and enthusiastic, open-air religious services attracted large numbers of men.[68] Migrants carried home a knowledge of the gospel that, however limited, laid the seed of belief in rural areas where missionaries intended to raise the fruit of Christianity.[69]

Alongside Christian teaching, Shangaans and other black workers acquired a general familiarity with European ways of seeing the world. Black and white churchmen preached a universal set of ethics that cut across the cultural diversity of Kimberley. Although philanthropically motivated, their teaching often attacked the cultural values of migrant workers and imposed upon them the beliefs of their employers. Church pronouncements on the evils of idleness, drunkenness, diamond theft, polygamy, the accumulation of bridewealth, and the frivolity born of high wages were not always well received.[70] This industrial morality was also propagated in the rural areas, where missionaries attacked the diamond fields as "Satan's nest" or "the country of Sodom" because so many of their converts returned home with stolen diamonds and a penchant for strong drink.[71] Evangelists at Kimberley frequently saw poverty as a moral problem to be righted through the adoption of a lifestyle marked by frugality, sobriety, discipline, punctuality, providence, and obedience. In this way work became both a moral and an economic necessity, and upward social mobility was justified as a fair reward for moral worth. These qualities were stressed by Christians whose religious views, through their experience with the working class in Europe, were based as much on social reform as on faith. Because of their concern with the material well-being of their spiritual charges, evangelists acted as a major channel through which the norms and values of industrialism permeated noncapitalist societies. To the Kimberley missionary, the Rev. Arnt, "to work with zeal" was "a fruit and blessing of Christianity, an internal civilizing," while on the coast the Rev. Junod believed "the gospel of work" to be "a blessing for the blacks as it is for any other race," as it transformed a "capricious existence" into "an orderly life."[72] The worker who accepted this cultural hegemony might become more prosperous, but only at the cost of applying to himself forms of surveillance and control that had once been a site of contestation. By incorporating the habits and values of his employers, regarding the sanctity of private property, the rhythm and discipline of industry, and the relationship between labour and spiritual salvation, the worker developed, in the words of E. P. Thompson, an "inner compulsion" to labour and became "his own slave driver."[73]

Christianity also influenced workers to accept their employers' notion of the passage of time. Prayer meetings and bells structured the day, the Sabbath marked the passage of the week, Christmas and Good Friday outlined the year, and a distinctive eschatology took this linear sense of time beyond the grave. An individualism was inculcated by the privacy of reading and by the stress on a personal accountability for salvation. Various denominations also divided the social world of the miner by enforcing a strong stand on temperance, and by seizing hold of ceremonies, such as baptism, confirmation, marriage, and death, that marked his passage through life. The churches further divided the work force through the practice of racial segregation and by encouraging most black converts to live in small locations under their own ministers. By separating Christians from the rump of the black labour force, the church attempted to foster and protect a distinct "respectability," created by distinctive forms of naming, dress, music, and other sensibilities, together with behaviour and comportment, that were essentially European. Through this geographical and cultural segregation ministers drove a wedge into the fledging black working class.

However, the church was not just the spiritual wing of industrial capitalism. It provided a small number of men with the fellowship of a bounded community and introduced a far larger number to a range of powerful new resources.[74] Migrant workers came from rural societies whose cultural expressions were above all oral, gestural, and visual. At Kimberley the power of the written word filled everything from travel and work passes to the chit of paper allowing the purchase of liquor. The church offered workers an education that permitted them to manoeuvre in the material world or climb out of it. Blacks who acquired a basic literacy and a rudimentary knowledge of arithmetic could occupy leadership positions in the local church and find relatively well-paid jobs as clerks, translators, or letter-writers. The school established by the St. Mattheus Anglican mission in the West End location was supported financially by the Cape government, school fees, and private funds. The congregants contributed £100 towards the construction of the mission and were responsible for the cost of repairs. In mid-1883 some 71 men and 15 women were on the books of the night school, while 57 boys and 64 girls were inscribed at the day school.[75] The churches' stress on self-improvement provided a training for community leadership, and the Kimberley locations were to produce political leaders such as Robert Mashaba, Sol Plaatje, and Z. K. Mathews. But for most migrants the encounter with Christianity was a youthful adventure of short duration. Few immigrants from the rural areas were willing to exchange basic elements of their culture, such as *lobola* and polygamy, for those of an alien industrial morality, and in 1889 only about five hundred blacks on the diamond fields claimed to be Christian.[76] However, as I shall show in later chapters, the limited number of converts does not reflect the important role played by the church in diffusing new ideas throughout rural southern Africa.

Ethnicity and Identity

The missionaries preached a universal brotherhood that was not restricted by ties of kinship, or loyalty to a chief and his followers, and they played a crucial role in stimulating an ethnic consciousness amongst workers at Kimberley. Most missions were rooted in a specific rural area and their pastors and priests had come to the diamond fields to watch over their converts. By the late 1870s several mission groups had assembled a grid of orthographies and dictionaries to cover the southeastern branch of what linguists had only recently determined as the Bantu language group. The process of "standardizing" and "codifying" these linguistic forms had created bounded languages linked to the missionaries and their converts, and it was largely through these vehicular languages that the migrants were introduced to the knowledge that accompanied the European vision of the world.

A desire for the power that accompanies literacy was to become an important factor drawing men to the diamond fields. Vernacular literacy was accompanied by a belief in the positive attributes of "tribalism" or "nationalism," what we would today call ethnicity. In the eyes of many missionaries and administrators, ethnicity was a bulwark against the forces of social decline induced by industrialisation; it was also a familiar form of social categorisation and a means of bringing order to the swirling mass of black workers. Shangaans were stereotyped as strong and capable workers, less sophisticated than colonial blacks and possessed of "curious habits," such as smoking cigarettes with the burning end in the mouth.[77] The civil commissioner at Kimberley had firm ideas, enhanced by their originality, on the social composition of the black work force. In 1883 he determined the Shangaans to be "a warlike tribe governed by Sothangana." Yet Shoshangane had been dead for a quarter-century and many east coasters came from areas free of Gaza rule. It is also unlikely that people from around Delagoa Bay, classified as "Portuguese Zulus," shared the civil commissioner's opinion of them as "a lazy and useless race." It was perhaps this unfortunate reputation that caused the classificatory term to disappear, as "Portuguese Zulus" chose to become Shangaans. Under the rough taxonomic system used by the civil commissioner, these two groups were covered by the label "Zulu," alongside the "British and proper Zulu, the Swazi and Matabele."[78] This elementary form of classification made Africans visible to Europeans and incorporated them into the image of colonial society. But these mental constructs were also forms of identification that could be adopted and exploited by migrants who shared a specific rural inheritance, a lived experience on the mines, and a certain cultural fluidity. Social relations are never static, and the diamond fields served as a crucible for ethnicity as a new and dynamic means of distinguishing self from others.

Migrants from the east coast had to compete for work with other, more established, and politically homogeneous peoples. It seems no coincidence that they surged onto the fields only when an exodus of Pedi and Sotho workers made this possible. The sudden arrival of men from the east coast threatened the status quo and caused vertical, ethnic divisions to crystalize in the working class. The fear of death, whether due to disease, mine accidents, at the hands of strangers, or on the way home, permeated the daily lives of migrant workers and was no doubt magnified as a precapitalist belief system was assaulted by an industrial environment. But perhaps most troubling for the migrant worker was his isolation from the structures of support provided by the extended family and the chiefdom. In a society without chiefs or families, and hence lacking the rural controls of patriarchy, kinship, and political patronage, workers had to create their own indices of hierarchy, respectability, and self-worth. Through the constant repetition of daily experience, black workers on the diamond fields created the congruities and traditions, values and expectations that gave an equilibrium to their existence. These daily rituals grooved and regrooved their beliefs, established and reconfirmed their membership of a group, and provided them with a place in the order of industrial life.[79]

On the coastal plain political identity was rooted in the chiefdom, although ties of obligation and assistance extended to kinsmen living as clients of other chiefs. The putative nature of kinship and the *kondza* system allowed the integration of outsiders into these bounded groups, whose membership was ascribed and delineated by various cultural traits, including an often pronounced antipathy to other kin groups. Allegiance to the kin group did not diminish loyalty to the wider chiefdom, and people found a political identity in both institutions. But in the cosmopolitan society of the diamond fields, these political identities were too narrow and restrictive to function effectively, and, gradually, the fictive element in kinship was extended to include a wider community in which the chief was replaced by culture as the focus of loyalty. At the same time, a society that accepted fictive kinship could easily extend this belief into a putative ethnicity built on the use of familial terms, such as "brother" or "uncle," to describe the relations between workers.[80] Ethnicity, like kinship, was based on myths of origin, ascriptive and putative belonging, as well as relations of reciprocity.

In an environment where the life of a black worker, according to Louis Cohen, had "about the same value as that of a tiresome fly,"[81] men were obliged to construct their own system of social assistance. Excessive heat, extreme cold, and poor living conditions encouraged pneumonia, fevers, and dysentery in the mining camps. This was particularly a problem in the early years, when few brick houses were constructed because of uncertainty over the longevity of the mines. Respiratory problems were caused by long hours in the open-cast mines and by the choking dust blown from the heaps of fine worked soil, or "tailings," scattered throughout the camp. Medical services were horribly inefficient, and the corpses of those who had died from disease or injury were frequently left in the street. Some of the sick were housed in the jail, but this did little to reduce the high mortality rate. "A dead nigger lying in some nook or corner on the open veldt at break of day," a resident was to remember, "was so ordinary an event as to be scarcely worth a paragraph."[82] A hospital was eventually constructed for blacks in 1883 with monies collected from their registration fees. Two wards were built, one for the sick and the other for accident victims; but even to a white resident of Kimberley, the "nigger's hospital" seemed "an outrageous place."[83] In 1883–1884, when Kimberley was infected by smallpox, about 600 black workers lost their lives. Inadequate sanitation increased the rapidity with which disease spread. In 1878 the black mortality rate was about 80 per 1,000; it was to rise to almost 100 per 1,000 a decade later. As William Worger has noted, this made Kimberley one of the most dangerous and pestilential towns in the world.[84] The brutality of existence in the mining camps drove black workers to create an "extraordinary freemasonry and rapidity of communicating information."[85] Kinsmen carried a sick man's food and medical costs and paid his burial fees. If relatives were not available, "companions or his people" shouldered the responsibility, which indicated, commented the Rev. Richter, "that they care for their sick people, not only during the journey but also while working."[86]

The formation of loose, corporate groups was also based on an exclusion of outsiders that sometimes developed into hostility, and the "tribal fights" between "Sotho" and "Zulu" that punctuated life in the isolated railway camps were repeated at Kimberley.[87] The communal brawls that disturbed Kimberley weekends and left large numbers of men unfit for work on Mondays were partly the result of shifts in the composition of the work force. These heightened competition for a limited and fluctuating number of jobs and destabilized the ethnic balance of power at specific mines. Migrants also looked to liquor and fighting as a means of relief from the tensions generated by their overcrowded living conditions and the unrelenting demands of their work.[88] But faction fighting was also concerned with forging community and gender identities. On the east coast, one of the ways in which boys learnt what was expected of them as men was by taunting and insulting neighbouring herdsboys and, often after a pitched battle, seizing their animals.[89] This socially sanctioned notion of violence, associated with masculinity, group identity, and the responsibility that comes with age, was carried to the diamond fields. Faction fights were a display of belonging through which men chose their own leaders and resorted to their own notions of justice. Through the blows from their pickhandles, knobkerries, and fighting sticks, atomised individuals broke the bonds of rural society and, as they battled against their opponents and depended on the leadership, courage, and solidarity of their comrades, asserted their masculinity, and forged the outlines of hesitant, new identities.[90]

It was in the turbulent and cosmopolitan atmosphere of labour centers such as Kimberley that men were introduced to the mental imagery of an overarching group identity. Migrants found a sense of security and a reassuring fellowship in meeting and mixing as the members of what Europeans or other Africans defined as a specific "tribe" or "nation." Excluded by established ethnic groups, classified as a group by the white authorities, and in search of the social and political stability and moral economy they knew at home, migrants from the east coast accepted the name "Shangaan," and then started to give this term of identification their own meaning and coherence. Men who possibly came from opposing and hostile chiefdoms found themselves part of a wide and shaky ethnic diaspora that included Shangaans and Portuguese Zulus at Kimberley, Amatongas in Natal, and Mozbiekers and Delagoa Bay men in the Cape. They also started to establish a wider identity based on a shared pigmentation and their interpretation of a specific class experience. A small number of migrants adopted the universalistic beliefs of Christianity, but the vast majority shared a pattern of behaviour, and a system of values, that set them apart from whites.

Workers constructed their own world, but they did so within the constraints of colonial society. In 1880 Griqualand West was incorporated into the Cape Colony and the Kimberley members of parliament succeeded in strengthening the police force and legalizing strip searching. Under the Diamond Trade Act of 1882, the penalties for illicit diamond dealing were increased and a dubious rapidity was introduced into court procedure. But the new level of cooperation between employers and the state was accompanied by a collapse in the price of diamonds, which, together with the heavy costs incurred by the development of underground works, speeded up the process of company amalgamation and the demise of competitive capitalism. Kimberley was gripped by depression after the collapse of speculative shares in mid-1881 was followed, in June the following year, by a 30 percent fall in the price of diamonds. The years 1882–1885 were marked by bankruptcies, takeovers, and an increasing amalgation of companies. As the De Beers and Kimberley Central Diamond Mining companies emerged as the two giants on the fields, employers were able to centralize their decision-making and strengthen their position vis-à-vis both labour and the state. At the same time, they attempted to recuperate their losses by cutting black wages to as little as 20s per month, and by inducing the police to clamp down sharply particularly on public drunkenness.

In January 1883, on the eve of the implementation of strip searching, Shangaans began leaving the diamond fields in large numbers.[91] While "old hands" returned home due to the downturn in conditions on the fields, new men were dissuaded from leaving home as African chiefs in the Transvaal, following the British withdrawal in 1881, attempted to reassert their independence. The principal labour route through the eastern Transvaal was closed entirely for several months in 1883 when Pretoria attacked Mapoch, and, in the northern Transvaal, where the Boers exercised little effective control, many Shangaans returning from Kimberley were attacked and stripped of their wages.[92] The route to Kimberley via Natal was also made more difficult by the folding of the Dunn scheme and by strict quarantine regulations introduced to combat the spread of smallpox.[93] With migrants fearful of contracting the disease on the mines, the number of Shangaan "new hands" registering at Kimberley declined sharply from 10,300 in 1882, when they composed more than half the work force, to 1,680 in 1883.[94] In 1884 fewer than 1,000 Shangaans signed on at Kimberley as new hands. Meanwhile, the depression accelerated the rise of De Beers, which was able to establish an effective monopoly over the diamond fields in 1888. The boardroom victory of Cecil Rhodes and his colleagues had an immediate impact on the daily lives of black workers, for monopoly capitalism modernised the system of management and initiated a new set of labour relations.

Closed Compounds and Industrial Morality

Through its monopoly, De Beers forced up the price of diamonds by cutting back on production. As hauling gear was dismantled and open-cast mining operations restricted, the number of workers on the fields dropped precipitously. The need for workers declined further when De Beers halted the surface excavations in the Dutoitspan and Bultfontein mines and extended the subterranean works, first started in 1885, beneath the Kimberley and De Beers mines. These actions caused the number of black workers on the mines to decline further, from 11,300 in 1887 to 6,000 in 1890.[95] Amalgamation concentrated political and economic power in the hands of a small number of mine owners who, no longer threatened by the com-

The De Beers' compound. The prototype of the closed compound.

petition for labour that had pitted one company against another, were able to over-rule the objections of local merchants and confine black workers within closed compounds. The first closed compound was constructed in 1885 at the height of the depression, and four years later there were seventeen of these structures on the fields. The large West End compound, belonging to De Beers, eventually enclosed over 3,000 men on four acres of land. The inspector of diamond mines described the compound in 1886 in the following terms:

> Within an enclosing wall are arranged sleeping huts along one and part of two sides. The huts are constructed of corrugated iron and wood, the walls lined inside with sun-dried bricks. At one flank of one side of the square are the meat and bread shops and the cooking-houses, on the op-posite side are the urinals etc. Along the end of the square unoccupied by huts are built the office, clothing and food shops, mess-room, recreation room and hospital. . . . At the centre of the square large tanks for washing and bathing are provided . . . [and] well supplied with river water.[96]

As a result of the takeover by De Beers and the continuing reduction in the size of the work force, by 1894 some 5,800 black workers were housed in ten compounds.

The progenitors of the compound system liked to argue that it was the only means of preventing the large-scale theft of diamonds. But Rob Turrell has shown that compounds also functioned to discipline and regulate a preindustrial work force.[97] Employers combatted the irregular movement of workers to and from the fields by creating a surplus of labour in the compounds. As Turrell pointed out, this local reserve army of labour, as well as that in the locations, provided a pool of workers familiar with the demands of underground mining. Workers incarcerated in closed compounds were coaxed into registering for periods of two to three months that, through regular renewal, could amount to nine and even eighteen months.[98] One indication of the extent to which the labour force had become stabilized was the disappearance of the old rough welcome or hazing that had formerly initiated migrants to life on the fields.[99] To persuade newly-arrived workseekers to accept the restrictions of life in the compounds, management initially provided a controlled amount of alcohol before and after the work shift and allowed men to go into town over weekends. But De Beers gradually replaced this brandy tot with a low-alcohol "ginger" beer and closed the compounds. As early as 1886, the inspector of diamond mines commented that "one material result of the compound system is that on Mondays the muster roll of capable Kafirs is nearly complete, whereas previously a company could not reckon on more than a half or a third of their Kafirs turning up every Monday morning in a sufficiently sober state to work."[100] The compound system suppressed the worker's practice of choosing when he would drink and how much he would consume. Another consequence was a sharp reduction in alcohol-related accidents in the mine and in faction fighting. The compound was "an undoubted success," wrote the protector of natives, "and a protection to the Natives from drink and robbery."[101] A survey conducted by the Alliance for the Prevention of the Deterioration of the Natives Through Drink indicated that the discipline enforced by the compound system raised worker productivity by 20 to 50 percent.[102]

The compounds restricted the emergence of a class solidarity by separating black and white miners and by isolating blacks from their peers in other compounds. Some companies separated underground and surface workers into different compounds. Workers who undertook any form of militant action were easily rounded up and could be starved of food and water. Degrading and humiliating body searches and tight controls over the worker's movements, extending to those of his bowels, reduced the level of diamond theft. The terrifying degree of surveillance inherent in this system of control has led several historians to find the inspiration for the compound in the prison.[103] The power of this argument is based on the immorality conjured up by the image of unfree labour. But this overestimates the strength of the employers and exaggerates their ability to impose their will on the work force. After all, the function of the compound, unlike the prison, was not to punish men convicted of misdemeanors by separating them from society; its function was rather to discipline a voluntary force of migrant labourers. To see mine owners as warders and mineworkers as prisoners obscures the nature of labour relations. The compounds had to attract men from competing areas of employment such as the gold mines, and, to do this, management and labour had to negotiate working conditions that were acceptable to both parties. Shangaans, Chopis, and Inhambane Tongas who, by the end of the 1880s, again made up the major part of the work force, came from an area almost entirely free of European control. As they were not yet compelled to sell their labour by a colonial government, they had to be attracted to the diamond fields by competitive working conditions. The mine owners were dealing with volunteers, not prisoners, and they were fully conscious of the need to modernize the work force by teaching men the skills and discipline of underground mining while creating conditions that would draw labour to the fields. It is not sufficient to explain how the compound system put money into the pockets of the mine owners; we also need to know why migrant workers chose to subject themselves to a voluntary and often lengthy incarceration in these confined spaces.

Under the De Beers' monopoly, the compound system exerted a downward pressure on wages, as workers were no longer able to sell their labour to the highest bidder. This has led to the belief that a major function of the compound was to depress wages, a point that, as it is a central element in the compound-as-prison argument, deserves some investigation.[104] Firstly it should be recalled that in 1882, when well over 17,000 blacks worked on the fields, their wages averaged about 30s per week without food. During the depression years, weekly wages in the Kimberely mine fell to as little as 20s but by 1890, when there were only 5,840 blacks employed on the fields, they had climbed back to 32s.[105] It was thus with some justification that the manager of De Beers claimed in 1888 that "our natives are better paid than the miners in any of the European countries."[106] The rise in black incomes had occurred despite the downward pressure on wages exerted by the forces of land alienation and taxation in the colonial territories, and despite the replacement of old hands, unwilling to accept the new compound regime, by cheap recruits imported from Gazaland and Inhambane.[107] It is clear that the mine owners, despite their growing monopsony, raised wages in an attempt to coax workers to give up their freedom of movement, accept the increased discipline and danger of underground labour, the new restrictions on the theft of diamonds, and the loss of St Monday.

The underground works initially consisted of a honeycomb of tunnels beneath the Kimberley and De Beers mines. Systematic mining only started in 1889 after the early tunnels collapsed and the last independent claims were amalgamated. At the De Beers mine the men clambered down the ladders to the working levels over four hundred feet below the surface. Long tunnels were driven off the shaft, at intervals of forty feet, through the hard rock at the edge of the mine. From these tunnels a large number of small, timbered galleries were dug through the diamondiferous blue ground to the opposite wall of the mine, where they were widened into stopes. Once these neighbouring galleries were joined, they formed chambers often as large as 100 feet long, 20 feet wide, and 20 feet high. Miners used long jumper drills sharpened at both ends to dislodge soft rock or hammered short drills into harder rock to create holes to be charged with dynamite. The ceilings of the upper working levels were then blasted and cut back through the blue ground to form a system of underground terracing. The loose rock was shovelled down tunnels to the main galleries, loaded into trucks, and railed to the shafts, from where it was conveyed to the surface in skips or elevators that took thirty-five seconds to be lifted over a thousand feet. Above ground the rocks and earth were placed in loading boxes, poured into tip trucks, and carried to the depositing floors.

Underground mining revolutionised the labour process. It required a greatly increased investment of capital to buy up the last individual claims; sink shafts; drive and timber galleries; install haulage equipment, electricity, telephones, and a system of subterranean railage; and to pay the high salaries required to attract the skilled labour needed to initiate this form of mining. To prevent their investments from falling idle, the mineowners introduced a system of continuous twelve-hour, back-to-back shifts. The men took about an hour to get to and from the rock face, an hour for lunch, and spent the remaining time drilling, shovelling, and carting. Shift work subjected the worker to the full intensity of industrial labour, as it stripped him of any control over when he worked and dominated his leisure hours and social life. Absenteeism was discouraged by the introduction of a ticket system according to which the worker's wage was noted on a card at the end of each shift. A miner who missed his shift received no pay for that day and, as he had to buy his own food, he had to carry the cost of absenteeism. Management sought to avoid the problem of disciplining, supervising, and controlling migrant mineworkers by turning to subcontractors, generally former miners, who fetched their men from the compound barracks. The subcontractor was remunerated according to the amount of blue ground raised to the surface by his team, and he in turn credited each of his men, apart from those working on the pumps, tracks, and timber supports, with a shift ticket only once the man had drilled a minimum number of inches or filled a designated number of trucks. Task work was revolutionised by this system, as it introduced the concept of a standard minimum rate of production, agreed to by both employer and worker. Many of these miners were children who were quick to learn and adopt the new pace of labour. Boys under the age of twelve were prohibited from working underground, but there was little way of verifying the age of young miners and the tradition of employing children continued well into the twentieth century.[108] The work rhythm was also driven by the new division of labour and a chain of dependency emerged as specialised drillers, shovellers, and trammers fought to keep up with the rolling trams and haulage skips and struggled to achieve the minimum output needed to earn a shift ticket.[109]

As the men accepted the need to subject themselves to this labour rhythm, experience was hammered into tradition, and employers were able to reduce the level of surveillance, cutting the ratio of overseers to workers from 1:6 to 1:30. The sober and disciplined pace of labour also contributed to the rapid fall in working costs, from 13s2d per load of 16 cubic meters in 1882 to 8s10d in 1890 and 6s7d in 1894.[110] Gardner Williams frequently attributed this improvement in production to the skills of the black workers employed by De Beers, 70 percent of whom were engaged underground by 1890–1891. Increased productivity was won at the cost of competitive wages, and in 1890 black workers on the diamond fields earned more than twice the wage of their peers on the Witwatersrand.[111] The result was that experienced miners chose to go to Kimberley, while even novices had to be recruited to labour in the shallow, outcrop mines of the Witwatersrand.[112]

The system of using high wages to attract skilled workers with minimal aid from recruiters proved successful only as long as it could be supported by the profitability of the diamond industry. But in 1890 the fortunes of the diamond magnates suffered a sharp and sudden reverse when a large part of their speculative investment in the Witwatersrand gold fields was lost following a crash on the Johannesburg share market. At the same time, profits on the diamond fields were adversely affected by a severe drought and, later that year, by a 30 percent slide in the value of diamonds. As in 1876 and 1883, a fall in profitability was immediately translated into a wage reduction. But this time black workers, who were more experienced and proletarianized than their fathers' generation, did not respond to the cut in their weekly wages, from 32s in 1890 to 24s in 1891, by emigrating from the fields. Instead, already angered by the reduction in their numbers, they turned on the white subcontractors and team leaders who were the symbol of their exploitation. As this new form of aggressive industrial action spread, the inspector of diamond mines reported that "racial non-cooperation and violence became the order of the day" and raised for the first time the spectre of "a Kaffir rising."[113]

As most underground workers were engaged in piecework, it is extremely difficult to assess the actual content of their wages, particularly as the worker had to negotiate his wage rate with a subcontractor who had won the tender to perform a specific task. The size of the wage was also influenced by whether a man worked overtime and on Sundays, by the richness of the section of the mine in which he laboured, its dangers, and the level of his skill. Thus even after the wage reduction of 1891, experienced underground drillers and trammers could still earn 5s per day, or up to 30s per week. However, even a weekly wage of 21s compared favourably with the 15s paid for similar work on the Witwatersrand.[114] But although black miners earned competitive wages at Kimberley, they experienced little upward mobility, partly due to pressures from European miners with a long history of opposition to deskilling, and partly because employers wished to divide the work force along racial lines. Black workers were locked into closed compounds, subjected to body searches, and precluded from working as blasters (in 1885) and team leaders (1889). These practices protected white workers but also restricted the emergence of an established and skilled black leadership. Nevertheless, the wages paid to workers in the compounds remained the highest in South Africa. The comparative financial advantage of living in the compound was stated simply and forcefully by a worker known only as Charlie. "I would prefer the outside," he reported in 1893, "if I could get the same wages there."[115] A miner like Charlie could increase his earnings by working overtime or by finding diamonds, which he handed to the overseer.[116] He could also participate in the informal economy of the compound as a cook, barber, or tailor, by taking in washing, or by making and selling objects ranging from horsewire and copper bangles to clothing and cakes. Penny capitalism flourished to such an extent that the De Beers compound was compared in 1895 to "a great bazaar in the East or an old English fair."[117] In the compounds Charlie was sure to receive his pay and there was little chance of it being stolen from him.

Industrial Paternalism

By restricting the size of the cash content of the wage, De Beers imposed a stability on traditionally volatile worker incomes. Although cash payments were reduced, a renewed effort was made to attract and hold workers, and increase their efficiency, by improving the social sector of the wage. The purpose behind this reorientation of managerial policy following the crisis of 1890–1891 becomes clearer if we abandon the analogy between the compound and the prison and see in it the logic, taken to its fullest extreme, of the mining village or company town. In Europe or the United States, management frequently had to attract workers to new centres of employment, particularly in rural areas, by means of a set of paternalistic labour relations that combined fair wages with a series of nontransportable benefits.[118] In return management expected loyalty, discipline, and acquiescence.

Much the same strategy was practised in the compounds of the diamond fields, where the willingness of men to re-engage for long periods of work, and hence effectively to reproduce the labour force despite the absence of women, was particularly dependent on benefits that did not fluctuate with market conditions.

The system of industrial relations emerging under monopoly capitalism at Kimberley was rooted in a specific mentality. Employers at Kimberley were members of a triumphant class that had conquered the world, and they were supremely confident that their dominance was as much the result of moral as of technological superiority. Industry was not only concerned with making profits; the industrialist, like the missionary, believed he had a civilizing mission, that of elevating blacks from barbarousness and savagery through the discipline of labour. Migrants who arrived on the diamond fields "in a wretched state of emaciation," it was frequently remarked, returned home "sleek, well-made and loaded with purchases."[119] Gardner Williams went so far as to assert that, for the migrant worker, Kimberley was a "field flowing with meat and porridge."[120] J. B. Currey noted in the 1870s that the Mahawas or Pedi who arrived on the diamond fields were "docile, ignorant, helpless creatures, the very raw material of the slave trade." The Makelakas, Currey remarked, were "a race said to be without chiefs or laws, organization of any kind whatever."[121] This discourse, with deep historical roots in the European perception of the other, linked the evolutionary progress of Africans as a race to the discipline of labour. More than elsewhere in the world, wage labor was perceived as a moral necessity.[122] The counterface of this belief in the civilising powers of work was migrant labour as a source of disorder or proletarianisation, with its stark social consequences. When black tribesmen were separated from their domestic economy and culture, it was feared, they were contaminated by the aggressive individualism and cupidity of industrial society and dragged down the ladder of evolution. In the language of employers, administrators, and missionaries, this resulted in a "demoralized," "decadent," and "degenerate" work force.[123] This evolutionist discourse portrayed "raw Kaffirs" as "children incapable of governing themselves," or as "absolute children, although fully grown."[124] Even a sympathetic observer such as Junod was to note in the 1890s that, "this child, this younger brother, the black, needs a sympathetic voice to instruct him and to put him on guard against the dangers of a civilization of which he attempts, all too often, to assimilate only the faults and the vices."[125] The discourse on the need to protect the "weaker races," which was later to underlay notions of trusteeship and separate development, was already current at Kimberley in the 1880s, where it exerted a strong influence on the relations between employers and labourers. Many philanthropists initially saw compounds as a means of protecting blacks from the uncertainties and insecurities of wage labour in a particularly volatile sector of the economy. While the employers saw the compound as a mechanism of social control, many missionaries lauded it as an alternative to the shanty towns, which they viewed as products of social degeneration and poor hygiene rather than poverty. They believed the compounds to be spaces in which tribesmen could be instilled with notions of discipline, frugality, sobriety, cleanliness, and other virtues, while being protected from the evils of industrialism. "Compounds offer many safeguards," wrote the Rev. Jackson, against "the natives deteriorating when brought into contact with the civilization of our larger towns."[126] The compound system was "a great protection to the natives," according to the evolutionist anthropologist and churchman, W. C. Willoughby, and a "vast improvement upon the condition of affairs existing at Kimberley before it was adopted."[127] Even the black editor and politician John Tengu Jabavu considered the compound system "as near perfection as it was possible to make it."[128] The compounds were not just the product of economic necessity or social control, they were also the result of confluent discourses that shape actions as much as material forces.

The amalgamation of claims concentrated workers on mining properties, and the accumulation of financial resources in fewer hands also provided employers with the political and economic power needed to implement a policy of industrial paternalism. This was most vividly expressed in the modern garden suburb of Kenilworth, built for white miners on the edge of Kimberley in 1889, where subsidized rents and a range of social and welfare facilities reduced the traditionally turbulent white workers of Kimberley to what Hobson called "the political and economic serfs" of De Beers.[129] The same policy, passed through the heavy filter of racism and colonialism, was also applied to black workers whom employers saw as children in need of paternal care and parental control. Through a system of what I shall call racial paternalism De Beers sought to build up a body of skilled miners without giving them cause to develop an aggressive class consciousness.[130] White colonists aped the paternalism of their social superiors in Europe when they called their workers "boys" and demanded to be addressed as "master," a discourse that infantilised black miners and locked them into the "natural" (biological) role of eternal children.[131] The compound was portrayed by management as a fictive chiefdom. This notion, I wish to suggest, was less a "mine owners' fantasy"[132] than a managerial strategy through which De Beers battened onto, reinforced, and fed off rural structures of authority in a way that was seen to provide workers with a sense of belonging and self-control that would prevent their "degeneration" into a proletariat in need of rights. Production in the homestead economy was marked by a set of social relations that included a strong sense of mutual rights and obligations, and a respect for authority, as well as a conceptualisation of the work unit as a relatively harmonious and integrated social entity. But these notions of authority and moral economy lost much of their meaning at Kimberley, where men were brought together as equals from unrelated localities. The authority structure within the compound provided uprooted individuals with leaders, the lineaments of a community, and a form of social cohesion that reduced their alienation from their fellows. In the discourse of racial paternalism, the compound manager was the "great white chief" who arbitrated in disputes between workers and investigated complaints raised about their treatment at the hands of sub-contractors.[133] He was portrayed, not as an exploiter of the workers, but rather as a natural intermediary in the dealings between capital and labour, the local equivalent of the rural chief whom Junod had referred to as "the master, but also the father" of the village.[134] As the compound manager, his police, and *indunas* were not involved in the production side of mining, their everyday relations with the miners were relatively benign and gave a human content to what was otherwise an alienating wage relationship. As an expression of trust many workers, who normally kept their wages in leather money belts until they could be entrusted to friends returning home, deposited their savings with the compound manager.[135]

Through this notion of the compound-as-tribe, management saw labour relations in terms that might be described as unitary rather than conflictual. The only legitimate form of dissent allowed in the compounds, from this perspective, was that caused by ethnic divisions. As the members of different tribes were considered "clannish," they were housed separately and their leisure time activities were structured on an ethnic basis, at least partly to prevent the "tribal jealousy and vanity" at the root of "occasional fights."[136] These vertical divisions in the labour force served to hamper worker solidarity and, on occasion, were manipulated by management. The state reinforced this managerial paternalism by separating the offices of registrar and protector of natives and by adding to the latter the duties of an inspector of compounds. The protector of natives and inspector of compounds was expected to visit compounds, check on the activities of the compound managers, and act as a court of appeal for the workers.

The labour relations forged under this form of racial paternalism were negotiated between capitalist employer and migrant worker on a daily basis. Some companies initially provided a ration of liquor and allowed their men to leave the compound on Sundays, attend funerals, or receive visitors from the outside. But as the compounds closed entirely, it became common for men to enter into short, repeated contracts of two to three months broken by extended periods in the locations. It was in these zones free of white control that married miners could rejoin their families, bachelors could bring an end to their enforced celibacy, and both could embark on heavy drinking sprees. Through this system of short contracts, miners continued to exercise a control over both the length of time they spent in the compounds and the intensity with which they worked.[137] The state attempted to limit drunkenness to the locations rather than eradicate it altogether. Thus although beer-brewing was outlawed, and the ratio of bars per inhabitant cut from 1:48 in 1874 to 1:300 in 1889, and despite extensive arrests for drunkenness (amounting to over two thousand per year after 1888), large amounts of liquor continued to flow into Kimberley. The logic behind this drinking pattern was perhaps best expressed by none other than the commissioner of police who held that "a man getting hopelessly drunk one day in the month is far better than a man soaking all the month through."[138] Thus while the compound system did not extinguish the workers' drinking culture, it passed the cost of St. Monday to the worker.

A bout of heavy drinking was not the only means devised by the black miner of breaking the monotony of an onerous job. The nature of piecework and even the ticket system gave black miners some control over the pace and rhythm of their work. The system of minimum piece rates required a concentrated burst of energy from the worker, but he could relax once he had completed the required amount of work. The ticket system allowed the black miner to determine when he was to work and, if tired or dispirited, he could forego his ticket, join the reserve army of labourers, and perhaps turn to the informal economy in the compound. "To work 900 men we want 1400 or 1500 men," remarked a compound manager, "for natives won't stay the whole week with the white miner."[139] By allowing a surplus of men in the compounds, management ensured a full complement of workers, but at the same time and at no extra cost, also allowed the miners to exercise a control over the pace at which they worked. In 1892 the subcontractors, under pressure from workers, succeeded in getting De Beers to reduce the double twelve-hour shift to three eight-hour shifts for underground workers. This was a momentous decision, particularly in view of the fact that the British parliament had in the same year rejected, by a large majority, a similar proposal made by the newly established Miner's Federation. The eight-hour shift was a supremely pater-

Dancers from Inhambane at Kimberley. A musician plays on a drum fashioned from a discarded wooden barrel.

nalistic managerial strategy, for it was restricted to experienced underground miners, the potential leaders of the work force, just as the average cash wage paid to blacks was cut sharply.[140]

In the compounds workers had the freedom to decide when, what, with whom, and how much they wished to eat. Public eating houses operated in the compounds, but men normally chose to share their meals with a more restricted group of friends, often in the form of eating clubs whose members contributed a weekly fee to a communal kitty. The men either cooked the food themselves or avoided the indignity of this female task by employing disabled or young miners. The company provided free fuel and water and, on special occasions such as Christmas, presented the men with rations of meat, bread, and ginger-beer.[141] The worker's leisure hours in the compound were spent at *chuba*, a popular backgammon-like game, or playing musical instruments like the *gora*, xylophone, or concertina.[142] Impressive dances were held on Sundays when they dressed and sang in the manner of what had become their ethnic group. The company also intervened directly in the miners' leisure hours in an attempt to instill the men with the moral values of industrial society. Cricket and football, jumping and wrestling were encouraged and, on festival days, workers competed for cash prizes against members of their ethnic group in events such as the three-legged race or the sack race, or battled on a greasy pole above the compound swimming bath. By promoting these distractions, the company hoped to infuse its employees with the virtues of teamwork, discipline, and a healthy competitiveness. Although the games provided participants with their own hierarchy of achievement, they also infantilized blacks in the eyes of whites, who considered many of these pastimes undignified and juvenile. A choral society was formed under white instructors to encourage the singing of concert hall and minstrel melodies that would tame indigenous songs and dances, the turbulence of which was so antithetical to industrial order. "Native chants are rarely heard," Gardner Williams wrote with obvious pleasure, "except when dancing."[143] But in the long term these culturally eclectic musical expressions made little impact on the traditions brought to the mines by migrant workers. The compound segregated black workers from foreign music and the miners continued to regulate the rhythm and pace of their work through songs whose lyrics pilloried the white "master" and highlighted his ignorance. Hymns were the only truly eclectic musical form, but they were confined to the respectable world of the Christian worker. Not all forms of acculturation were encouraged by the company and the thoroughly European occupation of card-playing was prohibited with such vigour that a pack of cards worth 6d could sell for £1–2 in the compounds. Gambling was suppressed because it both engendered violence and, like liquor, ate into the miner's income.[144] These employer controls over how men spent their wages nudged workers into a grudging respect for providence. Some compound managers estimated that under the regime of closed compounds, the amount saved by black workers rose by as much as 40 percent. This preaching of frugality and thrift amounted to a specific managerial strategy, for when the average worker saved £14.10s in six months or a driller like Charlie Lura returned home after twenty-three months with £50, the benefits of choosing to work on the diamond fields were clearly advertised.[145]

In the locations the various churches held tea meetings to raise money for mission activities and to provide a locus of socialising that was not based on alcohol. At these meetings missionaries "talked about saving, clothes, management of a household and other important questions concerning everyday life which cannot be addressed during a church service."[146] Mine managers encouraged mission work in the compounds because it imbued workers with an industrial morality and a sense of improvement. Missionaries targeted the compounds, where they preached the virtues of industry and respectability and taught the basic skills of literacy. Many workers attended night classes and in the De Beers' compound the church served as a school during the week. The compounds became centres from which literacy and Christianity spread throughout southern Africa. In the last six months of 1888 the 3,000 men in the four Bultfontein compounds bought some 535 Bibles, New Testaments, prayer books, hymn books, and readers in Xhosa, Sotho, Tswana, Zulu, Dutch, and English. The books were sold at cost price, and the Rev. Crosthwaite reported that "after the service the rush to buy [them] is somewhat staggering." In January 1889 he believed that two-thirds of the men in the largest Bultfontein compound were able to read.[147] By 1892 the Methodists held school classes four times a week in the De Beers West End compound and received substantial grants from the company.[148] Workers resting between contracts could also acquire an education in the locations, where, by the end of the 1880s, growing numbers of adults and children attended evening classes and day schools.[149] De Beers bought books printed in Bantu languages in Cape Town and sold them in the compounds, and the South African Bible Society remarked that the demand for Bibles in African languages at Kimberley outstripped the supply.[150] Religious works were the "pride and joy" of Christian workers from which they would "never be separated," wrote the Rev. Richter.[151] As the books sold to blacks were either religious or highly moral in tone, literacy was seen as a crucial means of both spreading the gospel into the remote corners of Southern Africa and teaching workers "to bear patiently whatever befalls them, looking to be rewarded in the next world."[152] However, as we shall see, black workers' readings of religious texts did not always conform to those of their missionary teachers.

The compounds presented the most visible part of a policy of social engineering aimed at bringing order to the process of industrialization. In the compounds, "the natives are taught cleanliness and sobriety," reported the protector of natives in 1895, "they are assisted to save considerable amounts of money and," he continued, "are kept from falling into many of the vices that they otherwise would if permitted to associate with what is known as the Town boy."[153] Shangaan workers were introduced to the virtues of soap on the diamond fields. On the coast, fats and oils were rubbed on the body to protect the skin and make it more supple. Many of these same fats and oils were exported to Marseilles where, mixed with an alkaline base, they were transformed into soap, a powerful cleanser of body and clothes, and a revolutionary means of personal hygiene. Men living in the compounds were quickly pressed into adopting the new, industrial habit of regularly washing themselves and their clothes in the compound swimming pool, showers, and wash tubs.[154] Cleanliness was not enough to prevent the high incidence of disease on the diamond fields, and in 1887 several hundred people died when typhoid swept through Kimberley and Beaconsfield. However the epidemic was short-lived, and the incidence of the disease dropped as the sanitary situation improved. Pneumonia had always been a major cause of death during the cold winter months, but it became particularly lethal when men started to work underground. The oppressive heat in the dark stopes encouraged miners to work naked, with the result that they experienced sharp fluctuations in temperature, particularly in winter, between their work at the rock face and their lives on the surface. Once pneumonia entered the severely overcrowded barracks, it passed quickly to other workers, to claim up to three-quarters of the lives of all black miners who died on the diamond fields.[155] Various measures were taken to improve the health situation. By mid-1889 about two hundred black patients filled beds in the Kimberley hospital every day. In an attempt to prevent migrants from bringing epidemic diseases to the fields, quarantine stations were constructed, and workers were subjected to two medical checks before entering the compounds. For those arriving on the fields "destitute and almost dying," a gaol hospital was constructed behind the Native Registry office. These men, many of whom walked to Kimberley from north of the Limpopo, continued to die in large numbers as they were "so starved and emaciated as to be beyond help."[156] In the mid-1880s fresh water was pumped for the first time from the Vaal River to Kimberley, and in the 1890s the protector of natives and inspector of compounds and medical doctors kept a check on the sanitary situation in the compounds. In 1891 the first mine hospital was built in the Kimberley mine compound.

While the system of preventative and curative health care resulted in a precipitous drop in epidemic diseases, as well as those caused by poor sanitation and malnutrition, underground mining resulted in a sharp rise in industrial diseases. The warmth and moisture in the underground works almost immediately attracted the ankylostomiasis worm. This parasite, which burrows into the intestines causing anaemia, internal haemorrhaging, debility, and death, spread quickly in these conditions and within a decade had become a serious threat.[157] Phthisis, caused by the lodging in the lungs of minute particles of rock dislodged by blasting, almost certainly made up a large part of the deaths from "pneumonia," particularly amongst miners who had worked underground for several years. But in the 1890s doctors were only vaguely aware that "the Kimberley pneumonia" was "an acute specific disease arising from or fostered by work in connection with the mines."[158] Because of their lack of experience with industrial conditions, they did not fully understand that pneumonia was aggravated by the lack of change houses at the shaft head, by over-ventilated barracks with earthen floors, and by a policy requiring workers to buy their own blankets and clothes. Nor were doctors convinced that the frequent plagues of scurvy were the result of the severe vitamin deficiency engendered by the prohibition of beer-drinking in the compounds. The slow and painful adaptation of management to the new social conditions brought by monopoly capitalism was most apparent in the high death rate from accidents of 6.2 per 1,000 in the 1890s. This was as much a problem of geology as of inexperience and exploitation; men not infrequently fell down mine shafts as they clambered up and down ladders, several hundred feet long, to the working level; they were trapped, injured, or killed by rock falls, or drowned as pools of mud, accumulated over time in the open cast pits, burst into the tunnels below and rushed through the works. Fire was another hazard that, in one single and terrible accident, claimed the lives of over two hundred men in 1888. Employers were not insensitive to these problems; electricity quickly replaced candles in the main works underground, new and safer forms of longwall and terrace tunneling were evolved, and ventilation shafts and pumps were installed in areas subject to flooding.[159]

Between 1878 and 1891 the death rate for blacks at Kimberley almost halved and, over the next three years, fell from 41 to 32.7 per thousand.[160] But what is often overlooked is that these figures made no distinction between the locations occupied by families and the all-male compounds, where the mortality rate was considerably lower. An appallingly high infant mortality rate in the locations indicates that these areas were, as the medical officer of health claimed, insanitary and disease-ridden. In contrast, despite the large number of accidents, "the death rate of persons employed on the mines is only about 24 per thousand, or 30 per cent lower than that of the coloured population of the town," wrote the medical officer of health in 1895. "The reason is sufficiently clear," he explained, for "in the compounds every care is taken to keep the men in good health, they have good food, good quarters, plenty of opportunities for personal cleanliness. Then there is the absence of liquor, and they enjoy proper care and attention during illness."[161] Although the veracity of this account requires further scrutiny, it does provide support for the claims made by De Beers to have improved the health and safety of their workers.[162] The miners can hardly have thought otherwise. Their position was a great improvement on that of their fathers and uncles, who, when injured or taken ill a decade earlier, had been thrown into the street to die. They were less threatened by epidemic diseases and the fevers caused by poor sanitation than their brothers working on the Witwatersrand, and, despite the transition to underground mining, the number of accidents at Kimberley had declined.

De Beers had improved the conditions under which company employers laboured, but this policy was not driven by purely philanthropic motives. Rather, it was the product of a subtle system of management aimed at stabilizing the work force and increasing production. "At one and the same time," writes the historian H. Newby, paternalism "may consist of autocracy and obligation, cruelty and kindness, oppression and benevolence, exploitation and protection."[163] Racial paternalism combined benevolence with authoritarianism in such a way as to persuade the worker to accept, of his own volition, the pace and discipline of industrial labour. A man who challenged this order of the world soon felt the heavy hand of the company. Black miners were increasingly isolated and secluded in a space constructed and controlled by management in the interests of order and surveillance. By the 1890s they were required to pass through a tunnel to get to work, they were not allowed out of the compound even to register at the office of the protector of natives, and only the most serious cases were taken to the town hospital. Under these conditions even the "grotesque and terror-inspiring" dances were thought to be rendered "harmless" by the "peace and order" that reigned in the compounds.[164] Blacks were subjected to harrowing searches and the judicial whim of their employers. By the late 1880s the compound had become a state within a state, where the manager could legally whip men (a practice stopped by De Beers in the mid-1890s), or sentence them to fines of up to 20s and periods of detention on bread and water. Despite warnings from the protector of natives that the abdication of the magistrate, as a neutral arbiter, was "open to grave abuse," the state sanctioned what might be termed "company justice." Under this system, recidivists and agitators were expelled from the compound, blackballed, and, in the eyes of management, excluded from the bounty of the company.[165]

A network of small communities underlaid and reinforced society in the compounds, where a worker was not only a member of a rural chiefdom and clan; he also belonged to a Christian denomination, an eating cooperative, a sports team, dance group, a circle of students, and an overarching ethnic group made up of fictive "brothers" and "uncles." Yet at the same time, workers had little space in which to organize, as De Beers took charge of their lodging, leisure, sources of food, fuel and clothing, and their access to physical and spiritual well-being. Miners were obliged to accept a unitary structure of labour relations that gave to the company the initiative for change. Nevertheless, they were not without the means to organize and, when wages in the newly opened Wesselton mine were cut, and hours extended in 1894, the black workers refused to work and demanded to leave the compound. Faced by a body of eight to nine hundred strikers, the compound manager called in the Kimberley police; when the strikers rejected the call to disperse, three men were shot dead, seven wounded, and thirty arrested.

But the Wesselton incident was unusual, and Gardner Williams's description of a similar occurrence in the De Beers compound is more representative of the tactics employed by management. In this case a combination of Kimberley and compound police succeeded in dispersing "the protesters." As management's view of labour relations denied the validity of a conflict of interest between capital and labour, agitators had to be held responsible for the unrest. "Ringleaders" were found, fined £3, and, in a move that displayed and reinforced the authority of the company, were obliged to work an unpaid eight-hour underground shift. The men were then exhibited before their work mates before suffering the ultimate punishment; expulsion from the compound.[166]

In 1969 Jack and Ray Simons commented on the remarkable achievements of De Beers in the decade after amalgamation: working costs had fallen by half, the price of diamonds had risen by 50 percent, and dividends had increased from 5 percent in 1889 to 40 percent in 1896. The profits that the Simons ascribed to the "exploitation" of workers and S. F. Frankel to "miraculous industry," I have attempted to trace to a modernized system of management that I have called racial paternalism.[167] This was a strategy of recruitment, a means of discipline and control, and a way of inculcating migrant workers with industrial values. I have also stressed that life on the mines cannot be severed from life in the rural areas. And it is to Southern Mozambique that I now wish to turn in order to examine the link between the development of the diamond mines and the sugar plantations, and the social and economic changes taking place on the coast.

4

A Certain Prosperity: Migrant Labour and Commodity Production

The Portuguese presence on the East Coast remained weak and divided throughout the 1870s and 1880s. Inhambane, which had supported Mawewe during the civil war and had sheltered some of his chiefs after their defeat by Umzila, was in a beleaguered position. The fort was "hardly worthy of description," wrote St. Vincent Erskine in 1871, "fifty men could take it without loss if properly led and directed."[1] British visitors frequently condemned the failure of the Portuguese to develop Lourenço Marques, and even the governor of the colony referred to the district around the town as "a national disgrace."[2] The garrison, made up of *degredados*, press-ganged Angolans, and slaves, was generally illiterate and always poorly trained and armed, and wages were invariably six months in arrears. The Portuguese were only able to exercise an influence in the region by supplying their allies with arms and by instituting trade blockades against their enemies.[3] This policy of intervention in local disputes was one of weakness and frequently misfired. The tribute collected by the Portuguese from what they called the "vassal chiefs" of the *terras de coroa* (crown lands) consisted mainly of a symbolic basket of millet or sorghum and rarely exceeded the taxes in kind paid by individual villages to their chiefs.[4] Tribute in kind or labour was paid irregularly, and, although the Portuguese equated tribute with the recognition of vassalage, this did not prevent "tributary chiefs" from simultaneously recognizing the overlordship of one or more other local suzerains. Vassal chiefs met Portuguese demands for *xibalo* forced labourers and military conscripts by supplying them with people on the margins of society, those whom one explorer referred to as "*umtagatis* (wizards), riffraff, the overclever and agitators."[5] The presentation of labour and the exchange of gifts served to reinforce ties of friendship and civility between the Portuguese and the chiefs. But the lines of domination in this relationship were so opaque as to lead one hostile critique to claim that the Portuguese were the vassals of the chiefs.[6] The exchange of *sagwati* or tribute, it seems to me, was a form of reciprocal gift-giving, albeit often

81

unequal, that confirmed a relationship of some mutual benefit to the *status quo*, as chiefs exchanged the labour or produce of their followers for the guns, ammunition, liquor, clothing, and other goods presented by the Portuguese.[7] Marriages between chiefs' daughters and the garrison officers or wealthy merchants served a similar function, as the transfer of a brideprice was both a means of accumulation for the chief and a way to create a reciprocal alliance between the two parties.

On two occasions in the late 1860s Lourenço Marques was threatened by neighbouring chiefdoms, but a more serious menace emerged in 1870, when the Maputo invaded the region to the south and west of the Bay. The conflict originated when, after the Tembe had refused to supply the Portuguese with labour, the garrison provided the Maputo with guns to raid Tembeland. But the ambitions of the Maputo chief Nozingile stretched beyond a punitive raiding party. His men were well-armed with firearms bought with wages earned in Natal and, having forced the Tembe from their land, he threatened to attack Lourenço Marques. The Portuguese tried to halt the Maputo advance by arming another chiefdom, the Mazwaya living to the north of the town, and by mounting a trade blockade. Nozingile then *hlasela'd* or invaded Matollaland, to the west of the Bay, and *cita'd* or ravaged the lower Nkomati. Maputo expansion was only halted when the Portuguese appealed to the Zulu for help, and Ceteswayo, who feared that Nozingile was acting as a surrogate for the Swazi, reimposed his rule over the lands to the south of the Bay.[8]

The political upheavals of the late 1860s and early 1870s influenced migrant labour in two important ways. Firstly, armed bands of Swazi, Maputo, and Zulu increased the danger of the overland routes and pushed men to use the vessels plying between Lourenço Marques and Durban. But in general the wars of the period restricted the flow of labour, as chiefs required their men to stay at home, serve in the army, and guard their families. Secondly, the political disturbances highlighted the weakness of the Portuguese, who were unable to control or even influence the rate of labour emigration. The most they could do was tax workers obliged to use the shipping facilities at Lourenço Marques and Inhambane. The hollowness of Portuguese claims to rule the Crown Lands was highlighted in October 1875 when all but one of the "vassal" chiefs refused to supply the governor of Lourenço Marques with labour. In the same year this official wrote despairingly of "the district of Lourenço Marques,"

> or speaking more correctly the fort of the same name—because we do not really rule except up to the range of the ancient guns of our tumble-down ramparts . . . surrounded by more or less powerful chiefs in whose loyalty but little trust could be placed, peace has been preserved since 1868 with them through a miracle of equilibrium. . . . in reality they live freely, at their own good pleasure.[9]

The enduring political instability underlined the importance of wages as a means of procuring food. The lung sickness epidemic in 1862–1863 had pushed men to concentrate on hunting as a source of meat and had forced many others, who had formerly supplied Lourenço Marques with food and cattle, to seek work in Natal.[10] Over the next few years the African population continued to supply food to the settlement and visiting ships, but little was left for export. Nevertheless, in a good year such as 1866–1867, rice valued at over £1,000 was exported to feed Indian plantation workers in Natal.[11]

The insecurity of food supplies becomes clear a decade later when the Portuguese started an annual, and at times monthly, report on agricultural conditions. In 1875 sufficient crops were harvested to allow the export of 44,100 kilos of cereals through Lourenço Marques to Natal.[12] But summer rains later that year were poor in most areas, except for Maputoland and the upper Nkomati, and the governor of Lourenço Marques feared a year of "disastrous famine." In March 1876 the situation became critical as the price of food soared; by December the region was in the grip of a widespread drought affecting the entire subcontinent.[13] Cereal cultivation came to a standstill as people fell back on mafureira almonds, fruit, roots, and venison, and men left to work in Natal, or bought imported food with their savings.[14] The situation changed later that year when sufficient rain fell to support a sizable agricultural surplus.[15] But the rains failed again at the end of 1878 and high summer temperatures killed the plant seed. When the rain finally arrived, crops were replanted and, in March 1879, maize was sold in the fertile river plains for a third of its price in Natal. But irregular rainfall continued to be a major problem and the final months of 1879 witnessed another drawn-out food shortage.

To offset the unpredictable nature of agricultural production, many men turned to the hunting of small game. The unrestricted slaughter of elephants in the years after the Gaza civil war had pushed the herds into the dry plains to the west and north of Inhambane. Wars in the Delagoa Bay area, and later in the Transvaal, severed Lourenço Marques hunters from the herds in the Zoutpansberg and in Mzilikazi's country beyond the Limpopo. Elephant hunting became too costly and dangerous, and exports through Lourenço Marques fell off rapidly, from almost 50,000 kilos in 1863–1864 to 2,800 kilos in 1877–1878. Portuguese merchants relinquished their hold over the ivory trade in the eastern Transvaal, and in 1875 even Albasini retired from the area. The *coup de grace* for the hunters operating from Lourenço Marques came in 1877, when otherwise liberal Portuguese tax reforms doubled the export duty on ivory. The following year the governor blamed the economic crisis in the town on the departure of the elephants, as the interior no longer produced enough commodities to pay for imports.[16]

The decline in elephant hunting affected not only the Lourenço Marques ivory merchants and their *amapisi* partners. The porters, gun carriers, and traders who accompanied the hunting expeditions, together with their extended families, were all affected. But many of these men carved a new existence for themselves by using their skills to hunt smaller game such as buck, wildcat, and monkey. An almost insatiable demand existed locally and in Zululand, Swaziland, and Natal for monkey skins and for civet and genet furs, which warriors attached to their shields and headdresses or cut into strips, which they twisted and hung from the waist, to form heavy kilts.[17] In the early 1870s the fur of a civet cat bought in Bilene on the lower Limpopo for one shilling could fetch three shillings in Natal.

Commerce and Consumerism

The driving force behind the transformation in hunting patterns was the compatibility of the trade in guns and skins. The small vessels leaving Durban for Lourenço Marques always included in their cargoes a good supply of gun powder, lead bars, and percussion caps. In the early 1870s, as men tramped to Natal to earn

money, and Delagoa Bay hunters turned increasingly to small game for their livelihood, Natal merchants like S. F. Beningfield and the Dutchman Dentzelman responded to the new demand for small-calibre guns; between 1872 and 1873 the
number of firearms landed at Lourenço Marques more than quadrupled, as vessels
carried migrant workers and firearms from Durban. Dentzelman joined another
Hollander, Lippert, to form a company selling guns in Zululand for buckskins, and
firearms at Kimberley for cash. The company carried a large part of the 7,228 guns,
worth over £7000, shipped from Natal to Lourenço Marques in 1874. The following
year, when guns were considered to be in "short supply" at Lourenço Marques,
5,336 were imported from Natal and perhaps as many as 6,000 from France and
Portugal; there was also a sharp rise in the importation of gun powder.[18] When the
British prohibited the trade in guns between Natal and Zululand in June 1875, Lippert and Dentzelman expanded their operations in the Delagoa Bay area. By 1877
the company's agent at Lourenço Marques, Oswald Hoffman, employed over one
hundred African compradores, who travelled as far west as the Spelonken, selling,
lending, and exchanging guns and ammunition for furs and skins, and combining
these activities with labour recruitment.[19]

Hoffman's agents handed firearms, percussion caps, gun fittings, and ammunition to bands of Zulus (sometimes numbering over two thousand) arriving on
the beaches south of the Bay. He boasted of having sold 800 guns in one day and
played such a central role in the trade as to be known to the Zulu as the "Portuguese leader."[20] British officials believed that 6,000–7,000 guns and about 20,000
barrels of gunpowder were imported annually through Lourenço Marques after
1875.[21] However, Portuguese officials were probably correct when they claimed
that the British inflated the importance of the gun trade as a justification for their
interference in the affairs of Lourenço Marques, a cornerstone of their schemes for
a South African confederation. And they were certainly correct in their estimations
that the gun trade at Lourenço Marques was far inferior to that at Kimberley.[22] The
arms trade with the Zulu brought little gain to the people of the Delagoa Bay littoral, for the Zulu paid the Natal gun suppliers in cattle driven south to the British
colony.[23] But the gun trade did boost the strategic importance of Lourenço Marques
and cement an alliance between the Portuguese and the Zulu that blocked Maputo
and Swazi expansion in the region. Zulu support also gave some credence to Portugal's rights, under the MacMahon award of 1875, to the southern shores of the Bay.

The commerce with Zululand was only one aspect of the trade in firearms
through Lourenço Marques. Guns formed a highly saleable item of European commerce, as Africans were familiar with firearms and prized them as weapons, a
means of hunting game, and a source of symbolic capital.[24] By entering into the
local system of value, European traders were able to use guns as a common means
of exchange with which to coax people into producing a surplus for the market. In
this manner a complementary trade emerged as Lippert and Dentzelmann, Beningfield, and other traders shipped hides, furs, and some ivory back to Natal in
vessels offloading guns and migrant workers. In 1877 some 25,000 cat and monkey
skins were exported through Lourenço Marques to Durban, and hides and horns
formed an important secondary export.[25] French steamships, visiting Lourenço
Marques in growing numbers in the 1870s, arrived with thousands of rifles and
returned to Marseilles with cargoes including oil-producing vegetable fruits and
seeds, and as many as 100,000 buck skins.[26]

The shift in exports, from ivory to cat furs, buck, and monkey skins, brought about a democratization of hunting and dissolved the caste-like group of skilled *amapisi* hunters. Hunting buck, civet cats, and monkeys merely required traps or the purchase of a small-bore shoulder gun that would not damage the animal's skin. These flintlock and percussion firearms were much cheaper than elephant guns and it became possible for large numbers of men to make a living from hunting. Most of the guns imported through Delagoa Bay were obsolete military firearms that, although costing almost £3 to make, had been remaindered for 2s in Europe. They were landed at Lourenço Marques for about 8s and sold in the interior for 10–30s.[27] As wages soared in Natal in the early 1870s, migrant workers invested their earnings in guns and their firepower grew accordingly. By 1874 buckskins had overtaken ivory as the most valuable product of the hunt and, over the economic year 1876/77, almost 95,000 animal skins were exported from Lourenço Marques.[28] It is clear that Amatongas saw wage labour as a means of buying guns at Lourenço Marques rather than at Kimberley, where muzzle-loading flintlock and percussion guns were considerably more expensive. The fact that Amatongas moved to Kimberley in large numbers only after the ending of the gun trade in Griqualand West further indicates that they were not attracted to the diamond fields by the prospect of purchasing a gun.

Porterage was another growing area in which people invested their labour and skills. The transport of goods from Lourenço Marques to the eastern Transvaal goldfields was particularly important in winter, when cold and snow on the Drakensberg cut the route linking the eastern Transvaal with Durban. During this season transport-riding from Lourenço Marques was relatively safe but in summer it was severely restricted by a virulent tsetse belt, weak oxen, and the bad state of the newly constructed roads. Although the mortality rate of draught oxen dropped as the trypansome-carrying game was shot out, the ease with which tsetse could suddenly infest an area remained a constant problem for transport riders. Malaria was another hurdle and as many as twenty-seven white diggers died in one summer, out of the thirty-five who attempted to get from Pilgrims Rest to Lourenço Marques. The safest way of getting goods to the gold fields, particularly in summer, was to have them head-loaded. Porters carrying up to eighty pounds took from eight to ten days to walk from Delagoa Bay to Lydenburg, for which they received 15s per 100 lbs, and a further 12s if they continued to Pretoria. There were about 750 men employed as porters on the Lourenço Marques route at any given time during the late 1870s. Road construction and porterage introduced many men to wage labour and offered carriers the opportunity of supplementing their incomes from porterage with several months on the gold fields before returning home.

An important innovation during the 1860s and 1870s, although only indirectly related to migrant labour, was the adoption of new foodstuffs. As people became familiar with the taste of cassava, and learnt how to cook and prepare the tuber, it gained in popularity.[29] As early as 1862 some 1,660 litres of cassava were exported from Lourenço Marques, and twenty years later the plant was grown throughout the Delagoa Bay region.[30] In 1871 millet was still considered "the staff of life of south-east Africa," but maize was cultivated in the fertile river plains on a sufficient scale to support an export trade.[31] Its seems likely that the sudden and rapid adoption of maize as a basic foodstuff was related to the diet of Amatonga workers in Natal, where maize was the staple food on the plantations. Even more important was the fact that the adoption of maize as a staple made up for a great deal of the labour lost to South Africa through migrant labour. Much energy was spent during the long growing season on guarding millet and sorghum crops, as their fruit, unlike that of the maize plant, is not protected by a hard husk. Maize only demands an intensive labour input over the harvesting period and most of the effort required to prepare maizemeal is invested in the crushing of the tenacious kernel, a task allocated to women. Maize also produces far more calories per acre than other cereals, and is therefore an important and ready source of energy. In fertile, well-watered regions, maize produced two harvests annually, and storage problems, which aggravated the pre-harvest hunger period, were partly overcome by the consumption of green maize in December.

The major problem with maize is its susceptibility to drought, a feature that was partly overcome by the widespread adoption of cassava. As a perennial, cassava need not be planted or harvested with other crops and, while it continues to grow for several years, it needs little attention, apart from desultory weeding during its early growing period. If properly tended, cassava will significantly outyield maize. The tuber is highly reliable as a source of food, since it is resistant to drought and disease and can withstand locust attacks, while the bitter strains are even immune to damage by rodents and monkeys. Cassava presents no storage problems as, after two to three years' growth, it may be stored in the ground for a further two to three years and harvested at any time. Furthermore, if the stalk is cut off, the tuber is effectively hidden from human and animal predators. As distinct from maize, cassava gives high yields on short-fallow fields and survives well in sandy soil. Thus although lacking in protein, cassava complements maize and spreads the production risks involved in cultivating the cereal as a staple. Most importantly, cassava and maize are both labour-saving crops, although the woman's task of preparing and cooking the tuber is time-consuming. The adoption of maize and cassava as basic foodstuffs released male labour from the domestic economy, which allowed men to work for longer periods in South Africa, anchored women more firmly to the homestead, and increased their importance within the domestic economy.

Another significant agricultural innovation to emerge largely as a response to an external stimulus was the production of vegetable oils, rubber, wax, and orchil lichen collected from rocks and trees. In the 1850s Augustin Fabre and Son, a major Marseilles trading company, had made substantial profits by purchasing West Africa palm oil with *annulus* cowrie shells shipped from Zanzibar and northern Mozambique. The profitability of this trade rose steeply as the shells took on the value of a currency and replaced the smaller *moneta* cowries imported from the Maldive Islands. Part of the gains made from the sale of palm oil in Marseilles was invested in cloth, guns, and other trade goods with which more cowries were purchased on the coast of east-central Africa. But the success of this triangular trade was seriously affected by a precipitous fall in vegetable oil prices in the 1860s. At the same time, the energy with which Fabre and Son, and their associate Victor Regis, oversupplied the West African market with "Zanzibar" cowries unleashed a spiraling inflation that sharply devalued the cowrie currency. Propelled by the desire to find more profitable terms of trade, and encouraged by the imminent opening of the Suez Canal, Fabre and Son extended their operation along the Mozambican coast in 1863–1870. Seven new stations were built, including one at Inhambane in 1867 and another at Lourenço Marques in 1869.[32]

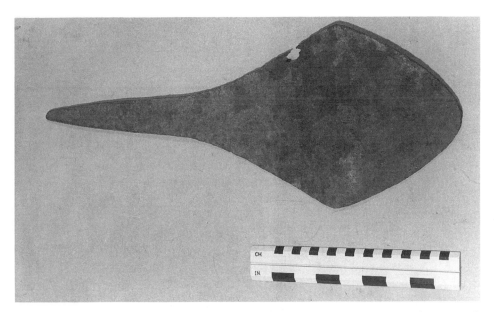

A *beja* marriage hoe. As the wages of migrant workers rose in the 1870s they bought imported, industrially-produced substitutes with their wages. This inflated local brideprices to such an extent that gold coins earned in South Africa replaced hoes as the medium of bridewealth in the early 1880s

At Lourenço Marques, Fabre and Son's operations were particularly successful because, as in West Africa, they were able to exploit the local system of value. In Chapter 1 I pointed out the importance of iron hoes as a bridewealth medium in the Delagoa Bay region.[33] These hoes measured about 45 centimeters along a ribbed spine leading to an elongated, thick shank, and 18 cms across the blunted lotus-shaped head. Although some marriage hoes were forged from salvaged iron in Matolloland and others were made by ironworkers around Phalaborwa, the vast majority were produced in the foothills of the Zoutpansberg. Known locally as *beja*, *landin*, or kaffir hoes, each marriage hoe, weighing about one and a half kilograms, had to be carried several hundred kilometers down to the coast.[34]

Industrially produced copies of *beja* hoes were imported from Lisbon by Lourenço Marques merchants who paid up to one hundred hoes for a large elephant tusk, and as early as 1859, migrant workers were returning home with hoes bought in Natal.[35] Men tramped south in increasing numbers as monthly wages in Natal rose from 6s3d in 1858 to 10s in 1860, for 20s bought a brideprice of ten hoes in Lourenço Marques. As migrants created a new demand for hoes, and annual Swazi raids prevented the recovery of the cattle herds decimated by lungsickness, the number of hoes imported through Lourenço Marques rose from about 1,500 in 1861 to well over 10,000 each year by the mid-1860s.[36] Manufactured hoes imported from Europe sold for 1s6d at Lourenço Marques or 25 percent less than their price in the northern Transvaal.[37] Natal hunter/traders quickly discovered the local value of *beja* hoes and, in the early 1870s, coastal vessels like the *William Shaw* and the *Roe* usually included several hundred in their cargoes.[38]

Once established in the region, Fabre and Son became by far the largest importer of industrially produced copies of the *beja* hoe. Before the arrival of the Marseilles company, ivory made up the majority of exports from Lourenço Marques and it was largely the *amapisi* hunters and their dependents who consumed foreign goods. Because of the narrow base of the consumer market, the fastest way to persuade people to produce crops with which they were unfamiliar and would not themselves consume was to enter into the local perception of value. By importing hoes, the value of which was widely accepted, Fabre and Son encouraged the production of saleable crops and drew a profit from the unequal exchange. The company purchased great quantities of hoes direct from factories in France and shipped them cheaply to south-east Africa in ocean-going steamers.

The demand for hoes was also dependent on the steadily increasing buying power of migrant workers. As the sugar boom pushed monthly wages in Natal up to 15s in the mid-1870s, Amatongas streamed into the colony via the new labour importation schemes. For the migrant worker, only a few months of hard work and saving in Natal was sufficient to buy a brideprice of ten to fifteen hoes. Natal hunter/traders also exploited this local currency. Between 1872 and 1874 the number of hoes imported into Lourenço Marques from Durban jumped from 2,150 to 51,270, and the volume of trade between the two settlements soared. In those three years, the value of exports from Lourenço Marques to Durban rose from £5,000 to £18,300, and imports soared from £5,430 to £29,500.[39] In 1874 some 255,000 hoes, weighing 400 tons and valued at £13,350 were offloaded at Lourenço Marques, where they raised more customs revenue than all goods imported just three years previously.[40] In November the governor noted that "the most considerable articles of Kafir consumption in the area are hoes, but of a special kind; if they do not conform to this pattern they will not sell."[41] The nipple or blunt tip of the marriage hoe could not be marked by field labour. As the governor General remarked, a *beja* hoe brideprice "was considered a sacred deposit in the hands of the father, brother or tutor of the bride, that could under no circumstances be used for agricultural purposes."[42] Buried in the ground and generally protected from rust, the hoes were stored as a means of paying future brideprices. Junod related that "hoes were kept as a sacred treasure. Those that a man had received for selling his daughter were to serve as a means of buying a wife for his son. Only the danger of death would push a starving family to touch this dowry buried in the soil."[43] Between 1869 and 1876, almost one million hoes were shipped to Lourenço Marques and sucked into the interior.

The profitability of Fabre's station drew Regis Aîné and Dunlop Mees of Rotterdam to establish branches at Lourenço Marques in 1873. The presence of these wholesalers brought a great improvement to commerce at the settlement where they joined hands with a new group of immigrant retailers, largely Muslims from Bombay and Cutch in British India. Professionally and culturally distinct from the local Hindu and Catholic Luso-Indians, these men drew Lourenço Marques indefatigably into a trading diaspora covering much of the western Indian Ocean. Migrant labour and the activities of European and Indian, or Banyan, merchants drew the Delagoa Bay hinterland ever more tightly into the world economy.

The importers at Lourenço Marques acted as wholesalers who provided itinerant merchants, the backlanders called *sertanejos*, with credit in the form of *beja* hoes and other goods.[44] These men, generally Banyans or former *degredados*, moved through the interior, establishing mobile and fixed markets, and entrusted their goods to African compradores. At the larger depots goods were traded, caravans rested, and retailers were sent out in all directions.[45] When sufficient produce had been collected at the depot, the goods were headloaded back to the coast under guard. The itinerant traders were dependent on credit and long-delayed returns. Overheads were high, profits precarious, and merchants had few guarantees. The governor wrote in 1875 that

> Merchants who venture to trade in the traffic in goods and spirits in the interior have to give at the villages where they wish to establish themselves a larger or smaller present to the king or headman of the village and to entrust part of their valuable property to Kafir buyers who travel on their account, and trade for them—they sometimes settle their accounts and sometimes do not settle them—it is necessary that this business must be most profitable to give a return.[46]

For the *beja* hoes and other goods peddled by traders, Africans exchanged such products as groundnuts, sesame seeds, and mafureira almonds, all of which were then sold by the traders to the wholesalers on the coast. As mafureira and sesame were gathered, they were inexpensive to produce. Groundnuts were also grown using family labour and traditional tools, and all three oil-producing plants could be grown on marginal agricultural lands. Mozambican groundnuts were particularly valued at Marseilles, where the first press produced a cooking and salad oil, and the second a lighting oil and grease. The *mafurra* tallow drawn from the mafureira almonds had been praised when first exhibited by Portugal in 1855 at the Paris Universal Exhibition, and the almonds were much sought after as a source of vegetable tallow for the manufacture of candles and soap, and as a machine grease. Sesame was especially valued after the invention of margarine by the French in the early 1870s, as it is odorless and has a rich oil content.[47]

Agriculturalists, like migrant labourers, responded rapidly to the opportunity to acquire marriage hoes and, by 1875, a "lively commerce based on vegetable oils" existed at the Bay.[48] Vessels like the *Endonne* arrived from Marseilles with tens of thousands of hoes and returned with a typical shipment of 5,340 kilos of groundnuts, 1,960 kilos of sesame and 2,210 kilos of orchil. During the financial year 1876/77, vegetable oils, hides, and maize made up the major exports from Lourenço Marques.[49] The trading companies bolstered the administration of Lourenço Marques by paying customs duties and by lending money to the irregularly and poorly paid garrison. Customs revenues that had remained stagnant for a decade increased from £1,750 in 1871 to almost £8,000 in 1874, and agricultural exports grew alongside migrant labour.[50] In 1876/77, over 264,030 litres of mafureira were exported; but the following year exports dropped to 37,574 litres, as drought caused producers to consume their crop.[51] Liberal customs reforms in 1877 encouraged the production and export of several thousand kilos of sesame, wax, rubber, and orchil.

The circulation of currency at Lourenço Marques was, as early as 1866, reckoned to be dependent on the gold brought home by migrant labourers. In 1868 it was estimated that a trader operating on the Usutho River could enjoy a cash turnover of £400–500 each month and the Maputo, who initially formed the majority of the Amatongas working in Natal, were thought to spend fully £4–5,000 on trade goods each year.[52] In 1872 the Natal government had to apply for £30,000 in specie, as migrants carried off the coinage of the colony and left planters without the means to pay wages.[53] Migrants grew to appreciate cash as a medium of exchange and coastal vessels included substantial amounts of specie on their voyages from Durban to Lourenço Marques.[54] Even before the large-scale movement of labour to the diamond fields towards the end of the 1870s, gold coins with the image of Queen Victoria constituted almost all the money in circulation in the Delagoa Bay hinterland, and sterling was the currency most used and understood by the African population. During the severe drought of 1876, when people were obliged to consume their vegetable oil crops, money was the only medium available to pay for imports. A large trade imbalance developed at Lourenço Marques as consumers started to pay for imported products with sterling.[55] This monetization of the economy had a circular effect. It pushed workers onto the labour market, as it was only in South Africa that they could earn appreciable amounts of specie and, by increasing their buying power, it stimulated a local consumerism. The demand for gold coins was to grow into one of the driving forces behind migrant labour.

The spread and acceptance of money as a means of exchange was limited by an unfamiliarity with general purpose currencies and by the undeveloped nature of the consumer market. During the 1860s and early 1870s, hoes remained the most acceptable means of exchange. But cracks in the dominance of this bridewealth medium were already noticeable in early 1875 when the governor of Lourenço Marques reported that "a notable surplus" had accumulated in the customs house and that their official price had fallen by half.[56] In December he explained this "great fall in the value of landin hoes" when he wrote that, their "fall is because the Kafirs have adopted the system of exchanging wives for gold instead of hoes."[57] At this stage hoes and gold were both used as bridewealth, and merchants continued to flood the market with industrial substitutes. In 1876 220,000 imported hoes were estimated to be worth more than the combined value of the two other major imports, cloth and liquor. To understand fully the effect of this change in the bridewealth medium requires a closer analysis of the structure of local society.

Marriage and Accumulation

From the perspective of our position in the late twentieth century, when inequality is immediately visible through the display of wealth and power and when revolutions transform society, the stratification and dynamics of precapitalist societies seem almost invisible. Nevertheless, there were profound contradictions in these societies. Part of the theme of this chapter is that, as the structure of social life was shaken by capitalism, age-old conflicts found new outlets, one of which was migrant labour.

For some time historians have been aware of the relationship between marriage and power in precapitalist Africa. In the nineteenth century the dominant position of most chiefs in southern Mozambique was entrenched by their marriages. Because chiefs married their official wives late in life, their heirs were generally young on their accession to the chieftaincy and had time to consolidate their power. While chiefs tended to marry members of the royal families of neighbouring clans, commoners were prohibited from marrying the offspring of a shared grandparent and, apart from a social pressure to marry within the clan, their marriages lacked any recognized pattern.[58] This meant that contrary to the repetitive marriage alliances centralizing wealth and power in the hands of the royal families, commoner marriages promoted an egalitarian spread of women and goods between families sharing the same clan patronym. Corporate political groups were formed by the chief, who placed his brothers, sons, or father's brothers as sub-chiefs in the various districts under his control. These groups had little opportunity to solidify into lineages and were generally dependent on the chief's patronage to maintain or expand their wealth and size. It was common practice for a chief to replace existing sub-chiefs with supporters or clients, generally drawn from his agnatic kin, on his accession to power. If a sub-chief accumulated sufficient followers to threaten the chief, the legal precedent existed for the latter to seize his property and replace him with a more tractable client.[59]

The power base of the chiefs also depended upon the support of the *numzane*, or homestead heads. These men controlled the homestead as a productive unit consisting of the "houses" of married sons and dependents. Junod referred to them as "gentlemen," "owners of cattle," "the important men of the country" who ranked "almost as petty chiefs."[60] The accession to power of a deceased chief's eldest son was far from automatic or ascribed, and in some cases the *numzane* found legal precedent for the seizure of the chieftaincy by the regent and his house, or by a brother of the heir who, as a charismatic sub-chief, had accumulated an important following. The council of elders drawn from the *numzane* confirmed the legality of the chief's position and could overrule and, in extreme cases, depose and even execute a chief for misrule.[61] The chief ensured the clientage of the *numzane* in several ways. He entered into a large number of marriage alliances with the most powerful *numzane* and he received from them his official wife. The *numzane* benefitted from the way the chiefs distributed land, farmed out livestock, blessed the crops, redistributed taxes, and appointed sub-chiefs. But it was the common role of the chiefs and *numzane* within the production process that linked them as a group. They organised production strategies, made political decisions, and interceded with the ancestors.

The dominance of the chiefs and *numzane* rested on their control of access to wives, land, tools, and social knowledge. The quality and amount of land received by a young man was dependent upon the generosity of the *numzane*, as was his access to iron tools, seeds, and livestock. In a manner antithetical to the missionaries' notions of providence, a man's prestige depended on his public display of largesse. A successful man aspired to attract up to one hundred dependents in a circular homestead and attempted to conclude his life with an ostentatious wake bringing together all those who had benefitted from his generosity and renown.[62] However, the patronage needed to attract such a following depended largely on a man's ability to marry. "The wife," wrote Junod, was "assuredly in a state of excessive inferiority." She laboured on the land, cooked the food and looked after the children, and, in the end, it was "the wife who supports her husband."[63] Folktales portray women as constantly planting, hoeing, or harvesting crops; they stamp maize, make beer, cook food, cut wood, draw water, and gather wild fruits, vegetables, and fuel from the commonage.[64] By giving birth to her husband's children, a woman also increased the size of his household and his right to land within the homestead. In a society frequently rocked by subsistence crises, food and drink were associated with respect, and the status of the *numzane*, like that of the migrant worker, was dependent on his powers of patronage.[65] The homestead was held together by circulating bridewealth as young men were dependent on the *numzane* for their access to wives. Bridewealth also served in extreme cases to prevent a family from starving, and, during times of famine, it was not unusual to *ganisela*, or

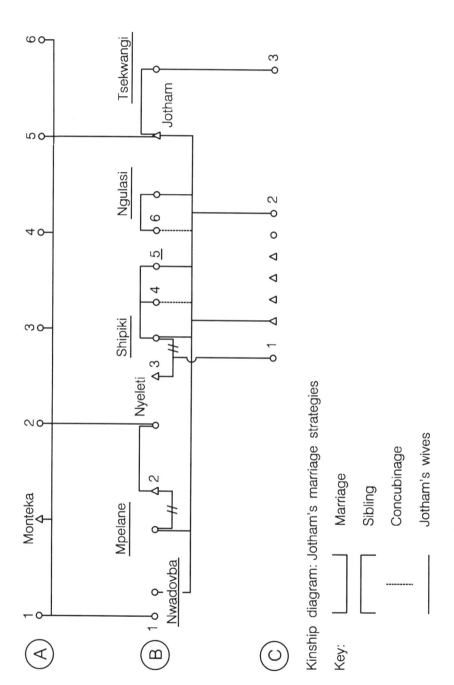

Kinship diagram: Jotham's marriage strategies

Key:

Marriage

Sibling

---------- Concubinage

——— Jotham's wives

marry off girls, even those unborn, and eat the cattle or sell the hoes received as brideprice. Bridewealth debts, or the promise of a brideprice, ensured that young sons or cadets remained dependent on the *numzane*.[66] "It is, of course," wrote Junod, "entirely in the interest of the *numzane* to keep his protégé on his land, for he adds considerably to its value by cultivating an otherwise useless bush (*nhoba*). He also helps to people his protector's tract of country, and thus to increase his strength; finally he makes certain payments in kind or rather in labour."[67] But marriages also provided young men with the means to break away from the *numzane* and to establish their own homesteads. A *numzane* generally had two or three wives, while powerful chiefs like Magude of the Khosa and Ngwanasi of the Maputo had "several dozen" and fifty-eight wives respectively.[68] Contemporary observers, proverbs, and folklore portrayed marriage as the engine of accumulation. Junod observed that

> to possess many wives is to have succeeded, to have made one's fortune, to have become someone. It is through the women that the village grows and prospers. The power and wealth of the master of the village grows with the children that they bring into the world. It is thanks to the pots that wives prepare each day for the husband that he is in a position to exercise hospitality on a large scale. Here is the basis of the black's reputation and glory. To always keep an open table, bowls full, an abundance of beer and you will quickly become famous![69]

Ambition was not the only element behind a world view that portrayed celibacy as intolerable and bachelorhood as despicable. A man without a wife had no one to tend his fields or prepare his meals; he was a parasite in a society living close to subsistence.

As the accumulation of wealth and power by males was heavily dependent on female domesticity, women were generally excluded from activities that took them far from the homestead. The pressures on women to remain at home became even stronger in the 1870s, as their role in the domestic economy became increasingly onerous. They gathered the fruit and seeds of oil-producing plants, orchil lichen, wax, and rubber, were obliged to engage in the time-consuming preparation of new foods, and had to shoulder many of the responsibilities of males absent in South Africa. It was largely through this sexual division of labour that men were able to realize a profit from hunting, trading, and labour migration for, while women increasingly provided most of the labour needed to feed and reproduce the family, men accumulated wealth through their involvement in the market economy. The importance of women as producers and reproducers of male power explains much of the logic behind the emigration of single males. The emigration of an unmarried woman entailed the possible loss of her brideprice, which, in turn, could endanger her brother's ability to marry, or even unravel the marriages of a string of male relatives. A married woman remained at home to ensure the productive and reproductive base of the domestic economy that provided migrants with a second source of accumulation, as well as a refuge in times of trouble.

After the epizootic of the early 1860s, cattle keepers found it difficult to replenish their herds because the tsetse belts continued to restrict the importation of animals. Under normal circumstances, cattle could only be acquired as *lobola* for a sister, on loan, through inheritance, or by raiding. The dependence of men of marriageable age upon their fathers was secured by a form of late inheritance as a father's goods passed on his death to his younger brothers and then to his eldest sons.[70] Heirs were obliged to distribute part of their inheritance only insofar as it consolidated the dependence of younger siblings, sons, and male dependents upon them for wives. The *numzane* were able to contract several marriages because of their monopoly of cattle bridewealth and because of the levirate through which they inherited the wives and children of their deceased elder brothers.[71] Marriage did not mean the automatic accession of the cadets and *nandja* (followers or subjects) to the ranks of the *numzane*, for a bridegroom remained dependent on his creditors until either he inherited a brideprice or the *lobola* of a daughter could be used to cancel his debt. The passage of the brideprice in its entirety created ties that were stronger than blood, and gave to the father and his family the inalienable right to the children of his wife. If the wife's kin were to demand the entire brideprice and the husband were unable to pay, they could theoretically reclaim their daughter and all the children of the marriage. One divorce and the demand that the brideprice be returned could cause the dissolution of a series of marriages as parents scrambled to find the bridewealth needed to secure an elder son's children. Even where, in the ideal instance, the full *lobola* was paid by the bridegroom's agnates, the young man remained in a state of indebtedness to these *numzane*. As bridewealth debts were contracted with the *numzane* of different houses and homesteads, good relations between a man and his elders were essential. As long as part of a man's brideprice remained outstanding or he remained indebted to the *numzane*, he was a legal minor, a *de facto* "cadet" dependent on the goodwill of the elders.

Both the status of the wife and that of the children was determined by the transfer of the brideprice. If we descend briefly from the structural to the specific, we may take the case of a *numzane* who attempted to secure the loyalty of a dependent by presenting him with a wife. In the eyes of the community this woman was a concubine, since the chief, and not her husband, had paid her brideprice. If the chief abandoned, and the progenitor claimed, the right of filiation, the children were technically barely legitimate. They were subordinate to the children of the most junior wife and would find it difficult to marry anyone of standing.[72] Other children of low birth were those born of slave concubines, women pejoratively termed *heads* or *nhloko*, a term pregnant with the anonymity of their origins. Their children were recognized as members of their father's clan but, because of the mother's low standing, were disadvantaged in terms of inheritance.[73] In general younger sons, particularly those of junior wives, were disadvantaged by their "low" birth. Whether a boy ever achieved the status of *numzane* was dependent on one major factor: his birth and consequent position in the chain of inheritance. For a man to escape the disadvantage of his low birth, he could attempt to earn a brideprice through hunting, trading, or raiding, by indebting himself to a powerful *numzane*, or he could *kondza* to another chief. As we shall see, the wages earned through migrant labour provided men with an independent source of bridewealth, a factor that was to shake the structure of society to its roots.

Let us move again from the abstract to the concrete, and take as representative of the complexities of marriage alliances the circumstances of a man known to us only as Jotham.[74] Jotham's father Monteka had six wives. When his principal or "official" wife (A1 in the kinship diagram) died, Monteka used the *lobola* of one of her daughters to procure a woman to serve as his fifth and "official" wife (A5). This woman mothered Jotham, who was later presented with a wife procured with the *lobola* received for his sister Tsekwanyi. As this wife (B5) died childless, Jotham had a legal right to her sister, Shipiki. But as Shipiki's parents were slow in giving her to Jotham, he eloped with the girl. Jotham then sought to raise her brideprice by working in Natal, Kimberley, and Cape Town. On his return home, he found that Shipiki had been betrothed by her parents to a man (B3) who had fathered her child (C1). Jotham was then presented by his father with a wife (Ngulasi) procured with the *lobola* received for Nyeleti, a daughter of Monteka's second wife. A year later Shipiki left her husband, and Jotham's brothers paid her *lobola* with the brideprice received for an illegitimate daughter (C3) of their sister Tsekwanyi. Both Ngulasi and Shipiki were accompanied by sisters (B4,B6) who helped with domestic chores and served as concubines. Some time later Nyeleti's brother (B2) died and Jotham inherited one of his wives, Mpelane. His final and fifth wife, Nwadouba, who was "too young to be married at the time," was procured with money earned in South Africa. After this marriage Jotham left to work in Pretoria; on his return, he found that Mpelane had died and that the two concubines had returned home. The young Nwadouba died a little while later, but Shipiki and Ngulasi, who had lived with one of Jotham's sisters while he was away in Pretoria, eventually presented him with a total of four boys and two girls. Jotham's history illustrates the way in which a man (the son of a principal wife), could use both his kin network and wages to marry and increase the size of his following. It also reminds us of the high mortality rate, as three of Jotham's five wives died before he reached old age. A similar story is that of Sirkomane who, as a disadvantaged younger son, left his home in Tembeland to find work in Natal. After spending several years in South Africa, he learnt of the death of his eldest brother and inherited his two wives. When he returned home, Sirkomane invested his wages in the bridewealth needed to procure another wife. These three women provided him with an economic base independent of his parents and, when he quarreled with them, he was able to move and establish his own homestead in southern Maputoland.[75]

The political subordination of the cadets was also based on the belief that the chiefs and *numzane*, as the direct descendants of the ancestors, could intercede with them and influence factors such as rainfall, health, the fertility of women and the soil, and the outcome of wars. Hence the elders both provided the cadets with wives and exercised an influence over the material forces of production. In return, they received a range of taxes. The *nhlengo* tax consisted of the payment to the chief of a basket of maize or millet by each village at harvest time. An irregular and voluntary form of taxation, considered as "an act of civility" (or *mashobo*), was to send beer or fruit to the chief's homestead. Other official taxes consisted of the payment to the chief of the skins and joints of certain slaughtered and hunted animals, the grounded tusk of an elephant, and the contents of a crocodile's stomach.[76] A tax was levied on communal fishing expeditions and on the use of fishing traps. Under the *djimo* labour tax, people were required to build and repair their chief's huts, clean his cattle kraals, public places, and roads, carry his goods, and hunt on his behalf. It was expected that the chief's followers would provide his soldiers with food and shelter. Outsiders attached to the clan, but not recognized as members, contributed a special tax when they agreed to *kondza* a chief; others paid a *huba* or *hlenga* tax as a sign of fealty. To *kunga* involved the payment of a fee to the chief by an initiate who wished to be reincorporated into society. The payment of *sagwati* had a strong element of reciprocity which, at the cost of commoners, strengthened the position of the royal families. Thus Chief Nozingile of the Maputo would present Mpande with up to 200 headloads of goods each year, collected from his followers, for which he received over 100 head of cattle.[77] It was common for chiefs to lend livestock to followers who were given part of their off-spring in return for looking after the animals.

Chiefs and *numzane* were also able to accumulate and redistribute wealth, and hence attract followers, in various other ways. Because a chief was married to numerous women, he normally fathered a large number of daughters who were a source of both financial and social capital as their marriages secured inflated, "royal" brideprices as well as political alliances. The goods confiscated from a man accused of witchcraft accrued to the chief, while chiefs and *numzane*, who acted as magistrates, were allowed part of any fine extracted from a defendant. The sale of slaves (*psikarawa*) was another source of wealth that peaked during periods of political upheaval. Although few slaves were shipped from Lourenço Marques after the 1840s, a limited market for captives continued to exist in Swaziland, the Transvaal, and parts of southern Mozambique.[78] The goods accumulated by a chief or *numzane* were frequently distributed to followers in such a way as to secure their loyalty and increase his renown. Work was rewarded with a slaughtered beast or beer, and food and drink was disbursed at festivals and parties. The relations between the dominant chiefs and *numzane* and the subordinate cadets were a complex interaction of patriarchal and filial bonds and patron-client ties. Labour relations were personal and intimate and stressed social rather than economic values, and corporate rather than contractual ties. Migrant workers travelled south with this concept of social relations of production. They interpreted social responsibility, justice, and work in terms of historical rights, obligations, and mutual benefits, and they built the contours of community on the girders of moral economy.[79]

The dominance of the chiefs and *numzane* was symbolised in various ways, such as the wearing of headrings and expensive cat and monkey skin kilts, the hierarchical distribution of the joints of a slaughtered beast, ritual drinking (when the ancestors were the first to be served), and the arrangement of households within the homestead.[80] The hierarchical structure of the social formation was particularly noticeable during first-fruits festivals when "the gods must be the first to enjoy the produce of a new year," wrote Henri Junod, "then the chiefs, the subchiefs, the counsellors, the headmen, then the younger brothers in order of age."[81] Junod described a stratified society in which the chief was

> all powerful . . . an autocrat with power over life and death. In every village the headman possesses similar power over his subjects and the elder brother reigns as a despot over the younger. . . . From the top to the bottom of the social ladder the strong dominate the weak and combine, in a powerful way, to assure the submission of the inferior.[82]

A cadet dissatisfied with his position could always leave the homestead and settle with his mother's brother (the *malume*), as his closest male blood relative with property outside his father's family, or *kondza* to a new chief. But a sister's son had no claim to the patrimony of the *malume*, and the nature of the *kondza* relationship was determined by the size and importance of the migrant's following; a single cadet would be beneath the youngest son of the most junior wife. Thus in the Delagoa Bay region segmentation was a measure of desperation rather than a mechanism for the resolution of conflict.

The cadets and women expressed their opposition to the dominant *numzane* through the medium of folk stories, proverbs and songs. The surface tranquility of the bucolic homestead masked various forms of oppression, everyday nastiness, and suspicion. The range of disputes that emerged in small-scale societies was encapsulated in riddles such as:

What is a calabash full of mosquitoes? *It is a quarreling village*

What is the buffalo with long horns that mutilates himself? *It is your village that you are busy damaging.*[83]

The village was infused with the tension that brews beneath the surface harmony of a small community. This general disquiet was partly a product of the opposition between juniors and elders, but it was also made up of the competition between households within the homestead, the antagonism between women vying for the approval of their husband and his mother, and constant fear of the witchcraft believed responsible for such everyday adversity as death, bad weather, or marital problems.

Several folk stories attack the egoism and selfishness of the husband who refuses to provide adequately for his family. Others teach caution in human relationships, for even one's husband could turn out to be a hyena or cannibal; nor should one speak openly of enchanted instruments, as even members of the family might steal them.[84] The young girl who is maltreated by her elder sisters eventually engineers their death and cruel relatives meet an untimely end. The despised junior wife, the *tshakalati*, produces an enchanted son who, after winning the love of his father, becomes his sole heir. People have constantly to be on their guard against thieves who come to steal crops or meat.[85] The stories reveal that, despite an outward conservatism and ascription, a deep strain of ambition ran through society. The characters in the tales frequently discover or produce enchanted wealth that allows them to marry into the family of the chief or governor. The alternative route to power is guile or good deeds.[86] But success attracts jealousy and envy. When the orphan boy who *kondzas* to a chief becomes his favourite, the local notables decide to kill him, as "he is only a foreigner!" But through the use of magic, the orphan overcomes his enemies and eventually becomes chief. In a similar story, the despised girl invokes the jealousy of the *numzane* when she marries the chief's son. A young boy frees a number of captives held by a cannibalistic witch but, instead of thanking and rewarding him, they try to kill him because of his success. In another story, jealousy leads a father to kill his son.[87]

Folktales reveal the deep-seated fissures within society and provide an indictment of power and injustice. They present what Junod referred to as "a discrete protest of the weak against the strong, of the spiritual against material force."[88] Many stories end with the death of a chief, a metaphorical lion or elephant, killed by the crafty hare or the astute frog. The hero of the tale often displays great guile in escaping from his persecutors, who end up killing their own chief.[89] Social antagonisms can run deep; when given an enchanted wish, a boy asks, not for wealth and power, but for the death of his cruel father and his brutal followers.[90] The hero is normally an insignificant shepherd boy, a despised younger sibling, or a junior wife. In the animal stories, characters of low status are portrayed by Mr. Hare, Mr. Frog, or Mr. Chameleon. But while the stories provide the disadvantaged in society with a means of coping with an oppressive situation, they do not present a strategy of revolution. The trickster does not challenge the system; he attempts to use it to his own advantage, and in so doing, ultimately confirms and strengthens the status quo. This was remarked on by Junod in the 1890s:

> They would never think to overturn the social order. Oh! far from that! But they feel a malicious pleasure in recounting the tricks of the hare and his companions. Why? Because Mr Hare is the everyman, the subject to whom nature and birth have given no advantage and who, nevertheless, succeeds against the notables, through his personal qualities.[91]

As Darnton, Levine, and others have shown, tricksterism is a strategy of defence, not attack. It does not reflect an assertive or aggressive group consciousness but rather a cautious and defensive attitude.

There were several reasons for the lack of open conflict between elders and juniors. Adelphic inheritance ensured that many cadets would eventually became *numzane*, even though at an advanced age. This dissuaded them from segmenting, and accounts for the large size of many homesteads. As males, all cadets were separated from women by their gender role, and even within the homestead, married women were separated from unmarried women, childless wives from mothers, and junior wives from senior wives and widows. Moreover, married women, like their sons, were of different status; and matriarchs exploited the labour of their daughters-in-law and female slaves. Due to the patrilocality of marriage, the adult women in the homestead were generally of diverse origins. The women and junior males were further divided by inadequate communications, kinship divisions and disputes, struggles over bridewealth debts, and by the various local problems whose resolution was often dependent on the *numzane*. Thus in contrast to the chiefs and *numzane*, the exploited cadets and women exercised little solidarity. Nevertheless, a structured opposition of interests existed between the two groups. The struggle between the cadets and *numzane* was an ever-present but undramatic part of life in the homestead. One of the expressions of this struggle was a centrifugal pressure on young men to leave their homestead. With the emergence of wage employment in South Africa, migrant labour became another expression of this struggle. Wage labour gave young men like Sirkomane, disadvantaged by their lowly birth or awaiting an inheritance, the opportunity to escape the dominance of the elders. By finding work in South Africa, men could accumulate enough money to purchase a brideprice without recourse to the *numzane*. Others made socially uncomfortable by an extended bachelorhood or widowhood could likewise move onto the labour market and avoid having to enter into a domineering relationship with a powerful *numzane*. A man who wished to "legalise" his rights to the children of his union with a woman "loaned" to him by a *numzane* could earn her brideprice in South Africa. Migrant labour provided a source of bridewealth for a young man without sisters or for brothers who had "eaten" the brideprice of a sister seeking to leave her husband.[92] Men were also able to procure in South Africa the money needed to ransom a wife or children seized by the Gaza king.[93]

The independence with which young men obtained bridewealth in South Africa challenged the foundations of the political dominance of the chiefs and *numzane*. The *numzane* fought to retain control over the value of their daughters by inflating brideprices from five hoes in the late 1860s to over fifty a decade later.[94] After the cattle epizootic of the early 1860s, they required hoes to maintain and extend their following. Failure to acquire sufficient hoes threatened the existing balance of power, not only between households and homesteads, but also between different chiefdoms. Thus it was not just poverty or the prospect of acquiring a wife that sent men south, and chiefs and *numzane* pressured young men to seek work, including their sons, as a means of extending their power base.[95] Chiefs leached money from migrant labour in various other ways. By the mid-1870s the Maputo chief received capitation fees varying from thirty-seven old Queen Ann guns in exchange for two hundred men, to the more common levy of £1 for each departing worker.[96] Under the so-called "Nozingile system," Maputo migrants were required to hand over a part of their earnings, often as much as five shillings, to their chiefs and *numzane*.[97] What we might perceive as the imposition of new and disagreeable taxes might not have been experienced by the migrant in this way. When a young man returned from South Africa, he was contaminated by foreign ideas and forces, and, to purge himself of this pollution, had to supplicate his superiors, through the payment of a fee, to perform the rites permitting his reintegration into society. The fee was also a form of compensation for the chief who had been deprived of the young man's labour. Hence the taxes paid by labour migrants to their chiefs were not entirely novel and had their roots in traditional *kunga* and *djimo* forms of payment.

The brideprice inflation initiated by the elders could not be maintained *ad infinitum*, particularly as hoes quickly lost their special-purpose exchange value and started to take on the attributes of modern money.[98] As the supply of imported hoes was elastic, the only way to halt the brideprice inflation was to cauterize demand. This the *numzane* successfully achieved by encouraging the adoption of another bridewealth medium, the gold coins earned by workers in South Africa. Gold coins started to replace hoes in the late 1870s, and by 1881 the director of customs at Lourenço Marques remarked that "sterling specie has replaced hoes as a means of *lobola*. Hoes are not imported to-day as they no longer serve in the marriage of blacks. Marriages are to-day made with goods and money. In this district only money is used and hoes are employed only in agriculture."[99] Unlike hoes, gold sovereigns were easily transportable, could be hidden without difficulty, and were not subject to rust. Most importantly, sterling specie had a constant scarcity value and could be exchanged throughout Southern Africa. As with a cattle brideprice, a *lobola* paid in coins was, in cases of dire need, easily convertible into food. The adoption of the gold brideprice was also assisted by the Portuguese, who viewed gold dowries as an index of civilization and as a means of attracting traders and raising customs revenues.[100] By imposing an import duty of 3d (60 reis) on each marriage hoe in 1877, the Portuguese attempted to encourage the importation of agricultural hoes that would increase exports, and hoped to discourage Africans from storing value in hoes that, unlike gold, had a restricted exchange value.[101]

A mild prosperity was brought to the Delagoa Bay region by the production and export of vegetable oils, animal skins, and furs. These commodities, together with the sterling brought back from South Africa, resulted in a rise in imports as hoes and guns, as well as cloth and liquor, were shipped into Lourenço Marques. The benefits of this commercial activity breathed life into the settlement. In 1876 Lourenço Marques was declared a *vila* (town) and the following year the neighbouring malarial swamp was drained, the administration embarked on a project of land reclamation, and the decision was taken to build a railway to Pretoria.[102] The improvement in the economy increased the number of ships visiting Lourenço Marques from fewer than 7 each year in the 1860s to 72 in 1877, of which 26 were steam-driven vessels.

The sudden prosperity that bathed the Delagoa Bay region was short-lived, for in 1878 the collapse in the trade in hoes was accompanied by a sudden drop in the price of vegetable oils.[103] By the late 1870s the piles of *beja* hoes accumulated in the warehouses of Lourenço Marques were worthless. Some were sent back to Durban, others were taken overland to Swaziland and Zululand, and a number were even carried to the iron-producing areas in the Zoutpansberg.[104] As the price of agricultural produce tumbled and the major item for which it had been exchanged evaporated, agriculturalists withdrew from the market. This process accelerated in February 1878 when, as war loomed between the Zulu and British, the gun trade was prohibited at Lourenço Marques. Unable to buy guns, and unwilling to purchase hoes, consumers rapidly shifted their money from the exchange sector of the economy to the sphere of circulating bridewealth. This retreat from the market economy had an immediate impact on trade at Lourenço Marques. The tonnage of shipping at the Bay fell in 1878 from 30,000 to 16,800 tons, the number of vessels visiting the settlement declined to forty-five, and customs revenues fell sharply. The value of exports diminished by £4,220, and there was a sudden shrinkage in the demand for imports, which fell fourfold in volume.[105]

The depression was also caused by British policy in the region. Many Lourenço Marques merchants suffered heavy losses when the annexation of the Transvaal in 1877 ended the railway speculation. Despite the MacMahon award, the British were determined to incorporate Delagoa Bay into their planned South African confederation, as the area was both an important source of labour and the natural port for the Transvaal, and its acquisition would effectively encircle Zululand. The British assault on Lourenço Marques was both economic and diplomatic, and it was to prevent them from using the gun trade as a pretext for invasion that the Portuguese prohibited the import of arms and ammunition.[106] The short-term result of the depression was the abortive Lourenço Marques treaty of 1879 that envisaged a direct British involvement in the running and administration of the town. In the event, the treaty was never ratified, as the South African confederation scheme evaporated with the re-establishment of Transvaal independence in 1881. However, the treaty did portend the extent to which Lourenço Marques was to be drawn into, and dominated by, British South Africa.

Underlying these surface events, a longer-term, more deeply rooted change emerged out of the economic depression of the late 1870s. Faced with bankruptcy, the wholesalers at Lourenço Marques were obliged to call in their credit and demand more securities and guarantees from roving traders. The high cost of porterage, the proclivity of compradores to disappear, and what the governor of Lourenço Marques referred to as the "wild revelries" of *degredado* backlanders had always thinned merchants' earnings. As the depression deepened and profits fell, Lourenço Marques traders started to accompany their goods into the interior. Itinerant trading was gradually replaced by fixed retail outlets and *sertanejos* gave way to a new wave of Banyan traders who bought goods offered by European companies directly for cash, produce, or letters of credit.[107] This new breed of Banyan trader was to play a crucial role in encouraging men to tramp south; by taking commodities out of Lourenço Marques to fixed and regular trading posts, they introduced imported goods into the everyday lives of people living in the interior. The slow and quiet consumer revolution that Banyan retailers brought to the region was to have a marked influence on the volume and flow of migrant labour.

A Slow Consumer Revolution

When migrancy was re-established after the unsettled years of 1879–1880, the consumer habits of the peoples of the Delagoa Bay region were gradually transformed. The depression that had gripped Lourenço Marques after the ending of the trade in hoes and guns lifted as migrants started to buy new articles of consumption. And as the level of consumerism rose, so too did the pressures to emigrate. Migrant workers acquired a new degree of consumer sophistication in South Africa and returned home, particularly by sea, with clothing, blankets, guns, cloth, wire, tins, tools, and beads that could not be found at the Portuguese settlements.[108]

Perhaps more importantly, local consumer awareness was heightened by the stories of well-stocked "Kaffir shops" in the towns and villages of South Africa, and by the sight of the luxuries carried home by migrant workers into even the most isolated areas of the coastal plain. In 1882 Shangaans spent roughly £30,000 at Kimberley every year, of which about half was invested in durables, and they carried home perhaps as much as £20,000 in cash.[109] On Saturday afternoons, when the two o'clock sirens announced the end of the working day, miners were assailed by vendors on the main streets who pressed on them all manner of objects. The DuToitspan Road was the English "High Street" in Africa, a dusty stretch of road lined on either side by a multitude of shops advertising a variety of wares. This nineteenth-century equivalent of the modern shopping mall was an emporium for imported and colonial goods, where migrants were introduced to the wonders of consumerism and credit.[110] The revolution in production that had brought mass-produced clothing and footwear to the working class in Europe created a large market for cheap second-hand clothes, and migrants willingly dressed themselves in the less fashionable cast-offs of white society. There was "pandemonium on Saturday afternoons" along the DuToitspan Road, wrote J. B. Currey, and the "hideous noise and tumult lasted far into the night."[111] Robberies provide some idea of the amounts of money carried home by individuals. After working for three years in the Western Cape, one Mosbieker lost £27 to bandits. Two others returning from Kimberley were robbed of £8 and £10. Another two men employed in the Transvaal were plundered of £102, a sum sufficiently large to indicate that they were carrying money home for friends.[112] Diamonds and gold nuggets swelled these earnings. At home workers were also able to increase their sterling wages by almost 10 percent by exchanging them at black market rates for Portuguese reis.[113]

The rise in the flow of migrant labour over the period 1880–1883 was immediately transformed into increased buying power in the labour-supply areas. Once they had arrived home, migrants invested their money in wives and, increasingly, in a narrow range of imported goods, particularly cotton cloth, distilled liquor, and sugar. Cloth was worn largely by women who evolved their own distinctive style of dress, clothing themselves entirely in imported cottons.[114] Between 1878 and 1883, the year in which labour migration peaked, the value of cotton goods imported through Lourenço Marques rose by 40 percent and distilled liquor by 60 percent.[115] Part of the money used to pay for these imports came from the sale of skins and oil-producing fruits and seeds. But the deficit in the balance of payments rose by 57 percent, or £46,670, over the decade 1874–1883, and the "invisible earnings" that paid for imports came almost entirely from migrants' wages.[116] By 1883 migrant labour brought into the Delagoa Bay area twice as much money as the produce exported by local agriculturalists and hunters.

Banyan retailers quickly sought to benefit from the gold coins repatriated by migrants, and by 1884 were oversupplying the market with cheap, imported goods.[117] In sharp contrast to the situation in Gazaland, where even the itinerant *sertanejos* operated with difficulty, retailers working through Lourenço Marques "established permanent trading stations in all possible places," and within the next few years they had "spread everywhere."[118] The economic depression of the late 1870s had started this process, but it was the buying power of migrants' wages that completed the crucial transfer of merchant capital from itinerant trading to fixed retailing. The profits of Banyan traders were particularly high in the Delagoa Bay area, where goods bought with depreciating silver rupees from old stock in India were exchanged for gold sovereigns. As the wages of migrant workers provided traders with an internationally stable currency, retailers increasingly demanded sterling specie as payment for imported trade goods rather than agricultural products that were costly to transport and depreciating in value.[119] At the end of 1885 there were about four hundred Banyans in the Delagoa Bay region, and their numbers grew steadily over the following decade.[120] They created a network of distribution outlets through which a range of imported articles filtered into the rural areas. Goods that at one stage could only be bought in Lourenço Marques or in South Africa were sold at their stores, and gradually articles that had been luxuries to a previous generation became everyday requirements.

This transformation in the demand and supply of foreign goods had a spiralling effect, for as traditional crafts were undermined and destroyed, people became more dependent on imports. The local weaving industry was one of the first casualties. Industrial cloths duplicated a large range of designs, reflecting the social standing of a man and his wife, and were cheaper to produce than cloths woven locally on the cumbersome horizontal loom. The increase in the importation of cotton cloth was an index of rising standards of living, as people chose to replace locally woven cloths with imported substitutes that were lighter, stronger, and more suited to a tropical climate than the heavy local weave. After the collapse of the trade in marriage hoes in the mid-1870s, cotton cloth quickly became the chief item of importation, and in 1883 almost 146,000 kilos of cotton goods, valued at £26,770, were shipped through Lourenço Marques.[121]

The effect of the importation of liquor on the local production of beverages is more difficult to calculate. I pointed out in Chapter 1 the dietary importance and social function of liquor in the rural areas and in Chapter 3 showed how this concept of alcohol became a major source of friction between employers and workers on the diamond fields.[122] The consumption of alcohol is often related to poverty or social malaise, but it also reflected a rise in the standard of living on the coastal plain, as rare and exotic drinks brought an added choice and richness to everyday life. Unlike local drinks that depended on the seasonal availability of cereals and fruit, imported brandies, gins, and wines lasted indefinitely, even in a tropical climate, and could be consumed all year round. As imported liquor was the product of European crop surpluses, its price and availability was not dependent on local climatic variables. These were vital factors for people whose productive relations, with both the living and the dead, depended on an easy social intercourse and who, without sophisticated storage facilities, were constantly threatened by famine. Restricted buying power had traditionally limited the demand for foreign liquor, and in 1863 Lourenço Marques had imported only 8,200 litres of Portuguese wine and 25,000 litres of distilled drink. This situation changed markedly towards the end of the 1870s, as migrants returned from Kimberley and the Cape with a new taste for distilled liquor (or the sugar from which it could be manufactured) and with the means to purchase it at the Banyan stores. By the early 1880s, more than half the customs revenues at Lourenço Marques came from imported alcohol, and well over 30 tons of sugar were brought through the settlement every year. "He who has no alcohol," wrote the director of customs in 1882, "does no business in this district."[123] As at Kimberley or on the Cape railways, this foreign liquor was diluted with water and then doctored to give it a special local appeal. As "European" liquor, the concoction was imbued with a certain status, the drink of important and respected men who had returned from South Africa with wealth, knowledge, and experience. Merchants encouraged this local perception of imported drink by supplying liquor to the chiefs, and French and Dutch wholesalers who had suffered severely from the collapse of the trade in hoes and guns in the late 1870s started to import brandies and gins. The taste for distilled liquor quickly spread into the rural areas through the capillary of Banyan shops, ubiquitous "canteens" that served as institutions, almost "schools," for the spread of new consumer habits. Run by foreigners, they were politically neutral areas where people could drink without becoming socially indebted; they also served as centers of news-distribution and became important places for the recruitment of workers. The amount of distilled liquor entering Lourenço Marques rose from just under 230,000 litres, worth about £6,770 in 1877–78, to almost 600,100 litres (worth over £18,000) in 1883.[124] One of the great benefits of imported alcohol—that it could be drunk throughout the year—was also one of its most pernicious flaws: consistent and steady drinking induced an alcoholism that undermined social stability and, by creating a need for money, pushed men onto the labour market. But it would be wrong to see drink merely as an "agent of proletarianization" that forced an unsavory addiction upon a naive and compliant consumer public. Alcohol consumption was, perhaps more than anything, a symptom of a little-developed level of consumerism, for its inspiration was rooted in the local drinking culture; it was by responding to an already existing demand for indigenous beers and wines that European and Banyan traders extracted a profit from their operations.

By the early 1880s, migrant labour had become an important branch of the homestead economy. But this widening of the economic base was won at the expense of a diminution in the export sector, a fact much remarked on at the time. From the early 1880s, numerous commentators observed that trade in the Delagoa Bay region was no longer dependent on the export of agricultural and hunting produce, but instead rested on the purchasing power of migrant worker's wages. Lourenço Marques merchants who had formerly exchanged their imported goods for ivory, vegetable oils, and skins were demanding payment in cash for their wares.[125] Already in 1882, the export of Lourenço Marques produce was considered "insignificant" in comparison with undeclared gold exports, which were estimated at over £100,000 each year.[126] By 1886 the total weight of sesame, groundnuts, and orchil exports had dwindled to under 8,000 kilos.[127] In 1887 the British consul in Lourenço Marques was struck by the comparatively large trade practised in an area largely devoid of cultivation. On asking a local trader how people could afford to pay for the imports entering the country, he was told that "the produce of this district is English gold. The native pays for everything here in hard cash." "This is strictly true," reported the consul, "the natural produce of the district is almost nil: its wealth consists in the savings of the natives from their earnings in one of our South African colonies. Sterling is the local currency."[128] For a large part of the population, migrant labour had become an important element in the struggle to survive.

The fragility of an economy increasingly reliant on external earnings became evident for the first time between 1883 and 1886, when migrants were pushed from South Africa by the depression. As the flow of repatriated wages declined to a trickle, the importation of consumer goods plummeted, and people who had become dependent on wage labour were faced with a serious crisis, as was the Lourenço Marques customs house.[129] Without wages entering the area, the spectre of a rootless lumpenproletariat emerged at Lourenço Marques for the first time. In March 1886 the governor cautioned that the suspension of emigration to Natal "could have a terrible effect on the Natives." Within months he warned that people were arriving every day at the town looking for work, and that this could have "grave consequences," as the local constabulary was not large enough to deal with a workless poor.[130] At Lourenço Marques imports dropped from £70,000 in 1883 to £33,550 in 1886.[131] But the following year, as South Africa emerged from the depression, men tramped to the Witwatersrand, and wages started to trickle back into the region.

At Inhambane the transformation brought to the economy by migrant labour was not so marked. The settlement's hinterland produced its own distilled liquor from sugar cane, and the region in general did not have the same history of dependence on migrant labour as the area south of the Limpopo. Nevertheless, although the export of agricultural goods through Inhambane continued to climb during the depression of 1883–1886, imports dropped marginally and continued to fall until wages from the Witwatersrand started to enter the area towards the end of the decade.[132] Meanwhile, when war and drought reduced the export of agricultural and hunting produce in 1886, the population around Inhambane resorted to paying for imports with sterling specie.[133]

The depression brought to southern Mozambique by the decline in migrant labour was accompanied by a string of ecological problems the seriousness of which serves to remind us of the fragile balance between preindustrial people and their environment. Good rains fell in the summer of 1884–1885, but by December part of the maize crop was lost due to insufficient rain, and the food situation became "precarious" as people fell back on hardier crops such as groundnuts, millet, sorghum, and beans.[134] Sowing was postponed because of late rains at the end of 1886, and agriculture was reported to be "completely stagnant" during the summer of 1886/87. The following summer the first crop was lost due to poor early rains.[135] When the governor of Lourenço Marques stopped his agricultural reports in 1888, the food exports of the previous decade were only a dim memory and his district was the poorest agricultural region in Mozambique.[136]

The precariousness of food supplies was made more serious by the shooting-out of game. The prohibition of the sale of guns at Lourenço Marques had pushed the trade in firearms with the Zulu northwards to Inhambane.[137] But when the ban was lifted in July 1882, migrants' wages rather than Zulu militarism attracted firearms back to Delagoa Bay. The general displacement of flintlock muskets by more modern percussion guns added to the decimation of game.[138] Without game protection laws, animals were a wasting asset, and the production of buckskin exports soon declined, from 143,000 kilos in 1877–78 to 42,200 kilos in 1883 and 32,600 kilos in 1890.[139] A similar decline took place in the export of monkey and civet skins, a process compounded by the disintegration of the export market with the demilitarization of Zulu society. In the Delagoa Bay region the shooting-out of cats and the availability of cloth brought home by migrants, or purchased locally, led men to discard skins in favour of a more Europeanized dress.[140] The shooting-out of game brought an indirect and unexpected benefit to the populace, as it rid the area of the ungulate vectors of trypansomiasis. Although this caused a reduction in porterage as a source of income, it allowed men to replenish their cattle herds, and, with peace firmly established over much of southern Mozambique, milk and beef once again became important components of the local diet.[141]

The historic trade with the highveld came under pressure when the border delineated between Mozambique and the Transvaal in 1869 was ratified six years later. As Boers occupied the northern Transvaal, they pressured Pretoria to implement laws requiring Mozambican merchants to buy government licences and pay import duties on goods carried across the border. "On my way to Delagoa Bay via Phalaborwa," wrote an incensed Boer trader in 1884, "almost every day I saw Kafirs and Banyans, the former as porters engaged by the latter, carrying guns and boxes filled with drink or gunpowder, and Kafir hoes, such that I myself saw . . . a party of 100 of which each Kafir carried rum or 8–10 guns or 25–30 hoes."[142] This commerce caused a Zoutpansberg veldkornet to complain that the Spelonken hills were being

> overrun with native traders from the Portuguese territory. The lowveld is full of them. Of course none of these traders have any licenses and consequently undersell the white traders here and defraud the government of import taxes and licence money. . . . the white traders here are complaining bitterly and in fact the trade is taken entirely out of their hands.[143]

In 1882 the newly independent Transvaal government gave a physical presence to a mental border when officials were stationed along the border to collect import duties.[144] Three years later "Asians" were prohibited from obtaining Transvaal citizenship or owning land, were required to purchase expensive trading licenses, and were soon to be prohibited from trading in liquor.[145] Banyan traders and African compradores, who for decades had linked the Zoutpansberg and eastern Transvaal with the coast, became poachers and smugglers almost overnight.[146]

Christianity and Colonialism

Numbers of workers returned to the East Coast with an element of literacy and a familiarity with European concepts of ethnicity, race, and religion. Robert Mashaba, the migrant worker who had gained an education in Natal and the Eastern Cape, returned to Lourenço Marques in 1885. He soon found a chief willing to help him open a night school. But as a Protestant trained by British missionaries, he received little support from the Portuguese; when his money ran out, Mashaba was obliged to seek work at the Komati Drift. With his savings he established a day school in May 1888 and succeeded in attracting sixty-six children on a regular basis. The popularity of European education was paralleled by a growth in the popularity of Christianity, and within three years Mashaba was assisted by four local preachers and five class leaders, and had two hundred people on trial for communion. He built a church at Nkasana and established nine out-stations along the Tembe River, four of which included day schools. In 1890 he was officially recognized by the Methodists as a minister, his church incorporated into their Transvaal District, and his converts baptised.[147]

Robert Mashaba was not the only migrant to return home with a proselytizing zeal. Andreas Honzwana established a small chapel-school near the mouth of the Tembe River, and Isaac Mavilo attempted, unsuccessfully, to bring Christianity to the capital of the young Maputo king.[148] Some migrants almost inadvertently spread the Christian message, since they had acquired religious training with their education, or had returned home with Christian wives.[149] For others, like Jim Ximungana, Christian beliefs lay dormant until they were activated by visiting evangelists. Ximungana had worked for several years in Natal, where he had learnt to read and write, and where, although he had not been converted, he had probably come into contact with Christian ideas. On his return to Tembeland, he invested his wages in the purchase of goods, particularly distilled spirits, and settled down as a trader. Ximungana established careful marriage alliances. His one sister married the Tembe chief Mabayi, while another married the Dutch manager of the successful Swiss firm, Widmer and Co. He himself had three wives and numerous slaves. Speaking fluent English and Portuguese, Ximungana was able to acquire credit from the European wholesalers in Lourenço Marques. He was converted to Christianity after reading the *buku*, a collection of hymns and passages from the New Testament translated and compiled by Swiss missionaries in the northern Transvaal into what they defined as the Gwamba or Thonga language.[150]

In 1882 three Swiss mission converts from the Transvaal, Yosefa Mhalamhala, his sister Lois, and her husband, Eliachib Mandlakusasa, established a mission at Rikatla, some 15 miles to the north of Lourenço Marques. Their independent and animated preaching soon sparked off a religious revival that Jan van Butselaar has described as "an African movement developing in the context of African culture, using African customs."[151] They adapted local customs to create their own terms of avoidance and greeting. They developed gestures, mannerisms, and dress that bound them together and they created their own structure of command, independent of local chiefs and white missionaries. Yosefa Mhalamhala was the head of the church, his sister Lois one of several prophetesses, and Jim Ximungana, who bought a house in Lourenço Marques for use as a chapel, was a *mufundisi*, or pastor.[152] They based their teaching on the *buku*, which gave them a freedom of interpretation, and they introduced their followers to a written language not far different from their own linguistic forms. Bible readings were combined with classes using the Gwamba (Thonga) reading primer published by the Swiss Mission in 1884. The small Christian community recognized a universal humanity that cut across the old tribal divisions; they were all "children of the Lord" and "children of the father." To suffer a mishap no longer implied the work of malevolent ancestors or witches, but was "to be beaten by God." They also imbued work with a new morality, for to cultivate the land was "to work for the flesh."[153] Thus the material changes that came to the Delagoa Bay region in the 1880s were accompanied by the stirring of new perceptions of self.

It was only at the Portuguese settlements on the coast that the brief prosperity of the 1870s had given way to a more traditional, tropical torpor. In the early 1880s

Robert Mashaba. The migrant worker and scholar who established Methodism in the Lourenço Marques area.

the Portuguese attempted to give coherence to their relations with local African allies by drawing up "treaties of vassalage." In December 1880 three chiefs to the north of Lourenço Marques signed treaties of vassalage, which bound them to supply the Portuguese with labourers, porters, and soldiers, and the sporadic gathering of taxes in kind was replaced by a fixed annual hut tax of 1s6d ($340). The Portuguese were reminded of the double-edged benefits of the vassalage system when in 1882 two chiefs, to whom they had supplied guns and ammunition, raided the peoples living south of the bend in the Komati River.[154] Moreover, when the officials at Lourenço Marques attempted to raise the hut tax to 3s6d ($800) in July 1883, and implement a decree on forced labour issued at Mozambique Island two years previously, they were met with armed opposition and had to rescind the move.[155] An evangelist employed by the Swiss mission, who visited Lourenço Marques in 1882, noted that

> The Portuguese have only the port where ships discharge their cargoes. Delagoa Bay is the only place that they occupy and dominate. Everywhere else they are entirely under the power of the native chiefs. The natives would be most astonished if one were to tell them that a treaty exists marking the frontier between the Portuguese possessions on the coast and the Transvaal.[156]

During the depression of 1884–1887, the number of ships calling at Lourenço Marques dropped, the letters received at the town fell by almost half, and shipping and trade remained firmly in the hands of foreign companies.[157] In 1886 the salaries of civil servants were about three months in arrears, officers entrusted with tax collection were provided with no clerical assistance, and the garrison was on the verge of mutiny. Despite the treaties of vassalage, the hut tax returns for the Lourenço Marques district amounted to a meagre £300 during the economic year 1883–84.[158]

At Inhambane the Portuguese succeeded in extending their territory southwards in the late 1870s and, within a few years, started to enter into "treaties of vassalage" with local chiefs.[159] A new and interesting discourse crept into their correspondence as they remarked on the detrimental effect of emigration overland, which pushed up the cost of labour at Lourenço Marques and Inhambane and brought no revenue to the colony in the form of taxes. As it became evident that there was no way to prevent what the Portuguese started to term "clandestine" emigration, they attempted to redirect the flow of labour through Inhambane by officially reopening the port to labour emigration in January 1885 and by arresting unlicensed recruiters.[160]

In October 1885 the Gaza became vassals of the Portuguese, a decision that provided them with the guns needed to seize slaves and provisions from the independent Chopi chiefdoms south of Inhambane.[161] The anomaly of Portuguese claims to rule Gazaland and rightfully tax or "sell" the labour of Gaza subjects was underlined when the Gaza king demanded that he be the recipient of all "passport fees" gathered at Inhambane and Lourenço Marques. Like his counterparts to the south, the Gaza king demanded financial compensation for the absence of his subjects in South Africa.[162] When the Portuguese finally turned from rhetoric to action in October 1886 and attempted to expand their control over the lands around Inhambane, they were resoundingly defeated by a Gaza army.[163] Because of the centralization of power in the hands of Umzila, the nature and function of trade in Gazaland was substantially different from the commerce practised south of the Limpopo River, in the Portuguese enclave around Inhambane and in the territory occupied by the Chopi bowmen. In Gazaland, trade was largely controlled and regulated by the king and his provincial chiefs; merchants could only enter the territory with their permission, and they, rather than the trader, determined what could be sold and fixed the price of imported goods.[164] Merchants tended to establish themselves at villages on the edge of Gazaland, to which such goods as wax, groudnuts, ivory, and cat skins were brought and exchanged for cloth, liquor, and beads.[165] By controlling the movement and circulation of foreign goods, the Gaza monarch restricted the level of consumerism in his kingdom. Labour migration from Gazaland was less responsive to economic factors than emigration from the chiefdoms south of the Limpopo River, and the spiral in hoe bridewealth that had shaken the social and economic structure of the southern chiefdoms was never duplicated in Gazaland.

By the mid-1880s the development of Lourenço Marques, and to a lesser extent that of Inhambane, had become tied to the economy of South Africa. The amount of traffic passing through Lourenço Marques to the eastern Transvaal gold fields had almost quadrupled during the depression. The recovery of diamond prices, and the discovery of gold on the Witwatersrand, were to bind the future of southern Mozambique ever more firmly to developments in the interior.

5

The Early Witwatersrand

Halfway between Pretoria and Potchefstroom, Shangaan workers on their way from Gazaland to Kimberley tramped past the western edge of a ridge of land called the Witwatersrand. It was in the heart of this area that gold was discovered in early 1886; in September the area was proclaimed a goldfield and three months later diggers were required to buy residential plots on the triangle of land that was to become Johannesburg.[1] The gold reef stretched over thirty miles from east to west, or roughly the distance between present-day Krugersdorp and Boksburg. The first systematic underground mining took place in 1887, and confidence in the mines soared as the reef was found to slope to the south and coal was discovered on the East Rand. Scores of claims were rapidly amalgamated to form companies like the Langlaagte Estate or the Crown Reef; many of these mines were then absorbed by syndicates such as Wernher, Beit and Co., Consolidated Goldfields, and Randfontein Estates.

The Mine Owners Organize

As development capital flowed into the Witwatersrand from Kimberley, the demand for labour rocketed; by 1889 there were almost ten thousand black workers on the gold fields, 60 percent of whom came from the East Coast.[2] Huge profits and speculation over the richness of the reef to the south of the outcrop produced a boom climate, but this evaporated in mid-1889 when pyrite was encountered in the reef at about 300 feet. Investors panicked as the gold recovery rate plummeted; fearing the gold fields grossly overvalued, they withdrew working capital. Recession deepened into depression as a severe drought caused food prices to treble and the lack of water restricted mining operations. With only the early outcrop mines in production, the need for labour declined; as the terms of employment moved against unskilled labour, the mineowners attempted to recoup their losses by introducing a wage cut. They were encouraged to take this step by the belief, common in industrializing countries, that preindustrial workers, because they had limited consumer needs, were less concerned with the length of time they laboured than with a specific target income; hence a cut in wages would induce men to work for longer periods of time.[3] What this ignored, of course, was that workers tied their earnings to calculated levels of voluntary absenteeism and that they opposed any sudden and unilateral adjustments to the informal contract that governed their conditions of employment.

In July 1890 the recently formed Witwatersrand Chamber of Mines gingerly introduced a system of monthly payments in an attempt to reduce the absenteeism and drunkenness that accompanied Saturday wages.[4] Later that year, as the traditional winter efflux of labour was turned around, black wages were cut from an average of just over 63s per month to 48s10d. But because producing mines required more skilled labour than mines at the development stage, the mineowners introduced a three-tier wage structure according to which at least half the work force on each mine was paid under 40s per month, semi-skilled workers received up to 50s, and no ceiling was set on the wages of the top 20 percent. Despite misgivings from the secretary of the Chamber of Mines that "the reduction is likely to have as a result a general strike," the employers' combination advised its members to institute a working month of twenty-eight days, divided into twenty ten-hour shifts and four Saturday shifts of roughly seven hours.[5]

Almost immediately, groups of workers defended their established working conditions by returning home.[6] Experienced and seasoned miners who could find work at Kimberley were the first to leave, but others quickly followed, and newly arrived workers refused to go underground. On the Meyer and Charlton mine, where several hundred miners were lodged in the company compound, large numbers of men left for home. Those who remained were "sullen" and "discontent" and sought revenge by gutting the house of the paymaster, the official held responsible for their plight.[7] The miners were in a weak bargaining position, however; with no exploratory work being undertaken and with several of the mines south of the outcrop closed down by the depression, those who remained on the Witwatersrand were obliged to accept the reduction in earnings. As the summer brought with it new waves of migrants, the average wage sank to 41s6d. But the nature of mining was revolutionized the following year, when the pyrites problem was solved, capital flowed back to the Witwatersrand, and new mines were opened. This caused the demand for labour to soar and in the winter of 1891, as workers left the mines in advance of the highveld cold, cracks appeared in the mineowners' combination.

The management of wealthy mines like the Langlaagte abandoned the Chamber's three-tiered pay system when they saw their experienced workers tramp off to Kimberley to earn an average monthly wage of 128s. Other mines sought to attract workers by reintroducing the weekly system of payment or raising the average monthly wage. Although these measures caused the number of black workers to almost double, from 14,000 in 1891 to 25,860 in 1892, the nature of mining on the Witwatersrand placed employers under strong pressures to reduce working costs. As Frederick Johnstone and others have shown, the profitability of mining the treasure house of low-grade ore deep beneath the Rand was dependent on the creation of a cheap labour force.[8] Yet at the same time, the labour-intensive nature of gold mining resulted in an almost untrammelled competition for workers. This was made more acute by the very uneven richness of the ore body, for the wealthy mines needed large numbers of skilled workers and were prepared to lure them from their competitors with high wages. The very existence of several of the poorer mines, on the other hand, was contingent on reduced working costs. This divergence of interests naturally introduced a fragility into employer combinations, as mineowners were under constant pressure to improve working conditions as a means of attracting labour, and to lower wages, so as to exploit the low grade ore at deep levels. To resolve this contradiction, they attempted to reduce the price of labour by flooding the market with recruited workers, a policy that was to make labour relations on the Witwatersrand very different from those operating under the monopoly conditions at Kimberley.[9] In the event, the mines were able to salvage the monthly payment system and hold down the wage rate only by buying workers from labour recruiters.[10] The success of this venture, and the refusal of government to become involved in the importation of labour, encouraged the Chamber to form its own Native Labour Department (NLD) in August 1893, an organisation that promised "to endeavour, while lowering the rate of native wages, to secure an ample supply of labour."[11] This was the first salvo in what was to be the long struggle between employers, free-lance recruiters, and tramping workers to control the labour market.

The Native Labour Department sought the assistance of the Portuguese in recruiting labour and in preventing or restricting the operations of independent recruiters who invaded southern Mozambique each winter.[12] In order to gain some return from the large number of workers who left Mozambique without passing through government controls, the Portuguese agreed in December 1893 to place the emigration of labour to the Transvaal on the same footing as the export of labour to Natal by sea.[13] Once the Transvaal government was assured that it would be placed under no financial obligation, it appointed agents at Lourenço Marques and Inhambane to act as co-witnesses, with Portuguese officials, to the signing of contracts by vaccinated emigrant workers. The Chamber of Mines guaranteed to pay a 15s passport fee to the Portuguese, undertook to transport workers along the newly built railway from Lourenço Marques to Ressano Garcia on the border, and constructed depots at Komati Poort and Nelspruit.[14] These attempts by the NLD to centralise the labour supply amounted to very little.[15] Despite a plethora of legislation regulating the emigration of workers, the Portuguese were almost entirely unable to pressure men into leaving Mozambique, or tax them on their departure. But the *ad hoc* agreement of December 1893 did lay the basis for cooperation between the Chamber and the Portuguese government. The Native Labour Department had very little financial backing and was unable to bring the numerous independent labour recruiters under its control. Nor could the Portuguese, hemmed into the enclaves around Lourenço Marques and Inhambane, restrict the operations of "touts" who were able to charge up to £5.10s, depending on the length of the contract, for a worker brought to the mines from the East Coast.[16] But although expensive, recruiting succeeded in uncoupling the black workers' income from the demand for labour to such an extent that, although the number of blacks employed in the mines increased by more than a third in 1893, the average wage remained static.[17] But at 57s6d, the average monthly wage of a black worker compared favourably with that of miners elsewhere in the world, particularly as they received free food, fuel, water, and quarters valued at 12s6d per month.[18]

As scores of claims were combined to form a company mine, the small camps of black workers, employed on individual diggings, were consolidated into communal barracks reminiscent of the old structures on the early diamond fields. Although these clusters of buildings were called "compounds," the make-shift structures had little in common with the closed compounds at Kimberley. Influential voices blamed "the want of proper quarters" for the seasonal efflux of labour, as workers fled the intense winter cold, and argued that improved living conditions would serve to attract and secure labour.[19] While the system of closed compounds at Kimberley functioned to regulate and discipline a migrant labour force, the early, open compounds on the Witwatersrand served merely to allow migrants to recover from their journey, housed them close to the mine, and protected them from the extremely high cost of living that afflicted the Witwatersrand.

As at Kimberley, managerial philanthropy on the Witwatersrand was based on sound economic principles. In early 1890 some of the larger mines had compounds housing as many as four to six hundred men.[20] The barracks were generally constructed of wood and iron, facing inwards towards a square housing the cooking quarters and administrative buildings. The compound manager lived in a more sturdy structure on mine property, generally within hailing distance of the compound. It was only in 1892–1894, when the huge influx of men inflated the price of housing and food, that barracks were constructed of brick and iron. These early compounds were not even fenced in, and the men could come and go as they pleased; the only restriction on their movements was that they were required by law to carry a travel pass if they wished to move beyond the limits of mine property. In fact, until the beginning of 1888 black workers were unhindered in their movements on the gold fields; it was only in that year that the old Kimberley system of monthly passes was applied to the Witwatersrand. This required the migrant, once he had found work, to exchange his travel pass for an employer's pass that had to be renewed every month for 1s. A worker found without either a travel or employer's pass was considered to be in the area illegally and could be fined 5s.[21] But these restrictions were seldom enforced, as mine managers were unwilling to impose on their workers a 1s tax that would encourage them to look for work elsewhere, and they hesitated to provide passes giving men the legal right to move freely on the Witwatersrand. In 1889 about half the work force had monthly passes and the meagre police force could only implement the law by mounting raids on the compounds, a form of action strenuously opposed by mine managers.[22] In 1892 it was estimated that only about one-third of the black mineworkers could produce a pass.[23]

The development of a system of closed compounds, advocated in some quarters,[24] was precluded by the competitive nature of capitalism on the Witwatersrand in the 1890s. Protected from violent fluctuations in profitability by a fixed gold price, the mine owners were not under the same pressures to amalgamate as their peers on the diamond fields. Hence they lacked the strength and unity of purpose needed to close the compounds in the face of opposition from merchants, who feared this would destroy their livelihood, and from a government unwilling to allow further economic power to fall into the hands of foreign capitalists.[25] Nor were the mine owners able to attract and hold workers by duplicating the Kimberley system of racial paternalism, as an inflexible gold price made the working of low-grade mines dependent on the reduction of wages and other working costs. Yet while profitability constraints restricted employers from luring workers to the mines by means of competitive wages and working conditions, or from holding and disciplining workers through the mechanism of closed compounds, the gold fields exhibited a voracious demand for unskilled labour. The mine owners' policy of resorting to large-scale recruitment was to require novel solutions to the old problem of disciplining a preindustrial, migrant labour force.

The Miners' Solidarity

Gold miners were able to supplement their formal earnings in various ways. The wealthier and more developed mines used high monthly wages of up to 80s to attract experienced and skilled workers. As Shangaans stayed on the Witwatersrand for longer periods than other workers, they were invariably better trained and, working underground, earned above-average wages. The men increased their earnings through various informal activities, stretching from selling food and firewood to making bracelets, musical instruments, and knives. Their cash wage was often substantially augmented by this penny capitalism, as well as by purloining tools such as iron files, knives, and piping, which, together with copper and iron wire, were considered wage bonuses by most workers. Files were reforged at home, bracelets were fashioned from wire, and piping was used to construct stills. What the mineowners saw as pilfering seems to have been condoned by many Europeans who, only a generation previously, had considered 'chips', 'clippings', and 'sweepings' and other by-products of the work process as a legitimate part of the wage. A form of appropriation not condoned by management was the theft of gold amalgam, but as this illegal bonus was only available in the surface works, it brought little benefit to Shangaans.[26] Miners could also augment their wages by deserting after receiving their monthly pay and "selling" themselves to a recruiter, particularly as the fine for travelling without a pass was only 5s. In the rural areas prospective workers were able to exploit the highly competitive nature of recruiting by selling their labour to the highest bidder. This pushed wages on the Witwatersrand up to an average of 63s6d in 1895 and ensured that recruiters continued to receive capitation fees worth several pounds.[27] Perhaps most importantly, migrant labourers were able to use their access to an alternative means of production in the rural areas to protect their wage level. As had been clearly demonstrated on the Witwatersrand in 1890–1891, and on the plantations and diamond fields in earlier years, workers who retained a subsistence base at home could withdraw their labour almost at will.

Miners also demanded financial compensation for the dangers involved in travelling to, and working on, the Witwatersrand. There were frequent smallpox scares in the mining camps, and particularly severe epidemics in 1893–1894 and 1897–1898 cost the lives of several dozen men. Dysentery and typhoid were common and could take on epidemic proportions.[28] These enteric diseases were caused by overcrowded and unsanitary living conditions, an inadequate water supply, and poor drainage.[29] Pneumonia and various lung ailments were particularly prevalent in winter. In Johannesburg the death rate for blacks stood at 30.8 per thousand in 1890 and 35 per thousand in 1893–1894, while in particularly insalubrious areas of the city it could reach 42 per mille.[30] As at Kimberley, the 1s worker registration fee was used to pay for medical facilities. Blacks seldom received any return from this tax, however, as the central Johannesburg hospital was too far from the mines and largely reserved for whites. In 1892 a health inspector started to visit the compounds, and in 1895 each mine was required, in theory at least, to build a hospital and provide training in first aid.[31] In the meantime black workers were expected to bear the cost of illness, and during the smallpox epidemic of 1893–1894, they were obliged to pay a tax of 10s in support of a vaccination campaign and a quarantine station.

The gender composition of the population on the Reef encouraged the spread of venereal diseases. Female immigrants to the Witwatersrand gravitated towards the residential areas of Johannesburg, where they lived in the back yards of their employers, or, more frequently, erected shacks on vacant plots. Few women migrated from Mozambique to the Witwatersrand, and in 1896 only ninety were registered as living in the city. It was only the hardiest and most intrepid who ventured to live out along the Reef in the small villages on mine property.[32] In the mining areas around Johannesburg, the ratio of black women to men was 1:63 in 1896; for the age group 25–39, it was a staggering 1:98. "It is painful to contemplate," warned the director of census, "the far-reaching results of this enormous disproportion between the sexes."[33] One of the earliest results was a flourishing market for prostitution as black and white prostitutes, pushed out of the Cape by the Contagious Diseases Act, flocked to the Witwatersrand.[34] They brought with them the occupational diseases of their profession, and these spread rapidly in the migrants' world of enforced celibacy. But formal prostitution was an unfamiliar and expensive practice for most miners, and it seems more likely that the venereal diseases from which they suffered were incubated less in the brothels than in the drinking places run by black women along the Reef. Of the 1,678 black women living in Johannesburg in 1896, less than 2 percent were married, and few had any formal employment in a world where even jobs like washing and domestic service were dominated by men. Many women lived by exercising skills, such as beer-brewing, learnt in the rural areas, and it was common for them to enter into temporary sexual relations with migrant workers whose gifts supplemented their informal incomes. For the miner far from home these women, particularly those living in the mine villages or locations called "married quarters," provided sympathy, support, an important leisure activity, and a crucial sexual outlet. But the gratification of a heterosexual relationship, however brief, was accompanied by the prospect of a more lasting venereal disease.

The injury and death of a frighteningly high proportion of miners may be traced to the low standards of safety in the mines. Checks on the conditions under which men worked were abysmal, and miners lived in constant fear of sudden death or crippling injury. In 1893, the first year in which accident mortality figures were kept, 5.9 black miners died out of every 1,000. This figure dropped to 4.6 over the next two years, but rose to 5.1 in 1896, three times the accident mortality rate in English mines. About a quarter of all deaths were caused by mishandling poor-quality explosives or by driving drills into misfired charges. Miners were also buried by rockfalls and trapped by collapsing shafts; they fell from rudimentary cages and ladders, and were killed by falling objects. They were crushed in the dark galleries by trams loaded with ore, drowned in flooded passages, and asphyxiated by gasses and smoke. Mining was the most remunerative of wage labour activities, but it was also the most dangerous.[35]

As the subterranean works were extended "hammer boys," or the drillers who made up about 60 percent of the underground labour force, rapidly became an élite. To enter the mines they either walked in their bare feet down an incline shaft or descended to the clatter and confusion of the working level in elevators or cages, an experience that was perhaps the most quotidian source of terror. Each driller was armed with a four-pound hammer, about five hand-sharpened steel drills of varying lengths, a supply of twelve-ounce candles, matches, an old cloth swab, and a can of water. After the white miner indicated to the men under his charge where they were to drill in the stope, the men fixed candles to the rock face or the nearby timbering and, because of the heat, removed much of their clothing. In the flickering light, the shadowy figures applied their hammers to the short starter drills, which they turned with the free hand after each blow to loosen the interior of the hole. Every few minutes the miner lubricated the drill by squirting a mouthful of water into the hole. The cloth swab was wrapped round the drill to protect him from the ensuing slush and this was removed, from time to time, with a wooden peg. The miner completed the hole, generally a meter deep, with a 1.7 meter-long "jumper" drill. Mechanical drills were employed in shaft driving and tunnelling but only rarely in the stopes, as their weight and bulk required an enlarged and uneconomical working face; since they produced large holes that were easily overcharged with dynamite, they also increased the danger of working underground. A skilled hand-driller was able to follow the gold seam more closely than a miner with a compression drill. He was able to work in a confined stope, and, because the holes he drilled were narrower and charged with less explosive, he kept the amount of waste rock to a minimum.[36] Once the drillers had completed their work, the holes were charged with explosives and the reef blasted. "Lashers" shovelled the broken rock through box holes down to the level below, from where it was transported to the shaft in trams or trollies and lifted to the surface in elevators. Drill men earned about 10s more than lashers and trammers. Experienced underground workers, as well as those employed in unhealthy and uncomfortable wet shafts, were paid more than novices and men working in dry conditions. As the mines deepened and the task of the underground worker became increasingly dangerous and skilled, the difference between the monthly wages paid to underground and surface workers jumped from about 1s6d in 1889 to 5s in 1896. The conditions under which black miners worked engendered a natural solidarity. Many of the accidents and mishaps in a mine were caused by human error or by lapses in worker discipline. A badly tended skip or tram, poor workmanship in the construction of tunnel props, and insouciance in the detection of gas, water, overhanging rock, or misfired charges could kill a miner as surely as bad luck or deficient safety standards. A man's life underground was thus often dependent on the diligence and discipline of his fellow workers. To the comradeship required by efficient, concerted action must be added a miner's pride in his physical prowess, skills, and experience.

On the Witwatersrand the natural cooperation required of workers was magnified by other factors. The miner's first challenge was to complete a long and dangerous overland journey. Men travelling to the mines were captured by farmers who demanded payments in cash or labour for the right to cross their lands. Police in the employ of labour contractors sometimes obliged migrants to work on the railway under construction in the eastern Transvaal. They were defrauded by bogus policemen and were preyed upon by unscrupulous recruiters, who offered false terms of employment and then sold the men for a capitation fee. Attacks by bandits and wild animals remained an ever-constant problem; the former caused many

(a) Drill men employed in an underground stope. As an occupational category hand drilling was dominated by Mozambicans.

men to shun established paths and travel at night.[37] After a stiff climb onto the escarpment and a tramp of 40–50 kilometers every day, many arrived at the mines in an exhausted physical condition, particularly in winter.

    The tramping workers' situation had not improved in over twenty years; as Lionel Phillips noted, the late 1880s and early 1890s at Johannesburg were "just like the early days on the diamond fields."[38] A. W. Baker, the head of the South African Compound Mission, described the hardships faced by a migrant from the East Coast on his 300-mile journey to Johannesburg:

> you are scorched by the sun, bitten by the frost, drenched by the rains, you tramp through the swamps, cross rivers infested by crocodiles, many fall ill and sometimes die on the roads. You arrive half starved and worn out and go down into the mines.[39]

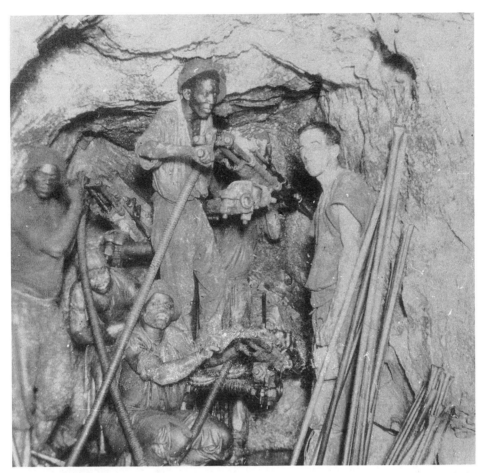

(b) Machine driving in a waterlogged tunnel. Long "jumper" and short "starter" drills lie against the tunnel wall.

John Hays Hammond, a leading mining engineer, wrote of the "hundreds who died on their march to Johannesburg, from pneumonia and other causes. When the boys finally arrived, always in an emaciated state, they had to be placed in the company's compound and conditioned for a month or more before they were fit to work."[40] The directors of a labour recruiting company were even more graphic, describing how the "skeletons of those who have died are frequently seen, and at almost every store and dwelling near the road can be found those whom sickness and fatigue have compelled to give up the road and either find a friend or perish."[41]

Shangaan migrants making their way to the Witwatersrand carried blankets, clothing, pots, sleeping mats, and a gourd filled with water. Cassava, maize flour, or *xigugu*, a nutritious mixture of roasted groundnuts, maize, and salt, was stored in a leather pouch. A knobkerrie furnished protection against snakes and bandits, as well as a means of stunning an unweary guinea fowl. Rolls of tobacco were used to buy food or pay the fee charged to cross a river.[42] Homestead elders were under an obligation to help members of their chiefdom or clan travelling to the mines, but men passing through foreign territory could expect little hospitality. Local people were particularly afraid that if a foreigner fell sick and died, the homestead would be contaminated by his malevolent spirit (*nuru*).[43] The alternative to tramping to the mines with a group of companions was to seek the protection of a recruiter. African labour agents in Mozambique often paid a chief 1s for each recruit and as soon as a few dozen men had been gathered at a bush compound, they were taken to a white recruiter and sold for a capitation fee of 5–7s. Workers considered by the Portuguese to be "clandestine" because they paid no passport fees were "run" across the border to Komati Poort and Hectorspruit and sold to the highest bidder for up to 15s. Licensed recruiters working for the Chamber of Mines tended to pay passport fees to the Portuguese at Ressano Garcia, under the 1893 agreement, or bought workers from independent recruiters in the Transvaal.[44] A migrant who travelled to the mines under the protection of a recruiter was saved much of the harassment and danger of the journey. Recruiters paid for the steerage passage of migrants on steamers like the *Lady Wood* plying between Inhambane and Lourenço Marques; they also provided their charges with food and shelter, paid their ferry fees, bought the travel passes required to cross the Transvaal, and fended off the unwanted attentions of bandits, farmers, and policemen. But signing on with a recruiter meant entering into a fixed contract with the mine to which the contract was sold. This was particularly the case with the Chopi who, because of their enmity with the Gaza, had little choice but to engage themselves with a recruiter. Hence "East Coasters" tended to be concentrated in underground work in the deepest and most dangerous mines.[45] Men who chose to make their own way to the Witwatersrand generally emigrated in stages. An individual would, for example, work as a stevedore at Lourenço Marques before moving to the Nkomati railway. At Barberton in 1893 he could earn a monthly wage of 33s3d, and a similar wage at Lydenburg. Because men were engaged in these places on a weekly basis, they were popular halting spots on the way to the Witwatersrand. The more desperate were constrained to work on farms, where they found shelter and the food, clothing, and money needed to continue the journey. Several thousand Mozambicans were employed on the gold mines of the eastern Transvaal, in scattered, smaller mines in the northern Transvaal and Swaziland, and in the coal mines of the eastern Witwatersrand, Vereeniging, and Middelburg. A few men still made their way to Natal, many continued to tramp to Kimberley, and substantial numbers worked on the construction of the railway linking Johannesburg and Pretoria with Komati Poort and Ressano Garcia.[46] Europeans quickly fitted these uprooted individuals into their system of classification by categorizing them as *padkaffirs*, wandering "road kaffirs."[47]

By the middle of the 1890s, the imprint of a new culture had emerged out of the tramping network. This culture combined and transformed elements of the old and new and bound workers together as a group. It also facilitated the relationship between young men, returning home with disturbing ideas, and their domestic communities. Migrants from the East Coast adopted various rites and rituals traditionally associated with hunting, trading, and travelling in a way that allowed them to tap into established sources of power while creating a new but comprehensible social order. By adhering to these customs migrants created a community of believers and exercised some control over events in unfamiliar areas. Various signs forewarned of trouble along the route and indicated possible forms of preventive action. If a *manupfana* bird flew across his path with widespread wings, or if the migrant saw a polecat, or a certain snail, this was an omen that he should return home and seek the blessing of his grandfather. Special rituals had to be performed to exorcise the misfortune brought to a group of migrants if a small red antelope crossed their path. When climbing the Lebombo hills they had, at certain places, to pick up a stone, spit on it, touch their knees and pitch it onto a cairn (*shititane*) that had been built up over time by previous travellers. This rite called a blessing on the journey and ensured a favourable reception for the men at the villages along their route.[48] Before crossing a dangerous river they could chew a special root to increase their courage and improve their chances of success. Some forests, lakes, and rivers were inhabited by spirits, and the traveller who wished to enter these areas had to request local inhabitants to propitiate their ancestors.[49] If a man died en route to the mines, he had to be properly buried or his spirit would wander through the bush, harassing and attacking other travellers. Tramping migrants feared being possessed or assaulted by these bush spirits, but as long as the migrant believed in the power of his rituals and talismen, and his ability to interpret omens and signs, he was able to exert some control over the dangers lurking on the way to the mines.[50]

The comradeship forged during a long and dangerous journey was strengthened on the Witwatersrand as Mozambicans gathered on specific mines and turned drilling into what was almost an ethnic specialisation. A wider sense of community was engendered by the ease with which they circulated between the mines. On Sundays workers travelled to other compounds to visit kinsmen and friends; at the end of a contract, it was not unusual for a man to move to another mine in search of better pay and working conditions. By tramping from mine to mine, workers passed on and exchanged information linking them in a shared community of interests and experiences. The complex of channels along which news spread was largely concealed from whites, but the efficiency with which workers mobilized, rapidly and *en masse*, bore testimony to a developed communications network. The miner's world stretched beyond the series of compounds to include the small locations established on mine property by managers anxious to attract and hold skilled workers. For most black miners, Johannesburg was a hostile place where, after 1894, they were forced off the pavements and subjected to a 9:00 p.m. curfew; but it was also an area of freedom from the rigours of mine discipline. Although it was difficult for East Coasters to find work in a world dominated by Zulu domestic servants, washermen, and policemen, and by Sotho labourers, several hundred moved into the towns and locations along the Reef.

Churches functioned as important community centres, providing workers with entertainment, a venue for social gatherings, and a bridge into the world beyond the mine. As at Kimberley, Christianity provided men with a stability and a security that was both tangible and intellectual. Once the future of the Witwatersrand had been secured, the Methodists seized on the area as a centre of evangelism and by the mid-1890s had sixty-five voluntary preachers operating in Johannesburg, Jeppestown, the Krugersdorp, and Boksburg locations, and the locations on the Langlaagte, Simmer and Jack, New Primrose, and George Goch mines.[51] But radicals quickly grew tired of the caution of Methodist beliefs and practices. A. W. Baker left the church to form the South African Compounds Mission, and Mangena Mokone, dissatisfied with the lack of opportunity for blacks, broke away to start the first Ethiopian church. This was not only the first of the independent churches to cut across tribal divisions; it also reached across the Atlantic to form links with churches run by African-Americans.[52] Anglican, Catholic, and other churches also established a presence on the Witwatersrand, and by mid-1896 Christians constituted about one-third of the 14,150 blacks living in Johannesburg.[53]

Eating houses also served as centres of communal life beyond the compounds. These cheap restaurants were directed at a working-class clientèle—a slice of bread and a cup of soup cost 3d, a slice of bread and meat 6d, and bread, meat, and coffee 9d. Clients sat around long benches on heavy stools and were frequently encouraged by hostesses to part with their money.[54] Like the eating houses, canteens were open from 6:00 a.m. to 9:00 p.m. Between 1888 and 1895, the number of licensed canteens on the Witwatersrand grew from 147 to perhaps as many as one thousand. Liquor outlets quickly became the most frequented centres of socialization; by 1892, the ratio of bars to people on the Rand stood at 1:60.[55] The white population alone could not support this proliferation of bars, and many publicans focused on blacks as their major clients. The profitability of the liquor trade, particularly when drink was adulterated and venal policemen were common, encouraged publicans to ignore closing hours and operate illegally on Sundays. In the towns and locations a more informal commerce in alcohol was dominated by female brewers.

In this demi-monde workers mixed and created new ties of friendship and loyalty, and constructed a common symbolism that cut across their social and political differences. The consumption of alcohol by black workers was marked by practices that, through constant repetition, had come to be viewed as traditional. Partly influenced by drinking patterns brought home from Kimberley, distilled liquor had become an important item of consumption on the coastal plain; this form of drinking was carried to the Rand, where a large-scale absenteeism on Mondays and Tuesdays became an intrinsic part of industrial life. In the absence of other leisure activities, miners spent an important part of their earnings in canteens where drink was a cheap diversion. A tot of liquor cost 6d; two tots induced "pronounced symptoms of intoxication," and three or four tots were sufficient to render the imbiber "blind drunk."[56] As at Kimberley, the men bought diluted "whiskeys," "brandies," and "gins" spiked with caustic and corrosive additives.[57] This liquor provided men with a common means of escaping from the monotony and dreariness of their work and, through familiar drinking rituals and the sharing of the cost and content of a bottle and a meal, workers entered into relationships of fellowship, patronage, and rivalry.

The worker's reassertion of an ingrained, irregular labour pattern marked by spurts of hard work and spells of leisure was abhorred by industrial capitalists, who equated drunkenness with indiscipline and absenteeism with larceny.[58] Missionaries were shocked by "appalling scenes on Saturday night" and wrote with dismay that Sunday was "the most riotous and dangerous day along the Witwatersrand." The Chamber of Mines reported that on Sundays the mine areas were "thronged with natives in all stages of intoxication."[59] Heavy bouts of drinking and revelry, beginning on Saturday night and continuing throughout Sunday, often incapacitated men or made them a danger to themselves and their fellows. On Mondays and even Tuesdays, some 25 to 30 percent of the black labour force failed to arrive for work. This absenteeism was costly to the mine companies; to keep the work force up to full strength, they had to increase the size of the reserve army of labourers in the compounds.[60] Missionaries estimated that the mines lost between £750,000 and £900,000 each year through Monday absenteeism.[61] On one mine alone, 1,300 work days were lost because of the large numbers of miners who had to attend court as witnesses in cases arising out of drunkenness, crime, and assault.[62] Equally serious, drink caused up to 90 percent of the accidents on the Rand mines, according to one temperance agitator. To mineowners and managers, these accidents were time-consuming to rectify and costly in terms of the recruiting appeal of a mine.[63]

As closed compounds were not a feasible solution to what they regarded as the liquor problem, the mineowners formed an alliance with church and temperance groups and pressurized the government to restrict the freedom with which blacks bought liquor. The government approached the liquor question with the hesitancy that characterized much of its dealings with the mining industry. The state benefitted from the payment of liquor licences, and Kruger and his colleagues were wary of alienating the powerful trading interests, Boer farmers, and manufacturers, whose efforts had created the local liquor industry. Caught between these interests and those of the mining industry, the government sought to restrict workers' access to liquor by requiring blacks to produce written permission from their employers before purchasing drink. A law passed in 1891 attempted to limit the amount of liquor sold to blacks to one drink, after which the employer's chit was to be cancelled. The following year the mineowners were given representation on the Johannesburg liquor licensing board, the number of licences issued in the city was restricted, and canteens' doors and windows had to be constructed facing the street.[64] These laws did little to dent the determination with which migrants held onto their established drinking patterns, and mine managers found themselves in an invidious position. Although some valued liquor as a means of attracting and holding men, most were obliged either to accept a work pattern dysfunctional to the running of an industrial enterprise or see their workers move elsewhere.[65]

Heavy drinking induced a lowering of moral restraint and, particularly in the narrow space of the canteen, generated a competitive social climate that could easily explode into "the fearful tribal fights that are common along the mines."[66] "The fights were regular standup battles," wrote W. Bleloch, "not single hand encounters, but opposing forces of from 500–1000 men a-side, in which kerries, stones and any handy weapons were used, the frequent result being that several would be seriously wounded and occasionally one or two killed."[67] Faction fighting had been clearly visible on the diamond fields and the railway works in the 1870s and 1880s. But a richer documentation provides a clearer picture of this phenomenon on the Witwatersrand. On Sunday, 13 November 1892, over one thousand workers clashed when men from the Simmer and Jack accused others, from the neigbouring New Primose mine, of stealing their blankets. The "curious feature" of this fight, according to the *Star*, was that "it was not a tribal one, but purely one company's boys against another, showing that Zulus and Shangaans will combine for a common object, a fact that should be noted by the authorities."[68] Because conflicts of this nature disrupted work and resulted in the death and incapacitation of miners, in May 1894 the government prohibited blacks from carrying weapons. This did little to reduce the level of faction fighting, however, and in 1895 another murderous conflict broke out between the Simmer and Jack and New Primrose workers. On Monday afternoon, 7 October 1895, a canteen brawl erupted into the biggest faction fight ever witnessed on the goldfields. As news of the battle spread, Zulus and East Coasters, including Shangaans, Chopis, and "Inhambanes," ran to the space bordering the Geldenhuys, Jumpers, and Treasury mines, where the leaders of the two sides eventually succeeded in mobilizing from two to three thousand men. The combatants were initially deployed in long lines behind the stone embankments of surface tramways that served both as battlements and a source of ammunition. But once they were reinforced, the Shangaans attacked the Zulu in a phalanx and hand-to-hand fighting took place with assegais, knobkerries, broken bottles, shovels, picks, and drills. Toward the end of the afternoon the Shangaans succeeded in entering the Jumpers compound, plundered the Zulu barracks, and stripped the dead of their belt purses and clothing. Chanting a victory song, the East Coasters returned to their compound as evening fell.[69]

In his novel, Back to the Mines, Fisher Vane, a mine manager, made a detailed analysis of two faction fights. He described how disagreements arose on the fictional Proprietary GMC due to a shift in the balance of power when three hundred Zulus were replaced by an equal number of "Delagoa Bay kafirs." The Zulus attempted to recoup the prestige and power that came with numerical superiority by mounting a faction fight, an event marked by a strong degree of ritual. The Zulus made no attempt to take the Shangaans by surprise and chose a Sunday afternoon, when most men were off work, to confront their opponents. After fortifying their courage in a nearby canteen, a group of Zulus, armed and in war dress, spent over ten minutes dancing and singing, gesticulating, beating on the ground with their knobkerries, and throwing insults at the Shangaan, a signal for "stragglers to come flying from all quarters of the veldt." During this phase of a fight, the participants displayed what one journalist called "a ferocious and blood-curdling attitude."[70] Through this ritual interaction, men displayed the borders of their community, expressed group solidarity, and recruited new members. The violence of the situation fused men into a physical community of interdependence reinforced by the strong emotional appeal made by recognizable and shared gestures, singing, and drumming. This ritual enactment of violence was also a prominent exhibition of hierarchy, as the champions from both sides encouraged their men and taunted their opponents. And perhaps most importantly, in a society without women, the fighters displayed the courage and bearing perceived to be signs and markers of masculinity. When the two sides eventually clashed, five men suffered broken arms, one had his jaw broken, two lost an eye, and twelve were left unconscious. The fictional battle was stopped by the mine manager and the men were persuaded to return to their barracks. Despite the subsequent death of two of the wounded, the faction fight was less about death than display. It was particularly about power, for, later that night, the Zulus "seeing themselves so greatly outnumbered and knowing that between them and the Bay 'boys' peace could not exist, quietly stole away in twos and threes," wrote Vane. "The Delagoa Bay 'boys' were left in undisputed

(a) Mine dancers in traditional dress.

possession of the compound, and the vacancies were quickly filled up by others of their own class, so that no more tribal fights took place on the Proprietary for the remainder of my stay."

The second faction fight described by Vane involved a different expression of local politics and identity assertion. This involved a fight between two mine compounds. As supporters from surrounding mines joined the fray, the mine managers found it difficult to suppress the fracas, even with the aid of mounted police. The fighting lasted for several days and involved up to four thousand men. The faction fights that marked Sundays and other holidays only gradually disappeared, and then only temporarily, at the beginning of the twentieth century.[71]

In Chapter 3 I underscored the importance of looking at the social institutions created by migrants on the mines in terms of the web of signs brought from the rural areas. From this perspective, the "indescribable orgies of drunkenness and tribal and faction fights" described by Lionel Phillips take on an internal logic.[72] Twenty years previously men from the East Coast had joined the "Zulu" faction in the fights on the diamond fields and the Cape Railways; by the 1890s they had developed an identity of their own and formed a conscious community. Group fighting was a concrete representation of the divisions within society; it was a prominent performance through which black miners constructed and advertized membership of an ethnic group, mobilised and asserted the territorial rights of a community occupying a specific space (such as a compound or a group of mine properties), and exercised the qualities required of "real," virile men. Faction fighting was also a means of releasing pent-up tensions and at times a way of striking at specific symbols, such as the concession stores and canteens on mine property.[73] But it was preeminently about erecting the social boundaries of inclusion and exclusion through which workers carved out and created a place for themselves in a turbulent and unpredictable world.[74] Faction fighting gave a physical content to their notions of community and a coherence to their sense of justice, hierarchy and self-respect.

Various other cultural markers and practices cut across the divisions between black migrant workers and separated them from European miners. Their dress code, like their drinking culture, was tailored by a desire to advertise social standing rather than conform to European norms. In the towns and compounds along the Witwatersrand, migrants were continually brought into contact with European music. The simple harmonium, carried from compound to compound on Sundays by evangelists, introduced them to new musical forms and rhythms. The boisterous hymn-singing, in which onlookers in the compound quadrangle were encouraged to participate, competed in a cacophonous uproar with men performing the music, dances, and songs of their home areas. Church brass bands played to all and sundry in the knots of settlement along the Reef. Men brought musical instruments from home, fashioned them from local materials on the Witwatersrand, or purchased them from general dealers. Instruments like the accordion, already familiar to some from the diamond fields, were retuned to conform to the migrants' understanding of tonality. As Western instruments and songs were adapted to express the experience of migrant black mine workers, a new musical form gradually emerged. Taken into the rural areas, these songs, dances, and tunes became an expression of the expanded space within which people lived and an advertisement for the mines.[75] Tribal dancing was encouraged by management as a means of releasing tension, but it also served to divide the workforce along tribal lines and restrict the development of a class solidarity. Management encouraged the ethnic and atavistic element in the dancing. When three thousand Shangaan, Chopi, Zulu, and Baca dancers were brought to the Simmer and Jack Mine in 1896 to entertain the visiting British rugby team, the effect was spoiled, according to one newspaper report, by the blankets and Western dress worn by many of the men. "The variety of costume was a conspicuous feature in the ranks of these mine boys," reported the Star, "and detracted from the value of the spectacle. Some were in European dress, in an infinity of colours or patterns, or the dilapidated remains of such dress. Some had blankets round their loins, others fur or feathers. One otherwise majestic black had a petticoat slung on behind."[76] Three years later, when six thousand dancers gathered on the Geldenhuys Deep to bid farewell to

(b) Mine dancers in "a variety of costume."

the general manager of the mine, their "pure" war dress was applauded by the four thousand spectators and the press. Stick fighting and a concertina dance formed part of the programme on both occasions.[77] The ground maize meal provided by the mines introduced a common diet that cut across regional differences. At home many Shangaans soaked maize in water before pounding it and looked down on people who ground maize between stones; but on the mines they were obliged to share the same maize meal diet as their colleagues from other parts of southern Africa. Although the workers generally added their own relish, and particularly meat, to the ground meal served by the compound kitchen, a new and more homogeneous diet was introduced on the mines.[78]

Cultural forms shared by large numbers of workers had been hesitantly emerging since the first men tramped to the sugar plantations and the diamond

The assertive self-definition displayed by mine dancers sometimes slid into aggressive armed clashes known on the mines as "faction fights."

fields. New and common patterns of drinking and eating, wearing clothes, playing music, and dancing all contributed to an emerging culture whose historical roots can be found in the old tramping diaspora. These cultural expressions were neither static nor distinctively bounded and cohesive. They were a product of the swirling intercourse between blacks drawn from a multitude of different areas, of their working experience, and their contacts with whites, together with the influence of previous generations and waves of newly arrived miners. As Mozambican workers seldom spent more than three years on the mines, this new and dynamic culture was firmly based on rural perceptions and values. But while they were divided by their origins, black workers were pushed together by their work and by a common racial oppression.

The skilled workers and supervisors who were the natural trade unionists and leaders of the working class were divided from the men in the compounds by the steel divide of race. During the 1890s the mineowners were in no position to attack the high wages of white workers, partly because qualified miners were in short supply and had to be enticed to the Witwatersrand from Europe, and partly because of the class solidarity of experienced workers. Most European miners were imbued with a pride in their labouring skills honed through generations of conflict with capital. As proletarians, their relationship with employers was essentially different from that of migrants who were able to fall back on a productive homestead, and whose families were protected from destitution by the kinship system and leviratical marriages.[79] Hence migrant workers had some protection from the insecurity, caused by cycles of prosperity, recession, and depression, that dogged the lives of mineworkers. In contrast, the proletarian and his family were entirely dependent for their survival on the breadwinner's mining skills. Attempts to devalue these skills engendered white hostility, as the prospect emerged of "permanent work on the mines producing a class of skilled boys," whose employment, the editor of the *Mining Journal* speculated, would eventually allow management "to discard with the white worker and his high-priced work."[80] But white supremacy also lay on a lexical foundation of familial metaphors that described blacks as "boys" and "children," natural biological inferiors, and in the femininization of the landscape.[81] It was also rooted in the discourse of slavery as recruiters "hunted," "purchased," "guarded," "sold," and "re-sold" "niggers," as "clandestines" were "run" across the border and "runaways" broke contract.[82] "Blackbirding" (recruiting) and "piccanin" (a child labourer) were other terms embedded in the lexicon of slavery.[83] This terminology was not only an expression of the inequality between blacks and whites; it also created those inequalities and locked whites into a discursive world in which black workers were permanent inferiors. The racism inherent in the European experience and structure of knowledge was given a visible content as white workers sought to protect their skills, and capitalists to divide their workforce, by implementing a battery of laws on the basis of pigmentation.

The mine owners continually sought to involve the state in their attempts to raise the efficiency, and bring down the cost, of black labour. One of their major concerns was to curtail the freedom with which men increased their wages by tramping from one mine to another.[84] Employers particularly saw an efficient pass system as the means to secure the heavy investment in the recruiting that was the key to cheap labour. However, as long as the state refrained from actively intervening in the labour market on the side of capital, this was an unequal struggle dominated by a migrant work force.[85] Soon after the establishment of the Chamber of Mines' Native Labour Department its manager, William Grant, the former chief recruiter for the Natal Planters' Labour League, drew up and presented to the Volksraad a special pass law for the Witwatersrand.[86] But the law was blocked, as it was considered too costly to implement, capable of provoking disturbances, and was of benefit to only one sector of the population.[87] This refusal by the Kruger government to aid the mining industry has been castigated by critics as the shambling incompetence of a preindustrial, agrarian society.[88] Elsewhere I have suggested that government ambivalence was less the product of ignorance and inefficiency than the result of a desire to ensure that political and economic growth occur in tandem—that a political structure emerge capable of controlling both economic development and the large concentration of foreigners, both black and white, on the Witwatersrand.[89] This policy became increasingly controversial as an improved gold recovery rate allowed the mineowners to sink shafts down to the low-grade ore in the Main Reef south of the outcrop.[90] One of the results of this expansion in the scale of mining was a sharp rise in the number of black workers, from 29,500 in 1893 to 70,000 in 1896, and an increase in the number and size of the compounds that gave the black workers' occupational community a clear geographical expression.[91] The potential damage that could be wrought by a large crowd of miners threatened the stability of the state for, by the mid-1890s, the black population on the Witwatersrand outnumbered the entire Boer population capable of carrying arms. The Kruger government had no reason to support wage cuts that would generate instability, and favour shareholders and the large population of Uitlanders, at the cost of local producers and merchants. Hence the government policy of restrictions and monopolies served to control and limit the development of the mining industry.

By the mid-1890s the Transvaal was no longer the rural backwater conquered, a little less than twenty years previously, by Sir Theophilus Shepstone and a handful of mounted policemen. The once-impoverished republic could boast an annual revenue of well over £4 million, almost 90 percent of which came from gold sales. The stability of the republican state and the well-being of the economy had come to rest firmly on the profitability of the gold mines. Mineral speculation and the mushrooming consumer market on the Witwatersrand caused a steady rise in land prices and farming profits.[92] Revenues drawn from the hut tax and import duties were largely dependent on mine wages, as were the taxes paid by traders and transport riders. Thus the funds required to pay the salaries of government officials, to purchase the weapons needed to conquer the remaining independent chiefdoms, and to defend the state against British imperialism came almost entirely from gold. Less than ten years after the discovery of gold, the unity, strength, and stability of the Boer state was dependent on the profitability of the Witwatersrand mines.

The impossible contradiction in the conservatism of government policy towards the mining industry was highlighted in late September 1895, when overspeculation in the stock market was followed by a sudden crash in the value of shares, followed by a sharp fall in the price of farm land. This threat to economic stability pushed the government grudgingly to start throwing its weight behind the interests of mining capital. As investors fled the Witwatersrand, the Volksraad accepted in its entirety the pass law drawn up two years previously by William Grant. Law No. 23 of October 1895 attacked the very basis of the tramping system by restricting the freedom with which black workers could withdraw their labour or move from mine to mine in search of better working conditions. Unlike the pass laws of the twentieth century, with which it is often confused, the 1895 pass law made no attempt to regulate the influx of men from the rural areas or to enforce an oscillating, migratory flow of labour. Its "cardinal aim," according to the *Mining Journal*, was "the reduction of the ridiculously high native wage."[93]

The law was applicable to only the mining districts of the proclaimed gold fields of the Witwatersrand and eastern Transvaal. When a migrant arrived in one of these districts, he presented his travel pass to the local mining commissioner and, on the payment of a 1s fee, received a numbered district pass and a corresponding metal arm badge allowing him to spend three days looking for work. With the permission of the mining commissioner, and having paid another 2s, the man could extend this period for a further three days. But if he failed to find employment during this time, he either had to move to another labour district or return home. Mine managers were prohibited from employing men unable to produce a district pass, and work-seekers found without this pass were fined 10s. Once he had secured work, the migrant handed his district pass to his employer and received in exchange a 2s pass renewable every month. Half of this amount was to be used to construct medical facilities for blacks in the labour district and the other half to pay for the running of a special department concerned with enforcing the pass law. District labour inspectors were appointed to check the employment books and registers of the mining companies and to arrest blacks found without passes.[94] When a black worker wished to return home at the end of his contract, his district pass was returned to him by his employer; when presented to the district labour commissioner, this pass was exchanged for a 1s travel document. The gold fields' pass law was aimed as much against mine managers as against workers. The law introduced the state into the labour market as both a neutral arbiter and regulator of competition between the mines, and as an ally of capital in its struggle with labour.

The Turning Years: 1895–1897

State intervention in the labour market initially went little further than shepherding the pass law through the Volksraad. It took two major events to propel the Kruger government to intervene actively in the labour market on the side of the mineowners: one was the Jameson Raid, which threatened the very basis of Boer rule, and the other was the Portuguese conquest of southern Mozambique, the area from which the Witwatersrand mines drew the majority of their labour.

The Kruger government's refusal to assist in reducing the production costs of mining was viewed by many as the cause of the stock market crash that had brought several low-grade mines to the brink of closure and had jeopardised the huge investments in deep-level mining. A group of Randlords involved in long-range mining programmes responded to this crisis by mounting an invasion and simultaneous *coup d'état* against the Transvaal government at the end of December 1895. But the Jameson Raid merely magnified the mineowners' labour problem, for, as the Witwatersrand seemed to slide into war, thousands of black miners fled from the gold fields and those arriving returned home at the sight of patrolling Boer commandos.[95] Nor did the Boer military victory resolve the tension between the government and the mining industry. Instead, the Jameson Raid demonstrated in a most forceful manner that a hesitant and restrictive mining policy had serious consequences for the political stability of the state. This was underlined as, following their subjugation of the chiefdoms of southern Mozambique in November 1895, the Portuguese acquired a stranglehold over the source of labour feeding the economic heartland of the Transvaal.[96]

The Portuguese consul was well aware that his country's control over the labour supplies for the gold mines was "a weapon that could be very useful to us."[97] Within weeks of the conclusion of the Luso-Gaza war, official recruiting was halted, and the transportation of workers along the railway from Lourenço Marques to Komati Poort was prohibited or subjected to exorbitant costs.[98] In February 1896 recruiters were "frantic" because the Portuguese would only allow workers to leave if they paid capitation fees, often amounting to over 20s. Labour agents who were not recognized by the Portuguese either left the country or were arrested; the price paid for clandestines at Komati Poort rose from 10s to 27s6d, and, on the Witwatersrand, to as much as 70s. The scarcity and high cost of Mozambican workers, as well as the exodus of labour following the Jameson Raid, pushed up monthly wages on some mines to 80s.[99] To defuse this situation, the government declared its readiness to help facilitate the supply of labour to the mines only three weeks after Jameson's surrender outside Klerksdorp.[100] A week later native commissioners were instructed to recruit workers, and the Transvaal consul in Lourenço Marques was ordered to enter into negotiations with the Portuguese on the basis of the defunct agreement of 1893.[101] In mid-February the Eckstein Group recognized that government was trying to facilitate the recruitment and importation of labour.[102] By May 1896 the native commissioner in the Zoutpansberg was assembling workers for the mines, and three months later even veldkornets were recruiting labour.[103]

The Transvaal government tried to bribe the Portuguese consul in Pretoria to use his influence to lift the restriction on labour emigration from Mozambique. Late in February the consul met President Kruger, who informed him that the need for a labour agreement with the Portuguese arose from his desire to rectify one the major causes of the dissent that had culminated in the Jameson Raid.[104] Members of the Kruger government voiced the same sentiment on several occasions.[105] The governor of Mozambique, Mousinho de Albuquerque, was later to remark that through Kruger's strategy

> The government of the South African Republic wished to make those concessions that it could to the Uitlanders in order to defuse the crisis provoked by them in Johannesburg, while avoiding, at the same time, to defer to the two most important demands of the Rand committee—the reduction of the railway tariffs and the abolition of the dynamite monopoly.[106]

Portuguese demands turned on the establishment of an official in Johannesburg to oversee the importation and taxation of labour and end the employment of "clandestines," and it was on this issue that negotiations between the two governments eventually foundered.[107] In September 1896 the Native Labour Department (NLD) of the Chamber of Mines came to a private agreement with the Portuguese, giving the former the right to erect shelters and recruit labour anywhere in Mozambique. An NLD compound was constructed at Ressano Garcia to attract workers away from the free-lance recruiters at Komati Poort, and the activities of these independent "touts" was declared illegal by the Portuguese.[108] From this position of strength, the Chamber proposed the establishment of a new organisation to recruit labour and enforce a uniform system of pay and working conditions in the mines. The Native Labour Supply Association (the NLSA) formed in October 1896 was wealthier and more organised than the old NLD, it was supported by almost all the mining houses, and had privileged access to recruiting in Mozambique. It promised to bring down the cost of labour by ending competitive recruiting and flooding the market with labour.[109]

The establishment of the NLSA marked a new stage in the struggle to control the labour market. Black workers continued to use the tramping system to defend their established working conditions. On a mine like the Wolhuter, management paid £2,520 in 1895 to labour recruiters of which only £234 was recuperated from the 1,105 workers. The mine owners claimed that up to 75 percent of recruiting overheads were lost through desertion and that this mobility of the black labour force pushed up the overall wage level.[110] The pass law only gradually came into operation; it was published in January 1896 but was only implemented, under continual pressure from the mining industry, towards the middle of the year. Worker resistance to the law made it both difficult and costly to implement. Until May 1896, when the law was amended to include Krugersdorp and Boksburg, men were able to desert and reappear in these districts, where they acquired the travel passes needed to re-enter the Witwatersrand. Workers who wished to move to a new mine had little fear of being imprisoned, as recruiters and mine managers were only too willing to pay the 10s fine extracted from men found without a district pass.[111] The limited success of the pass law was denounced by the mineowners as "a farce" and "merely an extra tax-collecting agency."[112] Yet the Transvaal pass law was far more stringent than those employed in Natal and Griqualand West and was a vivid indication of the extraordinary lengths to which the state was prepared to go to suppress the workers' tramping system. The Randlords saw government intervention as the crucial expression in the equation of migrant labour from Mozambique. If the pass laws were "properly administrated," stated Lionel Phillips, "it should be possible to enforce the fulfillment of contracts and in that case it will pay to import labour from long distances at considerable cost and at lower wages."[113]

Further government support for the mining industry came in the form of Law 17 of July 1896, which reduced absenteeism, fighting, accidents, and sickness by closing all canteens on mine property and by prohibiting the sale of intoxicants to blacks. Within a few months, the issuing of licences to liquor outlets and eating houses was restricted, and a number of bars were placed under strict police supervision.[114] While a blow to the fledgling local liquor manufacturing industry, this law was considered by the British Agent in Pretoria to be an "inestimable boon" to the mining industry.[115] "Mr Kruger has at last recognised that the mining industry is the backbone of the Republic," crowed the editor of the *Mining Journal*, "the fundamental element of the Republic's prosperity."[116] The mineowners believed that the implementation of liquor prohibition in January 1897 would terminate the St. Monday and the less saintly Tuesday that had traditionally broken the regularity of work. Sobriety would induce punctuality and discipline and result in a fall in the destruction brought to labour and property by the high accident rate. In September 1896 the government brought another reform to the mining industry when it passed legislation to curb the theft of gold amalgam.[117]

The mineowners were encouraged to cut black wages by their new-found support from the government, their ability to construct a united recruiting organisation, and their secure access to Mozambican labour. With a severe drought, locusts, and the aftermath of war pushing labour from Mozambique, they combined to introduce a staggered 30 percent cut in the wages of black miners. The first phase of this operation began on the 1st of October, 1896. It included both a nominal 20 percent reduction in wages and the introduction of a nine-hour shift for drill men. "Hammer boys" were the most important section of the underground work force. Their skill came with experience and, by the mid-1890s, it had become traditional on many mines to offer drill men piece work in an attempt to encourage them to re-engage.[118] On a mine like the Simmer and Jack, where lashers and trammers worked a ten hour shift in June 1896, drill men were expected to sink a hole of about 36 inches or two holes of 24 inches, depending on the hardness of the rock, during a shift of six to seven hours. After completing this task, the miner had his ticket signed by his supervisor and returned to the surface. From the managerial perspective, task work was a means of controlling absenteeism, speeding up the work rate, and dividing the black labour force. The object of this system was "to convince the boys that there are differences between them in respect of their value as labourers," wrote the editor of the *Mining Journal*, and to "induce rivalry and offer the reward of high wages only to those who deserve it."[119] By allowing the drill men to control the pace at which they worked and the length of their shift, the management of the Simmer and Jack succeeded in attracting large numbers of skilled workers. But not all the companies could afford this piecework system and a disparity in wages and the length of the shift quickly emerged between the different mines. Thus in October 1896 the maximum wage paid to blacks for a twenty-eight-day month on the Wolhuter mine was 63s, while on the George Goch they received only 58s. These differences in pay and working conditions encouraged men to desert, a tendency that the mine owners hoped to reduce by combining the introduction of the nine-hour shift for drillmen with the issuing of a common food ration on all mines and a strict application of the pass law.

The Assault on Black Labour

The October wage reduction was preceded by a meeting between members of the government and representatives of the Chamber of Mines, the Association of Mines, and the Association of Mine Managers. Government support for the mine-owners' assault on the working conditions of the black labour force was initially nervous. Fieldcornet H. S. Lombard reported that he had been informed by reliable sources that the black miners would leave their work and attack Johannesburg if their wages were cut. The fieldcornets at Krugersdorp and Klipriver and the commander of the Johannesburg Volunteer Corps were ordered to place their men on the alert, and on the 25th of September some five hundred police and volunteers started a massive search of the compounds for weapons.[120] But while the government believed these measures would forestall an "uprising," the Chamber of Mines believed they would frighten workers into leaving for home. After representation from the mining industry, the search was called off; instead, the superintendent of natives and the minister of mines visited the compounds, where they explained the wage cut and warned the men of the consequences of disobedience and desertion.[121]

The new conditions were accepted at first with such a degree of acquiescence that the *Standard and Diggers News* proclaimed that "the British working class might take a lesson from the coloured labourers of South Africa." But as soon as a section of the drillmen on the Crown Reef mine received their first depleted wage packet, they came out on strike in opposition to both the cut in wages and the lengthening of their shift.[122] They were followed the next morning by the rest of the underground work force. But the wage cut was only one of their grievances, for, as the working levels deepened, the miner's job had become more difficult and dangerous. He was persecuted under the pass laws, a cornerstone of his social life had been knocked away by the prohibition of liquor, and the selling of gold amalgam had been made more dangerous. It was this more structural downturn in the working conditions of black miners, combined with the sudden reduction in their wages, that brought them into conflict with the mine owners. By the 10th October the Treasury, Henry Nourse and Paarl Central, Pioneer, and other mines were affected by the strike. Groups of workers from Crown Reef were seen visiting the compounds of the Langlaagte Estate and Langlaagte Royal, while others followed the progress of the strike in the newspapers.[123] The miners were concerned with protecting established work practices rather than with defending their wages. The drillmen were less concerned with the wage cut than with the change to time work, longer hours and, particularly, the demands of white miners that they drill an extra hole, as this was seen as an unjust break with tradition. Their sense of justice led the miners to refuse to eat the food served in the compounds while on strike and, instead, they purchased their own supplies of maize, meat, and other food in neighbouring Fordsburg.[124]

The mineowners responded to the strike in various ways. On the Crown Reef, half the batteries were kept in operation by white miners, who worked the ore dumps stockpiled in expectation of a strike. A confrontation was narrowly averted on the mine when the compound manager prevented 1,700 strikers from attacking a group of sixty to seventy Basotho who wished to return to work. Here ethnic divisions within the work force overlapped with occupational interests as the Basotho, who were mainly shaft sinkers or lashers, were not directly affected by the new system of timework. The Langlaagte Royal turned to labour recruiters to hire a small number of contracted black miners. But these scabs had to be protected by a detachment of mounted police, whose presence caused the striking miners to retreat into Fordsburg and the mine location. On their return to the compound, the men were forced to work underground, even though many had been drinking heavily. The following day the leaders of the strike on the Langlaagte Royal and half their followers left the mine, while the rest of the work force, under police protection, returned to work.[125] It was not only on the Crown Reef that the soli-darity of black workers was undermined by imbricating ethnic and occupational loyalties. On the Worcester mine Zulus, who generally worked on the surface, and Basothos accepted the new conditions, while "East Coasters" came out on strike. On the Robinson mine East Coasters, "the best underground workers," also made up the bulk of the strikers.[126] On some mines, management succeeded in ending the strike by reinstituting the piecework system for drillmen, while on others the intransigence of management and the threat of force caused the most ardent strik-ers to desert. But the detachments of mounted police patrolling the Rand made this option difficult, and deserters often had to resort to buying expensive, illegal travel passes.[127] In some quarters it was suggested that white miners were responsible for the black miners' decision to strike.[128] However, it is far more likely that the strike was fomented by the drillmen, as they were the most aggrieved sector of the work force, and their experience and skill made them natural leaders. But it also seems likely that the drillmen, most of whom were Mozambicans, were pressed to strike, rather than opt for the more traditional response of mass desertion, by the devastation of their rural homes by war and ecological disaster.

The strike at one time mobilized about six thousand workers but petered out towards the end of the third week in October 1896, largely because many mine managers refused to enforce the nine-hour shift for drillmen.[129] Although the men returned to work, the number of migrants arriving on the Rand declined sharply, as knowledge of the wage cut spread along the tramping routes into the labour supply areas. When the bulk of the October wages were finally to be paid on the 1st of November, many managers avoided confronting their workers with the new rate. They either paid them "bonuses" or disguised the wage cut by increasing the wage month from four to five weeks.[130] In this way a skilled drillman who had received a "target" income of £3.10s for a twenty-four-day working month on the

Ferreira mine was presented, under the adapted system, with £3.18s for a thirty-five-day month. But when they received less than three sovereigns, workers expressed their dissatisfaction by going on strike or deserting. This action frequently resulted in confrontation between workers and management and, at the Star mine, blacks were forced into the cages by armed policemen and employers.[131] Most black miners responded to the wage cut by returning home. Within days of the first reduced wage payment, an exodus of labour took place and, with only recruited men arriving, several mines were unable to bring sufficient ore to the surface to keep the stamps working.[132] On other mines, strikers were replaced by heavy and uneconomical rock drills.

The exodus of black miners was not homogeneous. The men who deserted or returned home at the end of their contracts were mainly from Basutoland, the Cape, Natal, Zululand, and the northern Transvaal. Few Mozambicans returned home and, even more importantly, men continued to arrive on the Witwatersrand from the East Coast. On 19 November the *Star* reported that "the only source of supply which is reliable now is Gazaland."[133] But while political and economic upheavals at home made Mozambicans increasingly dependent on wage labour for their survival, they were not sufficiently proletarianized to make up for the large number of workers departing from the Witwatersrand. Mozambican labour was also very expensive, since, on top of the high cost of transport, the Portuguese had imposed onerous fees on both recruiter and worker.[134] By the end of November, some mines were losing ten workers for every new arrival, deep-level shaft sinking had halted at the Simmer and Jack, and on the 30th the Langlaagte closed down because of the labour shortage. On the Meyer and Charlton, where machine drills had been introduced into the stopes, the general manager declared the wage reduction of the previous month "an utter failure."[135] By the end of December 1896, Percy Fitzpatrick was forced to admit that the wage reduction had "utterly and hopelessly collapsed." The massive efflux of workers from the mines continued into the following year and, as managers scrambled for labour, the wage agreement of October fell apart.[136]

Rather than cut wages, suggested the editor of the investment journal *South Africa*, the companies should arrange "the concentration of every available agency on the flooding of Johannesburg with black labour. Then wages will come down of their own accord. . . ."[137] The importation of labour was severely hampered by widespread desertion and the malfunctioning of the pass law. Under the agreement with the Portuguese, the recruiting wing of the Chamber of Mines paid £225 for a recruiting license and a passport fee of 27s6d for each worker. This investment, together with the 42s6d that it cost to recruit, feed, and transport a man from the East Coast, was lost when he deserted. The mining industry blamed the deficiencies of the pass law for these losses and in December 1896 Law 31 raised the penalty for travelling without a district pass from 10 to 60s and condemned second offenders to a fine of £5, or four weeks' hard labour with the option of lashes. The number of people administering the pass law was increased, and a special body of police was formed to assist the Pass Department. The new pass law raised the level of violence employed by the state to discipline black labour. "The treatment of natives found without passes is nothing less than barbarous," the Natal labour agent on the Rand was to complain, "thousands of innocent natives are at present fined, imprisoned and lashed under the provisions of the pass law."[138] He and other critics saw the combination of pass law, contract, curfew, and compound as a new form of slavery.[139]

In November 1896 the regularity with which men were expected to labour was made more exacting when the government relaxed the law regarding Sunday observance. Under the mining regulations, Christmas, Good Friday, Dingaan's Day, and Sunday were observed as miners' holidays and companies found contravening this law were prosecuted.[140] The new law, No. 28 of 1896, allowed 5 percent of the labour force to work on Sundays at the pumps and in the reduction and crushing works. Although this legislation was not of direct importance to Mozambicans working underground, it did introduce a new relentlessness to the work rhythm by clearing the production bottleneck built up in the batteries over weekends. Workers living in the compound could also not help but notice that, while the pit head was silent on a Sunday, the surface works reverberated to the noise of creaking trollies, the thunder of the batteries, and the general din of a working day. The Sunday Observance Law was another victory for the mineowners who, at the cost of the government's Calvinist principles, raised productivity by perhaps as much as 15 percent, increased profitability by up to £1 million, and saved some of the marginal mines.[141]

With the implementation of the liquor prohibition law on 1 January 1897, the state threw its considerable weight further behind the mine owners and attempted to impose a new and confining discipline on the black labour force. But the miners fought to retain their old drinking habits, and the size and profitability of the consumer market encouraged the growth of a widespread illicit trade in liquor. Miners continued to buy alcohol from hawkers peddling goods in the vicinity of the compound, in near-by eating houses, through the back door of legal establishments, or in shebeens run by women in the towns, locations, and married quarters.[142] But, as Charles van Onselen has so graphically shown, most of the illegal liquor trade was run by members of powerful underworld syndicates from liquor dens equipped with warning devices, maze-like passages, and armed guards.[143]

The impressive and colourful activities of the illegal liquor lords, and the no less impressive statistics of the Chamber of Mines, have created the impression that prohibition was a failure. Members of the Chamber continued to claim that drunkenness resulted in the loss of from 20 to 30 percent of working hours, while Monday absenteeism could still reach as much as 40 percent.[144] The Chamber of Mines' Special Liquor Committee produced statistics showing a sharp rise in the importation of spirits from Mozambique in the years after prohibition. This was damning evidence of government bungling and inefficiency, and it was used to bludgeon the government into intervening more actively in the labour market. But other impressionistic and statistical evidence indicates that prohibition did indeed have a marked effect on the drinking habits of black mineworkers. In Mozambique, Mousinho de Albuquerque had envisaged that the production of alcohol for export to the Transvaal would provide a market for local produce and create an industry capable of attracting settlers from Portugal. Under an 1870 treaty, Mozambican produce was exempt from taxation on entering the Transvaal, while liquor in transit through the Portuguese colony was taxed at the rate of 4s per litre. But as imported liquor was often passed off as Mozambican produce in order to benefit from this preferential tariff, Mousinho recommended a 50 percent increase in the duty levied on imported alcohol and a reduction in the tax on locally manufactured spirits.[145] Although this implied a cut in government revenue and a reduction in a principal item of trade, Lisbon was eager to encourage the local manufacture of spirits and particularly to create a protected market for metropolitan wine. This protective tariff caused a sharp fall in the importation of distilled liquor through Lourenço Marques, from well over a million litres in 1890 to 195,000 litres in 1894.[146] The tariff change also resulted in a sharp rise in the importation of unrefined sugar, and particularly molasses, suitable for the local manufacture of rum. In 1894–95 the amount of unrefined sugar brought to Lourenço Marques from Durban almost doubled, and the following year, some 2,651 tons of molasses were shipped into the Portuguese port from Natal. At seven distilleries along the Transvaal frontier, this raw material was transformed into a biting alcohol.[147] Liquor was also manufactured at Mopea on the Zambezi and transported south in vessels like the *Induna*, involved in shipping workers to the railhead at Lourenço Marques. In 1896, the demand for liquor in the Transvaal caused over half a million litres of alcohol to enter Lourenço Marques from Europe and Quelimane. But when prohibition was enforced in January the following year, the importation of liquor immediately fell to 215,000 litres, the amount of unrefined sugar dropped by two-thirds, and the quantity of molasses taken through Lourenço Marques plummeted from almost 310,000 gallons in 1897 to just over 4,000 a year later.[148] At the same time, the production of alcohol in the Transvaal dropped sharply. Hence there seems little justification in the claims made by the Chamber of Mines that prohibition had little impact on the amount of alcohol consumed by black mineworkers in the Transvaal.[149] In 1900, with the outbreak of war in the Transvaal, profits from the liquor trade in Mozambique evaporated entirely and the long-established firms of Regis and Fabre finally closed their doors.[150]

In March 1897 the chairman of the Chamber of Mines praised the new liquor law. "The natives," he stated, were "better under control than they had been before, and more work had been got out of them in January than in any other previous month in the history of the Rand."[151] In other quarters, prohibition was believed to have cut the absentee rate on the mines to well under 20 percent and, perhaps not unconnectedly, it coincided with a fall in the accident rate from 5.1 to 3.9 per thousand.[152] But while the amount of liquor produced in the Transvaal and imported from neighbouring countries fell, and half the canteens on the Witwatersrand closed down, the number of men employed on the mines soared; the result was a three-fold rise in the price of drink. It is clear that workers struggled to retain customary drinking habits that were a focus of social life and a means of breaking the grind of mine labour; but what is also clear is that, with the help of the state, the mineowners had succeeded in intensifying the relentlessness of labour by curbing the workers' drinking pattern.

Mozambican mineworkers were caught in a vise: while the mineowners and the state struggled to shape their work habits and control their mobility, the Portuguese rapidly imposed their will over the labour supply areas. Lisbon viewed the defeated peoples of southern Mozambique as a welcome source of income and drew from them hut taxes, war reparations, and forced labour levies that exacerbated an existence already made tenuous by years of drought and locusts, and by the new scourge of rinderpest. In 1897 the old affliction of war reappeared, this time in a new guise as rebellion, and large numbers of men tramped to the Witwatersrand to save their families from starvation. As the winter of 1987 approached, intensive recruiting in Mozambique brought an oversupply of labour to the mines that was to undermine the bargaining position of black miners.[153]

Strikes, the Just Wage, and the Defeat of Labour

The abundance of Mozambican labour encouraged the mineowners to introduce the second phase of the wage cut, first started in October of the previous year. "We have an earnest and unanimous action in reducing native wages," declared Percy Fitzpatrick sanguinely on 8 May 1897, "I feel sure that the beginning of '97 will—like '90—be a date marking a fresh starting point in the industry."[154] Fitzpatrick could hardly have realized the full import of his prophecy; it was not until fifty years later that the wages of black mineworkers were to rise, in cash terms, above the level of 1897; in real terms they would not do so until the mid-1970s.[155]

The October wage cut had reduced working costs on the mines by an average of 4d per ton and it was only on very few mines, such as the Crown Reef, that management succeeded in holding anything like the envisaged reduction of 20 percent. Most mines had drifted back to the old wage level and were called upon by the Chamber of Mines to introduce the full 30 percent cut on 1 June 1897 and to extend the working month from twenty-four to at least thirty shifts. In recognition of the need for skilled labour, 7.5 percent of the black work force would not be bound by the new, uniform rates.[156] But for the average black miner, the new regulations marked a severe downturn in his conditions of employment: his working month was extended, sometimes by over 25 percent, and his wage reduced from 60s to 48s7d.

Black miners responded to the impending wage reduction in various ways. There was initially a "falling off" in the number of workers in April, followed by a "considerable exodus" in May.[157] On 3 May, some fifteen hundred workers went on strike at the Henry Nourse in response to the reintroduction of the nine-hour shift for drillers.[158] At the Knights and the May Consolidated, the miners came out in opposition to the prolongation of the working month from twenty-four to thirty-two shifts.[159] On the Randfontein mines, wage cuts pushed four hundred whites and one thousand blacks to strike.[160] "If there should be anything like a general strike," wrote Fitzpatrick in the face of these work stoppages, "we shall be dependent upon the government to carry out the pass law and to give the effective police supervision, or the labour will fail us."[161] When between three and four hundred men deserted from the Wolhuter in mid-May, they were arrested and their leaders imprisoned, measures that did not stop most of the men, mainly Basothos, from leaving the mine a month later when their contracts expired. By the end of May, miners were streaming from the Rand, and on 6 July, as they received their first full wage package under the new system, thousands of men left the mines.[162]

In order to undermine concerted action amongst workers and break the effect of a mass walkout, the mineowners had developed a strategy of paying miners their monthly wages in batches each week.[163] At the end of the first week of June, a section of the work force discovered that their pay consisted of three weeks under the old rate and a week under the new rate of pay. A week later a second batch of miners was surprised to learn that half their wage packet was paid under the new system and the following week a third group found that three-quarters of their pay had been cut. The size of the wage reduction also differed from mine to mine, for companies that had adhered to the October agreement were only required to introduce cuts of between 1s6d and 2s3d. On the Meyer and Charlton there was "grumbling and dismay" on 7 June, while at the City and Suburban mines there was "much murmuring amongst the boys instead of the usual jollifications, compound dances and inter-compound convivialities."[164] As the effects of the wage cut became increasingly apparent, large numbers of men left the mines and attempted to persuade their workmates to do likewise. In the first week of July, striking miners were arrested on the New Primrose, Robinson Deep, and Roodepoort mines, while four men accused of inciting workers to strike were arrested at the Robinson mine and two at the Spes Bona.[165] As the full import of the wage reduction was felt and newspapers speculated on an ultimate wage of 40s for thirty working days, workers fell back on their most effective defence and returned home. The large-scale departure of miners was "meant as a protest against the reduced wage," reported the Star, "for to a Kaffir, whatever is, is right and a wage once fixed is as sacred as an ancient 'doom.' "[166] Men returned home because they saw the cut in wages, together with the new level of state harassment, as a betrayal of working conditions entered into by, and considered acceptable to, both parties. As in October, most of those who left the mines were surface workers, for few Mozambicans were able to respond to the downturn in their working conditions by abandoning the mines.[167] With southern Mozambique under military occupation and its economy broken by war and ecological upheaval, Shangaans, Chopis, and Inhambanes could ill afford to abandon the wages needed to feed their families and reconstruct and rebuild their devastated homes. However, while few East Coasters left the mines, even fewer made their way to the Rand.[168]

Despite the conquest of southern Mozambique the Portuguese could not prevent "clandestine" labour emigration without the aid of the Transvaal authorities; nor could the mining industry maintain the wage cut of June 1897 without Portuguese assistance in the provision of cheap and continuous supplies of labour. In November 1897 the governments of Mozambique and the Transvaal reached a formal agreement over the emigration of labour to the Transvaal. Decree 109 attempted to minimize competitive recruiting by cutting out independent agents; only men representing "firms or bodies which are bona fide employers of natives" would be given a certificate of recommendation by the Transvaal's superintendent of natives. The cost of an annual recruiting licence was reduced to £200, and the worker's "passport" was to cost 7s6d, a reduction of £1 on the existing fee. In return, the major concession made by the Transvaal government and the mining industry was to permit a Portuguese protector or "curator" of natives to operate on the Rand. This official was the lynchpin in the system of surveillance and taxation introduced by the new labour agreement; he ensured the fulfilment of contracts, received complaints from Mozambican workers, and, in theory, sent home workers' savings through the district governors. The curator's major task was to suppress clandestine emigration by registering, keeping track of "Portuguese" labour on the Rand, and extracting from Mozambican workers various registration and endorsement fees. In this way, the worker was required to pay for the reproduction of the system of control that prevented his clandestine migration and restricted him from selling his labour to the highest bidder on the open market.[169]

The 1897 labour agreement was celebrated as a major government reform.[170] But it was a "sprat," reported the *Star*, in comparison with "whales" such as the railway and dynamite monopolies. The legislation was a "cleverly arranged scheme," according to which "the Republic is not called upon to sacrifice a solitary halfpenny," complained the editor. "The whole or nearly the whole pecuniary burden of the new labour scheme falls upon the hapless native himself."[171] However, as Mozambicans refused to emigrate or frequently deserted if they were obliged to pay these charges, the weight of the Portuguese fees, as well as recruiting costs, frequently fell on the mineowners.[172] But this heavy investment in recruiting, amounting to 2.4 percent of production costs in 1898, or over £3 per Mozambican worker, bore dividends in the form of reduced wages. In 1897 the NLSA succeeded in holding the June wage reduction by importing 14,510 Mozambican workers and, over the next twenty-one months (until the outbreak of the Anglo-Boer war), the organisation was able to import a further 27,538 men.[173] While the June wage reduction lopped 11s off the black miner's monthly salary, the cost of recruiting and re-engaging Mozambican workers, who spent an average of eighteen months on the mines, averaged less than 4s per month.[174] The success of a policy that combined the large-scale recruitment of migrants with a severe disciplinary code soon became apparent, as working costs plummeted. Between 1896 and 1897, while the wages of white miners experienced a marginal rise, the cost of black labour fell from 6s9.5d per ton of extracted ore to 5s4d and declined from 25 to 20.4 percent of total working costs.[175] The decline in black wages, together with improvements in both labour productivity and the gold reduction process, steadily brought down the average cost of working one ton of ore from 31s6d in 1896 to 27s6d in 1899. However the fall in production costs was much greater than these figures reveal, for several of the deep-level mines, some of which had sunk shafts to three or four thousand feet, were still at the development stage.[176] The reduction in working costs allowed the mines to extract increasingly low-grade ores. Between 1890 and 1898 the amount of ore brought to the surface rose from 702,828 tons to 7,308 million tons. Although there was a decline in the gold content per ton, the sheer volume of ore lifted the amount of gold produced from 73 tons in 1895 and 1896, to over 140 tons, valued at £15.141m, in 1898. This brought handsome dividends to shareholders, who had seen profits almost halve in 1895–1896; between 1897 and 1898 returns on their investments shot up from £2,817 to £4,827 million.[177]

The success of the gold mining industry was based, in large measure, on the cheap and ample flow of Mozambican labour secured under the labour agreement of November 1897. The Chamber observed in its report for 1898 that "the rapid growth of the industry has only been made possible by a corresponding increase in the supply of the labour." The rise in the number of workers employed on the gold fields, from ten thousand in 1889 to almost ninety thousand in 1898, had been obtained "without any appreciable rise in the rate of wages," the report noted. "Good work has been done, both in meeting as far as possible labour demands and especially in keeping down the scale of wages."[178]

The government continued to open the way for immigrant labour; in 1898, new pass offices and a depot for Mozambican workers were erected on government land in Braamfontein, and the following year, compounds were built at Krugersdorp, Johannesburg, and Boksburg to receive migrants arriving on the Witwatersrand. These constructions were "not on a magnificent scale," President Kruger assured his Volksraad, "but were only to prevent the natives deserting, which was the great trouble at present."[179] The number of Mozambicans employed on the Witwatersrand mines grew from 7,500 in 1890, when they made up half the black miners, to 20,000 in 1894. By 1898 their ranks had swelled to 55,220, and the following year, with over 70,000 men from the East Coast on the mines, they composed about 75 percent of the black labour force.[180] After reaching a peak of 63s6d in 1895, African wages stabilized at 49s9d in 1898, more than 40 percent less than was paid to black miners at Kimberley. The phenomenal success of management, in bringing through and holding a wage reduction of well over 20 percent while at the same time increasing the work force by 21 percent, depended on the recruitment of cheap Mozambican labour.

Mozambican workers on the Witwatersrand, constrained by a range of extraordinarily restrictive laws passed in the Transvaal in 1896–1897, and by the undermining of their productive base in the rural areas, had suffered a severe reverse. From the mineowners' perspective, Fitzpatrick stated simply in 1904 that "the East Coast has been the salvation of the Rand."[181] In the following chapter I examine how the mineowners' success was won at the cost of the long-term economic development of southern Mozambique and how, ultimately, events in the rural areas contributed to the defeat of labour.

6

Discretionary Migrant Labour and Standards of Living

Lourenço Marques and Inhambane developed in the slipstream of the Witwatersrand. Between 1887 and 1891, the number of letters received at Lourenço Marques multiplied twelve times, more merchandise passed through the port in the first six months of 1893 than in the five previous years, and in that year, government income amounted to more than £100,000.[1] In six short years, Lourenço Marques was transformed from a colonial backwater to by far the richest district in Mozambique. As a mark of its ascendence, the town was raised to the status of a city in 1887 and, eleven years later, it replaced Mozambique Island as the capital of the colony.[2]

The Growth of Portuguese Power

In 1887 the Portuguese reorganized tax gathering in the Lourenço Marques District, placed several chiefdoms near the town under military jurisdiction, and, the following year, established a magistracy in Mabotaland.[3] Beyond the Crown Lands, Residencies were established in the Gaza and Maputo capitals in 1886 and 1888. But the presence of the Portuguese in these powerful polities was little more than symbolic. They could neither expand the areas under their *de facto* control nor prevent the Gaza from raiding the Chopi. In 1889, the Portuguese were obliged to stand by idly as the Gaza moved their capital south to Mandlakazi on the lower Limpopo.[4]

The chiefdoms around Lourenço Marques were far smaller and weaker than the Gaza and Maputo, and it was in this area that the vigorous imperialist governor of Lourenço Marques, Mousinho de Albuquerque, raised the hut tax from 1s6d ($337) to 4s ($900) in 1891.[5] Military posts were built on the middle and upper reaches of the Nkomati and, in 1890–91, the first comprehensive tax, levied on 12,250 huts, produced £2,850 (12,826$000); two years later revenue from the hut tax

141

Lourenço Marques, c. 1891. The quadrangular Portuguese fort, constructed in the 1780s, looks over a bay brought to life by the trade with the Witwatersrand gold fields.

jumped to £4,500.[6] The same process was visible at Inhambane, where hut tax returns rose from under £500 in 1886–87, to over £3,000 the following year and climbed steadily.[7] As 10 percent of the hut tax went to the collector, it was often gathered with extreme brutality, including the torching of homesteads.[8] These methods of collection constituted an important cause of the Luso-Gaza war, which broke out in 1894 following an official rise in the hut tax from $900 to 1$350 (6s) in June and a further, perhaps unofficial, increase later that year to 12s-14s. Many people were unable to pay the tax because of the ecological and epidemiological upsets plaguing the area during the late 1880s and early 1890s. But according to Junod, the ability of the African population to pay tax was primarily marred by the demands of the Portuguese for forced labour (*xibalo*), "lasting weeks if not months," as this undermined agricultural self-sufficiency.[9] During the 1890s the crucial issue of contention that arose between the Portuguese and the population of the Crown Lands was that of labour rather than taxation. Both issues were intimately linked to the development of the Witwatersrand mines.

In the early 1890s, several thousand Mozambicans were employed on the construction and maintenance of sections and branchlines of the Lourenço Marques-Pretoria railway, and their wages compared favourably with those paid to miners on the gold fields.[10] Many men were also employed in porterage, shipping, landing, and forwarding goods, in customs clearance, public and municipal works, domestic service, and various other spheres of the local economy.[11] Because of the competition for labour between these different sectors and the gold mines, African workers in Lourenço Marques could earn as much as 1s6d-3s per day, high wages that were at the base of the *xibalo* system.[12] Following the abolition of slavery in 1878, vagabondage was considered a legal justification for compelling men to labour, and in May 1881 forced labour had been legalised.[13] Ten years later, the British consul in Lourenço Marques regarded *xibalo* as a form of employment that "seems to carry with it many of the component parts of slavery, while it ensures none of that protection which expensive slaves receive. . . . Workers get no food but are promised 'ordinary wages' of 1s to 4s per day. After 2 to 3 months they are sent home with a few shillings or in some cases nothing at all."[14]

Early in 1894 a particularly severe *xibalo* was imposed on the people of the Crown Lands when they were forced to construct the roads needed by the Portuguese to show effective occupation of the Delagoa Bay hinterland. Members of various small chiefdoms in the region, such as the Tembe, Matolla, Nwamba, Mabota, Mafumo, and Mazwaya, all worked on these roads and in some areas the villages were deserted of men.[15]

Forced conscription into the Portuguese army was another corollary of the high local cost of labour. The arrival in Delagoa Bay of a sinister black corvette, known as the *misi* or hyena, foreshadowed razzias throughout the streets of Lourenço Marques.[16] Pressgangs and *xibalo* levies invoked an understandable dread in the local population, for the unexpected loss of a father, brother, or son could deal a shattering blow to the productivity of the homestead. The disappearance of individuals confirmed the image of anthropophagous Europeans recounted in local folklore and many believed that the *misi* "called men and devoured them."[17] As the local demand for labour grew, the system of "vassalage" was transformed from a political alliance of some mutual benefit to one of exploitation; the chiefdoms around Lourenço Marques were the first actively to oppose the *xibalo* system. The brunt of *xibalo* and conscription demands fell on the young men of the Crown Lands, and it was from these cadets, replete with the independence and earnings associated with mine work, and fully aware of the market value of their labour, that revolt was to emerge.

When the youths of Matolla refused to supply labour to their chiefs for *xibalo*, the Portuguese seized the Matolla chief, his mother, and other notables, and held them hostage until the elders had produced the required workers. But as Junod recounted, "the young people persisted in refusing [to perform forced labour] by saying 'we have just returned from *xibalo*, how can we return so soon?'" and by "declaring that they did not have the time to repair their own houses." The young men continued to refuse to work for the Portuguese and the Matolla chief was only freed when "the mature men and those of headring status" offered themselves in exchange for their chief.[18] Hostilities started in August 1894 when Mahazule, the Mazwaya chief on the lower Inkomati, protested against Portuguese intervention in a succession dispute, refused to pay the augmented hut tax and, symbolically ending his vassal status, returned his government uniform.[19] The young men of Mafumo, who had suffered grievously from conscription, *xibalo*, and taxes, soon pressured their chief, Nwamantibyana, to join the rebellion.[20] After briefly besieging Lourenço Marques, the Mazwaya and Mafumo turned for aid to Gungunyana; as the war spread northwards, its effect was quickly felt on the Witwatersrand as Gaza subjects started to return home; in April 1895, as the war moved north of the Inkomati, more than one hundred fifty Shangaans left the Witwatersrand every day.[21] Several months previously, the Native Labour Department of the Chamber of Mines had constructed depots at Pietpotgietersrus and Zandfontein, and in May 1895 four new shelters were built so as to provide Gaza migrants with food and shelter every night on their way to the government depot in Pretoria.[22] In June-July 1895, soon after the opening of the Lourenço Marques-Pretoria railway, the NLD attempted to extend this system by constructing depots on the intersections of the major labour routes in Gazaland. About thirteen hundred men were sent out of Mozambique in this manner before the scheme ground to a halt as the war engulfed Gazaland.[23]

In August 1895, it was reported from Khosen that "masses of young people were leaving in a great hurry for the mines so as not to be called to fight."[24] But the following month the movement of labour from Gazaland was halted entirely as Gungunyana's soldiers patrolled the border in an attempt to prevent men capable of bearing arms from leaving the country.[25] "Gungunyana is reserving his strength for the Portuguese," reported the Johannesburg *Star*, "and naturally objects to his warriors foresaking the assegai for the drill hammer at a time like this."[26] With up to 50,000 Gaza soldiers gathered at Mandlakazi the mines began to suffer from an acute shortage of "the most acceptable and best class of natives for underground work"; in an attempt to draw drillmen, wages were increased on the wealthy mines.[27] Inhambane and Chopi migrants, whose passage across Gazaland was dangerous in the best of circumstances, could no longer be taken overland, while Gaza workers, who normally migrated without paying fees to the Portuguese, were prevented from leaving the country. Independent labour recruiters, fearful that a Portuguese victory would exclude them from Gazaland, supplied Gungunyana with arms, and offered to lead a Gaza attack on Lourenço Marques.[28] A group of mine managers attempted unsuccessfully to bring about a peaceful settlement to the conflict by introducing Gaza ambassadors to the imperial secretary in Cape Town.[29] The Chamber of Mines was also to make several attempts to end the war, and delegations from Johannesburg frequently arrived at Mandlakazi.[30] In August 1895 Gungunyana made a final attempt to win over the Portuguese by offering them £10,000 in cash—but when this strategy failed, a decisive battle became unavoidable.[31] Hemmed in by two Portuguese columns, the Gaza soldiers were unable to resort to raiding for their provisions and turned for days on end to locusts, which they roasted and ground into a sauce. Dietary problems and unsanitary conditions caused epidemics of dysentery to break out in the bivouacs. The Portuguese also suffered from the climate, but with their modern logistics they were not obliged, like the Gaza, to live off the countryside. The hunger and sickness depleting the Gaza ranks widened the political divisions within Gungunyana's heterogeneous army and, on the 7th of November 1895, a severely depleted Gaza army was resoundingly defeated at the battle of Coolela.[32] The Gaza king was finally cornered at Chaimite where, in a gesture that again indicated how successful he had been in appropriating part of the earnings of Gaza migrant workers, he presented his captors with eight diamonds and more than £1,500.[33]

In Johannesburg the mineowners greeted the end of the war with relief, for the shortage of labour had contributed to a 30 percent fall in the production of gold during the final six months of 1895.[34] The Portuguese victory had been achieved at the cost of a scorched-earth policy that, together with drought and locusts, had devastated much of the area north of Delagoa Bay. The defeated chiefdoms in the Lourenço Marques district were rapidly regrouped into five circumscriptions, each under a Portuguese administrator, the coastal districts of Lourenço Marques and Inhambane were declared Crown Lands, and Gazaland was placed under military rule.[35] Chiefs and sub-chiefs who had taken up arms against the Portuguese were exiled and replaced by native commissioners. The Mafumo chiefdom was disbanded and incorporated into the growing town of Lourenço Marques, while the Maputo, who had refused to help the Portuguese in the dark days of 1894, were obliged to pay a war "indemnity" of £1,800 and 2,500 head of cattle.[36] The removal of the chiefs left the peoples of southern Mozambique politically leaderless. The chief was "the forest into which we retreat; without him," remarked one man, employing the ultimate metaphor of powerlessness, "we are but women."[37] The loss of the traditional leaders left rural communities unprotected in their dealings with foreign agents such as labour recruiters and traders. In Gazaland the Portuguese abolished the restrictions and controls placed by Gungunyana on the level of commerce and consumerism. Within months of the king's defeat, nine hundred Banyan merchants had entered the area "to suck the country dry," in the prose of one Portuguese administrator, "taking from it the gold the native brings from the Transvaal."[38] The collection of hut tax was extended throughout southern Mozambique, and in December 1895 all adult males were obliged to provide the state with seven days of unpaid labour annually.[39] War, drought, locusts, hut taxes, and *xibalo* dealt a crippling blow to the independence of the people of southern Mozambique and compelled large numbers of men to seek work in the Transvaal, where, as we have seen, they were prepared to accept a decisive cut in wages. Gungunyana's "starving and impoverished people," reported the *Star* in January 1896, "are only too anxious to come down to the mines."[40] For the first time, the Portuguese were able to draw a comprehensive revenue from, and exercise a direct pressure on, the flow of migrant labour.

Environment, Money, and Survival

An almost continual spate of ecological upheavals facilitated the advance of the Portuguese into the interior. It was almost as if, following the discovery of gold on the Witwatersrand, nature were waging a final titanic struggle to maintain her hold over a people increasingly liberated from her tyranny by wage labour. A group of Swiss missionaries carefully recorded this contest from their hill station at Rikatla, just to the north of Lourenço Marques. The thoroughness of their reports provides moving testimony to the unequal struggle between a preindustrial people and their environment.

Unseasonably early rains in August 1887 were followed by a harrowing drought that destroyed three-quarters of the cereal crop in 1888 and caused the price of maize imported from Natal to quadruple.[41] When the rains failed again in 1889–1890, people were reduced to scavenging for food while others travelled in search of food to the fertile, maize-producing areas on the lower and middle Nkomati.[42] The missionaries attributed the shortage of maize in Khosen partly to the capricious climate and partly to the cyclical sense of time of local agriculturalists, who frequently sold their crops to Banyan merchants speculating in grain. As a combination of migrants' wages and a scarcity of food quadrupled the price of cereals, maize was imported from the United States.[43] This famine, part of a more widespread drought affecting most of southern Africa, ended suddenly with heavy downpours in February 1890.[44] Yet, little more than a year later, drought was again threatening much of Southern Mozambique. In Khosen the situation was particularly bad as the arrival at Mandlakazi of eighty thousand Gaza settlers had placed enormous strains on supplies of cultivable land and fuel. In 1891 Arthur Grandjean remarked on the "cruel suffering" brought to the Nkomati bend by drought and a cattle epizootic related to redwater or Texas fever; in June 1892 the area was again in "dire straits."[45] By September most people were "reduced to eating only grass and wild fruit or to preparing the pith of certain trees," wrote Grandjean, "over half the population is constantly travelling in order to buy provisions where they are still available." All supplies of maize had been consumed and no seed was left for planting.[46] Around Lourenço Marques the entire maize crop failed and the population was "on the verge of starvation."[47] Even at Mandlakazi, the new capital of the Gaza empire, famine was declared to be the rule.[48]

The drought finally ended in December of the following year, when seeds planted in the riverine areas produced an early crop.[49] In January 1893 Khosen celebrated the end of the famine but, within days, torrential rains inundated the plains bordering the Nkomati, and the country experienced the worst floods in living memory.[50] In Lourenço Marques over 1500 mm of rain (almost 60 inches) fell in the next three months; communications were broken, and part of the harvest was lost when fields, roads, and river banks disappeared in the flood waters.[51] Malaria spread with the pools of stagnant water; in Lourenço Marques alone the annual mortality rate from fever jumped from 153 to 228.[52] In Khosen the crops produced by the good seasonal rains at the end of 1894 were destroyed by swarms of locusts (*Acidius pereginus*) in December.[53] In February 1895 twelve consecutive days of rain resulted in floods throughout the country.[54] Matters were made worse as five waves of locusts invaded Khosen in April to ravage the fields freshly sown after the flood.[55] Around Lourenço Marques, war, locusts and drought caused the price of maize to treble. But in Khosen the famine was so bad that parents pawned their children for £4–5, while men left for Lourenço Marques and the Transvaal to earn money with which to buy food.[56] Rain failed to fall over the summer of 1895/96, locusts and soldiers continued to plague the area, and, because of the drought, wild animals were drawn to settlements where they pillaged even hardy crops like sweet potatoes.[57] In the south the Tembe and Maputo, whose maize crops had been destroyed by drought and locusts, subsisted on cassava, sweet potatoes, fowls, and eggs, and fathers were reduced to *ganisela* or pledging their young daughters to husbands in return for meagre brideprices paid in cash. The drought continued after the establishment of peace, and in most areas people were obliged to live from hunting, fishing, and gathering while they bought expensive, imported food with the money earned from wage labour.[58] The drought was eventually broken by rain in the late summer of 1897.[59] But a new source of morbidity soon emerged as the Portuguese established themselves throughout southern Mozambique and, through their hut tax and *xibalo* levies, precipitated the second Luso-Gaza war.

In April 1897 the British consul reported that in the Lourenço Marques district, "the greater portion of the revenue is contributed by the direct hut tax on natives"; he warned that martial law and the collection of an estimated £22,000 in hut tax by the military authorities would lead to rebellion. In Khosen and Bilene the Portuguese demanded a war tax of £1 per inhabitant, or one head of cattle, together with a hut tax of 10s. Each petty chief was also expected to supply a contingent of *xibalo* workers.[60] The tribulations of this period caused hundreds of families to cross the border into the Transvaal and pushed large numbers of men to the Witwatersrand. The missionaries wrote with horror of children crippled by malnutrition and of starving people sifting through their compost heaps and subsisting on locusts and a meal of wild grass every two days.[61] Famine and relentless waves of locusts caused even the population in the fertile region on the Nkomati bend to subsist on sweet potatoes, eventually pressing Gungunyana's old general, Maguiguana, to join with the Khosa in a revolt against the Portuguese.[62] The food situation worsened over the next few months when rinderpest destroyed large numbers of cattle and wild animals. "When I arrived in Khosen the life led by the natives, simple, without worries, so close to nature under the great blue sky or a shining African moon seemed to me to be full of poetry," wrote Rev. Eberhardt in late September 1897, "a quick look moved one to agree with the opinion of Rousseau. But stay and, believe me, all the charm disappears. These great children of nature are often her victims."[63] Maguiguana was defeated in August 1897, the Khosa chiefdom was broken up, most remaining Gaza Ngoni fled to the Transvaal, and refugees scoured the land for food.[64]

The rural economy was no longer able to absorb large numbers of internal migrants. While the Portuguese demanded taxes in cash, kind, or labour, and imposed *xibalo*, the country was devastated. The population of Lourenço Marques grew from just over one thousand to almost five thousand between 1894 and 1897, as people turned to the town as a possible source of earnings.[65] But men had little alternative other than to seek work in the mines; the cash value of cultivated and gathered crops had fallen by 30–50 percent during the long depression of 1877–1895, and the export of skins and horns declined by 70 percent in the last decade of the century.[66] With the completion of the railway linking Johannesburg to the coast, both navvies and porters lost a traditional means of income. Migrants' wages had, on the other hand, multiplied several times during the depression, from just over 10s per month in Natal in the early 1870s to over 63s on the Witwatersrand in the mid-1890s. Emigrating to the mines was an economically rational solution to the continuous problems raised by war and environmental upheaval.

While mining offered a better cash return than cultivating or gathering produce for the market, large-scale migrant labour undermined agricultural self-sufficiency. Men played an important role in the cultivation of crops and performed various domestic duties, particularly in the Chopi areas.[67] It was common for a man in the southern and central Delagoa Bay hinterland to work his own field (*mpashu*) and to assist his wife in planting and harvesting the maize crop.[68] Probably the major agricultural task undertaken by males was the breaking of new ground; they also made and repaired all tools and utensils (except pots) used in the homestead, built drying tables, dwelling huts in winter, and granaries in summer, and cut the poles and grass used in their construction. Only men looked after the cattle, cultivated tobacco, and opened new fields. They constructed fishing traps, mounted fishing expeditions, and contributed to the food supply by hunting extensively and by trading for cattle. It is obvious that men made an important contribution to the home economy.[69] Yet a strong school of thought holds that, with the decline in hunting and trading, men had more time to spend on the mines. "On the whole, men have but little to do," remarked Junod at the turn of the century. "We can fairly estimate at three months the time required for the work which they have to do for the village and for the community. The remaining months are devoted to pastimes and pleasure."[70] However, this overlooks the productive nature of many of these pastimes, and assumes that the absence of male labour was not particularly disruptive of food-producing activities as men worked on the Witwatersrand during the agricultural off-season. This was patently not the case, as migrants spent an average of eighteen months on the gold mines. In local terms, a

A hunter carrying a firearm and wearing cat tails. He is accompanied by a young boy holding a plunge basket used in fishing.

mine contract involved the loss of the labour of a male member of the family for at least two consecutive agricultural seasons. Nor was labour migration adjusted to the agricultural season; most men travelled to Natal in winter, when malaria and jiggers were less virulent, and to Kimberley and the Transvaal in summer, when the highveld cold proved less of an obstacle. Hence an important and large part of the male population was constantly working in the gold mines during the agricultural season.

There was also a steady demographic drain from rural southern Mozambique, as young men left their homes to settle permanently in South Africa. In 1887 British officials remarked that half the male population was employed beyond the borders of Maputoland, a view supported by population and hut tax returns for the early 1890s.[71] Travellers confirmed this impression, one reporting from the south in 1896 that "the Amatongas who remain in the country were either home from the Rand for the holidays or belonged to that class content to live without work."[72] Statistics suggest a permanent emigration out of the coastal areas of 15–20 percent, and a temporary loss of a further 30–35 percent of the adult male population.[73] Together with the dangers encountered travelling to and from labour centres and the high mortality rate in the mines, this must have resulted in a permanent loss, of as much as a quarter of the adult men in some villages. This constant outflow of male labour was partly responsible for the decline in exports from Lourenço Marques.[74] As early as the mid-1860s, the governor of Lourenço Marques had complained that the capacity of the Maputo to produce food and articles of tribute had been impaired by the emigration of men to Natal.[75] In 1878 the governor general expressed his concern that emigration would "impoverish the interior of labour" and "be fatally translated into a decline in the flow of products from the coast."[76] In the same year, the Portuguese secretary for native affairs stated that labour emigration had caused a fall in agricultural surplus. "Emigration," he stated, "is nothing but a real cancer for this province, from which the Blacks get very little."[77] In 1880 he complained that while migrants were away, their lands were left uncultivated, and that on their return they squandered their wages instead of investing them in the development of the land.[78]

There were two strands in this opposition to labour migration. Most Portuguese officials had good economic reasons for being opposed to the flow of labour out of the colony. Unlike slaves, most of whom had been channelled through the coastal settlements, workers crossed the hypothetical border separating Mozambique from South Africa without passing through Portuguese controls. Thus, whereas the export of slaves had brought a considerable profit to Portugal and her officials, the emigration of workers, apart from a trickle through Lourenço Marques and Inhambane, merely drained the colony of labour. This perspective had long been held by Portuguese abolitionists, who believed that, following the independence of Brazil, Lisbon should turn from the slave trade to the development of her African colonies. The notion that manpower should be employed locally to produce raw materials and provide consumer markets for the metropole, rather than be sold, was a central argument behind the abolitionist legislation of the 1830s and the prohibition in 1855 of the shipment of *emigré* labour from Mozambique to the French islands of the Indian Ocean.[79] The opponents of labour emigration rapidly developed a racial discourse, blaming the lack of development on Indian merchants. "In Inhambane there is a real swarm," wrote one official,

> hunting the blacks who return from Natal or Lourenço Marques, because of the pounds they can send to India, where they are greatly prized. The native returning to his homeland is immediately besieged by a horde of Moors and Banyans who seduce him by every means until he lets go of his money. Lourenço Marques belongs to this caste.[80]

From this perspective, emigration deprived the economy of agricultural labour, forced up local wages, and was of benefit only to Indian traders who sent their profits out of the country.[81]

A string of Lourenço Marques' governors, ever eager to find an immediate source of revenue, opposed the anti-emigration policy of the liberals. Augusto

Castilho, governor of the settlement in the late 1870s, stated frankly that "emigration takes away a large amount of labour that otherwise would be of little use to the country." As long as Portugal could tax both the workers and the goods on which they spent their wages, their emigration was of value to the colony.[82] Mousinho d'Albuquerque compared Mozambicans working in the Transvaal with Galician migrants in northern Portugal and Portuguese immigrants in Brazil. Through the sale of their labour, people who were otherwise "useless to the public interest" brought money into the colony, paid taxes, and purchased imports on which the government levied duties. Mousinho believed labour emigration to be a positive element in the economy, for it was "only by aiding and enabling the Johannesburg mines to work and by developing the Transvaal trade in general that Lourenço Marques itself can be developed."[83]

The liberal-conservative controversy over labour emigration revolved around the question of how best Portugal could benefit from her African colony. The liberals believed that the development of Mozambique's natural resources would yield the largest returns for the metropole, while the conservatives sought to sell the colony's major means of production, the labour of its black male population. But until the 1897 labour agreement with the Transvaal, which marked an overwhelming victory for the conservatives, this remained a largely theoretical debate. The decision to export labour rather than develop the domestic economy had in fact been taken many years previously by the people of southern Mozambique when they invested their energies in labour emigration rather than in the less profitable production of goods for export.[84]

The effects of this decision were visible well before the Portuguese conquered southern Mozambique. After a brief hiccup in exports when migration was restricted by the depression of 1883–1886, the production of saleable crops in the Delagoa Bay region withered away to almost nothing. The same process was observable at Inhambane, where the emigration of workers to the Witwatersrand was largely responsible for a drop of almost 60 percent in exports over the years 1889–1891.[85] The growing dependence on wages was partly reflected in the mounting disparity in the balance of trade. Without a parallel rise in exports, the increase in imports was only possible because of the purchasing capacity of workers' wages. By 1894 some twenty-five thousand migrants returned home every year with savings of about £20–30 each, resulting in an annual influx of well over £500,000.[86] A growing dependence on migrant labour was inevitable in a situation where men could choose between investing their energy in mining, with its dangers but relatively high and steady wage, or the export sector of the domestic economy, with its uncertainties and falling prices. The people of southern Mozambique depended on the earnings of their tramping workers to purchase imports; but import statistics are notoriously imprecise as an index of improved living conditions. It would also be wrong to see migrant labour as bringing an egalitarian distribution of wealth to the people of southern Mozambique.

Banyan merchants continued to expand the network of small shops through which imported commodities filtered into the interior. Three years after the discovery of gold on the Witwatersrand, the number of traders operating in the Delagoa Bay hinterland had almost doubled; some two hundred fifty lived in Lourenço Marques and another five hundred in the interior.[87] They were regarded by the Standard Bank as a respectable clientèle; punctual in meeting payments, they had not suffered one bankruptcy in twenty years and were "large purchasers" of drafts on London for remittance to Bombay.[88] Although traders were not obliged to declare the amounts of specie exported, at least £16,500 was sent from Lourenço Marques in 1885. Some 58 percent went to Bombay, 37 percent to London, and 3 percent to Zanzibar. In 1890, of a total of £12,700 in specie exports declared at the Lourenço Marques customs house, 81 percent went to "British possessions," 15 percent to Britain, and 4 percent to "Portuguese possessions."[89] Banyan traders seldom sank roots in Mozambique (their average age was estimated in 1894 to be 28), and they tended to take temporary wives.[90] But although they did not invest their profits in Mozambique, they were a vital element in the economy. Their rural stores were centres of labour recruitment, where the consumer articles exchangeable for mine wages were on open display. They provided the administration with customs revenues and bought trading permits; by providing outlets where migrants could spend their earnings, they played a crucial role in reproducing the work force on the distant Witwatersrand mines. By importing, purchasing, and selling surplus food, and frequently speculating with harvests, Banyans played an important role in distributing food to needy areas.

As early as 1886 the governor of Lourenço Marques believed that many people were dependent on earnings from migrant labour to purchase food. The British consul reported in 1891 that men chose to live on their earnings rather than cultivate the soil. "They find it more profitable to work for Europeans and buy from them food as they require," he remarked. "With the high rate of wages obtained they are both able to live better in this way than they could by cultivating the ground, and to have a surplus with which to drink or buy such luxuries as they may desire."[91] An Anglican missionary wrote at roughly the same time that high wages and a poor environment pushed men to sell their labour rather than invest it in the domestic economy. "On account of the poverty and dryness of the soil," of the Delagoa Bay region, he wrote

> which in appearance is just like sand, the natives in the least drought are often in a starving condition, through failure of their crops. The appearance of the soil to an ordinary European would lead him to believe that nothing could possibly grow in it, yet it is surprising how the natives do produce from it pumpkins, melons, sweet potatoes, beans, bananas, mealies etc., if they get the rain in its season. The uncertainty of the food crops is, of course, a great incentive to the natives to offer themselves for work, and the rate of wages offered in the labour market is a great attraction.[92]

In 1892 Arthur Grandjean lamented over the fate of Khosen, which was normally a maize-exporting area. Due to the fertility of the area, the Khosa had retained an independence of wage labour and had remained dependent on agriculture for their subsistence. But, he argued, this reliance on nature's bounty caused the ecological upheavals of the early 1890s to take on a far more serious aspect on the Inkomati bend than in those areas where people had supplemented agricultural production with wage labour.[93] Henri Junod, writing in 1895 of the continuing famine and locust plague, believed that

> For the blacks, the necessity to work for the whites in order to produce their food is a great tragedy, a calamity of the first order. For centuries the

families have lived from the product of their fields—and if one earned money, the last few years, it was to buy clothes and luxuries. All is now changed.[94]

The ecological crises of the period had more than merely widened the gap between real and desired standards of living. Despite a deep disapproval of migrant labour, Junod claimed that wages had "saved" the people of the southern and central Delagoa Bay region from the effects of drought, locusts, war, and rinderpest.[95] Paul Berthoud commented on the "detrimental" effects of this proletarianization when he wrote with consternation that "they eat everything they earn."[96]

To many families wage labour was no longer just a supplement to agricultural production; it had become a means of subsistence. European observers quite clearly believed that the people of Southern Mozambique had come to rely on money for their livelihood. Although I have found it difficult to obtain the point of view of the people themselves, I have some clues. Junod remarked in 1894 that, when visiting a famine-struck community, his offer of spiritual assistance was rebuffed by an elderly woman who "pulled a small coin from its hiding place" and inveighed "here is my cock."[97] To this woman money had become a symbol of wealth in which she could place her trust, rather than in the vagaries of religion or agriculture. Money, brought home by migrant workers and circulated locally, was her means of survival. The same metaphor was employed in the songs of young migrants who defined themselves as "cocks" while deriding the stay-at-home *mamparas* as "hens." Johannesburg was known as *Nkambeni* (a wooden bowl), a term that evokes the image of a receptacle that holds food. This positive interpretation of wage labour would be expressed more generally some twenty years later, when the followers of the millenarian Murimi movement symbolically replaced the word for rain (*mpfula*), with the term for a returned migrant (*gayisa*).[98]

The repatriation of migrants' wages unleashed a consumer revolution that was to transform the society of Southern Mozambique. As wages poured in, the amount of distilled liquor imported through Lourenço Marques rose from 91,600 litres in 1886 to well over a million litres in 1890. It seems hardly coincidental that the Brussels Conference of 1890 prohibited the importation of alcohol into the African continent north of 22 degrees south, a decision leaving southern Mozambique, an area awash with the earnings of migrant workers, open to the unrestricted ingress of European alcohol. A good deal of the alcohol imported through Delagoa Bay found its way to the Witwatersrand, but a great deal was also consumed in southern Mozambique. European visitors frequently remarked on the large number of canteens, and extensive trade in liquor, in the Delagoa Bay hinterland. In 1892 there were 147 canteens serving a population of forty thousand in the Crown Lands; by 1896 there were eighty-two licensed canteens within a 1.5-kilometre radius of Lourenço Marques, supplying a population of five to six thousand.[99] On the Inkomati bend, thirteen Banyan liquor traders prospered in an area of two square miles, one merchant importing from eight hundred to one thousand five-gallon carafes every month.[100] In Gazaland the king exerted a limited control over the consumption of imported liquor. When a great reunion of men and women at Mandlakazi in 1890 blamed the drop in the birthrate on widespread drunkenness, Gungunyana prohibited the sale of alcohol.[101] But the interdiction did not last more than a few months, and the king was to prohibit the importation of liquor on at least two further occasions. Part of the reason for his prevaricating attitude was based on the divisions within his council over whether liquor was a foodstuff or an intoxicant.[102] Gungunyana himself had come to believe that "drink is not a foodstuff as we think. It is wood," he told Dr. Liegme, "wood that burns. . . ."[103]

Consumer tastes were sensitive to price fluctuations. When the Portuguese imposed a high tariff on the importation of distilled liquor in 1892, the consumption of spirits fell sharply and there was a marked rise in the importation of rough, metropolitan wines unsuitable for the European market. Variously termed kaffir or colonial wine, or "wine for blacks" (*vinho para pretos*), the Portuguese beverage benefitted from a nominal import duty of one *real* per litre. The cheapness of the product was ensured by bulk imports of a concentrated article highly fortified with cheap brandies and industrial alcohol. In Mozambique the volume of the wine was multiplied through adulteration with water and, very often, additives ranging from glycerine and pepper to battery acid. The colonial wine sold in barrels was generally a 15–17 degree proof spirit, while bottled wine could reach 20 degrees in strength. As such, this vinous concoction was not far different from the adulterated, distilled liquors to which people had become accustomed. From a rough annual average of 50,000 litres in 1882–1890, the amount of wine imported through Lourenço Marques rose to over 3 million litres, worth almost £80,000, in 1897–1898.[104] The importation of cotton cloth through Lourenço Marques was quickly driven into second place by colonial wine but nevertheless experienced a steady growth, doubling in value in a decade to amount to over £40,000 by 1897.

In 1892 Henri Junod made an inventory of the goods sold by a Banyan general dealer, a Goanese Hindu named Nala, at his shop on the lower Inkomati. The number of articles arranged on the shelves showed a quite highly developed consumer consciousness and a dynamic integration of European fabrics and beads into the local forms of dress. A large range of cloths was stocked and sold by the arm-lengh. The most popular were white, red, red and black, black with white stripes, navy blue and red (a special mourning cloth), and dark blue cloth with white flowers (a courting garment). Other favorite materials were white blankets, costing 3–4s, thicker coloured blankets priced at 5–7s, handkerchiefs and towels, and overcoats at 15s each. At least twelve different kinds of beads were on sale in the store. Other items included rings, fish-hooks, buttons and general haberdashery, snuff boxes (worn in the ear-lobe), knives, spoons, balls of string, little chains (hung from the belt), bracelets selling at ten for a shilling, wooden spoons, combs, coils of fine iron wire, animal skins, sardines at 6d a tin, and English biscuits. The cask of diluted German brandy remarked on by Junod in 1892 was soon to be replaced, following the tariff changes of that year, by three barrels of colonial wine fortified with spirits.[105] Also found on the shelves were padlocks with which, increasingly, men fastened their doors and barred access to their private property.[106]

In Mozambique the buying capacity of workers' repatriated savings was inflated by a growing black market for gold specie. Although officially valued at 4$800 in 1882, the open market exchange rate for the pound sterling rose to 5$200 in 1892 and 6$000 in 1896.[107] Sterling became the accepted currency of southern Mozambique, as merchants, railway workers, and the African population in general refused to deal in Portuguese bank notes.[108] Migrants also returned home with "bonuses" ranging from gold nuggets and amalgam to diamonds, as well as smaller objects such as iron files, piping, and copper wire. They spent their money on goods bought in the mine concession stores, town shops, or in the small trading stores erected along the paths home. As a young transport rider, Percy Fitzpatrick wrote of lines of Shangaans returning from the mines with "gaudy blankets, collections of bright tin billies and mugs, tin plates, three-legged pots, clothing, hats and even small tin trunks painted yellow."[109] The range and diversity of purchased articles was to smother local craftwork and build a growing dependence on manufactured imports.[110] But apart from a handful of missionaries, few people were concerned with the negative side of this consumer revolution. Even fewer were concerned with the distribution of power and wealth that migrant labour brought to southern Mozambique.

Migrancy, Marriage, and Power

Mozambican migrant workers accumulated wealth in two areas. A stable rural family presented a bulwark against the social assault of industrialisation and proletarianisation and served as a vital security net for a miner constantly threatened with unemployment and physical injury; an alternative source of income was also a powerful weapon in the hands of workers unwilling to accept a cut in wages. Thus the rural and industrial economies were intimately linked, and the migrant worker exploited both in the process of extracting a livelihood. In the less fertile areas wage labour became the nutrient for survival and, through the acquisition of wives and goods, a crucial means of reproducing the family and attracting a following. Hence sterling wages were imbued with both an exchange and a social value; during the 1890s, wages became an integral means through which the people of southern Mozambique survived and prospered from one year to the next. But the benefits of migrant labour were distributed in a highly unequal manner, and, in order to maintain the cohesion of the home community, migrants had to bolster the very political structure that was threatened by the freedom and independence with which they sold their labour.

When sterling specie replaced *beja* hoes as the bridewealth medium in the late 1870s, the control exercised by the *numzane* over the circulation of women became increasingly contingent upon their ability to accumulate gold coins. The introduction of a sterling brideprice was initially opposed by fathers of marriageable women who sought a return to cattle as a medium of bridewealth.[111] Cattle produced "interest," in the form of calves; they were not "eaten up" in the buying of consumer goods; and, most importantly, the elders controlled the herds. Cattle were an unpredictable alternative to sterling, however, as diseases and tsetse continued to plague the area.[112] Well before the rinderpest epidemic of 1897, some of the chiefdoms around Delagoa Bay were still largely without cattle and the elders had no alternative other than to accept brideprices paid in sterling. But in order to retain a hold over the circulation of bridewealth, the *numzane* had to control the major part of the "liquid capital" (workers' wages) flowing into southern Mozambique. This they partly achieved by continually raising brideprices above the level of the returning migrants' earnings; a strategy that prevented the "devaluation" of brides and held the cadets in a relationship of dependence upon the *numzane* for their access to wives. In the early 1860s ten hoes, worth 20s, were sufficient to obtain a wife. During the early years of the reign of Chief Zihlala (1867–83), the Mafumo brideprice was fixed at £8 but soon rose to £15. The chief of the Mazwaya on the lower Nkomati, Maphunga (*ca.*1860–1890), tried to limit to £15.10s the claims of *numzane* to brideprices of £20–30. Brideprices continued to rise and by the 1890s stood at £15–20; in the Lourenço Marques area, where there was a larger circulation of sterling, they could amount to as much as £30.[113] The cost of a concubine in Khosen in the late 1880s was about £10, or roughly two-thirds that of a normal brideprice, and remained relatively constant, perhaps because of the large numbers of Chopi women enslaved by the Gaza and Khosa in the early 1890s.[114] In Gazaland brideprices ranged in 1894 from £20 in the area near Inhambane to £30 in the dry area north-east of the bend in the Limpopo River.[115] Around Inhambane they stood at about £20 in 1897, although the size of the dowry depended on the status of the bride's family.[116]

The chiefs and *numzane* also demanded a part of the workers' wages, frequently in the form of "labour taxes," when they returned home. This form of taxation generally amounted to about £1 paid to the chief and 2s to the *numzane*. Taxes differed according to the chiefdom and the chief. Chief Nozingile had received up to 5s from returning migrants, a tax that his wife, the queen regent who succeeded him, increased to £1. Her son, Ngwanasi, who used his regiments to plant and weed his fields, levied a fee of £5–10 on all males who avoided military service by emigrating to South Africa.[117] During the late 1880s young migrants, who returned to Gazaland with sums of between £12 and £15, gave diamonds or a part of their savings to their chiefs.[118] At the Gaza capital, "all those who have earned some money working for the whites," remarked George Liengme in 1892, "when they return to the country must give the larger part to their chief for the King."[119]

Men returned from the mines with new consumer habits and requirements. But the chiefs and *numzane* also contributed to the demand for imported goods by dressing their wives in European cloths and by using liquor as a libation, a reward, and as an integral part of many social rituals.[120] It was in the interests of the chiefs to encourage trade because of the numerous taxes they extracted from merchants. A chief such as Magude of Khosen levied death duties on Banyan merchants, taxed traders, and then resold the goods on his own account. This was a common practice in Gazaland, where the king and his chiefs exercised a strict control over trade.[121] It was common for traders to provide chiefs with gifts, licence fees, and transit, ferry, and shipping taxes, and to extend to them considerable amounts of credit.[122] In this way migrant labour contributed indirectly to the accumulation of the wealth needed by the chiefs and *numzane* to attract a large political following.

The emigration of labour simultaneously threatened to undermine the power of the chiefs and *numzane*. Only powerful rulers such as the Gaza and Maputo chiefs were able to exert a pressure on their followers to return home. In Maputoland permanent emigration reached such a high level in the 1880s that the queen regent sent an embassy to Natal requesting that "the government [make] it compulsory for her subjects to return home after two or three years service as many of them forsake their homes, wives and children and never return."[123] But no colonial government was prepared to oblige migrants to return home, as this would push up wages, deprive the colony of skilled labour, and, in some cases, deprive the government of revenue.

To make matters worse, new diseases threatened to reduce the rural population. Syphilis had existed at Lourenço Marques for many years but only became endemic when carried into the interior by workers returning from the Witwatersrand. Syphilis and gonorrhea proliferated in southern Mozambique with the development of a rootless work force and a growing market for commercialized sex.[124] In 1887 syphilis crossed the Nkomati, entered Khosen, and, within a few years, had spread throughout most of the Delagoa Bay region.[125] Highly infectious, syphilis was greatly feared as it not only led to physical disfigurement and death, but also destroyed female powers of procreation. Gonorrhea was also introduced in the mid- to late 1880s, reportedly at the time of the construction of the Delagoa Bay railway. Because of its effect on the fertility rate, it soon acquired the epithet of "the disease that crushes the villages."[126] With large numbers of young men employed and settling in South Africa, and with venereal diseases raising the incidence of female infertility, the already low population growth rate fell further.[127] The loss of dependents was a serious blow to chiefs and *numzane* who depended on the loyalty and labour power of a small community for their social and political dominance. The threat posed to the elders by the downturn in the birthrate and the emigration of young men should be seen in conjunction with the general shrinkage of the domestic economy and their fragile hold over the bridewealth system. In short, the reproduction of the established relations of dominance and subordination was dependent on the repatriation of the worker and his wage.

The chiefs and *numzane* encouraged their followers to return home in various ways. By dropping the marriage age, the elders pressed youths to become wage-earning adults, anchored them to their rural families, and, ultimately, raised the birthrate. Instead of marrying in their mid-twenties, girls were married increasingly at the age of eleven or twelve and boys when they reached early puberty. At the same time *gangisa*, the traditional form of sexual socialization for adolescents, seems to have been restricted.[128] "It is not uncommon," wrote the Anglican bishop of Lebombo, "for a father to buy a wife for his boy before he has reached the age of puberty. These boys therefore are already provided with wives before they go to the mines."[129] The reduction in the marriage age served to attract adolescent migrants home, as they had experienced the security, respect, affection and sexual gratification of family life and had established a stake in the domestic economy. If a young man was not married when he left for the mines, he had the prospect of receiving a wife or an inheritance from the *numzane* when he returned home.

In a society where the term "recruiter" was synonymous with "swindler" and "perjurer,"[130] the elders played an increasingly important role in controlling the operations of recruiters and looked after the migrant's interests during his absence. In the case of a man going to South Africa without having paid the full *lobola* for his bride, it was expected that she would return to her paternal homestead, as this reduced the chance of her eloping with another man and depriving her father and brothers of her *lobola*. But in most cases a migrant left his wife and family in the charge of his father, his brother, or, if he were old enough, his heir. The protective role extended by the elders to the migrant's homestead came to be known as *basopa*, a word perhaps derived from the Afrikaans or Fanagalo term *pasop*, to watch out. Under this system, the welfare of the migrant's family and property was assured during his stay in South Africa and the man was expected, on his return home, to repay any costs incurred in safeguarding the prosperity of his homestead. An integral part of the emerging *basopa* system was the protection of the migrant's rights to the sexuality and procreativity of his wife.[131] However, here again I am aware of an adjustment in socially accepted patterns of behaviour. By the early twentieth century, it was not uncommon for a miner to return home to find his wife living with another man, in which case it was possible to acquire an automatic divorce and the custody of his children by simply demanding the repayment of her *lobola*. If the wife had given birth to her lover's son, the migrant could claim the boy as his own; if the illegitimate child were a daughter, the husband had the right to her *lobola*.[132] Migrants' attempts to control the sexuality of their wives reached a peak during the First World War, when the high god Murimi supplied them with a snuff capable of eradicating adulterers, witches, and thieves from society. It was also claimed at the time that a man deserted by his spouse needed only invoke the name of Murimi for the errant woman to be returned to him.[133]

During the last two decades of the nineteenth century, migrant labour came to be incorporated into the world view of the peoples of southern Mozambique as a normal part of their lives. This notion was particularly entrenched in the *mentalité* of people who marked the passage of time in the short term by the agricultural seasons and in the long term by the special occasions, such as births, initiations, marriages, and deaths, that measure the social development of the individual. As the novelty of tramping to the mines wore off, and repatriated wages became an important pillar of the local economy, migrant labour was viewed increasingly as a stage in a boy's passage to manhood, and young men were expected to spend time in *xilungu*, the white man's town.[134] Labour recruiters described migrancy as a rite of initiation, and Swiss missionaries viewed it in the same light as the European journeyman's ritual *tour de compagnonnage*.[135] The term *gayisa*, applied to men returning from work, seems to have originated in much the same way as similar forms of identification in Europe. In the Basque and Alpine regions of France, migrants who returned after a long period of residence away from home were called "Parisians," "Lyonnais," or "Americans," people whom the Portuguese labelled "Brazilians," or "Californians."[136] The *gayisa* were those who returned from the land of the *ngisi*, the English, who were called *Ingleses* in Portuguese.[137] In much the same way as the professional hunters and traders of earlier times, the *gayisa* were respected for their wealth, experience, and generosity and were markedly superior in status to men who refused to work on the mines.[138] These latter were denigrated and looked down upon as *mamparas* or inexperienced and ignorant provincials, or as Augusto Cabral remarked, "stupid blockheads who had never seen anything."[139] Men tramping to the mines expressed these ideas forcefully through the gendered imagery in songs such as

> *Nha mae ne xongola*
> *mikuko to sal nimbaa.*
>
> The cocks are going
> and the hens are staying.[140]

But all novice miners were *mamparas* when they arrived on the mines, and it was only on their return home that they could claim the status of *gayisa*.[141] The stories, songs, dances, and dress of the *gayisa* conveyed the miners' experience to both new recruits and home audiences, and names such as Jack, Tom, Sixpence, and Shilling set them apart as men of experience.[142]

The gender socialisation of most young boys on the coastal plain had come to be strongly dominated by their mothers. Extended postpartum rites, polygamy, and a high degree of migrant labour encouraged boys to identify with mothers, whose importance in the homestead was magnified by the absence of adult males. While the father inspired "fear and respect," wrote Junod, he did "not take much trouble with his children." In contrast, the mother-son relationship was "very deep and tender," and fathers often accused their wives of spoiling the children.[143] As the Shangaans in Mozambique did not practice initiation, there was no traumatic break in the emotional control exercised by a mother over her son. Instead, the boy gradually learnt a distinctively male gender role as he graduated, at the age of ten or eleven, from herding goats to looking after his father's cattle. This socialisation continued when, after his first emission of sperm, rites were performed, the boy had his ears pierced, and he was given permission to *gangisa;* the acquisition of a wife in his mid-twenties had traditionally marked the end of a long period of gender socialisation and the attainment of adulthood.[144]

As the marriage age fell in the 1890s and young boys entered the mines in their early teens, the most important phase in the process of learning a masculine identity was shifted from the rural areas to the mines; the boy left home as his mother's child and returned a man. Prohibitions on sexual intercourse during pregnancy and breast-feeding had served as a traditional method of contraception that could last up to eighteen months and even three years.[145] But with the development of migrant labour, men were encouraged to go to South Africa during this period of sexual abstinence. Tramping was institutionalized and incorporated into the local belief structure in songs and stories and through specific "rites of departure," performed by the elders, that offered protection to a young man leaving for the mines.[146] It was likely that the young man would pray at the ancestral altar with his grandfather or father, appease the shades with beer and snuff, and ask one of them to protect him from aggressive, wandering spirits. He was then visited by a diviner who, by throwing the bones, decided whether it was a propitious time to undertake a long journey. The diviner then prepared a number of protective medicines, which he sprayed over the man while praying to both his own and the migrant's ancestors. He invited the ancestors to address the young man through his person and cleansed him of any malefic spells; protective powders were sprinkled on his baggage, he was given talismen to hang around his neck and waist, and was told to refrain from sexual intercourse for the duration of these rituals. It was vital to secure the aid of the ancestors, as they protected the migrant from accidents, disease, and bewitchment, and assured financial success by promising him a well-paid position. These rituals also ensured that, if the young man died far from home, his spirit would enter into the world of the ancestors.[147]

Ritual practices also limited the disruption brought to rural society by the return of young men who had acquired a new status as *gayisa* and a potentially dangerous knowledge of foreign societies and unknown customs. By incorporating migrant labour into social life as a form of initiation, the chiefs and *numzane* normalized what otherwise might have been a disruptive force. Following the same pattern as well-established, local rites of passage, migrant labour was marked by rituals of separation and a period of marginalisation followed by rites of incorporation. Junod related the case of a man who, having returned from the Witwatersrand, had to sit outside the village while his father, squatting at the entrance, cut the neck of a chicken, spattered its blood on the migrant's baggage, and addressed the ancestors.

Here is your son. He has returned home safely because you have accompanied him. Perhaps he has brought back pounds sterling with him to lobola. Perhaps he will now take a wife! I do not know, the great thing is that he is healthy, and you have brought him back safely.[148]

In another account, a migrant who had returned from Kimberley was brought to the clan altar, where the ancestors were offered ritual beer and thanked for his safe return. A few days later quantities of beer were brewed, an ox killed, and further prayers offered to the ancestors.[149] Through these rites the migrant was ritually reincorporated into his home community and system of belief.

While many cadets could look forward to the day when they themselves would become *numzane*, for women the situation was far bleaker. By marrying earlier, they were initiated at a younger age into childbearing and childrearing activities. The adoption of new foods required a greater investment of energy from women in terms of cooking (cassava) and grinding (maize) than the old sorghum staple. With their fathers, husbands, brothers, and sons away on the mines, women had to perform many of the administrative and manual duties formerly undertaken by their menfolk. They were not only obliged to work in the fields, cook, and bring up their children; they had also to open up new fields, construct huts, cut grass and poles, and perform other traditionally male tasks.[150] The new importance of women as producers was reflected in soaring brideprices and a new freedom to marry, but it brought little change in their status.[151]

The subordination of women was deeply embedded in everyday discourse. Proverbs asserted that "women have no court," that their word did not have the same value as that of men, or simply that "marriage makes a man happy."[152] The gendered use of metaphor entrenched this image of womens' inferiority; an old woman was a synonym for cowardice, cocks and *gayisa* were a metaphor for wealth, while *mamparas* were ridiculed as hens, and men without their chiefs were said to be like women.[153] Gendered dictums were common: the chief was "the cock by which the country is sustained," recorded Junod. "He is the bull; without him the cows cannot bring forth. He is the husband; the country without him is like a woman without a husband. He is the man of the village."[154] Men not only refused to accord women the status warranted by their increased role within the domestic economy, they also systematically repressed female sexuality. When the husband handed over his wife's brideprice, he acquired the exclusive rights to her sexuality. Hence a wife was prohibited from entering into extramarital sexual relations, while her husband was encouraged, by custom and precedent, to find other unmarried sexual and marital partners. With the growth of migrant labour, women had to repress their sexual instincts for periods often lasting over two years. "Adultery" was considered the theft of the husband's rights to his wife's sexuality and was punished by the extraction of as much as a full brideprice from the guilty male while the woman was merely chastized. Divorce was even less acceptable than adultery, for it entailed the repayment of the *lobola*, an action that could involve the dissolution of the wife's brother's marriage.[155] Consequently migrant labour increased the workload and responsibility borne by women, while at the same time causing an often severe sexual repression.

It was not only women who suffered a setback as migrant labour became rooted in social practice. The position of the cadets deteriorated as they lost their fathers and elder brothers for long periods, saw their childhood truncated by the hard life of the miner, and, pushed into early marriages, were expected to take on the responsibility of a family. The constant inflation of brideprices paid in sterling obliged men to work for ever-increasing periods far from home and, as the Portuguese spread into the interior, the weight of the hut tax and labour conscription fell particularly heavily on the cadets and women. While the chiefs and *numzane* benefitted from the presents and payments made by the Portuguese to the *regulos* or government chiefs, it was the cadets and women who provided their leaders with the hut tax and *xibalo* paid to the Portuguese. Earlier in this chapter I traced a major cause of the Luso-Gaza wars of 1894–1895 to the social division between chiefs and *numzane* on the one hand and cadets on the other. The conflict between these two groups manifested itself in various other ways, as a general decline in cadet respect for their elders was paralleled by a refusal to wear headrings.[156] Another sign of social upheaval was the growth of widespread alcoholism, as migrants spent their wages on cheap liquor.[157]

Misfortune, Consolation and Explanation

The popularity of new religions was another expression of social change. The Christian Revival brought to the Delagoa Bay region in the early to mid-1880s by Swiss-trained black evangelists did not survive the arrival of the first European missionaries. The first Swiss missionary established himself at Rikatla to the north of Lourenço Marques in July 1887 and immediately set about bringing under his control the Transvaal catechists whose independent interpretation of Christian tenets had sparked off the Revival. But the "correction" of the "aberrations" in the teaching of the revivalists caused large numbers of people to leave the mission.[158] Many found a greater familiarity in the Methodist Church established by Robert Mashaba. In 1893, five years after the establishment of his school and chapel, Mashaba was ordained as a church minister. In the same year he published a *Shironga Vocabulary* and, a little later, a *First Shironga Reader*. Mashaba also started on a number of other books and produced a collection of hymns in what he defined as Ronga, the local language.[159] This posed a particular problem for the Swiss missionaries and their catechists, who, grounded in the Gwamba language of the church in the north-eastern Transvaal, were greeted everywhere as foreigners from the north.[160] Alarmed by the success of his Methodist rivals, Junod published a Ronga reading primer in 1894 and a Ronga grammar in 1896. The following year he published a collection of folktales and songs and, in 1898, a long ethnographic monograph. In this work Junod portrayed the Ronga as a culturally homogeneous group, easily distinguishable from the Gwamba of the Transvaal and the Thonga to the north of the Inkomati River. It was only later that he expanded the Thonga "tribe" to include both the Ronga and what he initially referred to as "the northern clans."[161]

Migrants returned from the mines with a range of intellectual tools and a bricolage of images with which to make sense of the world. On the Witwatersrand they had taken on additional identities as Christians, *gayisa* migrant mine workers, literate members of a compound community, members of an ethnic group, and even, perhaps, as Mozambicans. As their world expanded, many men moved from communicating with ancestors, who were associated with the narrow physical world of the clan and chiefdom, and gave a new value to the Supreme Being whose powers, although distant and vague, were not constrained by kinship and geography.[162] Until the defeats of the mid-1890s, the Christianity purveyed by the Swiss had largely attracted marginalized members of society.[163] But defeat on the battlefield was accompanied by an equally severe spiritual collapse, as the ancestors seemed powerless to stop the climatic excesses, the plagues of locusts, the rinderpest, or the exactions of the Portuguese.[164] The number of students attending the Swiss mission night school in Lourenço Marques soared in October 1895, on the eve of the Gaza defeat, as people showed a sudden and seemingly inexplicable interest in the Supreme Being of the Christians and in the skills of literacy. Even more novel was the growing size of church collections, as people paid for the security and power offered by a new religion.[165] To the beleaguered missionaries, whose chapels were suddenly overflowing, it seemed that "the sufferings of the war had favourably disposed the hearts" of the people to Christianity.[166] But this wave of conversion was as much the result of a need for consolation as it was the product of a desire for a new or adapted, and in many cases supplementary, system of belief. Perhaps most importantly, this "second wave of evangelisation," as it has been called by Charles Biber, was sustained, strengthened, and finally spread beyond the confines of the mission stations by Christian converts returning from the mines.[167] But, as the Comaroffs have reminded us, Christianity is not synonymous with conversion.[168] In Southern Mozambique concepts such as hell's fire, a punitive God, and monogamy, along with what one minister called "all symptoms of church wisdom," had spread for many years by migrants returning from South Africa.[169] The defeat of the chiefs, who formed the focal point of local folk religions and social relations, created a new demand for a system of knowledge and power capable of explaining and controlling the expanded political and social space in which people lived. Christianity in southern Mozambique was planted by miners returning home with vague ideas of the gospel; it was fertilized by the arrival of converts and consolidated by the labours of isolated evangelists.[170] Much of the early work undertaken by the Swiss Presbyterian, independent Methodist, and newly established Anglican missionaries was aimed at sustaining the ideas brought home by migrants and, particularly, at supporting and keeping alive the various communities founded by Christian miners in southern Mozambique.

Christian miners frequently acquired a modicum of literacy on the Witwatersrand and returned home to establish schools, often with the encouragement of local chiefs, where they conducted religious meetings, preached, baptised, and converted friends and relatives.[171] A knowledge of the tenets and principles of Christianity, together with a basic literacy, spread with the cheap English and Zulu Bibles carried home from the mines. Other migrants applied reading skills acquired in the mine compounds to the Gwamba *buku* or the Ronga works of Mashaba and Junod. The "second wave of evangelisation" was different from the revival of the early to mid-1880s; it was conducted by important people, male migrant workers, and was associated with the skills of literacy. After the Portuguese victories of 1894–1895, Christianity rapidly lost its stigma as an ideology of the marginalized and acquired the status of a discourse of power. The Swiss missionaries sought to fertilize the seeds of Christianity implanted by migrant workers by sending evangelists north of the Limpopo to Bilene. They also spread southwards to establish ties with a migrant converted on the Witwatersrand, named Likhapeni, who had started to preach in Maputoland. On the Maputo border with Swaziland, they entered into contact with Jothan Khatwane and his friend Thomas, both of whom had been converted at Pretoria. By 1895 these two men had gathered around them twenty-six converts and two hundred adherents interested in Christianity or wanting to attend school.[172] The gradual growth of Christian communities received an enormous impetus when the Anglo-Boer War broke out in October 1899 and a wave of sixty thousand miners returned home in one month. A large number of these men were converts whose energy fanned the embers of faith in many corners of Southern Mozambique.[173] The European missionaries had a fixed image of black Christians, demanding a respect for punctuality, sobriety, and the virtues of disciplined labour.[174] The inflexibility of their views on the cultural content of conversion nudged many people towards what many Europeans viewed as syncretic religions. Imported from the Transvaal or emerging locally, these forms of Christianity were imbued with a deep respect for local traditions.

Elements of Christian teaching were sometimes appropriated to bolster the power of local eradiction cults. In late 1897, diviners in the lands west of Delagoa Bay blamed famine, war, locusts, and rinderpest on ancestors who had been offended by their descendents; the only way to propitiate the shades, they declared, was to refuse to work on Sundays. Christians on the mines and elsewhere had for many years linked rituals such as Sunday observance, hard work, and the prohibition of liquor to the moral and material improvement of society. From this perspective, ritual was a source of power and the observance of Sunday as a day of rest was a means of appropriating the strength associated with Christianity, the religion of the white conquerors. People besieged by misfortune grasped at this new source of power and, for some months, and in the face of Portuguese opposition, the sabbatarian movement enjoyed a growing following.[175] But propitiation of an angry body of ancestors was only one of a series of mechanisms used to explain adversity and alleviate misfortune. In various areas cults flared up, as the elders promised to eradicate evil if their followers propitiated the ancestors by slaughtering their goats, fowls, and dogs.[176] At the same time there was a significant rise in witchcraft accusations, as people turned to diviners to smell out the *baloyi* who were at the root of their misfortune.[177] It is difficult for those of us brought up within the constraints of Western logic and reasoning to grasp the extent to which fear was embedded in the psyche of the people of southern Mozambique. The unpredictability of climate and disease, mine accidents, plagues of insects and invaders, and the extortions of rulers rendered life tenuous indeed. In a society equipped with little notion of the scientific laws of nature, these constant upheavals were frequently explained in terms of supernatural agency. As much as people feared the capriciousness of the visible world, they equally feared the unpredictability of the supernatural world. By propitiating the ancestors, they were able to intercede with the forces influencing the human condition.

While the ancestors generally became angry and malevolent only when provoked by actions such as the failure to adhere to local customs, the *baloyi* practitioners of black magic were motivated by purely negative sentiments of hatred and jealousy. Witchcraft explained why some individuals or communities prospered while others suffered, and offered a remedy for the misfortunes made visible by disparities in wealth and fortune. Once diviners had traced the cause of the problem to black magic, the *baloyi* or witches were smelt out or uncovered by means of a magic potion. In this way the blame for conflict within small-scale societies was removed from human agency and ascribed to the evil influence of the antisocial *baloyi*, who could hardly be classed as clan members. As colonialism challenged the accepted givens and certainties of preindustrial society, and as young men returned from the mines to confront their elders with a new wealth and confidence, the number of witchcraft accusations soared. Seen in terms of the web of local beliefs, the disputes causing the dissolution and dispersion of the old homesteads of up to thirty huts were the product of witchcraft rather than a heightened level of conflict between cadets and *numzane*. The tenacity with which many people clung to a belief in the ancestors, even after the defeats suffered at the hands of the Portuguese and the removal of their chiefs, also served to render new and disturbing changes comprehensible and normal.

Spirit Possession and the Marginalisation of Women

The growth and spread of spirit possession in the 1890s was perhaps the most spectacular sign of social upheaval. The notion that the body could be possessed physically by foreign spirits seems to have emerged in the Delagoa Bay region in the 1860s. The intellectual origins of this new belief can probably be traced to the Zulu/Ngoni concept of a possessing ancestral spirit and, perhaps, contact with the Christian notion of demoniacal possession.[178] The earliest foreign spirits to take possession of people in the Delagoa Bay area were picked up, Junod postulated, by young men passing through Zululand on their way to Natal and Kimberley. When the migrant worker returned home, the Zulu spirit entered the body of another, generally female, member of the community. A later and more powerful possessing spirit came from the lands north of the Sabie River where the destitute spirits of Ndau who had died at the hands of Gaza soldiers invested the bodies of their killers' descendents. These *ndiki* spirits were carried south in 1889 when Gungunyana moved his capital to the lower Limpopo. Four years later the disease was diagnosed by the Swiss missionary doctor at Mandlakazi, George Liengme, as hysteria.[179]

Ndiki spirit possession took an epidemic form and spread rapidly south of the Limpopo, entering Swaziland, northern Zululand, and, probably, the eastern and northern Transvaal.[180] The belief in *ndiki* was also carried to the mines, where the frequency of death and the ritual impurity of burial produced a plethora of uneasy and displaced spirits awaiting incorporation into the world of the ancestors.[181] Miners often served as unsuspecting vectors for these rootless shades by spreading them in the compounds and carrying them back to their rural homes.[182] The symptoms displayed by *ndiki* were clearly similar to those marking the hysteria epidemics sweeping through much of the industrialized world in the late nineteenth century.

Spirit possession, like hysteria, was largely confined to women.[183] Its characteristic symptoms were a persistent pain in the chest or side, consistent weight loss for no apparent reason, swollen and distended legs, and noisy and continuous hiccuping or frequent and unusual yawning. Fits of aggression, in which the afflicted person would indiscriminately beat people around her, were accompanied by bouts of amnesia.[184] A bone-thrower (*babula*) had to diagnose the cause of the problem as either physical, in which case a doctor (*nanga*) was called, or due to witchcraft, which rerquired the attention of a person skilled in smelling out (*xi-nusa*). If the patient's ailments were traced to the ancestors, a diviner (*mungoma*) was called; but if a possessing spirit was held responsible, an exorcist or *gobela* was summoned to treat the disease. The exorcism of the spirit was performed by initiates of the cult under the direction of the *gobela*. These people, who themselves had once been possessed by a spirit, joined the local villagers in an attempt to persuade the spirit to expose itself. The object of the ceremony, which included drumming, incantations, and offerings, was not to drive away the spirit but to enter into a dialogue with it and harness its powers. The ultimate aim of the ceremony was to convert hostile forces into benevolent ones, and it was hoped that the male or female spirit or spirits could be persuaded to assist rather than torment the person it had possessed.

As the "lord of the spirit," a medium was invested with supernatural powers of healing and detection. The exorcism ceremony was marked by rites of initiation, including the symbolic washing of a patient and a long period of sexual abstinence. After a period of apprenticeship with the *gobela*, the initiate acquired the skill and knowledge needed to cure afflictions that, by incapacitating their victims, disturbed social harmony and curtailed productivity. Initiates became skilled in creating charms, amulets, and medicines, and in performing rites that provided protection against the *baloyi*. They entered into a special, individual communion with their spirits that was closer and more powerful than the relationship with the ancestors. An initiate who showed special powers of prophesy or other aspects of white magic could become a *gobela* or even a diviner, while rank-and-file initiates entered guilds whose leaders were often women. The members of these guilds were widely respected for their supernatural powers.

What is less clear is the reason for the growth of these possession cults at the end of the nineteenth century.[185] As in other parts of Africa, epidemics of spirit possession in southern Mozambique may be related to the tensions produced by rapid changes in the "normal" flow of life. By the end of the century, large-scale migrant labour had increased the domestic workload of women and subjected them to new levels of psychological stress. Not only were they required to take on more responsibility within the home and to undertake tasks that did not conform to the accepted propriety of their sex; they were also forced into sexual asceticism and a state of insecurity provoked by the fear that the male members of the homestead would stop remitting money or fail altogether to return home. Yet while the physical and mental pressure on women increased, they became more dependent on the wages earned by males for access to imported commodities, and even, through the purchase of food, for the reproduction of the household. While males earned increasing amounts of money in South Africa, women were squeezed from cash-producing activities by the fall in the profitability of local exports and by their increased role in the subsistence sector. This shift in the sexual division of labour had a profound effect on gender relations. Concepts of female worth, defined both subjectively and objectively, suffered a relative decline and patriarchal authority was increased, at a time when women were required to shoulder a heavier load within the domestic economy. As there were no accepted social conduits for the tensions generated by this gender conflict, feelings of aggression harboured by women had to be suppressed. Women were trapped within a culture that, in a contradictory manner, required both obedience and a commanding strength. Unable to express their powerful libidinal and aggressive sentiments, women manifested their dissatisfaction, in a way that was not consciously admissible, through the medium of a possessing spirit. And in so doing, they protested actively and sometimes violently against their situation, while retaining an essential passivity. It was the foreign spirit, and not the person possessed by the spirit, who was responsible for attacking people with her ceremonial axe or invective. Initiates were also able to express some of the thoughts and feelings, not admissible to their consciousness, in songs decrying the shabby treatment they received from their husbands.[186]

The etiology of spirit possession in southern Mozambique might, I believe, bear comparison with Jan Goldstein's description of hysteria in Europe. The latter was "a protest," he writes, "made in the flamboyant yet encoded language of the body by women who had so thoroughly accepted that value system that they could neither admit their discontent to themselves nor narrow it in the more readily comprehensible language of words."[187] Spirit possession was both a protest, made by women against their disadvantaged position and powerlessness, and a means of exercising emotional control within the family. The foreign spirit was a metaphor for the new and alien forces that had destabilized society but that, if correctly propitiated and controlled, could be of benefit to the community. To harness the forces of the spirit, the homestead head had to show his concern for the "victim" by purchasing the services of an exorcist, and the recovery of the woman was won at the cost of establishing a more positive relationship between her and the spirit. In achieving a cure for the woman, the male had to accept her new status and power as an initiate of a spirit possession cult. Membership of this cult provided women and disadvantaged males with an alternative political structure that was, at once, a mutual aid group and an arena for individual advancement. Thus, while accusations of witchcraft revitalized traditional power structures, by calling on diviners and chiefs to protect the community from the *baloyi*, the new spirit possession guilds grouped together marginalized people unable to exert an influence on the centres of power. While the fight against witchcraft reasserted a basic conservatism, spirit possession allowed a controlled experimentation. It was noticed, for instance, that several of the women who had joined the Christian Revival movement in the early to mid-1880s were members of possession guilds and that they had been brought to the new religion by their spirits.[188] But while the spirit possession guilds provided a greater freedom of action, they did not challenge the basic structure of society; they were an institutionalised means of coping with an oppressive situation rather than a mechanism of resistance opposed to the increasing domination of males.

By the end of the nineteenth century, there was an increase in the fission of households from homesteads.[189] In areas like Lourenço Marques, the established structure of society started to dissolve, as cadets and women asserted their independence, preferential endogamous marriage patterns broke down, and women married to wealthy merchants in the town purchased Chopi slaves.[190] Some widows were able further to build up their own personal following by contracting marriages with outsiders who, because they were unable to supply a brideprice, surrendered their rights of filiation to their wives' deceased husbands' kin.[191] But for marginalized members of society perhaps the most effective response to an oppressive situation was to emigrate permanently to South Africa. For males at least, a less drastic option was to work for wages until sufficient money had been earned or inherited to establish an independent homestead. In strictly material terms, migrant labour brought about a general rise in the standard of living in pre-colonial southern Mozambique. Benefits were unequally distributed and tended to reflect and reinforce the existing *status quo*, as the chiefs and *numzane* appropriated an increasingly large part of the earnings brought home by the cadets. For many young men their period of wage labour was merely a long-term investment, for one day they themselves would rise to become *numzane*. Others remained cadets all their lives, as their ascribed position excluded them from the ranks of the *numzane*. These impoverished dependents, or young sons of junior wives and slave concubines, could only improve their position by working in South Africa. Their standard of living was affected by migrant labour in much the same way as was that of women; while it gave them a more secure access to food, wage labour imposed on them a heavier and more demanding workload. Although wages provided people with a powerful weapon in the daily struggle against the forces of nature, the ability of migrant labour to stimulate long-term development was more dubious. When workers returned home, a large part of their savings was soon encapsulated in a circulating bridewealth system, and much of what remained flowed into the pockets of merchants who channelled gold out of Mozambique. Nor did the policies of metropolitan Portugal encourage grass roots development, as Lisbon was more concerned with stimulating consumerism and the export of labour, both of which were highly taxable, than with protecting and developing the colonial economy. After the final subjugation of the independent chiefdoms, the Portuguese were able to exert a firm grip over the labour-supply areas. The product of that grip was the flow of workers into South Africa under the labour agreement of November 1897. Portuguese colonialism was drastically to alter the nature of migrant labour from Mozambique.

7

Colonialism and Migrant Labour

Nature seemed to smile favourably on the first years of colonial rule. Rinderpest had decimated the ungulate vectors of the *morsitans* species of tsetse fly and had almost ridded Southern Mozambique of trypanosomiasis. The export of agricultural produce from Gazaland was encouraged by the large number of traders entering Gungunyana's old kingdom, and by the construction of a rudimentary economic infrastructure.[1] The regular subsistence crises were softened by the importation of food, and, when a serious drought descended on southern Mozambique in 1902–1903, the amount of maize brought through Lourenço Marques increased five-fold.[2] A certain ecological stability then settled on the region, and it was only in 1908 that the cycle of bad times returned when the crops failed and locusts reappeared. In 1910 the recovery of the cattle herds, always rendered fragile by the depredations of tax collectors, suffered a severe setback when Texas fever broke out and the Portuguese, in an attempt to arrest the spread of the disease, slaughtered the surviving beasts. In 1911 and 1913 drought resulted in famine, and people fell back on mineworkers' wages in an attempt to avoid starvation.[3] Hunger continued to push migrants to the Transvaal. "If the families had the means to sustain themselves," wrote the Portuguese curator in Johannesburg, "their able-bodied men would not abandon them to work in the Transvaal, where they know they are subject to hardships, die crushed by stones, buried by rock falls, blinded by explosions or asphyxiated by silicosis."[4] Ecological instability continued into the twentieth century, but the spread of colonialism subjected the peoples of southern Mozambique to what was essentially yet another plague—the colonizers.

Xibalo, Taxes, and Wine

In the years before the Luso-Gaza war of 1894–1895, the severity of *xibalo* had been restricted by the limited local need for labour and by the unwillingness of the Portuguese to antagonize their African allies. Once they had conquered southern Mozambique, the Portuguese were held back by no such constraints, and in November 1899 blacks were made subject to the "moral and legal obligation" to work for the state or private individuals. The duration of the *xibalo* was normally about one month and official wages were set at $80 per day for field work and $200 for porterage. The forced labour decree of 1899 was altered, adapted, and abused in various ways. It became common practice for *xibalo* labourers to work for contractors, who profited from their services by hiring them out to private employers. Children were obliged to work for civil servants, and women were pressed into forced labour, particularly as a means of getting their menfolk to come out of hiding and report for *xibalo*.[5] Forced labourers were employed on a large scale by the government in road construction and cleaning, stone-breaking, porterage, on the railways, and in the harbour. Men were also forced to work for white landowners and to serve as carriers for merchants or travellers.[6] As Jeanne Penvenne has graphically illustrated, Lourenço Marques' prosperous façade was built by forced labour drawn from throughout southern Mozambique.[7] But while *xibalo* was heartily disliked, military service was regarded with a dread that bordered on terror, as it resulted in the expatriation of individuals for much longer periods of time. Conscripts frequently failed to return home at all, and if they did, it was with very little to show for their years of service.[8] The Swiss missionaries frequently commented on the profound sense of fear and insecurity that pervaded Southern Mozambique as the seizure of men for forced labour and military service became institutionalized. "In January the authorities conducted a razzia in the villages," wrote Paul Berthoud from Lourenço Marques in 1899, "and kidnapped 600 men to create a police force on the West Coast, taking fathers from their wives and children, who were then left without protection."[9] Towards the end of that year he wrote that

> The evening schools still suffer, from time to time, from panics. All goes well for weeks, perhaps even months then suddenly one learns that the razzias have started again, that masses of men and young people have been kidnapped by the police and taken away for ever; then everyone hides, and they sleep in the bush.[10]

Henri Berthoud perhaps best conveyed the popular perception of Lourenço Marques when he described it as "an enemy town where one runs the risk of being plucked and exported like a piece of common merchandise."[11] A more influential voice of protest was raised by native administrators who saw the razzias sour their relations with the local population and strip the area of taxpayers and able-bodied workers.[12] Governor-general Freire d'Andrade considered *xibalo* "an industry in reality exercised by various individuals who draw benefit from it at the cost of the blacks, whom they frequently do not pay"; he attempted to curb its worst abuses in December 1906 by restricting *xibalo* to government departments.[13] But the implementation of this decree was blocked in the rural areas by the beneficiaries of *xibalo*: a network of chiefs, policemen, and employers. In the Manhica district in 1911–1912, of a population of about eight thousand able-bodied adult males, some thirteen hundred were employed under forced labour.[14]

The demand for *xibalo* workers and conscripts grew with the development of the region. In 1908 Henri Junod remarked on the increasing sophistication of the methods used to press-gang young men into military service

> The Portuguese have again started to catch young people and men in order to conscript them into their African armies in Angola and Mozambique. Formerly they would raid around Lourenço Marques—now the

administrators in the interior simply order the small chiefs to furnish them with x amount of men. Black policemen accompany the chief's envoys and they merely take the individuals indicated. They are told it is only for forced labour. But at the police station the old are sent home and the young are locked up. They will be sent off in a few days time—where to or for how long, they do not know. As most of those who had been apprehended in the same way in previous years have never returned, these arrests are the equivalent of a life service in the eyes of the natives, which is for them an intolerable idea.[15]

The desperation of two of these young men at being conscripted led them to disable themselves for military service by amputating their index fingers at the last joint. It was common for people to try and escape military service by bribing the police and indunas with money and livestock or by unofficially buying themselves out of the army. Others deserted, but at great cost, for they had often to travel thousands of miles to get home.[16]

These actions indicate the degree to which young men abhorred serving in the colonial army. But in general we have little access to the perceptions of the colonized. A snapshot is provided by A. W. Baker, who, during an evangelical tour of southern Mozambique in 1899, frequently employed a picture of the crucifixion to illustrate his lectures. A certain amount of secular symbolism was not lost on the missionary when one of his auditors cried out "I know who crucified him—the Portuguese!"[17] The same sentiment infused a song overheard by Augusto Cabral,

The whites killed Gungunyana because he was bad *but the whites are no better.*[18]

In 1904 Junod recorded the following "plaintive, sad and resigned" lament of boatsmen on the Nkomati:

They believed in Gungounyane
Mahazoule, and Nuamantibyane
They dared to kill some whites
They have been defeated
They fought for a long time
And now forced labour has fallen on me
It has fallen on me
forced labour.[19]

Another song, recorded in the Chopi area, conveyed some of the sense of fear, vulnerability, and disorientation felt by black women during the early years of colonialism. They had become dependent on the wages of males in the family to pay the hut tax and buy food and clothing. Hence the disappearance of a husband or son into the colonial army or the *xibalo* gangs threatened women with arrest for tax evasion, as well as with the loss of their livelihood and security:

The commandant ordered Nandelo to go and catch the women and throw them in the prison.
They have killed my husband and where is the money that made up my brideprice?[20]

Other songs, representing the precolonial period as a golden age, formed an implicit critique of society under Portuguese rule.[21] But perhaps the most telling denunciation of Portuguese colonial rule was the swelling current of people leaving southern Mozambique. During the late 1880s and early 1890s, the native policy of the Republican government in the Transvaal had pushed numbers of people to move eastwards into Gungunyana's empire. But the Portuguese conquest of the Gaza and their allies reversed this migration. Administrators frequently remarked that at the first signs of a razzia, many young men would retreat into the forests or into uninhabited, dry bushland areas and, if the harsh exactions of xibalo and conscription did not abate, entire families would move across the border into the Transvaal or British Amatongaland.[22] Another common and frequently remarked-on response to the pressgangs was for men to seek refuge on the Transvaal gold mines. "The natives of this district emigrate to the Transvaal on a large scale," reported the administrator of the Guija circumscription in 1912, "especially when the period of recruiting approaches, with the result that at this time, it becomes difficult to get half a dozen able-bodied men for military service."[23] "This system of forced conscription causes much harm," remarked Junod after the razzias of 1908. "At the moment the entire male population is sleeping in the swamps at night in order to avoid being arrested, and many are leaving for the Transvaal."[24] Many also delayed their return home as long files of workers trudging home, weighed down by goods bought on the Rand, and even men alighting from trains, constituted easy targets for the xibalo pressgangs.[25] It was also possible for xibalo workers to find themselves shanghaied to Lourenço Marques and then contracted to work on a Witwatersrand mine. The venality of Portuguese officials at Inhambane was well known; on at least one occasion, they sent xibalo workers to unpopular collieries in Vereeneging.[26]

By the late 1890s xibalo, conscription, and emigration had become intimately linked in a continually reinforcing spiral; the more labour the gold mines drew from Mozambique, the more Portugal, a weak colonial power, was compelled to rely on cheap, compulsory labour. But forced labour also served to push increasing numbers of men to South Africa where, as "volunteers," they could earn far higher wages than at home. While this drained Mozambique of labour, it provided the government with a durable source of income, as most of the provisions of the 1897 labour agreement were incorporated into the Anglo-Portuguese modus vivendi of December 1901. Under this agreement the Portuguese succeeded in increasing the passport fee paid by each worker from 7s6d to 13s. Secondly, by formally linking the number of Mozambicans employed in the mines to the amount of Transvaal traffic passing through Lourenço Marques, they retained the old preferential tariff structure and the prewar volume of goods handled at the port. Under the agreement, twenty truckloads of goods entered the Transvaal each day in exchange for an annual total of thirty thousand recruits; and for every additional ten thousand workers sent to the Transvaal, five trucks were added to the daily trains leaving Lourenço Marques. This served as a strong inducement to the Portuguese to manipulate the flow of migrant labour. Forced labour was also of direct benefit to the Transvaal mining industry, as it killed the old, discretionary migrant labour and drove men to "volunteer" to work on the Witwatersrand. This was viewed in a positive light by employers in the Transvaal; just as their predecessors had "saved" Mozambicans from slavery and famine, employers believed that wage labour "rescued" workers from the xibalo exactions and military conscription of the Portuguese.[27]

The hut tax also forced men onto the labour market. After the defeat of Gungunyana, the hut tax was raised from 6s to 10s and extended into the conquered

FIGURE 2.   Hut Tax From Southern Mozambique[30]

Years	LM dist	Gaza dist	Inham dist	Total
1897–1898	34,290$	29,147$	297,106$	360,543$
1898–1899	38,526$	77,674$	278,193$	394,393$
1899–1900	57,136$	95,150$	300,361$	452,647$
1900–1901	28,054$	44,760$	184,016$	256,830$
1901–1902	66,953$	7,734$	196,921$	271,608$
1902–1903	68,937$	1,329$	286,327$	356,593$
1903–1904	77,577$	100,232$	344,248$	522,057$
1904–1905	176,066$	117,280$	368,586$	661,932$
1905–1906	143,206$	190,932$	355,560$	689,698$
1906–1907	161,297$	308,622$	373,638$	843,557$
1907–1908	168,744$	433,856$	644,919$	1247,519$

areas. Between 1897–1898 and 1906–1907, the amount of hut tax gathered in southern Mozambique more than doubled, from £87,643 to £187,457. The money brought home by migrant workers was channelled directly into these payments, a situation reflected by the 40 percent drop in hut tax receipts that occurred when workers were forced to abandon the mines during the Anglo-Boer War. The provenance of the hut tax was clear to Augusto Cabral when he wrote in 1910 that "the government lives from emigration and the hut tax."[28] It was also clear to a mother who exclaimed to Cabral, when informed that her two sons had died in the Transvaal, "and now I have no-one to pay the hut tax!"[29] Beneath what the Portuguese official saw as the callousness of this remark was the despair of a woman who would have to throw herself on the mercy of her relatives.

After the Anglo-Boer War the hut tax was extracted with growing efficiency and was increasingly paid in gold.[31] As is reflected in Figure 2 above, the Portuguese were initially more successful in gathering the hut tax in the densely populated coastal areas around Inhambane than in newly conquered Gazaland. The manner in which the hut tax was collected was often brutal, for soldiers continued to be paid out of the money extracted from the population.[32] In 1908 the hut tax was doubled to 20s, an increase initially largely restricted to Inhambane, as this district was furthest removed from the border and offered less opportunity for the disaffected to emigrate. The jump in the hut tax pushed a fresh wave of workers to the Transvaal, which in turn secured a rise in the amount of Witwatersrand traffic passing through Lourenço Marques. By 1914, the Portuguese were strong enough to demand a hut tax of 22s6d in many areas.[33]

The common response of those unwilling or unable to pay tax was to hide from its collectors, but this became increasingly difficult as the chiefs were drawn into the colonial system of control.[34] After the wars of 1894–1897, the Portuguese broke up many of the larger chiefdoms and exiled their leaders, some of whom returned home in early 1902 in the police uniforms that were to symbolize the duality of their new role in the colonial state.[35] They were no longer allowed to raid, hold slaves, or impose heavy sentences in the tribal courts, but they were permitted to demand and keep fines paid in sterling.[36] The chiefs retained much of their customary and ritual power and added a monetary tax, of about 4s, to the annual basket of maize paid by each homestead.[37] Their powers of land distribution were generally not undermined, as southern Mozambique attracted few settlers until the 1950s. However, in some fertile riverine areas the indigenous population was expelled or transformed into labour tenants.[38] But while the chiefs retained some of their prewar powers, they were required to serve as paid state functionaries who performed policing duties, helped collect the hut tax, and furnished the army with conscripts. In many cases, if a man deserted from a forced labour contingent, a member of his family or the chief would be punished in his stead. It was also common practice to fine, or in extreme cases, to replace or exile a rebellious chief.[39] Caught between loyalty to his followers and the demands of the state, the position of the chief as protector of his people became highly ambiguous, and it became common for men and boys to seek refuge from conscription, xibalo, and the hut tax on the Witwatersrand.[40]

Men were also pressured to work on the mines by a growing consumerism, most notably a demand for Portuguese wine. The sharp rise in the tariff on imported spirits in 1892 had created a protected market for metropolitan wines. As the price of distilled liquor rose, imports fell off sharply and by 1902 were valued at less than £500. In that year the Portuguese attempted to quash the last vestiges of a competitive market by prohibiting the manufacture of all distilled and fermented brews in the colony. Although they soon relaxed the interdiction on bukanye beer and a weak sorghum beer, women brewers were frequently fined and imprisoned.[41] As metropolitan wine replaced gins and brandies, Portugal became, for the first time, the largest supplier of Mozambican imports. The popularity of the vinous concoction sold as vinho para pretos was in large measure secured by its low price; colonial wine was sold by wholesalers at about 6d per litre and retailed to the public at less than 11d.[42] The popularity of colonial wine was partly due to its cheapness and strength; but it was also the result of a sophisticated distribution network. Protective tariffs and a low tax of just over £2 levied on "third class taverns" encouraged the proliferation of canteens. These structures, often consisting of only a few sheets of zinc and two or three barrels of wine, mushroomed wherever people gathered; at crossroads, drifts, labour recruitment camps, villages, and towns. Between 1896 and 1906, the number of licensed canteens in Lourenço Marques grew from eighty-two to perhaps over one thousand, with almost fourteen hundred in the outlying parts of the district, about one canteen for every fifty individuals. The ratio was considerably lower in the Gaza district, where 1,563 canteens served a population of about 220,000.[43] The retailers scattered throughout the countryside diffused wine even further by selling carafes to individuals who hawked drink by the glassful. Wine was absorbed into the fabric of society through this capillary of retail outlets; it was employed as a libation and often replaced beef, made scarce by epidemics and tax collectors, in social rituals and festivals.[44]

During the Anglo-Boer War, the amount of colonial wine flooding into the Lourenço Marques district fell sharply, as the fighting ended emigration and sliced the buying power of families dependent on migrant workers' wages. But by 1905 almost 10 million litres of wine were shipped through the town, more than three times the volume imported before the war. The prohibition on the manufacture and importation of spirits had an even more marked effect at Inhambane, where distilling was an important economic activity. The volume of wine imported through the settlement almost trebled between 1902 and 1903 and doubled yet again over the next two years, to reach 557,000 litres in 1905. In the same year, about 4 million litres was shipped into the Gaza district through Xai Xai, a village on the lower Limpopo that had grown into a bustling commercial centre.[45] The wine trade acted as both an agent of proletarianization, in that a heightened consumerism pulled men onto the labour market, and as a means of channeling migrants' wages to the metropole. The complaints of missionaries and administrators who attacked the "deadly influence of the canteen" that "constitutes the most pernicious agent of physical and moral deprivation," were brushed aside by the powerful viticultural lobby in Lisbon.[46] By 1909, Mozambique absorbed some 43 percent of Portuguese wine exports.[47]

An integral part of Lisbon's strategy was to impose heavy duties on goods imported on foreign ships from areas outside the Portuguese empire. This policy successfully replaced distilled liquor with Portuguese wine, but, as it also suppressed other imports, it restricted the range of goods available in Mozambique and encouraged migrants to purchase durable goods on the Witwatersrand. The owners of the poorly capitalized but ubiquitous canteens had little money to spare on expensive imported goods like wire, knives, and mirrors, that men could obtain more cheaply in the Transvaal. Despite a growing buying power, there was a fall in the purchase of even cotton cloth, once the most popular item of purchase in southern Mozambique, in the face of competition from cheap colonial wine.[48] In the Inhambane district, where wine was unfamiliar to the local palate, the Portuguese imposed *vinho para pretos* on reluctant consumers with such force that, in the space of four months in 1906, some 885 brewers were arrested and four hundred stills dismantled.[49] But the suppression of the production of distilled liquor merely reduced the range of articles consumers were prepared to buy. Agriculturalists in the Inhambane district responded to the narrowing of the range of goods available for sale locally by cutting back on the production of saleable crops by 15 percent between 1897 and 1906. Consumers, rather than turn to wine, increasingly purchased their requirements in the Transvaal. After the opening of the railway between Johannesburg and Lourenço Marques in January 1895, men were able to cart home heavy trunks packed with items bought cheaply on the Rand, ship them up the coast to Xai Xai and Inhambane, and headload them overland to their homes.[50] In 1906 the governor of Inhambane estimated that mine workers returned to his district alone with goods worth £120,000 every year.[51] On the Rand Mozambicans were "reputed to be the largest purchasers of store goods" and "rather spendthrift," as they handed over between a third and a half of their monthly wages to local storekeepers, fully twice the amount spent by other migrant workers.[52]

Consuming Wages

There was a marked difference between the scale of mercantile enterprise on the Witwatersrand and in Southern Mozambique. In the Portuguese colony the canteens were reduced to selling large amounts of wine, a few dyed or stamped cloths, and little else. On the Witwatersrand well-stocked shops, catering specifically to black migrants, grew up next to the compounds, in the towns along the Reef, and on the main footpaths leading home. Men travelling by rail to or from Johannesburg were offered an array of goods at each stop. When they alighted in Johannesburg, they were harassed and cajoled by merchants selling glittering watches, razors, ostentatious mirrors, brightly coloured neckties, polished brass rings, knives, pipes, and "a thousand and one" other articles. By 1918 there were almost a thousand stores on mine properties, the annual turnover of which amounted to over £1 million. Here, the Portuguese curator of natives remarked, the "Kafir truck" reached "extraordinary proportions."[53] Only the mines closest to the mining villages and towns did not have at least one general dealer on mine property for whom black mineworkers presented an enormous consumer market. Under a system whose roots can be traced back to the early days at Kimberley, Mozambicans demanded to be paid in gold sovereigns, which they kept in money belts fastened around the waist or upper arm and which they never took off.[54] Miners invariably bargained with storekeepers over the price of goods displayed on their shelves. Most storekeepers extended credit to Mozambicans and kept their purchases in locked trunks at the back of the shop. At the end of his contract, the miner settled his remaining debt and left for home with his trunk.[55] Some miners kept their boxes in their sleeping quarters, but this was difficult as there was little space in the dormitories and the trunks were subject to the unwelcome attention of thieves. Independent hawkers also frequented the vicinity of the compounds, vending their wares from small barrows. If a miner could not acquire what he wanted from the local general dealer or the hawkers, he made his way to the neighbouring villages and towns where retailers packed their shops with "Kafir truck." Whites often ridiculed or were baffled by the purchases of migrant workers. To Portuguese administrators, miners from the East Coast wasted their money in spending 20s on leather boots, worn without socks and often without trousers, that were discarded within days of returning home. Frock coats and especially waistcoats and smoking jackets were often worn without a shirt; hats and bonnets were popular, as were canes and umbrellas. Men who could not write or tell the time bought pens and nickel and silver watches.[56]

Europeans and colonials, who had a different system of values, could not comprehend how these objects fitted into the migrants' conception of the world. To the miner returning home, these articles were symbols of his success; they had been luxuries to his parents and many had been unknown to his grandparents. In the rural areas, watches and pens were symbols of an acquired knowledge and of the power that accompanied new concepts of time and writing.[57] European clothing that was rare and exotic at home marked a man as a *gayisa*, and exotic pomades and oils replaced local animal fats and *mafura* as a body cleanser. A man was imbued with the quality of *vugayisa* for as long as he was seen to have returned from work. An analysis made of the trunks of ten Mozambican workers indicates that their buying patterns were determined as much by questions of symbol and status as by practical concerns. The average value of the trunks' contents amounted to just under £10. Over three-quarters of this sum was spent on knives, boots, cloth, and blankets, the diversity and cheapness of which could not be matched in Mozambique. The presence of table knives and spoons, bedspreads and table cloths, brushes and combs, vests, waistcoats, shirts, jackets, socks, and belts suggest a new comportment. Most of the men had bought mirrors and knives of various shapes and sizes and several carried iron files to reforge at home. Half the trunks contained up to 12 kilos of soap in rough bars, a salubrious indication of a new concern with personal hygiene and the secular causes of disease.[58] *Gayisas* not only returned with goods unavailable in Mozambique; they also sent money back to their families with comrades returning home, with recruiters and missionaries,

Miners leaving the Witwatersrand. The range of goods available to migrant workers in southern Mozambique was restricted by the massive importation of cheap, protected colonial wine. This caused Mozambican mineworkers to spend a large part of their wages on the Witwatersrand where they quickly earned the reputation for being "spendthrift."

and later through the Portuguese curator's office.[59] At the end of their contracts, they themselves returned home with savings of perhaps £15, out of which they were expected to pay a labour tax of about 30s to the chief, a hut tax of over 20s, and provide the gifts, beer, and food required to confirm their new status and ease their reintegration into the home community.[60] Although the repatriation of wages brought to the Mozambican economy an annual boost of well over £500,000, Portugal was the chief recipient of the profits of migrant labour.[61] In 1906 the colony sent almost £107,000 to the metropole in payment for wine. In the same year it was estimated that the protective duties on metropolitan goods cost Mozambique £114,450 and the subsidy on Portuguese shipping a further £107,780. Freire d'Andrade complained that, in the space of ten years, over £5.5 million in gold had been sent from Mozambique to Portugal.[62] This leaching to Lisbon of the profits of migrant labour held back the development of southern Mozambique. So too did the high tariffs placed on foreign articles, as they depressed the quantity and range of goods imported into the colony and persuaded migrants to buy their goods in the Transvaal. "From a commercial point of view," wrote Freire d'Andrade, "Inhambane is less a Portuguese district than one of the Transvaal." While imports worth £25,335 were shipped into the district in 1906, migrants returned from the Transvaal with goods valued at almost five times that amount.[63] The Portuguese did little to protect traders in the colony from this competition. The fee paid by the Transvaal government after 1908, as compensation for lost customs duties, went directly to the colonial treasury, and the question of deferred wage payments, aimed at obliging workers to spend their wages in Mozambique, was first raised in 1909 but only implemented some twenty years later.[64]

While traders and members of the colonial administration could criticize elements of metropolitan policy, they were too dependent on miners' wages—as the source of the hut tax and the purchasing power of the colony—seriously to oppose migrant labour as an institution. Mozambique's prosperity had come to settle on the revenues brought to the colony by migrant labour.[65] This was noticeable as early as the turn of the century when, during the Anglo-Boer War, a fall in the number of migrant workers resulted in a drop in imports, hut tax payments, and even church collections.[66] In 1900 at least 163 Mozambicans, driven by the unemployment caused by the war, left Lourenço Marques on three-year contracts to work on the sugar plantations of Reunion for monthly wages of less than 30s.[67] At the same time, unrest in the Xai Xai area was blamed on the hardships caused by a combination of drought and the war, as the latter had halted the repatriation of mine wages. By working in the Transvaal, men earned the money needed to acquire a wife, help the family pay the hut tax, and tide over the loss of a son, father, or brother conscripted into the army or *xibalo*.[68] The *gayisas* also provided the money needed to buy food when epidemics destroyed the cattle herds and drought ruined the harvest, or when alcoholism ate up the family reserves and deprived the homestead of able-bodied workers.

"For the blacks of this area," wrote the administrator of the Manyisa district, "the Transvaal is a promised land and the greatest propagandists are those who return with money and the large number of knick-knacks they buy there cheaply; they exaggerate everything and avoid recounting the privations they have suffered. The Transvaal is for the black what Brazil is for our *minhoto*."[69] This parallel was often drawn, for, in the eyes of a colonial official, Brazil and the Transvaal were both lands of opportunity where an industrious individual could acquire the fortune needed to live like a gentleman at home. The *gayisa* returned from the mines with rare and exotic clothes, a knowledge of foreign languages, perhaps the ability to read and write, and names that advertized their status. *Gayisas* gained praise and prestige as they distributed patronage and acquired the social capital needed to marry. But they also developed obligations to dependents whose insistent demands, I noted in the previous chapter, prompted the popularity of padlocks. "They are moneyed folk these magayiza," wrote an Anglican missionary:

> whenever they land, or leave a train, there is someone on the *qui vive* to make something out of them, a drink shop keeper, an official, a low "white" pretending to some authority, a low woman, in places even footpads who attack and rob by force. Friends most unexpectedly appear to ask a loan or to share in some expenditure and when home is reached there is the customary gift to be paid to his chief—probably a feast to be given.[70]

Workers returned home with a spiritual, as well as a material, assurance. In one of the ten trunks mentioned earlier, a man had packed seven bottles of ink, pens, and pencils, a packet of envelopes, and a writing slate; he and another traveller each carried home two bibles. In southern Mozambique, missionaries such as Henri

Guye marvelled at "the almost continual procession" of migrants returning home. "Many have converted to Christianity and wish to practise it here," he wrote, "others have already opened Bilene to Christianity."[71] Many migrants started their own churches. James Ngonyama had been converted by A. W. Baker's Compounds Mission in 1896 but had later gone on to join the Zulu Congregational Church. In 1908 he established the African Gaza Church, a denomination based on the Witwatersrand with numerous branches in Mozambique.[72] Levi Magwebu returned to his village from Johannesburg in 1908 and, within weeks, had constructed a school serving one hundred pupils.[73] Others acquired elementary reading skills on the mines, bought reading charts and other teaching aids, and then returned home to minister to their rural communities.[74] That there were no colporteurs wandering between villages, or books in the Banyan shops, indicates that reading lost much of its attraction in rural areas cut off from the literate world of the colonizer. Nevertheless, the strength of the flow of ideas was such that Pierre Loze believed the Swiss mission had to take charge of "these [independent] sorts of schools," or they would "fill the country."[75]

While many Christian miners founded their own schools and chapels, others worked for missions straddling the divide between the Witwatersrand and Southern Mozambique.[76] In 1901 George Mandlati took the gospel to the area south of Bilene, where he founded an important Swiss mission at Chikhumbane. Titus Kunita established a church at Guija in 1907, and several other miners succeeded, in a similar way, in spreading the work of the Swiss and other mission churches.[77] A. W. Baker saw Mozambique as fertile ground for the gospel and encouraged his followers in the compounds to undertake mission work when they returned home; by 1910, members of the South African Compounds and Interior Mission were able to congregate at about thirty churches and as many meeting places in Southern Mozambique.[78] Competing Christian denominations used literacy as an important instrument in the battle to win souls and increase church membership.[79] While the missionaries employed the literature of the Ronga, Thonga, and Tswa languages that they themselves had codified, the "independent" schools and chapels tended to use English and Zulu reading skills acquired on the Witwatersrand. The Portuguese feared that these languages were the thin edge of British imperialism and in 1907 attempted to limit the number of schools opened by Protestant and "independent" churches. Anyone wishing to open a school had to receive permission from the district administrator; languages indigenous to Mozambique could be employed during the first three years of schooling, but any further education had to be conducted in Portuguese, and teachers were required to pass an examination in that language.[80] This legislation closed impecunious schools and pushed struggling independent congregations to join mission churches;[81] it also deepened the distrust of Catholicism that migrants acquired with Christianity on the mines, and laid the foundations of the Protestant missions' future role as bunkers of opposition to Portuguese colonialism.[82]

While the pressures on males to migrate to the Transvaal grew under colonialism, the Portuguese exercised increasingly tighter control over the movement of labour out of Mozambique. In their attempt to stamp out what they decreed to be "clandestine" migration, the Portuguese gave the Chamber of Mines monopoly recruiting rights to Mozambican labour on the eve of the Anglo-Boer war. This policy was informally adhered to after the war, when the Witwatersrand Native Labour

Mozambican workers in open railway trucks on the Lourenço Marques–Johannesburg line. Travelling by train was far safer and quicker than the journey by foot but it placed migrants more firmly under the control of recruiters and employers.

Association (WNLA), the new and strengthened recruiting wing of the Chamber of Mines, established a recruiting network in Southern Mozambique. The WNLA monopoly was a major setback for the independence with which workers sold their labour under the old tramping system. The solidarity of the employers' combination, challenged only briefly in 1906–1907, achieved a major victory for the Chamber of Mines in its struggle to control the labour market.[83] It succeeded in both pushing down the workers' wage rate, and swept away the enormous difficulties workers had experienced in tramping to the mines. Jeeves, Katzenellenbogen, and Duffy have provided an excellent picture of the politics behind WNLA and of the size and extent of the organisation's operations in Mozambique.[84] With the financial backing of virtually all the mining houses, and the support of the Portuguese administration, WNLA reintroduced the system of shelters for migrants tramping to and from the Transvaal. By 1905 a total of sixty-five receiving stations fed men to the fourteen camps run by white recruiters. With one station to every 300 square miles and almost fifteen hundred employees, WNLA exerted an influence over Southern Mozambique that was rivalled only by the Portuguese administration. The controlled recruiting undertaken by WNLA provided the Portuguese with well over £100,000 every year.[85]

Prospective mineworkers were generally recruited in their villages by black "runners," clad in gaudy jerseys, who were paid on a capitation basis. The men were assembled at receiving stations and then funnelled to camps run by white recruiters, where they were fed and provided with wine; at these camps, at least in theory, Portuguese officials checked their hut tax receipts, explained their contracts, and provided them with passports. The recruits were then marched off in a body to an embarkation point. Men from the north were taken to Inhambane, where nearly twenty-six thousand passengers entered and left the port in 1906. From the Gaza district, migrants were taken to Xai Xai on the coast and shipped south on the packed decks and in the crammed holds of small coastal steamers.[86] In Lourenço Marques they were housed in compounds before being entrained for Ressano Garcia, where, in practice, the great majority of the migrants were processed by Portuguese officials. Men from the districts of Lourenço Marques and western Gaza were generally marched to the nearest railway station or to the nearest border post. Some WNLA recruits crossed the border at Namahasha and later at Pafuri in the north, but the vast majority followed the conduit formed by the railway to Ressano Garcia, where they were lodged in a large compound, subjected to a medical inspection, and provided with passports. On the other side of the border, in Komati Poort, the passports were validated by the Native Affairs Department (NAD) for travel in the Transvaal. Workers were liable for the cost of the passport, its validation, and the rail ticket, a sum amounting to over 25s. However, in the early years of the century recruiters generally bore these costs, since deductions from workers' wages gave them good cause to desert once on the Rand. At Ressano Garcia the recruits were loaded into open sheep trucks, or closed luggage vans, and provided with baked bread rations for the trip to Johannesburg. The coaches were sufficiently overcrowded to prevent the men from lying down during the overnight trip, and their discomfort was increased by the constant harassment from guards employed to prevent their escape. They were seldom allowed to leave the train and the sleepless two-day voyage was broken only once, at Waterval Boven, where the men were supplied with blankets and overcoats in an effort to prevent pneumonia. In 1905 this station was abandoned when third-class coaches were introduced and the journey was reduced to twenty-six hours. But in winter the cold drove the train to stop at Witbank, where the eight hundred voyagers were provided with cocoa. The men were initially detrained at Braamfontein in central Johannesburg on Wednesdays and Saturdays. But as Park Station became over-congested, their point of arrival was moved to Booysens from where they were marched to the WNLA receiving compound in Eloff Street (named "Mzilikazi" after the autocratic Ndebele ruler) and the office of the Portuguese curator of natives.[87]

The curator's major task was to tax Mozambican workers and, by controlling their movements, to suppress clandestine and permanent emigration. Between 1903 and 1906 an average of 7,750 Mozambican migrants failed to return home each year.[88] The Inhambane district was particularly badly hit. In the late 1890s steamers left the bay with from two to three hundred passengers each month and returned with only half that number; during the period from 1902 to 1907, some 18,500 able-bodied men disappeared on the Witwatersrand, almost 8 percent of the entire population of the district.[89] In 1907 the governor of Inhambane warned that if this demographic trend continued, his district would be reduced to a "nursery for blacks that benefits only the Transvaal."[90] The governor-general was also aware of this danger, for a fall in population meant a decline in "the principle source of our present revenues." If migrants refused to return home, the hut tax went unpaid, and customs revenues declined with the level of consumerism.[91] For men like

Freire d'Andrade, the problem lay not with migrant labour as an institution but with the mineowners' need for an experienced work force of skilled, proletarian miners. To prevent the permanent emigration of Mozambique's major economic resource, the curator's office was expanded and strengthened. The revenue accruing to the curator, much of which was drawn from recruiters and employers rather than migrants, increased with the growth in the number of Mozambican miners, the efficiency of border patrols, and the competency of his staff. By 1913, on the eve of the repatriation of workers from north of 22° south, the curator's office received a total of almost £80,000 from Mozambican workers.[92] Each migrant had to pay the curator a 2s6d registration fee before exchanging his passport for a district pass. To prevent him from discarding his Mozambican identity, the man's passport number and his employer's name were printed in red ink in the district pass and he was lodged in the compound adjoining the pass office until claimed by his employers. Men who had financed their own way to Johannesburg were given a district pass, valid for three days, enabling them to look for work. Once engaged, the worker was required to exchange his district pass for an employer's pass, for which he had to pay 2s every month. This monthly pass was a constant source of grievance, as it served merely as a tax-gathering mechanism used to fund the system of pass controls. Workers who wished to leave mine property were generally provided with "special passes" issued by their employers on weekends. But not all employers were willing to allow men to travel to town where they could buy illegal liquor or look for better-paid work. Hence many of the workers who left the mine "to visit their brothers," or purchase goods, courted arrest under the pass and curfew laws.[93]

At the end of his contract the worker was re-issued with his district pass, which allowed him to make his way to the pass office to retrieve his passport. A Mozambican who wished to extend his contract had to pay a 10s endorsement fee to the curator and, after 1901, a fee of 6d for every month he extended his one-year contract. If he chose to return home, the curator stamped his passport for a 10s fee, endorsing the expiration of his contract. Many workers attempted to avoid paying this fee by breaking contract and returning home early and illegally. But this well-established pattern of resisting poor conditions of employment became more difficult after 1897, for if a miner returned home without an endorsed passport, he was liable to a fine of between two and three months' *xibalo*. On his return home he was required to present his endorsed passport and pay the hut tax.[94]

The 1897 labour agreement had a far-reaching effect on the worker's life. His ability to sell his labour to the highest bidder was curtailed as the system of recruitment strictly controlled his freedom of movement, both at home and on the Witwatersrand. At the same time, prohibition on the Witwatersrand suppressed the canteens as information-gathering centres and the British administration tightened the system of worker surveillance and control. In February 1899 the Johannesburg, Krugersdorp, and Boksburg pass offices were equipped with detention rooms, where men suspected of desertion could be identified by mine managers. Detainees were kept in these lock-ups for six days before being transferred to the main detention centre in Johannesburg for a further six days.[95] At the end of the Anglo-Boer War the pass commissioner's office was brought under the NAD, a fingerprint section was established at the central pass office in October 1901, and two years later pass offices were opened in Germiston and Roodepoort. By 1908 the administration of the pass system had been sufficiently expanded for some two hundred thousand men to be registered at the Fordsburg pass office each year. The introduction of single entrance compounds restricted the movements of the miner, and in 1911 all black workers were required by law to be fingerprinted when registering at a pass office.[96]

Workers fought a continuous battle to preserve their freedom to socialise and to sell their labour. Many found employers who considered the payment of a deserter's fine of 60s preferable to the investment of money in recruiting and transporting workers from the East Coast. Others deserted from Johannesburg only to reappear in another district, where there was little chance of being discovered and where they could obtain travel passes to re-enter the Witwatersrand. Black workers were still able to exploit some chinks in the armour of legislation that controlled their movement and forced down their wages. Collective bargaining by desertion remained, through experience and tradition, the worker's major weapon in dealing with management. "There is one thing with the Kaffir in which he is different to the white man," declared J. Ware of the Trades and Labour Council in 1907. "If things do not suit him he goes home and stays there, he does not go on strike, that is better than any strike."[97] But the conquest and colonisation of southern Mozambique had significantly undermined the independence of East Coast workers. Caught between the pass laws and the curator's office on the Witwatersrand, and *xibalo*, conscription, and a rudimentary pass system in Mozambique, migrants found it increasingly difficult to leave the mines at will.[98] Their rate of desertion fell from 34 per thousand in 1908 to 18 in 1914, most deserters were recaptured, and it became increasingly difficult to settle permanently on the Witwatersrand.[99] As the bargaining position of East Coast workers shrank, they were progressively funnelled by WNLA towards the collieries and deep-level mines, where working conditions were disagreeable and dangerous, and where there was no guarantee of falling among friends and relatives. A WNLA contract, according to one old retired miner, entailed being "sold to Mzilikazi," the company's receiving compound.[100]

Increasing numbers of Mozambicans attempted to retain their freedom to select their employers, to choose their occupation on the mine, and set the length of their contracts by making their way to the gold fields independently of WNLA. While many of these "volunteers" passed through Portuguese border controls and paid their own passage to the Witwatersrand, many others entered the Transvaal "clandestinely" under the guidance of freelance recruiters operating illegally in Mozambique. Other "clandestines" made their way to recruiting camps in the Transvaal or, braving the dangers of the route, struck out independently for Johannesburg.[101] Because of the extent and open nature of the frontier, the Portuguese were unable to prevent this "illegal" outflow of labour. But they were able to clamp down on clandestines on the Witwatersrand, especially after 1912 when the curator established inspectorates in every labour district.

The British victory in the Anglo-Boer war had encouraged the mineowners to reduce the pre-war wages of black miners by 23 percent and to severely "clip" their earnings. In September 1902 the working month was extended from twenty-eight to thirty shifts, creating a five-week month that obfuscated customary wage expectations and undermined worker solidarity. As men joined at different times and lost tickets through illness and absenteeism, they did not all receive a wage on the same payday, with the result that those who had completed a number of shifts were less willing to enter into combined action than those who had just received their wages. In late 1902 it was possible for a man who had earned 63s per month in 1890 to see his son earn 24s for the same period of work.

Negotiating the Conditions of Work

"It went through the country like a telegram that the wages had been reduced" after the war, remarked H. F. Strange, the president of the Chamber of Mines.[102] Many Mozambicans responded to the downturn in their working conditions on the Rand by simply refusing to return to the Witwatersrand.[103] Towards the end of 1902 a critical shortage of labour emerged, as less than half the workforce had returned to the mines and the production of gold had failed to rise above 45 percent of output in 1898.[104] To attract Mozambicans back to the mines, the mineowners raised wages in April 1903 and gave almost one-third of the men recruited in the Portuguese colony the freedom to choose where they wished to work. But at the same time the Chamber sought to reduce the competition for labour by attempting, as in 1890, to standardize working conditions. Individual mines were prohibited from surpassing a maximum average wage of 50s; they could pay an unrestricted wage to only 5 percent of the work force, and a minimum daily wage of 1s6d was introduced for men and 1s for children ("youths and boys"). The maximum average wage allowed employers to attract a limited number of skilled workers by means of high wages, and it divided older, more experienced workers from their juniors. But from the workers' perspective, this drive for uniformity reduced the attraction of the richer mines by limiting the payment of bonuses and piece rates.[105] The overall improvement in wages had the desired effect, and by December 1903 the number of black miners had risen to fifty-eight thousand. Earnings continued to climb, to a peak of 57s in September 1904, and workers' rations and living quarters were improved. In that year the number of black miners on the Witwatersrand stood at 77,600, of whom 67 percent were Mozambican.[106]

As the old dependence on Mozambique reemerged and wages started to supersede pre-war levels, the mineowners persuaded the British administration to allow the importation of Chinese workers; held by long indentures and housed in new closed compounds, they would provide the mines with a stable, disciplined work force. The first Chinese arrived in mid-1904 and, by the end of the following year, almost fifty thousand were employed on the Witwatersrand. This flooding of the labour market with poorly paid indentured workers reversed the upward movement in black wages and reduced the mining industry's reliance on foreign, Mozambican labour.

The importation of Chinese labour also allowed the Chamber to again clip black wages by introducing, in September 1905, a minimum standard of individual productivity that required drillmen to produce a hole, depending on the mine and the hardness of the rock, of between 18 and 48 inches in depth, and lashers and trammers to remove a defined amount of ore. A novice had a specific period of grace, generally a month if he were under a six-month contract, in which to acclimatize himself to the rigours of piecework. Once the shift had been successfully completed, the day's ticket and counterfoil were marked by the white shiftboss and sent to the time office. This widened the racial divide in the mine and increased the level of surveillance and control, as only the white miner was empowered to measure the amount of work completed by the blacks in his team. If the black worker failed to achieve the minimum standard set by the mine, he was credited with a specially coloured "loafers' " ticket. At the end of the month, the signed counterfoils in his book were matched with the tickets received by the time office; on some mines the worker was credited with some of the work he had completed, but on others he received only porridge for a cancelled shift.

The number of cancelled shifts varied from one mine to another.[107] In 1909, fully 21 percent of shifts were cancelled on the Simmer Deep; four years later the rate of cancelled shifts on the Cinderella Deep stood at 23 percent and, on the Witwatersrand Deep, 17 percent. But these were exceptionally high cancellation rates and when a "fair minimum" of about 30 inches was established on most mines, the average drillman lost perhaps slightly less than 10 percent of his shifts.[108] Although piecework demands varied from one mine to another, for many workers the "ticket system" amounted to an appreciable reduction in earnings, as their wages were tied strictly to individual productivity and their contracts were subjected to an unauthorized lengthening. Due to sickness, absenteeism, and cancelled shifts, it was quite normal for a Mozambican miner to complete fewer than twenty-five shifts per month. This meant that he would often take six weeks to complete the thirty shifts making up the "five-week ticket," and more than fourteen months to finish the maximum contract period of one year (313 shifts) set by the Portuguese.[109] Despite the new relentlessness with which the system of minimum standards stoked the pace of labour, it also served to reduce worker militancy as science, rather than management, was seen to regulate the workload.

Along with these new strategies to improve labour discipline, the Chamber attempted to entrench the divisions within the work force by setting differential daily wages for drillmen (2s), trammers (1s8d), lashers (1s6d), and surface workers, and in 1909 the wages paid to novice drillers in their first three months was dropped to 1s per day.[110] By the end of the first decade of the twentieth century, many mines had also tied food rations to productivity; men who surpassed the minimum task were rewarded with extra portions of meat, while those who failed were penalized by the withdrawal of their food ration for the day. This system of penalties and rewards increased peer pressure on the individual's productivity for, in the tradition of their home culture, most black miners shared their meat ration with their companions.

Various forms of peer pressure were also applied to the daily negotiation of working conditions. Migrants who made their way to the Witwatersrand independently of WNLA, or who re-engaged after their contracts ended, frequently agreed to engage themselves in a body if they were exempted from the mine's medical examination and were guaranteed work of their choice.[111] As we shall see in the following chapter, the miners' solidarity was frequently based on the sense of mutuality that emerged out of occupying the same quarters, eating together, entering into a web of social debts and rights, and constructing a meaningful symbolism. Part of this communality was constructed at the workplace, where men relied on each other for their safety and sometimes even agreed to complete the contract of a "brother" obliged to break contract because of an emergency at home.[112] The miners forged a collective pattern of work underground. Novices were instructed in the skill, rhythm, and pace of labour by the older, more experienced men.[113] Gangs worked in unison, singing and hitting their drills in a rhythmical pattern that urged on the inexperienced, restrained the over-ambitious, and created a commonly accepted work pace. Over time, the definition of work negotiated with management hardened into precedent and precedent into tradition.

Yet at the same time, the expected rhythm of labour was a matter of constant bargaining, as working conditions depended on the nature of the mine concerned and even on the conditions in a specific stope (opening on to the workface). The "hammer boy's" ability to drill a hole was not just dependent on the hardness of the rock; it was also influenced by the steepness of the stope, his access to an adequate supply of candles and drills, the angle of the hole (vertical holes being more difficult to drill than horizontal ones), and the amount of unauthorized work, such as the shovelling away of debris, that he was required to engage in. Tramming was particularly difficult to undertake on a piecework basis due to great differences in the length and slope of the haul, the size and mechanised nature of the trucks, the condition of the tracks, and the amount of loose rock in the stopes. Hence the quantity of work agreed upon was always subject to bargaining and negotiation.[114] In some cases management succeeded in breaking the miners' collective control practices by rewarding individual effort with bonuses of food and money; but the miners were wary of "departing from established custom," reported the *Star*, and refused to be duped into establishing higher and more onerous work standards.[115] J. H. Johns, a consulting engineer, recounted that he had once tried to implement a system of incentives to speed up the work rhythm at the Ferreira mine where he

> persuaded several boys to drill two holes instead of one. They were paid twice as much for their work and we were well pleased, but they suddenly stopped, and when the mine foremen wanted to know why, they said: "It is alright putting these two holes now, but presently the boss will think these two holes is the days work. . . ." They saw what we were working up to. They saw as well as some of the white men we have had to deal with, only the native was more honest about it. He stuck to it too.[116]

Johns was correct in pointing out the resistance of these men to a more demanding work rhythm, but he might have added that the men had agreed, after negotiation with management, to accept one hole as the standard amount of work to be accomplished by a driller. The workers' communal notion of fair labour practices was remarked on by H. F. Strange, who found it difficult to control what he described as "idling," for a miner was "associated with a gang of his brothers and the discharge of one or more of them as idlers would frequently lead to the others leaving as soon as possible."[117] Miners who worked under the ticket system were not obliged to work every day; to ensure sufficient labourers for their needs, mine managers were obliged to house and feed a surfeit of men in the compounds.[118] To draw and hold men, managers also introduced the notion of a "fair minimum," and many were obliged to allow sick employees to take off a day in which to consult their own doctors and herbalists.[119]

But migrancy itself was to remain the most important and visible means of breaking the unremitting pace of labour demanded by the mineowners. S. Reyersbach, the chairman of Rand Mines, complained of the black miner that "any attempt to improve his efficiency is only likely to result in a native strike, in which the native must win."[120] At the heart of the grievances of migrant workers was the impersonal way in which men like Reyersbach equated them with machines by wishing to "improve their efficiency." While the legitimacy of this approach rested on an appeal to the pragmatism of profit, the workers' demands were informed by a morality rooted in a preindustrial sense of mutual exchange and obligation, and ultimately in an interpretation of the labour process dominated by human relations rather than economic forces.

Management responded to the workers' solidarity and resistance to innovation by pushing the work rhythm through fear and pulling it by means of incentives. The mineowners' interpretation of labour discipline was backed by law, for, although compound managers were no longer allowed to punish black workers for breaches of discipline, the NAD could impose fines of up to £3.[121] As at Kimberley, subcontracting was used by management to drive and divide the work force. By supplying black mine workers under hire to subcontractors, many mines were absolved from having to train and discipline inexperienced migrants. But many subcontractors also attracted skilled workers by allowing them more freedom in the compounds, more humane conditions underground, and regular bonuses that raised their wages above the maximum average.[122] Subcontracting was also a means of dividing skilled and experienced workers from the rump of the workforce, a strategy that exempted management from constructing married quarters, depressed the expectations of the majority of the miners who were herded into company compounds, and separated them from their natural leaders. Yet at the same time it helped to stabilize the skilled work force by providing experienced black miners with the opportunity to earn up to £12 per week as subcontractors.[123]

If these managerial strategies failed to impress upon workers the urgency and discipline of the work rhythm, they were driven in the stopes by the brutality of the white gangers. Beating and flogging workers was officially frowned upon by management, at least partly because it gave a company a bad reputation with recruits, but it was seen as an unavoidable evil. Workers could report assaults to NAD inspectors, but it was difficult to get a conviction in the encapsulated world of the mine.[124] The inspectors appointed by the NAD in 1902 "spend much of their time in chatting with the mine officials," complained J. M. Makhotle, "and neglect the people whom they are supposed to look after." He had never heard of the inspectors' superior, the protector of natives.[125] Some black miners found an outlet for their oppression in songs that mocked and derided their overseers, while others settled for rough justice. A black miner "will often stand a blow or kick, if he deserves it," wrote W. C. Scully, who implicitly recognized the workers' notion of rights and duties, "but not otherwise. There are recorded instances of European bosses and overseers having been found unconscious in some dark stope, with wounds that had evidently been inflicted from behind."[126] It was in these various ways, ranging from the subtle discipline of bonuses, to fingerprinting and the fear of physical violence, that managers and the state attempted to force black miners to adopt a new and exacting notion of work as their own.

While miners negotiated, contested, rejected, and accepted aspects of this new labour discipline, other changes were imposed on them by developments in the mining industry.[127] The scale of mining operations changed rapidly in the first decade of the twentieth century. As early as 1897 the Simmer and Jack had established a world record for monthly shaft sinking of 127 feet; by 1906 shafts were being sunk at the rate of 250 feet a month and the Robinson Deep had become, at

2,600 feet, the deepest producing mine in the world. By 1910 a spate of mergers had caused a company like Crown Mines to swallow seventeen competing properties while ERPM had grown to absorb over twenty rivals. Randfontein Central, the biggest operating mine on the Witwatersrand, consisted of over twenty-one hundred original claims and stretched over 11 kilometers.[128] The postwar expansion was built on foreign investment, which in turn was dependent on the lowering of working costs. The price of coal, explosives, and railway rates fell appreciably when the old Republican monopolies were abolished. Technical innovations such as tube mills, heavier stamps, and hand drills increased the tonnage and recovery rate, while electricity replaced steam power in driving the winding gear, pumps, and stamps, and provided lighting and ventilation, as well as compressed air for the drills.[129] The fall in working costs, from 25s9d per ton in 1902 to 17s7d in 1910, propelled the mines further into the low grades. But the demand for labour soared as enormous amounts of ore had to be extracted to make up for the fall in grade and the decline in profitability per ton.[130] Between 1902 and 1910 the amount of ore hauled to the surface by black and white miners rose from 3.4 million tons to 21.4 million tons. A year later, if the amount of tunneling beneath the Witwatersrand had been extended into a single passageway, ten feet high and wide, it would have stretched from Johannesburg to Bulawayo.[131] By 1913, on the eve of the opening up of the fields on the Far East Rand, the Transvaal produced 40 percent of the world's gold.

Underground working conditions became more onerous and difficult as the easily worked reefs were exhausted and miners tunnelled at ever-increasing depths. The deeper the mine, the longer it took for the men to get to the rock face, the more water they encountered, and the greater the temperature under which they laboured.[132] The miners generally worked in two shifts, for ten hours every week day and six hours on Saturday. The British administration showed less respect for Sunday observance than their predecessors and a new relentlessness was introduced into mining as, for the first time, men were obliged to work underground on Sundays.[133] This particularly affected Mozambicans, who made up from 70 to 75 percent of underground labour.[134] Machines were used to open the tunnels leading from the main shaft to the rock face, but drillers hewed out the stopes and cut into the gold reef in such a way as to follow it to the next level. Ore dislodged on one level was passed down to the level below, where it was shovelled into cocopans and railed to the shaft. Work was uncomfortable and dangerous. "Walking along the levels, you come to the opening of a stope and look down at the men at work, perhaps two hundred feet below," wrote Edward Bright to his mother in 1903.

> The most interesting sight I saw was one stope where 50 boys were working. They were perched along the side of the excavation, each boy with a hand drill ("jumper") and hammer. The chamber was probably 150 feet wide by 50 feet deep and about six feet high, more like a slit than anything else. The boys were all singing in their monotonous way and striking in time. They were all naked and the flickering candle light on their black skin made a weird scene. To go down this stope, two chains are provided, about two feet apart, fastened securely to the top. On these chains, with a candle in your mouth, you slide down or pull yourself up.[135]

Accidents plagued the life of the black miner. Subcontracting, piecework, incentives, and penalties encouraged miners to rush through their work. Poor safety standards and deep-level mining also contributed to an accident rate of between 4 and 5 per thousand.[136] In 1905 a voluntary system of compensation was introduced; for an annual insurance of 2s, the miner received £5 in the case of incapacitation, and, in the case of death, £10 was paid via the curator's office to his family in Mozambique. Child miners ("piccaninnies and umfaans") were eligible for half these amounts.[137] In 1911 compensation payments were legally enforced by the Native Labour Registration Act and three years later the amount paid for total incapacitation was increased to £50. By forcing the mineowners to take responsibility for the large number of deaths, the state reduced the accident mortality rate to 3.5 per thousand by 1914, an improvement in working conditions of indirect benefit to employers, as it made the mines more attractive to labour.[138]

If life was dangerous in the stopes, it was not much safer above ground. The mines were unprepared for the wave of black workers who arrived on the Witwatersrand in 1903 and many of the compounds still reflected an uncertainty about the longevity of the outcrop mines. On some of the poorer mines, men were housed in single lean-tos, but in most cases they were billeted in windowless, wood-and-iron sheds with low roofs and earthen floors. Even the more modern compounds had become dilapidated during the war, and they were so severely overcrowded that miners had to sleep on floors that turned to mud in bad weather. Large tin drums packed with burning coals provided heating and cooking facilities but filled the overventilated huts with smoke.[139] These overcrowded and insalubrious conditions, and a frequently inadequate diet, caused a sharp jump in the winter mortality rate, from 51.25 per thousand in 1902 to a horrifying 110.2 a year later.[140] The death rate on the large, deep-level mines, where Mozambicans contracted by WNLA made up a large majority of the work force, was the heaviest on the Rand.[141] About thirty-four Mozambicans out of every thousand died each year between 1905 and 1912, more than double the mortality rate for miners drawn from the Cape and Natal/Zululand.[142] Mozambicans could retain a certain freedom of mobility by avoiding WNLA contracts and certain mines, and by engaging with independent recruiters. "In their rustic and primitive simplicity," remarked the Portuguese curator, "the natives observe the facts and draw conclusions long before investigations of a scientific nature explain them."[143] "The native knows very well," he was later to remark, "where he will find comfort, protection, and a better salary."[144] It was partly in order to compete with the clandestine operations of independent recruiters in Mozambique that WNLA introduced the system of "specials" in 1903. This allowed about 50 percent of Mozambican recruits to choose the mine on which they wished to work. A hospital was built at the Ressano Garcia compound in 1905, and WNLA recruits were in theory subjected to three medical inspections: in their district of recruitment, at Ressano Garcia, and at the receiving compound in Johannesburg, where they were held for two days to weed out the physically unfit and prevent the spread of epidemics.

As the case of Mechelisse shows, by 1905 it was far easier for recruits to get to Johannesburg than in their fathers' day. But an easier voyage to the Rand was won at the cost of lower wages and a more intense degree of surveillance and control. Mechelisse, whose European name was Messajo (from the Portuguese *mensageiro* or messenger), was registered as worker No. 48049 by WNLA and No. 2230 by the Portuguese. He was recruited at Inharrime near Inhambane and left there, at 4:00 a.m. on 6th January 1905, after receiving a blanket. He took five days to walk to Magude on the Nkomati River, where he camped for the night, and another five days to get to Ressano Garcia, where he was issued with a sweater on the 15th or 16th January. Mechelisse was then entrained for Waterval Boven, where he was supplied with "the balance of his clothing." After two days on the train, he arrived at "Mzilikazi" on the 19th January. The following day he was sent to the compound of the Lancaster mine and housed in a barrack with twenty-one other men.[145] Mechelisse had less to fear from smallpox, typhoid, or bubonic plague than had his father a generation before. Typhoid, and especially dysentery and diarrhoea, had initially flourished in the overcrowded and unhealthy post-war compounds.[146] But these enteric diseases were brought under control as conditions were improved through a mixture of state intervention, the increased profitability brought about by company mergers, and the opening of the Far East Rand. New barracks were built of masonry or stone and equipped with impervious floors and sufficient partitioned shelving, built in three tiers, to provide bunks for most workers. Mine hospitals were constructed; standards were set for ventilation and space, water, food, and sanitation; and the miners were taught the values of soap and a basic personal hygiene.[147] A severe outbreak of scurvy in 1903 was quickly checked when workers were supplied with vitamin-rich beer made from millet and sorghum.

Pneumonia remained the single largest killer, partly because Mozambicans from south of the 22nd parallel, who had little natural immunity to the disease, tended to work long contracts in the deepest mines, and partly because of the conditions in which they lived and worked. On bitterly cold winter mornings the first bell in the Simmer Deep compound sounded at 3:15 a.m. and the men were required to walk one mile to the shaft head. On other mines workers commonly walked several hundred meters from their barracks to the mine entrance where, in long queues, they waited for the two or three cages, or elevators, to take them down to the working levels. On many mines the hauling gear was unable to cope with the growing numbers of men, and workers were obliged to wait for long periods before descending into the mine. At 2,000 feet underground the temperature stood at 73.5 degrees and increased by one degree every 208 feet. Men working in the narrow stopes were soon bathed in sweat or soaked by water in tunnels and shafts. In this condition they quickly fell prey to pneumonia, either because the ventilation shafts sent drafts of cold air onto their near-naked bodies, or because of the cold highveld air encountered on the surface. After standing around in their wet clothing waiting for their tickets to be marked, the miners returned to draughty barracks and muddy, earthen floors. Pneumonia accounted for the death or repatriation of four out of every hundred southern Mozambicans in 1908 and, five years later, 45 percent of the 2,213 Mozambicans who died of disease on the Rand.[148]

Veteran miners were familiar with pneumonia and enteric and venereal diseases, but few had any experience of the new industrial maladies that emerged as the physical effects of underground mining, particularly at deep levels, were felt for the first time. Tuberculosis (TB) had already reached the coast by the early 1890s, when it was diagnosed in Khosen, Mandlakazi, and Lourenço Marques.[149] The sudden explosion of pulmonary tuberculosis on the mines in the early twentieth century can probably be traced to its earlier diagnosis, on the diamond and gold fields, as pneumonia.[150] Between 1903–1906 and 1906–1909, the incidence of the disease on the Witwatersrand rose by 42 percent and by a further 50 percent between 1910 and 1912.[151] The miners passed on tuberculosis as they coughed and spat infected sputum in the overcrowded barracks and damp stopes. The disease spread particularly rapidly among men whose physical condition was weakened by exhaustion, hookworm, and poor food.[152] In 1912 TB killed 7.6 out of every 1,000 Mozambicans employed on the mines and caused another 18.3 to be repatriated. In 1913–1914, well over a quarter of the Southern Mozambicans who died on the Rand succumbed to tuberculosis. As the disease most characteristic of overwork, TB was particularly rife in the Witbank collieries, where Mozambicans under WNLA contracts worked twelve-hour shifts and took from six to eight weeks to complete a thirty-shift ticket book.

While there are figures on the incidence of mortality and repatriation caused by TB on the mines, there is little on the devastation caused by the disease as it spread into the rural areas. It is clear, however, that the rural community was required to carry a large part of the costs of industrial health. Mozambicans infected with tuberculosis were sent home on the Thursday train. They were given a loaf of bread and a ration of brandy for the trip. "Boys who are too sick to walk are taken to the station in trolleys," reported the Chamber of Mines, and "the really sick ones are put into one carriage and made as comfortable as possible." Those who were too sick to walk on their arrival at Ressano Garcia were housed in the WNLA hospital.[153] At least one sick Khosa miner was wheeled home from the Transvaal by his comrades in a makeshift barrow.[154]

In 1907 a Mozambican doctor reported a "great increase" in the incidence of TB and the "inundation" of the Lourenço Marques and Inhambane districts with this and other contagious diseases brought from the mines.[155] In the same year the administrator of the Sabie district related that the area was "full of tuberculosis," and five years later his colleague in the Gaza district complained that people in his area were "wasting away" due to the TB and pneumonia brought from the mines and the alcoholism induced by metropolitan wine. In moving detail he described how men, their lungs ravaged by TB, collapsed on the road home or died at seedy, bush canteens.[156] Others noted that tuberculosis had become a part of everyday life to such an extent that people had developed their own rituals and methods for restricting the spread of the disease.[157] The fatalism with which tuberculosis was greeted in the rural areas was captured in songs that recounted

> There is a sickness!
> The doctors can do nothing.
> It's *ndéré* (TB).
> The sun has set for me.
> Oh, my father,
> I am dying.[158]

Phthisis was another industrial disease about to become a major killer on the mines. It was caused when angular, microscopic atoms of stone, dislodged during drilling, blasting, and shovelling, fixed in the lung tissue. As the disease was aggravated by the length of time spent in the mines, proletarianized white workers were its principal victims. But Mozambicans, because they worked underground on long contracts, also suffered terribly from phthisis. The seriousness of the disease was at first disguised when men returned to the mines fresh from their enforced sojourn at home after the Anglo-Boer War. It was also initially obscured as sick miners were repatriated or returned home to die; many of the 9,251 men repatriated in 1912 (some 48 per thousand) suffered from phthisis, and a shocking 26 percent of all workers showed signs of the disease. The incidence of phthisis increased with the introduction of machine drills, and in 1916 the disease claimed the lives of 4.7 workers out of every thousand, and about 10 percent of all Mozambicans who died of illness on the Rand.[159] Under the Miners' Phthisis Act of 1912, blacks received £50 compensation for "permanent disablement" and £20 for less serious cases. This was far less than the amount paid to whites and did not cover phthisis sufferers who commonly died of TB, a disease defined as nonindustrial and hence not covered by the act. "Only a very small percentage of the monies surrendered to the Portuguese Curator is ever paid out," reported the Transvaal's director of native labour in 1914, as "the heirs are seldom if ever traced."[160] Nevertheless, employers were obliged to install underground sprays and more efficient ventilation in an attempt to cut down on compensation payments and attract labour.[161] Within a short time the gold mines were to lead the world in the development of dust-control programmes and workers' compensation legislation.[162]

Better food and housing, as well as improved medical conditions and sanitation, lowered the black miner's mortality rate from 48.2 per thousand in 1904, to 35.7 in 1910, and 14.9 in 1914.[163] An improvement in working conditions played an important part in bringing down the mortality rate. Changing houses were built at the pit head on some mines, and sections of the work force were sometimes served with soup, coffee, and bread before the start of the working day. An underground shift of eight hours had first been suggested on the Witwatersrand in 1893, a year after its introduction at Kimberley.[164] But as shorter working hours would have entailed a drop in wages, the scheme was shelved until 1906, when eight-hour shifts were introduced underground on the Wolhuter, New Unified, and Knights Deep mines, and, the following year, on other mines in the Consolidated Gold Fields group. By working in three shifts, a skeleton staff was able to blast at night and in this way improve the purity of the air for the men working the two day shifts. The success of this experiment persuaded the newly formed Union government to override objections from the Chamber and, under the Mines and Works Act of 1911, limit the length of time spent underground by any individual to eight hours in twenty-four, or forty-eight hours per week.[165] But despite these improvements, as late as 1913–1914, of the approximately 85,000 southern Mozambicans officially employed in the various labour districts of the Transvaal, 2,124 died of disease, 314 died through mine accidents, and an even greater number were repatriated as unfit for work.[166]

The position of the migrant Mozambican miner had deteriorated significantly in the decade after 1897. He was subject to new and fearsome industrial diseases; his working conditions worsened as the mines deepened and grew in extent, and his wages were cut and clipped by state involvement in the labour market. In addition, prohibition and new technologies of surveillance curtailed his freedom of movement, and scientific measurement brought a new ruthlessness to the work regime. Mozambican workers were at a severe disadvantage under colonialism— for they were confronted by the exploitative, and often concerted, demands of both the mineowners and Portuguese officials.

The Profits of Proletarianisation

In April 1907 the Portuguese attempted to take advantage of the imminent phasing-out of Chinese labour by imposing an *ad valorem* import duty of 25 percent on the goods taken home by mineworkers; further, to give Mozambicans something to spend their money on at home, they lifted the prohibition on the manufacture of fermented and distilled liquor.[167] The result was a sharp rise in the sale of locally manufactured liquor, an equal growth in imports, and a corresponding increase in the earnings of the colony's traders and customs department. But for the Transvaal the new tax caused a shortage of underground workers and a sharp fall in commercial revenue. Negotiations resulted in a compromise that bound the Transvaal government to pay 7s6d for every Mozambican worker returning home with a maximum of 60 kilos of baggage.[168] The Portuguese then sought to replace the departing Chinese by doubling the hut tax, a measure that succeeded in forcing a new wave of ten thousand Mozambicans to enter the mines. The 7s6d import fee brought the Portuguese almost £20,000, while passports and recruiting fees provided the treasury with a further £40,000 every year.[169]

Both the Transvaal government and the mining industry were aware of the political dangers arising from an overdependence on Portuguese labour. In May 1907 the newly elected Het Volk government established a Government Native Labour Bureau (GNLB) to oversee recruiting in the South African colonies. The Botha government was anxious to recompense the mineowners for the loss of Chinese labour and for promising to employ increasing numbers of Afrikaners; but they also wished to regulate the fratricidal competition for labour between the mining houses and avoid an overwhelming dependence on the Portuguese. The establishment of the GNLB marked a turning-point in the history of the struggle to control the labour market, for, ever since the early days of cane growing in Natal, employers had called for the direct participation of government in the recruitment of labour. Black South Africans were offered far more favourable conditions of employment than WNLA's Mozambicans. Through various incentives, such as allowing recruits to choose their occupation and the mine on which they wished to work and, especially, through the payment of substantial cattle or monetary advances for entering into short-term contracts, the GNLB was able to recruit large numbers of workers in the Cape, Natal, and Zululand. Hence, although the number of Southern Mozambicans employed in the mines rose from 57,300 in 1905–1906 to 76,000 in 1912, their numbers dropped from 59 to 34 percent of the overall work force, while that of black workers from the Cape Colony rose from 5.2 to 30 percent between 1904 and 1910.[170] The relative decline in the importance of Mozambican labour was reinforced as small machine drills replaced large numbers of "hammer boys" in the stopes. Government intervention in recruiting also helped undermine the wages of black miners, which fell from 51s11d in 1905–1906 to 48s7d in 1909–1910. Real wages continued to decline after 1912, when the Chamber attempted to reintroduce monopsonistic recruiting in British South Africa through the establishment of the Native Recruiting Corporation. All Mozambican workers brought to the Rand by WNLA were sold to the NRC, which then distributed the men to the mines and required them to repay the cost of their recruitment, a total of about 67s divided into monthly payments. The NRC also enforced the low ceiling on piecework rates by strictly overseeing the application of the maximum average.[171]

While the Mozambican worker's wage declined after 1897, the time he spent on the mines progressively lengthened. Under the *modus vivendi* of 1901, workers recruited in Mozambique were obliged to enter into twelve-month contracts. Once they had completed this initial "join," they normally chose to move, either directly or via the WNLA compound, to a specific mine or a subcontractor's compound. Men who volunteered to re-engage received bonuses that could, depending on the length of the contract, amount to several pounds.[172] In contrast to the three to six months spent on the mines by most migrants in the early twentieth century, Shangaans worked for an average of eighteen months.[173] By 1913–1914 the amount of time spent by Mozambicans on the Rand had climbed to well over two years, eighty-six out of every one hundred men recruited by WNLA on the East Coast decided to re-engage, and large numbers of men failed to return home.[174] Employers benefitted in various ways from this process of proletarianisation; Mozambicans were expensive to get to the Witwatersrand, but they did not absorb the same level of recruitment, transport, and training costs as other workers. Perhaps most importantly, they spent enough time on the gold fields to acquire the skills, experience, and discipline needed to work under pressure in the deep levels. Veteran workers also tended progressively to return to the mines; between 1906 and 1914 the number of experienced workers, as a percentage of all men recruited by WNLA in Mozambique, rose from 56 to almost 80 percent.[175] These qualities led some mine-owners to state that one Mozambican miner was worth six to twelve men drawn from other areas of Southern Africa.[176]

With the aid of the colonial governments in Mozambique and the Transvaal, the mine owners succeeded in reducing black wages from 23 percent of total costs in 1896 to 16 percent in 1911.[177] In cash terms, the wages of black workers remained lower than in 1896; but in real terms they were more than halved, particularly by the rampant inflation unleashed during World War I. Thus the pressures of scientific management had brought little profit to the miner, who had a far smaller disposable income than the men of his father's generation. The black miner's earnings had slipped steadily downward from the late 1880s at Kimberley, when he earned one of the highest mining wages in the world, and were only finally to turn upwards in real terms in the mid-1970s. Thanks to the large supply of labour from Mozambique, the Chamber had achieved its original aim, when setting up the Native Labour Department in 1893, of increasing the number of workers while reducing their wages. The qualities of Mozambican workers were frequently referred to. In 1898 the Chamber of Mines reported that

> The East Coast native pays us better in every respect than any native of South Africa, or, indeed, any class of coloured labourers we can get as far as we are now aware. He certainly comes farther and takes more trouble to collect, but when we get him he stays longer, and after he has once learnt his business, he almost invariably comes back again after he has gone to his kraal. The greatest advantage of employing the East Coast native is that you have no difficulty with him underground as compared with natives from other sources.[178]

H. F. Strange regarded men from the East Coast as "the best miners," while J. M. Makhotle thought them "the best hammer boys."[179] In 1904 the WNLA chairman, F. Perry, remarked that in terms of efficiency, Mozambicans represented "four-fifths of the whole native labour on the mines before the war. They were the backbone of the industry. . . .as long as the mines rely on black labour, they stand or fall by the supply of Portuguese natives."[180] In 1911 another Chamber of Mines representative remarked that Mozambicans were "the mainstay of the industry."[181] Because of the profound belief of the mineowners in the importance of Mozambican labour to the Witwatersrand, they imbued workers from the East Coast with "racial" qualities such as honesty, loyalty, reliability, and discipline.[182] They were believed to "take well" to mining and to "work harder," and, above all, they were associated with drilling. The stereotype of the East Coaster as a hard-working, underground miner legitimated the mineowners' need for, and indeed dependence on, cheap and experienced labour drawn from outside the Transvaal. The stereotype was reinforced as Mozambicans adopted it and built upon it as a means of increasing their self-worth, their competitiveness in the labour market, and their visibility in the world of their employers. Over time, the stereotype took on a force of its own, and its characteristics came to be perceived as the natural, biological attributes of an ethnic group or nation. "Shangaans were notably intelligent and practical," writes Anthony Hocking in a recent company history, "and white miners often chose them as their deputies or 'bossboys.' "[183] The Witwatersrand was a crucible in which blacks acquired new and sometimes conflicting identities.

8

Mine Culture

When the eponymous hero of Henri Junod's novel *Zidji* arrives in Johannesburg, he is confronted by the "horrible monotony . . . of industrial disorder." The train rushes past the dumps, tall black smoke stacks break the horizon, and shanties tear past, huddled together in little villages. Piles of beams and masses of scrap iron lie discarded alongside discoloured pools of stagnant water. This bleak industrial landscape moves at a pace and rhythm that is hurried and unsettling. The chimneys belch smoke, the railways multiply, the flywheels spin continuously, and trucks lumber unceasingly along their narrow-gauge tracks. The air is heavy with smoke and grime, a deafening roar comes from the battery, there is the scream of steam, the creak and groan of trucks, and the dull rumble of discharged ore.[1]

It was in this discordant environment that migrant workers like Zidji had to carve an existence. In the absence of records left by workers, our picture of life on the mines has depended on the descriptions of whites who attempted to speak for them. Philanthropists had initially viewed the compounds as places of protection for blacks torn from the traditional structures and codes that sustained rural society. The compounds provided a solution to the dangers of proletarianisation, as they maintained the "old restraints" and prevented the breakdown of tribal controls. This ideology lived on in the racial paternalism of the mine owners. "Like any grown up children released from the effective restraints of a rigorous home control," wrote Lionel Phillips in 1905, blacks "are apt to imbibe the vices and ignore the virtues of civilizaton."[2] Phillips and others continued to stress the benefits of wage labour; men arrived on the mines thin and in poor health and returned home fat and strong.[3] But as liberals became familiar with the living conditions of black workers, many came to see the compounds as centres of environmentally determined racial degeneration. To Junod, for whom the mine headgear conjured up the image of "antediluvian monsters," the mines represented an atavistic degeneration, and the compound was "the most complete triumph of modern industrialism," a process that had "impaired the character of [the native] race."[4]

Charles Bourquin, a Swiss missionary working amongst Mozambicans on the Rand, wrote in 1912 of

> Those dreadful compounds where everything speaks of misery, where everything shouts of exile, tribulation, vice, the exploitation of the weak by the strong. In certain compounds one sees men wandering around with-

194

out clothes; here man's decency and self-respect are assaulted; all the senses are offended and revolted. One is led to ask how our blacks can leave their forests, their lakes, their lovely rivers, to live for perhaps one, two, three, four years in these horrible conditions.[5]

This engulfing industrial landscape was frequently portrayed in the narrative imagery of Coketown and Montsou, the fictional industrial towns created by Dickens and Zola. The constant contrast with the pastoral veld served to intensify the picture of urban squalor and corruption. This was the "town and country" perceived by George Eliot to have "no pulse in common." The sprawling city was an aberration, an infraction of nature, and was condemned in biblical metaphors. By consigning Johannesburg to the status of a new Nineveh, Babylon, or Sodom, writers evoked the worldliness and greed of the new industrial social order. But this representation, as powerful as it was stark, obscured as much as it revealed. Liberal evolutionists like Junod and Bourquin saw African workers in terms of the image of the European proletariat; caught in an inescapable void between town and countryside, migrant workers suffered an inevitable decline in their level of civilisation. In his anthropological work, Junod contrasted the picture of a pristine tribal civilization, untroubled by colonialism or capitalism, with that of a brutalized and degenerate working class.[6]

Many mine owners and state officials used the same discourse but clung to the belief that the compound insulated the tribesman from the "demoralising influences" of urban communities "alien to his way of life." Well into the 1920s, they would perceive the compounds as "the best compromise possible in the difficulties of this transitional stage in the natives' economic development."[7] The binary opposition in the representation of rural and urban areas, synonyms for the traditional and modern, was later to imprint itself on the history of the period, as social scientists portrayed migrant workers as "men of two worlds."

However, black miners were not aware of their precarious position on the ladder of evolution or of the separate spheres into which their experiences were classified; nor were they concerned with their employers' preoccupations with cleanliness, sexual restraint, providence, and order. Black migrants were strongly tied to both their land and their culture and they were not the unrelenting victims of the environment portrayed by the industrial novelists of the nineteenth century. When critics assigned the cultural expressions of black workers in the cities to the realm of the abnormal or the degenerate, they obscured whole areas of life in the compounds. Beneath the surface, behind closed doors, and hidden within the intimacy of the worker's daily life lies another picture. This "hidden" world was alluded to by Junod when he wrote, "and yet, in the middle of this general ugliness, the blacks succeed in creating a good deal that is picturesque."[8]

Living Conditions

The compounds on the Witwatersrand were not closed institutions or panopticons, and were as much centres of worker organisation and expression as they were institutions of social control. As the mine companies grew and the work force expanded, increasing numbers of men were brought together in compounds. By 1910

The compound of the New Primrose Mine, c.1894. This compound, one of the biggest on the early Witwatersrand, held 3000 men in 1895. The kitchens are in the center of the quadrangular space formed by the barracks. Behind the mine hospital (visible in the right-hand corner) are the battery and reduction works, the headgear above the shaft, and the dump of excavated earth. Other mines are visible on the horizon. In 1916 the sixty compounds on the Witwatersrand housed an average of 4000 men.

the compound of an important deep-level mine such as the Simmer and Jack housed over four thousand men; within six years this was to be the average size of the sixty mine compounds on the Witwatersrand.[9] The new model compounds built to house the influx of African and Chinese workers after the war incorporated innovative ideas on hygiene, sanitation, and social order. "A typical compound," wrote Henri Junod in about 1910, was composed of "a vast square courtyard, surrounded on four sides by iron structures that served as dormitories with a single entrance, the dark alley that is closed at night."[10] Workers were supplied with maize meal from the steam pots housed in the compound kitchen, normally a tin roof structure supported by wooden beams in the centre of the courtyard. The men cooked their meat rations in the compound courtyard and, in a public statement of communal inclusion, clubbed together to buy food and drink in the compound or at neighbouring eating houses.[11] In an attempt to encourage miners to stay in the compounds over weekends, especially on outlying mines, compound managers frequently supplied their men with raw meat on Saturdays, Sundays, and Mondays.[12] On special occasions such as Christmas and Good Friday, companies presented the men with several bullocks. To a European observer, the butchering of these animals in the compound might have seemed a way of "gratifying the savage instincts of the natives and providing them with an exciting spectacle."[13] But for the miners the distribution of the joints of the slaughtered beast was an expression and exhibition of their own sense of hierarchy and belonging, with the head, liver, and tongue going to senior men and indunas, and hooves to the youths. For the compound manager, the slaughter of the bullocks was a festive display through which he reinforced the paternalistic image of the compound-as-tribe.[14]

In the early part of the century, miners received only a part of their nutritional requirements in the form of rations.[15] Even after attempts to standardise the miners' diet in 1906 and 1911, there was little way of controlling the equitable distribution of rations, and the men, particularly Shangaan miners working long contracts, were obliged to supplement their diet in various ways. Commensal groups of workers brought pigs, goats, sheep, and chickens into the compound where they slaughtered, cooked, and divided up the animals. Small cakes, fruit, bread, tins of meat, fish, and fruit, together with wood fuel, were sold by hawking miners and neighbouring concession stores.[16] Illegal supplies of liquor, brewed and sold in the vicinity of the compounds, became a cornerstone of the workers' informal economy. In these ways, miners both continued the tradition of penny capitalism and determined when, what, with whom, and where they ate and drank.[17] Like food, liquor was an important signpost of identity. To many Mozambicans drink was a physical necessity, a social lubricant, a quick source of energy, an escape from boredom, and a marker of masculinity. The men made up for the low alcohol content (less than 3 percent) of the sorghum beer served in the mines by mixing treacle with flour and water to obtain *skokiaan*. Others concocted *sigwagwa* from a mixture of ingredients dominated by brown sugar, or brewed *khali* from golden syrup and a powdered root.[18] Commercial methylated spirits were also consumed and, at one stage, a pile of empty *eau de cologne* bottles provided testimony to the popularity of this 67 percent proof spirit. Dagga (cannabis or *mbange*) was a familiar stimulant, and miners would frequently share a pipe in their leisure hours.[19]

The ties of solidarity linking workers caused the labour recruiter J. S. Marwick to marvel at their "freemasonry," and their willingness to entrust their savings with their "uncles," engage in extensive lending and borrowing, and send money home with their "brothers."[20] The concept of fictive kin was reluctantly recognised by management, as doctors were prohibited from performing amputations without the permission of the injured worker's "brothers." It was also accepted that "brothers" of a deceased miner might share his savings, rather than see them transferred to Mozambique by the Curator's Office.[21]

By exploiting the competition between mines for labour, workers were able to force mine managers to allow a restricted amount of commercial alcohol into the compounds. As Blackburn and Caddell remarked, "the average manager is prepared to put up with the trouble of dealing with a percentage of drunken natives, so long as he can send an average and sufficient number on shift."[22] Compound managers regarded the operations of liquor merchants with ambivalence, for drink was both a disruptive agent and a means of attracting workers to a mine. "Where irregularities are condoned or winked at," wrote W. C. Scully, "a compound is apt to become popular at the expense of others which are well conducted. Many of the natives . . . will cheerfully endure bad food and general discomfort for the sake of occasionally obtaining poisonous spirits, or of not having their conduct too closely scrutinized."[23] Compound dwellers bought liquor from, or worked as agents for, whites miners and itinerant traders. Others swelled their wages by, for example, purchasing three bottles of brandy for £1 and then selling glassfuls for 6d each to their comrades. Men who were unable to leave the compound to frequent illegal canteens or shebeens might pool a certain amount of money and send two of their number to buy drink from a liquor seller who had established himself, after nightfall, in a dip near a route leading to the compound.[24] Eating houses sold cheap food, such as offal and tripe, and served as meeting places and recreation centres. To attract labour and discourage workers from going into the local towns to find entertainment, mine managers encouraged the building of eating houses on company property, generally next to the concession stores, and often tolerated a limited amount of prostitution and liquor-selling.[25] Prohibition and an increased control over the workers' movements and habits served to reduce the incidence of drunkenness on the mines, but these measures did not completely suppress the miners' drinking culture and St. Monday was to linger on for many years.[26]

The locations on mine property were areas free of white control. The Chamber of Mines had initially called for the construction of permanent housing for skilled black workers and their families, at least partly because of the recurrent costs of migrancy.[27] But the construction of these quarters, I would suggest, was also a means of encouraging a hierarchical stratification of the work force. The skilled workers who lived in mine locations paid a rent of 6–12s per month for their wedge-like, wood-and-iron dwellings, or for small rooms built near the compound. Their wives and concubines increased the family income by brewing and selling illicit beer and by running illegal bars or shebeens. On a few mines, a majority of the workers were housed in these married quarters,[28] but the early enthusiasm showed by the mine owners for this form of housing died away in the twentieth century. Although some mining officials and members of the Native Affairs Department (NAD) still viewed them as a solution to the skilled labour shortage, the married quarters or mine locations declined in size and importance as the mineowners abandoned their attempts to stabilize a part of the black work force.[29]

During the nineteenth century, most blacks had fought proletarianisation by working in South Africa for limited amounts of time before returning home. By developing a system of migrant labour, they had benefitted from both the sale of their labour and the productive energy of their wives and children at home. This form of accumulation on two fronts increased the wealth and status of the migrant and provided him with a strong home community to which he could return in case of physical disability or a downturn in his conditions of employment. The workers' pattern of labour migration had been supported by the Republican government, which feared the growth of a proletariat of foreign extraction, and later by the Portuguese, who wished to ensure the repatriation of the labourers who formed Mozambique's major economic asset. But the Chamber had every reason to support migrant labour after 1897, as the wage reduction of that year had been achieved by flooding the market with Mozambican migrants. As colonialism added taxes, forced labour, military conscription, and land alienation to the forces pushing men to the mines, and as the state restricted their ability to sell their labour to the highest bidder, desert, or even drink, migrant labour was transformed from a weapon in the hands of the worker to the means of his subjugation.

The alliance between capital and the state that had crystalised in 1897 had succeeded in cutting, clipping, and containing black wages; but it had also succeeded in widening the division between black and white workers. To protect their high wages, white workers organised on a racial basis and any attempt to stabilise black labour was seen as a prelude to undermining the white monopoly of mining skills.[30] The Het Volk government discouraged the stabilisation of black mineworkers by prohibiting uncontrolled squatting on mine property. After 1908 only married couples and their families were allowed to live on mine property, and any shacks erected without company permission were demolished by government representatives; three years later all plans for the erection of locations had to be approved by the NAD. By 1914 only a fraction of the black work force, some 4,740 men, together with 7,108 women and children, was housed in these areas.[31] While the married quarters on some mining estates were broken down, in other areas their management was transferred to the local municipality and they became the "native locations" of towns like Germiston, Boksburg, and Benoni.[32] This lack of suitable housing for black mineworkers' families, and not legislation, pressured men to migrate. Workers were encouraged to renew their contracts, and some lived in the compounds for as long as ten years; but if a man wanted to build and maintain a family, he was compelled to leave his wives and children in the rural areas, as it became increasingly difficult to house them on mine property. Thus government housing policy pushed blacks to remain migrant workers long before the establishment of influx control.

The social world of the black miner reached beyond the borders of the mining estate. On the eve of the Anglo-Boer war, up to thirty thousand blacks were employed on the Witwatersrand as messengers, cooks, domestic servants, washermen, and brickmakers, and in a range of other occupations only indirectly related to mining. Many Mozambicans were attracted to settle beyond the confines of the mine by higher wages, better working conditions, and the prospect of establishing a family in the town locations. In 1903, when about fifty thousand Mozambicans lived and worked on the mines, perhaps as many as eleven thousand were employed in other sectors of the economy. But Mozambicans were disadvantaged by Portuguese controls and were stereotyped as less "civilized" than the martial Zulu and the more studious Sotho, who consequently tended to dominate urban employment.[33]

By 1909 almost forty thousand blacks lived beyond the compounds in the urban world of Johannesburg. Those who wished to escape from the back yards of their employers or the slum yards of the city lived in the Klipspruit native location south-west of Johannesburg or in the racially mixed areas, Alexandra and Sophiatown, on the northern and western fringes of the city. On weekends and between contracts, mineworkers left the cloistered world of the mine property, with its compound, concession stores, and eating houses, and made their way into town. This brought them into contact with the new urban communities clustered around churches, schools, political associations, and shebeens.

Industrialisation gave a new freedom to women. But it seems that it was only the most marginalised Mozambican women, such as Chopi ex-slaves, women dissatisfied with their marriages, or rebellious daughters, who took advantage of this new freedom.[34] Partly because of the high rents demanded by rackrenters in the slums (as much as 70s per month), many women were forced into beer brewing and the commercialised sex that often accompanied liquor selling. Others escaped the poor conditions and physical dangers of the slums by moving out to the mine locations. But there they were considered by men like H. O. Buckle, the chairman of the Natives Grievances Inquiry, to be "temporary concubines, often locally picked up, who contribute to the household the proceeds of liquor selling and prostitution."[35] With this unsavory reputation for moral turpitude and ill discipline, women were pushed away from mine property. Thus while there were 91,500 black males and 4,000 females in the Johannesburg area in 1910, in the knots of population along the reef the sexual imbalance was even more pronounced.[36] Pass laws and an alien outside world pushed workers back towards the mine company estate. At the centre of this world was the compound enclosure and the miners' sleeping quarters. Beyond the compound, but still on mine property, lay the concession stores, eating houses, married quarters, and perhaps a church hall. This was an insulated and self-contained community turned in on itself as a means of defence and of control; but it was perhaps most markedly a community without women.

Sex and Gender

A part of the battery of disciplinary legislation passed by the Republican government after the Jameson Raid had repressed both beer brewing and the commercialized sex with which it was often related. In an attempt to undermine illicit beer brewing and curb venereal disease, an Immorality Ordinance was passed in 1903 and "married quarters" were subjected to stricter controls. By confining workers to single-sex barracks and restricting their access to women, the mineowners attempted to channel their libidinal energy into work. But without women, the miners soon turned to their comrades to construct their notions of gender and satisfy their sexual needs. The migrants' pattern of sexuality was merely one of a wide range of cultural expressions strongly influenced by the social environment of the mines.

The practice of *bukhontxana*, or mine marriages, seems to have emerged amongst Mozambican workers in the early twentieth century. In 1904, the head of the C.I.D. on the Witwatersrand reported that "unnatural offences are very prevalent on the mines among the natives," particularly the Shangaan.[37] In 1906 Swiss missionaries claimed that homosexual activities were engaged in by three-quarters of the young men in some compounds and, through the Transvaal Missionary Association, called on the government to prohibit the practice. They regarded "drunkenness and immorality" as "the two major wounds that eat at our Christians."[38] In 1907 H. M. Taberer, at that stage in the NAD, ascribed the importation of the "unnatural vice practiced throughout all the mines on the Witwatersrand" to a Shangaan worker, Sokisi, employed on the Brackpan Mine. Within a few years, missionaries, journalists, and compound managers confirmed the existence of *bukhontxana* and, tracing its importation to the Shangaans, reported that it was rapidly spreading to other ethnic groups.[39] "When this custom became known, it spread like a powder-fuse, it invaded the dormitories like an irresistible prairie fire," wrote Junod, "it reigns in the compounds and it reigns in the prisons."[40]

In Southern Mozambique, young adolescents often played together "like husband and wife," a form of gender socialisation that sometimes included the practice of external coitus, or penetration between the thighs (inter-crural sex).[41] Boys and girls lived in special huts at the entrance to the homestead, and it was easy for them to meet at night; the only proviso to *gangisa* was that it should conform to local rules of exogamy and that the young couple should not stay together until morning; full and uninhibited sexual relations were tied to marriage. Thus sexuality bound boys and girls into gender roles that were distinctly masculine and feminine and marked the passage from childhood to adulthood. *Gangisa* formed part of the primary sexual imagery of young men arriving on the mines. As they came from a society that placed great value on children, and discouraged sexual practices that did not lead to pregnancy, the only acceptable forms of sexual release to which they could turn, within their cultural code, were variations of the intercrural sex practised during *gangisa*.[42]

By the beginning of the twentieth century, as men from the East Coast worked longer and more frequent periods on the mines, they became increasingly divorced, not only from their means of production and their culture, but also from their womenfolk. But many Mozambicans, who made up a high proportion of the most historically proletarianized miners, were little more than children. Children had frequently been employed on the Natal plantations, as well as at Kimberley, where managers had the legal right to employ males over the age of eleven.[43] The gold-mining industry followed the Kimberley example, and in 1896 boys under the age of twelve, as well as women, were prohibited from working underground.[44] In 1902 there were 132 boys under the age of fourteen on the Bonanza Mine, and 111 on the Crown Reef Mine, and Witwatersrand Native Labour Association (WNLA) members officially employed almost two thousand of these "piccanins."[45] In 1903 the British raised the minimum age for underground miners to fourteen years.[46] Portuguese officials estimated that most Mozambican miners started work at the age of fifteen or sixteen, and that most of the Shangaans employed on the mines were from fifteen to twenty-five years old.[47] "It is the custom" with Mozambican workers, wrote the secretary of the Chamber of Mines in 1911, "to come out to work on the mines at the earliest possible age, and a considerable proportion of the gangs coming up consist of youths who have just reached the age of puberty." When the Mines and Works Act of that year threatened to prohibit the employment of children underground, he warned that "difficulties might arise," particularly if the law were applied to Shangaans, as this "would affect a considerable number of natives who are at present employed on drill work on the mines."[48]

The low grade and depth of the mines required narrow stopes in which children could work more efficiently than adults, they were easier to train and discipline, and were paid less than the established minimum wage and half the compensation benefits available to adults. Under pressure from the Chamber, the law was finally modified to prohibit the employment underground of miners who were "apparently under the age of 16 years." This legal imprecision allowed mine managers to continue employing children underground and merely limited to eight hours the shifts worked by children noticeably under the age of sixteen, employed in the surface works. In 1915 the Portuguese curator was still able to note that "many workers on the Rand are really children," while the head of the Native Recruiting Corporation remarked that many recruits were "not over the age of twelve."[49]

However, it was not just the mineowners who created and perpetuated the employment of low-cost child labour. In the rural areas of southern Mozambique,

(a) Children employed in the surface works of the Premier Diamond mine east of Pretoria.

work was considered an integral part of a child's moral upbringing and gender so-cialisation and boys were expected to contribute to the homestead economy from an early age. As migrant labour became a crucial aspect of family income, boys were pressed into wage work by their elders and, particularly in years of famine, were frequently impersonated by older men when signing on with recruiters.[50]

These young boys had been brought up to regard their elders with deep re-spect. As the young recruits shared their quarters with up to fifty seasoned and experienced workers, and were almost entirely under their power in the dark un-derground tunnels, it is tempting to see *bukhontxana* solely as the product of an en-forced celibacy and as yet another aspect of a brutalised existence. But this is to ignore the strong ties of affection that bound the partners. Nor does it explain why the relationship was strictly intergenerational, impermanent, governed by specific rituals and laws, and readily accepted and practised by large numbers of miners, most especially Shangaans from Mozambique.

Bukhontxana bears many of the hallmarks of a rite of passage from the status of boy to man and from inexperienced provincial, or *mampara*, to respected *gayisa*. As an institution, it has many parallels with the initiatory homosexuality practised in many parts of the world.[51] While migrant labour abruptly severed the close rela-tionship between a boy and his mother, the initial stage of the homosexual rela-tionship marked a traumatic imposition of male authority. This amounted to a

(b) Young adolescents assisting senior miners in machine driving or tunnel cutting.

symbolic offer, made by an adult male, one day to share his power and authority if the boy agreed to give up his identification with his mother. Through the establishment of a close bond with a successful adult male, the boy was gradually detached from his mother and incorporated into the community of men. The relationship between the young adolescent and his mine husband was based on paternal respect. "The boy used to call his husband 'father,' " according to one informant, "and never anything like 'darling' or 'husband.' Respect was very important." In return, the older man frequently addressed his "wife" as "my child," and taught him not only how to survive but also what was expected of a man.[52]

The initiatory aspects of the *bukhontxana* relationship included an informal apprenticeship. One of the husband's first acts was to take his wife to the concession store on mine property, buy for him clothes, soap, and other everyday necessities, and guard him from the inflated prices charged of novice miners. Many experienced miners were dormitory prefects, or *indunas*, who frequently used their position of power to exact sexual favours from young boys; but they were equally able to protect their charges and allocate them light work. Underground husbands taught the new arrivals to recognize the sound, smell, and sight of danger and, by instructing them in the skills of mining, increased their earning power. Far from reflecting an ambiguity in sexual identity, *bukhontxana* introduced boys to an influential network of male friends and fictive kin and taught them the principles of masculine identity. By reproducing a hierarchical concept of gender, *bukhontxana* served to strengthen male identity at a time when women, due to migrant labour, were playing a growing role at home.

Bukhontxana was fundamentally tied to the exercise of power. At home, social order was represented in terms of male domination and female subordination, and it was on this familiar pattern that gender relations were modelled in the mine. In the compounds, the young wives performed domestic tasks that, in the rural areas, were perceived to be strictly female. "An *inkotshane's* duty appears to be," stated Taberer, "to fetch water, cook food and do any odd work or run messages for his master."[53] Informants remember that an *nkhontxana* would also wash and iron the clothes of his *nuna* (husband), clean his shoes, prepare his tea and make his bunk.[54] They sometimes wore womens' cosmetic oils, greeted their husbands by clapping hands in the manner of women, and, at feasts, were presented with the soft meat generally saved for women. In return the *nuna* was expected to be open-handed, his generosity being encouraged by the heated gossip of the *nkhontxana*. He was expected to organise a marriage feast at which a goat was slaughtered, meat distributed to his friends, and a brideprice of £10–15 lodged with the boy's "brother" or "guardian."[55] The gift-giving boosted the prestige of the elder and reinforced his masculine role as the provider in the gender relationship. According to Junod, the *nkhontxana* were

> treated with greater kindness than the others. Their husbands will give them 10s to woo them (*buta*) and will choose for them easy occupations, as, for instance, sweeping the dormitories, whilst the others will have to go to the hard underground work . . . But the "husband" will have not only to woo this peculiar kind of *nsati* (wife); he must also *lobola* her, and a feast sometimes takes place when as much as £25 is put on the ground, a goat is killed, and a real contract made which binds the *nkhontxana* to his master for the whole time he remains in the compounds. The elder brother of the boy will receive the money in this disgusting parody of the Bantu marriage. Sometimes the husband pays his *nkhontxana* at the end of each month as much as £1.10s, and this represents a big increase in the earnings of the boy.[56]

Bukhontxana provided the young miner with an emotional and financial security in a harsh, adult, and masculine world. The young miner accepted the custom "as a way of life and even derived a sense of security from it because he knew he wouldn't have to struggle over acquiring property," stated one informant, while another explained that *bukhontxana* "reduces the culture shock" of those unfamiliar with life and work on the mines. Yet another remarked that those who did not practice it were likely to remain lashers, shovelling ore all their lives.[57]

Gender roles were often advertised at parties where men drank heavily, swore, and engaged in bouts of horseplay, bravado, and generosity, while singing explicit erotic songs celebrating their sexual dominance over boys and women. The young "wives" displayed markers of femininity at these parties by wearing imitation breasts fashioned from wood or cloth, strong perfumes, skirts, and tight jackets. They further masked their masculinity by donning head-scarves and creams that hid their need to shave. The *nkhontxana* advertized their sexual role at these gatherings by sometimes greasing their inner thighs and by dancing in a suggestive manner while the older men exhibited their power and generosity by providing the boys with food and drink. The symbolism of this ritual inversion provides a point of entry into the hidden world of the compound dweller and allows us to unravel some of the unconscious social relations of dominance that are intertwined with sexuality.[58]

These parties were held during the worker's spare time when he was freed from the disciplined, chronologically regulated rhythm of mine labour. Because he was far from home, and less constrained by kinship obligations or the demands of the agricultural cycle, the worker had a new freedom of cultural expression. During his leisure hours, that specifically "private time" created by wage labour, he was able to experiment with new ideas and powers of creativity that would have been stifled at home. In rural society men were obliged to participate in public ritual, but on the mines they could choose to retreat into the "private space" created by wage labour or enter into public space in roles that ranged from actor to audience. Nor were the cultural expressions of most miners constrained by the notions of sin and guilt preached by missionaries and their converts; indeed, it might be argued that the individualism experienced by men on the mines allowed them to fall in love to an extent that was rare at home, where the function of marriage was often more social and political than affective. Informants today remember the loving and deep ties that a husband often developed for his mine wife, deep emotions that at times led to suicides, murders, and beatings if the boy left his husband for another man.[59] Through their leisure time activities, migrant workers made symbolic statements about their lives on the mines. Mine dances, singing, and fighting, language, music, and the more sedate consumption of food and drink formed part of this new symbolic order. So, too, did rites of sexual inversion.

Negation is a primary means of delineating identity, as it defines normality in terms of both what is acceptable and in opposition to what is viewed as abnormal. By ritually inverting the gender of the young *nkhontxana*, the husbands or *nuna*, who had convened and paid for the party, reinforced their masculinity. The transvestism served as a political act aimed at reasserting the virility and power of the *nuna*, whose masculine identity was emphasised when contrasted with the femininity of their mine wives. At the same time, the dance displayed the powerlessness and marginality of the *nkhontxana* and, I would suggest, expressed the ambiguity and uncertainty of initiates who have entered a liminal phase on their passage from one status to another.[60] This was noticeable in the rough greeting extended to migrants on their arrival in Kimberley in the 1870s and early 1880s, a custom abandoned with the erection of the compounds; but the distinction lived on in the terms *gayisa* and *mampara*.

It is possible that the transvestism of the *nkhontxana* formed a ritual element in the progression of a male from the status of boy, bachelor, and novice miner to that of married man and *gayisa*. Because of their marginality as "women," the *nkhontxana* were reduced to a status that symbolised their willingness to acquire the set of signs and codes associated with the senior status of the *nuna* or *gayisa*. By dressing as women, they advertised, in a symbolic form, their female role in the gender relationship. But at the same time, by an inversion of the normal, as represented by the transvestism, a border or threshold was created that had to be crossed for initiates to become "husbands," and hence "men." As at home, one of the distinguishing features of a male's attainment of adulthood, and the masculinity that accompanied it, was to take a wife with whom he could openly have full sexual relations. Thus at the same time that the transvestism buttressed the masculinity of the elders, it reflected the liminal or marginal position of the young men. In this way, the symbolic inversion of the gender of some men perhaps served to portray the *nkhontxana's* progression to becoming a *gayisa*. In much the same way as adopting an innovative name or new ways of dressing, eating, dancing, and drinking, the transvestism served to separate a man from his former status and proclaim his entry into the community of workers. Like most rites of reversal, the transvestism of the *nkhontxana* was a political rather than a sexual or aesthetic statement. The female role of the *nkhontxana* was reinforced during the sex act as the boy was not allowed, under threat of a heavy fine, to "breathe" into the thighs of his husband or take lovers. Here again, it is possible to discern the outlines of a rite of passage as sperm was considered a life-giving and strengthening force in southern Mozambique, and was associated with life passages. Sperm was employed in ritual ways to furnish an infant with the life force necessary to become a recognized member of society; it also provided evidence of the virility needed for a boy to enter adolescence.[61] Hence it seems possible that the sperm of the mine husband augmented the strength and vitality of his "wife" and in this way assisted the boy's progression to manhood. Once the boy felt himself sufficiently adult, masculine, and wealthy he was entitled, through the mediation of an "uncle" or the *indunas*, to be released from his marriage and acquire his own mine wife.

Bukhontxana was a channel for the acquisition of status and power. Junod noted that the *indunas* and the native police were the first to *humutsha* or make proposals to the newly arrived novices. As one man explained, by marrying an *nkhontxana*, "you put yourself on the same level as the *induna*. [A man's] maturity . . . was demonstrated by acquiring a boy."[62] The only restriction on *bukhontxana* relationships seems to have been that they should follow the patterns of exogamy practised at home. Thus mine marriages reinforced kin and gender identities and, ultimately, gave a familiar and comprehensible structure to life. For adult miners *bukhontxana* resolved the assault on gender definition brought about by males being obliged to perform domestic duties that they had been socialized to perceive as traditionally female. Although women were excluded from the compounds, those qualities regarded by the miners as female were incorporated into the culture of the mines. For the young men who switched gender, *bukhontxana* provided a means of entering, and adapting to, an environment that was at once foreign and yet familiar. Perhaps even more importantly, as Dunbar Moodie has pointed out, males who became "wives" on the mines succeeded in earning the bridewealth needed to become husbands, and hence adult "men," both at home and in the compounds.*

The acceptance of *bukhontxana* as a normal part of life in the compounds separated miners from the wider society. In 1915 Junod remarked that "the immense majority of the natives themselves do not consider this sin of any importance at all. They speak of it with laughter." As one informant recently explained to me, "in the beginning they were ashamed, but as time went on they became very well acquainted with mine culture."[63] Others stated simply, "it was a way of life on the mines," or "it is regarded as a mine activity." One possible reason for the rapid acceptance of *bukhontxana* was that, due to the scarcity of women, the value of sex as a means of reproduction declined and other (non-reproductive) forms of sexuality took on a new validity and legitimacy. But to an outside observer like Junod, *bukhontxana* was a repellent and "unnatural vice" and tangible evidence of the degeneration effected by industrialisation upon black tribesmen.

Mine managers turned a blind eye to *bukhontxana*. For the sake of missionary opinion, they ordered the migrants to remove the curtains enclosing their bunks and the state threatened men with twelve months' imprisonment for "unnatural vice."[64] But, apart from moving Christian workers, whose religion disapproved of the practice, into separate dormitories, little action was taken. In reality, compound managers had to put up with, if not encourage, *bukhontxana* if they wished to reproduce the labour force at their disposal. As the deputy commissioner of police in the Transvaal stated, "a compound manager who cracks down on vice and drink makes his compound less attractive," and NAD inspectors reported that active measures against *bukhontxana* were likely to produce a walkout, a strike, "or even a riot."[65] Mine managers were also aware that, by spending large amounts of money on their *nkhontxana*, the most experienced and skilled workers on the mines were obliged to renew their contracts, for it was unthinkable to return home empty-handed.[66] They must also have been aware that *bukhontxana* was an important form of tension release for men living in an all-male environment. That the dominant partners in the relationship were the politically important men, capable of mobilizing a large following in the compounds, must have heightened the manager's willingness to condone the institution. While *bukhontxana* acted as an agent of orderly proletarianization, it also reinforced the structures of control in the compound. "Sokisi's law," or the set of rules and customs regulating the practice, was enforced by the senior men, *indunas*, compound police, and, occasionally, the compound manager. Disputes frequently arose because of the adulterous behaviour of an *nkhontxana*, his desertion of his *nuna*, the husband's failure to pay the boy's brideprice, or the "eating" of the *nkhontxana*'s *lobola* by his "guardian." Through this arbitration, *bukhontxana* bolstered and reinforced, and hence was integrated into, the power structure of the compound.[67]

While an acceptance of Sokisi's law required men to submit themselves to the rules of the compound, *bukhontxana* also unified workers in a set of beliefs that were radically distinct from those of their European employers. *Bukhontxana* was a forceful rejection of the employers' demand that miners should value the virtues of sexual restraint and invest their libidinal energies in their work. It con-

*Moodie, "Migrancy and Male Sexuality on the South African gold mines" *JSAS* 14, 2, 1988.

tradicted the imposed morality of industrialism and established an alternative propriety. The gender relationship provided the workers with their own sense of
hierarchy and status, and with their own indices of prestige, power, and pride.
Bukhontxana gave men a sense of security, upward mobility, and self-worth in the
constrained world of the colonist. This initiatory homosexuality served as a strategy of social inclusion and difference that, although it did not directly resist capital,
could be mobilised politically. *Bukhontxana* also served to create a social space in
which the miner could assert a personal and communal autonomy and a male
identity and solidarity. By creating and sustaining gender distinctions in a world
without women, men retained their dominance over women at home. And ultimately, it was through their control over women's productive and reproductive ca-
pacities that men fought their own proletarianisation. Their vision of reality also
encompassed the supernatural.

Symbolic Space

Since the early days at Kimberley, black miners had adopted European names
which they incorporated into their cognitive world. By the turn of the century,
many boys started to add a European name to other forms of address adopted
when they reached puberty. These names could contain an element of snobbery
when the individual called himself after a symbol of authority such as Muxadora
(administrator), Mandante (commandant), Captain, Office, or Secretario. Some
men "replaced" a lost member of the family by taking the name of a relative who
had died or disappeared on the mines, while others sought to invoke the protection of an ancestor or godfather-like figure by taking on his European name. Men
who called themselves Sixpence, Tickey, Cemende, Correio (post), Parato (plate),
Djass (jacket), Fifteen, or Quartorze (fourteen) were situating themselves, in a traditional manner, within their environment. Even men called Go to Hell! Mais
Nada ("that's all"), Just Now, or God Damn! used a traditional system of naming
that recalled an event or frame of mind surrounding the young man's initiation
into a new status in life. Names like Xibalo (forced labour) or Kokamisaba (to carry
earth in the making of terraces, generally under the regime of forced labour) reminded men of the conditions existing at the time of their birth. Even the numerous Jims, Sams, Bobs, and Jacks returned home with what Guye called "a slight air
of the exotic." The names taken by black workers might have evoked derision
amongst whites, but for the workers themselves their pattern of naming had an
inherent logic and function, situating young men firmly within the turbulent
world on the mines. A European name was the sign of a *gayisa* in much the same
way as biblical names and surnames were markers of Christianity.[68]

A knowledge of Fanagalo was also a badge of achievement. This pidgin probably evolved in Natal where, as *isikula*, it served as a medium of communication
between blacks, Indians, and whites. It was carried to the diamond and gold fields
where, as *xikafula*, it evolved into a local pidgin.[69] Fanagalo reinforced white stereotypes of blacks as "ignorant child-like figures"; but the fact that whites were
obliged to learn an African-based pidgin is a mark of the strength and resilience of
this language form. Nor does it follow that what whites saw as a "bastard tongue"
was seen in the same light by all blacks.[70] Indeed, most men believed, as is com-

mon when speaking a pidgin, that they spoke the language of the "other," their European employers.[71] Augusto Cabral noted that young men returning from the mines remained conceited as long as their money and largesse lasted and that they expressed their new-found vanity through the frequent use of *xicafula* terms and an insistence on their English, Portuguese, or Dutch names.[72] On the mines men developed a system of naming, almost an *argot de métier* or occupational language, rooted in the old tramping system, through which they created places of reference in their own spatial and temporal world. Johannesburg was "Nkambeni," Kimberley "Dayiman," and Pietermaritzburg "Umgungundhlovu." African names were given to individual compounds and mines; Mzilikazi, the WNLA receiving compound, invoked the peremptoriness with which most Mozambicans were designated to a specific mine; the Bonanza was named Spensile after its mine manager (Spencer); the Primrose was called the Sinquangan after the "fierce temper" of its manager; the deep-level North Randfontein was the Gebuza (to dig a big hole), the Paarl Central the Majombolo (rock drill); and the City Deep, a mine made unpopular with Mozambicans because of its poor working conditions, was called "the insufficient supply of drills."[73] Men sometimes applied this symbolism to the rural areas, where a landmark such as a chapel might be known as "Number Four" after a shaft on a particular mine.[74] Through the act of naming, the miners seized control of the mental imagery of Europeans, turned it into their own, and created their own representation of the world.

Miners also attempted to arrange their living quarters in a manner that conformed to their customary conceptions of space and comfort. They frequently objected to being housed in the impersonal model compounds constructed in the early part of the century, as these restricted traditional freedoms and contradicted customary conceptions of space and comfort. "A curious fact," remarked the Portuguese curator, was that the old compounds, particularly those on the early outcrop mines, were "preferred by the natives," and that their "mortality rate was appreciably lower than that of the more hygienic compounds."[75] In a manner that had little to do with calculated interest or rational intentionality, the miners attempted to recreate the sensory world to which they were accustomed by ordering the arrangement of the barracks' interior.[76] Much against the desires of the medical personnel, the men plugged up the ventilation points, and nailed wood, cloth, or cardboard over their bunks in such a way as to turn them into cabins, protecting their privacy and possessions. Through these attempts to shape their habitat, the miners struggled to retain control over their lives in the compounds. "The authorities do not wish to interfere," wrote the Portuguese curator, "by imposing standards of discipline and cleanliness on the private lives of the natives and, in order to avoid friction and difficulties, they do not disturb their customs and traditions."[77]

Customs and traditions were also created and confirmed during the workers' leisure hours, when they incorporated elements of the industrial environment into the webs of signification that made up local culture. Men played *tchouba*, a form of backgammon employing four rows of holes, with pawns made of nuts and bolts. They used lengths of copper and brass wire to plait belts and bracelets. Planks of pinewood and cleaned-out oil or golden syrup tins served as calabashes in the construction of xylophones, the bottom of an old barrel was often replaced by a skin so as to form a drum, and the heads of beater sticks were made of solid india rubber obtained from the stamps.[78] The songs, dances, and music that formed a central

(a) Fashioning bracelets from copper and iron wire.

element of cultural life at home were similarly fused with elements of industrial life. Unicord harps impala horn trumpets, and small xylophones brought from the coast mixed on the mines with concertinas, harmoniums, harps, and guitars.[79]

Like all elements of culture, music invokes a system of symbols arranged in such a way as to constitute meaning for the performers.[80] The cultural code that constitutes music was inherited by migrant workers and reforged, improvised, and adapted on the mines. The result was a song genre, built on a specific tonality, a rhythmical call and response, as well as a shared set of tropes that were frequently incomprehensible to outsiders. These songs constituted an acquired knowledge and were an important, and exclusive, medium through which miners represented their world to themselves and others, and passed on this representation to novices. Songs provide a useful index of the sentiments and concerns of migrant workers. But very few mineworkers' songs were recorded at the turn of the century, and we are obliged to turn to those collected from men employed on the mines in the 1920s and 1930s to gather an impression of what interested their fathers.[81] The music and lyrics of the songs gave a tangible and emotional content to the notion of community.

> Take off your skins!
> There is no relish left, you Shangaans!
> It has been eaten by the Sotho and Xhosa
> And we will not get it.[82]

(b) Men sharing out meat.

Here Shangaan dancers are advised to take off their dancing costumes and claim their rightful share of the wealth (relish) found on the mines. Other songs referred to the miners' human and geographical points of reference and found a resonance in the compositions of women at home who sang of the departure of their menfolk and of their longing for their return.[83] Songs bound the rural homestead, the mine, and the city into one indissoluble space. One man was greatly moved when he sang of how the miner was caught between the tax collector and *xibalo* in Mozambique, and death underground in the Transvaal. The lyrics recorded the performers' overlapping identities; as Gazas (Shangaans), as miners, and as blacks. The song is filled with resignation as the miners bewail their fate; caught between starvation in the rural areas and the dangers of mining, there can be "no survival." Many songs were melancholic, expressing a deep resignation;[84] but others asserted

(c) Musicians playing Chopi xylophones of pitch pine and discarded tin drums.

the independence and strength of the miner by recalling his courage or by ridiculing and insulting white foremen. One song expresses resistance in flight from the mines, while another recalls the *xibalo* at home and calls on miners to "remain and *giya*," or dance in a warlike manner.[85]

Coordinated singing and dancing created an assertive display of power and discipline, an expression of the solidarity with which men confronted the fear and anxiety pervading life on the mines.[86] Men moved together in a tightly regimented and drilled manner, while their foot-stamping, hand clapping, and singing created a high degree of rhythmic complexity. Like faction fighting, tribal dancing was a performance—a highly competitive and visible demonstration of political recruitment and affiliation. Dancing and faction fighting existed on either side of a sliding scale of competition, ranging from symbolic confrontation to a direct physical trial of strength. But by 1913 faction fights were "practically extinct."[87] These public assaults on the colonial sense of order had been temporarily suppressed by the prohibition of liquor, the disarming of blacks under the 1905 Prevention of Crime Ordinance, and the general tightening of control over that "very dangerous class" of men who inhabited the compounds.[88] Dancing served to produce a more peaceful factionalism. Various styles of dancing were amalgamated to produce a visceral representation of ethnic belonging, along with a recognizable tonality and emotive lyrics. In the 1930s Hugh Tracey would remark that Chopi mineworkers "appear to dance as well as they do at home, but I understand they are inclined to stick to simpler routines on account of the fact that they are drawn from many different villages and they have to learn new steps to fit in with the others." Tracey would also recognise a growing uniformity as miners attempted to contain their music within an ethnic repertoire.

> The players of the mine orchestras, unlike those of the village orchestras, are not all drawn from the same district. Individual players have certain loyalties to particular mines to which they return again and again. Then once on the Reef, they play with whatever musicians happen to be up with them. In this way the music of the Chopi has become common national music and no longer exclusively village or district music.

Mine musicians also suppressed the tonal diversity found in the rural areas by using discarded tins, barrels, and pinewood in the construction of their xylophones.[89] This reduction of complex cultural traditions into recognizable ethnic genres reinforced a similar intellectual operation undertaken by individuals such as Junod and Mashaba who sought to conquer diversity and disorder by delineating "standard" languages and by isolating "pure" customs and traditions. It was on the mines that men, coming from geographically, culturally, and politically distinct regions, found a community of interests. Bounded groups that had been part of the imagery of folklore brought from the Transvaal by grandfathers, fathers, and uncles, became tangible as successive generations of young migrants returned home. Enmities that were deeply rooted in history were submerged as the members of different chiefdoms found a shared identity as Shangaans, Chopis, or Tongas.[90] This sense of belonging to a bounded ethnic group coexisted with other identities, as miners classified by others as East Coasters or "Potekees" gradually adopted this wider concept of self.[91] Many workers also came to see themselves as Christians.

Religion

The growth of the compounds was paralleled by the expansion of missionary activity on the Witwatersrand. Methodists, Anglicans, Presbyterians, Lutherans, Baptists, Congregationalists, Calvinists, and Catholics viewed the gold fields as an ideal centre from which to spread the gospel throughout southern Africa.[92] By 1904 over eighteen thousand blacks were affiliated to churches on the Witwatersrand.[93] When A. W. Baker left the Methodists, he first built a cottage for his family on the land of the City and Suburban mine and then, in February 1896, erected a church hall next to the mine compound. Over the next two years Baker's South African Compound Mission established schools, halls, and cottages on five other mines and regularly visited neighbouring compounds and hospitals.[94] When the Swiss Presbyterians extended their operations from Mozambique to the Witwatersrand in 1904, they built a school chapel on the Village Main Reef, a mine employing predominantly Shangaan workers.[95] The Anglicans began their Rand Native Mission in the Brickfields in 1903 and, by the end of the year, were operating in forty-three compounds. Three years later they had established twenty-seven churches, many on mine properties, and they preached regularly each Sunday to mine workers at over seventy places on the Rand. Anglican religious services and Sunday schools were run by 27 black catechists, 35 sub-catechists, 2 deacons, 13 theological college students, and 20 regular volunteers.[96] By the end of the decade the Swiss Mission operated from ten centres on the Rand, employed eleven evangelists, about twenty voluntary workers, and an equal number of church elders.[97] The South African Compounds Mission (SACM) followed a policy of constructing simple quadrangular buildings, consisting of a hall and two small rooms, on mine properties. At night and during the day these halls served as schools and, on Sundays, as religious meeting places capable of housing up to sixty worshipers.[98] The SACM eventually operated from twenty-four halls on the Rand and six on the coal mines. The Dutch Reformed Church worked in at least ten compounds.[99] Together with the Methodists, the Anglicans were to dominate the mission field on the Rand in the early twentieth century.[100]

Ministers adopted a strident working-class evangelism. On Saturday afternoons they combed the barracks, persuaded men to attend Sunday services in the compound square, organised passes for communicants wishing to attend church in the neighbouring town, and looked for Christians recently arrived on the mines. Migrants who left home with an elementary education and letters of commendation from their missionaries were often given the task of starting catechism classes. Others established their own Christian communities in the barracks and then called on the missionaries for assistance. Open-air services held in the compounds were a novel source of entertainment for the miners and drew large crowds. The boisterous hymn-singing, preaching, and praying competed with the workers' leisure-time activities and intruded into their world. Methodists, Anglicans, and Calvinists relied, to a varying degree, on hell-fire sermons and a belief in God's direct intervention through the Holy Spirit, visions, and dreams. Black miners were attracted by the simple and direct language and the animated style of these compound preachers, and they found a resonance in the puritanical simplicity of the mission churches whose rites of baptism and communion provided a passage into a new fellowship.[101] Through their sermons, Bible readings, catechism classes, and magic lantern shows, evangelists continued to introduce miners to a new system of causality, and an expanded view of the world; they also introduced a new musical tonality based on the portable harmonium and the strident hymns of composers like Moody and Sankey.

Conversion was accompanied by an industrial ethic that promoted punctuality, discipline, and obedience, and denounced drinking and gambling.[102] "Only Christianity will make of the black a servant content with his place," wrote Junod; it "will communicate to the African tribe the intelligence, the submission, the resignation and the flame of hope without which its evolution will amount to nothing."[103] Mine managers were quick to appreciate these attributes of Christianity. As the directors and managers of the mining companies "began to see and acknowledge the vast amount of good done to the characters of the boys" by Christianity, wrote the Rev. Bennet, they gave increasing support to mission work. The churches were provided with free sites on which to erect halls, schools, and cottages for their evangelists. Companies often supplied church halls with electricity, gave missionaries the use of old buildings, and even constructed new halls for their Christian workers. "As an experiment in promoting the welfare of mine boys," one company contributed £200 towards the construction of a church on mine property and undertook to pay a catechist's salary.[104] By 1912 the Anglican church on the Witwatersrand received direct grants amounting to £655 annually from mining companies. Four years later these contributions, largely made by Rand Mines and the recruiting agencies of the Chamber of Mines, had almost doubled.[105] Compound managers frequently patronized groups of Christian workers and often housed these men in separate barracks.[106] By encouraging Christian workers to live in their own social and geographical space, the churches restricted the opportunities for backsliding; but this policy also divided the work force. As Christians took biblical names, and refused to drink liquor, gamble, or participate in heathen dancing, they separated themselves from the rump of their fellows and even from non-Christian members of their family.[107]

Christianity had spread rapidly in southern Mozambique after the military defeats of the mid-1890s. On the mines conversion provided men with a universal creed that cut across tribal differences. It inculcated a discipline, a sense of time, a morality and a system of explanation that was more functional to industrial life than popular religions tied to a narrow environment and community. Scripture and prayer unions provided workers with a daily fellowship reaffirmed at Sunday church services. Many of the early churches were established by rural missionaries seeking to minister to their migrant congregants, and the Witwatersrand rapidly became a centre of evangelical energy as Christian miners collected money to support mission activity in their home areas. Churches served not only as a conduit for the passage of ideas and new forms of learning; they also provided workers with a place of safe keeping for their money, a channel for the repatriation of their earnings, and a network used by rural elders to trace young men who had "disappeared" on the Witwatersrand. For many miners the church was a source of spiritual strength, ritual power, and material security, as well as an introduction to new forms of understanding and behaviour.[108] Membership of a Christian community provided men with organisational skills, a sense of hierarchy, and a means of upward mobility. The Anglican missionaries on the Rand advocated a Trinitarian creed of "education, self-help, and responsibility," and many churches viewed lay preaching as a central element in evangelical work.[109]

Most missionaries believed that their churches should be self-financing and at least partially run by the congregants. Members were encouraged to form fundraising associations and hold tea-meetings to pay for building programmes, the salaries of evangelists and teachers, or an education into the ministry of one of their members.[110] In 1906 the Swiss Mission on the Rand introduced a system of fixed monthly contributions and later required those attending school to pay fees. By 1916 the annual income of the church amounted to just over £1,000, some 40 percent of which came from school fees. The SACM extracted a tithe from its members and encouraged those who attended school to pay monthly fees of 2s.[111] By 1912 Baker's Witwatersrand mission ran twenty-one schools and five classrooms, most of which were financially self-supporting.[112]

The churches were also involved in social reform; bodies such as the Witwatersrand Church Council, founded in 1908, and the Transvaal Missionary Association coordinated social work and criticised the pass laws, the destruction of mine locations, the racial barrier to worker mobility, the lack of political representation, and other matters affecting the social condition of black miners.[113] The missionaries spoke as representatives of black Christian workers, but did little to provide these men with the intellectual tools needed to defend their class interests. Missionaries like A. W. Baker were aware that, "in order to get the confidence of mine and compound managers," the education provided by his mission should contain "no influence in connection with disputes as to wages and terms of service," and he carefully limited teaching in the compounds to the skills of reading and writing in the vernacular.[114] Yet this political pragmatism did not prevent missionaries from preaching equality, and Baker sometimes published articles by African politicians in his mission's journal.[115] More than two generations of Mozambican migrants had been exposed to the tandem of Christianity and education in South Africa. Partly for political reasons and partly because few black workers stayed on the Witwatersrand long enough to learn English, most religious instruction was conducted in vernacular languages. But vernacular education was also a powerful means of censorship. It was a bulwark against what Baker called "the flood of filthy cheap literature" in English and, for the Swiss missionary linguist Henri Berthoud, a means of shaping and leading "a new people emerging from darkness." As late as 1938, G. P. Lestrade was to note of the Swiss Mission's school readers that "everything Thonga, except the language, seems to have been carefully banned from these books."[116] Until the Swiss missionaries and Free Methodists brought some of the languages spoken on the east coast to the mines, most Mozambicans attended Methodist, Anglican, or Compound Mission services in Zulu or Sotho. Even Robert Mashaba, the pioneer Ronga linguist, preached in Zulu when he joined the Methodist ministry to the compounds in 1902.[117]

Both preaching and literacy work were conducted in the linguistic forms classified and codified, and elevated to the status of "pure," "standard" languages by the missionaries. By the end of the nineteenth century, Mozambican workers were able to read religious works in Tonga (the language spoken around Inhambane), as well as in Ronga, Thonga, and Tswa, the three languages of the Thonga (or Tsonga) language cluster.[118] Literacy was particularly linked to Christianity by those missionaries who used the Bible as a textbook and basic reader. The Foreign Bible Society supplied cheap Bibles; a New Testament cost 1s6d and a complete Bible 2s6d. In 1908 some thirty-two thousand Bibles, almost three-quarters of which were in vernacular languages, were sold to blacks by the Christian Literature Depot in President Street. Cities like Johannesburg became centres of literacy, where migrants from the rural areas were able to join church libraries and buy spelling books, primers, and a variety of religious magazines and prayer books. "The bookshop," reported the Anglican ministry on the Rand, "is more than a centre of trade—it is a valuable evangelistic agency."[119]

The missionaries saw schooling as an essential element of evangelisation and encouraged the establishment of literacy groups run by workers. In 1910 the evangelist in charge of the Johannesburg presbytery of the Swiss mission noted that about thirty young men had started a school in the Meyer and Charlton compound. They had been given the use of a small room and their regular meetings attracted a number of dormant Christians to come forward. At one of the Randfontein compounds on the Far West Rand, a young miner from Bilene had started classes for twenty of his work mates; in another, a worker from Lourenço Marques, who had been engaged in literacy work, had recently been replaced by a migrant from Khosen; in a third Randfontein compound a new convert from Tembeland had placed himself at the head of a class of workers. At the Clydesdale Collieries, a Shangaan named Daniel witnessed to 400 men and taught night classes. Small literacy groups proliferated in the compounds; most worked under the guidance of church elders, but many laboured independently, or had only loose ties with neighbouring compound missions.[120] Shift workers learnt to read and write at schools run during the day, and at night they attended classes run by catechists, church elders, and other literate workers. At the Compound Mission school on the Crown Reef mine, an average of about forty men attended the night classes held six days a week. Between 7:00 and 8:00 p.m., newly arrived miners learnt to read with the aid of wall charts, while the more advanced students practised their writing. For the next half-hour, the beginners turned to writing on slates, and the more advanced students read the Bible aloud and posed questions. The final fifteen minutes were taken up with roll call, hymn-singing, and prayers.[121] The worker's voracious demand for a basic education often outstripped his predilection for Christianity. While the Swiss Mission on the Witwatersrand grew from 350 members in 1906 to over 1,000 in 1916, the enrollment of students multiplied about six times over the same period. Less than 20 percent of the 1200 students on the Swiss Mission books in 1916 were practising Christians.[122]

A mission such as that run by the Swiss Presbyterians was never defined in ethnic terms, and classes were held in Zulu, Sotho, English, and Portuguese, as well as in Tswa, Chopi, and Tonga, the languages of the coastal districts north of the Limpopo. But the mission had been intimately involved in the delineation of the Ronga and Thonga languages, and the catechism and literacy groups in the compounds crystallized around converts fluent in these church *linguas franca*. By targeting the "Tsangaan and Baronga" as "our young people," the Swiss attempted to appropriate an enormous mission field.[123] This association between language and church was also encouraged by missionaries who, in the Romantic tradition, saw a strong "national" or ethnic identity as an antidote to the social ills caused by the disintegration of tribal society.[124]

Literacy allowed the worker to fit more easily into the expanded and complex society on the Witwatersrand, and it provided him with a new source of power. The ability to read enabled him to comprehend the printed words that made up his work ticket, the various passes controlling his movements, and the sign-posted instructions that regulated his life. Letter-writing enabled the migrant to respond swiftly to appeals for help from home, and it provided a conduit for the information and knowledge that brought home and work into a single geographical space.[125] On the Witwatersrand the imagined community created by a standard vernacular literacy was made tangible as, confronted by competing ethnic groups, membership of a bounded linguistic group became a cornerstone of the worker's sense of security and belonging. In the rural areas many chiefs and commoners attributed supernatural powers to the written word. Writing was believed to be a source of the authority of the colonial conquerors; it was understood that a literate individual, merely by sending "the paper that speaks" to whites, "would receive everything he asks for"; writing was also associated with the "medicine of knowledge."[126] Literacy provided Christians with the wisdom needed to avoid damnation on judgement day, a convincing argument in an environment reeking of death. An ability to read in the vernacular, and particularly in English, gave the miner access to worlds that were both spiritual and secular, while a familiarity with the symbols and codes of whites allowed him a certain upward mobility. The literate worker could become a dormitory scribe, writing dictated letters for 1s, or move into domestic service, clerical posts, or other forms of service beyond the

Clients consulting the bones thrown by a compound diviner. The man on the right plays a unicord harp.

mine.[127] Some men were able to attend the various training colleges for evangelists, and a few graduated to further their education at missionary institutions such as Lovedale, Adams College, and Lemana. Literacy separated the reader from his peers in the compounds, and provoked an individualism encouraged by the private world of reading; it also adjusted perceptions of the world, as the worker increasingly mused upon and classified the soaring amount of knowledge available to him and as he replaced a mutable, functional concept of the past with an inflexible and written truth.[128] Yet there was no clear divide between orality and literacy, and the aspects of knowledge that came with reading were selected, reassembled, and dispersed by individuals in various ways. Some accepted the evolutionistic world view of missionaries who believed black miners would "grow to manhood by responsibility" and who sought to "uplift" these "debased and demoralised heathens."[129] Andrew Reid Ngayika, a minister in the Ethiopian movement, sought to educate "boys" in the compounds as a means of defeating the "barbarism" found in "raw places" in the rural areas. Levi Thomas Mvabaza opposed the ease with which "raw natives" mixed with Christians, and Saul Msane, the manager of the Jubilee and Salisbury compound, believed that it was only "educated and well-conducted people . . . brought up under the influence of the Europeans" who should be allowed to vote.[130] Men of this class were concerned to assert the signs and virtues of "respectability" that raised them above "savages." On the Witwatersrand, as well as in Mozambique, they constructed their own social space around the tea meetings *(timitis)* where people sang and danced to the accompaniment of musical instruments, put on pantomimes, or simply discussed events.[131] In the *timitis* the socially mobile collected money for their causes and separated themselves from the less well to-do in the shebeens and the compounds.[132] And they found a political voice in the Transvaal Native Congress, an organisation that, according to J. M. Makhotle, the mining subcontractor who served as its secretary-general, represented "educated natives and some chiefs."[133]

Preachers praised discipline, self-sacrifice, the dignity of labour, and thrift in their sermons, and inveighed against drunkenness, "unnatural vice," dancing, and superstition. They demanded that their followers enter into a visible community marked by a new respectability codified in dress, naming, behaviour, and a widened sense of social responsibility.[134] But preachers on the Witwatersrand were under pressure to temper their attacks on the miners' culture, for, like the mine-owners, the missionaries competed for followers. They had to beware of the willingness of Ethiopian, and particularly Zionist, preachers to make Christianity conform more closely to the tenets of indigenous folk religions.

As with other aspects of culture, religious belief was a product of struggle, and the Christian vision of the world was neither unanimous nor uniform. Popular religion explained the world in concrete and precise terms; diviners predicted the future and protected believers with magic potions and charms, while witchcraft personalised and explained misfortune. Miners were familiar with the explanations and symbolism of folk religion and the fellowship of a loose community of believers. While popular religions confronted worldly dangers, Christianity tended to transcend the secular and offered vague assurances of spiritual salvation. Yet the universalism and industrial morality of Christianity was in many ways more functional to life in a world dominated by capitalism and colonialism; for people caught between these two systems of belief, a bricolage of religious beliefs and practices provided a compromise, a way of entering into a new and unfamiliar society without fully embracing it. Church dissidents used powerful medicines, charms, prayers, and other rituals, and found a demonology and spiritualism in the Bible that accorded with popular beliefs but contradicted their employers' definitions of religiosity and scientism. The Ethiopian movement challenged the European monopoly of Christian interpretation but did not fundamentally change Protestant teaching. The Zionist churches that emerged in Johannesburg at the beginning of the century, under the influence of the American apostolic movement, were far more syncretic in their approach and incorporated many aspects of popular religion, such as a belief in healing, speaking in tongues, rites of purification, passage, and protection, and a sturdy symbolism that appealed to oral societies. But although the various Zionist churches were marked by a backward-looking traditionalism familiar to their adherents, they also propagated a gradual acceptance of the morality and ethics of industrial society.[135]

The missionaries on the Witwatersrand were not dealing with proletarians or slaves permanently cut off from the culture of their parent societies and in need of a new, fortifying morality. Instead they were obliged, in many ways, to mould themselves to the cultural demands of their migrant congregations; as many missionaries were to discover, to rail against the miner's morality was to push him into the arms of Ethiopianism.[136] Nevertheless, for many missionaries, the church replaced the old tribal structures and provided blacks with an avenue for leadership, responsibility, and respect in a colonial world. Through the church, miners acquired a literacy and a world view that enabled them to organize and mobilize themselves in new ways. Dissident churches were able to create an important space, a cultural airlock, in which blacks had some control over their destiny.

Despite the fears and suspicions of whites, the independent churches were, for blacks, more an escape from the mine than a means of rebellion.[137] Ethiopians and Zionists held Sunday school and literacy classes in the compounds, and most organized tea meetings at which participants were regaled with thick slices of bread, tea, and transparent sweets, and talks on the virtues of temperance and self-improvement.[138] Money raised at these functions was used to evangelize the rural areas. The Ethiopians also created mutual aid societies to help workers on the Rand and raised money in order to spread literacy and the gospel at home. In 1907 Ethiopians from Mozambique played a leading role in creating a benevolent society "to provide a purse for East Coast natives working on the Rand, out of which sick boys will be helped, boys dying friendless will be decently buried and boys preaching and teaching in Gazaland will be supported."[139] The compound missionaries struggled against the rebellious independent churches and waged war against the ancestor cults. One of their main objects was to burn "the paraphernalia of demons" kept by the miners, "such as horns, spoons for dipping up human blood, medicines for hypnotising girls, charms, sacred garments, anklets, and the things used in the worship of spirits."[140]

Before Moses Hongwana left for the mines, his father prayed to the ancestors and employed a diviner to provide his son with protective medicines and talismen.[141] Migrants like Hongwana brought with them a belief in the power of magic that provided a rationality and predictability in a world without secular insurance. Just as at home, or on the way to the mines, folk beliefs furnished miners with hope, assurance, and a sense of control over the unknown. On the mines workers frequently turned to their own medical practitioners, whose herbal remedies and medicines they knew and respected. The professionalism of these men must often have seemed superior to that of the company mine doctors, who stripped men naked in public and processed over a thousand workers in an hour.[142] Black mineworkers particularly feared being separated from their "brothers" and being sent to anonymous hospitals and quarantine stations, institutions they must have regarded as akin to death camps and charnel-houses.[143] On the other hand, the miners were thoroughly familiar with diviners who could read signs and omens and who could supply them with love potions and protective charms. These visionaries seemed able to acquire a promotion for their clients, recover their stolen goods, forecast the future, uncover causes of illness and accident, and even bring about the death of an enemy. At the end of his contract, a man would learn from an *inyanga* what to expect on his return home.[144]

Supernatural protection was vital in a society that ascribed misfortune to the practices of *baloyi* who bewitched workers both at home and on the Witwatersrand.[145] This belief was compounded by the anonymity of death on the mines. The corpses of black workers were wrapped in blankets and buried in shallow, often collective, graves in the "pagan native" section of the mine or municipal cemetery.[146] The corpses were seldom protected by a coffin and were believed to be subject to the nocturnal depredations of the *baloyi*. "Most natives are very superstitious about dead bodies," reported the head of the Native Recruiting Corporation, and "East Coast natives obliterate all signs of a grave."[147] The cause of death generally remained unclear, as family or friends were unable to employ a diviner to examine the corpse. If a migrant were buried on the mines without the knowledge of his family, and hence without the requisite rituals being performed to allow his incorporation into the world of the ancestors, his wandering spirit was considered easy prey for the *baloyi*.

Witchcraft practitioners carried their skills to the mines. As at home, they were able to enter locked rooms, "open up" their occupants, and devour their internal organs or force their life essence to labour on the *baloyi's* account as zombies in the mines' closed-off underground galleries. The *baloyi* were also considered responsible for misfortune, ranging from *xifulana*, a crippling swelling of the feet, to the sudden fall from favour of a powerful *induna*. Workers were constantly threatened by the spirits of deceased miners inhabiting the worked-out sections of the mine. They were captured by these spirits and, transmogrified into the zombies called *dlukula*, were forced to labour for several days without pay on a diet of mud. For migrants brought up in a nonscientific milieu, this explanation for the wasted condition of colleagues suffering from tuberculosis, phthisis, or the swollen feet caused by labouring in water-logged shafts, was probably more convincing than the unfamiliar diagnoses of an alien medical taxonomy.[148]

New beliefs emerged on the mines through contact with European notions of the supernatural, or as a pragmatic response to explain the unfamiliar. Thus it was probably after the introduction of compensation payments for miners' phthisis that the *dlukula* were believed to return to the mine's surface with a number chalked on their backs by the spirits. After being sent to the hospital for treatment, the men were paid the amount inscribed on their backs; if a mine manager refused to make this payment, the spirits would cripple the mine. This belief explained why certain unhealthy miners returned home with sufficient money to keep them from returning to the mines. "It was generally believed," explains Nyero Sithadi, a retired miner living in Vendaland, "that the Shangaans and the Pokutees from Mozambique had medicines to call the mine spirits to take them so that they might retire from the mines and relax at home with their pockets full of money."[149]

In rural southern Mozambique, Junod noticed around 1910 that the *baloyi* had recently acquired the ability to enslave the spirits of those improperly buried. These *shipoko* (from the Afrikaans or Fanagalo, *spook*) took the form of little children during the day when, hidden in forests and swamps, they were fed by the *baloyi*. At night they emerged to labour in their masters' fields.[150] This continuity of belief ascribed the ability of wealthy and powerful individuals to prosper, despite a general decline in rural affluence, to a new and virulent form of witchcraft rather than to capitalist exploitation; and it envisaged redress in terms of the eradication of witches, rather than in terms of class struggle.[151]

These folk beliefs also supported the structure of power on the mines, for *indunas* reported thieves, witchraft practitioners, and other wrongdoers uncovered by the diviners to the compound manager, who was then expected to dismiss the malefactor or transfer him to another part of the mine. The compound manager had to bend to the wishes of the workers' representatives and in so doing gave his support to the miners' belief system. Similarly, the power and efficacy of the miners' system of explanation was reinforced by stories of compound managers who consulted diviners and healers, and whose naked wives periodically descended into the shafts at dead of night with the money needed to propitiate the mine's spirits.

Class and Identity

During World War I, the disposable incomes of Mozambican mineworkers were more than halved by inflation and an augmented hut tax. This reduction in real earnings was made all the more remarkable, as it was achieved at a time when European and American workers were winning appreciable gains from management.[152] In contrast to the militancy of their homologues in the northern hemisphere, black workers on the Witwatersrand maintained a singular quiescence in their relations with capital. "Mine Natives," the mining editor of the *Star* was to write in 1936, "have a fine record of loyal service."[153] This "fine record of loyal service" has not held much appeal for labour historians concerned to document the grievances and rising class consciousness out of which grew the trade union movement and the prospect of a socialist future. Nor has it proved easy for radical historians to break from the antiindustrial narratives of their intellectual ancestors. The concentration on grievances and defiance has tended to repress a complex and contradictory working-class discourse that included apathy, collaboration, and a bundle of identities at best only obliquely related to resistance. Nor has there been much interest in the complicity of the working class in their own subordination or in their highly gendered responses to the threats and opportunities of industrial capitalism. In the compounds men exercised power over their colleagues through the metaphor of gender and the concept of community, while in the rural areas the labour of women and children provided male migrants with an additional source of livelihood. It might even be argued that the exclusion of women, but not boys, from the stopes, and even the surface works, served to ensure a male monopoly over the cash wages entering the rural areas. By representing working-class culture as bounded and unified, and the product of resistance, historians have created a positive image of the harbingers of socialism.[154] But they have also avoided the depressing task of analysing the long defeat of black labour on the Witwatersrand in the years after 1896. Worker consciousness grew in a fractured and fitful manner and only sporadically did it fuel a hesitant class conflict.

It is sometimes argued that workers created a common class consciousness through the everyday, "largely silent and unorganised" forms of resistance mounted in opposition to their shared exploitation.[155] But workers deserted, drank, stole, and loafed more as a means of protecting the rhythms of their noncapitalist work culture than as a means of expressing their opposition to a class of capitalists. The class cohesion created through their struggle against their employers' notions of work discipline, punctuality, and sobriety was only dynamic in the sense that it created a resistance to the moving force of capitalism. By defending these customs, workers manifested their desire to escape the mine rather than transform it; they exhibited a distinct unwillingness to join an uprooted proletariat and looked backward to what they knew rather than forward to a new social order. The black miners' life experience was not confined to the realm of exploitation, or even to the mine, and his relations with his employers were far from merely conflictual. Finally, even the concept of exploitation has to be understood in its cultural context, for what is interpreted as exploitation by today's historians was not necessarily perceived in the same manner by migrant workers at the turn of the century. Proletarianisation was an objective process, entailing a growing dependence on the sale of labour power for survival; but it was also a subjective process, an experience that was construed by people in a specific manner and to which they gave expression in various concrete ways. Class consciousness was not merely structurally determined by the political economy; it was also inherited, shaped, and adapted by individuals who wished to give meaning and order to their lives. It is an assessment of the symbolic content of the workers' culture that alerts us, I would suggest, to the very weakness of class as a source of group consciousness linking black miners on the Witwatersrand.

The exploitation suffered by migrant workers was muted by their independent means of production in the rural areas. Because their fate, and that of their families, was not indissolubly linked to a wage income, migrant workers were not in the same structural position as proletarians; their security lay at home, in a traditional network of rights and obligations, and the moral economy they built on the mines impeded the growth of individual freedoms, as well as the welfare associations that are their corollary.

Severed from their chiefs, the mineworkers recreated their own network of authority based on traditional values of patriarchy and gerontocracy that, in the rural areas, they accepted as the normal and legitimate structure of society. Rather than constructing a new social order through confrontation with their employers, workers tended to build their own society on the basis of what was comprehensible and familiar. Rather than looking forward to a class solidarity, they strengthened their ties with the "brothers" and "uncles" constantly arriving on the mines, kinsmen who channelled and directed the miners' gaze towards their rural homes. The noncapitalist social controls that men had been taught to respect were harnessed and appropriated by the mineowners. The despotism and benevolence of racial paternalism left workers little space in which to organize, while the vertical ties of patronage established between managers, *indunas*, and elders defused class consciousness and reinforced notions of mutual obligation.[156] The struggle over the rhythm of labour, liquor consumption, and leisure activities, the length of the contract and working day, remuneration, the state of the compounds and hospitals, the workers' leisure hours, and other aspects of their daily lives, was marked as much by compromises and concessions as by contestation and conflict. Working conditions were established through the everyday, informal struggles between labour and capital. These constant and unspectacular negotiations created a set of customary expectations that, as long as they were adhered to, reinforced the sense of moral economy on the mine. But a sudden change in the wage rate, the length of the shift, the pace of work, the cost of living, or diet could precipitate a direct response from the workers. Action was often aimed at the individual held responsible for the rupture in expected, "traditional" conditions of employment; the paymasters' house was torched, the compound manager's office stoned, a mine concession store burnt down, or a white worker attacked underground, all in a manner serving to remind the authorities of their duties and responsibilities. A cut in the wage rate was met by a wave of desertion, a work stoppage, or a walk-out as men defended their customary work conditions. But this unity of purpose was exceptional. Class cohesion was as ephemeral as the crisis that produced it; as soon as the antagonism between labour and capital subsided, class was quickly submerged by the multiplicity of identities through which black miners gave a dignity and meaning to their working lives.

The compound as a community was reinforced, divided, and sometimes linked to other compounds by overlapping bonds of occupation, gender, age, literacy, and orality as well as ethnicity, kinship, religious beliefs, and loyalty to a mine compound or rural chief. Migrants created these identities through a network of signification that included ways of dressing, eating, drinking, fighting, and dancing, naming and talking, sexuality, ways of arranging their living quarters, creating music, and expressing masculinity. The network of signs available to migrant mineworkers was rooted in their rural culture, not least because of their growing isolation in the compound. The fellowship and conviviality experienced by the miner had shrunk from the canteen and location to the compound, eating house, and concession store on mine property. Black workers were forced from the towns by night curfews, and legislation barring them from the pavements; hunted by the pass laws, regimented by prohibition, and separated from the colonists by their own leisure activities, they retreated into compounds where their gaze was further turned inwards. Their main contact with the European world was through the mine concession stores, but even these were generally run by East European Jews who themselves lived on the margins of colonial society. The modernisation that came with the development of the Rand increased the ghettoisation of the black miner; and his restricted access to European ideas and behaviour distanced him from the organisational skills of white proletarians and from the intellectual tools that construct a mental imagery of class.

The system of signification through which the black miner defined his social reality was interpreted in a very different manner by the mineowner or the immigrant English worker. The series of signs that distinguished a miner as a Shangaan, a skilled underground driller, respected member of a Zionist church, and a powerful *induna* were perceived by most contemporary Europeans as signs of barbarousness or racial decadence. Black miners were tribesmen, boys who could not claim the rights of the sturdy proletarians of Europe. Hence black miners did not see themselves reflected as a class in the eyes of their employers and constructed narrower identities bound by a conformity to their own norms and standards, values, beliefs, and ideals.[157] These identities fitted workers into a number of overlapping communities and, in a society without chiefs, provided them with pride, respect, and security, a degree of mobility, and power. Political conflict over working conditions was often based on these identities, as men mobilized on a situational basis as Shangaans, consumers, or drillmen, or as the members of a compound. Many whites saw the strengthening of ethnic differences as an important means of social control, but, as I pointed out earlier, ethnicity was a double-edged sword that could mobilize large numbers of workers in ways that contradicted the interests of employers.[158] Nationality also became a rallying point for miners, as migrants from the East Coast discovered the frontiers, constructed by Europeans, that gave them a common fatherland. As early as July 1902, about seven hundred Mozambican workers on the Durban Roodepoort demonstrated in support of fulfillment of their contracts.[159] And it was the East Coasters or "Pokutees," the major purchasers at mine concession stores, who responded to war-time inflation by leading the 1918 consumer boycott and picketing stores on the Witwatersrand.[160] Perhaps most importantly, Mozambican workers saw their presence on the mines as a rite of passage and a temporary break from a more fulfilling existence in the rural areas. Nevertheless, a number of Mozambicans sought to construct a more durable future on the mines and exercised their new-found nationality to establish benevolent societies and an African Union of Natives of Mozambique.[161]

On the mines tribesmen temporarily repressed their differences and asserted a range of new identities, of which class was perhaps the most foreign and intangible. But as customary forms of defence such as desertion, absenteeism, loafing, and inebriation were suppressed, and traditional solidarities proved unable to protect the black miners' working conditions, and as men lengthened their stay on the mines, a fledgling class solidarity emerged. In July 1913, during the white miners' strike, about nine thousand blacks stopped work on the deep-level mines clustered on the southern edge of Johannesburg. By demanding a doubling of their wages, these men exhibited a new class aggression. The suppression of the strike by the army did little to repress the halting and episodic growth of a class consciousness. This was reflected in the fears of men like the Portuguese curator who believed that black workers were forming a combination, a "Native Workers Union," in opposition to their employers. "There is no doubt that deliberate attempts are being made to liberate the natives of different tribes and to unite the bantu races in order to obtain better conditions from the Europeans," he wrote in the aftermath of the strike,

> the spirit of discord between the tribes is going to disappear. . . . it did not help to have different tribes on these mines, such as Zulus, Basutos, various Cape tribes, Shangaans and other natives from the East coast; all co-operated without distinction in the movement of subversion even though some were motivated by the force of intimidation exercised by the dominant tribe.[162]

In South Africa these fears have been slow to materialize. What were far more visible, in the early part of the twentieth century, were the continuing reverses suffered by black labour and the related growing inequality in the distribution of wealth in colonial Southern Mozambique.

CONCLUSION

In 1907 Freire d'Andrade saw the economic malaise affecting Mozambique as an "organic sickness" caused by "*the lack of production* and the exportation of its life force—the natives."[1] The vicious cycle of forced labour and emigration, the one fuelling the other, was the result of Portugal's policy of developing Southern Mozambique as a protected market for metropolitan produce and as a service economy for South Africa. But the Portuguese did more than just sell Mozambique's basic means of production to the mines in exchange for hard currency; they sold Mozambican labour at bargain-basement prices and passed on the costs to the miners and the homestead economy. The Portuguese conquest of Southern Mozambique had transformed the terms on which migrants sold their labour. In the mid-nineteenth century, the situation had been considerably different. For generations, people had responded to a harsh environment and unpredictable climate by moving either within the coastal plain or out, onto the highveld. Mobility was a traditional resource in a region plagued by seasonal food shortages and cyclical, often devastating famines that brought war and disease in their wake. Hence when the opportunity arose to earn wages in Natal in the 1850s, migrant labour was perceived as a new and welcome resource in the struggle against nature.

Wages introduced a new ferment into established social relations. Money provided men with new freedoms, as they were able to procure wives independently of their elders, buy an increasing range of consumer goods, and build up a separate political following. Migrant labour was integrated into economic and social life long before the imposition of colonialism. A moderate prosperity was generated in the south when, during the 1870s, agriculturalists exchanged oil-producing fruit and seeds, cereals, buckskins, and wages earned in South Africa, for guns, cloth, food and iron hoes, the local medium of bridewealth. But a massive importation of hoes resulted in rampant inflation, and fathers demanded that bridewealth be paid in gold coins. At the same time, consumerism experienced a quiet revolution as the old, wandering *sertanejos* were replaced by Banyan traders who established a network of small shops in the interior. But while wages in South Africa grew appreciably after the discovery of diamonds, the economy on the coast suffered a long-term reverse as the price paid for vegetable oils fell sharply, game was decimated, and an international frontier ended long-distance trade. From the early 1880s on, men increasingly found it more profitable to invest their energies in migrant labour rather than in a declining export economy.[2]

226

Chiefs and elders drew a profit from the wages repatriated by their young men, and gradually, despite the perils of a long journey, the dangers of mine work, and the alienation of wage labour, a period of work in South Africa became an almost obligatory life passage for young men. Women, or at least respectable women, remained at home. This was partly because colonial governments opposed the permanent establishment of immigrant African proletarians, and prohibited women from occupations such as mining. But the emigration of women was particularly restricted because their labour reproduced the homestead, the key element in the cycle of accumulation dominated by men. While labour migration caused the responsibilities of women within the rural areas to increase, and eventually give rise to epidemics of spirit possession or hysteria, men reinforced their dominance by controlling the circulation of money. Several years before the opening of the Witwatersrand mines and, it needs to be stressed, long before the small Portuguese garrisons on the coast could exert a pressure on men to sell their labour, a diaspora of about fifteen thousand Mozambican workers stretched across Natal and the Transvaal to Griqualand West and the Cape Colony. But the active recruitment of labour was expensive and was discontinued when large numbers of Mozambicans broke contract and returned home during the depression of the mid-1880s. It was only at the end of the decade that the discovery of gold revitalized the economy and drew East Coasters back to South Africa; by 1894, on the eve of the Luso-Gaza war, more than twenty-five thousand southern Mozambicans were employed in various parts by South Africa.

The earnings of Mozambican mine workers remained high and attractive well into the 1890s. The sheer need for unskilled labour on the mines drove up wages, but, as I have attempted to show, workers also developed a consciousness of their common interests and defended what they determined as their established, customary rights. This solidarity rested on culture as a web of signification that bound workers into interlocking and imbricating social networks, and separated them from their employers, as well as on a sense of conflictual interests. But conflict was combined with cooperation as management and miners negotiated the conditions of employment, even in the closed world of the Kimberley compounds. Thus in the 1870s migrants from the East Coast had first been lured from the plantations of Natal to the mines of Kimberley by the prospect of high incomes in cash and kind. They left the diamond fields when wages fell, and had to be coaxed, by means of cash, welfare, and other incentives, to accept the restrictions of the closed compounds. On the Witwatersrand, where structural pressures required a reduction in working costs, wages were deflated by large-scale recruiting. In this world of competing economic interests and divergent cultural perceptions, management and labour painfully forged a rudimentary system of labour relations, based on notions of tribal cohesion and racial paternalism, that would endure well into the twentieth century.[3]

In the Transvaal the mineowners had called unceasingly on the government to emulate the authorities in Natal, who, in the 1870s, had brought down the cost of plantation labour by aiding the recruitment of labour. But the Kruger government refused to allow an uncontrollably rapid economic growth to destabilise the state. However, when the Jameson Raid threatened to topple the government in early 1896, the Kruger regime showed a new willingness to intervene directly in the labour market. Migrants were shackled by the pass laws, their drinking patterns were suppressed by prohibition, and a new relentlessness was introduced as the surface works were kept running throughout the week. The importation of Mozambican labor was systematized and, for the first time, police, soldiers, and government officials assisted mine managers in effecting substantial wage cuts. Workers fought these laws tenaciously, most notably by turning to illegal liquor sellers and by deserting and reappearing in other districts. But it became far more difficult for Mozambicans to break contract and return home after their lands were conquered by the Portuguese in 1895–1897.

The workers' informal social networks, through which they had traditionally defended their interests, were no match for the combined forces of Portuguese colonialism, an interventionist state in the Transvaal, and the mineowners. The wage cuts of the period initiated a decline in the real earnings of black mineworkers that was to last almost eighty years. Hut taxes, forced labour, military conscription, and, initially to a limited degree, land alienation, obliged men to sell their labor to the mines for a wage well over 20 percent lower than that once earned by their fathers and grandfathers. Under the protection of the Portuguese, a new wave of retailers entered the rural areas to persuade migrants to part with their wages, particularly in the purchase of substandard Portuguese wines. At the same time, the WNLA established a network of camps that drained the countryside of able-bodied men. Despite the deterioration in the wages and working conditions of mineworkers, the factors pushing Mozambicans to the mines under colonialism were sufficiently strong to cause their number to more than treble in the first fifteen years of Portuguese rule. By 1910 some 77,500 men from southern Mozambique were employed on the Witwatersrand mines.

Migrant workers from Southern Mozambique played a central role in developing the Witwatersrand into the greatest centre of gold production in the world. Their industry and courage were frequently praised by mining officials. They were the "saviours of the Rand," remarked Fitzpatrick, the "pioneer coloured labourers," recalled the Chamber of Mines, without whom "the opening up of the gold fields and the development of South Africa would have been very greatly retarded."[4] While real earnings in the manufacturing and construction sectors of the economy increased steadily during the twentieth century, cheap immigrant labour pushed down the wages of gold miners and ensured the profitable exploitation of the deep level mines.[5] Under colonial rule, pull factors had little influence on the growth in the number of Mozambicans employed on the Witwatersrand, or on the frequency with which they returned to the mines. Wages fell, the mines grew deeper and more dangerous, tuberculosis and phthisis emerged as new scourges, the compounds became more restrictive, and prohibition, the work ticket, minimum standards of productivity, and subcontracting curbed the controls that workers had formerly exercised over the pace of labour. Yet at the same time, hospitals were built, the length of the working day was reduced, compensation was paid for injury and death, and the dangers incurred by tramping to the mines diminished. Despite the unequal struggle with management into which they were locked after 1897, migrants exerted sufficient strength to establish, with varying degrees of success, and often in opposition to management, their own notions of sexuality, leisure, providence, work, community, justice, and self-worth.

In South Africa, men from the East Coast were introduced to new ways of seeing the world. Contact with literacy and Christianity extended the borders of community and introduced men to new notions of individual responsibility, causation, organisation, and authority. Men from different regions met on the mines and constructed, through a series of rites and rituals, innovative and imbricating identities as Shangaans, Mozambicans, underground drillers, and mine workers.[6] Wage labour inculcated concepts of work and time that were dissociated from the natural ryhthm of the seasons.

Migrant workers carried these ideas home alongside the commodities and cash with which they filled their trunks. Despite the drain of men and money from southern Mozambique, migrants' wages brought a relative prosperity to the region. As Portugal was a weak imperial power, the central and northern sections of the colony were rented out to concessionary companies, which practised an unbridled form of exploitation. It was only in the south that sufficient income circulated to attract capital investment, entice a trickle of settlers (most of whom gravitated towards the towns), and, in some areas, stimulate the growth of a modest peasantry.[7]

Migrant labour was largely responsible for turning the population south of the Save River into by far the most literate in Mozambique.[8] The evangelical Christianity brought back from the Transvaal, and spread within Mozambique by the Protestant missions, provided early nationalists with a broad ideology and practice of resistance and, in the form of Robert Mashaba, their first martyr.[9] The development of a colonial administration and an economic infrastructure in the south aided a European-educated intelligentsia and a number of "great families" to take root and grow in the coastal towns.[10] These men were later, together with migrants returning from South Africa, to turn the region south of the Save into the cradle of Mozambican nationalism.[11]

Migrant labour drew southern Mozambique indefatigably into the modern world. But beyond the towns, mission stations, railways, roads, and the posts set up by WNLA or the colonial administration, the pace of change was less insistent. Notions of work and time driven by the clock and calendar were submerged in a world still dominated by the rhythm of the seasons. Literacy lost a great deal of its spell when the only texts available were didactic and moral, and the importance of a universal God and rational explanation seemed less pressing in the company of clansmen and ancestors. In a society still dominated by social values, providence was measured less by the accumulation of wealth than by spending it on others.

After fifty years of labour emigration, few areas were undisturbed by the tax collector, labour recruiter, and the Banyan store, symbols of a dubious modernity. Regional differences declined as imported items replaced distinctive local cloths, liquor, and pottery, and a uniform system of currency displaced older, local means of exchange. Literacy in the vernacular, and sometimes in Portuguese and English, created new communities that stretched across tribal, district, and even national borders. The footpaths of pilgrims making their way to the Transvaal gave a new unity to the geographical space south of the Save. For many, migrant labour had become a pillar of survival, but for others it was associated with fear rather than fertility, and affliction rather than abundance. The trepidation and ambivalence with which progress was embraced is perhaps best summed up by the private thoughts of an anonymous domestic servant employed by Henri Junod on an evangelical tour. One evening while washing the dishes, he quietly recited a poem in which he employed the image of a train, visible on the horizon, as a metaphor for modernity:[12]

> The one who roars in the distance. . . .
> The one who crushes in pieces the braves and leaves them
> The one who debauches our wives:
> They abandon us, they go!
> The seducer!
> And we remain alone.

NOTES

CHAPTER 1
Environment, Culture and Migration

1. Transvaal Archives (TA), A.33, GLM (Governor of Lourenço Marques) to GGM (Governor General of Mozambique), 20 September 1843; GGM to Overseas Ministry (MSMU), 16 April 1844. On the early nineteenth century history of the Delagoa Bay region, see D Hedges, "Trade and Politics in Southern Mozambique and Zululand in the 18th and Early 19th Centuries" (Ph.D. thesis, University of London, 1978); P. Harries, "Ethnicity, History and Ethnic Frontiers: The Ingwavuma District in the 19th Century," *Journal of Natal and Zululand History*, 6 (1983).
2. In 1849 the governor of Inhambane and a detachment of soldiers were killed in a skirmish on the outskirts of the town. F. Bordalo, *Ensaio sobre a estatistica de Moçambique e suas dependencias na Costa oriental da Africa ao Sul do Equador*(Lisbon, 1859), IV, 281; J. J. Texeiro Botelho, *História Militar e Política dos Portugueses em Moçambique* (Lisbon, 1934), 174-75; E. de Noronho, *O Districto de Lourenço Marques e a África do Sul*(Lisbon, 1895), 38. For slavery at Inhambane, see Public Records Office, London (PRO) Foreign Office (FO) 312/14, Mixed Commission, Cape Town to Earl of Aberdeen, 30 March 1849; British Parliamentary Papers (BPP) 1850, IX, *Report from the Select Committee of the House of Lords, 1850*, Appendix 1, 229. British Commissioners, Cape Town, to Lord Palmerston, 3 March 1849, in BPP LV, 1850, Correspondence with British Commissioners Abroad (No. 1290); B. H. Bunce to the select Committee on Slave Trade Treaties (No. 920) in BPP XXXIX, 1852–53.
3. João de Andrade Corvo, *Estudos sobre as provinciais Ultramarinos* (Lisbon, 1884), II, 265-66, 276; E. de Noronho, O Distr de Lourenço Marques e a Africa do Sul (Lourenço Marques, 1985), 72, 192; *Boletim Oficial de Moçambique (BO)* 23, 7 June, 1862; E. Noronho, *O Districto de Lourenço Marques e a Africa do Sul* (Lourenço Marques, 1895) 72, 192.
4. G. Liesegang "Beiträge zur geschichte des reiches der Gaza Nguni im südlichen Moçambiek 1820-1895" (Ph.D. thesis, University of Cologne, 1967); P. Bonner, *Kings, Commoners and Concessionaires: The Evolution and Dissolution of the Nineteenth-Century Swazi State* (Cambridge and Johannesburg, 1983), Ch. 6.
5. On the centralised political structure of Khosa society, see Swiss Mission Archive, Lausanne (SMA) 503b Grandjean to Council, 9 September 1891.
6. On Chopi ethnicity, see D. Earthy, *Valenge Women* (London, 1933), 9-10; H.-P. Junod, "Some Notes on Tshopi Origins," *Bantu Studies*, III, 1 (1929); L. Vail and L. White, "The Development of Forms: The Chopi *Migodo*," in their *Power and the Praise Poem: South African Voices in History* (Charlottesville, Va., 1991). On Tsonga ethnicity, see Harries, "Exclusion, Classification and Internal Colonialism: The Emergence of Ethnicity among the Tsonga-speakers of South Africa," and, for the Shona, T. Ranger, "Missionaries, Migrants and the

Manyika: The Invention of Ethnicity in Zimbabwe," both in L. Vail, *ed., The Creation of Tribalism in Southern Africa* (London and Los Angeles, 1989).

7. St. Vincent Erskine, "Journal of a Voyage to Umzila; King of Gaza, 1871-72," *Journal of the Royal Geographical Society,* 45 (1875), 259; Junod, *La Tribu et la langue thonga avec quelques échantillons du folklore thonga* (Lausanne, 1896), 3-4. For a more general discussion of early ethnicity in south-east Africa, see P. Harries, "The Anthropologist as Historian"; *idem,* "History, ethnicity"; *Idem,* "Exclusion, Classification"; *idem,* "The Roots of Ethnicity: Discourse and the Politics of Language Construction in South-East Africa," in *African Affairs,* 346 (January 1988).

8. J. Amselle, *Logiques Métisses: Anthropologie de l'identité en Afrique et Ailleurs* (Paris, 1990), 9-10ff.

9. Harries "Exclusion, Classification," 85.

10. St. V. Erskine, "Journal of Mr. St. V. Erskine, Special Commissioner from the Natal government to Umzila—King of Gaza, 1871 and 1872," MS in Royal Geographical Society (RGS); A. A. Caldas Xavier, "Reconhecimento do Limpopo: os territorios ao sul do Save e os Vatuas," in *BSGL,* 3 (1894).

11. SMA 1254/B, G. Liengme, "Rapport sur l'expédition et le séjour à Mandlakazi," May-September 1893; Junod, *La Tribu et la Langue Thonga,* 22.

12. *BO* 6, 11 February 1888; *BO* 20, 18 May 1889. On the structure of Gaza society, see J. K. Rennie, "Christianity, Colonialism and the Origins of Nationalism among the Ndau of Southern Rhodesia, 1890-1935" (Ph.D. thesis, Northwestern University, 1973), Ch. 3. And, especially, G. Liesegang, "Notes on the Internal Structure of the Gaza Kingdom of Southern Mozambique, 1840-1895," in J. Peires, ed., *Before and After Shaka: Papers in Nguni History* (Grahamstown, 1981).

13. Harries, "History, Ethnicity," 2, 4; Rennie, "Origins of Nationalism among the Ndau," 145.

14. *BO* 6, 11 February 1888, "Relatorio do Residente chef dos terras de Gaza, 1886-87"; Natal Archives (NA), Secretary for Native Affairs (SNA), 1/1/96 Erskine to SNA, 23 February 1872.

15. St. V. Erskine, his 1872 journal.

16. SMA 1255/B, H. Berthoud, "Rapport sur l'expédition à Gungunyana en 1891."

17. SMA 436/A, G. Liengme to conseil, 27 June 1893.

18. St. V. Erskine, his 1872 journal, 144-45, 159, 197; A. Freire d'Andrade, "Exploraçoes Portugêses em Laurenço Marques e Inhambane," *Boletim da Sociedad de Geografia de Lisboa* (BSGL), 5, 13, 1894.

19. Junod, *The Life of a South African Tribe (Life),* I, 358-59; II, 388.

20. *Ibid.,* II, 6-7.

21. *Ibid.,* II, 262, 581 n.1, 582. See also Ch. 4.

22. *Ibid.,* II, 581 n.1; SMA 437/A, Liengme to Leresche, 20 July 1894. On the brutal treatment of new (socially dead) Gaza slaves, see Earthy, *Valenge Women,* 198; SMA 438/B, Liengme to Leresche, 31 August 1895; Fondation pour l'Histoire des Suisses à l'étranger (FHS), Liengme diary, 20 July 1893 and 24 December 1893.

23. St. Vincent Erskine, "To the Limpopo Mouth and Back on Foot" (Manuscript (MS) in the Royal Geographical Society (RGS) dated 1868), 66; Erskine, "Fourth Journey, 1874-75" (MS in RGS), Ch. 2, 6.

24. *Ibid.;* Junod, *Life,* I, 356-440; II, 388. SMA 1760, Grandjean diary, 1891. For Gazaland, where George Liengme referred to the term as "khodzile," see his diary entries for 20 July and 19 August 1893, in the Liengme papers, FHS.

25. Junod, *"Les BaRonga," Bulletin de la Société Neuchâteloise de Géographie* (BSNG), X (1898), 382; Junod, *Life,* I, 382; SMA 513/b, Grandjean to Leresche, 5 September 1894.

26. These terms were also used as polite forms of address by foreigners. Killie Campbell Library, Durban (KCL), James Stuart Archive (JSA) File (F) 25, 260; F 74, 66; A. Delagorgue,

Voyage dans l'Afrique Australe (Paris 1847), 462-63; KCL, Erskine Papers (4) misc. notes, n.d. (approx. 1870-75); Junod, *Life*, II, 360-61; Doke and Vilakazi, *Zulu Dictionary*; Sa Nogueira, *Diçionario Ronga*.

27. A. Grandjean, "La Mission Suisse à la Baie de Delagoa," *Le Chrétien Evangélique* XL (September 1897), 434; *idem*, *La Race Thonga et la Suisse Romande* (Lausanne, 1921), 34; Junod, *Life*, I, 356; *idem*, *Cinquante ans après* (Lausanne, 1925), 14-15.

28. SMA 1256/A, Grandjean, "Rapport sur l'oeuvre missionaire," 1890.

29. Junod, *Life*, I, 470.

30. SMA 467, Grandjean 1890; *Bulletin de la Mission Suisse en Afrique du Sud (BMSAS)*, 1890, 122; Arquivo Histórico Ultramarino, Lisbon (AHU), Mocambique 2ª Repartição (Rep.), Pasta (folder) 9, Freire d'Andrade, 1891; E. Schaefli-Glardon "De Valdezia à Lourenço Marques, journal de voyage," *BSNG*, VII (1893), 156; Grandjean, "L'Invasion des Zoulou dans le sud-est Africain: une page d'histoire inédite," *BSNG*, XII (1900), 74; Junod, *Life*, II, 9.

31. This probably refers to the lower Nkomati area, *Life*, II, 315-16; see also Seidel, "Die Ba-Ronga an der Delagoa Bay," *Globus*, 74, 12 (1898), 188; C.G.Coetzee, "Die Stryd om Dela-goabaai," (Ph.D. thesis, University of Stellenbosch, 1954), 140, 144.

32. H. A. Junod, *Life*, II, 413, n.1.

33. These areas were more thickly inhabited than the valleys of Zululand according to St. V. Erskine. See the typescript (TS) of his 1871-1872 voyage in the RGS, Ch. 6, 4. The Shangane River was also known as the Shohozoli.

34. Witwatersrand University, Cullen Library (WUL), AB 867/Aa5 Zululand, Bishop McKenzie to Archibishop, Cape Town, 21 August 1889; Natal Archives (NA), Zululand Government House (ZGH) 796.Z233/96, Stephens to Res. Comm., 3 March 1896.

35. SMA 497/B, Paul Berthoud, "L'Etat du Littoral, Sept., 1887"; Junod, *Life*, II, 5; Grandjean, "La Mission Suisse," *Le Chrétien Evangélique*, XL, 9 (1897), 426; Junod, "Rikatla à Mara-kouène," *BSNG*, VI (1891), 323; AHU, Moc., 2a Rep., Pasta 3, Machado memo., 10 November 1885.

36. Junod, *Life*, I, 32, 358-59; Harries, "Exclusion, Classification," 83-85.

37. Harries, "Labour Migration from Mozambique to South Africa," 239-40.

38. St Vincent Erskine, his 1872 journal, 140, 197; *BO* 44 (1886), 538-48.

39. Junod, *Life*, II, 16.

40. *Ibid.*, I, 341-43, 609-11; SMA 598/D, Junod to council, 27 March 1914. For similar reports from areas to the north, see Society for the Propagation of the Gospel (SPG), 1897 B, Reports, Inhambane, Salfey, March 1897; Augusto Cabral, *Raças, usos e costumes dos indigenas do districto de Inhambane* (Lourenço Marques, 1910), 96. See also Earthy, *Valenge Women*, 39-40.

41. Junod, "BaRonga," 205-206.

42. Junod, *Les chants et les contes des Ba-Ronga* (Lausanne, 1897), 32.

43. Jeannert, "Les Ma-Khoca," *BSNG* (1895), 127; Junod, *Life*, II, 85-88; see also H. P. Braatvedt, *Roaming Zululand with a Native Commissioner* (Pietermaritzburg, 1949), 106.

44. J. Dias, "Qual seria o status glossinico no territorio de Moçambique, ao sul do rio Limpopo anteriormente à grande panzootia de peste bovine de 1896?," In *Boletim da Sociedade de Estudos da colónia de Moçambique* (BSEM) (1961), 128; H. E. Horny, "Report on Tsetsefly Problems of Maputo," *Anais do Instituto de Medicina Tropical* (1947), IV; D. Bruce, *Preliminary Report on the Tsetse-fly Disease or Nagana in Zululand* (Ubombo, 1895).

45. St. V. Erskine, 1874-75 MS., Ch 1, 3; SMA 1255/A, E. Rosset, "Voyage au Limpopo," July-August 1894; C. Fuller, *Louis Trigardt's trek across the Drakensberg 1837-38*, Cape Town, 1932 ed. L. Fouche, 141-42, 367, 333.

46. In 1861 and 1862, some 250 bushels (333 *panjas*) of "kaffir foodstuff" were exported from Lourenço Marques. *BO* 20, 18 May 1861; *BO* 22, 31 May 1862.

47. AHU,Moç., Correspondência de Governadors (CG), Pasta 21, GLM to GGM, 8 February 1863; Fernandes das Neves, "Notícia de uma caçada em Inhambane," *Annaes do Conselho*

Ultramarino (ACU), 1864, 61; *Ibid.*, "Notícias do ano 1862," 59; *BO* 32,27 December 1862, Governor of Inhambane (GInh) to GGM, 21 November 1862; *BO* 22, 30 May 1863; SMA 467, Grandjean diary, 1890.

48. *BO* 40, 5 October 1861; *BO* 42, 17 October 1863; *BO* 42, 15 October, 1864; *BO* 19, 13 May 1865. The price per panja of *meixoeira* (millet) and maize fell to $135 and $128 in 1866-1867, *BO* 22, 22 May 1869. The Portuguese currency was the real. At the official rate of exchange some 4$500 = £1 sterling. In 1913 the new Republic government introduced the escudo valued at 1$000 (1,000 reis).

49. It was reported that the white cattle taken from Umzila alone filled the Swazi king's cattle kraals, H. Merensky, *Erinnerungen aus dem Missionsleben im Transvaal* (Berlin, 1899), 83; AHU, Moc., CG., Pasta 19, GGM to MSMU, 28 May, 1862.

50. AHU, Moc., CG, Pasta 21, GLM to GGM, 8 February 1863.

51. AHU, Moc., CG, Pasta 21, GLM to GGM, 13 August 1862, encl. in CG to MSMU, 14 October 1862; St. V. Erskine, 1871-1872 ms. in RGS., Ch. 8, p. 7.

52. Natal Archives (NA) Secretary for Native Affairs (SNA) 1/1/96, encl. in No. 73, "Statement of Umzila's Messengers," 16 August 1870.

53. SMA 514, Grandjean to Leresche, 11 February 1895; Junod, "Les BaRonga," 206.

54. SNA 1/1/96, Erskine to Shepstone, 30 November 1872.

55. St. V. Erskine, 1869 typescript, 40; St. V. Erskine, 1871-72 typescript, Ch. 9, p. 17; NA, ZGH 796.2233/96, Dr. Stephens to Res. Comm., 3 March 1896. On impaludism, see NA, Colonial Secretary's Office (CSO) 665.4069/78, Statement of Umango . . . messenger to Nozingile, 4 June 1875; SMA 1256, A. Grandjean "Rapport sur l'oeuvre missionnaire," 1892; KCL, JSA 74, 67, Evidence of Majuba.

56. ZGH 796.2233/96, Dr. Stephens to Res. Comm., 3 March 1896; ZGH 796.892/96, Foxon to Res. Comm. "Information Regarding the Portuguese Protectorate of Maputoland"; E. and W(ilkinson), *Soldiers of the Cross in Zululand* (London, 1906) 111.

57. AHU, Moc., CG, Pasta 21, GLM to GGM, 13 August, 1862, in GG to MSMU, 14 October 1862; SNA 1/1/12, Foohey to SNA, 13 November 1862; H. A. Junod, "Native Customs in Relation to Smallpox amongst the Baronga," *South African Journal of Science* (July 1914), 1; Junod, *Life*, II, 463.

58. Eduardo de Noronho, *O Distrito de Lourenço Marques e a Africa do Sul* (Lourenço Marques, 1895), 157; *BO* 21, 25 May 1863.

59. SMA 435, Liengme to Leresche, 27 July 1891; SMA 82/H, Liengme, "La Conference du Littoral," 1892; A. M. Duarte Ferreira, "Relatório de Serviço de Saude de Lourenço Marques, 1886," *Archivos Medico-Coloniaes* 4 (1890), 60, 70; E. Noronho, *O Districto de Lourenco Marques*, 158; Junod, *Life*, II, 474.

60. BPP 1890,c.6200, C. R. Saunders to SNA, 17 November 1887.

61. E. Cohen, "Erläuternde Bemerkungen," 3u L routenkarte einer reise von Lydenberg . . . nach der Delaqoa Bai." *Zweiter Jahresbericht der Geographischen Gesellschaft in Hamburg, 1874–1875.* 228.

62. Junod, *Life*, I, 99.

63. *Ibid.*, I, 41, 57-58, 192; II, 439.

64. Africana Museum, Johannesburg, Junod collection (1) 39/220-661; H. Seidel, "Die Ba-Ronga an der Delagoa Baai," in *Globus*, 74, 12 (1898), 186-87; F. Elton in *Natal Mercury* 10 October 1871; Comprehensive descriptions of military dress are in SMA 1760, Grandjean diary, 27 January 1894 (for the Khosa) and Junod "Ba-Ronga," 161-62 (for the Mazwaya).

65. *BO* 20, 18 May 1861.

66. PRO FO 63/698, Parker to Palmerston 18 February 1848; *BO* 32, 11 August 1860.

67. Robert Struthers, "Hunting Journal in Zululand and Tongaland 1852-56" (private MS), 84, 124, 128, 132-33; AHU, Moç., Diversos, 2, Texeira Report, 1856.

68. SNA 1/6/2.87, Panda to Grey, 16 January 1856. See also "Statement of the Messengers of Panda, 27 October 1848," in *South African Archival Records*, Natal, 2, 359. Onofre de

Andrade, *O Presídio de Lourenço Marques no periodo de 24 de Novembro de 1859 a 1 Abril de 1865* (Lisbon, 1867), 10.

69. JSA File 25, Evidence of Mahungane and Nkonuza, 259. But for an earlier origin of the *amapisi*, see D. Hedges, "Trade and Politics," 57.

70. TA, A.1266, Braz Pereira Collection (BPC), No. 1, Simoes to Paiva de Rapozo, 6 December 1860; D. Das Neves, *A Hunting Expedition to the Transvaal* (London, 1879), 11; AHU, Moc., 2ᵃ Reparticao, Pasta 9, Freire d'Andrade report, 1891; Junod, *Chants et Contes*, 54-55, and *Life*, II, 68-69.

71. Das Neves, *A Hunting Expedition*, 7-14, 47-48, 267; W. H. Drummond, *The Large Game and Natural History of South and South-east Africa* (Edinburgh, 1875), 16, 28, 131, 201-202, 223, 271; Struther's "Hunting journal," 44, 45, 62; Junod "BaRonga," 88, and *Life*, II, 59-63, 72-74.

72. TA.SS, 45. 9/62, Albasini to Schoeman, 8 January 1862; TA, Albasini Letterbooks (ABB), Albasini to Portuguese consul, Natal, 17 August, 1869; Onofre de Andrade, *Presidio de Lourenco Marques*, 19, 26, 28. See J. B. deVaal "Die Rol van Joao Albasini in die Geskiedenis van die Transvaal," in *South African Archival Yearbook* (1953), I, for an excellent introduction to the topic.

73. British Parliamentary Papers (BPP) 1876 Consular report, C 1421, 1875; Anon., "Le Commerce de l'Ivoire Africain," in *L'Afrique Explorée et Civilisée*, VI (1885), 242.

74. *De Zuid Afikaan*, 28 January 1864; *Staats Courant*, 15 November 1867. R. Wagner "Soutpansberg: The Dynamics of a Hunting Frontier, 1848-67," in S. Marks and A. Atmore, eds., *Economy and Society in Pre-Industrial South Africa* (London, 1980).

75. TA, A.17 J,Fleetwood-Churchill; TA.W179, Glynn, "Game"; De Vaal, "Albasini," 15, 77; Hattingh, "Die Trekke," 400-415; F. V. Kirby, *In Haunts of Wild Game*.

76. KCL, Alexander Anderson Papers, "Gunrunning at Port Natal"; SNA 1/1/12 Koch to SNA 23 January 1862; Ministério dos Negócios Estrangeiros (Foreign Office), Lisbon (MNE), Caixa 697 Blandy to GLM, 20 May 1870; FO 63/1046, Lt. Gov., Natal to FO, 30 October 1863; Bishop of Zululand, *Mission Field* (April 1873), 106; *Natal Mercury*, 2 May 1871.

77. NA SNA 1/1/10, Statement of Mabulawa, 12 January 1860; Onofre de Andrade, *Presidio de Lourenço Marques*, 18. See also Das Neves, *Hunting Expedition*, 1-2; TA.ABB, Albasini to Governor of Lourenço Marques (GLM), 1 December 1859.

78. AHU, Moç., CG,Pasta 21,GLM to GG, 8 February 1863; GGM to MSMU, 8 May 1863; GGM to MSMU, 19 September 1863; BO 22, 30 May 1863. AHU, Moç., CGPasta 21, GLM to GG, 13 August 1862, in GGM to MSMU, 14 October 1862; *ACU*, 1863, 72 Report of GLM; BO 17, 1863. GLM to GGM, 2 October 1862.

79. BO 20, 18 May 1861; AHU, Moc., Pasta 20, Governor General (GG) to MSMU, 10 October 1862; BO 42, 17 October 1863; F. M. Bordalo, *Ensaio Sobre a Estatística de Moçambique e suas Dependencias na Costa Oriental da Africa* (Lisbon, 1859), 282.

80. FO 63/1047,Dickson, Munro and Co. to FO., 18 August 1863; BO 39, 26 September 1863; Fernandes das Neves in *ACU*, 1864, 66; BO 42, 17 October 1863; *ACU* 1866,2ᵃ serie, 45.

81. Junod, *La Tribu et la Langue Thonga*, 22. Travel is often associated with knowledge, and knowledge with power. J. Fabian, *Time and the Other: How Anthropology Makes Its Object* (New York, 1983), 6.

82. P. Harries, "Production, Trade and Labour Migration from the Delagoa Bay Hinterland in the Second Half of the nineteenth Century," in *Collected Papers of the Africa Seminar*, University of Cape Town, 1978, 30-31.

83. CO 48/62, Philip to Somerset, 13 April 1824; J. Thompson, "From Cape Town to Cape Correntes," in C. A. Walckenaer, ed., *Histoire des Voyages* (Paris, 1826-31), XXI, 17; I. Schapera, ed., *Livingstone's Private Journals 1851-3* (London, 1960), L. M. Thompson, *Survival in Two Worlds; Moshoeshoe of Lesotho, 1786-1870* (Oxford, 1975), 10; A. Smith, "Trade of Delagoa Bay," 179.

84. PRO, Admiralty (ADM) 1/2269, Captain Owen, "Report on the Portuguese Settlements, 15 April 1823"; P. Davison and P. Harries, "Cotton Weaving in South-east Africa: Its History and Technology," in D.Idiens and K.G.Ponting, *eds.*, *Textiles of Africa* (Bath, 1980).

85. G.Theal, ed., *Records of South East Africa*, VI, 434, 460, 495; *Cape Monitor*, 16 July 1853; JSA 14, File 25, , Evidence of Ndaba, 26; Junod, *Life*, I, 275.

86. *BO* 13, 26 March 1864, 81; AHU, Moç., 2ª Rep, Pasta 1, Director Inhambane Customs to GG, 26 June 1885; American Board Mission Archives, Harvard University (ABM) ABC.15.4. Vol 12, Ousley to Smith, 1 May 1886; Junod "BaRonga," 88; *idem*, *Life*, I, 276; Grandjean, *La Mission*, 57; Cabral, *Racas, Usos e Costumes*, 98.

87. E. Krige, *The Realm of a Rainqueen* (Oxford, 1943), 36, 45. The Tsonga and Venda words for "groundnut" are almost identical (N. J. van Warmelo, *Venda-English Dictionary*), as are the Venda and Ronga words for cassava, the Venda word for tobacco, and the Portuguese word for leaf. The *tshivalo* and *tshivedyane* strains of millet in Vendaland were introduced by Tsonga-speakers. Oral Testimony (OT), Edward Mabyalane, Kurulen, north-eastern Transvaal, 30 March 1979. E. E. Burke, ed., *The Journals of Carl Mauch* (Salisbury, 1969), 120; Grandjean, *La Mission*, 59; Kirby, *In Haunts of Wild Game*, 361; TA.179, H. T. Glynn, "Game and Gold," 214.

88. Cf. R. Darnton, "Peasants Tell Tales: The Meaning of Mother Goose," in his *The Great Cat Massacre*; L. Levine, *Black Culture and Black Consciousness* (New York, 1977); R. B. Bottigheimer, "Fairy Tales, Folk Narrative Research and History," *Social History*, 14, 3 (1989).

89. H. Junod, *Grammaire Ronga* (Lausanne, 1896), 102; *Les Chants et les Contes*, 131, 158-59; *Life*, II, 222 n.1, 248, 251.

90. Junod, "Les BaRonga," 313; "L'épopée de la Rainette," in *Revue des Traditions Populaires* 1898, 2; *Life*, II, 233, 240-41, 247.

91. Junod, "BaRonga," 299, 313, 317, 321; "L'épopée de la rainette," 5; *Life*, II, 225-27, 243-45.

92. Junod, *Chants et Contes*, 158-59; *Life*, II, 264.

93. Junod, *Chants et Contes*, 122, 163-64; *Life*, II, 222 n.1, 229.

94. Junod, *Chants et Contes*, 200, 211, 270; *Life*, II, 203-204, 254, 312.

95. H. P. Junod and A. Jacques, *The Wisdom of the Tsonga-Shangaan People* (Cleveland, Transvaal, 1935), 93-95.

96. Junod "Baronga," 88.

CHAPTER 2:
The Politics of Sugar and Labour

1. I stress this point in Harries, "Plantations, Passes and Proletarians: Labour and the Colonial State in Natal," *Journal of Southern African Studies* (JSAS) 13, 3 (1987).

2. NA SNA (Secretary for Native Affairs) 1/3/4, Resident Magistrate (RM) Tugela to SNA , 14 November 1855; SNA 1/3/8, Verulam magistrate to SNA, 29 November 1859; RM Inanda to SNA, 29 November 1859; Legislative Council, Sessional Document No. 33, 1865; SNA 1/1/8, Draft letter entitled "Refugees," n.d. See N. Etherington, "The 'Shepstonian System' in the Colony of Natal and Beyond the Borders," in A. Duminy and B. Guest, eds., *Natal and Zululand: From Earliest Times to 1910* (Pietermaritzburg, 1989), 181; D. Welsh, *The Roots of Segregation: Native Policy in Colonial Natal, 1845-1910* (Cape Town, 1971), pp 1-3 above. On the origins of the term *Amatonga* see Chapter 1.

3. G. Russel, *The History of Old Durban and Reminiscences of an Emigrant of 1850* (Durban, 1899), 311-12.

4. SNA 1/1/12, Lt.-Gov. to all RMs, n.d. (approx. November 1862); SNA to Greig and Umgeni Memorialists, 30 October 1862.

5. NA SNA 1/1/7, Shires and others to SNA, 10 December 1857. See also the correspondence in this File by Jeffels, Foxon, and Robinson.

6. NA SNA 1/1/8, Jeffels to SNA, 20 June 1858; SNA 1/1/9, Middleton to ANS, 3 September 1859, and Jeffels to SNA, 28 September 1859. Average wage rates for African labourers are in the "Agriculture" section of the Blue Books.

7. *Natal Mercury,* 25 September and 13 October 1863; *Natal Government Gazette* (*NGG*), Notice 130, 6 October 1863; SNA 1/1/13, Dunn to SNA, 27 September 1863; 1/1/14 Dunn to SNA, 10 January 1864.

8. PRO Colonial Office (CO) 179/90, No. 101/12269, Keate to Buckingham, 24 September 1868.

9. SNA 1/6/3, "Statement of the Messengers Sent by the Government to Ceteswayo and Panda," 23 March 1863. See also BPP 1875 C.1137, Shepstone's "Report of the Expedition Sent by the Natal Government to Install Cetewayo," August 1873, 20-21.

10. *BO* 21, 27 May 1865; *BO* 41, 22 September 1866.

11. KCL, JSA, File 25, p. 261, Evidence of Mahungane and Nkonuza, 8 November 1897.

12. L. M. Thompson, "The Zulu Kingdom and Natal," in M. Wilson and L. Thompson, eds., *The Oxford History of South Africa* (London, 1969), I, 389. Thompson, *A History of South Africa* (Johannesburg, 1990), 99-100.

13. *Natal Mercury,* July summary 1869; Natal Legislative Council Sessional Paper, No. 12, 1872, "Report of the Select Committee on the Introduction of Native Labourers from beyond the Borders of the Colony," 6; NLC, Sessional Paper No. 4, 1874, "Report . . . on the Best Means of Introducing Labourers from Beyond the Colony," 20 August 1874. It was expected that, as the Natal sugar industry expanded, the number of foreign African workers on the plantations would grow to anywhere from fifteen to twenty thousand. CO 179/99.1367/71, Memo to Earl of Kimberley, 20 October 1871; SNA 1/7/8, Memo signed by SNA, 18 December 1871.

14. P. Richardson, "The Natal Sugar Industry in the Nineteenth Century," in W. Beinart, P. Delius, and S. Trapido, eds., *Putting a Plough to the Ground* (Johannesburg, 1986), 149; A. Graves and P. Richardson, "Plantations in the Political Economy of Colonial Sugar Production: Natal and Queensland, 1860-1914," *JSAS* 6, 2 (1980), 221.

15. *Natal Almanac,* 1867, 149

16. C. T. Sauer in *Natal Mercury,* 19 February 1876.

17. This was in the space of less than ten years. CO 179/108 No. 50, Musgrave to Kimberley, 20 November 1872. For reports favouring the black peasantry, see annotation by Colonial Undersecretary, CO 179/99.86, Keate to Kimberley, 24 October 1870; and *Natal Witness,* 26 September 1865; 14 December 1866; 1 April 1870; 26 August 1870; 21 March 1871; 20 and 23 June 1871; 30 April 1872.

18. CO 179/102.61/7820, Keate to Kimberley, 22 June 1871.

19. Ministry of Foreign Affairs, Lisbon (MNE), Caixa 697; J. B. Blandy to MNE, 21 December 1868; *BO* 27, 9 July 1869. *Natal Mercury,* 24 June 1870; FO 63/1047, Keate to Kimberley, 8 December 1870.

20. SNA 1/1/19, Leslie to SNA, 25 July 1871; SNA 1/1/21, Elton to SNA, 20 September 1871; GH 845, GLM to Elton, 23 October 1871; FO 63/1049, GLM to Elton in Keate to Kimberley, 7 November 1871; AHU, Moc., CG, Pasta 28, Ablett to GLM, 27 June 1872, in GLM to MSMU, 3 December 1872. See also AHU, Moc., diversos, Pasta 1.

21. MNE, Caixa 663, W. Peace to MNE, 29December 1873 in Duprat to MNE, 17 February 1874; *Natal Mercury,* 19 August and 23 September 1873.

22. CO 179/110 No. 18.3423, Keate to Kimberley, 21 February 1871.

23. CO 179/102, No. 69.7819, Kimberley to Keate, 22 June 1871; No. 85, Keate to Kimberley, 12 September 1871.

24. *Natal Mercury,* 21 March 1871; CSO 379.535, Border Agent Zululand to Col. Sec., 28 February 1871; see also *Natal Mercury,* 5 September 1871.

25. CO 179/105 No. 28, Memorandum by Attorney General of 8 February 1872, in Keate to Kimberley, 8 February 1872.

26. *Natal Witness*, 9 May 1871 and 30 January 1872; *Natal Mercury*, 11 July and 21 November 1871.

27. CO 179/107, Confidential Despatch 10921, Musgrave to Kimberley, September 1872; CO 179/108, Confidential Despatch 1056, Musgrave to Kimberley, n.d.

28. The cost of introducing one Indian labourer was £15-17 in the early 1860s, and £22.10s in the early 1870s. The capitation fee for Amatongas was seldom more than 20s. L. M. Thompson, "Indian Immigration into Natal 1860-1872," in *South African Archives Yearbook 1952*, II (Pretoria, 1952), 13. African wages averaged 8s to 12s, and Indian, 15s to 19s monthly. SNA 1/1/21, Clarence to SNA, 24 April 1871; *Natal Mercury*, 31 August 1871.

29. *Ibid.*; SNA 1/1/22, "Memorandum on the Importation and Control of Native Labourers from Inland Tribes," Shepstone, 5 November 1872.

30. G. Stedman Jones remarks on the "waves of anxiety" at this period, which, due to a spate of social reform, haunted the propertied classes in Britain, "Working Class Culture and Working Class Politics in London, 1870-1900: Notes on the Remaking of a Working Class," *Journal of Social History* 7 (1974), 467. On colonists' fears of an African uprising, see E. Brookes and C. Webb, *A History of Natal* (Pietermaritzburg, 1965), 114; S. Marks, *Reluctant Rebellion: The 1906-8 Disturbances in Natal* (Oxford, 1970), 16, 144-45.

31. *Natal Mercury*, 25 September 1863; 19 February 1876; 29 February 1876; 27 February 1883. N. Etherington, "Natal's Rape Scare of the 1870s," *JSAS* 15, 1 (1988).

32. R. C. Alexander in Report of the Indian Immigrants Commission, 1885-87.

33. CO 179/104, Shepstone Memo of 18 December 1871, in confidential despatch Keate to Kimberley 20 December 1871. SNA 1/7/8 "Memorandum on the Supervision and Control of Native Labourers from Inland Tribes," n.d.

34. CO 179/108, Confidential Despatch No. 156/73, n.d., Musgrave to Kimberley; CO 179/111 No. 9/1573, Annotation by Under Secretary Herbert of 20 February 1873 on Musgrave to Kimberley, 6 January 1873; CO 179/95 No. 13706, Keate to Earl Granville, 22 October 1869.

35. Sessional Papers of the Legislative Council, No. 12, 1872. "Report of the Select Committee into the Introduction of Native Labourers from beyond the Borders of the Colony," Memorandum by SNA dated 5 November 1872. See also *Natal Witness*, 26 August 1870. SNA 1/1/22, "Memorandum on the Importation and Control of Native Labourers from Inland Tribes," 5 November 1872; SNA 1/7/8, "Memo on the Supervision and Control of Native Labourers from Inland Tribes."

36. British intercession had successfully halted Zulu raids into Swaziland. SNA 1/1/96 No. 73, "Statement of Umzungulu and Dubule, Messengers from Umzila," 16 August 1870.

37. SNA 1/1/96 No. 73, "Reply of the Lt.-Governor to the Message of Umzila," 19 August 1870.

38. As in 1868, the Gaza king demanded that, in return for labourers, the British should convince the Swazi to cease their raids into the northern Delagoa Bay hinterland and Bilene. SNA 1/1/96, Erskine to Shepstone, 23 February 1872; SNA 1/1/26 R1187, minute papers, Erskine to Shepstone 1873. See particularly Erskine's MS journal, 1871-72, in the Royal Geographical Society, London.

39. *BO* 9 (1871), 37; *BO* 10 (1871), 41; Delius, *The Land Belongs to Us, The Pedi Polity, the Boers and the British in the nineteenth century Transvaal* (Berkeley, 1984), 100; P. Bonner, *Kings, Commoners and Concessionaries*.

40. Sessional Paper of the Legislative Council No. 12, 1872, "Report of the Select Committee into the Introduction of Native Labourers from Beyond the Borders of the Colony."

41. CO 179/111 No. 9.1573, Musgrove to Kimberley, 6 January 1873.

42. CO 179/111 No. 45.3832, Memorandum by SNA of 3 March 1873, enclosed in Musgrave to Kimberley, 10 March 1873; *British Parliamentary Papers* 1875, C.1137, Shepstone's "Report of the Expedition Sent to Install Cetewayo," August 1873, 20-21.

43. SNA 1/1/23, Dunn to SNA, 16 September 1873 and 24 October 1873.

44. CO 179/123 No. 85.760, Bulwer to Colonial Office, 30 April 1877.

45. Etherington, "Labour Supply and the Genesis of South African Confederation in the 1870s," Journal of African History (JAH) 20, 2(1979), 249-50; *idem,* "Frederic Elton and the South African Factor in the Making of Britain's East African Empire," *Journal of Imperial and Commonwealth History* IX, 3 (1981).

46. Portaria No. 152 of August 1875, in BO 32 (7 August 1875); Immigration Notice No. 4 of 1875 in *NGG*, 6 July 1875. For the vilification of this scheme by French and other humanitarians, see GH 837, Elton to Brackenburg, 4 August 1875; FO 63/1026, Elton to FO, 9 August 1875; *Anti-Slavery Reporter,* 1 April 1876; V. Schoelcher, *Restauration de la traite des Noirs à Natal* (Paris 1877); Renault, *Libération d'esclaves,* 133-35.

47. Government Notice No. 3, 1878, in *NGG,* 1 January 1878; NA, Indian Immigration (II), 1/4.515, Railway Contractors to Protector of Immigrants (PI), 30 April 1878.

48. NA.II 1/16, Memorandum headed "Col. Sec." (n.d.). For a breakdown of the numbers per vessel see NA.II 1/4, various correspondence.

49. On the recruiting activities of hunter-traders like Beningfield and Henry Shires, see NA, Government House (GH) 829, Elton to PI, 25 October 1875; NA, II 1, SNA to PI, 24 January 1876; NA, Colonial Secretary's Office (CSO) 677.2882/78 Bennet to PI, 6 August 1878. On Lipperts and Dentzelman, see NA.II 1/4, Ed Cohen to Colonial Secretary, 12 January 1878; II 1/16 O, Hoffman to PI, 28 February 1877.

50. AHU, CG, Pasta 32, Curadoria Geral dos Individuous sujeitos a tutella publica to GG, 17 August 1877; *BO* 14, 2 April 1877. See also chapter 3, notes 20–21. On the slave trade at Inhambane, see FO 84/1169 G. Frere and F. Surtees to Earl Russel, 18 September 1862; FO 312/17, Mixed commission to Earl Russel, 20 September 1864; C. P. Rigby before the Select Committee on the Slave Trade (East Coast of Africa) in BPP XII, 1871, No. 420, p. 626. See also ch 1 n 2.

51. NA.II 1/3.558, Col. Sec. to PI., 22 December 1877: CSO 787.3031, PI to Col.Sec., 26 September 1878.

52. See notes 90–94 below.

53. *Natal Mercury,* 3 October, 8 October 1874; 5 February, 15 February, 19 February, 29 February 1876. These complaints were first raised in the late 1860s. See SNA 1/1/19, annot. Lt.-governor on Goodliffe to SNA, 7 June 1869.

54. SNA 1/1/27 No. 15, PI Memorandum, 18 January 1876; NA.II 1/16.819, Thompson to PI, 4 February 1877.

55. SNA 1/3/26, R233/76, RM Upper Tugela to SNA, 25 February 1876 and enclosures.

56. About 6,000 men, mainly Pedi and Sotho, left Kimberley at this time. Turrell, *Capital and Labour,* 24.

57. A. J. Purkiss, "The Politics, Capital and Labour of Railway Building in the Cape Colony, 1870-85" (D.Phil. thesis, Oxford, 1978), 330-31, 334; P. Harries, "Mosbiekers: The Immigration of an African Community to the Western Cape, 1876-82," in C. C. Saunders, ed., *Studies in the History of Cape Town* I (Cape Town, 1979).

58. *Natal Mercury,* 29 November 1878.

59. SNA 1/1/96, Erskine to Shepstone, 23 February 1872.

60. The chiefdoms were situated north of the Hluhluwe and were tributary to the Zulu chiefs Somkeli and Zibhebhu. CSO 817.809, PI to Col. Sec., 17 March 1883.

61. Leslie, *Among the Zulus and Amatongas,* (Edinburgh, 1875) 288; BPP, South African Correspondence 1878-79, C.2220 No. 66. See also CSO 656, Natal Government Railways (NGR) contractors to PI, 5 March 1877; NA.II 1/5, NGR Contractors to PI, 1 August 1878.

62. CSO 787.3373, British Resident to High Commissioner, 10 November 1880.

63. NA.II, 1/16.R238, Pollinghorne to Colonial Secretary, 16 April 1877; Legislative Council, SP No. 38, 1877; *Natal Mercury,* 12 February 1876; Harries, "Mosbiekers." The citation is from an 1879 newspaper cutting in the Leigh papers, RGS.

64. Turrell, *Capital and Labour,* 92-94; Worger, *City of Diamonds,* 88-99.

65. W. Campbell in *Natal Mercury,* 29 February 1876.

66. GH 1050, Case of Agnew vs Van Gruning in Registrar of Supreme Court to GH, 14 May 1875; NA, Umsinga Magistracy Files, 1876-78, Magistrate to Attorney Gen., 26 November 1877; *ibid.*, Annual Report for 1877; FO 84/1539, Vice Consul, Lourenço Marques to O'Neill, in O'Neill to FO, 10 October 1879.

67. Immigration Notice No. 1, 1876.

68. CSO 665.4069/78, Statement by Umango, the messenger sent by Nozingile, 7 June 1875.

69. SNA 1/3/21, RM Umvoti to SNA, 6 November 1871; *Natal Mercury*, 16 November 1871; Natal Legislative Council, SP. No. 12, "Report of the Select Committee on the Introduction of Native Labourers from Beyond the Border of the Colony," No. 12, 1872; SNA 1/1/27, Memo by P. E. Ridley, n.d., 1872.

70. R. Sieborger, "The Recruitment and Organisation of African Labour for the Kimberley Diamond Mines, 1871-1885" (MA thesis, Rhodes University, 1976), 39; *Natal Mercury*, 23 November 1883; SMA 8.10.B, H. Berthoud to council, 24 April 1890. A graphic description of the problems faced by migrants on this route is found in C. Richter, *Berliner Missionsberichte*, 1882, 46-59.

71. Louis Cohen, *Reminiscences of Kimberley* (London, 1911), 291, 293.

72. A. Wilmot, *The Life and Times of Sir Richard Southey* (London, 1904), 259.

73. *The (Kimberley) Independent*, 15 February 1876.

74. Transvaal Archives, Pretoria (TA) W179, H. T. Glynn, "Game and Gold," 205.

75. A. Mavanyici, *De la Course aux Diamants à la Recherche des Ames*, ed. P. Rosset (Lausanne, 1928), 3-6.

76. R. Berthoud-Junod, *Du Transvaal à Lourenço Marques: lettres de Mme R. Berthoud-Junod* (Lausanne, 1904), 81, 91-99.

77. J. Angove, *In the Early Days: The Reminiscences of Pioneer Life on the South African Diamond Fields* (Johannesburg, 1910), 190.

78. E. W. Feildon, *My African Home* (London, 1887), 255; B. Buchanan, *Natal Memories* (Pietermaritzburg, 1941), 229, 231; A Lady (J. Robinson?), *Life at Natal a Hundred Years Ago* (Cape Town, 1972), 31.

79. Legislative Council, SP No. 12, 1872, "Report of the Select Committee on the Introduction of Native Labourers"; SNA 1/1/27, Memo by P. E Ridley, n.d., 1872; SNA 1/3/21, RM Umvoti, 6 November 1871; CSO 179.104 SNA., Memo 18 December 1871, enclosed in Keate to Kimberley, 20 December 1871.

80. TA.A180, Cape Public Works Department (CPWD), Elliot to Tew and Co., 6 November 1875; McNaughton to Few and Co., 30 March 1876; TA, State Secretary (SS) 185.R54, Colonial Secretary, Cape Town, to SS, 27 February 1875; SS 186. R652; SS 188. R1103; SS 192. R1810; SS1193. R1822; NA, SNA 1/1/27, F. B. Fynney to SNA, 19 January 1876; TA, Native Affairs (SN), Merensky to Osborne, 25 July 1877; TA.SN 1, Acting Native Commissioner (NC) Waterberg to SNA, 8 May 1879; SN 2, H. Shepstone, Minute No. N309/1879 of 13 December 1879; *Ibid.*, Barlow to SNA, 3 September 1870; SN.4A, NC Spelonken to SNA, 2 July 1881; SS 490 Lddst. Lydenburg to Col. Sec., 25 November 1880; SN 173 R179/83, NC Spelonken to NC Zoutpansberg, 9 October 1883.

81. L. Phillips, *Some Remininscences* (London 1924) 18; Turrell, *Capital and Labour,* 25. Southey estimated that a migrant had to consume £2-3 in food so as to regain the strength needed to undertake heavy mine labour.

82. E. de Weber, *Quatre ans au Pays des Boers, 1871-1875* (Paris, 1882), 124; J. Angove, *In the Early Days: The Reminiscenses of Pioneer Life on South African Diamond Fields* (Johannesburg, 1910), 69; W. J. Morton, *The South African Diamond Fields and the Journey to the Mines* (New York, 1877), 15; G. F. Williams, *The Diamond Mines of South Africa*, 2 vols (London 1902), I, 53, 189.; R. W. Murray, *The Diamond Fields Keepsake for 1873* (Cape Town, 1886), 37.

83. C. Warren, *On the Veldt in the Seventies* (London, 1902), 125-26.

84. Phillips, *Some Reminiscences*, 18.

85. Cohen, *Reminiscences*, 292.

86. NA.II 1/1 R174/76, Jackson to PI, 13 March 1876; W. Peace, *Our Colony of Natal: A Handbook* (London, 1884), 43-44.
87. SNA 1/3/26 R233, RM Upper Tugela to SNA, 25 February, 1876.
88. On whites as cannibals, see Junod, *Life*, II, 266, 269, 506. This was a common belief on the slave coasts of Africa, see P. Curtin, *Africa Remembered* (Madison, 1967), 92-93, 215, 313, 331; Joseph Miller, *Way of Death: Merchant Capitalism and the Angolan Slave Trade, 1730-1820* (London, 1988), 4, 157-58. Alfred Aylward, a severe critic of British imperialism, claimed that at least one cargo of migrant workers bound for Natal had been shipped to Madagascar to be enslaved, *The Transvaal To-day* (London, 1877), 359.
89. NA.II 1/4 751/78, Deposition of Mondisa in Bennet to Lt.-Gov., 16 February 1878.
90. SNA 1/1/27 No. 47, Supt. Police to SNA, 2 March 1876. See also No. 60, DuBois to SNA, 3 April 1876; *Natal Mercury*, 29 February 1876. SNA 1/1/27 No. 47, Supt. Police to SNA, 2 March 1876. See also *Ibid.*, No. 60, Du Bois to SNA, 3 April 1876; *Natal Mercury* 29 February 1876.
91. Legislative Council, SP No. 12, 1872; *Ibid.*, No. 4, 1874, "Report of the Select Committee to Consider the Best Means of Introducing Labourers from Beyond the Colony," 20 August 1874; NA.II R211/75, Jackson to PI, 12 May 1875.
92. *BO*, 14 April 1877, 84; *Natal Mercury*, 29 February 1884. Slave ships averaged 2-2.5 slav₁ ₃ per ton, D. Eltis, *Economic Growth and the Ending of the Transatlantic Slave Trade* (New York, 1987), 136-37.
93. T. Costello, *1874! The Exciting True Story of the Early Days on the Caledonian Gold Fields, Transvaal* (London, n.d.), 9-10.
94. The *Boletim Oficial de Mocambique* recorded the number of "black passengers" or "free blacks" embarking at Lourenço Marques. See also NA.II 1/4.751/8, Bennet to Lt.-governor, 16 February 1878; *Natal Mercury*, 29 February 1876 and 7 March 1876.
95. W. Campbell in *Natal Mercury*, 14 March, 18 March 1876.
96. Purkiss, "Railway Building," 390-93; Turrell, *Capital and Labour*, 166-68.
97. SNA 1/3/26 R233/76, RM Upper Tugela to SNA, 25 February 1876 and 29 March 1876.
98. MNE C 663, Forsman to MNE, 22 March 1875, in Duprat to MNE, 4 May 1875.
99. Cory Library, Rhodes University, Grahamstown. MS 15774 by Rev E. Botrill. See also the typescript by Mr. Choat in the Cory Library; James Stewart, *Lovedale: Past and Present* (Lovedale, 1887), 183; Amos Burnett, *A Mission to the Transvaal* (Cape Town, 1919), 13-24; G. Mears, *Methodist Torchbearers* (Cape Town, 1955), 20-22; *South African* (Weekly), 18 March 1949; J. van Butselaar, *Africains, missionaires et colonialistes: les origines de l'église Presbytérienne du Mozambique (Mission Suisse), 1880-1896* (Leiden, 1984), 167. There are numerous contradictions in these different sources. I have compiled what seems to me the most logical chronology of Mashaba's life.
100. B. Willan, *Sol Plaatje: A Biography* (Johannesburg and London, 1984), 28-32.
101. On the "accredited ministers" who kept their chiefs informed of conditions at Kimberley, see J. B. Currie, "Half a Century in South Africa," TS in South African Public Library (SAPL), Cape Town, Ch. XII, 23. On the workers' communication networks in Natal, see NA.CSO 787.3373, Border Agent to Col. Sec., 17 August 1880; Report by RM Tugela of 31 March 1876 in *Natal Government Gazette*, 4 April 1876; C. Parsons in *Natal Mercury*, 26 February 1876.
102. The following description is drawn from, Natal Land and Colonization Company, *Twenty Seven Queries . . . with Reference to the Capabilities of the Colony of Natal, More Especially as Regards the Culture and Manufacture of Sugar Cane* (Durban, 1867); J. Robinson, *Notes on Natal* (Durban and London, 1872); W. Campbell, "Sugar Planting in Natal," in *Natal Almanac and Register*, 1874, 157; W. Campbell, "Central Sugar Factories in Natal," in *Natal Almanac*, 1875; A. F. Hattersley, *The British Settlement of Natal* (Cambridge, 1950).
103. T. W. Lampert before the *Coolie Commission*, SP No. 1 of 1872, reprinted in *NGG*, 17 September 1872.

104. On milling, see Robinson, *Notes on Natal*, 92-100; *Natal Mercury*, 20 November 1882; W. R. Ludlow, *Zululand and Cetewayo* (London, 1882), 13-14; Richardson, "Natal Sugar Industry," 167-68, notes 63-64; D. Lincoln, "The Culture of the South African Sugar Mill: The Impress of the Sugarocracy" (Ph.D. thesis, University of Cape Town, 1985).

105. R. F. Osborn, *Valiant Harvest: The Founding of the South African Sugar Industry, 1848-1926* (Durban, 1964), 54, 61.

106. "A Lady," *Life at Natal a Hundred Years Ago* (Cape Town, 1972), 38.

107. Robinson, *Notes on Natal*, 9; Richardson, "Natal Sugar Industry," 133, 154.

108. Richardson, "Natal Sugar Industry," 139.

109. R. J. Mann, *The Colony of Natal* (London, 1859), 79; Robinson, *Notes on Natal*, 5-6, 71, 83.

110. Osborn, *Valiant Harvest*, 85.

111. R. Williams, *Keywords; A Vocabulary of Culture and Society* (London, 1976).

112. C. Parsons in *Natal Mercury*, 26 February 1876; W. Listner before the *Coolie Commission*, 1872.

113. Natal Legislative Council, SP. No. 12, 1872; "Report of the Select Committee to Consider the Introduction of Native Labourers from Beyond the Borders of the Colony," 1; SNA 1/1/22, Memorial by the SNA on the Importation and Control of Native Labourers from Inland Tribes," 5 November 1872.

114. Natal Legislative Council, "Report of the Select Committee to Consider the Introduction of Native Labourers from beyond the Border of the Colony," SP No. 12, 1872; NA.II 1/1 R815/76, Parsons to Col. Sec., 18 March 1876; *Natal Mercury*, 26 February, 14 March 1876; C. Parsons in *Natal Mercury*, 26 February 1876.

115. W. Listner before the *Coolie Commission*, 1872; H. Shepstone before the *Indian Immigration Commission*, 1885-87, 78.

116. B. Buchanan, *Natal Memories* (Pietermaritzburg, 1941), 230; W. Peace, *Our Colony of Natal*, 153. But for remarks on the lack of tension between blacks and Indians, see E. Beater before the *Coolie Commission*; S. F. Beningfield before the *Indian Immigration Commission*, 211.

117. Natal Land and Colonisation Company, *Twenty-seven Queries*, 2, 5; Campbell, "Sugar Planting," 48; Robinson, *Notes on Natal*, 6, 56-57.

118. E. T. Phillips before the *Coolie Commission; Indian Immigration Commission*, Evidence of Rev. Stott (p. 172), W. Arbuckle (p. 134), W. Palmer (p. 183), R. Jameson (p. 188).

119. Report of the *Coolie Commission*, 1872.

120. E. T. Phillips before the *Coolie Commission;* Report of the *Natal Native Commission*, 1881-82, 5; Evidence of Rev. Stott and Messrs. Arbuckle, Palmer, Jameson, and Shepstone before the *Indian Immigration Commission*.

121. *Natal Mercury*, 29 February 1876; C. Behrens in the Natal Land Company's *Twenty-seven Queries*, 4.

122. Robinson, *Notes on Natal*, 15; Natal Land and Colonization Co., *Twenty-seven Queries*, 5-6; H. Shepstone before the *Indian Immigration Commission*, 30; W. Peace, *Our Colony of Natal*, 50; Osborn, *Valiant Harvest*, 167-68.

123. Natal Land and Colonization Company, *Twenty-seven Queries*, 5-6; Peace, *Our Colony of Natal*, 100.

124. Robinson, *Notes on Natal*, 105.

125. Report of the *Coolie Commission* and Evidence of Lamport, Lean, Dawson; Thompson, "Indian Immigration into Natal."

126. G. Clarence, "Notes on the Cultivation of Sugar Cane," in *Natal Almanac*, 1870, 80; Robinson, *Notes on Natal*, 57.

127. See pp 6-8, 16-17, above.

128. *Natal Mercury*, 29 February 1876.

129. *Ibid.*

130. Saunders, in the Natal Land Co.'s *Twenty-seven Queries*, 4.

131. CO 179/104, Shepstone Memo of 18 December 1871, in Keate to Kimberley, 20 December 1871; See also SNA 1/7/8, "Memorandum on the Supervision and Control of Native Labourers from Inland Tribes," n.d.
132. *Natal Mercury,* 6 April 1876.
133. SNA 1/1/59.65, RM, Lions River, to Advocate, Pietermaritzburg, 19 February 1883 and enclosures; Circular, Col. Sec. to Res. Magistrates, 13 November 1878. See also SNA 1/1/59.77, SNA to RM, Pietermaritzburg, 28 February 1888.
134. AHU, Moc., CG., Pasta 32, GLM to Conselheiro Diretor general do Ultramar, 25 December 1878. In his district report for the previous year the governor had written of "numerous caravans" going overland to Natal and the eastern Transvaal goldfields, BO 52, 30 December 1878.
135. *BO* 50, 15 December 1879; NA, GH 837, Br. Consul to Lt. Gov., 12 January 1880; PRO FO 84/1539, Br. Consul to FO, 10 December 1879; FO 84/1616, Azvedo to Nunes (n.d.) in Br. Consul to FO, 14 February 1882.
136. CSO 2555.C32, Dunn to Acting SNA, 8 September, enclosed in RM Lower Tugela to Col. Sec., 13 July 1881; CSO 897.809, PI to Col. Sec., 17 March 1883; SNA 1/1/68.936, PI to Col. Sec., 9 January 1884.
137. SMA 8.10.B, P. Berthoud to Cuenod, 16 March 1884. For the conditions of migrant workers on board the *Dunkeld Castle,* see Rapier (pseud.), *To the Transvaal Goldfields and Back* (Cape Town, 1885), 7. See also W. Joest, *Um Afrika* (Cologne, 1885), 204-205.
138. SNA 1/1/25, PI to Border Agent, 24 November 1881; PI to Col. Sec., 14 December 1881; CSO 2555 C32, RM Durban to SNA, 27 July 1881; SNA 1/1/53.144, Fynney to SNA, 31 March 1882. For similar statements about Amatongas at Kimberley, see TA A180, CPWD, McNaughton to De Coster, 4 October 1881; McNaughton to De Coster, 24 October 1881.
139. NA.II 1/24.163, D. C. Andrews to PI, 8 January 1885 and annotation PI to Col. Sec., 9 January 1885.
140. Act 48 of 1884, later amended by Government Notice 217 of 1886. CSO 2555 C32, RM Durban to SNA, 27 July 1881; SNA 1/1/53.1144, Fynney to SNA, 31 March 1882.
141. SNA 1/1/106.416, SNA to Governor, 21 June 1888. See also Government Notice in *NGG,* 255 of 1888.
142. SNA 1/1/78.812, SNA to Attorney General, 21 November 1884, and Att. Gen., enclosure of 21 November 1884; Government Notice No. 323, 1884; SNA 1/1/78.832, Tatham and Edmonstone to SNA, 19 November 1884.
143. NA.II 1/17/17, CSO to PI, 4 January 1884; SNA 1/1/68.936, Col. Sec. to SNA, 9 January 1884; SNA 1/1/68.936, SNA to Bulwer, 21 January 1884.
144. Harries, "Plantations, Passes," 394-98.
145. AHU, Moc., 2a Repartiçao, Pasta 1, G. Inh. to GGM, 13 June 1884, in GGM to MSMU, 28 June 1884; American Board Mission (ABM), ABC 15.4 Vol. 12, Richards to Mean, 24 August 1884; E. Creux, "Une tournee Missionaire," *BMSAS* 40 (1881), 231, 234.
146. NA.II 1/57.816, Gen. Manager, NGR, to Col. Sec., 13 August 1890, enclosed in PI to Col. Sec., 19 August 1890.

CHAPTER 3

Kimberly: The Cradle of a New Working Class

1. Sieborger, "Recruitment and Organisation," 4; Turrell, *Capital and Labour,* 20 n.3.
2. Phillips, *Some Reminiscences* (London, 1924), 30; Sawyer, *Mining at Kimberley,* 21; W. Nelson, "Some Letters—Extracts from the *Masbro Advertiser* from 19 May 1877," *Africana Notes and News* 20, 5 (1973), 181; J. Couper, *Mixed Humanity* (Cape Town, 1892), 20; W. C. Holden, *A Brief History of Methodism* (London, 1887), 514.
3. Cape Archives, Cape Town (CA), Griqua Land West (GLW) 100.442, Report of the Native Labour Department for 1876 by J. D. Coleman. See also pp.26, 33, 45, above.

4. SMA 8.10.B, H. Berthoud to Grandjean, 9 October 1883; SMA 8.10.B, H. Berthoud to conseil, 24 June 1890. See also Delius, *The Land Belongs to Us*, Ch. 3.

5. Cape Parliamentary Papers (CPP), G 102-'83, Report on the Diamond Mines of Kimberley and De Beers, 1883; Turrell, *Capital and Labour*, 12-14.

6. Turrell, *Capital and Labour*, 13.

7. *Hard Times* (London, 1969 ed.) 102-3.

8. Turrell, *Capital and Labour*, 128-29.

9. Phillips, *Some Reminiscences*, 18-20; J. Angove, *In the Early Days*, 191.

10. A point particularly made by Worger, *City of Diamonds*, 73, 99, 101.

11. Trollope, *South Africa* (London, 1877), I, 359; Nelson, "Extracts from the *Masbro Advertiser*," 179.

12. C. Payton, *The Diamond Diggings of South Africa* (London, 1872), 139; CPP.A9-'82, S. Marks before the Select Committee on Illicit Diamond Buying.

13. W. Morton, *The South African Diamond Fields*, 5, 78, 674; Cohen, *Reminiscences of Kimberley*, 112.

14. Morton, *Diamond Fields*, 4, 78, 563; K. Shillington, *The Colonisation of the Southern Tswana, 1870-1900* (Johannesburg, 1985), 66, 92.

15. A. Connyngham, *My Command in South Africa, 1874-78* (London, 1890), 197; Couper, *Mixed Humanity*, 74-75.

16. Couper, *Mixed Humanity*, 108, 153-55.

17. Warren, *On the Veldt*, 125-26. See also CA.GLW 17, Lanyon to Acting Administrator, Griqualand West, 22 August 1880.

18. Cape Blue Book, 1885, 209.

19. SMA 467, Diary of Arthur Grandjean, 1890, p. 12; SMA 8.10.B, H. Berthoud to A. Grandjean, 5 July 1886. See also pp. 61, 144, 153, 155, below.

20. FO 84/1616, Consul O'Neill to FO, 14 February 1882.

21. NA.II,1/10.79, Supt. Police to Mayor and Council, Durban, 6 January 1882.

22. NA.CSO 841, RM Durban to PI, 2 February 1883; CPC, Packet marked "Various Documents," 1890.

23. The origin of these workers, who were described as "Zulu," is uncertain; that they would accept abysmally substandard working conditions and that they were "under their own captains" indicates they were a subject people hired out to white recruiters. It is probable that Arthur Shepstone used his old contacts as a Natal Government Railways recruiter to procure the workers from the Zulu chief Zibhebhu, who was at that time supplying Natal planters with cheap, coerced Amatonga labour. Harries, "History, Ethnicity," 23. See also chapter 2, notes 60–61.

24. *Griqualand West Directory*, 1884, 19; Baring-Gould before the IDB Commission, 118; Turrell, *Capital and Labour*, 168.

25. J. Smalberger, "The Role of the Diamond Industry in the Development of the Pass-law system in South Africa," in *International Journal of African Historical Studies* 9, 3 (1976).

26. Turrell, *Capital and Labour*, 27-28; Worger, *City of Diamonds*, 115-17.

27. Smalberger Papers, University of Cape Town (SP).GLW 163, Protector and Registrar of Natives to Acting Col. Sec., 15 September 1880; CA.NA 448, Protector and Registrar of Natives to SNA, 14 September 1880.

28. A1-'90,. Evidence of J. MacKenzie.

29. Worger, *City of Diamonds*, 123-30; Turrell, *Capital and Labour*, 98ff, 181-82.

30. H. H. Curson, *The History of the Kimberley Regiment* (Kimberley, 1963).

31. Turrell, *Capital and Labour*, 53-55.

32. SP, GLW 153 Manager, Vooruitzich Estate Office to Acting Col. Sec., 31 March 1880; SP.NA 186, Civil Commissioner, Kimberley, to SNA, 24 March 1881; Turrell, *Capital and Labour*, 98-102.

33. SP.GLW 139, Draft Bye laws in Native Locations, 8 July 1879; Government Notice 151 of 1879.

34. E. de Weber, *Quatre ans au pays des Boers: 1871-1875* (Paris, 1882), 127.

35. Morton, *Diamond Fields*, 77. See also Angove, *In The Early Days*, 60.

36. G. Williams, *The Diamond Mines of South Africa* (London, 1902), I, 218-19.

37. V. Turner, *The Ritual Process* (Chicago, 1969); E. Goffman, *Asylums* (Harmondsworth, 1968).

38. On the concept of liminality, see Turner, *Ritual Process*, 95; *idem*, "Betwixt and Between: The Liminal Period in Rites of Passage," in his *The Forest of Symbols* (Ithaca, 1962).

39. Payton, *Diamond Diggings*, 140, 145; R. W. Murray, *South African Reminiscences* (Cape Town, 1894), 36.

40. H. Schlesinger before the Liquor Laws Commission, CPP.G1-1890, 426.

41. See p. 9 above, and pp. 91, 93, 229, below.

42. See M. Douglas, "Deciphering a Meal," in C. Geertz, ed., *Myth, Symbol and Culture* (New York, 1971); Douglas, "Standard Social Uses of Food," in her *Food in the Social Order* (New York, 1984); J. Goody, *Cooking, Cuisine and Class* (Cambridge, 1982), 29-32.

43. Newbury, *The Diamond Ring*, 60.

44. CPP.A9-1882, Matthews before IDB Commission, 132. See also much of the evidence before the Liquor Laws Commission, CPP.G1-1889-90.

45. Angove, *In the Early Days*, 195; Matthews, *Incwadi Yami, or Twenty Years Personal Experience in South Africa* (New York, 1887), 187-88. For a breakdown of the function of these different additives, see O. Robert "Les vins falsifiés au XIXe siècle: image d'un certain quotidien vaudois?" *Revue Historique Vaudoise* (1989).

46. On liquor as a stimulant and foodstuff, see J. R. Scrutton before the Transvaal Liquor Commission, C 41 of 1908, 24, 30; A. T. Bryant, *The Zulu People* (Pietermaritzburg, 1949), 289. More generally, see J. Roberts, *Drink, Temperance and the Working Class in Nineteenth-century Germany* (London, 1984).

47. The social aspect of drinking is stressed by M. Douglas, ed., *Constructive Drinking: Perspectives on Drink from Anthropology* (Cambridge, 1987), and by many historians; cf. Roberts, *Drink, Temperance and the Working Class*, and T. Brennan, "Towards the Cultural History of Alcohol in France," *Journal of Social History* 23, 1 (1989). The rural influence on social drinking in industrial South Africa is stressed by J. Crush and C. Ambler eds., *Liquor and Labor in Southern Africa* (Athens and Pietermaritzburg, 1992), 2, 4ff.

48. G. Mitchell in the *Quarterly Paper of the Bloemfontein Mission* (QPBM), 55 (November 1881), 14.

49. CPP.A9-1882, Tracey, Hornby, and Baring-Gould before the IDB Committee.

50. W. Crisp, *Some Account of the Diocese of Bloemfontein in the Province of South Africa, 1863-1894* (Oxford, 1895), 94.

51. Note 48 above.

52. CPP.G1-1890, Evidence before the Liquor Commission of RM, Beaconsfield, J. Brunton, S. Mvambo, RM Kimberley, Commissioner of Police, pp. 436, 448, 874, 876; J. Arnt, "Die eingebornen-frage auf den Diamantenfeldern von Kimberley in Sudafrika," in *Beiblatt zum Berliner Missions-freund*, 13, 5/6 (1887), 42.

53. TA, C41, Scrutton before the Transvaal Liquor Commission, 23.

54. CPP.G40-'86, General Report of the Inspector of Diamond Mines.

55. Cf. D. Reid, "The Decline of St. Monday, 1776-1876," *Past and Present* 71 (1976); H. Gutman, *Work, Culture, and Society in Industrialising America* (New York, 1976) 20-1, 38-9; R. Church, *The History of the British Coal Industry* (Oxford, 1986), III, 241-46.

56. W. Morton, "To South Africa for Diamonds," in *Scribner's Magazine* XVI (1878), 673; R. Murray, *The Diamond Field's Keepsake for 1873* (Cape Town, 1873), 36; Williams, *The Diamond Mines*, I, 219.

57. See pp. 210-213, below.

58. Couper, *Mixed Humanity*, 153; Warren, *On the Veldt*, 111.

59. Matthews, *Incwadi Yami*, 422.

60. See p. 6, above. On naming in other contexts, see Geertz, *Local Knowledge*, 63-67; Comaroff and Comaroff, *Of Revelation and Revolution*, 216-19; H. Gutman, *The Black Family in Slavery and Freedom, 1750-1925* (New York, 1976), 217-23.

61. C. Richter, "Wanderende Bassuto," *Berliner Missionsberichte* 3/4 (1882), 56. See also p. 208, below.

62. Connyngham, *My Command*, 194; L. Phillips, *Reminiscences*, 20. Civilians were later prohibited by from wearing military uniforms, Phillips, *Transvaal Problems: Some Notes on Current Politics* (London, 1905), 103.

63. Morton, "South African Diamond Fields," 15.

64. Mrs. Monteiro, *Delagoa Bay, Its Natives and Natural History* (London, 1891), 74; Report of the Governor of *Lourenco Marques for 1876, in *BO* 45, 5 November 1877; *BO* 52, 30 December 1878.

65. Junod, "Ba-Ronga," 211, and *Life*, II, 96-97. On dress as a system of signification and meaning, see J. M. Cordwell and R. A. Schwarz, eds., *The Fabrics of Culture: The Anthropology of Clothing and Adornment* (The Hague, 1979).

66. On the notion of symbolic capital, see P. Bourdieu, *In Other Words: Essays Towards a Reflexive Sociology* (Stanford, 1990), 22, 93, 111-12.

67. G. P. Fergusson, *CUSA: The Story of the Churches of the Congregational Union of South Africa* (Pretoria, 1940), 42, 217.

68. Wesleyan Methodist Church of South Africa, Ninth Annual Report, 1890, 101; *ibid.*, Twelfth Annual Report, 1893, 116.

69. Wesleyan Methodist Church of South Africa, Sixth Annual Report, 1887, 92; *ibid.*, Seventh Annual Report, 1888, 102-103. W. C. Holden, *A Brief History of Methodism*, 514-16; Crisp, *Diocese of Bloemfontein*, 39-40.

70. One man informed the missionary A. Grandjean that "we cannot accept to live in poverty, to have only one wife and to no longer drink beer." SMA 872 Grandjean to Council, 24 August 1892. Junod feared high wages would make Africans "haughty and lazy" when they returned home, "BaRonga," 244; *QPBM*, 45 (August 1879), 25; BPP.A1-90, Evidence of Rev. Mvambo.

71. SMA 8.10.C, Creux to Council, 5 June 1880; SMA 8.10.B, H. Berthoud to A. Grandjean, 5 July 1886. South African Native Races Committee, eds., *The Natives of South Africa* (London, 1901), 142.

72. Arnt, "Die Eingebornen-frage," 36-37; SMA 517/B, Junod to Renevier, 10 October 1895; Junod, "BaRonga," 116, and *Life*, II, 630; Methodist Episcopal Church, East Central African Mission Church, 8th session, 1911, report of P. W. Keys. See also Trollope, *South Africa*, II, 171-72.

73. Thompson, *Making of the English Working Class*, 393.

74. Junod was to note that Christianity transformed the idea of charity by introducing broader notions of community than the clan and chiefdom, *Life*, II, 581 n.1.

75. *QPBM*, 54 (October 1881), 205-206; *ibid.*, 55 (December 1881), 14; *ibid.*, 56 (January 1882); *ibid.*, 57 (July 1883), 191.

76. CPP.A1-'90, Evidence of S. Mvambo, 448.

77. Wesleyan Methodist Church of South Africa, Ninth Annual Report, 1890, 101; *ibid.*, Thirteenth Annual Report, 1894; Williams, *Diamond Mines*, I, 218, II, 64: Turrell, *Capital and Labour*, 172. See also pp. 192-193 below.

78. SP.NA 195, Report of the Acting Registrar of Natives for 1882, in Civil Commissioner to SNA, 27 March 1883; Williams, *The Diamond Mines*, 421.

79. On this process elsewhere in the world, cf. E. P. Thompson in H. Kaye, *The British Marxists*, 206.

80. For similar processes from elsewhere in the world, see Gutman, *The Black Family,* 220; D. Horowitz, *Ethnic Groups in Conflict* (Berkeley, 1985) 61; Johnson, *Peasant and Proletarian,* 95.
81. Cohen, *Reminiscences,* 293.
82. Native Races Committee, *Natives of South Africa;* CA GLW 126, annotation by C. M. Bult on J. E. Dyer to Lt-Gov., 17 December 1878.
83. Cohen, *Reminiscences,* 293.
84. Worger, *City of Diamonds,* 100-104; Sieborger, "Recruitment and Organisation," 279, 300; Turrell, *Capital and Labour,* 97.
85. *Diamond News,* 20 April 1880, cited in Worger, *City of Diamonds,* 127-28.
86. C. Richter, "Wanderende Bassuto," in *Berliner Missionsberichte* 33/4 (1882).
87. Europeans perceived the major protagonists in the early railway camps as "Basutos" and "Zulus," although "Delagoa Bay men" formed a distinct category. CA.CO 3276, RM Worcester to Col. Sec., 7 and 10 February 1877; CPP, H. Pauling before the Cape Liquor Laws Commission, G 1-'90, 429-30; H. J. and R. E. Simons, *Class and Colour in South Africa, 1850-1950* (Harmondsworth, 1969), 46.
88. See the pioneering article by C. van Onselen and I. Phimister, "The Political Economy of Tribal Animosity: A Case Study of the 1929 Bulawayo Location 'Faction Fight,' " *JSAS* 6, 1 (1979).
89. Junod, "BaRonga," 23. See also *Life,* I, 82-85.
90. Phillips, *Reminiscences,* 22-23; Crisp, *Diocese of Bloemfontein,* 94; Payton, *Diamond Diggings,* 165.
91. *Natal Mercury,* 22 January 1883.
92. SMA 8.10.B, H. Berthoud to Grandjean, 9 October 1883; TA.SN 173.179/83, Native Commissioner, Spelonken to Native Commissioner, Zoutpansberg, 9 October 1883; CA. G3-'84, Division of Kimberley, Native Registrar and Protector to Civil Commissioner, 18 January 1884.
93. NA.CSO 927.3812/83, annot., Col. Sec., 27 September 1883; CSO 936.5730, Memorial of Farmers in the County of Weenen (1884); CSO 974.3915, Col. Sec. to Cmdt. Natal Mounted Police, 27 September 1883.
94. Turrell, *Capital and Labour,* 43, 52, 59; Worger, *City of Diamonds,* 104-107, 131, 136.
95. Turrell, *Capital and Labour,* 228; Worger, *City of Diamonds,* 249-52.
96. CPP.G40-'86, Report of the Inspector of Diamond Mines for 1885, 13. For later reports, see also *Cape Times,* 1 April 1895; Williams, *Diamond Mines,* II, 53; Turrell, *Capital and Labour,* 146-47, 161.
97. Turrell, "Kimberley: Labour and Compounds, 1871-1888," in S. Marks and R. Rathbone, eds., *Industrialisation and Social Change;* Turrell, *Capital and Labour,* 49, 143, 148, 172-73.
98. Most men chose to enter into two-month contracts although some agreed to sign on for four months, because they had to pay a 1s fee each time they registered. R. Turrell, "Kimberley's Model Compounds" *JAH* 25, 1 (1984); A. Mabin, "Labour, Capital, Class Struggle and the Origins of Residential Segregation in Kimberley, 1880-1920," *Journal of Historical Geography* 12, 1 (1986), 18.
99. Williams, *Diamond Mines,* 413.
100. CPP.G40-'86, Annual Report of the Inspector of Diamond Mines. See also CPP. C22-'89, p. 6.
101. CA.NA 411, Protector of Natives (PN) to SNA, 7 October 1889.
102. CPP.G1-'90, Report of the Liquor Laws Commission, 410.
103. Turrell, *Capital and Labour,* 155-58; Johnstone, *Class, Race and Gold,* 35, 38-39; C. van Onselen, *Studies in the Social and Economic History of the Witwatersrand,* II, *New Nineveh* (Johannesburg, 1982), 179; B. Bozzoli, *The Political Nature of a Ruling Class: Capital and Ideology in South Africa, 1890-1933* (London, 1981), 72-74. This argument was first used by Kimberley merchants and anti-trust politicians, cf. S. Cronwright-Schreiner, *Some Vital facts about Kimberley and Johannesburg* (London, 1900).

104. Perhaps most forcibly expressed by Turrell, "Kimberley's Model Compounds," and *Capital and Labour,* 172.
105. Figures are drawn from the *Cape Statistical Register;* see Appendix I in Turrell, *Capital and Labour,* 228.
106. Williams, cited in CPP.G2-'89, Report of the Inspector of Diamond Mines for 1888.
107. In April 1885 some four hundred recruited Inhambane workers were housed in the closed compounds of the Kimberley Central DMC. *Diamond Fields Advertizer,* 24 April 1885. See also p. 54 above.
108. Williams, *Diamond Mines,* 422. See also QPBM, 33 July (1876), 37.
109. Williams, *Diamond Mines,* Chs. 8 and 11; CPP.C22-'89, 9; CPP.G5-'96, p. 34; Worger, *City of Diamonds,* 248-49.
110. Turrell, *Capital and Labour,* 237, 239.
111. Wages at Kimberley remained consistently higher than those on the gold fields. *Chamber of Mines Annual Reports* 1907, 539. Native Races Committee, *Natives of South Africa,* 148; TG2-1908, Transvaal Mining Industry Commission of 1908, Evidence of Makhotle; UG 12-1914, Report of the Economic Commission, January 1914. Compensation payments were also consistently higher at Kimberley, see TA.K358-1, S. Pritchard, Transvaal Director of Native Labour, to the Native Grievances Commission, 1913-14.
112. Pritchard to the Native Grievances Commission, 1913-14.
113. Erskine to Rhodes, 29 May 1890, cited in Worger, *City of Diamonds,* 269 n.98.
114. Newbury, *The Diamond Ring,* 74, 116, 117-19.
115. Before the Cape Labour Commission, CPP.G3-'93, 366. See also Lepelo, Mshavu, Dallas, Liefelt before this commisssion, 366, 368, 392-93, 397. Williams, *Diamond Mines,* 405.
116. CA.NA 411, Protector of Natives to SNA, 10 September 1889; Williams, *Diamond Mines,* 341.
117. R. W. Murray, "Sunday in the De Beers Compound," *South Africa* (2 November 1895), 236; Williams, *Diamond Mines,* 68.
118. G. Noiriel, *Longwy, immigrés et prolètaires, 1880-1980* (Paris, 1984), 13; D. Perrot, "The Three Ages of Industrial Discipline in 19th Century France," in John M. Merriman, ed., *Consciousness and Class Exploitation in 19th Century Europe* (New York, 1979), 160.
119. J. B. Currey, "The Diamond Fields of Griqualand West and their Probable Influence on the Native Races of South Africa," *Journal of the Society of Arts* XXIV (1876), 378; Phillips, *Some Reminiscences.*
120. Williams, *Diamond Mines,* 413.
121. Currey, "The Diamond Fields," 378.
122. A point made by P. Brantlinger, "Victorians and Africans: The Genealogy of the Myth of the Dark Continent," *Critical Inquiry* 12 (1985). See also D. Kidd's influential *The Essential Kaffir* (London, 1904), 66, 405.
123. CPP.G1-'90, Evidence of J. Sivewright, A. H. Watkins, S. Mvambo, Archdeacon Gaul, before the Cape Liquor Commission, 408, 410, 445, 451.
124. Lt.-Col. Crossman on the Affairs of Griqualand West, May 1876, cited in Turrell, *Capital and Labour,* 29. The second citation is from J. H. Hofmeyer before the Cape Liquor Commision, CPP.G1-'90, 453. See also Williams, *Diamond Mines,* 436; R. Rotberg, *The Founder: Cecil Rhodes and the Pursuit of Power* (New York, 1988), 225, 470.
125. "Baronga," 8-9. See also *Life,* II, 609-11, 633.
126. QPMB 74 (1886), 84.
127. Cited in Native Races Committee, *Natives of South Africa,* 141, 149. See also Rev. Crosthwaite in QPBM, 83 (15 January 1889); Wesleyan Methodist Church of South Africa, 10th Annual Report, 1891, 100; *ibid.,* Eleventh Annual Report, 1892, 106.
128. Cited in Simons and Simons, *Class and Colour,* 46.
129. J. A. Hobson, *The War in South Africa* (London, 1900), 239. On Kenilworth, see Williams, *Diamond Mines,* 471-78; Mabin, "Residential Segregation in Kimberley."

130. The notion of industrial paternalism is discounted by Turrell (*Capital and Labour*, 163) but finds a strong echo in Worger (*City of Diamonds*, 284-91). According to W. James, paternalism emerged as "a coherent managerial discourse" only in the 1940s and 1950s, "The Erosion of Paternalism on South African Gold Mines," *Industrial Relations Journal of South Africa* 12, 1 and 2 (1992), 1. There is an extensive literature on industrial paternalism, cf. P. Joyce, *Work, Society and Politics: The Culture of the Factory in Later Victorian England* (Brighton, 1980); D. Reid, "Industrial Paternalism: Discourse and Practice in 19th Century French Mining and Metallurgy," *Comparative Studies in Society and History* [27] (1985), and note 118 above.

131. A. R. Sawyer, *Mining at Kimberley* (Newcastle-under-Lyme, 1889), 34; Williams, *Diamond Mines*, 416, 418, 423. On the use of the same terms in Britain, see S. Meacham, *A Life Apart: The English Working Class 1870-1917* (London, 1977), 20-21. This colonial complex was reinforced by a black petty bourgeoisie eager to distance itself from those considered backward and uncivilized, B. Willan, *Sol Plaatje: A Biography* (Johannesburg, 1984), 33. For the contemporary discourse on "barbarian" and "superior races," see *Imvo Zabantsundu*.

132. N. Levy, *The Foundations of the South African Cheap Labour System* (London, 1982), 39. On the benefits of treating the compound as a tribe, see *South African Mining Journal*, 22 September 1894. An obvious parallel is the system of Indirect Rule, which Sir Philip Mitchell qualified as the application of "old tribal forms and authorities to modern needs and conditions." See his *African Afterthoughts* (London, 1954), 52.

133. Williams, *Diamond Mines*, 416; G5-'96, Report of the Protector of Natives; Worger, *City of Diamonds*, 284-85.

134. Junod, "BaRonga," 118. See also the Natal Native Affairs Commission of 1906-1907, whose members felt black tribesmen lived under "a paternal despotism" and that Native administration should combine "the autocratic principle of control" with the perspective of "a benevolent and sympathetic father," cited in Marks, *Reluctant Rebellion*, 13.

135. Sawyer, *Mining at Kimberley*, 35; CPP.G1-'90, Schlesinger before the Cape Liquor Laws Commission, 425; Cape Blue Book 1899, Protector of Natives, 32; Arndt, "Die Eingebornen-frage," 39; Native Races Committee, *Natives of South Africa*, 143.

136. Williams, *Diamond Mines*, 406; Times Correspondent, *Letters*, 17; *South Africa*, 2 November 1895, pp. 236-37.

137. CPP.G39-'93, Evidence of S. B. Liefeldt, 399-400; CA.NA 411, PN to SNA, 19 May 1896; Blue Book, G5-'96, p. 35.

138. CPP.G1-'90, Cape Liquor Laws Commission, Evidence of G. Hudson, 445, 875. On drink in the locations, see *ibid.*, Evidence of Peiser, 304-306; Kosani, 451; Haarhoff, 439; MacKenzie, 417; Brunton, 436, and appendix R, p. 1073.

139. Cited in Turrell, *Capital and Labour*, 171.

140. CPP.G38-'94, Report of the Inspector of Diamond Mines for 1893, 13; Williams, *Diamond Mines*, 408; De Beers Consolidated Mines, Report for 1893, 6. The Eight Hours Act was finally legislated in Britain in 1908.

141. CPP.G3-'93, Evidence of Charlie and Charlie Lura before the Cape Labour Commission, 367-68; Williams, *Diamond Mines*, 428.

142. J. Bryce, *Impressions of South Africa* (London, 1897), 151; Couper, *Mixed Humanity*, 108, 153; Weber, *Quatre Ans*, 127.

143. Williams, *Diamond Fields*, 416, 433-38, 446; *Diamond Fields Advertiser*, 28 December 1898.

144. CA.NA 411, Protector Of Natives to SNA, 6 June 1891; Williams, *Diamond Mines*, 431.

145. CPP.G3-'93, C. Lura before the Cape Labour Commission, 367; Turrell, "Kimberley's Model Compounds," 73.

146. Arndt, "Die Eingebornen-frage," 46.

147. *Quarterly Paper of the Bloemfontein Mission*, No. 83 (January 1889), 18-19, and No. 86 (July 1889), 159; Wesleyan Methodist Church of South Africa, Eighth Annual Report, 1893, 90.

148. Wesleyan Methodist Church of South Africa, Ninth Annual Report, 1890, 101; *ibid.*, Eleventh Annual Report, 1892, 106; *ibid.*, Thirteenth Annual Report, 1894; *ibid.*, Sixteenth Annual Report, 1897; Sawyer, *Mining at Kimberley*, 35; Williams, *Diamond Fields*, 413, 416, 432.

149. In 1889 over one thousand black children were registered at government-assisted schools, CPP.G8-'89, Report of the Superintendent for Education. See also Arndt, "Eingebornen-frage," 45-46.

150. *British and Foreign Bible Society*, 73 (1877), 156.

151. Richter, "Wanderende Bassuto," 50.

152. Hamilton Fyfe, *South Africa To-day with an Account of Rhodesia* (London, 1911), 76.

153. *Cape Times*, 1 April 1895.

154. This new standard of hygiene was often imposed on workers (Gardiner Williams, *Diamond Fields*, 416), yet Hamilton Fyfe was to write a decade later, that "most of these natives are of far cleaner habits than the city poor of home." *South Africa To-day*, 75.

155. Worger, *City of Diamonds*, 265; Turrell, *Capital and Labour*, 163.

156. SP.CA Native Affairs (NA) 195, Civil Commissioner to Under SNA, 27 March 1883; CPP.G22-'89, Inspector of Diamond Mines, 10; Williams, *Diamond Fields*, 417.

157. J. Mathias, "An Epidemic of Ankylostomiasis," *South African Medical Journal* VI, 5 (1898), 108-109.

158. CPP.G74-'96, Report of the Medical Officer of Health, 1895, 19; Worger, *City of Diamonds*, 265; F.C.Kolbe, "A Visit to Kimberley," *South African Catholic Magazine*, May 1892, 252.

159. Archives of the University of Cape Town, Judge Papers, Autobiography, 42, 442; *QPBM* 86 (15 July 1889), 161; *South African Catholic Magazine*, May 1892, 250; Williams, *Diamond Mines*, 413, 417; Worger, *City of Diamonds*, 315, 335.

160. CPP.G14-'93, "Report on Public Health for 1892"; G74-'96, Report of MOH for 1895, Appendix IV.

161. CPP.G74-'96, Appendix N. See also the Report of the Protecter of Natives in G5-'96, p. 35.

162. The MOH report stands in marked contrast to the evidence gathered by Turrell and Worger on the mortality rate in the mine hospitals of between thirty and fifty per thousand in the 1890s. Turrell, *Capital and Labour*, 162-63; Worger, *City of Diamonds*, 265. But many mine hospital fatalities can probably be traced to the "starved and emaciated" migrants who, on their arrival at Kimberley, were "beyond help." See Newbury, *The Diamond Ring*, 76, 117, 121.

163. Newby, *The Deferential Worker* (London, 1977), 425.

164. South African Native Races Committee, *Natives of South Africa*, 143.

165. NA 411, Protector of Natives to SNA, 7 October 1887 and 10 September 1889; PN to GM of Anglo-African DMCo., 31 August 1889; PN to SNA, 13 July 1896; CPP.G3-'93, Evidence of S. Dallas before the Cape Labour Commission; Blue Book 1896, 34; *Cape Times*, 1 April 1895.

166. Williams, *Diamond Mines*, 442.

167. Simons, *Class and Colour*, 43.

CHAPTER **4**

A Certain Prosperity:
Migrant Labour and Commodity Production

1. SNA 1/1/96, Erskine to SNA, 3 July 1871. For a fuller description, see the journal kept by Erskine during his "second journey," 1871-72 (MS in RGS), 5-12.

2. Joao de Andrade Corvo, *Estudos sobre as provinciais ultramarinas*, II, 267; Augusto de Castilho to Joao de Andrade Corvo, 17 May 1875, in *Moçambique. Documentario trimestral,*

68 (December 1951), 73; FO 63/1026, Elton to FO, 25 October 1875; BPP, 1876 LXXIV, Cons. rep. for Mozambique, 1875.

3. SNA 1/1/21, D. Leslie to SNA, 9 and 24 August 1871; *Natal Mercury*, 2 November 1878.
4. This form of "hut tax" was considered "more a sign of vassalage or feudality than a source of revenue for the state." *BO* 32, 6 August 1877, Lourenço Marques District Report, June 1877; *BO* 11, 17 March 1879, Lourenço Marques District Report for the financial year 1877-78; see also FO 63/1026, Elton to FO, 25 October 1875; Junod, "Les Baronga," 140.
5. SNA 1/1/27 No. 55, R. du Bois to SNA, 22 March 1876.
6. *Natal Mercury*, 2 November 1878.
7. FHS, Liengme Diary, 19 August 1893. SMA 840, Liengme to Rossel, 3 January 1896.
8. The Swazi exercised an influence over the central Delagoa Bay area well into the 1880s and on at least one occasion, in 1881, were paid tribute by the governor of Lourençco Marques. Harries, "History, Ethnicity," 10-13.
9. *BO*, 22 May 1875, GLM to GGM, 24 April 1875, reprinted in *Mocambique*, December 1951, No. 68, 73. Also AHU.Moc.CG., Pasta 29, GLM to MSMU, 19 January 1874.
10. *Annaes do Conselho Ultramarino*, GLM, 15 April 1865, Report for 1864, p. 97; *BO* 41, 14 October 1866, GLM, 13 September 1866. *BO* 22, 22 May 1869.
11. P. Manso, *Memoria sobre Lourenço Marques* (Lisbon, 1870), 28-35; BO 22, 22 May 1869.
12. An amount valued at £5,400. Natal *Blue Book* (NBB) 1875, "Imports and Exports." The total maize exports for 1875 were declared as 10,000 *panjas* (277,100 litres, or 7,864 bushels), *BO* 27, 3 July 1875.
13. *Natal Mercury*, 21 March 1876; *BO* 7, 14 February 1876; *BO* 15, 10 April 1876; *BO* 46, 13 November 1876.
14. *BO* 6, 5 February 1877; *BO* 47, 19 November 1877.
15. NBB 1877, "Imports and Exports," *BO* 13, 25 March 1877; *BO* 45, 5 November 1877; *BO* 11, 18 March 1878; *BO* 20, 20 May 1878; *BO* 22, 3 June 1878; NBB 1878, "Imports." The official amount of maize exported was 300,588 litres (about 8,500 bushels).
16. *BO* 4, 27 January 1879. District Report for Lourenço Marques, 1877-78.
17. On local dress, see Ch. 1, n.64.
18. *BO*, 18 May 1875; *BO* 21, 22 May 1876; Natal Blue Books.
19. NA.II 1/4, Edward Cohen to Col. Sec., 12 January 1878; NA.II 1/16, Hoffman to PI, 28 February 1877; Hoffman to Col. Sec., 3 March 1877; SS 263 R250/78, Veldkornet Grieve to Landdrost Zoutpansberg, 8 January 1878.
20. Webb and Wright, *James Stuart Archive*, I, 63, Evidence of Bikwayo. See also FO 84/1539, O'Neill to FO, 5 August 1879.
21. Harries, "History, Ethnicity," 16. For Portuguese estimates, see *BO* 4, 27 January 1879.
22. MNE Caixa 664, Duprat-MNE, 29 February 1879; CPC. Cdo 1878-1879, Carvalho to MSMU, 15 October 1878. See also MNE Caixa 697, Vice Cons. Durban to MNE, 21 October 1874.
23. Customs revenues from the guns going to Zululand only amounted to about £1,700 annually. On the gun trade, see C. Ballard, *John Dunn, The White Chief of Zululand* (Craighall, Johannesburg, 1985), 114-21.
24. CSO 525.2461/75, Lipperts and Dentzelman to Firearms Board, Durban, 30 June 1875.
25. Fynn, *Diary*, 47; NA/GH 1050, Supreme Court case Agnew vs. Van Grunning, 24 May 1875; NA/SNA 1/7/9, "Passes Issued," 10 June 1874, 20 May 1876. See also *BO* 29, "Report of Lourenço Marques Customs House for 1881," 29 August 1882; ZGH 736.249, Statement of Faku, 20 March 1891; Junod, "Baronga," 242; NBB, "Imports" for 1877.
26. For one year, see *BO* 7, 13 February 1875; *BO* 10, 6 March 1875; *BO* 40, 2 October 1875; *BO* 43, 6 November 1875; *BO* 50, 11 November 1875.
27. MNE 664, Duprat to MNE, 30 April 1879; GH 829, Purvis to Lt. Gov., 20 March 1878; FO 84/1539, O'Neill to FO, 5 August 1879.

28. *BO* 45, 5 November 1877; *BO* 47, 19 November 1877.
29. On the early history of cassava, see H. B. Ross, "The Diffusion of the Manioc Plant from South America to Africa: An Essay in Ethnobotanical Cultural History" (Ph.D. thesis, Columbia University, 1954); Heweson, *South African Commercial Advertiser,* 20 April 1839; Jose Antonio Texira, "Descriçao dos rios da Bahia de Lourenço Marques" (September 1838), in *Arqivo das Colonias,* II, 1918.
30. *BO* 34, 22 August 1863; *BO* 21, 27 May 1865; Junod, *Life,* II, 15; BPP 1890 c. 6200, Martin to Natal Governor, 21 July 1888, 87. Carl Mauch, *Journal 1869-72,* ed. E. Burke (Salisbury, 1969), 120.
31. Elton in *Natal Mercury,* 10 October 1871; *BO* 14, 1871, 61; Owen, *Narrative,* 100, 117, 129.
32. E. Isnard, *Dix Générations de Marins Provencaux: Les Fabre* (Marseilles, 1927), 160; B. Schnapper, *La Politique et le Commerce français dans le Golfe de Guinée de 1838 à 1871* (Paris, 1961), 190-91; BPP XC, 1881 C. 2945, Consular Report for Mozambique, 1880; M. Johnson, "Cowrie Currencies in West Africa," Part II, *JAH* XI, 3 (1970), 338; L. Vail and L. White, *Capitalism and Colonialism in Mozambique* (London, 1980), 64. See also Hogendorn and Johnson, *The Shell Money of the Slave Trade* (Cambridge, 1986), 71-77.
33. See pp. 15–16, above.
34. On smelting in the northern Transvaal, see Berthoud and Scharfli, "Voyage d'Exploration" in *BMSAS* 77 (April 1888), 55; Anon., "Eine Bawenda-schmieden," in *BMB* 1889, 562-63.
35. SNA 1/3/8, RM Inanda - SNA, 29 November 1859; Junod, "Baronga," 87-89.
36. *BO* 35, 29 September 1863; *BO* 42, 15 October 1864 Manso, 28-35.
37. Compare prices in *BO* 40, 5 October 1861 ($460) with *BO* 42, 17 October 1863 ($345).
38. See the shipping lists in the *Natal Mercury.*
39. Natal Blue Books.
40. BPP, 1883 XLVII e 3533, Report of the Mozambique Tariff Commission, April 1877, in Morier to Derby, 11 May 1877.
41. *BO* 1, 2 January 1875, Lourenço Marques District Report for November 1874.
42. Neves, *Hunting Expedition,* 280; UNISA/JC Junod, "Litteratures - Coutumes," 27.
43. Junod, *Chants et Contes,* 260 n.2.
44. *BO* 4, 27 January 1879; District Report for 1877-8.
45. *BO* 45, 5 November 1877, 324.
46. GH 837, GLM to GGM, 24 April 1875, in British consul to C.O., 27 May 1875. Also in *Mocambique,* December 1951, p. 77 and in *BO* 22, May 1875.
47. Louis Pierrein, *Industries traditionnelles du port de Marseille: le cycle du Sucre et des Oléagineux, 1870-1950* (Marseilles, 1975), 197, 200-201; Francisco M. Bordalo, *Ensaios sobre a Estatistica das Possessoés Portuguezas no. Ultramar,* IV: *Moçambique,* 266.
48. *BO* 15, 10 April 1875; GH 837, GLM to GGM, 24 April 1875, in Br. Cons. to FO 27 May 1875.
49. A good record of ships' manifests was kept in the *Boletim Oficial de Mocambique,* especially for 1875-76. *BO* 45, 5 November 1877; *BO* 4, 27 January 1879.
50. AHU Pasta 29, GG to MSMU, 17 August 1875; G. Liesegang, H. Pasch, A. Jones, eds., *Figuring African Trade* (Berlin, 1986), 468-69.
51. *BO* 45, 5 November 1877; *BO* 52, 30 December 1878. These and the following statistics are drawn from the *Boletim Oficial.*
52. GLM to GG, 11 April 1866, in *BO* 41, 22 September 1866; SNA 1/1/21, Leslie to SNA, 28 July 1871; Leslie, *Among the Zulus and Amatongas* (Edinburgh, 1875), 392.
53. NA.CO 179/108 No. 42, Musgrave to Kimberley, 5 November 1872.
54. *Natal Mercury,* 19 July 1870; *BO* 47, 19 November 1877; Leslie, *Zulus and Amatongas,* 274.
55. This is difficult to assess, as traders were not obliged to declare the amount of sterling exported. *BO* 47, 19 November 1877; BPP 1876 LXXIV, Consular Report 1875.
56. *BO* 7, 13 February 1875.

57. *BO* 50, 11 December 1875, District Report for October-November 1875.
58. Junod, *Life*, 234, 253, 369-70, 376-77. Marriage to men living in distant districts was discouraged, ostensibly due to the problem of retrieving brideprices, Junod, "BaRonga," 387.
60. Junod, "BaRonga," 187-88.
61. Junod, *Life*, I, 376, 410-13.
62. Junod, "BaRonga," 54; H. F. Fynn, "Delagoa Bay," in *RSEA*, II, 480; *Cape Monitor*, 16 July 1853; BPP 1890 C. 6200, Saunders to SNA, 17 November 1887, 45; M. Morris, "Ronga Settlement Patterns," *Anthropology Quarterly* 45 (1972), 233.
63. Junod, "BaRonga," 91.
64. Junod, *Chants et Contes*, 96-140; "BaRonga," 105-106; *Life*, II, 248-51, 255-57, 261-62, 266.
65. Junod, *Life*, I, 128-29; Leslie, *Zulus and Amatongas*, 170.
66. *James Stuart Archive*, IV, 267, 162, 171-72.
67. Junod, "BaRonga," 188.
68. JSA File 74, 66, Evidence of Majuba; Mission Romance, *Chez les Noirs*, 7; Junod, *Life*, I, 283.
69. Junod, "BaRonga," 95; SMA 8.10.B, P. Berthoud to Conseil, 23 September 1879; SMA 1760, Grandjean Diary, p. 272; Grandjean, *La Mission*, 79; H. P. Junod, *The Wisdom*, 121, 137, 145, 149.
70. Junod, *Life*, I, 211, 278-79, 322-333.
71. *Ibid.*, I, 201-211, 247, 262, 288-89, 509; H. A. Junod, "The Fate of the Widows Amongst the Ba-Ronga," in *Report of the South African Association for the Advancement of Science*, 1908. See also FHSE, Liengme Diary, 19 August 1893.
72. SMA 5.10.B, P. Berthoud to Council, 25 March 1885.
73. Junod, "BaRonga," 96.
74. SMA 543/B, P. Loze to Grandjean, II December 1899.
75. SMA 543/D, P. Loze to Grandjean, 25 February 1900.
76. Junod, *Life*, I, 401-402, 405-407; "BaRonga," 140-44.
77. Webb and Wright, *James Stuart Archive*, I, 67-68; *ibid.*, III, 157.
78. *Cape Mercantile Advertizer*, 16 July 1886; ZGH 699.252, Umbandeni to SNA, 19 August 1886; FO 84/2224, Br. Cons. to FO, 4 April 1892; Junod, *Life*, I, 450, 471. See also SMA 8.10.B, H. Berthoud to Council, 28 October 1886; SMA 497/BP, Berthoud to Council, September 1887. Harries, "Free and Unfree Labour," 312-18, 322.
79. Junod, *Life*, I, 332-33, 437.
80. *Ibid.*, I, 312, 329-30, 321.
81. *Ibid.*, II, 404.
82. *Ibid.*, II, 224-25. The power of the chief was not always and everywhere the same.
83. Junod, "BaRonga," 121 n.1.
84. Junod, *Chants et Contes*, 260-64; *Grammaire Ronga*, 102; "BaRonga," 283, 311.
85. Junod, *Chants et Contes*, 122, 160; "BaRonga," 285-87; *Life*, II, 223, 229, 237, 241, 275.
86. Junod, *Chants et Contes*, 88, 122, 164, 180, 278, 300; "BaRonga," 303, 351; *Life*, II, 230, 246, 273.
87. Junod, *Chants et Contes*, 276-81; "BaRonga," 329.
88. Junod, *Chants et Contes*, 82-83.
89. *Ibid.*, 82, 86 n.1, 88, 108, 122; *Life*, II, 223, 233-34; "L'Epopée," 16.
90. Junod, "BaRonga," 337.
91. Junod, *Chants et Contes*, 82.
92. Cf. SMA 502/H, P.Berthoud to council, 26 February 1889.
93. FHS, Liengme Diary, 20 July 1893.
94. Junod, "BaRonga," 35-36.
95. *Ibid.*, 168.
96. *BO* 45, 5 November 1877; GH 1050, Supreme Court case, Agnew vs Van Gruning, 14 May 1875.

97. SNA 1/1/96, St. V. Erskine to Shepstone, 23 February 1872; J. R. Saunders, *Natal and Its Relation to South Africa* (London, 1882), p.9. See also pp. 17, 18, above.

98. BPP 1883 XLVIII C 3533, Report of the Mozambique Tarriff Commission, April 1877, enclosed in Morier to Derby, 11 May 1877.

99. Augusto de Castilho, *O Distrito de Lourenço Marques, no presente e no futuro* (Lisbon, 1881), 13; AHU.Moc., 2a Rep., Pasta 3, GG to MSMU, 8 October 1886; JSA File 74, Evidence of Mahungane, Nkonuza, and Ndaba.

100. AHU.Moc., 2a Rep., Pasta 1, GG to MSMU, 28 April 1884; BPP 1883 C3533, Report of the Mozambique Tariff Commission, 1877; BO 33, 16 August 1884, portaria 199.

101. BPP 1883, Report of the Mozambique Tarriff Commission.

102. Castilho, *O Distrito de Lourenço Marques*, 12-13; S. E. Katzenellenbogen, *South Africa and Southern Mozambique: Labour, Railways and Trade in the Making of a Relationship* (Manchester, 1982), 12-20.

103. Chambre de Commerce de Marseilles: situation commerciale et industrielle—1896-98 et tableau des prix moyens, 1875-98. See also A. G. Hopkins, *An Economic History of West Africa* (London, 1975), Ch. 4.

104. NBB, "Imports," 1,073 were exported to Durban in 1877, 1,250 in 1878, and 7,575 in 1880. SS 919 R1634/84, Lddrst Lydenburg to SS, 10 September 1883; Raddatz, "Das Kaffernland," 54; ZGH 736.249, "Statement of Faku, a Tongaland Induna," 20 March 1891.

105. These figures are taken from the *Boletim Oficial.*

106. Hoffman was left with thirty tons of gunpowder in the Lippert and Dentzelman storehouse. Webb and Wright, *James Stuart Archive*, I, 63, Evidence of Bikwayo; FO 84/1539, O'Neill to FO, 5 August 1879. On the Portuguese interpretation of British strategy, see MNE Caixa 664, Duprat-MNE 29 February 1879. CPC.Cdo 1878-1879, Carvalho to MSMU, 15 October 1878. See also MNE Caixa 697 Vice Cons. Durban to MNE, 21 October 1874. CPC.Cdo 1878-9, Carvalho to Frere, 20 April 1878; Carvalho to MSMU, 27 October 1878.

107. BO 4, 27 January 1879, District Report for 1877-78, p. 22; Corvo, *Estudos*, II, 265-66.

108. BO 52, 30 December 1878.

109. CPP.A100-'82, Petition of Kimberley Merchants. CPP.G86-'82, p. 72a; SP.NA 190, Protector and Registrar of Natives to SNA, 12 January 1882; J. B. Currey, "The Diamond Fields of Griqualand West and Their Probable Influence on the Native Races of South Africa," *Journal of the Society of Arts* XXIV (1876).

110. Angove, *In the Early Days*, 61. On consumer practices learnt at Kimberley, see *QPBM*, July 1883, 191; Warren, *On the Veldt*, 126; Phillips, *Reminiscences*, 20-21; J. B. Currey, "Half a Century in South Africa" (TS in South African Public Library), Ch. 12, 22.

111. CPP.A7-'91, J. B. Currey to the Griqualand West Select Committee on Trade and Business, 1891, 275.

112. CA.IAC - 1, Swellendam Magistrate to Contracting Officer, 15 February 1884; TA.SS 490, Lydenburg Landdrost to Col. Sec., 25 November 1880; TA.SN 173.R179, Native Commissioner, Spelonken, to Native Commissioner, Zoutpansberg, 9 October 1883; Letter from Fernandes das Neves to GLM, 13 June 1882, printed in *Moçambique*, 69, 1952.

113. PRO.FO 63/127, O'Neill to Granville, 13 June 1882.

114. "They were much more covered" than women in Switzerland, SMA 1760, Grandjean Diary, 27 January 1894. See also *The Net*, May 1893, 70; Junod, "BaRonga," 115.

115. Figures are drawn from the *Boletim Oficial de Moçambique.*

116. BPP, Accounts and Proceedings (A + P), XCIX 1895, Consular Report for Mozambique, 1893.

117. A. Vasconcellos, "Dos mappos estatisticos com relação ao movimento commercial No. distrito de Lourenço Marques, durante o ano de 1884" in *Bol. da Soc. de Geogr. Commercial do Porto*, 1886, 53.

118. A. Longle, "De Inhambane à Lourenço Marques" *BSGL*, 6, 1 (1886), 36; Letter from P. Berthoud in *L'Afrique Explorée et Civilisée*, 1889, 92; SMA 435, Liengme to Leresche, 27 July 1891; AHU.Moc., 2a Repartiçao, Report by Freire d'Andrade, 1891.
119. Captain Chaddock, "L'Exploration du Limpopo," *L'Afrique Explorée et Civilisée* VI (1885), 186. Indian rupees were legal tender in most countries bordering on the western Indian Ocean. But from 1873 the value of the rupee declined, and companies with branches in Mozambique started to pay government taxes and customs duties in rupees, while selling their wares for gold coins which they remitted to India.
120. *BO* 4, 22 January 1887.
121. *BO* 4, 27 January 1879.
122. See pp. 9, 57ff, above.
123. *BO* 29, 1882, 223. The figures are drawn from the *Boletim Oficial*.
124. *BO* 21, 22 May 1876; *BO* 4, 27 January 1879; AHU.Moc., Pasta 1382, Alfandegas 1836-1890.
125. Bishop McKenzie in *The Net*, December 1881; P. Berthoud in *L'Afrique Explorée et Civilisée* VII (1886); Freire d'Andrade to GLM, 8 July 1891, in *Mouzinho: Governador de Lourenço Marques*, ed. C. Montez (Lourenço Marques, 1956).
126. This is probably an exaggeration. *BO*, 30 July 1882, 232.
127. *BO* 6, 11 February 1888.
128. FO 84/1846, O'Neill to FO, 26 February 1887. For a similar statement, see the Report of the Consul of the South African Republic for 1894, in TA.SS 155 R1358/95.
129. Vasconcellos, "Mappos estatisticos," 59.
130. *BO* 19, 18 May 1886; *BO* 28, 1886, 331.
131. BPP (A + P) XCIX 1895, Consular Report for Mozambique, 1893. The importation of distilled liquor fell from over 600,000 to less than to 92,000 litres. AHU.Moc., Pasta 1376, Alfandega stats.; AHU. 2ª Repartiçao, Alfandega de Moçambique, p. 7; Monteiro, *Delagoa Bay*, 77.
132. *BO* 19, 1886, 219; *BO* 28, 14 July 1888; *BO* 6, 7 February 1891.
133. *BO* 31, 1887, 343.
134. *BO* 2, 10 January 1885; *BO* 7, 13 February 1886; *BO* 11, 13 March 1886; *BO* 16, 17 April 1886; *BO* 23, 5 June 1886.
135. *BO* 42, 16 October 1886; *BO* 40, 2 October 1886; *BO* 49, 3 December 1887; *BO* 2, 14 January 1888; *BO* 3, 21 January 1888; SMA 497/B, Paul Berthoud to Leresche, 7 October 1887; Berthoud to Leresche, 14 November 1887; SMA 497/D, Paul Berthoud to Leresche, 4 February 1888.
136. AHU. Moc., Diversos, Caixa 2, "Relatório acerca de alguns portos de Província de Moçambique," Augusto Castilho 12 March 1883; AHU.Moc., 2a Rep., Pasta 3, Machado Memo, 10 November 1885.
137. AHU.Moc., CG Pasta 31, GGM-MSMU 20 July 1878; GH 829, Menlove to Lt. Gov., 9 June 1878; GH 845, GGM to Lt. Gov., 30 July 1878; G. Inhambane to Lt. Gov., 2 August 1878; *James Stuart Archives*, I, 64, Evidence of Bikwayo.
138. FO 84/1539 Vice-consul O'Neill to FO, 10 October 1879; BPP C-6200, 1890, Saunders to SNA, 17 November 1887.
139. AHU.Moc., Alfandega, Pasta 1382; AHU.Moc., 2ª Rep., Pasta 7, Alfandega de Mocambique.
140. H. Seidel, "Die Ba-Ronga an der Delagoa Baai," in *Globus*, 74, 12 (1898), 186. Nineteen photographs taken by George Liengme of the 1895 Gaza mobilisation show most soldiers wearing a cloth sarong under a kilt of skins. A majority also wear shirts or a cloth worn over the shoulder, SMA 2001/B. See also SMA 2001/A for photographs of men wearing waistcoats, red military jackets, pith helmets, shirts, and sarongs. See also SMA 515/D, Jacques to Renevier, 24 November 1896; SMA 1760, Grandjean Diary, entry for 24 January 1894.

141. *BO* 22, 14 May 1887. Provincial Agronomist, "Excursao Agricola do districto de Lourenço Marques," March 1887.
142. SS 919 R1634/84, "Verklaring van Louis Kaufman."
143. SS 263 R250/78, Grieve to Zoutpansberg Landdrost, 8 January 1878.
144. SS 919 R1634, Lydenburg Landdrost to SS, 16 September 1883; Sanitary Inspector, Lydenburg, to Landdrost, 10 October 1883; R2208/84, Gold Commissioner to SS, 6 May 1884. Volksraad Decision 146, 23 June 1884, 86; Law 4 of 1882.
145. TA.State Secretary, Foreign Affairs (SSA), 384 Ra 2892/96, M. J. Farrelly, "Opinion on the Treaty with Portugal and the Coolie Laws," 29 May 1897. See also the various enclosures in Ra 2892/96 and MNE 709, Pretoria consul to MNE, 17 November 1896.
146. For arrests under these laws, see MNE 707, Consul to MNE, 19 November 1883; Schlaefli, "Valdezia à Lourenço Marques," 150; *Zoutpansberg Review,* 26 February 1890; A. Schiel, *Drei und Tzwantzig Jahre Sturm und Sonnenschein in Sudafrika* (Leipzig, 1902), 263.
147. UCT.BC 106, Mashaba to Stewart, 18 May 1902; J. Whiteside, *A History of the Wesleyan Methodist Church of South Africa* (London, 1906), 447-48.
148. SPG, Bishop MacKenzie's journal for July, 1889; SPG, C. Johnson's "Amatongaland Trip," Part I, 1895; *The Net,* November 1889.
149. SMA 497/E, P. Berthoud to conseil, 11 October 1888; SMA 513/A, Grandjean to Leresche, 21 August 1893; O'Neill, "Journeys in the District of Delagoa Bay, December 1886-January 1887," *Proceedings of the RGS* IX (1887), 502-503; SPG, Bishop MacKenzie, Letter of 31 July 1889.
150. SMA 8.10.B, H. Berthoud to Grandjean, 28 October 1886. On the delineation of the Gwamba or Thonga language, see Harries, "The Roots of Ethnicity."
151. J. van Butselaar, *Africains, Missionnaires et Colonialistes: Les origines de l'Eglise Presbytérienne du Mozambique (Mission Suisse), 1880-1896* (Leiden, 1984), 47-56, 70-71; Junod, "BaRonga," 483.
152. H. Junod, *Ernest Creux et Paul Berthoud* (Lausanne, 1933), 144-45.
153. Van Butselaar, *Africains, Missionnaires et Colonialistes,* 53.
154. FO 84/1616, O'Neill to Governor of Natal, 22 July 1882.
155. Unrest was reported, presumably over the new taxes, in Xerinda. In 1886 the Mazwaya and Mafumo, in an engagement referred to as a "skirmish," quelled a minor tax rebellion. E. de Noronho, "Lourenço Marques e as suas relacoes com a Africa do Sul," *BSGL* 15, 2 (1896); H. A. Junod, "Les Causes de la rebellion dans le district de Lourenço Marques," letter to V. Rossel, 4 September 1896 in the Junod Collection, University of South Africa (UNISA), Pretoria.
156. E. Creux, "Voyage de Yosepha Ndjumo . . . à la baie Delagoa," *BMSAS* (1882), 42. See also SMA 1255/B, P. Berthoud, "Rapport sur l'expédition à Magude," 6 October 1885.
157. Noronho, *O Districto de Lourenço Marques,* 181.
158. *BO* 19, 8 May 1886; SMA 497/E, P. Berthoud to Leresche, 30 Occtober 1888; Noronho, *O Districto de Lourenço Marques,* 183, 189.
159. R. Pelissier, *Naissance du Mozambique* (Orgeval, 1984), II, 558-61.
160. AHU.Moc., 2a Rep., Pasta 1, GGM to MSMU 28 March 1884; B.O. 38, 1884, 176; B.O.2, 10 January 1885; B.O.18, 17 June 1885.
161. Starting in 1886, these razzias were mounted on an annual basis; after 1889, sometimes with arms supplied by the Portuguese. SMA 1254/B, G. Liengme, "Rapport sur la visite faite à Gungunyana," July 1892; FHS, Liengme Diary, 23 May 1893; Vail and White, "The Chopi and their Migodo," in *Power and the Praise Poem,* 116 ff.
162. AHU.Moc., 2a Rep., Pasta 3, GGM to MSMU 22 March 1886; ibid., GGM to MNE, 27 December 1886. See also Chapter 6, note 133.
163. ABM (American Board Mission): ABC: 15.4, Vol. XII. Ousley to Smith, 25 October, 15 November 1886; SMA 6007D, D. Prideaux, "A Short Biography of E. Richards," 28-31; Pelissier, *Naissance du Mozambique,* 567-69.

164. In his negotiations with the British in the early 1870s, Umzila stressed that he did not want traders "invading" and "overrunning" his lands. SNA 1/1/96 Memorial on the mission of Mr. St. V. Erskine to Umzila, 14 January 1873; CO 179/102.61, Statement of Umzungulu and Dubule, messengers of Umzila, 18 August 1870, in Keate to Kimberley, 22 June 1871; SNA 1/1/26. R1187, SNA Minute Paper, Erskine to Shepstone, 1873; ABM. Richards to Means, 15 June 1881.

165. A. Freire d'Andrade and J. Serrano, "Exploraçoes Portugueses em Lourenço Marques e Inhambane," *BSGL*, 5, 13 (1894), 366; J. Serrano, "De Makiki a Inhambane pelo Ualuize," *BSGL* 6 (1894), 400, 417; H. Berthoud, "Voyage chez Magoude," *BMSAS* 64 (1886), 6; A. Grandjean, "Antioka, 11 Decembre 1893," *BMSAS*, 114 (April 1894); E. Schlaefli-Glardon, "De Valdezia à Lourenço Marques," *BSNG* VII (1893).

CHAPTER 5

The Early Witwatersrand

1. On early Johannesburg, see particularly B. Kennedy, *A Tale of Two Mining Cities: Johannesburg and Broken Hill, 1885-1925* (Johannesburg, 1984).
2. Archives of H. Eckstein and Co. (HE) 149, L. Phillips to Wernher, Beit and Co., 13 September 1890; *Chamber of Mines Annual Reports (CMAR)* 1891, 49, 50, 76.
3. Europeans clung tenaciously to this idea in Africa where they believed the natives' housing, clothing, fuel, and food requirements were limited by the climate. HE 149, Phillips to Werner, Beit and Co., 9 August 1890. *The Press*, 24 March 1890. *CMAR*, 1889, 9-10; *CMAR*, 1893, 44; *Standard and Diggers News*, 17 July 1891; Transvaal Industrial Commission of Enquiry (ICE), 1897, Evidence of G. Albu, E. Way, and H. Jennings, 43, 219. For the same views at Kimberley, see Newbury, *The Diamond Ring*, 124. For the same ideas elsewhere, see Harrison, *British Coal Mining Industry*, 238-50; E. Hobsbawm, *Labouring Men* (London, 1964), 352-58.
4. *Diggers News, and Witwatersrand Advertizer*, 18 July 1889.
5. *Star*, 25 and 26 September, 11 October 1890; *CMAR*, 1890, 65-70.
6. TA.SS 2273.5596/90, Secretary of the Chamber of Mines to Superintendent of Natives, 22 September 1890; HE 149, Phillips to Werner, Beit and Co., 13 December 1890.
7. *Star*, 21 October 1890.
8. The South Reef lay close to the surface and, although thin, was the richest source of gold. Below it lay the larger Main Reef Leader, of a lower grade and more expensive to extract. At a much greater depth lay the Main Reef—in quantitative terms the richest of the gold deposits. C. W. B. Jeppe, *Gold Mining on the Witwatersrand* (Johannesburg, 1946), 419-21; Johnstone, *Class, Race and Gold*, 17-20; J. van Helten and P. Richardson, "Labour in the South African Gold Mining Industry" in Marks and Rathbone, eds., *Industrialisation and Social Change*.
9. This was alluded to in the *Diggers News*, 23 January 1890; Newbury, *The Diamond Ring*, 367.
10. *Standard and Diggers News*, 10, 17, 25 July 1891; 11, 25 September 1891.
11. *CMAR*, 1893, 43.
12. TA.SSa 263 Ra 3309/95, Supt Natives to SS, 26 October 1893; SSa 264 SS to GGM, 3 November 1893; SMA 483, Grandjean to Leresche, 7 October 1891; SMA 513/A, Grandjean to Leresche, 21 August 1893; SMA 81/I, Grandjean "Report to Antioka," 1893.
13. MNE 698, Portuguese Consul to MNE, 10 November 1893. On the exportation of labour to Natal by sea, see pp. 24–25, above.
14. TA. Leyds Archive (LA) 455, Secretary of Chamber of Mines to SS, 18 October 1893; LA 463, Consul, Lourenço Marques to GGM, 14 November 1893; SS 3924.15520, Telegram, ZAR Consul, Lourenço Marques to SS, 6 December 1893.
15. LA 455, GGM to ZAR Consul, Lourenço Marques, 22 December 1893; SS 3924 R2002/94, GGM to SS, 10 February 1894.

16. Several schemes existed for the recruitment of labour in Mozambique, especially "from tribes not acknowledging Portuguese authority." *CMAR*, 1893, 29, 31, 34-36; *CMAR*, 1894, 26, 29; SS 3925 R10295, Wilhelm to Supt. Natives, 26 January 1893.
17. *South African Mining Journal (SAMJ)*, 11 February 1893.
18. For favorable comparisons of black miners' wages on the Witwatersrand with those of miners in Europe, see *SAMJ*, 24 October 1891, 28 January 1893. See also *Star*, 26 September 1890; G. Albu before the ICE, 15; Milner to Chamberlain, 6 December 1901, in the *Milner Papers*, II, ed. C. Headlam (London, 1933), 313; *CMAR*, 1891, 49, 50, 76; *CMAR*, 1895, 36-37. See also *SAMJ*, 11 February 1893; E. G. Rathbone, "Economic Features of Mining on the Witwatersrand," *Engineering and Mining Journal (EMJ)*, 13 February 1897, 161; W. Y. Campbell "The Witwatersrand Goldfields and its Working: Labor," *EMJ*, 7 August 1897, 160. M. Newitt (*Portugal in Africa*, 114) was correct to drawn attention to the relatively high earnings of black miners, but, as I outline below, he overestimated the longevity of their high wages.
19. *Diamond Fields Advertizer*, 2 June 1888; C. Duval, in the *Irish Weekly Times*, 13 October 1888, reprinted in M. Fraser, ed., *Johannesbourg Pioneer Journals, 1888-1909* (Cape Town, 1985), 24-25; *The Press*, 29 March 1889; *Diggers News, and Witwatersrand Advertizer*, 18 July 1889, 13 January 1890.
20. *SAMJ*, 20 April 1892; *Star*, 25 February 1890.
21. J. J. Fourie "Die Koms van die Bantoe na die Rand en hulle posisie aldaar, 1886-1899," in *South African Archives Yearbook*, I (1979), 208, 258.
22. *Star*, 16, 26 November 1889.
23. *CMAR* 1892, 45, 106. See also *CMAR* 1890, 52, 73, 189.
24. Cf. *SAMJ*, 12 November 1892; 20 April 1895.
25. *SAMJ*, 21 November 1892; J. J. Fourie "Die Koms van die Bantoe na die Rand en hulle posisie aldaar, 1886-1899," in *South African Archives Yearbook*, I (1979), 224.
26. *SAMJ*, 12 November 1892; ICE, Evidence of G. Albu and C. S. Golman, 22-23, 96; D. Blackburn and W. Waithman Caddell, *Secret Service in South Africa* (London, 1911), 129-30. See also J. W. Haley, *Life in Mozambique and South Africa* (Chicago, 1926), 122.
27. Transvaal Labor Commission, 1904 (TLC), Evidence of Dyer, 284, and Annexure A, Exhibit No. 1, Native Wages; A. Richardson, *The Crowded Hours: The Story of Lionel Cohen* (London, 1952), 137; J. H. Bovill, *Natives under the Transvaal Flag* (London, 1900), 48.
28. *Star*, 9 January 1893.
29. On poor conditions in the compounds, cf. *SAMJ*, 20 April 1895.
30. Such as the Brickfields. Kennedy, *Tale of Two Mining Cities*, 39; Fourie, "Bantoe aan die Rand," 259. Bryce gave a mortality of 58 per 1,000 in late 1896, *Impressions of South Africa*, 382.
31. *SAMJ*, 21 November 1896; Fourie, "Bantoe aan die Rand," 225-26.
32. Fourie, "Bantoe aan die Rand," 42, 247-49.
33. *Standard and Diggers News*, 22 October 1896.
34. *Ibid.*; Charles van Onselen, "Prostitutes and Proletarians 1886-1914," in *Studies in the Social and Economic History of the Witwatersrand*, I, *New Babylon* (Johannesburg, 1982), 103-114.
35. The mortality rate from accidents on the Witwatersrand was almost certainly underestimated, as many deaths went unreported. See *SAMJ*, 5 January 1892; 8, 15 October 1892; 12 January 1895; 22 June 1895.
36. F. C. Kolbe, "The Golden City," *South African Catholic Magazine*, July 1892, 363-64; Jeppe, *Gold Mining*, 51, 674; D. Jacobson, *Fifty Golden Years of the Rand, 1886-1936* (London, 1936), 123; P. C. Grey, "The Development of the Gold-mining Industry on the Witwatersrand, 1902-1910" (Ph.D. thesis, University of South Africa, 1969); A. Hocking, *Randfontein Estates: The First Hundred Years* (Bethule, South Africa, 1986) 78-79; Campbell "Witwatersrand Gold Fields," 36-37.

37. LA 462, Portuguese Consul to SS, 7 May 1888; Glynn, "Game and Gold," 205; R. Berthoud-Junod, *Du Transvaal à Lourenco Marques* (Lausanne, 1904), 81, 92-99; E. Smithers, *March Hare* (Oxford, 1935), 55; MNE 697, Portuguese Consul to MNE, 28 September 1891.
38. HE 149, Phillips to Werner, Beit and Co., 20 June 1890.
39. A. W. Baker, *Grace Triumphant: The Life Story of a Carpenter, Lawyer and Missionary in South Africa from 1856 to 1939* (Glasgow, n.d. 1939?), 307.
40. J. H. Hammond, *The Autobiography of John Hays Hammond* (New York, 1935), 304. See also Campbell, "Witwatersrand Gold Fields," *EMJ*, 7 August 1897.
41. Best and Williams, *CMAR*, 1894, 35.
42. *Star*, 26 January 1891; Cabral, *Racas, Usos*, 99; Junod, "BaRonga," 163; P. Fitzpatrick, *Jock of the Bushveld* (London, 1907).
43. Junod, *Life*, I, 354-55, 400, 478.
44. SMA 438/A, Liengme to Leresche, 18 February 1895; Richardson, *The Crowded Hours*, 137-46, 160, 317; Bovill, *Natives Under the Transvaal Flag*, 47-48, 67; *SAMJ*, 14 September 1895; *CMAR* 1895, 37, 40; *CMAR* 1898, 4.
45. *CMAR* 1893, 38; *CMAR* 1894; 34; *CMAR* 1895, 33, 37, 43-44, 55; *CMAR* 1898, 459; Transvaal Labour Commission, 1904, Evidence of F. de Mello Breyner, 99-100; Ferraz, 246, Perry, 47, Report, 37.
46. SMA 503/A, Grandjean to Leresche, 15 November 1889; BPP LXXVI, 1890, Br. Consul, Report for 1889; *ibid.*, XCIX; *CMAR* 1894, 29; *A Voz Publica*, 13 October 1894; Cabral, *Racas, Usos*, 86, 102; MNE 697, Portuguese Consul, Durban, to MNE, 28 September 1891; Evidence of Wirth and Holterhoff before the Transvaal Labour Commission, 1904, 107, 161; Crush, *The Struggle for Swazi Labour*, 39.
47. *The Daily News* (Bloemfontein), 31 August 1886; *South Africa*, 14 November 1891, 281.
48. Junod, *Life*, II, 393 n.1. This was a common ritual in south-east Africa, see E. Gottschling, "The BaWenda: A Sketch of Their History and Customs," *Journal of the Royal Anthropological Institute* 35 (1905), 381; Paula Dlamini, *Servant of Two Kings*, compiled by H. Filter, translated and edited by S. Bourquin (Pietermaritsburg, 1986).
49. Junod, *South Afican Tribe*, II, 324.
50. Junod, "BaRonga," 478 n.1; Junod, *Life*, II, 374-75. For the rituals practised by a migrant worker on leaving and returning home, see pp. 158–159, above.
51. Transvaal Methodist Mission Society Archives, London (MMS), South Africa, Transvaal (SA-T), Box 330, Hudson to Hartley, 16 December 1897; B. Sundkler, *Bantu Prophets in South Africa* (London, 1948), 39.
52. Sundkler, *Bantu Prophets*, 38-40; Baker, *Grace Triumphant*.
53. *Star*, 22 October 1896; B. Kennedy "Missionaries, Black Converts, and Separatists on the Rand, 1886–1910: From Accommodation to Resistance" *Journal of Imperial and Commonwealth History* 20, 2, 1992.
54. *Star*, 8 September 1898.
55. Jacobson, *Fifty Golden Years of the Rand*, 173; *Diggers News*, 24 December 1889; *Standard and Diggers News*, 22 October 1896; Charles van Onselen, "Randlords and Rotgut," in *Studies*, 57. In France the ratio was 1:82 at this time, although far higher in urban centres.
56. Blackburn and Caddell, *Secret Service*, 43.
57. *Ibid.*, 44; Van Onselen, "Randlords and Rotgut," I, 56.
58. *Diggers News, and Witwatersrand Advertizer*, 30 April 1889; 24 December 1889; *SAMJ* 29 October 1892; 31 August 1895.
59. A. W. Baker, *Grace Triumphant*, 166; Transvaal Methodist Mission Society Archives, London (MMS), South Africa, Transvaal (SA-T), MMS, Box 329, J. Morris to Mission HQ, 30 April 1893; *CMAR* 1891, 50.
60. *CMAR* 1895, 14; *South Africa*, 1 August 1896.
61. Baker, *Grace Triumphant*, 107; MMS, SA-T, Box 329, Lowe to HQ, 24 April 1896.

62. Baker, *Grace Triumphant*, 107; Blackburn and Caddell, *Secret Service*, 27.
63. Hammond, *Autobiography*, 305; Baker, *Grace Triumphant*, 107.
64. Fourie, "Bantoe aan die Rand," 228-35.
65. Blackburn and Caddell, *Secret Service*, 47-48.
66. MMS, Box 328, Weavind to Hartley, 9 August 1889; Box 329, Lowe to HQ, 25 April 1896; Morris to HQ, 30 April 1893.
67. Bleloch, *The New South Africa* (London, 1902), 229.
68. *Star*, 14 November 1892. See also *CMAR* 1892, 5.
69. *Star*, 8 October 1895; *Standard and Diggers News*, 9 October 1895.
70. *Johannesburg Times*, 9 October 1895.
71. Vane, *Back to the Mines*, 155-68. See also the *Star*, 27 March 1899. Other references to widespread faction fighting in the 1890s are found in *Africa's Golden Harvest*, January 1914, 54, and December 1915, 44.
72. Phillips, *Some Reminiscences*, 127. See p. 65 above. This approach to faction fighting is stressed by D. Moodie, "Ethnic Violence on South African Gold Mines," and W. Beinart "Political and Collective Violence in Southern African Historiography," *JSAS* 18, 3 (1992), 474-80, 593-600.
73. *Star*, 14 November 1892; *Star*, 22 July 1897.
74. This form of group fighting was present in many industrialising communities; cf. R. W. Malcolmson, *Popular Recreation in English Society, 1700-1880* (Cambridge, 1973), 84; P. Bailey, *Leisure and Class in Victorian England* (London, 1978), 8, 21; M. Sonnenscher, "Mythical Work: Workshop Production and the Compagnonnages of Eighteenth-century France," in Joyce, ed., *Meanings of Work*, 46.
75. Blackburn and Caddell, *Secret Service*, 145.
76. *Star*, 24 September 1896.
77. *Star*, 27 March 1899.
78. Junod, *Life*, II, 37-38.
79. However, if the brideprice had not been completed before the death of the husband, the wife would leave his family and return to her father; see the Evidence of B. G. Lloyd before the Natives' Grievances Commission, 1913-14 (TA. K358-1). On the levirate, see p. 94 above and p. 253 n. 71 below.
80. *SAMJ*, 4 May 1895. See also *SAMJ*, 29 June 1895. This point has been stressed by R. Davies, *Capital, State and Labour in South Africa, 1900-1960* (Brighton, 1976), and Johnstone, *Class, Race and Gold*.
81. See pp. 57, 58, 72, 73 above. Comaroff and Comaroff, *Of Revelation and Revolution*, 105; A. McClintock, "Maidens, Maps and Mines: King Solomon's Mines and the Reinvention of Patriarchy in Colonial South Africa," in C. Walker, ed., *Women and Gender in Southern Africa to 1945* (Cape Town and London, 1990).
82. HE 146, L. Phillips to H. Eckstein, 20 February 1891; Association of Mines, *Annual Report*, 1896, 40; *CMAR* 1895, 53, 75, 111; FO 63/1317, British Consul to FO, 2 September, 26 November 1896; *South Africa*, 17 October 1896.
83. "Blackbirds" were African captives aboard a slaver, E. Partridge *The Penguin Dictionary of Historical Slang* (Harmondsworth, 1972); C. Lloyd *The Navy and the Slave Trade* (London, 1949), 201, 290.
84. It was often remarked that the best area of labour recruitment was the Witwatersrand itself. *Diggers News*, 23 January 1890.
85. *Star*, 15 October 1895; *SAMJ*, 6 April 1895.
86. SS 3924, Ballot to Grant in Ballot to Supt. Natives, 2 November 1893.
87. Fourie, "Bantoe aan die Rand," 210.
88. Critics included the mine owners as well as socialists like J. A. Hobson. This perspective has been supported by various influential studies, see A. Atmore and S. Marks, "The Imperial Factor in South Africa in the Nineteenth Century," *Journal of Imperial and Com-*

monwealth Studies (1974), 127, 131; S. Marks and S. Trapido, "Lord Milner and the South African State," *History Workshop Journal* 8 (1979), 60-61; Van Onselen, "Randlords and Rotgut," in his *Studies,* I, 45.

89. P. Harries, "Capital, State and Labour on the Nineteenth Century Witwatersrand: A Reassessment," *South African Historical Journal,* 18 (1986). I would suggest that the politics of the Kruger government were influenced by a neo-Romantic *völkisch* idealism, a philosophy particularly strong in Germany, see R. Stackelberg, *Idealism Debased: From Völkisch Ideology to National Socialism* (Kent, Ohio, 1981), 11-12, 85.

90. By 1895 a ton of ore yielded over 40 percent more gold than in 1890, a factor helping to push down mining costs from about 40s per ton in 1888 to 31s6.9d in 1896. A fall in production costs was the equivalent of a rise in the gold price. Bleloch, *The New South Africa,* 19; S. J. Truscott, *The Witwatersrand Gold Fields Banket and Mining Practice* (London, 1898), 443; Jeppe, *Gold Mining,* 25.

91. In 1895 some 3,600 men were concentrated within the compound of a large mine like the Simmer and Jack. *SAMJ,* 25 May 1895.

92. C. G. W. Schumann, *Structural Changes and Business Cycles in South Africa, 1806-1936* (London, 1938), 88, 91.

93. *SAMJ,* 19 January 1895.

94. *Ibid.*

95. *Johannesburg Times,* 17 January 1896.

96. *Star,* 11 and 13 December 1895. See also P. Fitzpatrick, *The Transvaal From Within* (London, 1899), 105.

97. MNE 709, Consul to MNE, 23 February 1896; Consul to MNE, 16 May 1896.

98. *CMAR* 1896, 35. See also Mousinho de Albuquerque, *Moçambique 1896-1898* (Lisbon, 1934), 146-48; *SAMJ,* 6 February 1897. The secretary of the pro-Kruger Robinson group considered the 26s6d charged to carry workers on the train from Lourenço Marques to Johannesburg "enormous considering that the niggers are conveyed in open trucks and packed like herrings." SSA 329 R1959, Secretary of the Robinson Group to Assistant SS, 7 February 1896.

99. *SAMJ,* 6 February 1897; SS 329 R1959, Sec. Robinson Group to SS, 7 February 1896, in Ra607; HE 171 Rouliot to Beit, 29 March 1896; ICE, Evidence of T. H. Leget, J. H. Johns; D. M. Wilson, *Behind the Scenes in Transvaal* (London, 1901), 196-97.

100. *Staatscourant,* 27 January 1896. Historians who stress the intransigence of the Kruger government normally portray the failure of the Jameson Raid as a setback for mining capital. Cf. L. M. Thompson, *A History of South Africa* (New Haven, 1990), 139.

101. SS 929, pp. 2-3, SS to ZAR Consul, 8 February 1896. SS 329 Ra139/66, SS to SN, 30 January 1896, and circular of 4 February 1896, enclosed in R607. See also *CMAR* 1896, 141.

102. HE 171, Eckstein and Co. to Beit and Co., 17 February 1896. See also HE 171, Eckstein and Co to Beit and Co., 22 February 1896; 9 and 18 March 1896.

103. *Zoutpansberg Review,* 11 May and 3 August 1896. In March 1899 the Rev. Creux, a cautious missionary, wrote of "the reappearance of slavery" as state officials in the Spelonken, encouraged by a capitation fee of £2, forced men to volunteer for the mines. SMA 8.11.C, Creux to Mission Council, 7 March 1899.

104. MNE 709, Consul to Ministry of Foreign Affairs, 23 February 1896.

105. MNE 709, Consul to Ministry of Foreign Affairs, 16 May 1896; Consul to GLM, 2 December 1896, enclosed in Consul to FO, Lisbon, 9 January 1897; Archives of the Portuguese Consulate, Pretoria, Consul to Ministry of Foreign Affairs, 23 February 1896.

106. Mousinho, *Moçambique,* II, 148.

107. Harries, "Capital, State, and Labour," 38-40.

108. MNE 709, Consul to GLM, 2 December 1896; Consul to MNE, 9 January 1897; *South Africa,* 31 October 7 November 1896.

109. HE 171, Rouliot to Beit, 6 June 1896. On the crisis of confidence in the NLD, see *CMAR*, 1895, 31-32, 53.
110. C. S. Goldman, J. B. Robinson, and T. H. Leggett before the Industrial Commission of Inquiry, 104, 109-112, 246, 268.
111. The pass law could not prevent the desertion of 5,175 men, from seven companies, in the space of less than one year. During this time, thirty-three companies experienced an average of fifty-five desertions per month. J. H. Johns before the Industrial Commission of Inquiry, 257; *South Africa*, 1 May 1897.
112. The secretary of the Robinson Group complained that the revenue from the pass law was enough to create a neutral native labour department under government control. SSA 329 R1959/96, Secretary of the Robinson Mines to Acting SS, 7 February 1896 in RA 607; Association of Mines, *Annual Report* 1896, 75-76.
113. HE 62, L. Phillips to Eckstein and Co., 12 September 1896.
114. *Standard and Diggers New*s, 14 October 1896; *Star*, 28 July 1897.
115. PRO.CO 417/185, British Agent to High Commissioner, 31 December 1896, enclosed in High Commissioner to Colonial Office, 8 January 1897.
116. *SAMJ*, 9 January 1897.
117. Blackburn and Caddell, *Secret Service*, 130.
118. *Standard and Diggers News*, 12 October 1896; *Star*, 24 August 1897.
119. *SAMJ*, 25 May 1895, 712; South Africa, 14 November 1896.
120. Fourie, "Bantoe aan die Rand," 219-21.
121. *Star*, 1 October 1896; *Standard and Diggers News*, 2, 10, October 1896; *South Africa*, 3 October 1896.
122. *Star*, 10, 13 October 1896; *SAMJ*, 10 October 1896; *CMAR* 1896, 161; South Africa, 10 October 1896.
123. *Standard and Diggers News*, 10 October 1896; *Star*, 12, 14 October 1896.
124. *Star*, 9, 10, 13 October 1896; *South Africa*, 14 November 1896.
125. *Star*, 13 October 1896. The Basotho were also fully capable of mounting a strike when their interests as lashers were threatened; see D. W. Robertson before the Native Grievances Commission, 1913-14 (TA K358).
126. *Star*, 13 October 1896.
127. *Star*, 12, 13 October 1896.
128. *Star*, 12, 14 October 1896.
129. *Standard and Diggers News*, 9 November 1896; *Star*, 13, 24 October 1896; *South Africa*, 14 November 1896.
130. *Standard and Diggers News*, 9 November 1896; *Star*, 30 November 1896.
131. *Star*, 4, 5 November 1896.
132. *Standard and Diggers News*, 26 October 1896; *SAMJ*, 7, 28 November, 5 December 1896; *Star*, 14, 19, 26 November 1896.
133. See also the *SAMJ*, 7, 21 November 1896; *SAMJ*, 19 December 1896.
134. *Star*, 18 December 1896; *Standard and Diggers News*, 19 December 1896.
135. *Standard and Diggers News*, 12 November 1896; *Star*, 30 November 1896.
136. *Star*, 18, 23, Dec., 1896; *Standard and Diggers News*, 19 December 1896; Truscott, *The Witwatersrand Gold Fields*, 455.
137. *South Africa*, 17 October 1896.
138. NA.SNA 1/46, Confidential paper C22/1899, Marwick to SNA, 28 June 1899. See also *CMAR* 1898, 463, and Jeeves, *South Africa's Mining Economy*, 51.
139. Marwick, cited in D. Denoon, *A Grand Illusion* (London, 1973), 128; L. de Launay, *Les Mines d'Or du Transvaal* (Paris, 1896), 90. Johnstone is more temperate when he refers to this combination, during the 1910s and 1920s, as a "system of forced labour," *Class, Race and Gold*, 46.

140. Under Article 131 of the Mining Regulations, despite an earlier amendment (Law 16 of 1894) to the original Sunday Observance Act of 1888; see *Star*, 1, 15 October 1896; *South Africa*, 24 October 1896.
141. *SAMJ*, 17 October 1896. See also the debate over the Sunday Observance clause in the 1911 Mines and Works Act, Union of South Africa, House of Assembley, *1910-11 Debates*, 1092.
142. *Star*, 17 May 1897.
143. Van Onselen, "Randlords and Rotgut," in *Studies*, I.
144. C. S. Goldman before the ICE, 114; *Standard and Diggers News*, 4 May 1897; *South Africa* 1 May 1897.
145. Montez, ed., *Mouzinho*, 179-84; Mousinho, *Moçambique*, II, 185-89.
146. AHU.2a Rep., Pasta 7; Alfandega de Lourenço Marques, Mappa estatisticos, 1890; Freire d'Andrade, *Relatorios Sobre Moçambique*, I, 40.
147. *Natal Blue Books*, statistical sections. Mozambican alcohol cost 3s per gallon to produce, was taxed 5d per gallon by the Portuguese, and sold for 9s per gallon in the Transvaal. BPP 1896, LXXXVIII, Consular Report for 1895; TA *Leyds Archive* (LA) 464, LM Consul to SS, 18 November 1895 and 6 February 1896. According to both Junod and the Transvaal consul in Lourenço Marques alcohol manufactured in Mozambique for export to the Transvaal was manufactured solely from unrefined Natal sugar and molasses, "Une course au Tembé," *BSNG* 1894, 117-18.
148. Freire de Andrade, *Relatorios Sobre Moçambique*, I, 40; TA. LA 465, "Certificaten afgeven voor alcohol vanaf 1 Januari tot 1 September 1897"; *Natal Blue Books*, statistical sections.
149. "Report of the Special Liquor Committee," in *CMAR*, 1898. I have found no evidence to suggest that sugar or alcohol produced in the Quelimane District in 1898 was sent to Lourenço Marques, Vail and White, *Capitalism and Colonialism*, 127-28.
150. On the outbreak of war in 1899, the Société française de distillerie de Lourenço Marques et Ressano Garcia was left with 85,000 litres of alcohol. Ministère des Affaires Etrangères (MAE), Paris, CCC, A-25-7 Interêts français dans le Mozambique, 1901.
151. *South Africa*, 6 March 1897.
152. Between 1896 and 1898. *SAMJ*, 20 March 1897; J. S. Marais, *The Fall of Kruger's Republic* (Oxford, 1961), 25-27; Fourie, "Bantoes aan die Rand," 235, 271.
153. *SAMJ*, 20 March 1897; HE 62, Beit to Eckstein, 10, 30 April 1897; HE 172, Eckstein to Beit, 30 April 1897; SMA 501/A, Eberhardt to Grandjean, 5 April 1897; *CMAR* 1897, 107.
154. Duminy and Guest, eds., *Fitzpatrick; Selected Papers*, 103.
155. F. Wilson, *Labour in the South African Gold Mines* (Cambridge, 1972), 46, 141.
156. *Star*, 6 May 1897; *Standard and Diggers News*, 10 May 1897.
157. HE 172, L. Phillips to Beit and Co., 8 May 1897; *CMAR* 1897, 116.
158. *Standard and Diggers News*, 3, 8 May 1897.
159. *Star*, 8 May 1897
160. *Standard and Diggers News*, 3, 5, 6, 8, 10 May 1897.
161. Duminy and Guest, eds., *Fitzpatrick; Selected Papers*, 100.
162. *Standard and Diggers News*, 31 May, 3, 12 June 1897; *Star*, 25 May, 3 June, 1897.
163. *Star*, 3, 7, June 1897; *Standard and Diggers News*, 9 June 1897.
164. *Star*, 7 June 1897.
165. *Star*, 9 June, 1, 8 July 1897.
166. *Standard and Diggers News*, 8 July 1897.
167. *Star*, 3 June 1897; *Standard and Diggers News*, 12 June 1897.
168. *Star*, 13 July 1897; *Standard and Diggers News*, 24 July 1897.
169. *Boletim Oficial* 50, 11 December 1897; *Staatscourant*, 8 December 1897. See also Mousinho de Albuquerque, *Providências Publicadas pelo Commissário Régio na Província de Moçambique desde 1 Dezembro até 18 Novembro 1897*, 694-703

170. *Natal Witness*, 8 November 1897; *Standard and Diggers News*, 22 November 1897; *De Pers* 10 November 1897.
171. *Star*, 24 November 1897. See also reports of 22, 23 November.
172. *Star*, 23 March 1898.
173. *South Africa*, 11 September 1897; S. Katzenellenbogen, *South Africa and Southern Mozambique* 39.
174. Mozambicans spent an average of eighteen months on the mines, and recruiting, transport, and government fees cost roughly 68s.
175. *Annual Report of the Association of Mines*, 1896, 19; Evidence of Albu, Way, Seymour, Jennings, and Shanks before the Industrial Commission of Inquiry, 1897, 14, 38, 149, 200, 366; *Star*, 24 March 1898.
176. In some of the deep-level mines it cost 34s6d to extract and process a ton of ore. *SAMJ*, 20 March 1897; *CMAR* 1898, 24; Bleloch, *New South Africa*, 16 n.2, 23.
177. L. von Praagh, *The Transvaal and its Mines* (London, 1906), 506; Bleloch, *New South Africa*, 15-16.
178. *CMAR* 1898, 407, 458. *CMAR* 1897, 129.
179. *Standard and Diggers News*, 5 November 1897; *Star*, 5 November 1897.
180. SSa Ra 1358, ZAR Consul Lourenço Marques, Report for 1894; *CMAR* 1898, 458, *CMAR* 1899, 68; Evidence of F. de Mello Breyner before the Transvaal Labour Commission of 1904, 27; Hobson, *The War in South Africa*, 232.
181. Fitzpatrick to the Transvaal Labour Commission, 1904, 119.

CHAPTER 6

Discretionary Migrant Labour and Standards of Living

1. Noronho, *Lourenço Marques*, 181-82; *BO* 8, 24 February 1894; MNE Caixa 698, enclosure in Natal Consul to MNE, 9 November 1894.
2. BPP (A + P) XCIX 1895, Consular Report for Mozambique, 1893; E. Medeiros, "L'Evolution démographique de la ville de Lourenço Marques, 1894-95," in M. Cahen, ed., *Bourgs et Villes en Afrique Lusophone* (Paris, 1989), 64. By far the best treatment of the history of Lourenço Marques is Jeanne Penvenne's *Engineering Inequality: The Indigenato and the Develoment of an African Working Class, Lourenço Marques, Mozambique, 1877-1962* (forthcoming, Heinemann).
3. Noronho, *Lourenço Marques*, 55, 183, 198; UNISA, Junod Collection (JC), "Les Causes de la guerre."
4. See chapter 4, notes 161–163.
5. FO 84/2224, Consul to FO, 4 April 1892. Grandjean, "La Mission Suisse à la Baie de Delagoa," *Le Chrétien Evangélique* XL (9 September 1897).
6. GLM to GGM, 18 August 1891, in *Mousinho*, 227; Noronho, *Lourenço Marques*, 54; Grandjean, "Notices," in *BSNG*, 1893, 120; A. Grandjean, "Notice relative à la carte du Nkomati," *BSNG* VII (1892-93), 120.
7. *BO* 33, 18 August 1888; *BO* 38, 21 September 1889; *BO* 10, 8 March 1890.
8. Cf. FO 84/2224, De la Cour to FO, 4 April 1892; *BO* 2, 21 January 1888.
9. SMA 1127/E, Junod, "L'Histoire du différend entre Mahazoule et Mobvesha."
10. SMA 503/A, Grandjean to Leresche, 15 November 1889; BPP LXXVI 1890, Consul's Report for 1889; BPP, 1895 XCIX; *CMAR*, 1894, 29.
11. Penvenne, Engineering Inequality.
12. AHU.Moc., 2a Rep., Pasta 9, Freire d'Andrade, "Relatorio do Reconhecimento do Rio Incomati, 1891"; Richardson, *The Crowded Hours*, 163; Grandjean, "Voyage de Lourenço Marques à Rikatla," *BMSAS*, 104, 1892.
13. A. Enes, *Mocambique: Relatorio Apresentado ao Governo* (Lisbon, 1946), 40; F. d'Andrade, *Relatorio*, II, 10.

14. FO 84/2224, Consul to FO, 4 April 1892; BPP XCIX 1895, Consular Report for 1893; UNISA/ JC, Junod, "Les Causes de la guerre."
15. Junod, "Les Causes de la rebellion dans le district de Lourenço Marques," letter to V. Rossel, 4 September 1896, in the Junod Collection (JC), University of South Africa (UNISA); SMA 519/B, Loze to Leresche, 17 May 1894; SMA 516/B, Junod to Leresche, 3 September 1894; Junod, "Tembe," in *BSNG*, 1895, 115.
16. UNISA/JC, Junod, "Les Causes de la rebellion"; BPP 1895 XCIX, Consular Report for 1894.
17. Even Robert Mashaba, the Methodist preacher, thought that when the Portuguese "have arrested a man they tie stones to him and sink him in the Bay." Mashaba, letter of 22 October 1894 in the *Mission Field*, 1895, 38; SMA 8.10.B, H. Berthoud to Grandjean, 28 October 1886; Junod, *Life*, II, 269, 353-354.
18. UNISA/JC, "Les Causes de la rebellion."
19. SMA 1127/E, Junod, "L'histoire du différend"; SMA 1127/B, Junod, "La Correspondence entre le régule Nouamantibyana et H. A. Junod"; Junod, *Life*, I, 409-10.
20. Junod, *Life*, I, 514. On the Luso-Gaza war, see W. Rodney, "The Year of 1895 in Southern Mozambique: African Resistance to European Colonial Rule," *Journal of the Historical Society of Nigeria* V, 4 (1971); Pelissier, *Naissance du Mozambique*, II, 527-645. Junod, "Lettre du chef Nouamantibyana à M Junod, 10 Octobre 1894," in *BMSAS*, 18 December 1894.
21. *CMAR* 1895, 41-42.
22. *Ibid.*, 12, 33, 42; *South Africa*, 10 October 1896.
23. *SAMJ*, 29 June 1895.
24. SMA 514, Grandjean to Leresche, 4 August 1895; Grandjean to Renevier, 21 October 1895.
25. SMA 514, Grandjean to Leresche, 13 August 1895; *CMAR* 1895, 54; *South Africa*, 28 December 1895.
26. *Star*, 15 October 1895.
27. *CMAR* 1895, 37.
28. PRO FO 63/1281, British Consul, Lourenço Marques to FO, 11 June 1895; FO 63/1281, Bernal to FO, 11 June 1895; SMA 840, Liengme to Leresche, 3 January 1896; FHS, Liengme to M. Noguera Soares, n.d. [1898].
29. MNE 709, news cutting enclosed in Consul, Pretoria, to MNE, 23 December 1895.
30. FHS, Liengme Diary, 6 January 1894; SMA 840, Liengme to Leresche, 3 January 1896.
31. SMA 438/A, Liengme to Council, 9 August 1895.
32. Liengme, "Un Potentat Africain," 115-16, 132; Liengme, "Journal de M. Liengeme," *BMSAS*, February 1895, 262-63; SMA 540, Liengme to Rossel, 3 January 1896; Grandjean, "La Mission," 156.
33. R. Martins, *História das colonias portuguesas* (Lisbon, 1933), 572. Gungunyana and Nwamantibyana were exiled for life to the Azores, and Mahazul ended his life as a Portuguese soldier in Timor. Pelissier, *Naissance de Mozambique*, II, 619.
34. *CMAR* 1896, 265.
35. Portarias 78 A and B, *BO* 52, 28 December 1895.
36. SMA 519/C, Loze to Leresche, 23 August 1895; SMA 504/A, Eberhardt to Grandjean, 18 April 1902; Junod, *Life*, I, 388, 542, II, 5, 542; *Natal Witness*, 17 December 1898; Natal Blue Book, Magistrate's Report for Maputa District.
37. Junod, *Life*, I, 542. See also pp. 5, 96 above.
38. Gomes da Costa, *Gaza 1897-98* (Lisbon, 1899), 128.
39. Portaria 78-A, *BO* 52, 28 December 1895.
40. *Star*, 16 January 1896.
41. SMA 497/B, P. Berthoud, "L'état du littoral," September 1887; P. Berthoud in *BMSAS*, February 1888; Grandjean in *BMSAS*, April 1889.
42. SMA 502/A, P. Berthoud to Leresche, 28 August 1889; P. Berthoud in *L'Afrique Explorée et Civilisée*, X (1889); BO 27, 6 July 1889; SMA 503/A, Grandjean to Leresche, 15 November 1889; SMA 503/B, Grandjean to conseil, 9 September 1889.

43. Grandjean, "Voyage à Antioka," in *BMSAS*, December 1889, 337; Grandjean, Letter of 16 November 1889, in *BMSAS*, February 1890; SMA 1256/A, P. Berthoud, "Marche sur l'oeuvre," 1889.
44. SMA 502/B, Grandjean to Leresche, February 1890; SMA 502/C, Junod to Leresche, 13 February 1890.
45. SMA 467, Grandjean to Leresche, 12 June 1892; SMA 1256/A, Grandjean, "Rapport sur l'oeuvre missionnaire, 1892"; Grandjean, "Voyage à Antioka," in *BMSAS*, 1892, 119; P. Berthoud in *L'Afrique Explorée et Civilisée*, XIV (1893); SMA 513/B, Grandjean to Leresche, 7 March 1894. On the epizootic, see SMA 484/B, P. Berthoud to Leresche, 9 March 1892; SMA 485/B, Junod, "Rapport sur Rikatla," 1891; AHU.Moç., 2a Rep., Pasta 9, Freire d'Andrade Report, 1891, 46.
46. SMA 872/E, Grandjean to Leresche, 9 September 1892.
47. FO 84/2224, Consul to FO, 4 April 1892.
48. SMA 1254/B, G. Liengme, "Rapport sur l'expédition à Mandlakazi," May-September 1893.
49. SMA 484/B, P. Berthoud to Leresche, 7 September 1892; SMA 484/B, Berthoud to Leresche, 14 October 1892; SMA 872/E, Grandjean to Leresche, 22 October 1892.
50. SMA 467, Grandjean to Leresche, 1 October 1893.
51. P. Berthoud, in *L'Afrique Explorée et Civilisée*, 16 March 1893.
52. BPP 1895, Trade Report for Lourenço Marques, 55; SMA 1254/B, H. Berthoud, "Rapport de la Conférence du Littoral, 1893"; SMA 528/A, P. Berthoud to Leresche, 19 June 1893. See also J. Machado, "Le Chemin de fer de Lourenço Marques à Prétoria," *BSGL* 5, 2 (1885), 226.
53. SMA 513B, Grandjean to Leresche, 3 December 1894; SMA 573/B, Grandjean to Leresche, 5 December 1894; Junod, "BaRonga," 206.
54. Perrenoud, "Antioka," 10 February 1895, in *BMSAS*, June 1895. See also SMA 438/A, Liengme to Leresche, 18 February 1895; SMA 514, Grandjean to Leresche, 4 April 1895.
55. SMA 514, Grandjean to Leresche, 27 May 1895; Grandjean, "Antioka," 25 May 1895, in *BMSAS*, August 1895, 362.
56. SMA 517/B, Junod to Leresche, 28 June 1895; SMA 514, Grandjean to Leresche, 27 May 1895; Junod, *Life*, II, 444.
57. SMA 514, Grandjean to Leresche, 27 May 1895, Grandjean to Renevier, 21 October 1895; SMA 515/C, Jacques to conseil, 1 October 1895; SMA 515/D, Jacques to Renevier, 24 June 26 December 1895.
58. SMA 517/B, Junod to Leresche, 10 October 1895; SMA 519/D, Loze to conseil, 25 September 1896; Webb and Wright, eds., *James Stuart Archive*, IV, Evidence of Ndukwa, 267.
59. SMA 515/D, Jacques to Renevier, 11 January 1897.
60. FO 63/1336, R. Casement to FO, 9 April 1897; SMA 515/D, Jacques to Renevier, 24 January, 24 June, and 24 November, 1896.
61. SMA 8:10:B, H. Berthoud to conseil, 14 December 1896. See also SMA 496/A, P. Berthoud to Grandjean, 19 January 1897; SMA 496/A, Reminiscences of Pastor Dan Malunpane (edited by P. Fatton in 1951); Cabral, *Raças, Usos*, 9.
62. SMA 501/A, Eberhardt to Grandjean, 22 March, 3 May, 3 July, 6 August 1897; SMA 496/A, P. Berterhoud to Grandjean, 15 July 1897; Junod, *Chants et Contes*, 64; SMA 542/A, 5 June 1897.
63. SMA 501/A, A. Eberhardt to Grandjean, 29 September 1897.
64. SMA 1760, Grandjean Diary, 274; Junod, *Life*, I, 358-59, 537; II, 586; Transvaal Native Administration, *Annual Report*, 1904-5, B22; J. Stevenson-Hamilton, *The Low Veld: Its Wild Life and Its People* (London, 1929), 179-81.
65. SMA 501/A, Eberhardt to conseil, 31 August 1897; C. S. Reis, *A Populaçao de Lourenço Marques em 1894* (Lisbon, 1973), 33-34.
66. AHU.Moç., Alfândega, Packet 1382; AHU.Moç., 2a Rep., Pasta 7, Alfândega de Lourenço Marques.

67. W. C. Baldwin, *African Hunting from Natal to the Zambezi, 1852-1860* (London, 1863), 84; A. Longle, "De Inhambane à Lourenço Marques," *BSGL* 6, 1 (1886), 19; BPP 1890, C6200, Saunders to SNA, 17 November 1887. Cabral, *Raças, Usos*, 85.

68. JSA, File 74, Evidence of Mahungane and Nkonuza; Junod, *Life*, II, 23.

69. JSA, File 12, Evidence of Ndaba; File 74, Evidence of Mahungane and Nkonuza; NA.ZGH 796.z892/96, Foxon Report on "The British Protectorate of Maputoland"; Junod, "BaRonga," 106-109; Junod, *Life*, II, 14-15, 86-87, 338.

70. Junod, *Life*, I, 340. See similar statements, see BO 21, 27 May 1865; AHU.Moç., 2a Rep., Pasta 9, Freire d'Andrade Report, 1891. A modern variant of this argument is A. Rita Ferreira, "Labour Emigration among the Mozambican Thonga," 143.

71. NA.ZGH 708.z288/87, Saunders, "Supplementary Report on the Character of the Amatonga People, 1887"; FO 84/1846, O'Neill to FO, 26 February 1887. Population returns for 1884-88 are in BO 4, 23 January 1886; BO 4, 22 January 1887; BO 3, 21 January 1888. Compare with Noronho, *Lourenço Marques*, 54-55, and *Circumcriçoes de Lourenço Marques, 1909* (Lourenço Marques, 1909), 142.

72. NA.Zululand, Commissioners Archives (ZA) 27, "Report of the Amatongaland Boundary Commission," 24 December 1896.

73. TA.SSa 330, "Aantal Naturellen vertrokken . . . ," 183; Transvaal Labour Commission, Evidence of Ferraz and Wirth, pp. 112, 246; *CMAR* 1895, 56; SPG, Lebombo diocese, W. Smythe to SPG, 5 January 1899.

74. Several observers viewed migrant labour as the reason for the collapse in exports; see Monteiro, *Delagoa Bay*, 145; BPP 1896 LXXXVIII, Consular Report No. 1760 for 1895; BPP 1897 XCII, Consular Report No. 1904 for 1896; A. Freire d'Andrade, "As minas de ouro do Transvaal e sua influencia sobre Lourenço Marques," *Revista de Obras Publicas e Minas*, 1898, 331; P. Berthoud, "Lourenço Marques," *BSNG*, 1895, 105, 108.

75. BO 21, 27 May 1865.

76. AHU.Moç., CG, Pasta 31, GLM to GG, 11 March 1876, in GGM to MSMU, 15 March 1878.

77. AHU.Moç., CG, Pasta 31, Report of the "Curadoria Geral dos individuos sujeitos a tutela publica de Moçambique," 21 January and 8 February 1878.

78. AHU.Moç., CG, Pasta 32, Report of the Curadoria to MSMU, 30 October 1880. See also BO 46, 15 November 1880, 238.

79. *Africa Oriental*, 11 December 1879. On the slave trade, see J. Duffy, *A Question of Slavery* (Cambridge, Mass., 1967), 71-72, 87; V. Alexandre, ed., *Origens do Colonialismo Portugues* (Lisbon, 1979), III, 103-104; G. Clarence-Smith, *The Third Portuguese Empire, 1825-1975* (Manchester, 1985), Ch. 2. See also A. K. Smith, "The Idea of Mozambique and Its Enemies, c.1890-1930," *JSAS* 17, 3 (1991).

80. J. Serrano, "Exploraçoes Portugueses em Lourenço Marques e Inhambane," *BSGL* 6 (1894), 436; Freire d'Andrade, "As minas de ouro," 330-31.

81. A view with which the British and Transvaal consuls concurred. BPP 1893-94, Consular Report (No. 1153) for Lourenço Marques, 1892; SSa 155 Ra 1358/95, Verslag van de Consulaat in Mozambique, 1894. See also Note 35 above.

82. Castilho, *O Distrito de Lourenço Marques No Presente e No Futuro* (Lisbon, 1880), 163.

83. Mousinho, *Moçambique*, 105ff., 146-48, 150. NA.GH 830, Report in British Consul, Lourenço Marques, to Governor of Natal, 6 June 1898. See also F. Renault, *Liberation d'esclaves et nouvelle servitude* (Abidjan, 1976), 146.

84. Mousinho had recognised this when he wrote that "it was neither possible nor convenient to prohibit" the emigration of labour to South Africa, *Moçambique*, 105.

85. AHU.Moç., Mapas das Alfândegas, Pasta 1654; BO 9, 27 February 1892.

86. Mousinho, *Moçambique*, 105ff.

87. BO 4, 22 January 1887; BPP 1890-91, Consular Report No. 855 for 1889.

88. Std. Bank 1/1/102, Lourenço Marques 1895-1900, Position and Prospects of the Branch and the Post, 12 October 1895; Inspector's Report, 26 July 1897. See also liabilities reports.

89. In 1892, some £170,000 was officialy exported in the form of specie. These figures are in no way complete, and merely indicate the direction and flow of sterling exported from Lourenço Marques. AHU.Moç., Alfândega, Packet 1382, 1885 exports; AHU.Moç., 2a Rep., Pasta 7, Alfândega de Lourenço Marques; BPP 1893-4, Consular Report No. 1153 for 1892. See also BO 4, 27 January 1879; BO 3, 28 July 1888; Estatistics das Alfândegas.
90. SMA 502/A, P. Berthoud to Leresche, 20 August 1889 and 23 November 1893; SMA 516/B, Junod to Leresche, 3 December 1894; Junod, Life, I, 279.
91. BPP 1892 LXXXII, Consular Report No. 955 for 1891.
92. J. H. Bovill, Natives under the Transvaal Flag (London, 1900), 64.
93. SMA 1256/A, Grandjean, "Rapport sur l'oeuvre missionnaire, 1892."
94. SMA 517/B, Junod to Renevier, 16 October 1895.
95. Junod, "BaRonga," 207, 244.
96. SMA 493, P. Berthoud to conseil, 17 May 1900. On the purchasing of Swazi cattle by Mozambican migrants, see Crush, Struggle for Swazi Labour, 36.
97. SMA 516/A, Junod to Leresche, 26 June 1894.
98. Junod, Life, II, 311. See also R. Honwana, The Life History of Raul Honwana (Boulder, 1988) ed. A. Isaacman, 106 n.3. For the song, see note 141 below.
99. This figure excludes many unlicensed canteens and wine shops. SMA 350, P. Berthoud, "Rapport sur la baie de Delagoa," 1887; SMA 497/B, P. Berthoud, "Etat du Littoral," September 1887; R. Berthoud-Junod, Lettres, 119-20, 236; D. Doyle, "A Journey through Gazaland," Proceedings of the Royal Geographical Society, XIII (1891), 114; FO 63/1317, Casement to FO, 4 August 1896; Noronho, Lourenço Marques, 54; Junod, "BaRonga," 206, 363.
100. D. Doyle, "With King Gungunhana in Gazaland," Fortnightly Review, July 1891, 114.
101. SMA 1255/B, H. Berthoud, "Rapport sur l'expédition à Gungunyana," 27 October 1891. FHS, Liengme's first visit to Mandlakazi, 27 June to 9 July 1892.
102. SMA 840, G. Liengme to V. Rossel, 2 January 1896; SMA 437/A, G. Liengme to P. Loze, 9 March 1895.
103. SMA 840, Liengme to Rossel, 2 January 1896.
104. Mousinho, Moçambique, 185-87.
105. Junod, "BaRonga," 244 n.1. Compare with Junod, Life, II, 146 n.1.
106. Junod, "BaRonga," 222.
107. FO 63/1127, O'Neill to Granville, 13 June 1882; BPP 1893-94, Consular Report No. 1153 for 1892; SMA 528/C, P. Berthoud to conseil, 20 December 1896.
108. AHU.Moç., 2a Rep., Pasta 6, GLM to MSMU, 27 September 1889. See also the enclosed petition from the Lourenço Marques Municipal Council, 13 August 1889.
109. Fitzpatrick, Jock of the Bushveld (London, 1907), 216.
110. Junod, "BaRonga," 244-45; Earthy, Valenge Women, 20-21.
111. SMA 502/A, P. Berthoud to Leresche, 26 February 1889; 1760, Grandjean Diary, p. 232; SMA 513/B, Grandjean to Leresche, 8 March 1894; ZGH 796.892/96, Foxon Report, 31 August 1896. See also Webb and Wright, James Stuart Archive, II, 146, Evidence of Mahungane.
112. Junod, "BaRonga," 199; Cohen, "Erläuternde Bemerkungen," 286; ZGH 796.892/96, Foxon Report; JSA File 74, 9; Mackenzie, The Net, 1881.
113. SMA 528/A, Berthoud to Leresche, 23 November 1893; SMA 1642/A, "Confessions des Negres," 1896; WUL.A.170, American Zulu Mission, Pinkerton Diary, July 1880; ZGH 708.2288, Saunders Report; ZGH 796.892, Foxon Report; BMSAS, 116 (1894), 143; BMSAS, 122, 1895, 361; Castilho, Districto de Lourenço Marques, 13.
114. Cape Mercantile Advertizer, 16 July 1886; Harries, "Free and Unfree Labour," 322 n.55, 56.
115. Serrano, "De Makiki à Inhambane," 418; F. d'Andrade, "Relatorio da Commissao de Limitacao da fronteira de Lourenço Marques," BSGL, 1894, 343.

116. SPG, 1897 Reports, Rev. Selfey.
117. NA.GH 1050, Supreme Court case, Agnew vs Van Gruning, 14 May 1875; *BO*, 5 May 1877; *BO* 45, 11 November 1877; ZGH 708.z288/87, Saunders Report of 17 November 1887; FO 63/1316, Consul to FO, 14 February 1896; Junod, "BaRonga," 141; Junod, *Life*, I, 407.
118. *BO* 20, 18 May 1889, 322.
119. SMA 1255/B, G. Liengme, "Rapport sur la visite faite à Gungunyane," July 1892.
120. Junod, *Life*, I, 148, 216; II, 382, 385, 390.
121. E. Creux, "Voyage de Yosepha Ndjumo," *BMSAS* 45 (1882), 40; SMA 1760, Grandjean Diary, entry for 23 February 1893; Junod, "Rikatla," *BMSAS*, 98 (August 1891).
122. BPP 1887, Consular Report No. 60 for 1885; SMA 497/B, P. Berthoud to Leresche, 14 November 1887; SSa 155 Ra 1358/95, Consular Report 1894; ZGH 795.2131, Consul to Salisbury, 25 January 1896; KCL, Richter in Von Wissel, 4.
123. ZGH 702.33/87, "Statement of Grantham and the Deputation from Zambile," 27 January 1887. See also *Natal Mercury*, 15 January 1887.
124. SMA 1256/A, Grandjean "Rapport sur l'oeuvre," 1892; Junod, *Life*, I, 204-206, 355, II, 610; Earthy, *Valenge Women*, 151.
125. SMA 497/B, P. Berthoud, "L'état du littoral," September 1887; SMA 484/A, P. Berthoud to Leresche, 26 May 1891; Junod, *Life*, I, 206.
126. Junod, *Life*, II, 476.
127. SMA 497/B, P. Berthoud, "L'état du littoral," 1887; SMA 82/H, Liengme, "Rapport de 1892"; SMA 513/B, Grandjean to Council, 8 March 1894; Junod, *Life*, I, 203. See also p. 4.
128. SMA 497/B, P. Berthoud, "L'état du littoral," September 1887; SMA 1642/A, "Premières confessions des Negres"; ZGH 708.z288/87, Saunders Report of 17 November 1887; ZGH 796.157, Foxon Report of 31 August 1876. Robertson, July 1890, in Wheeler, *Soldiers of the Cross*, 113; *Natal Witness*, 17 December 1898; Junod, "BaRonga," 29-30, and *Life*, I, 99; Cabral, *Raças, Usos*, 83. On *gangisa*, see p. 12 above.
129. SPG, Correspondence 1905, Report of the Bishop of Lebombo for 1904. See also *Relatorio das Terras de Coroa*, 1907, 25; Earthy, *Valenge Women*, 139, 149-50. In Gazaland the marriage age only seems to have dropped after the defeat of Gungunyana; see L. Cohen before the Transvaal Labour Commission, 1904, 163.
130. Sa Nogueira, *Dicionario*, "Ba-Galantzana."
131. A. Grandjean, *La Mission Romande* (Lausanne, 1917), 199; Junod, *Life*, I, 330, 440; *Relatorio das Circunscipçoes de Lourenço Marques*, 1911-12, 17. See ZGH 708.z288, Saunders to SNA, 17 November 1887.
132. Cabral, *Raças, Usos*, 99-100; Earthy, *Valenge Women*, 150.
133. Junod, "Native Customs in Relation to Small Pox Amongst the Ba-Ronga," *South African Journal of Science*, July 1919; Junod, *Life*, II, 531-33.
134. Junod, *Life*, II, 147.
135. Also known as a *tour de France*. SMA 8.10.B, H. Berthoud to Cuenod, 4 May 1888; SMA 1255/B, H. Berthoud, "Rapport sur l'expédition à Gungunyana," 1891; FHS, Liengme Diary, 12 February 1893. Best and Williams, *CMAR* 1894, 34.
136. A. Chatelain, *Les Migrants temporaires en France de 1800 à 1914* (Lille, 1977), 50; Rodrigo de Sa Nogeira, *Da Importancia do estudo Cientifico das Linguas Africanas* (Lisbon, 1958) 169.
137. Sa Nogueira, *Dicionario Ronga-Português*, 220-21.
138. *Star*, 26 January 1891.
139. Cabral, *Raças, Usos*, 182; Honwana, *Life History*, 106 n.3.
140. Cabral, *Raças, Usos*, 114.
141. See the term "momparra" used by the members of the Native Trading on Mines Committee to a Shangaan miner called "One" (TA. K409).
142. SMA 8.10.B, H. Berthoud to Cuenod, 4 May 1888; Cabral, *Raças, Usos*, 107. See also Junod, *Life*, II, 187-89.

143. Junod, *Life*, I, 226, 230. If we follow Emmanuel Todd, the Shangaan form of inheritance through brothers also distanced sons from their fathers. See his *The Explanation of Ideology: Family Structures and Social Systems* (Oxford, 1985), 192-93.

144. Junod, "BaRonga," 28-30, 127, and *Life*, I, 71-72, 85, 95-97.

145. Monteiro, *Delagoa Bay*, 89; *Relatoria das Terras de Coroa*, 1907, 141. See Chapter 1, note 63.

146. On rites of departure, see P. McAllister, "Work, Homestead and the Shades: The Ritual Interpretation of Labour Migration among the Gcaleka," in P. Mayer, ed., *Black Villagers in an Industrial Society* (Cape Town, 1980).

147. Junod, "BaRonga," 381, 383, and *Life*, II, 82, 347, 547; Honwana, *Life History*, 148 n.26. Many of these rituals were still practised by miners in the 1940s and 1950s, see OT, Johannes Sibuyi, Mgukawa Ngonyama, Madambi wa Ntimane, and Nyedze Ntukudzi.

148. Junod, *Life*, I, 398-40.

149. *Ibid.*, I, 401, 414.

150. S. Young, "Fertility and Famine: Women's Agricultural History in Southern Mozambique," in R. Palmer and Q. N. Parsons, eds., *The Roots of Rural Poverty in Central and Southern Africa* (London, 1977), 73-74. See also Earthy, *Valenge Women*, 22-27.

151. Webb and Wright, eds., *James Stuart Archive*, IV, Evidence of Ndaba, 172.

152. H. P. Junod, *The Wisdom of the Tsonga-Shangana People* ([1936], Morija, 1957), 189, 195.

153. Junod, *Life*, I, 464.

154. *Ibid.*, I, 382.

155. Junod, "BaRonga," 64-65; Junod, *Life*, I, 196-98.

156. Richardson, *Lionel Cohen*, 159-160; Junod, *Life*, I, 130-32, 157. SMA 1760, Grandjean Diary, 1889.

157. SMA 1255/B, H. Berthoud, "Rapport sur l'expédition à Gungunyana," 27 October 1891; SMA 1254/B, G. Liengme, "Rapport sur l'expédition à Mandlakazi," May-September 1893; SMA 840, Liengme to Rossel, 2 January 1896; Doyle, "With King Gungunyana," 113.

158. Van Butselaar, *Africains, Missionnaires et Colonialistes*, 70-71.

159. UCT.BC106, Mashaba to J. Stewart, 18 May 1902. See also A. Burnett, *A Mission to the Transvaal* (Cape Town, 1919), 14. There is mention of Mashaba's *Second Reader*, but I have been unable to trace this work. See Noronho, *Lourenço Marques*, 169; Junod, *Grammaire Ronga*, 25.

160. Harries, "The Roots of Ethnicity." See also SMA 840, Liengme to Rossel, 3 January 1896; Van Butselaar, *Africains, Missionnaires et Colonialistes*, 55, 167-73.

161. Harries, "The Anthropologist as Historian."

162. On the Supreme Being, see Junod, *Life*, II, 372, 429; D. Earthy, "Customs of Gazaland Women in Relation to the African Church," *International Review of Missions* XV (1926), 662. This Supreme Being was of course close to the Christian concept of God. But he was equally close to other High Gods such as Mwari (called Dumaphansi in chiNgoni and Murimi in Tsonga), who attracted a large following, almost a "revival," in Southern Mozambique during the years 1913-1917. SMA 558/A, Guye to conseil, 10 January 1916; Junod, "BaRonga," 407, 483.

163. On the tenacity of local custom on the eve of the war, see SMA 513, Grandjean to Council, 8 March and 30 July 1894; SMA 1256/A, Grandjean, "Rapport sur l'oeuvre missionnaire," 1890. At the Swiss mission stations in Nondwane and Lourenço Marques, the ratio of males to females was, respectively, 85:556 and 19:53. See SMA 1256/C, Statistiques de 1890; R. Berthoud-Junod, *Lettres*, 140-41.

164. After the war, one of Nwamantibyana's aids remarked that "our gods are dead." FHS, Tandane's account collected by Leresche, January 1896.

165. Van Butselaar, *Africains, Missionnaires et Colonialistes*, 183, 197.

166. SMA 501/A, A. Eberhardt to Grandjean, 29 September 1897.

167. Charles Biber, *Cent Ans au Mozambique* (Lausanne, 1987), 48. On conquest and conversion, see J. Peel, "Conversion and Tradition in Two African Societies: Ijebu and Buganda," in *Past and Present* 77 (1977).
168. *Of Revelation and Revolution*, 219, 249-50.
169. SMA 1760, Grandjean Diary, entries for 8 December 1889 and January 1890; SMA 484/B, P. Berthoud to Leresche, 23 June 1892; SMA 543/B, P. Loze to conseil, 22 November 1897, 2 September, 12 October 1899; FHS, Liengme's first voyage to Mandlakazi, 27 June to 9 July 1892; SPG, Reports 1898B, J. Bovill, 30 June 1898; Smyth in *Mission Field*, 2 May 1898, 169, and in *Lebombo Leaves*, 14 July 1900, 10. The citation is from Rev. E. H. Richard's Report before the Methodist Episcopal Church, East Central African Mission Conference, 5th session, 1907, 20
170. Smyth in the *Mission Field*, 1 February 1895, 67; Robertson, *Soldiers of the Cross*, 157-58; SMA 543/E, P. Loze to conseil, 27 October 1900.
171. On the chiefs' desire for schools, see SMA 516, Junod to Council, 3 September 1894; FHS, Liengme's first voyage to Mandlakazi, 27 June to 9 July 1892.
172. Van Butselaar, *Africains, Missionaires et Colonialistes*, 179, 181.
173. Bennet, *Romance and Reality*, 11.
174. SMA 467, Grandjean, 1890; SMA 517/B, Junod to Renevier, 10 October 1895; SMA 1128/F, Grandjean to Portugal's Ambassador to Berne, 7 November 1896; Junod, "BaRonga," 116. See also pp. 61–63, 76 above.
175. SMA 542/B, P. Berthoud to Grandjean, 27 November 1897. See also Grandjean's diary entry for 11 September 1892 (SMA 1760), where he remarks that he has persuaded people to stop working on Sundays as an act of contrition aimed at ending the famine. Grandjean frequently threatened misfortune if people continued to work on Sundays. SMA 872, Grandjean to Leresche, 9 September and 31 October 1892.
176. Natal Blue Book, 1898, Magisterial Report for Ingwavuma District, BB21; Marks, *Reluctant Rebellion*, 167.
177. SMA 513b, Grandjean to Council, 5 September 1894; SMA 542/B, Loze to Grandjean, 27 November 1897; Junod, *Life*, II, 504-509, 522-24, 535, 550; Earthy, *Valenge Women*, 217-20. See also Junod, "The Theory of Witchcraft amongst South African Natives," in *Report of the South African Association for the Advancement of Science*, 1905-6.
178. Junod, "BaRonga," 440; Junod, "Deux cas de possession chez les Ba-Ronga," in *BSNG* XX (1909-10), 393. But see also Junod, *Life*, II, 480.
179. SMA 1254/B, Liengme's "Rapport sur l'expedition à Mandlakazi," May-September 1893; Liengme, "Notice de géographie médicale: Quelques observations sur les maladies des indigènes des provinces de Lourenço Marques et Gaza," in *BSNG* VIII (1895), 183-85. A. Bryant, *Zulu Medicine and Medicine-men* (Cape Town, 1920), 71-72; J. K. Rennie, "Christianity, Colonialism and the Origins of Nationalism among the Ndau of Southern Rhodesia" (Ph.D. thesis, Northwestern University, 1973), 99, 157; Earthy, "Customs of Gazaland Women," 663.
180. Webb and Wright, eds., *Stuart Archive*, II, Evidence of Majuba, 158; *ibid.*, III, Evidence of Mnkonkoni, 287; H. Filter, ed., *Paulina Dlamini: Servant of Two Kings* (Pietermaritzburg, 1986), 94-95; Ingwavuma Magistracy Records, "The Historical Record of the Ingwavuma District Tribes" (1932); H. Stayt, *The BaVenda* (London, 1931), 302-307; W. Hammond-Tooke, *Boundaries and Belief* (Johannesburg, 1981), 104.
181. Junod, *Life*, I, 374-75, 487-88. A derivative form of spirit possession, the epidemic of *amafufunyama*, was to spread in this way in the 1920s and 1930s; cf. F. Edwards, "Amafufunyana Spirit Possession," *Religion in Southern Africa* 5, 2 (1984).
182. C. E. Fuller, "An Ethnohistoric Study of Continuity and Change in Gwambe Culture" (Ph.D. thesis, Northwestern University, 1955), 203-204; A. Ferreira, "An Anthropological Analysis . . . Chronic Disease . . . Thonga" (Ph.D. thesis, Columbia University,

1952), 27, as cited in G. Waite, "The Indigenous Medical System in East-central Africa" (Ph.D. thesis, UCLA, 1982), 81.

183. Junod, "Deux cas de possession," 388; Liengme, "Les maladies des indigènes," 183-85; FHS, Liengme Diary, 12 February 1893; Augusto da Cunha Rolla, "Relatorio sobre as principais doençes do indigena dos distritos de Lourenço Marques e Inhambane," in *Relatorio acerca das Circumscripçoes das Terras da Coroa, 1907* (Lourenço Marques, 1908). On hysteria, cf. E. Shorter, *From Paralysis to Fatigue: A History of Psychosomatic Illness in the Modern Era* (New York, 1991).

184. Junod, "BaRonga," 441, and *Life*, II, 481-82.

185. The following analysis draws on Junod, "BaRonga," 440-50; Junod, "Deux cas de possession"; Junod, *Life*, II, 479-504; Earthy's evidence collected in the 1920s, *Valenge Women*, 196-208; Young, "Fertility and Famine," 77-78. For the pioneering work in this area, see E. Alpers, " 'Ordinary Household Chores': Ritual and Power in a Nineteenth-century Swahili Women's Spirit Possession Cult," in *International Journal of African Historical Studies* 17, 4 (1984).

186. Junod, "BaRonga," 444; Earthy, *Valenge Women*, 48.

187. J. Goldstein, "The Hysterical Diagnosis and the Politics of Anticlericalism in Late Nineteenth-century France," in *Journal of Modern History*, 5, 4 (1982), 212.

188. Junod, "Deux cas de possession," *BSNG* XX (1909-10), 393-94; Earthy, "Customs of Gazaland Women," 670; Junod, *Ernest Creux et Paul Berthoud* (Lausanne, 1933), 144-45.

189. Junod, *Life*, I, 318, II, 535; Earthy, *Valenge Women*, 27.

190. Junod, "Deux cas de possession," 399.

191. Junod, *Life*, I, 213, 253, 509-10.

CHAPTER 7

Colonialism and Migrant Labour

1. See for instance the effects of the railway built in 1910 from Mutamba to Inharrime, J. Nunes, "Inspecçao das circunscriçoes do distrito de Inhambane," *BSGL* 38 (1920), 90.

2. Freire d'Andrade, *Relatorios sobre Moçambique* (Lourenço Marques, 1907), I, 30-31.

3. Nunes, "Inspecçao das circunscriçoes," 87, 118; B. G. Lloyd before the Native Grievances Commission (TA.K358-1); A. Manghezi, "Ku thekela: Estratégia de sobrevivência contre a fome no sul de Moçambique," *Estudos Moçambicanos* 4 (1983), 35-36.

4. J. Serrão de Azevedo, *Relatório do Curador, 1913-14* (Lourenço Marques, 1915), 173.

5. Freire d'Andrade, *Relatorios*, II, 10-11; A. Cardoso, *Relatorio do Governador (de Inhambane)*, 135.

6. *Relatorio das Circunscriçoes de Lourenço Marques, 1911-12*, Manhiça, 22, 25; *Relatorio das Circunscriçoes de Lourenço Marques, 1913-14*, Sabie, 28-29; Cabral, *Raças, Usos*, 99; J. Penvenne, "The Impact of Forced Labour on the Development of a Working Class: Lourenço Marques, 1870-1962," Boston University African Studies Center, 1978. See also Lisa Brock's important thesis, "From Kingdom to Colonial District: a political economy of social change in Gazaland, Southern Mozambique, 1870–1930." Ph.D. thesis, Northwestern University, Illinois, 1989, 185ff.

7. Penvenne, *Engineering Inequality*, Ch. 3, *passim*.

8. SPG, Report of the Bishop of Lebombo for 1909; *Relatorio das Terras do Coroa, 1907*, 25; SMA 548, Junod to council, 15 May 1908.

9. SMA 493/A, P. Berthoud to Grandjean, 19 July 1899.

10. *Ibid.*, 9 December 1899.

11. SMA 548/D, H. Berthoud to council, 14 December 1899.

12. *Relatorios das Terras da Coroa, 1907*, Marracuene, 24-25, 69, Maputo, 111; *Relatorios da Circumscriçao de Lourenço Marques, 1911-12*, M'Chopi, 105, Guija, 127; Cabral, *Raças, Usos*, 11-12.

13. *BO*, 8 December 1906, 683; Freire de Andrade, *Relatorio*, II, 11.

14. *Relatorios das Circunscriçoes de Lourenço Marques, 1911-12,* 22-25. See also SMA 8/17/J, Junod to Mission Council, 17 August 1904.

15. SMA 548, Junod to council, 15 May 1908.

16. *Ibid.; Relatorio das Terras de Coroa, 1907,* 25; *Relatorios das Circumsciçoes de Lourenço Marques,* M'Chope, 105.

17. Baker, *Grace Triumphant,* 125.

18. Cabral, *Raças, Usos,* 112.

19. SMA 8/17/J, Junod to Mission Council, 17 August 1904.

20. Cabral, *Raças, Usos,* 115.

21. SMA 548, Junod to Council, 7 December 1908; H.-A. Junod, "Le Mouvement de Mourimi: un réveil au sein de l'animisme Thonga," *Journal de Psychologie Normale et Pathologique* (December 1924), 872; H. P. Junod, "L'Exploitation colonial dans l'Afrique du Sud," *Le Christianisme Social* 5 (July 1930), 2.

22. SMA 8/10/B, H. Berthoud to Leresche, 27 February 1891, 9 March 1892, and 12 August, 14 October 1897; Nunes, "Inspecçao das Circunscriçoes," 118.

23. *Relatorios das Circunscricoes de Lourenço Marques, 1911-12,* 127.

24. SMA 548, Junod to conseil, 15 May 1908; SMA 8/17/J 1903, Junod to A. d'Oliveira, 2 November 1903. For the early 1920s, see H. Guye's annual reports in SMA 14/172B and SMA 14/172F.

25. SMA 9/114/F, "Rapport sur la station du Tembe pour l'année 1911-12," L. Perrin.

26. Duffy, *A Question of Slavery,* 161-62; CPP G 3993, Cape of Good Hope Labour Commission, 1893, Evidence of G. Stevens, 62.

27. B. G. Lloyd, General Manager of WNLA, to the Native Grievances Commission (NGC), 1913-14.

28. Cabral, *Raças, Usos,* 12; *Relatorios das Terras de Coroa, 1907,* Sabie, 83.

29. Cabral, *Raças, Usos,* 127.

30. Freire d'Andrade, *Relatorios,* I, 16; III, 368; *Relatorio das Circunscriçces de Lourenço Marques, 1911-12,* Maputo 51; J. Capela, *O Imposto de Palhota e a Introduçao do Modo de Produçao Capitalista nas Colonias* (Oporto, 1977), 100.

31. T. de Almeida Garrett, *Um Governo em Africa—Inhambane, 1905-1906* (Lisbon, 1907), 153-54.

32. Cardoso, *Relatorio do Governador,* 131.

33. Cabral, *Raças, Usos,* 12; *Relatorio do Circumscriçao, 1913-14,* Maputo, 56.

34. SMA 597, H. Junod to conseil, 11 March 1914; Cabral, *Raças, Usos,* 99; *Relatorio do Curador, 1913-14,* 163; Evidence of Breyner before the Transvaal Labour Commission, 1904, 100; Junod, *Life,* I, 407.

35. SMA 545/C, P. Loze to Council, 27 June 1905; Earthy, *Valenge Women,* 153; Pélissier, *Naissance de Moçambique,* II, 637-38.

36. Junod, "BaRonga," 426, 439. On the prohibition of slavery, see SMA 881B, Benoit to Grandjean, 4 October 1906; *ibid.,* Sechaye to Grandjean, 4 October 1906.

37. Evidence of Breyner before the Transvaal Labour Commission, 1904; Junod, *Life,* I, 407.

38. SMA 585/C, H. Junod to conseil, 19 November 1913; SMA 586, D. Benoit to conseil, 3 June 1913; Nunes, "Inspecçao das circunscriçoes," 124.

39. SMA 542/D, P. Loze to conseil, 12 September 1898; SMA 543/E, Loz to conseil, 27 October 1900; SMA 505/A, Eberhardt to conseil, 17 September 1900; F. d'Andrade, *Relatorio,* I, 258-59. For a more general discussion on the role of colonial chiefs, see M. Newitt, *Portugal in Africa: The Last Hundred Years* (London, 1981), 104-106.

40. SPG 1907, Inhambane Reports, S. J. Harp, 31 November 1907; Reports for 1908, J. C. Salfey; Cabral, *Raças, Usos,* 99.

41. SMA 544/D, P. Loze to conseil, 25 June 1903.

42. Garrett, *Um Governo em Africa,* 113-16; F. d'Andrade, *Relatorio,* I, 4.

43. Serrao de Azevedo's report to the Transvaal Liquor Commission of 1908 (Pretoria, 1910), 116. Freire d'Andrade gave figures of 669 and 395 canteens in Lourenço Marques and the

circumscriptions, *Relatorio*, I, 5-6. For Gazaland, see Garrett, *Um Governo*, 113. The number of canteens in Gazaland was to rise to two thousand by 1909, D. da Cruz, "Agricultura e a emigraçao em Moçambique," *Portugal em Africa* (1909), 307.

44. *Relatorio das Terras de Coroa, 1907*, Manyisa, 39-40; Cabral, *Raças, Usos*, 96.

45. Freire d'Andrade, *Relatorio*, I, 17; Cardoso, *Relatorio do Governador de Inhambane, 1906-7*, 72-73; Azevedo's report before the Transvaal Liquor Commission. On the wine trade in Lourenço Marques, see Penvenne, *Engineering Inequality*, Ch. 2. On Gazaland, see Brock, "From Kingdom to Colonial District," Ch. 5.

46. Azevedo's report before the Transvaal Liquor Commission; SMA 598/D, Junod to Council, 22 August 1915.

47. Clarence-Smith, *The Third Empire*, 94.

48. Freire d'Andrade, *Relatorio*, 32-33; III, 198; *Relatorio das Circunscriçoes de Lourenço Marques, 1913-14*, Sabie, 14; *Relatorio das Terras de Coroa, 1907*, 46-47.

49. Andrade, *Relatorio*, I, 239; Cabral, *Raças, Usos*, 94-98.

50. *Africa's Golden Harvest (AGH)*, February 1911, 4.

51. Cardoso, *Relatorio do Governador, 1906-7*, 43-44, 73-74, 86; Andrade, *Relatorio*, I, 235; III, 212.

52. Evidence of Taberer and Makhotle before the Mining Industry Commission of 1908 (MIC), 1312, 1451; B. G. Lloyd to the NGC; P. Mitchell before the Native Trading on Mines Committee, 1919 (TA K409); Report of the Special Commissioner Appointed to Enquire into the Boycotting of Rand Storekeepers by Natives (UG4-'19), 1.

53. Azevedo, *Relatorio do Curador, 1913-14*, 175-76; UG4-'19, Report of the Special Commissioner Appointed to Enquire into the Boycotting of Rand Storekeepers, 2.

54. A. Hocking, *Randfontein Estates*, 117; J. S. Marwick to the NGC; OT, J. Khosa to Harries, Tulumahanxi, 9 July 1987 (Tape 21).

55. TA K409, Evidence of P. Mitchel, J. Sundu, A. H. Stanford, and "Sixpence" before the Native Trading on Mines Committee, 1919. For the same "box system" on the mines of Southern Rhodesia, see Van Onselen, *Chibaro*, 163-64.

56. *Star*, 22 July 1897; Cabral, *Raças, Usos*, 98-101; *Relatorio das Circunscriçoes de Lourenço Marques, 1913-14*, 16; Azevedo, *Relatorio do Curador, 1914-15*, 205.

57. See pp. 62–63, 217–218 below.

58. Freire d'Andrade, *Relatorio*, I, 229-31.

59. The amount repatriated by the curator rose from £12,800 in 1914 to £48,400 in 1917; see UG4-'19, 7.

60. Junod, *Life*, I, 407. See also Freire d'Andrade, *Relatorios*, I, 236; *Relatorio dos Terras de Coroa, 1907*, 65.

61. The Portuguese estimated each man returned with about £15, a sum inflated by the British consul to £20. The settlers who opposed the emigration of labour because of its inflationary effect on wages thought each migrant returned with £8-10. The annual sum of repatriated wages was believed to amount to between £300,000 and £1 million. TA.GOV 18.441/02, MacDonald to Lansdowne, 2 June 1902; TA.GOV 41.307/03, Gosselin to Lansdowne, 6 February 1903; B. G. Lloyd to the NGC; Freire d'Andrade, *Relatorios*, I, 123-24, 128, 236; III, 267, 274; Cabral, *Raças, Usos*, 97; Da Cruz, "Agricultura e a emigraçao," 307; Azevedo, *Relatorio do Curador 1914-15*, 204-205.

62. Freire d'Andrade, *Relatorios* III, 281, 297, 299, 305; R. J. Hammond, *Portugal and Africa, 1810-1915: A Study in Uneconomic Imperialism* (Stanford, 1966), 294; Pélissier, *Naissance du Moçambique* I, 138-43.

63. Freiere d'Andrade, *Relatorios*, I, 228, 235, III, 212; *Relatorio do Governo, 1906-7* (Inhambane), 43-44, 73-74, 86.

64. Katzenellenbogen, *South Africa and Southern Mozambique*, 113-17.

65. Cd 786-115 in BPP 1902, 109; Freire d'Andrade, *Relatorios*, III, 280, 380; Cabral, *Raças, Usos*, 12.

66. SMA 493/B, P. Berthoud to Grandjean, 17 May 1900, 1 November 1900; SMA 505/B, A. Eberhardt to conseil, 11 January 1911.

67. Renault, *Liberation d'esclaves*, 148-49.

68. *AGH*, April 1917, 80.

69. An inhabitant of the northern, Minho province of Portugal. *Relatorio das Terras de Coroa, 1907*, 65.

70. *Lebombo Leaves* 14, 1 (January 1916). See also Junod, "Ba-Ronga," 211; Da Cruz, *Em Terras de Gaza*, 201, 214, 218; Cabral, *Raças, Usos*, 101; *Relatorio das Circumscriçoes de Lourenço Marques, 1913-14*, 14, 53.

71. SMA 547/A, H. Guye to conseil, 25 July 1904.

72. *AGH*, December 1913, 44, October 1916, 22; A. J. Potgieter, "Die Swartes aan die Witwatersrand, 1900-1933" (Ph.D. thesis, Rand Afrikaans University, 1978), 272.

73. Grandjean, *La Mission*, 187.

74. Baker, *Grace Triumphant*, 124; *AGH*, May 1912, 3, see also Rennie, "Christianity, Colonialism," Ch. 8.

75. SMA 543/E, Loze to conseil, 27 October 1900; 544/B, Loze to conseil, 12 February 1901. See also SPG, Lebombo, Report of Bishop Smyth, September 1900.

76. Methodist Episcopal Church, East Central African Mission Conference, 6th session, 1909, Report of W. C. Terril from Inhambane; Haley, *Life in Mozambique*, 22, 34; J. Dexter Taylor, "The Rand as a Mission Field," *International Review of Missions* XV (1926), 648.

77. Biber, *Cent Ans au Mozambique*, 48; Potgieter, "Swartes aan die Rand," 261.

78. On the South African Compounds and Interior Mission in southern Mozambique, see *AGH* (April 1907), 15-16, April 1910, 3; June 1910, 4; March 1911, 4-6; November 1911, 52; December 1913, 44; January 1914, 54; April 1915, 76; May 1916.

79. The Anglican bishop of Lebombo went so far as to refer to schools "simply as bait," places from which to "turn out Christians," First General Missionary Conference, *Report* (Johannesburg, 1904), 93.

80. Grandjean, *La Mission*, 230-31; Methodist Episcopal Church, East Central African Mission Conference, 6th session, 1909, Report of W. C. Terril from Inhambane, 24-26; L. Fuller, *Light on the Lebombo* (London, 1920), 4.

81. *Ibid.*

82. For an example of the religious prejudices with which migrants returned home, see SMA 544/B, P. Loze to conseil, 12 February 1901. A history of the relations between the Portuguese, African nationalists, and the Protestant churches has yet to be written, but Biber provides a start in Chapters 11 and 12 of his *Cent Ans au Mozambique*. See also B. Munslow, *Mozambique; The Revolution and Its Origins* (London, 1983), 66-67; I. Christie, *Machel of Mozambique* (Harare, 1988), 4; and A. Clerc's biography of the young Mondlane, *Chitlangou: Son of a Chief* (London, 1950).

83. TA.GOV 210.33/06, Lourenço Marques Consul-General to Selbourne, 27 June 1906; PRO FO 367/19, Minutes of Barrington and Grey, 14 November 1906; FO 800/71, Grey to Soveral, 24 November 1906.

84. Jeeves, *South Africa's Mining Economy*; Katzenellenbogen, *South Africa and Southern Mozambique*; Duffy, *A Question of Slavery*.

85. This sum included payments made to chiefs, runners, and recruiters, and the salaries of management. It also included the running of camps and compounds, and the transportation, feeding, and clothing of workers. *Star*, 15 December 1906; *CMAR*, 1905, 14, 316.

86. *Lebombo Leaves* 14, 1 (1916), 24; Richardson, *The Crowded Hours*, 137; Cardoso, *Relatorio do Governador*, 79. On emigration from Xai Xai, see particularly Brock, "From Kingdom to Colonial District," 239-45.

87. *South African Mining Journal*, 14 September 1895; *Star*, 11 December 1897; S. A. M. Pritchard and B. G. Lloyd to the Native Grivances Commission, 1913-14.

88. Freire d'Andrade *Relatorios*, I, 58, 232.

89. SPG, Bishop of Lebombo, report "On the State of East Coast Labourers at the Gold Fields," January 1899; *Relatorio do Governo, 1906-7*, 45.

90. *Relatorio do Governo*, 45.

91. Freire d'Andrade, *Relatorios*, III, 280-88, 367.
92. Azevedo, *Relatorio do Curador, 1913-14*, 109, and *Relatorio do Curador, 1914-15*, 38, 171; Freire d'Andrade, *Relatorios* I, 52.
93. Evidence of Makhotle to MIC, 1042, 1044.
94. Evidence of Breyner and Ferraz before the *Transvaal Labour Commission*, 99, 248.
95. Fourie, "Bantoe aan die Rand," 215-16.
96. Potgieter, "Swartes aan die Witwatersrand," 49, 71-81.
97. Ware before the MIC, 1425; also Reyersbach, 97. See also C. Villiers to the NGC.
98. Identity passes or cards were introduced in the Gaza District in 1906-1907 and the Inhambane District in 1913. See Brock, "From Kingdom to Colonial District," 249; Nunes, "Inspecção das circunscriçoës," *BSGL* 39 (1921), 66.
99. P. Grey, "Gold Mining Industry," 169; TG 16-'10, Native Affairs Department Report, 1908-9, 122. Between 1909 and 1916 the average number of southern Mozambicans lost each year on the mines fell to 2,642—little more than the number of men who died on the mines as a result of disease or accidents. Eduardo Saldanha, *João Belo e o Sul do Save* (Lisbon, 1928), I, 328.
100. OT, M. Ntimana to B. Subuyi, Tulumahanxi, December 1989. On the advantages of ethnic groups dominating particular mines, see Crush, *Struggle for Swazi Labour*, 197-98.
101. Jeeves, *South Africa's Mining Economy*, Ch. 6.
102. H. Strange before the South African Native Affairs Commission (SANAC), IV, 783.
103. Evidence of Cohen, Donaldson, and Dyer before the Transvaal Labour Commission, 163, 166, 281, 603; TA, SNA 14 Na 172/02, WNLA Circular, General Manager to Other Directors, 1902.
104. Levy, *Cheap Labour System*, 154, 259.
105. J. MacFarlane to SANAC, 1903-5, IV, 735-45; Levy, *Cheap Labour System*, 157.
106. Grey, "Gold Mining Industry," 123-26; *CMAR* 1905, 355.
107. Potgieter, "Swartes aan die Witwatersrand," 201; Azevedo, *Relatorio do Curador, 1912-13*, 87-88.
108. The average number of shifts worked in 1913 was 283, out of a possible 313 per annum, see C. W. Villiers to the NGC; Minister of Native Affairs in House of Assembly, *debates 1910-11*, 1123; Azevedo, *Relatorio do Curador, 1913-14*, 148-49; S. Moroney, "Industrial Conflict in a Labour Repressive Economy: Black Labour in the Transvaal Gold Mines, 1901-1912" (B.A. hons. thesis, University of the Witwatersrand, 1976), 94.
109. Evidence of Enoch, a Shangaan driller, B. G. Lloyd, and J. S. Marwick, to the NGC; Azevedo, *Relatorio do Curador, 1912-13*, 85; *ibid.*, 1913-14, 149; Moroney, "Industrial Conflict," 81-91. See also H.-A. Junod, *Zidji: Etude de moeurs sud-africains* (Lausanne, 1911), 264. An exceptional case seems to have been that of a Mozambican miner who took eight months to complete four tickets, see B. T. Hertzel to the NGC. Mozambicans employed by WNLA had to complete 313 shifts before renewing their "join" or returning home. *CMAR* 1904, 65; J. M. MacFarlane, General Manager of WNLA, before SANAC, IV, 740.
110. *CMAR* 1910, 13-17.
111. C. W. Villiers, B. G. Lloyd, and Dr. Watt to the NGC.
112. C. W. Villiers to the NGC.
113. *CMAR* 1907, 456.
114. H. W. Stockett and C. W. Villiers to the NGC.
115. *Star*, 29 October 1897; L. Phillips, *Transvaal Problems: Some Notes on Current Politics* (London, 1905), 100.
116. Cited in Moroney, "Industrial Conflict," 100. For similar remarks, see H. M. Taberer (before the MIC, 1908, 1316) and T. Lane Carter, "Mining Methods at Johannesburg," *EMJ*, 18 April 1903.
117. Strange before the SANAC, IV, 780.

118. As early as 1897, up to 20 percent of the men in the compounds were not directly employed; Campbell, "The Witwatersrand Gold Fields: Labor," 160.
119. C. W. Villiers and C. L. Butlin to the NGC.
120. Reyersbach before the MIC, 97.
121. SANAC, IV, Evidence of S. Pritchard, Chief Inspector NAD, 732.
122. T. Lane Carter, "Mining Methods at Johannesburg," *EMJ* (18 April 1903); J. S. Marwick, B. G. Lloyd, C. W. Villiers, and C. Marx to the NGC.
123. J. Makhotle before the MIC, 1445-47.
124. Moroney, "Industrial Conflict," 102.
125. Makhotle before the MIC, 1444.
126. Scully, *Ridge of White Waters*, 229; Hammond, *Autobiography*, 305.
127. Phillips, *Transvaal Problems*, 100; J. M. Makhotle before the MIC, 1444.
128. Hocking, *Randfontein Estates*, 87.
129. Grey, "Gold Mining Industry," 411-15.
130. The grade fell from £2.2s per ton in 1902 to £1.4s5d in 1910; profitability fell from 16s6d per ton in 1902 to 10s 1/2d in 1910, Grey, "Gold Mining Industry," 422.
131. House of Assembly, *Debates 1910-11*, 1095.
132. *CMAR* 1904, 21.
133. Under Ordinance 54 of 1903 and later under the Mines and Works Act of 1911. See also the evidence of H. Pookhe, a CID detective, before the MIC, 1082.
134. *CMAR* 1907, 456
135. Edward Bright to Mrs. Bright, 2 October 1903, in M. Fraser, *Johannesburg Pioneer Journals 1888-1909* (Cape Town, 1985), 141-42.
136. Jacobsson, *Fifty Golden Years*, 181.
137. *CMAR* 1905, 27-28, 35.
138. Potgieter, "Swartes aan die Witwatersrand," 241-42; *CMAR* 1914, lx.
139. *CMAR* 1904, 24-40; Cd 2401, Further Correspondence Relating to Labour in the Transvaal Mines, 1905; Jeeves, *South Africa's Mining Economy*, 21ff.; Potgieter, "Swartes aan die Witwatersrand," 156.
140. *CMAR* 1904, 394; Grey, "Gold Mining Industry," 174.
141. Grey, "Gold Mining Industry," 171, gives the average mortality rate as 80.9; L. G. Irvine thought it 71.16, in SANAC, IV, 720, 724. The figure given by the South African Native Races Committee in *The South African Natives*, 27, was 71.25 per thousand.
142. A. Pratt, *The Real South Africa* (London, 1913), 160; Azevedo, *Relatorio do Curador, 1914-15*, 133.
143. Azevedo, *Relatorio do Curador, 1913-14*, 167.
144. *Ibid., 1914-15*, 138. See also Makhotle before the MIC, 1442.
145. *CMAR* 1905, 67.
146. Irvine before the SANAC, IV, 727.
147. Cf. Mines and Works Regulations of 1903, the Labourers Health Ordinance (No. 32) of 1905, and Ordinance 569 of 1906; Jeeves, *South Africa's Mining Economy*, 51-52.
148. Azevedo, *Relatorio do Curador, 1912-13*, 22; ibid., *1913-14*, 26, 30, 126-28, 130, 144; *ibid., 1914-15*, 15, 25, 128.
149. FHS, Liengme Diary, 22 November 1892; Liengme, "Notice de géographie médicale," 186. TB was also visible at Lourenço Marques, Penvenne, *Engineering Inequality*, Ch. 2.
150. See pp. 78, 113 above.
151. R. Packard, "Tuberculosis and the Development of Industrial Health Policies on the Witwatersrand, 1902-32," *JSAS* 13, 2 (1987), 200; Packard, *White Plague, Black Labor: Tuberculosis and the Political Economy of Health and Disease in South Africa* (London, 1990), 74-75, 83-84, 88-89.
152. In Johannesburg, four to five times more blacks succumbed to TB than whites, Kennedy, *Johannesburg and Broken Hill*, 55, 64.

153. *CMAR* 1905, 368-69.
154. SMA 514, Grandjean to Council, 5 January 1895.
155. Augusto da Cunha Rolla, "Os principaes doenças do indigena," 124-25, 140.
156. *Terras de Coroa, 1907,* 140; *Relatorio das Circunscripçoes de Lourenço Marques,* 94, 102; *Relatorio do Curador, 1913-14,* 132; *ibid., 1914-15,* 30, 119, 131-38.
157. Jeeves, *South Africa's Mining Economy,* 214; Cabral, *Raças, Usos,* 87. Followers of the millenarian Murimi movement believed that a magic snuff could cure "chest ailments" such as tuberculosis and phthisis. SMA 556/A, Junod to conseil, 13 June 1916; Junod, *Life,* I, 465.
158. H. P. Junod, "L'exploitation coloniale de l'Afrique du Sud," *Le Christianisme Social* 5 (July 1930), 10; Packard, *White Plague, Black Labour,* 94, 101-103.
159. Grey, "Gold Mining Industry," 318-21; Potgieter, "Swartes aan die Witwatersrand," 321-26.
160. S. A. M. Pritchard to the NGC.
161. Kennedy, *Johannesburg and Broken Hill,* 64; Jacobsson, *Fifty Golden Years,* 120; G. Burke and P. Richardson, "The Profits of Death: A Comparative Study of Miner's Phthisis in Cornwall and the Transvaal," *JSAS* 4, 2 (1978).
162. A. Derickson, "Industrial Refugees: The Migration of Silicotics from the Mines of North America and South Africa in the Early Twentieth Century," *Labour History* 29, 1 (1988), 76, 85-86.
163. *CMAR* 1914, lx; South African Native Races Committee, *The South African Natives,* 28.
164. *SAMJ,* 14 January 1893.
165. Act No. 12 of 1911; *CMAR* 1911, 50-52; Potgieter, "Swartes aan die Witwatersrand," 204; Grey, "Gold Mining Industry," 312-14. See the interesting debate on this issue in Union of South Africa, House of Assembly, *Debates 1910-11,* 1092ff.
166. Azevedo, *Relatório do Curador, 1913-14,* 13.
167. In 1912-1913 the production of liquor was only allowed under government licence; Nunes, "Inspecçao das circumscripçoes," 99-100.
168. *Star,* 23 December 1908.
169. Katzenellenbogen, *South Africa and Southern Mozambique* 74-76, 88.
170. Jeeves, *South Africa's Mining Economy,* 71-80, 122, 135, 265.
171. B. G. Lloyd and C. W. Villiers to the NGC.
172. Azevedo, *Relatorio do Curador, 1912-13,* 96, 98.
173. *CMAR* 1905, 396; Grant before the Transvaal Labour Commission, 58; Pritchard before the SANAC, 745; Hallimond before the MIC, 612.
174. Azevedo, *Relatorio do Curador, 1913-14,* 189.
175. *Ibid., 1914-15,* 13, 147-48.
176. Chairman's Report, WNLA Report, 1906, 6; Azevedo, *Relatorio do Curador, 1914-15,* 129, 146; Transvaal Labour Commission, Report, 4, 20.
177. Grey, "Gold Mining Industry," 115. As a percentage of total working costs, black wages fell to 8.8 percent in 1970 and stood at 15 percent in 1984, *Weekly Mail,* 25 April 1986. Jennings before the Transvaal Labour Commission, Report, 4, 20. See also p. 139 above.
178. *CMAR,* 1898, 459.
179. Strange, cited in WNLA Report 1904, 1; Makhotle before the MIC, 1450.
180. Perry before the Transvaal Labour Commission, 30.
181. *CMAR,* 1911, ix.
182. *CMAR* 1904, 64; T. Lane Carter, "The Kaffir Mine-workers," *EMJ,* 18 February 1904; Potgieter, "Swartes aan die Witwatersrand," 375.
183. Hocking, *Randfontein Estates,* 114.

CHAPTER 8
Mine Culture

1. Junod, *Zidji* (Lausanne, 1911), 255ff.

2. Phillips, *Transvaal Problems*, 102.

3. *Ibid.*, 102; South African Native Races Committee, *The South African Natives*, 27.

4. Junod, *Zidji*, 255, 267; *Life*, I, 543-44; II, 110, 630-31.

5. SMA 550/A, Bourquin to council, 10 February 1912.

6. Harries, "The Anthropologist as Historian," 41, 45.

7. *Report of the Economic and Wages Commission*, 1925, 157. These ideas formed a pillar of early liberal segregation, cf. E. Brookes, *History of Native Policy in South Africa* (Cape Town, 1924), 423ff.

8. Junod, *Zidji*, 267.

9. *Africa's Golden Harvest (AGH)*, June 1910, 4; Potgieter, "Swartes aan die Witwatersrand," 156, 161.

10. Junod, *Zidji*, 257. For other, fuller descriptions, see Azevedo, *Relatorio do Curador, 1912-13*, 74; Moroney, "Labour Repressive Economy," 62, 67-68; L. Fuller, *The Romance of a South African Mission* (Leeds, 1907), 16-19. The panopticon model was not without its advocates, see J. S. Douglas before the Native Grievances Commission (NGC) (TA.K358-1), 1913-14.

11. J. Sundu before the Native Trading and Mines Committee (TA.K409); *AGH*, June 1910, 4; *AGH*, January 1914, 3.

12. B. G. Lloyd before the NGC; Jim Sundu before the Native Trading on Mines Committee, 1919.

13. *AGH*, April 1916.

14. OT, M. Ngonyama, P. Sihlangu, and Madaubi wa Ntimane, to B. Sibuyi, 1989. On the hierarchical distribution of meat, see Junod, "BaRonga," 117-18.

15. Lionel Phillips estimated the cost of rations per shift as 3.52d for black workers and 6.85d for Chinese, *Transvaal Problems*, 105.

16. *Mining Industry Commission* (MIC), Evidence of J. M. Makhotle, 1449.

17. Junod, *Zidji*, 258-59, 267; SMA 8.11.C, Creux to council, 4 April, 16 April 1907; Azevedo, *Relatorio do Curador, 1913-14*, 136-37, 176; *Relatorio do Curador, 1914-15*, 142; Haley, *Life in Mozambique*, 125.

18. *MIC*, Evidence of A. S. Edmunds, 1042. For this period, see J. Baker, "Prohibition and Illicit Liquor on the Witwatersrand, 1902-1932," and Dunbar Moodie, "Alcohol and Resistance on the South African Gold Mines, 1903-1962," in Crush and Ambler, eds., *Liquor and Labor*.

19. *SANAC* 1903-5, Evidence of S. Pritchard, 735; Report of the Transvaal Liquor Commission, 1908, 14-17. For dagga-smoking in the rural areas, see Junod, *Life*, I, 343-45.

20. Marwick and R. W. Currin before the NGC; "Fifteen," "One," Sixpence Hiteydene, and J. Sundu before the Native Trading on Mines Committee, 1919.

21. Dr H. A. Loesner and J. S.Marwick before the NGC.

22. Blackburn and Caddell, *Secret Service*, 32, 49.

23. Skully, *Ridge of White Waters*, 238.

24. Junod, *Zidji*, 280; Blackburn and Caddell, *Secret Service*, 50-54.

25. S. Pritchard, Chief Inspector, NAD, before the SANAC, 745; C. Rogerson, " 'Shishanyama': The Rise and Fall of the Native Eating House Trade in Johannesburg," *Social Dynamics* 14, 1, 1988, 25-27.

26. Report of the MIC, 1910, 84-86; Baker, *Grace Triumphant*, 104; K. Eales, " 'Jezebels,' Good Girls and Married Quarters, Johannesburg 1912," paper presented to the African Studies Institute, University of the Witwatersrand, 1988, 10.

27. TA.SN 23 R2470, Secretary of the Chamber of Mines to Superintendent of Natives, December 1893; SS 3924 R16105, W. Grant to SS, 19 December 1893; *Standard and Diggers News*, 8 July 1897; *South Africa*, 10 July 1897; *CMAR* 1897, 24; *Star*, 20 January 1898; Bozzoli, *Nature of a Ruling Class*, 96.

28. *Standard and Diggers News*, 3 June 1897. The coal mines seem to have used married quarters on a far larger scale than the gold mines. UG12-1914, *Report of the Economic Commission*, January 1914, 36.

29. Evidence of Hammond and Pritchard before the SANAC, IV, 744; Evidence of Makhotle, Jennings, and Hammond before the MIC 258, 304, 1447-48; South African Native Races Committee, *The Natives of South Africa*, 139.

30. The structural insecurity of white workers has been treated by Jeeves, *South Africa's Mining Economy*, 31-32, 71-72; Johnstone, *Class, Race and Gold*, 57-64; and R. Davies, *Capital, State and White Labour in South Africa, 1900-1960* (Brighton, 1980), 69-70.

31. S. Moroney, "Mine Married Quarters: The Differential Stabilisation of the Witwatersrand Workforce, 1900-1920," in Marks and Rathbone, eds., *Industrialisation and Social Change*, 267.

32. Potgieter, "Swartes aan die Witwatersrand," 127-29, 135-38; D. Humphriss *et al.*, *Benoni, Son of my Sorrow: The Social, Political and Economic History of Benoni* (Benoni, 1968), 93-95.

33. P. C. Grey, "Gold Mining Industry," 126. But see the evidence of Breyner and Wirth before the TLC, 102, 112. On stereotypes, see Taberer and Makhotle before the MIC, 1908, 1313, 1444.

34. H. Bennet, *Romance and Reality: The Story of a Missionary on the Rand* (Leeds, 1912), 72-74; Earthy, *Valenge Women*, 151. In 1928, eighty Chopi women were repatriated after having kept shebeens for "many long years," Potgieter, "Swartes aan die Witwatersrand," 370, 246. In the 1930s there were perhaps sixty-five hundred black Mozambian women on the Rand, Rita-Ferreira, *O Movimento Migratorio*, 113-14.

35. Cited in Azevedo, *Relatorio do Curador, 1913-14*, 138. See also *Relatorio do Curador, 1912-13*, 81-84; Fuller, *South African Mission*, 45; Junod, *Life*, I, 493.

36. Potgieter, "Swartes aan die Witwatersrand," 39.

37. Movrogordato before the SANAC, 863. However in 1898 Junod wrote of the existence in the compounds of "immoral customs that paganism has never known," "BaRonga" 481. This was perhaps a reference to *bukhontxana*.

38. Archives of the Swiss Mission (ASM), University of the Witwatersrand, 25.2, Johannesburg Presbytery, Reports for 1904, 1910-11.

39. Van Onselen, *New Nineveh*, 179; Scully, *Ridge of White Waters*, 234-37; SMA 598, P. Loze to conseil, 6 April 1915.

40. Junod, *Zidji*, 259-60.

41. Junod, "Baronga," 29; Junod, *Life*, I, 97-99. On *gangisa*, see pp. 12, 156, 158 above.

42. TA.GNLB (Government Native Labor Bureau), 229. Native Affairs Department (NAD) Inspector, Boksburg, to Director of Native Labour (DNL), 15 February 1916; NAD Inspector, Benoni, 10 October 1919; "Statement: Remarks on Unnatural Vice among British Basothos," 16 February 1916, in GNLB 229. Sodomy seems to have been practised but was much less acceptable, see NAD Inspector, Johannesburg Central, to DNL 16 February 1916 in GNLB 229. Junod, Schapera, and Laydevant were convinced that homosexuality was a foreign custom. See Junod, *Life*, I, 98; Schapera, *Tswana Law and Custom*, 278; and Laydevant, "Etude sur la famille au Basutoland," *Journal de la Société des Africanistes* 1, 2 (1931), 255.

43. For Natal, see p. 4 above. For Kimberly, see p. 70 above. Women were barred from British coal mines in 1842, but the employment of boys under the age of twelve was only effectively stopped in 1887. On child labour in the mines of Southern Rhodesia, see Van Onselen, *Chibaro*, 124-25.

44. Under Law 12 of 1896.

45. A. J. Potgieter, "Die Swartes aan die Witwatersrand," 202; Grey, "Gold Mining Industry," 123; Jeeves, *South Africa's Mining Economy*, 147-49.

46. Under Ordinance 54 of 1903.

47. Cabral, *Racas, Usos e Customes*; Junod, *Zidji*, 258-60; *Relatorio das Teras de Coroa, 1907* (Lourenço Marques, 1908), 140; F. de Mello Breyner to the Transvaal Labour Commission, 1904, 99.

48. Secretary of the Chamber of Mines to Department of Mines, 20 January 1911, 49.
49. *Relatorio do Curador*, 1914-15, 144; TA.K358-1, NGC, Evidence of C. W. Villiers, 3 March 1914.
50. The importance of child labour to rural families was an enduring problem for the missionaries, cf. SMA 72/794.E, Annual Report of the Rikatla Church, 8 March 1942.
51. The term "homosexual" was a neologism of the 1880s, a legal definition rather than a label of identity. On initiatory homosexuality, or pederasty, in pre-Christian Europe, see B. Sergent, *L'Homosexualité initiatique dans l'Europe ancienne* (Paris, 1986). For New Guinea, see G. Herdt, *The Sambia: Ritual and Gender in New Guinea* (Chicago, 1987).
52. M. Ngonyane to B. Sibuyi, December 1989.
53. Cited in van Onselen, *New Nineveh*, 179.
54. GNLB 229, NAD Inspector, Randfontein South, to DNL, 16 February 1916; *ibid.*, NAD Inspector, Germiston to DNL, 16 February 1916; P. Sihlangu to B. Sibuyi, Namahale, 12 February 1987 (Tape G2); John Baloyi to Sibuyi, 14 July 1987, Mambedi (Tape 22A).
55. GNLB 229. "Private Statement," 1915; NAD Inspector, Germiston, to DNL, 16 February 1916.
56. Junod, *Life*, I, 493.
57. OT, Sihlangu, Shadrack, and an anonymous Mozambican refugee, Lulekani, 10 July 1987 (Tape 1A).
58. GNLB 229, NAD Inspector, Boksburg, to DNL, 15 February 1916; *ibid.*, NAD Inspector, Eastern District, 15 February 1916. I have been influenced in the following interpretation by the essays of Babcock, Zemon Davis, and Turner in B. Babcock, ed., *The Reversible World: Symbolic Inversion in Art and Society* (Ithaca, 1978).
59. Movrogordato to South African Native Affairs Commission, 863; GNLB 229, "Private Statement," 1915; *ibid.*, NAD Inspector, Springs, to DNL, 16 February 1916; OT, Philemon Sihlangu to B. Sibuyi, Namakgale, 12 February 1987.
60. Turner, *Ritual Process*, 95-111.
61. Junod, *Life*, I, 40, 56-57, 95, 518-9.
62. Junod, *Life*, I, 493; Shilangu, Joe, and Jackson Khosa to Harries, July 1987 (Tape 21A).
63. Junod, *Life*, I, 494; Mr. Shadrack to Z. Nofemela, Indwe, January 1987.
64. GNLB 229, NAD Inspector, Eastern District, to DNL, 15 February 1916; Junod, *Life*, II, 494; Scully, *Ridge of White Water*, 237.
65. *Delagoa Bay Gazette* 3, 4 (April 1911); GNLB 229, NAD Inspector, Eastern District, to DNL, 15 February 1916; *ibid.*, NAD Inspector, South Randfontein, 16 February 1916; *ibid.*, NAD Inspector, Benoni, to DNL, 10 October 1919.
66. SMA 599/C, P. Loze to Consul, 6 April 1915.
67. Junod, *Life*, I, 493; OT, Baloyi, Shilangu, and an anonymous Mozambican refugee.
68. Junod, *Life*, I, 38-39, 490-94; Junod, *Wisdom of the Tonga-Shangaan*, 271; Henri Guye, "Des Noms propres chez les Ba-Ronga," *BSNG* XXIX (1920).
69. T. Lane Carter, "The Kaffir Mine-workers," *EMJ*, 18 February 1904; O. Trapp "Die Isikula Sprache in Natal, Südafrika," *Anthropos* III, 3 (1908), 508-11; Cabral, *Raças, Usos*, 188; R. Mesthrie, "The Origins of Fanagalo," *Journal of Pidgin and Creole Languages* 4, 2 (1989); D. Brown, "The Basements of Babylon: English Literacy and the Division of Labour on the South African Gold Mines," *Social Dynamics* 14 (1988).
70. The quotes are from Van Onselen, *Chibaro*, 152.
71. D. T. Cole, "Fanagalo and the Bantu Languages in South Africa," *African Studies* 12, 1 (1953), 7; Mesthrie, "Origins of Fanagalo," 225.
72. Cabral, *Raças, Usos*, 101.
73. *South African Mining Journal*, 14 September 1895, 1063-64; *Star*, 24 November 1899; TA.K 358-2, B. G. Lloyd before the NGC, 1913-14; Cabral, *Raças, Usos*, 98; Junod, *Life*, II, 311; Moroney, "Labour Repressive Economy," 5, 42.
74. SPG Reports 1902, Bishop of Lebombo, 2 September 1902.

75. Azevedo, *Relatorio do Curador, 1914-15*, 140. See also the evidence to the MIC of H. M. Taberer and A. S. Edmunds, 1043, 1316-17; Packard, *White Plague, Black Labour*, 78.
76. This is best explained by Bourdieu's notion of "habitus," which refers to forms of practice dominated by "natural," learnt dispositions rather than conscious interests. *The Logic of Practice* (Cambridge, 1989).
77. Azevedo, *Relatorio do Curador, 1913-14*, 132.
78. UCT, Kirby Collection, BC750, Box II, "Native Musical Instruments in Johannesburg Mine Compounds," 1929; Junod, *Life*, II, 282; Junod, *Zidji*, 267-68, 272; Fuller, *South African Mission*, 17.
79. ASM, Johannesburg Presbytery, 25.2, Report 1909-10.
80. J. Blacking, ed., *The Performing Arts: Music and Dance* (The Hague, 1979), 6; Ranger, *Dance and Society*, 73-75, 122. On the anthropological analysis of workers' songs, see D. Coplan, *inter alia*, "Eloquent Knowledge: Lesotho Migrant Songs and the Anthropology of Experience," *American Ethnographer* 14, 31 (1989).
81. See particularly A. Manghezi, "The Voice of the Miner," *Estudos Moçambicanos* 1 (1980), and collections by Manghezi in R. First, ed., *Black Gold: The Mozambican Miner, Proletarian and Peasant* (Brighton, 1983), and H. Johnson and H. Bernstein, eds., *Third World Lives of Struggle* (London, 1982), 31-35, 103-104, 164-75; Penvenne, "African Labour in Lourenço Marques," 483-488, and her forthcoming book, *Engineering Inequality*; H. Tracey, *Chopi Musicians: Their Music, Poetry and Instruments* (London 1948); and especially Vail and White, *Power and the Praise Poem*. During the 1980s I collected, and supervised the collection of, miners' songs, a very few of which relate to the late 1920s and early 1930s.
82. Tracey, *Chopi Musicians*, 30.
83. Earthy, *Valenge Women*, 178-80.
84. Junod, *Life*, I, 187-89; SMA 544/D, P. Loze to conseil, October 1903.
85. OT, J. Sibuyi, 10 January, 1987 (Tape B., side 2); on *giya*, cf. Junod, *Life*, I, 463-64.
86. Earthy, *Valenge Women*, 172; Junod, *Life*, II, 201; Haley, *Life in Mozambique*, 125-26.
87. G. Cross and D. Robertson before the NGC, 1913-14; Vane, *On the Mines*, 168.
88. The Commissioners Report, NGC.
89. Tracey, *Chopi Musicians*, 114-16.
90. On pan-Shangaan identity, see Van Onselen, *Chibaro*, 196, and Harries, "Exclusion, Classification, and Internal Colonialism."
91. Vane, *Back to the Mines*, 164.
92. *AGH* June 1911, 1. See also p. 61.
93. Potgieter, "Swartes aan die Witwatersrand," 269-70.
94. *AGH*, December 1913, January, May, August 1914.
95. Baker, *Grace Triumphant*, 102; Grandjean, *La Mission*, 207.
96. Diocese of Pretoria, *Annual Report*, 1 (1903), 46-47; *Transvaal Mission Quarterly*, 2, 1906, 3-7.
97. ASM 25.2, Johannesburg Presbytery 1906, *Annual Reports*, 1910-1916. And more generally, G. Cross before the NGC.
98. Halls were established on the properties of mines such as Randfontein (1897), ERPM (1898), Langlaagte Deep (1899), Driefontein (1903), Simmer and Jack (1903), Crown Reef, and elsewhere. See *AGH* February 1912, 79; January 1913, 60; March 1914, 68; May 1914, 83; September 1914, 115-16; March 1915, 64; June 1915, ii.
99. Potgieter, "Swartes aan die Witwatersrand," 261, 267; Baker, *Grace Triumphant*, 110.
100. G. Mears, *Witwatersrand Methodist Mission* (Rondebosch, 1954), 5-7; Bennet, *Romance and Reality*, 20-25; Diocese of Pretoria, *Annual Report*, 1903, 47.
101. Bennett, *Romance and Reality*, 30-31, 57, 89; Baker, *Grace Triumphant*, 104; Archives of the Swiss Mission, Johannesburg, Annual Reports, 1907, 1908-9, 1909-10, 1915, 1916; *AGH*, May 1914, ii.
102. Bennet, *Romance and Reality*, 32; Baker, *Grace Triumphant*, 104.

103. Junod, "BaRonga," 481-82.
104. Bennet, *Romance and Reality*, 59, 61.
105. Diocese of Pretoria, *Annual Report*, 1912, 86; *ibid.*, 1916, 39, 74.
106. ASM 25.2, Johannesburg Presbytery Reports, 1910-11, 1915, 1916, 1917.
107. See, for example, a Christian converted on the mines who was expelled from his family when he refused to inherit one of his father's wives. *AGH*, June 1915, 111. According to the letter columns of *AGH*, major problems emerged in rural communities as migrants returned home with a Christian respect for temperance and monogamy, and refused to enter into the network of bridewealth exchange.
108. ASM 25.2, Johannesburg Presbytery 1906, 1911-12, 1915, 1916; Haley, *Life in Mozambique*, 120.
109. Diocese of Pretoria, *Annual Report*, 1905-6, 78-80.
110. Bennet, *Romance and Reality*, 83-84, 88; Haley, *Life in Mozambique*, 115, 120; Diocese of Pretoria, *Annual Report*, 1918, 78; C. B. Hamilton, *Report of the Transvaal Native Mission of the Presbyterian Church of South Africa for 1916* (Dundee, Natal, 1916), 112.
111. *AGH*, December 1913, 45.
112. *AGH*, June 1910; 1912, 15; December 1913, 45; January 1914, 54; March 1914, 67.
113. Potgieter, "Swartes aan die Witwatersrand," 259, 269-70; ASM 25.2, Johannesburg Presbytery, *Annual Reports*, 1909-10; Diocese of Pretoria, *Annual Report*, 1914, 85.
114. *AGH*, January 1914, 3.
115. *AGH*, April 1907, 9; October 1908, 8.
116. Baker in *AGH*, July 1910; Harries, "The Roots of Ethnicity," 42-43.
117. Mashaba had been implicated by the Portuguese in the first Luso-Gaza war and spent the years 1895-1902 in prison on the Cape Verdes. Transvaal Methodist Missionary Society Archives, London (MMS), Box 330, R. Mashaba to J. Morris, 16 April 1896; SMA 544, P. Loze to conseil, 17 October 1902.
118. See Harries, "Roots of Ethnicity," and Fuller, "Continuity and Change in Gwambe Culture," 39.
119. Diocese of Pretoria, *Annual Report*, 1904-5, 96, 106; Baker, *Grace Triumphant*, 106, 110; Potgieter, "Swartes aan die Witwatersrand," 352-53; Bennet, *Romance and Reality*, 60, 80. In 1916 the Swiss Mission spent £576 to expand its library holdings, ASM 25.2, Johannesburg Presbytery 1916.
120. ASM, 25.2, Johannesburg Presbytery, *Annual Reports*, 1909-10, 1910-11; *AGH* 1907, 17 September 1912; Fuller, *South African Mission*, 15; Diocese of Pretoria, *Annual Report*, 1904-5, 106. See also Honwana, *Life History*, 102-3.
121. *Africa's Golden Harvest*, October 1911, 38; Baker, *Grace Triumphant*, 106; Haley, *Life in Mozambique*, 114-15; S. Msane before the SANAC, 857; Junod, *Zidji*, 242, 276; ASM 25.2, Johannesburg Presbytery, Annual Reports, 1904; 1906; 1908-9; Biber, *Cent Ans au Mozambique*, 47.
122. ASM 25.2, Johannesburg Presbtery, Annual Reports, 1906, 1911-12, 1916.
123. *Ibid.*, 1904, 1906, 1907, 1910-11.
124. Harries, "Exclusion, Classification and Internal Colonialism," 98.
125. Jaas, a Shangaan informant (Native No. 627) before the NGC.
126. SMA 8.10.B, P. Berthoud to Council, 2 September 1886; Junod, *Life*, I, 339; SMA 513, Grandjean to Council, 11 December 1893; SMA 467, Grandjean Diary, 1890, 7.
127. Junod, *Zidji*, 242, 298; Biber, *Cent Ans au Mozambique*, 47.
128. See J. Goody, *The Domestication of the Savage Mind* (Cambridge, 1977). For a critical approach to Goody's thesis, see R. Finnegan, *Literacy and Orality: Studies in the Technology of Communication* (Oxford, 1988).
129. Terms used in the Annual Report of the Anglican Diocese of Pretoria, 1905-6, 78; Bennet, *Romance and Reality*, 29; Baker, *Grace Triumphant*, 101.
130. Ggayika and Mvabaza before the NGC; Msane before the SANAC, 856-57.

131. On *timitis* in Mozambique, see Honwana, *Life History*, 102-103.

132. G. Mears, *Witwatersrand Methodist Mission* (Rondebosch, 1954), 9; Honwana, *Life History*, 97-98; Haley, *Life in Mozambique*, 119; D. Coplan, *In Township Tonight!* (London, 1985), 76.

133. Makhotle before the MIC 1908, 1442, 1445. On the early politicization of this petty bourgeoisie, see Potgieter, "Swartes aan die Witwatersrand," 385ff.; for its radicalisation, see P. Bonner, "The Transvaal Native Congress, 1917-1920," in Marks and Rathbone, eds., *Industrialisation and Social Change*.

134. *AGH* January 1907, 9; GNLB 229 "Statement"—Remarks on Unnatural Vice among British Basutos, 16 February 1916.

135. B. Sundkler, *Bantu Prophets in South Africa* (London, 1948), 41-54; Potgieter, "Swartes aan die Rand," 277-300. See especially A. Vilakazi, *Shembe: The Revitalization of African Society* (Johannesburg, 1986), 30ff.

136. Cf. MMS Box 330, Lowe to Hartley, 6 December 1897.

137. MMS Box 837, Lowe to Hartley, 5 July 1901.

138. Junod, *Zidji*, 293.

139. *AGH*, October 1907, 2.

140. *AGH*, April 1907, 14-15; March 1915, 6-7. See also Methodist Episcopal Church, East Central African Mission Conference, 6th session, 1909, report of C. Runfeldt, 26.

141. *AGH*, 1915, 76.

142. Azevedo, *Relatorio do Curador, 1913-14*, 174; Doctors Watt and Loesner before the NGC.

143. Richardson, *Crowded Hours*, 71-72; J. S. Marwick before the Native Grievances Commission, 1913-14; Haley, *Life in Mozambique*, 122.

144. *AGH* 1907, 3; August 1909; February 1911, 9; Honwana, *Life History*, 148 n.26.

145. FHS, Liengme Diary, 30 July 1893; Junod, *Life*, II, 513; Earthy, *Valenge Women*, 153.

146. *CMAR* 1905, 25; *Rand Daily Mail*, 9 September 1903; Potgieter, "Swartes aan die Witwatersrand," 323, 327; Fourie, "Bantoe aan die Rand," 258-59; G. Cross before the NGC.

147. C. W. Villiers before the NGC.

148. L. Cohen before the Transvaal Labour Commission, 241-43. On witchcraft in the mines of Southern Rhodesia, see Van Onselen, *Chibaro*, 197-98.

149. Nyero Sithadi to R. Madzonga, Milaboni village, Vendaland, December 1989. For other oral evidence on supernatural beliefs, see B. Sibuyi's interviews with J. Baloyi, P. Sihlangu, J. Sibuyi, and M. Ngonyama, and P. Harries' interview with J. Khosa. See also various similar interviews conducted in other parts of South Africa and stored in tapes and transcripts in the possesion of the author.

150. Junod, *Life*, II, 299, 488 n.1, 513-15.

151. *Ibid.* 599. For a similar explanation of an outbreak of zombies in the Camerouns, see E. Ardener, "Witchcraft, Economics, and the Continuity of Belief," in M. Douglas, ed., *Witchcraft Confessions and Accusations* (London, 1970). On the 1913-17 epidemic of witchcraft eradication in southern Mozambique, see p. 157 above.

152. In Britain, workers' wages kept ahead of a similar wartime inflation rate, J. Benson, *The Working Class in Britain* (London, 1989), 55.

153. Jacobson, *Fifty Golden Years*, 89.

154. Particularly Johnstone, who prefaced *Class, Race and Gold* with the stirring but millenarian image of a triumphant working class drawn from Zola's concluding paragraph to *Germinal*. Van Onselen's approach is more subtle, but sometimes leans toward hagiography, cf. *Chibaro*, 226, 243.

155. Van Onselen, *Chibaro*, 244; R. Cohen, "Resistance and Hidden Forms of Consciousness Amongst African Workers," *Review of African Political Economy* 19 (1980); Freund, *The African Worker*, 58-59. For an important criticism of this notion, see Vail and White, "Forms of Resistance: Songs and Perceptions of Power," *American Historical Review* 88, 4 (1983).

156. Levy, *Cheap Labour System*, 37-41; Moroney, "Labour Repressive Economy," 42.

157. See, for example, the expulsion of men from their community of friends in the compound when they converted to Christianity, *AGH*, 1910, 4; 1914, 3.

158. On ethnicity as a means of social control, see Report of the Native Grievances Enquiry, 1913-14, 64; Azevedo, *Relatorio do Curador, 1913-14,* 159; Taberer to the Native Grievances Commission; *CMAR* 1904, 64. On ethnicity as dysfunctional to capitalism, see pages 54–55, 133, 135, 137, 262 n. 125.
159. P. Warwick, "Black Industrial Protest on the Witwatersrand: 1901-2," in E. Webster, ed., *Essays in Southern African Labour History* (Johannesburg, 1978), 27, 30.
160. UG.4-'19. Report of the Special Commissioner Appointed to Enquire into the Boycotting of Rand Shopkeepers by Natives; TA.K409, Taberer and Jakame before the Native Trading on Mines Committee, 1919.
161. P. Bonner, "Transvaal Native Congress," 274. See also Van Onselen, *Chibaro,* 219-20.
162. *Relatorio do Curador 1913-14,* 159-60. See also Taberer before the NGC; for a more general view on the breakdown of tribal differences and the rise of a common racial nationalism, see Harries, "Exclusion, Classification, and Internal Colonialism," 98-99, 102.

CONCLUSION

1. Freire d'Andrade, *Relatorios,* III, 282; italics in the original.
2. This was still the case in the 1967-1991 period discussed by O. Roesch, "Migrant Labour and Forced Rice Production in Southern Mozambique: The Colonial Peasantry of the Lower Limpopo Valley," *JSAS* 17, 2 (1991), 266-67, 269.
3. For the 1970s, see H. Alverson, *Mind in the Heart of Darkness: Value and Self-identity among the Tswana of Southern Africa* (New Haven and Braamfontein, 1978), 100; J. M. McNamara, "Brothers and Work Mates: Home Friend Networks in the Social Life of Black Migrant Workers in a Gold Mine Hostel," in P. Mayer, ed., *Black Villagers in an Industrial Society: Anthropological Perspectives on Labour Migration in South Africa* (Cape Town, 1980), 309-10; T. Dunbar Moodie, "The Formal and Informal Social Structure of a South African Gold Mine," *Human Relations* 33, 8 (1980), 558.
4. P. Fitzpatrick before the Transvaal Labour Commission, 1904, 119; Transvaal Chamber of Mines, *The Gold of the Rand* (Johannesburg, 1927), 58; *CMAR* 1911, lxx; *CMAR,* 1922, 77.
5. Wages in manufacturing and construction almost trebled in real terms between 1916 and 1970. M. Lipton, *Capitalism and Apartheid: South Africa 1910-1986* (London, 1985), 44-45.
6. For the 1970s, see T. Dunbar Moodie, "Mine Culture and Miners' Identity on the South African Gold Mines," in B. Bozzoli, ed., *Town and Countryside in the Transvaal* (Johannesburg, 1983), 185-87, 194, 197 n.24. See also J. K. McNamara, "Social Life, Ethnicity and Conflict in a Gold Mine Hostel" (M.A. thesis, University of the Witwatersrand, 1978), 31, 37, 39, 107-109, 120-21; P. Pearson, "The Social Structure of a South African Gold Mine Hostel" (B.A. Hons. thesis, University of the Witwatersrand, 1975) 10, 13-15.
7. Ruth First et al., *The Mozambican Miner,* 130, 135, 140ff., 183; J. van den Berg, "A Peasant Form of Production: Wage-dependent Agriculture in Southern Mozambique," *Canadian Journal of African Studies* 21, 3 (1987), 384-85; Roesch, "Migrant Labour and Forced Rice Production," 268; A. Isaacman, "Peasants, work and the labor process: forced cotton cultivation in colonial Mozambique, 1938–61," *Journal of Social History,* Summer, 1992, 833.
8. Rita-Ferreira, *O Movimento Migratório,* 152; M. Cahen "Le Mozambique: Une Nation africaine de langue officielle portugaise?" *Canadian Journal of African Studies* 24, 3, (1990) 317.
9. Penvenne remarks that Robert Machaba's photograph was displayed, alongside those of João and José Albasini and the high commissioner, Brito Camacho, in the offices of the *Grêmio Africano,* see her *Engineering Inequality.* Machaba is remembered in Honwana, *Life History,* 103-104.
10. Isaacman, *From Colonialism to Revolution,* 73-75; Penvenne, *Engineering Inequality,* Ch. 6; M. Cahen, *Mozambique: La Révolution implosée* (Paris, 1987).
11. L. White, "The Revolution Ten Years On," *JSAS* 11, 2 (1985), 329; Honwana, *Life History,* 22-23; Munslow, *Mozambique: The Revolution and Its Origins,* 79-80.
12. Junod, *Life,* II, 197.

SOURCES

I. Unpublished Sources

1. *Official*

a. Arquivo Histórico Ultramarino (AHU), Lisbon.
   Moçambique. Correspondênçia de Governadors (Moç., CG).
   Moçambique. Primeira Repartiçao (Moç., 1a Rep.).
   Moçambique. Segunda Repartiçao (Moç., 2a Rep.).
   Moçambique. Alfândegas.
   Moçambique. Diversos.

b. Ministério dos Negócios Estrangeiros (MNE), Lisbon.
   Portuguese Consulates: Cape of Good Hope; Natal and Saint Helena; Transvaal; London.
   British Legation in Portugal.

c. Portuguese Consulates, Cape Town (CPC) and Pretoria (CGP).
   Copybooks and registers of correspondence.

d. Public Records Office (PRO), London.
   Foreign Office. FO 63; FO 84; FO 97.

e. Natal Archives (NA), Pietermaritzburg.
   Secretary for Natal Affairs (SNA).
   Indian Immigration (II).
   Colonial Secretary's Office (CSO).
   Government House (GH).
   Zululand Government House (ZGH).
   Zululand, Commissioner's Archives (ZA).

f. Ingwavuma Magistracy Records, Ingwavuma, Kwazulu.
   Magistrates' records.

g. Transvaal Archives (TA), Pretoria.
   State Secretary (SS).
   State Secretary, Foreign Affairs (SSa).
   Secretary for Native Affairs (SN).
   Leyds Archive (LA).
   Governor's Office (Gov).
   Government Native Labour Bureau (GNLB).
   Native Grievances Commission, 1913–14 (K358-1).
   Native Trading on Mines Committee, 1919 (K409).

2. *Missionary and Business Records and Diaries*

a. Swiss Mission Archives (SMA), Lausanne.
   A large number of files and boxes containing photographs, diaries, station reports and correspondence between individual missionaries and mission headquarters.
b. Archives of the Swiss Mission (ASM), University of the Witwatersrand.
c. United Society for the Propagation of the Gospel (USPG), Oxford.
   Correspondence and reports from missionaries.
d. American Board of Commissioners for Foreign Missions, Harvard University, Cambridge, Mass.
   Letters from Missions. ABC 15.4. Volume 12.
e. University of Cape Town, Manuscripts division, Jagger Library. BC 106. James Stewart Papers.
f. Witwatersrand University Library, Johannesburg.
   A.170. American Zulu Mission. "Our Lamented Pinkerton's Story: Diary of an Expedition (July-Nov., 1880) from Durban up the East Coast."
   Archives of the Anglican Church
g. University of South Africa (UNISA), Pretoria.
   Junod Collection, Original MSS and letters.
h. Archives of H. Eckstein and Co. (HE) of the Wernher-Beit Group.
   Held by Barlow-Rand, Johannesburg.
   Correspondence of H. Eckstein, P. Fitzpatrick, L. Phillips, and G. Rouliot.
i. Standard Bank Archives (SBA), Johannesburg.
   Lourenço Marques 1895–1900 and Lydenburg 1878–1879.
j. Chambre de Commerce, Marseilles (CCM).
   File 157, Compagnie de Navigation, Cyprien Fabre.

3. *Unpublished Private Papers*

a. Transvaal Archives (TA).
   Albasini Letterbooks.
   Henry T. Glynn, "Game and Gold."
   Mariano Luiz de Souza, "Herineringe van Lydenburg 1872."
   Braz Piedade Pereira Collection (Portuguese original).
   Cape Public Works Department, correspondence.
b. Royal Geographical Society, London (RGS).
   St. V. Erskine, "To the Limpopo Mouth and Back on Foot," 1868; *idem*, "Journal of Mr. St. V. Erskine, Special Commissioner from the Natal Governement to Umzila—King of Gaza, 1871 and 1872."
c. Killie Campbell Africana Library, Durban (KCL).
   James Stuart Archive.
   St. V. Erskine Papers.
   Alexander Anderson Papers.
d. South African Public Library, Cape Town.
   J. B. Currie, "Half a Century in South Africa," typescript.
e. Fondation pour l'histoire des suisses à l'étranger. Geneva.
   Papers of Dr. G. Liengme.

II.   Published Papers and Reports

a. *British Parliamentary Papers (BPP).*

   Consular Reports for Mozambique:
   LXXI, 1877, C.1662 - 1876; LXXIV, 1876, C.1421 - 1875; XC, 1881, C.2945 - 1880; LXXI, 1881, No. 45 - 1882; LXXXV, 1887, No. 60 - 1885; LXXVI, 1890, No. 742 - 1889;

LXXXVII, 1890–91, No. 855 - 1890; LXXXIII, 1892, No. 955 - 1891; XCV, 1893–4, No. 1312 - 1892; XCIX, 1895, No. 1463 - 1893; XCIX, 1895, No. 1537 -1894.
Consular reports for Lourenço Marques District:
   XCV, 1893–4, No. 1153 - 1892; XCII, 1897, No. 1904 - 1896.
Other reports:
   C.2220 South Africa. Correspondence No. 66, 1878–79.
XLVIII, 1883. C.3533 Correspondence with Respect to Tariffs in the Portuguese Possessions in Africa, 1877–1883. LXXV, 1883, C. 3587 Report by Consul O'Neil on Agriculture and Labour in the Province of Mozambique.

b. *South African Republic and Transvaal Colony.*

Industrial Commission of Enquiry, 1897
Transvaal Labour Commission, 1904
South African Native Affairs Commission, 1904–5
Mining Industry Commission, 1908. 4 vols.
Transvaal Liquor Commission, 1908.

c. *Cape Parliamentary Papers (CPP).*

Annexures to Votes and Proceedings of the House of Assembly:
1880 - G.71. Report on Native Immigration to the Colony from Extra-colonial Territories for the Year 1879.
1882 - A.9282. Select Committee on Illegal Diamond Buying.
1882 - G.86. Report on the Working and Management of the Diamond Mines of Griqualand West, 1881–2.
1883 - G.101. Report on the Diamond Mines of Kimberley and DeBeers.
1890 - G.1. Report of the Liquor Laws Commission.

d. *Natal Legislature.*

Sessional Papers
1872, No. 1. Report and Evidence of the Coolie Commission. Also in *Natal Government Gazette*, 17 September 1872.
1872, No. 12. Report of the Select Committee into the Introduction of Native Labourers from beyond the Borders of the Colony.
1874, No. 4. Report of the Select Committee on the Best Means of Introducing Labourers from Beyond the Colony.
1881–82. Report and Evidence of the Natal Native Commission.
1885–87. Report and Evidence of the Indian Immigrants (Wragg) Commission.

e. *Mozambique.*

Estatisticas das Alfândegas, 1884; 1899.
Relatório das Circumscrições, 1911–1912; 1913–1914

f. *Almanacs, Periodicals and Newspapers.*

Africa's Golden Harvest.
L'Afrique explorée et civilisée. Monthly, Geneva.
Bulletin de la mission suisse en Afrique du sud.
Bulletin de la Société Neuchâteloise de Géographie.
Boletim Oficial de Moçambique.
Boletim da Sociedade de Geografia de Lisboa.
Engineering and Mining Journal
Methodist Episcopal Church. East Central African Mission Conference. *Annual Reports.*

Missionary Herald. Proceedings of the American Board of Commissioners for Foreign Missions. 1880 to 1883.

Natal Almanac and Register, 1867 to 1874.

Natal Mercury.

Natal Witness.

South African Mining Journal.

Standard and Diggers News.

Star.

Transvaal Chamber of Mines, *Annual Reports*, 1889–1910.

III. Selected Books

Angove, John. *In the Early Days: The Reminiscences of Pioneer Life on the South African Diamond Fields*. Johannesburg, 1910.

Axelson, E. *Portugal and the Scramble for Africa*. Johannesburg, 1967.

Azevedo, J. Serrao de. *Relatório do Curador, 1912–13*. Lourenço Marques, 1913.

———. *Relatório do Curador, 1913–1914*. Lourenço Marques, 1914.

———. *Relatório do Curador, 1914–1915*. Lourenço Marques, 1915.

Baker, A. W. *Grace Triumphant: The Life Story of a Carpenter, Lawyer and Missionary in South Africa from 1856 to 1939*. Glasgow, 1939.

Baldwin, W. C. *African Hunting from Natal to the Zambezi 1852–1860*. London, 1863.

Ballard, C. *John Dunn: The White Chief of Zululand*. Johannesburg, 1985.

Bennet, H. *Romance and Reality: The Story of a Missionary on the Rand*. Leeds, 1912.

Berthoud, H. *La Mission romande à la baie de Delagoa*. Lausanne, 1888.

Berthoud, P. *Les Nègres Gouamba*. Lausanne, 1896.

Blackburn, D., and W. Waithman Caddell. *Secret Service in South Africa*. London, 1911.

Bleloch, W. *The New South Africa*. London, 1902.

Bovill, J. H. *Natives under the Transvaal Flag*. London, 1900.

Bozzoli, B. *The Political Nature of a Ruling Class*. London, 1981.

Buchanan, B. *Natal Memories*. Pietermaritzburg, 1941.

Bundy, C. *The Rise and Fall of the South African Peasantry*. London, 1979.

Cabral, A. *Raças, Usos e Costumes dos Indígenas do Districto de Inhambane*. Lourenço Marques, 1910.

Capela, J. *O Vinho para o Preto: Notas e Textos sôbre a Exportação do Vinho para Africa*. Porto, 1973.

Cabral, J. *Relatório do Governador de Inhambane, 1911–12*. Lourenço Marques, 1913.

Castilho, A. *O Districto de Lourenço Marques no Presente e no Futuro*. Lisbon, 1880.

Clarence-Smith, W. *The Third Portuguese Empire, 1825–1975: A Study in Economic Imperialism*. Manchester, 1985.

Cohen, L. *Reminiscences of Kimberley*. London, 1911.

Coplan, D. *In Township Tonight! South Africa's Black City Music and Theatre*. London, 1985.

Corvo, Joao de Andrade. *Estudos sôbre as provinciais Ultramarinas*. Vol. II. Lisbon, 1884.

Costello, T. *1874! The Exciting True Story of the Early Days on the Caledonian Gold Fields, Transvaal*. London, 1931.

Costa, Gomes de. *Gaza 1897–1898*. Lisbon, 1899.

Costa Leal, Fernando da. *Uma Viagem na Africa Austral do interior da República do Transvaal para o porto de Lourenço Marques em 1870*. Lisbon, 1943.

Couper, J. *Mixed Humanity*. Cape Town, 1892.

Crisp, W. *Some Account of the Diocese of Bloemfontein 1863–94*. Oxford, 1895.

Crush, J. *The Struggle for Swazi Labour 1890–1929*. Montreal, 1987.

Crush, J., and C. Ambler, eds. *Liquor and Labor in Southern Africa*. Athens and Pietermaritzburg, 1992.

Cruz, Daniel da. *Em Terras de Gaza*. Porto, 1910.

Cunnyngham, A. *My Command in South Africa 1874–1878*. London, 1890.

Denoon, D. *A Grand Illusion: The Failure of Imperial Policy in the Transvaal Colony During the Period of Reconstruction 1900–5*. London, 1973.

De Vaal, J. B. "Die Rol van João Albasini in die Geskiedenis van die Transvaal," *South Africa Archives Yearbook, 1953*, I. Pretoria, 1953.

Duffy, J. *A Question of Slavery: Labour Policies in Portuguese Africa and the British Protest, 1850–1920*. Oxford, 1967.

Duminy, A. H., and W. R. Guest. *Fitzpatrick Selected Papers 1888–1906*. Johannesburg, 1976.

Earthy, E. Dora *Valenge Women: The Social and Economic Life of the Valenge Women of Portuguese East Africa*. London, 1933.

Enes, A. *Moçambique: Relatório Apresentado ao Governo*. Lisbon, 1946.

Ferrao, F., ed. *Circumscipções de Lourenço Marques: Repostas aos Quesitos Feitos Pelo Secretario dos Negocios Indígenas*. Lourenço Marques, 1909.

Fernandes das Neves, D. *A Hunting Expedition to the Transvaal*. London, 1879.

First, R., et al. *Black Gold: The Mozambican Miner, Proletarian and Peasant*. Brighton, 1983.

Fourie, J. "Die koms van die Bantoe na die Rand en hulle posisie aldaar, 1886–1899." *South African Archives Year Book, 1979*, I. Pretoria, 1979.

Freire de Andrade. *Relatoriós sôbre Moçambique*, Vols. I-III. Lourenço Marques, 1909.

Fraser, M. *Johannesburg Pioneer Journals 1888–1909*. Cape Town, 1985.

Fraser, M., and A. Jeeves. *All that Glittered; selected correspondence of Lionel Phillips. 1890–1920*. Oxford, 1978.

Fuller, C. *Tsetse in the Transvaal*. 9th-10th Reports of the Veterinary Education Association, South Africa, 1924. Pretoria, 1924.

Fuller, L. *The Romance of a South African Mission*. Leeds, 1807.

Garret, T. de Almeida *Um Governo em Africa. Inhambane 1905–1906*. Lisbon, 1907.

Gool, S. *Mining Capital and Black Labour in the Early Industrial Period in South Africa: A Critique of the New Historiography*. Lund, 1983.

Grandjean, A. *La Mission romande*. Lausanne, 1917.

Haley, J. W. *Life in Mozambique and South Africa*. Chicago, 1926.

Hammond, J. H. *The Autobiography of John Hays Hammond*. New York, 1935.

Hammond, R. *Portugal and Africa, 1815–1910: A Study in Uneconomic Imperialism*. Stanford, 1966.

Henry, J. A. *The First Hundred Years of the Standard Bank in South Africa*. London, 1963.

Hocking, A. *Randfontein Estates in the First Hundred Years*. Bethuli, Transvaal, 1986.

Honwana, R. *The Life History of Raúl Honwana*, edited and with an introduction by A. Isaacman. Boulder, Colo., and London, 1988.

Isaacman, A., and B. Isaacman. *Mozambique: From Colonialism to Revolution, 1900–1982*. Boulder, Colo., and London, 1983.

Isnard, E. *Les Fabre*. Marseilles, 1927.

Jeeves, A. *Migrant Labour in South Africa's Mining Economy: The Struggle for the Gold Mines' Labour Supply 1890–1920*. Kingston and Montreal, 1985.

Johnstone, F. *Class Race, and Gold*. London, 1976.

Junod, H.-A. *La Tribu et la langue Thonga*. Lausanne, 1896.

———. *Grammaire et manuel de conversation Ronga*. Lausanne, 1897.

———. *Les Chants et les contes des Ba-Ronga*. Lausanne, 1898.

———. *Zidji: Étude de moeurs sud-africaines*. St. Blaise, 1911.

———. *Life of a South African Tribe*, 2nd ed. London, 1927. 2 vols.

———. *Cinquante ans après*. Lausanne, 1925.

———. *Ernest Creux et Paul Berthoud*. Lausanne, 1933.

Katzenellenbogen, S. E. *South Africa and Southern Mozambique: Labour, Railways and Trade in the Making of a Relationship*. Manchester, 1982.

Kennedy, B. *A Tale of Two Mining Cities: Johannesburg and Broken Hill, 1885–1925*. Johannesburg, 1984.

Kirby, F. V. *In Haunts of Wild Game.* London, 1896.

Lady, A. *Life at Natal a Hundred Years Ago.* Cape Town, 1972.

Leslie, D. *Among the Zulus and The Amatongas: With Sketches of the Natives, Their Language and Customs* . . . . Edinburgh, 1875.

Levy, N. *The Foundations of the South African Cheap Labour System.* London, 1982.

Liesegang, G., H. Pasch, and A. Jones, eds. *Figuring African Trade.* Berlin, 1986.

Lobato, A., ed. *Quatro Estudos e uma Evocação para a História de Lourenço Marques.* Lisbon, 1961.

Longden, W. H. C. *Red Buffalo: The Story of Will Longden.* Cape Town, 1950.

Lourenço de Andrade, Onofre. *O Presídio de Lourenço Marques no periodo de 24 de Novembro de 1859 a 1 de Abril de 1865.* Lisbon, 1867.

Mackenzie, A., ed. *Mission Life among Zulu-Kafirs: Letters of Henrietta Robertson.* Cambridge, 1866 and 1875.

Malton, W. H. C. *The Story of Lebombo.* London, 1902.

Mann, R.J. *The Colony of Natal.* London, 1866.

Marks, S., and R. Rathbone, eds. *Industrialism and Social Change in South Africa: African Class Formation, Culture and Consciousness, 1870–1930.* London, 1982.

Mathers, E. P. *The Goldfields Revisited.* Durban, 1887.

Mathews, J. W. *Incwadi Yami, or Twenty Years Personal Experience in South Africa.* New York, 1887.

Mavanyici, A. *De la Course aux diamands à la recherche des ames.* Lausanne, 1928.

Mission Romande. *Chez les Noirs. Glanures dans les champs de la mission romande.* Neuchâtel, [1894?].

Monteiro, R. *Delagoa Bay, Its Natives and Natural History.* London, 1891.

Montey, C., ed. *Mouzinho: Governador de Lourenço Marques.* Lourenço Marques, 1956.

Morton, W. J. *The South African Diamond Fields and the Journey to the Mines.* New York, 1877.

Mouzinho de Albuquerque, J. *Moçambique 1896–1898.* Lisbon, 1899. Vol. II.

Murray, R. W. *The Diamond Field's Keepsake for 1873.* Cape Town, 1873.

Natal Land and Colonization Company. *Twenty Seven Queries . . . with Reference to the Capabilities of the Colony of Natal, More Especialy as Regards the Culture and Manufacture of Sugar Cane.* Durban, 1867.

Newbury, C.*The Diamond Ring: Business, Politics and Precious Stones in South Africa, 1867–1947.* Oxford, 1989.

Newitt, M. *Portugal in Africa: The Last Hundred Years.* London, 1981.

Noronha, E. de. *O Districto de Lourenço Marques e a Africa do Sul.* Lisbon, 1895.

Noronha, E. de. *Augusto de Castilho.* Lisbon, 1895.

Osborn, R. F. *Valiant Harvest: The Founding of the South African Sugar Industry, 1848–1926.* Durban, 1964.

Payton, C. A. *The Diamond Diggings of South Africa.* London, 1872.

Paiva de Andrada, Joaquim Carlos. *Relatório de uma Viagem ás terras dos Landins.* Lisbon, 1885.

Paiva Manso, Levy Maria de. *Memória sôbre Lourenço Marques.* Lisbon, 1870.

Packard, R. *White Plague, Black Labor: Tuberculosis and the Political Economy of Health and Disease in South Africa.* London, 1990.

Peace, W. *Our Colony of Natal: A Handbook.* London, 1884.

Pélissier, R. *Naissance du Mozambique: Résistance et révoltes anticoloniales (1854–1918).* Orgeval, 1984. 2 vols.

Penvenne, J. *Engineering Inequality: The Indigenato and the Development of an African Working Class, Lourenço Marques, Mozambique, 1877–1962.* Portsmouth, N.H. (forthcoming).

Phillips, L. *Some Reminiscences.* London, 1924.

Pierrein, L. *Industries traditionelles du port de Marseilles: Le Cycle des sucres et des oléagineux 1870–1950.* Marseilles, 1975.

Quintinha, J., and F. Toscano. *A Derrocada do Império Vátua e Mousinho d'Albuquerque.* Lisbon, 1935. 2 vols.

Rapier [pseud.]. *To the Transvaal Gold Fields and Back*. Cape Town, 1885.

Reis, C. S. *A População de Lourenço Marques em 1894*. Lisbon, 1973.

Renault, F. *Libération d'esclaves et nouvelle servitude*. Abidjan, 1976.

Richardson, A. *The Crowded Hours: The Story of Lionel Cohen*. London, 1952.

Rita Ferreira, A. *O Movimento Migratório de Trabalhadores entre Moçambique e a Africa do Sul*. Lisbon, 1963.

———. *Povos de Moçambique: História e Cultura*. Lisbon, 1975.

Robinson, J. *Notes on Natal, an Old Colonist Book for New Settlers*. Durban and London, 1872.

Saunders, J. *Natal and Its Relation to South Africa*. London, 1882.

Sawyer, A. W. *Mining at Kimberley*. Newcastle-under-Lyme, 1889.

Schumann, C. G. W. *Structural Changes and Business Cycles in South Africa 1806–1936*. London, 1938.

Shillington, K. *The Colonisation of the Southern Tswana, 1870–1900*. Johannesburg, 1985.

Thompson, L. M. "Indian Immigration into Natal 1860–1872," in *South African Archives Yearbook 1952*, II. Pretoria, 1952.

———. *A History of South Africa*. New Haven, 1990.

Tracey, H. *Chopi Musicians*. Oxford, 1970.

Trollope, A. *South Africa*. 2 vols. London, 1878.

Turrell, R. V. *Capital and Labour on the Kimberley Diamond Fields 1871–1890*. Cambridge, 1987.

Van der Horst, S. *Native Labour in South Africa*. London, 1942.

Van Butselaar, J. *Africains, missionnaires et colonialistes: Les Origines de l'église presbytérienne du Mozambique (mission suisse), 1880–1896*. Leiden, 1984.

Vail, L., and L. White. *Power and the Praise Poem: Southern African Voices in History*. London and Charlottesville, Va., 1991.

Vail, L., and L. White. *Capitalism and Colonialism in Mozambque: A Study of Quelimane District*. London, 1980.

Van Onselen, C. *Chibaro: African Mine Labour in Southern Rhodesia 1900–1933*. London, 1976.

———. *Studies in the Social and Economic History of the Witwatersrand, I: New Babylon, and II: New Nineveh*. Johannesburg, 1982.

Warhurst, P. *Anglo-Portuguese Relations in South-Central Africa, 1890–1900*. London, 1962.

Warren, C. *On the Veldt in the Seventies*. London, 1902.

Weber, E. de. *Quatre ans aux pays des Boers: 1871–1875*. Paris, 1882.

Webster, E., ed. *Essays in Southern African Labour History*. Johannesburg, 1978.

Welsh, D. *The Roots of Segregation: Native Policy in Colonial Natal 1845–1910*. Cape Town, 1971.

Wilkinson, E., and H. Wilkinson. *Soldiers of the Cross in Zululand*. London, 1906.

Willan, B. *Sol Plaatje: A Biography*. Johannesburg, 1984.

Williams, G. *The Diamond Mines of South Africa*, 2 vols. London, 1902.

Wilson, D. M. *Behind the Scenes in the Transvaal*. London, 1901.

Wilson, F. *Labour in the South African Gold Mines, 1911–1969*. Cambridge, 1972.

Worger, W. *South Africa's City of Diamonds: Mine Workers and Monopoly Capitalism in Kimberley 1867–1895*. Craighall, S.A., and New Haven, Conn., 1987.

Xavier, A. A. Caldas. *Reconhecimento do Limpopo—Os Territórios au sul do Save e os Vatuas*. Lisbon, 1894.

IV.   Selected Articles

Arnt, J. "Die eingebornen-frage auf den Diamantenfelden von Kimberley in Südafrika." *Beiblatt zum Berliner Missions-freund* 13, 5/6 (1887).

Association of Mines. Reports of the Executive Committee, 21 May 1896, July 1896, 23 February 1897. *Annual Report of the Association of Mines*, 1896.

Berthoud, H. "Exploration de H. Berthoud entre le Spelonken et Lourenço Marques." *L'Afrique explorée et civilisée*, VII (1886).

————. "Quelques remarques sur la famille des langues bantoues et sur la langue tzonga en particulier." *Xeme Congrès International des Orientalistes. Session de Genève 1894*. Leiden, 1896.

Berthoud, P. "Lourenço Marques." *Bulletin de la Société Neuchâteloise de Géographie (BSNG)*, 1895.

Bonner, P. "The Transvaal Native Congress, 1917–1920." In Marks and Rathbone, eds., *Industrialisation and Social Change*.

Brown, D. "The Basements of Babylon: English Literacy and the Division of Labour on the South African Gold Mines." *Social Dynamics* 14 (1988).

Burke, G., and P. Richardson. "The Profits of Death: A Comparative Study of Miner's Phthisis in Cornwall and the Transvaal." *Journal of Southern African Studies* 4, 2 (1978).

Campbell, W. "Sugar Planting in Natal." *Natal Almanac and Register*, 1874.

————. "Central Sugar Factories in Natal." *Natal Almanac*, 1875.

Cardosa, A. M. "Expedição ás terras do Muzilla em 1882." *Boletim da Sociedade de Geógrafia de Lisboa (BSGL)* 3, 7 (1887).

Castilho, A. de. "Acerca de Lourenço Marques." *BSGL*, 1895.

Clarence, G. "Notes on the Cultivation of Sugar Cane." *Natal Almanac and Register*, 1871.

Coqui, J. "Journey from Ohrigstadt to Delagoa Bay." *Proceedings of the Royal Geographical Society*, 1859.

Creux, E. "Voyage de Yosepha Ndjumo . . . à la baie Delagoa." *Bulletin de la Mission Suisse en Afrique du Sud (BMSAS)* 45 (1882).

Cunha Rolla, A. da. "Relatório sôbre os principaes doenças do indigena dos districtos de Lourenço Marques e Inhambane." In *Relatórios das circumscripções das Terras da Coroa*. Lourenço Marques, 1907.

Currey, J. B. "The Diamond Fields of Griqualand and their Probable Influence on the Native Races of South Africa." *Journal of the Society of Arts*, 24 (March 1876).

Da Cruz, D. "Agricultura e a emigração em Moçambique." *Portugal em Africa*, 1909.

Delius, P. "Migrant Labour and the Pedi, 1840–1880." In S. Marks and A. Atmore, eds., *Economy and Society in Pre-Industrial South Africa*. London, 1980.

Derickson, A. "Industrial Refugees: The Migration of Silicosis from the Mines of North America and South Africa, in the Early Twentieth Century." *Labour History* 29, 1 (1988).

Dias, J. "Qual seria o status glossinico no territorio de Moçambique, ao sul do Rio Limpopo anteriormente à grande panzootia de peste bovine de 1896?" *Boletim da Sociedade de Estudos de Moçambique* 128 (1961), 55–65 and map.

Doyle, D. "With King Gungunhana in Gazaland." *Fortnightly Review*, July 1891.

Elton, F. "Journal of an Exploration of the Limpopo River." *Journal of the Royal Geographical Society (JRGS)* 42 (1873).

Erskine, St. V. "Journey of Exploration to the Mouth of the River Limpopo." *JRGS* 39 (1869).

————. "Journey to Umzila's, South-east Africa in 1871–1872." *JRGS* 45 (1875).

Etherington, N. "Labour Supply and the Genesis of South African Confederation in the 1870s." *Journal of African History (JAH)* 20, 2 (1979).

Fernandes das Neves, D. "Noticia de uma Caçada em Inhambane." *Annais do Conselho Ultramarinho*, 1864.

————. "Exploraçao do Rio Bembe." *BSNG* 3, 6 (1882).

————. "Cinco cartas de Diocletiano Fernandes das Neves ao Governo de Lourenço Marques, 8 Junho 1879; 18 Janeiro 1882; Junho 1882; Julho 1882; 31 Julho 1882." *Moçambique* 69 (1952).

Ferreira, A. M. D. "Relatório de Serviço de Saude de Lourenço Marques, 1886." *Archivos Medico-Coloniaes*, 4 (1890).

Franco, A. de M. "Relatório de facultivo da Expediçao as terras do Muzilla, 1882." *BSGL*, 1887.

Freire de Andrade, A., and J. Serrano. "Exploraçoes Portugueses em Lourenço Marques e Inhambane." *BSGL* 5, 13 (1894).

Freire de Andrade, A. "As minas de ouro do Transvaal e sua influência sobre Lourenço Marques." *Revista de Obras Publicas e Minas*, 1898.

——. "Exploraçao Portuguêse en Lourenço Marques e Inhambane." *BSGL* 5, 13 (1894).

——. "Relatório da Commissao de Limitaçao da fronteira de Lourenço Marques." *BSGL*, 1894.

Grandjean, A. "La Mission suisse à la baie de Delagoa." *Le Chrétien Evangélique*, XL, 9 (September 1897).

——. "L'invasion des Zoulous dans le sud-est africain: une page d'histoire inédite." *BSNG* XI (1899).

Guy, J., and M. Tabane. "Technology, Ethnicity and Ideology: Basotho Miners and Shaft Sinking on the South African Gold Mines." *Journal of Southern African Studies* 14, 2 (1988).

Harries, P. "Mosbiekers: The Immigration of an African Community to the Western Cape, 1876–82." In *Studies in the History of Cape Town* I, edited by C. C. Saunders. Cape Town, 1979.

——. "Slavery, Social Incorporation and Surplus Extraction: The Nature of Free and Unfree Labour in South-east Africa." *JAH* 22 (1981).

——. "The Anthropologist as Historian and Liberal: H. A. Junod and the Thonga." *Journal of Southern African Studies*, 8, 1 (1981).

——. "Kinship, Ideology and the Nature of Pre-colonial Labour Migration from the Delagoa Bay Hinterland to South Africa up to 1895." In *Industrialization and Social Change*, edited by S. Marks and R. Rathbone. London, 1982.

——. "Ethnicity, History, and Ethnic Frontiers: The Ingwavuma District in the Nineteenth Century." *Journal of Natal and Zululand History*, 1983.

——. "Plantations, Passes, and Proletarians: Labour and the Colonial State in Nineteenth-century Natal." *Journal of Southern African Studies* 13, 3 (1987).

——. "The Roots of Ethnicity: Discourse and the Politics of Language Construction in South Africa." *African Affairs* 346 (1988).

——. "Exclusion, Classification and Internal Colonialism: The Emergence of Ethnicity among the Tsonga-speakers of South Africa." In *The Creation of Tribalism in Southern Africa*, edited by L. Vail. London, Berkeley, and Los Angeles, 1989.

——. "Symbols and Sexuality: Culture and Identity on the Early Witwatersrand Gold Mines." *Gender and History* 2, 3 (1990).

Harris, M. "Labour Emigration among the Mozambican Thonga: Culture and Political Factors." *Africa* 29 (1959).

Hedges, D. "O sul e o trabalho migratório." In *Historia de Moçambique*, II, edited by Carlos Serra et al. Maputo, 1982–1983.

Jeannert, Ph. "Les Ma-Khoça." *Bulletin de la Sociètè des Sciences Naturelles de Neuchâtel* VIII (1895).

Junod, H.-A. "Les Baronga." *BSNG* X (1898).

——. "L'Epopée de la rainette." *Revue des Traditions Populaires* (1898).

——. "The Ba-Thonga of the Transvaal." *Addresses and Papers of the South African Association for the Advancement of Science*, 3 (1905).

——. "The Theory of Witchcraft Amongst South African Natives." *Report of the South African Association for the Advancement of Science*, 1905–6.

——. "Deux cas de possession chez les Ba-Ronga." *BSNG* XX (1909–10).

——. "Native customs in Relation to Small Pox Amongst the Ba-Ronga." *South African Journal of Science*, July 1919.

——. "Le Mouvement de Murimi: un réveil au sein de l'animisme thonga." *Journal de psychologie normale et pathologique*, December 1924.

Liengme, G. "Notice de géographie médicale: Quelques observations sur les maladies des indigènes des provinces de Lourenço Marques et de Gaza." *BSNG* VIII (1895).

————. "Un Potentat africain: Goungounyane et son règne." *BSNG* XIII (1901).

Liesegang, G. "Notes on the Internal Structure of the Gaza Kingdom of Southern Mozambique, 1840–1895." In *Before and After Shaka*, edited by J. Peires. Grahamstown, 1981.

Longle, A. "De Inhambane à Lourenço Marques" *BSGL* 6, 1 (1886).

Mabin, A. "Labour, Capital, Class Struggle, and the Origins of Residential Segregation in Kimberley, 1880–1920." *Journal of Historical Geography* 12, 1 (1986).

McNamara, J. K. "Migrant Routes to the Gold Mines and Compound Accommodation, 1889–1912." *South African Labour Bulletin* 4, 3 (1978).

Moodie, T. Dunbar. "Migrancy and Male Sexuality on the South African Gold Mines." *Journal of Southern African Studies* 14, 2 (1988).

————. "Ethnic violence on South African gold mines." *JSAS* 18, 3, 1992.

Moroney, S. "The Development of the Compound as a Mechanism of Worker Control." *South African Labour Bulletin* 4, 3 (1978).

————. "Mine Worker Protest on the Witwatersrand, 1901–1912." In *Essays in Southern African Labour History*, edited by E. Webster. Johannesburg, 1978.

————. "Mine Married Quarters: The Differential Stabilisation of the Witwatersrand Workforce, 1900–1920." In *Industrialisation and Social Change in South Africa*, edited by S. Marks and R. Rathbone. London, 1982.

Morton, W. J. "To South Africa for Diamonds." *Scribner's Magazine* 4, XIV (1878); 5, XIV (1878).

Nelson, W. "Some letters—Adventures of a Local Traveller in South Africa." *Africana Notes and News*, 20, 6 (1973).

————. "Some Letters—Extracts from the *Masbro Advertiser* from 19 May 1877." *Africana Notes and News*, 20, 5 (1973).

Newitt, M. "Mine Labour and the Development of Mozambique." Institute of Commonwealth Studies, *Collected Seminar Papers*, Societies of Southern Africa, 1974.

Noronha, E. de. "Lourenço Marques e as suas relaçoes com a Africa do Sul." *BSGL* 15, 2 (1896).

Nunes, J. "Apontamentos sobre a tribu dos ba-Thonga." *Boletim da Sociedade de Estudos da Colónia de Moçambique*, 3, 1 (1932).

————. "Inspecção das circumscrições civis do distrito de Inhambane" and "História dum caso singular de Politica supertição indigenas." *BSGL* 37 (1919).

O'Neill, H. "Journeys in the District of Delagoa Bay, December 1886-January 1887," *PRGS*, IX (1887).

Paiva de Andrada, Joaquim Carlos. "A Manica e o Musila. Exploraçao Paiva de Andrada." *BSGL* 1 (1882).

Penvenne, J. "Labor Struggles at the Port of Lourenço Marques, 1900–1933." *Review* 8 (1984).

Perrings, C. "The Production Process, Industrial Labour Strategies, and Worker Responses in the South African Gold Mining Industry." *JAH* 18, 1 (1977).

Richter, C. "Wanderende Bassuto." *Berliner Missionsberichte* 3/4 (1882).

Richardson, P. "The Natal Sugar Industry in the Nineteenth Century." In *Putting a Plough to the Ground*, edited by W. Beinart, P. Delius, and S. Trapido. London and Johannesburg, 1980.

Richardson, P., and A. Graves. "Plantations in the Political Economy of Colonial Sugar Production: Natal and Queensland, 1860–1914." *JSAS* 6, 2 (1980).

Rita Ferreira, A. "Labour Emigration among the Mozambican Thonga: Comments on a Study by Marvin Harris." *Africa* 30 (1960).

Ferreira, A. R. "Os Africanos de Lourenço Marques." *Memorias do Instituto de Investigaçao Cientifica de Moçambique*, 9, series c (1967/8).

Rogerson, C. " 'Shishanyama': The Rise and Fall of the Native Eating House Trade in Johannesburg." *Social Dynamics*, 14, 1 (1988).

Schaefli-Glardon, E. "De Valdezia à Lourenço Marques, journal de voyage." *BSNG* VII (1893).

Turrell, R. V. "Kimberley: Labour and Compounds, 1871–1888." In *Industrialisation and Social Change in South Africa*, edited by S. Marks and R. Rathbone. London, 1982.
———. "Kimberley's Model Compounds." *JAH* 25, 1 (1984).
Van Onselen, C. *Chibaro: African Mine Labour in Southern Rhodesia 1900–1933*. London, 1976.
Vasconcellos, A. de C. N. de. "Dos mappos estatisticos com relaçao ao movimento commercial no Districto de Lourenço Marques, durante o anno de 1884." *Boletim da Sociedade de Geógrafia Commercial do Porto*, 1886.
Warwick, P. "Black Industrial Protest on the Witwatersrand, 1901–02." In *Essays in Southern African Labour History*, edited by E. Webster. Johannesburg, 1978.
Webster, D. "Migrant Labour, Social Formations and the Proletarianisation of the Chopi of Southern Mozambique." *African Perspectives* 1 (1978).
Xavier, A. A. C. "O Inharrime e as guerras Zavallas." *BSGL*, 1881.
———. "Reconhencimento do Limpopo: Os territorios as sul do Save e os Vatuas." *BSGL* 3 (1894).
———. "Os territorios ao sul do Save e os Vatuas." *BSGL* 13, 2 (1896).
Young, S. "Fertility and Famine: Womens' Agricultural History in Southern Mozambique." In *The Roots of Rural Poverty*, edited by R. Palmer and Q. N. Parsons. London, 1977.

V.   Unpublished Theses and Papers

Brock, L. A. "From Kingdom to Colonial District: A Political Economy of Social Change in Gazaland, Southern Mozambique, 1870–1930." Ph.D. thesis, Northwestern University, Illinois, 1989.
Eales, K. " 'Jezebels,' Good Girls and Married Quarters, Johannesburg 1912," paper presented to the African Studies Institute, University of the Witwatersrand, 1988.
Fuller, C. E. "An Ethnohistoric Study of Continuity and Change in Gwambe Culture." Ph.D. thesis, Northwestern University, 1955.
Grey, P. C. "The Development of the Gold Mining Industry on the Witwatersrand, 1902–1910." Ph.D. thesis, University of South Africa, 1969.
Harries, P. "Labour Migration from Mozambique to South Africa; With Special Reference to the Delagoa Bay Hinterland, c.1862–97." Ph.D. thesis, University of London, 1983.
Hedges, D. "Trade and Politics in Southern Mozambique and Zululand in the 18th and Early 19th Centuries." Ph.D. thesis, University of London, 1978.
Liesegang, G. "Beiträge zur Geschichte des Reiches der Gaza Nguni im Südlichen Moçambiek 1820–1895." Ph.D. thesis, University of Cologne, 1967.
Lincoln, D. "The Culture of the South African Sugarmill: The Impress of the Sugarocracy." Ph.D. thesis, University of Cape Town, 1985.
Monnier, N. "Stratégies et tactiques d'appropriation: Etude de cas: Un Mouvement missionnaire au sud-mozambique." Mémoire en science politique, Université de Lausanne, 1992.
Moroney, S. "Industrial Conflict in a Labour Repressive Economy: Black Labour in the Transvaal Gold Mines, 1901–12." B.A. honours thesis, University of the Witwatersrand, 1976.
Penvenne, J. "A History of African Labor in Lourenço Marques, Mozambique 1877–1950." Ph.D. thesis, Boston University, 1982.
Pirio, G. "Commerce, Industry and Empire: The Making of Modern Portuguese Colonialism in Angola and Mozambique, 1890–1914." Ph.D. thesis, University of California at Los Angeles, 1982.
Potgieter, A. J. "Die Swartes aan die Witwatersrand 1900–1933." Ph.D. thesis, Rand Afrikaans University, 1978.
Rennie, J. K. "Christianity, Colonialism, and the Origins of Nationalism Among the Ndau of Southern Rhodesia." Ph.D. thesis, Northwestern University, 1973.
Sieborger, R. "The Recruitment and Organisation of African Labour for the Kimberley Diamond Mines, 1871–1885." M.A. thesis, Rhodes University, 1976.

VI.   Oral Testimony

Mgubane Ngonyama
John Baloyi
Joe Tihuhlu Khosa
Jackson Majaji Khosa
Madaubi wa Ntimane
Johannes Sibuyi
Philemon Sihlangu
Nyero Sithadi

INDEX